ANARCHISM, REVOLUTION AND REACTION

Catalan Labour and the Crisis of the Spanish State, 1898–1923

Angel Smith

Berghahn Books
NEW YORK • OXFORD

First published in 2007 by

Berghahn Books
www.berghahnbooks.com

Library of Congress Cataloging-in-Publication Data

Smith, Angel, 1958-
Anarchism, revolution, and reaction : Catalan labour and the crisis of the Spanish state,
1898-1923 / Angel Smith.
  p. cm. -- (International studies in social history ; v. 8)
Includes bibliographical references (p.) and index.
ISBN 1-84545-176-7 (hardback : alk. paper)
1. Labor movement--Spain--Catalonia--History. 2. Anarchism--Spain--Catalonia--History.
3. Syndicalism--Spain--Catalonia--History. 4. Confederación Nacional del Trabajo (Spain).
Comité de Catalunya--History. 5. Spain--Politics and government--1886-1931. I. Title.

HD8589.C32S64 2006
331.88'60946709041--dc22

2006019695

British Library Cataloguing in Publication Data

A catalogue record for this book is available from the British Library
Printed in the United States on acid-free paper

ISBN -10: 1-84545-176-7   ISBN -13: 978-1-84545-176-9   (hardback)

To my wife, Marga, and my daughter, Anna

CONTENTS

List of Figures and Tables   viii

Acknowledgements   ix

List of Acronyms   x

A Note on Language Usage   xi

Introduction   1

Part I: The Roots of Industrial Militancy

1. Industrial Structure, Technological Change and the Labour Process   11
2. Gender, Skill and Class: Hierarchy and Solidarity within the Catalan Working-Class Community   36
3. The State, Employers and Organised Labour: Political Marginalisation, Social Control and Resistance   67

Part II: Building the Anarchist-Syndicalist Movement, 1898 to 1914

4. Anarchism, Socialism and the General Strike, 1898 to 1909   103
5. Workers against the State: Anarchism, Republicanism, Popular and Working-Class Protest, 1898 to 1909   146
6. The Foundation of the CNT, 1910 to 1914   189

Part III: The Gun and the Sword: The Catalan CNT from Revolution to Repression, 1915 to 1923

7. The War-Time Economy and the Rise of the Sindicats Unics, 1915 to 1918   225
8. Between Reform and Revolution: The Catalan CNT and the Left-Wing Challenge to the Restoration Regime, 1915 to 1918   259
9. 1919: The Apogee of the Catalan CNT and the Employer-Military Counteroffensive   290
10. The Road to Dictatorship: The Destruction of the Catalan CNT and the Fall of the Restoration Regime, 1920 to 1923   323

Bibliography   361

Index   379

LIST OF FIGURES AND TABLES

List of Figures

1.1. The Geographical Location of the Catalan Textile Industries   13

1.2. The Ter and Freser Valleys   15

2.1. Percentage of non-Catalan Spanish Population by District in 1900   46

2.2. The Neighbourhoods of Barcelona in 1911   52

2.3. Percentage of Industrial Workers by District in 1900   57

4.1. Front Page of the First Number of *Solidaridad Obrera*   133

List of Tables

1.1. The Geographical Location of the Catalan Cotton Textile Industry in 1919   16

1.2. Number of Industrial Workers in the Principal Barcelona Industries in 1905 and 1920   20

1.3. Number of Industrial Workers per Unit of Production in Barcelona City and Province in 1907 and 1923   21

2.1. Population Change in Barcelona, 1890–1920   44

2.2. Wages and Expenditure of a Working-Class Family (Husband, Wife and Two Children), 1905–1917   48

2.3. The Social Structure of Barcelona by Neighbourhoods in 1900   55

3.1. Comparison of Strikes, Strikers and Working Days Lost in Barcelona and the Rest of Spain, 1899–1914   84

3.2. Propensity of Workers in Barcelona to Strike by Industry, 1899–1914   86

7.1. Comparison of Strikes, Strikers and Working Days Lost in Barcelona and the Rest of Spain, 1915–1923   227

A Note on Language Usage

It is difficult to decide whether to write names in Catalan or Castilian-Spanish. Most workers in Catalonia during the period of this study would speak in Catalan but usually write in Castilian-Spanish. From the late nineteenth century Catalan nationalist publications would largely be written in Catalan, but most of the working-class Left's press was in Castilian-Spanish. In these circumstances, I have taken the (inevitably arbitrary) decision to, in general, write the names of people born in Catalonia, Catalan organisations and place names in Catalan, and the names of non-Catalan Spaniards, non-Catalan Spanish organisations and places in other parts of Spain in Castilian-Spanish. However, I have excepted those Catalan bodies which included the word 'Spain' (España) in their title, and Catalan organisations which took an overtly Spanish nationalist (*españolista*) stance. In this case I have used Castilian-Spanish.

INTRODUCTION

The aim of this book is to study the relationship between Catalan workers, the anarchist-syndicalist movement and the development of the Spanish polity between the years 1898 and 1923. Following the injunction of Geoff Eley and Keith Nield, I wish to write a work covering, on the one hand, the social history of labour and its organisational manifestations, and, on the other, its broader political impact.[1] In this way I hope not only to deepen knowledge of the Catalan working class and its institutions, but also to contribute to the overall understanding of early twentieth-century Spanish history.

The reasons for choosing this topic are twofold. First, anarchism showed great vitality in Catalonia – along with several other parts of Spain, most notably Andalusia – during the early twentieth century. In 1919 the anarchist-syndicalist labour confederation, the CNT, would, albeit briefly, attain over half a million members in Spain as a whole, about 60 percent of whom were Catalan. Second, the growth of labour protest, and of the CNT in particular, was perceived as a massive challenge by business, and by the military and political elite of the Restoration regime, who between 1919 and 1923 spent much of their time searching for strategies to either contain or destroy the organisation. Catalonia and especially Barcelona were at the heart of these struggles. The period ended with a coup d'etat against the Restoration regime in September 1923. It is my contention that its origins cannot be understood without taking into account the violent social conflict which had racked the city over the previous four years.

I have divided the book into three parts. In Part One I have focused on several major and closely interrelated themes. First, I have studied economic and social change and its impact on workers' lives: industrial development, the recasting of the labour process, the stratification of labour, migration, urban development and living conditions. Second, I have turned to the attitude of the state and business towards labour, and the strategies which they put in place to maintain social control, 'integrate labour' and head off subversive threats. Finally, I have begun to chart how labour adapted to and criticised this changing world, through the discourses used in meetings and within the press, and through associational initiatives. With respect to the latter, for reasons to be explained, the chief area of concern has been union organisation and strikes.

Within this section I shall be posing a key question which puzzled contemporaries and taxed historians. Catalan industry was, when compared with that of the major European powers, small-scale and in some respects technologically backward. Middle-class contemporaries and some more recent commentators have suggested that in these circumstances the country 'should have' enjoyed quite cordial labour relations. And yet it spawned what was, at certain times at least, an aggressive labour movement, prone to the use of violence.

In order to address these issues I will centre my attention on the key industries and centres of labour unrest. This means that Barcelona will be the focal point of my study. By the first years of the twentieth century around half the Catalan working population was to be found in the city. Furthermore, almost invariably attempts to construct general workers' confederations were launched from Barcelona and it was at the heart of the majority of labour struggles. Nevertheless, by this time much of the territory's textile industries had vacated Barcelona and were located either in the medium-sized industrial towns which surrounded the Catalan capital and dotted Catalonia's central and southern coastline, or in the smaller centres which straddled its northeastern river valleys. Hence the discussion of textiles will include areas outside Barcelona. In particular, the woollen textile town of Sabadell and the cotton textile towns in the Ter and Freser valleys were key centres of labour organisation and will be subject to considerable attention.

In the second part of the work my focus will shift to the relationship between workers and the anarchist-syndicalist movement. A key area of discussion will be the reasons behind the growth of anarchism in Catalonia and, concomitantly, the difficulties other labour organisations, especially the Socialist party and its union, the PSOE and UGT, found in establishing themselves.

This has already been a subject of much speculation. One set of explanations has stressed the supposedly radicalising impact of rural migrant labour from southern and eastern Spain. Such interpretations tend to make a causal linkage between the growth of anarchism in Andalusia and Catalonia. What might be called the 'classic' explanation of Spanish anarchism sees it as particularly suited to the latifundia agrarian structure of southern Spain. Anarchism was, it is often claimed, rooted in the vast inequalities of income and wealth in the region, with impoverished landless and land-hungry peasants on the one hand, and rich and powerful landowners on the other. The power of the local political bosses or *caciques* made local elections a farce, hence the popularity of anarchist 'antipoliticism'. The isolation of the local villages from the state, with only the hated rural police or Civil Guard and tax collectors as evidence of its existence, lent credibility to anarchist calls for its disappearance. This isolation also formed the basis of support for the anarchists' decentralised vision of the society of the future, with the commune or collective as the centre of social life. Finally, this line of interpretation sees peasant anarchist protest as backward or, to use Eric Hobsbawm's phrase, millenarian, because the mythical anarchist revolutionary General Strike, which was supposed magically to usher in the new world, substituted other more rational forms of struggle.[2]

Anarchist-inspired labour organisations have, on the other hand, often been seen as unsuited to the needs of urban workers. These workers, according to some, tended towards reformism, and were at home in the more centralised trade unions and political parties of the Socialists. This left the tricky problem of anarchist success in Catalonia. The simple answer was to argue that it was the result of the migration by 'unassimilated' peasants from rural areas (often seen as anarchist hotbeds), who became highly militant within their new surroundings.

This was an idea which, in the early-twentieth century, had already found favour within the Catalan nationalist middle classes, shocked that anarchism had penetrated what they believed was an inherently moderate and practical working class, which could not possibly be tempted by revolutionary adventures. It was then developed by Catalan historians, most notable Jaume Vicens i Vives, who maintained that the *patuleia*, a floating, semi-employed *classe dangereuse* of rural extraction (in this case largely from rural Catalonia) was the insurrectionary element in the popular struggles of the period between 1833 and 1868. From the 1900s, however, migrants were increasingly drawn from Aragón and they were to have a radicalising impact on the Catalan CNT.[3]

The theory that 'uprooted' peasants were a radicalising influence in early twentieth-century urban areas became popular with many historians, most particularly in the United States, after the Second World War. And subsequently, in the 1960s and 1970s, either through the American or Catalan route, the idea that there was a connection between rural migrant workers and Catalan anarchism appeared in the works of a number of English-speaking historians. In these studies particular attention was paid to the growing numbers of southern *murcianos* within the Catalan working class after 1914.[4]

A second set of explanations emphasise the importance of the small-scale nature of Catalan industry. This has at its origin the Marxist claim that anarchism was an individualist, 'petty bourgeois', phenomenon, and that whereas Marxism attracted support amongst the industrial factory proletariat the anarchists could only gain that of workers employed in more marginal sectors of the economy.[5] Thus, for example, the leading Catalan Trotskyist theoretician, Andreu Nin, stated in the 1920s that 'petty bourgeois' anarchism had prevailed in Catalonia as a result of the high degree of subdivision within its agriculture and scattered nature of its industry.[6] It may immediately be noted that there is a logical slippage here, given that if anarchism was 'petty bourgeois' its supporters should presumably have been elements of the lower-middle class (clerks, office workers, shopkeepers etc.) rather than skilled workers and artisans. This reflected the fact that the phrase 'petty bourgeois anarchism' was, in reality, more a term of abuse than a fully worked-out analysis.

Nevertheless, the idea that anarchism and small-scale industry went together has been developed by historians, with such interpretations stressing that the anarchists' ideal of decentralised labour federations, with each individual union retaining a large degree of autonomy, was well suited to the disperse artisanal nature of much of Catalan industry. This is compared to the more centralised, bureaucratic, nature of the Socialist labour confederation, the UGT, whose strength, it is often stated, lay amongst the industrial workers in the big iron and steel, and coal-mining industries of northern Spain.[7]

A third set of what may be called approximations to anarchism – in that they do not always centre exclusively on the movement or attempt to offer a full account of its rise – can be grouped under the rubric of 'populist'. These studies tend not to treat anarchism as an exclusively class-based phenomenon and dwell on the links between anarchist ideology and more widely disseminated discourses on the political Left. They focus, above all, on the development, in nineteenth-century urban Catalonia, of what they see as a popular, interclass, cultural milieu and argue that the political language which bound workers, artisans, and the lower-middle class together, was based on liberal rationalism, which championed 'progress', education and science, and demonised the Roman Catholic Church and 'reaction'. Such ideas, they maintain, penetrated deeply into working-class and popular culture, and were behind the large number of free-thinking clubs, lay schools, Masonic and spiritualist associations which sprang up during the second half of the nineteenth century. Bourgeois rationalism was, from the mid-nineteenth century, the staple of republican ideology, which gained a wide-ranging popular following in this period. Anarchists, much more than Marxist Socialists, subsequently bought into this world view and, therefore, shared many of the same presuppositions as the republicans.[8]

An offshoot of this interpretation is that developed by a group of historians formed around the student of labour and nationalist movements, Josep Termes, who has argued that there was a close relationship between popular protest movements and the national question in nineteenth-century Catalonia. He maintains that with the Catalan bourgeoisie linked, albeit in a subordinate position, to the dominant Castilian-Andalusian ruling oligarchy, the fight against an alien centralising state was conducted by the 'popular classes'. It was in the context of this struggle that these classes developed a national identity and, therefore, tended to form specifically Catalan unions and political parties. This remained a crucial feature of Catalan political life through to the twentieth century and a party which, like the PSOE, did not take it into account was doomed to failure.[9]

In at least two respects such interpretations have a more 'modern' ring than the alternatives previously discussed. First, they echo claims, made recently in 'post-structuralist' circles above all, that the significance of class as an interpretative tool has been overemphasised. Second, as in the case of the proponents of the 'linguistic turn' in labour history, much more attention is given to political discourse in its own right, though Enric Ucelay Da Cal, for example, gave his argument a socio-economic twist by claiming that the disperse nature of Catalan industry provided the economic underpinning for this interclass alliance.[10]

There are, in my estimation, difficulties with all three interpretational strands. The key shortcoming of the first two explanatory models is that they are not based on any serious social history and, in fact, do not interrogate the anarchist movement in any detail. Hence, the radicalising influence of migrant labour and the impact of small-scale industry is stated rather than empirically explored. At the root of the problem is that Catalan historiography has, until recently, continued to focus on political history, and, with respect to labour organisation, centre its attention on the top echelons rather than the rank and file. By studying in some depth the interrelationship between the world of work, the neighbourhood, and organised labour I hope to shed further light on these matters. Furthermore, these studies lack any strong comparative perspective. Thus, for example, the extent to which urban Catalan anarchism was a unique phenomenon is open to question. Syndicalism attained considerable influence on both the European and American continents until at least 1914 and there was a marked similarity between this movement and pro-union Catalan anarchist currents. The major anarchist-syndicalist labour confederation, the CNT, formed in 1910, from the first referred to itself as syndicalist. Similarly, comparative work very much calls into question the link between Socialism and big industry, even in Spain itself. I will introduce such comparative perspectives when their usage may prove fruitful.

The third set of what I have termed approximations, by to an important degree shifting discussion onto the cultural and discursive field, do not suffer from these drawbacks. Their focus has without doubt been productive. I will endeavour to provide a careful analysis of the political languages employed by labour activists and study links between anarchism, republicanism and Catalanism. Language is, as 'post-structuralists' have reminded us, an important field of study in its own right. People do not 'read off' their understanding of the world from 'the social'. A human being's mental universe is linguistically constructed. And the cultural baggage picked up and passed from one generation to the next provides people with the raw material through which they interpret their world.[11]

Nevertheless, my focus will be rather different from that of the proponents of more 'populist' readings of anarchism in a number of respects. First, I shall forcefully argue that it was above all a movement based on industrial labour. Second, I will try to show how factors rooted in workers' real experience, such as changes in the world of work and the community, recast social relations, the strategies pursued by employers and the policies of the state, along with new ideological inputs (in this case above all class-based ideologies), deeply impacted on their cosmographies, on the type of organisations they built and on the protest movements they undertook. Furthermore, it is my contention that such elements help us to understand the anarchists' ability to gain followers among Catalan workers.

As a result, worker discontent and its manifestations will be at the heart of this study. The type of protest movements on which I should concentrate is not, however, unproblematic. In recent years the claim has been made that social and labour historians have been too centred on the industrial disputes of (largely male) workers to the detriment of other forms of dissent, often centred on issues related to consumption and frequently led by women workers.[12] It is an issue which I have taken on board. And in order to approach the varied forms taken by worker activism I have used Charles Tilly's concept of 'repertoires of collective action'; that is the specific forms of protest utilised by workers and other social groups in particular contexts.[13] For example, I shall be looking not only at strikes, but also at protests against clerical influence and the war in Morocco during the first decade of the century, and against rising food prices in 1918. In all these cases women were to the fore; in the latter men were almost totally excluded.

Indeed, I have striven to fully integrate gender relations into this study. In this respect, I have analysed the role that women workers played in early twentieth-century Catalan working-class society; taken care to understand how both the labour movement as a whole and the anarchist-syndicalist organisations in particular perceived women's place in the world of work, the neighbourhood and home, and within their associations; and studied women's own reactions and self-perceptions. Labour unions and anarchist confederations after all claimed to represent the entire working class and to be struggling for its emancipation, and it is crucial to study the extent to which they were in reality working to benefit all workers.

Nevertheless, most emphasis has been placed on labour unions and strikes. There are two good reasons for this. First, unions were the central core of the anarchist-syndicalist confederations. Second, it was the growth of union organisation and strikes which was at the heart of the explosive crisis of the Restoration regime between 1919 and 1923. It should be emphasised in this respect that such a focus does not exclude women to the extent that has sometimes been claimed. As we shall see, there was more overlap between strikes and other forms of protest, and between protests by working-class men and women, than some authors have realised.

I shall argue that it was in good measure the type of labour organisation and the 'repertoires of collective action' which emerged in urban Catalonia which made possible (though not inevitable) the rise of anarchism-syndicalism. Nevertheless, while I recognise that anarchism was born in the cauldron of social conflict and that languages of class were predominant within the movement it is not my intention to defend a simplistic class-based reading of either Catalan society or, indeed, anarchism itself. The 'populist school' was right to draw attention to the fact that anarchism was a child of liberal rationalism as well as socialism, and, as we shall see, this created tension within the movement between languages of class (workers versus industrialists) and languages of the people (anticlerics and freethinkers against the reactionary elite), and both opportunities to align with the liberal Left (as representatives of the forces of 'progress') and bitterly criticise them (as middle-class 'bourgeois'). I aim to tease out the political implications of these tensions and linkages both with respect to the development of Catalan labour and also, crucially, in relation to the possibility of constructing alliances against the Restoration regime.

In order to undertake these tasks it will be necessary to analyse in some detail the links between the anarchist-syndicalist movement and the broader working class, its real strength, component parts and ideology, and also its relations in different conjunctures with the liberal Left. As part of this endeavour a key question I will seek to answer will be how a movement which saw itself as forging a new world which liberated human potential for good came to incorporate bombers and gunmen, and, in the years of the First World War, operate what can only be described as a terrorist wing.

To do this I shall study grass-roots struggles and conflict as well as the reaction of the Spanish polity to protest movements and to the growth of anarchism. All social and labour historians now realise how important it is to place working-class history within the context of state policies. This will form a backdrop to the entire study and will be foregrounded in the third part of the book, in which I analyse the rise and fall of the CNT in the final crisis of the Restoration regime between 1917 and 1923. The period began in 1917 with a reforming, interclass, push to replace the Restoration regime by a liberal-democratic regime, but, in Catalonia above all, quickly escalated into class-based confrontation. It is a dramatic story, in which the CNT grew totally to dominate organised labour and was then largely destroyed in a counteroffensive launched by an alliance of industrialists and the military, and in which Barcelona became 'the Mediterranean Chicago' *avant la lettre*,[14] as fierce gun battles and shootings tinged the city's streets red.

My first concern will be to understand how such a dramatic conjuncture developed. Was it the result of totally new conditions created by the First World War: rapid economic development and inflation, an influx of 'uprooted peasants', the rise of a new class of hard-line *nouveau-riche* businessmen, or are pre-war developments of key importance in explaining subsequent events? I shall also be looking at the response of the CNT to the new opportunities for political and social change, and how the counteroffensive would impact on the organisation's strength, practice and ideology. In particular, from 1916 a reforming current developed in the Catalan CNT under the greatest labour leader of the period, Salvador Seguí. Its aim was to strengthen the organisation, build alliances against the regime, and, from 1919, rein in the gunmen. I shall study in some depth the policies Seguí pursued and attempt to answer the question as to whether, had the conditions been more favourable, he could have taken the CNT away from its roots in aggressive class-confrontational politics to play a part in shifting the balance of power towards labour while supporting democratic construction.

The story is often violent and the ending is not a happy one. Perhaps Seguí's spirit would be lifted by the thought that the strategy he advocated would, to an important degree, subsequently be taken up by the working-class opposition to Franco in Catalonia, and that labour would play an important role in laying the foundations of today's democratic Spain.

Notes

1. Geoff Eley and Keith Nield, 'Why Does Social History Ignore Politics?'.
2. Juan Díaz del Moral, *Historia de las agitaciones andaluzas*; Gerald Brenan, *The Spanish Labyrinth*; Eric J. Hobsbawm, *Primitive Rebels*, 74–92.
3. Jaume Vicens i Vives and Montserrat Llorens, *Industrials i polítics del segle XIX*, 142–5 and 165–6; Jaume Vicens i Vives, 'El moviment obrerista català (1901–1939)'.
4. See, for example, C.A.M. Hennessy, *The Federal Republic in Spain*, 67; Richard Kern, *Red Years, Black Years*, 69–71; Murray Bookchin, *The Spanish Anarchists*, 69–71; Gerald Meaker, *The Revolutionary Left in Spain, 1914–1923*, 2–3.
5. K. Marx, F. Engels, I. Lenin, *Anarchism and Anarcho–Syndicalism*.
6. Andreu Nin, '¿Por qué nuestro movimiento obrero ha sido anarquista?'.
7. Albert Balcells, 'Introducción', p.18; Pierre Vilar, *Historia de España*, 105–6; Manuel Tuñón de Lara, *El movimiento obrero en la historia de España*, vol. 1, 307–8.
8. José Alvarez Junco, *La ideología política del anarquismo español*, 204–14; Enric Ucelay Da Cal, *La Catalunya populista*; Angel Duarte i Montserrat, *El republicanisme català a la fi del segle XIX*.
9. Josep Termes i Ardévol, 'El nacionalisme català: per una nova interpretació'.
10. Ucelay Da Cal, *Catalunya populista*, 52–6.
11. See, for example, Gareth Stedman Jones, *Languages of Class*, 1–24. I do not, however, agree with Stedman Jones that class can be seen in purely linguistic–discursive terms.
12. In a Spanish context see, Pamela B. Radcliffe, *From Mobilization to Civil War*.
13. See Charles Tilly, *From Mobilization to Revolution*, 151–66.
14. The expression is taken from Colin M. Winston, *Workers and the Right in Spain*, 105.

Part I

The Roots of Industrial Militancy

1

INDUSTRIAL STRUCTURE, TECHNOLOGICAL CHANGE AND THE LABOUR PROCESS

As was noted in the introduction, for some contemporary observers there was a paradox at the heart of Catalan labour relations. Catalan industry was, they maintained, in western European terms, backwards and small-scale, so one would expect close relations to exist between masters and men. Yet, industrial militancy was a serious concern, with extensive and often violent conflicts hitting the major sectors of the economy. This question will be central to the present chapter and, in order to tackle it, I will be looking at three interrelated areas. First, I intend to provide an outline of the area's economic development. Issues such as the rate of growth, industries' international competitiveness and tariff policy have an obvious bearing on labour relations. Second, I will discuss in greater depth the economy's evolving industrial structure, focusing on the extent to which capitalist development was making its presence felt. In this context I emphasise the formation of a pronounced hierarchy in Catalan industry, in which both relatively large and marginal businesses had their place. This, as we shall see, provides an important key to resolving the apparent paradox, noted above. Finally, I shall tackle the issue of technological change and the restructuring of divisions of labour. Over the past forty years social historians have paid particular attention to how industrialists' attempts to recast the labour process have stimulated workers to mobilise in defence of their position on the shop floor. Within this tradition, I will examine the type of technological and structural changes Catalan industry underwent in the late nineteenth and early twentieth centuries and the impact that this had on workers' lives.

The Catalan Economy: Growth, Crisis and Diversification

During the early twentieth-century Catalonia, and in particular the area which to a large extent coincided with the province of Barcelona, stood out from much of Spain because of its high level of economic development. This was reflected in the structure of its active population. Thus, while in Spain as a whole between 1900 and 1920 the percentage of the active population working on the land only fell from 63.5 to 57.3 percent, in the province of Barcelona this figure was already under 40 percent in 1900, and by 1920 over 60 percent of the active population was to be found in industry and transport.[1] The relatively rapid industrial expansion also comes through in the balance between rural and urban population. In 1900 66.9 percent of the inhabitants of the province of Barcelona lived in urban areas of over 5,000 inhabitants and by 1920 the figure had increased to 71.8 percent.[2]

The territory's urban and industrial structure showed a number of specific characteristics. First, Barcelona, the 'Spanish Manchester',[3] had grown spectacularly throughout the nineteenth century and by 1900 had emerged as a major urban hub. Including in the statistics those neighbourhoods incorporated between 1897 and 1903, according to official figures its population had risen from 249,590 in 1861 to 607,170 in 1914, and, following rapid economic development during the First World War, it stood at 710,335 in 1920. This represented, by the end of the first decade of the twentieth century, close to 30 percent of Catalonia's total population and around 50 percent of its industrial labour force. As a result, Barcelona came to rival Madrid as Spain's principal urban centre, with the difference that while Madrid was the country's administrative capital Barcelona was her major industrial power house.

Far behind in 1900 were fifteen medium-sized towns with between 10,000 and 30,000 inhabitants, of which nine were significant industrial centres. Most of these were located in an area known as the Pla, either on the coast or within a radius of thirty kilometres of Barcelona. However, Catalan industry was not limited to these larger urban conurbations. From the late eighteenth-century industrial plants also grew up in the so-called Muntanya, particularly on the banks of the rivers Ter and Llobregat, to the north and north-east of Barcelona, where they were able to take advantage of water power (see figure 1.1.).[4]

Figure 1.1. The Geographical Location of the Catalan Textile Industries

The 'leading sector' in Catalan industrial growth from the early-nineteenth century through to the First World War was textiles. Uniquely in the Spanish context, from the early-nineteenth century a large factory-based, mechanised, cotton textile industry developed and several important centres of woollen textile production also sprang up. At the turn of the century there were approximately 80,000 workers employed in cotton, and 30,000 in the territory's other textile industries, representing at least a third of the Catalan active industrial working class.[5] The origins of textiles' preeminence were to be found in the resurgence experienced by the Catalan economy in the late eighteenth century as commerce with the American colonies grew rapidly. Led by cotton textiles, from the mid-nineteenth century the economy then experienced sustained economic growth, with the boom conditions of the decade between 1875 and 1883 known as the 'Gold Fever' or *febre d'or*. At the same time, in the early and mid-nineteenth century, as spinning and then weaving were mechanised and the use of steam power made rapid strides, much of the industry moved to the coastal plain in and around Barcelona in order to be close to the supply of British coal imported through its port. The

old city of Barcelona proved too cramped to accommodate the rapidly growing industry, and it was the surrounding towns which attracted most of the
factories. In particular, Sant Martí de Provençals, Sants and Hostafrancs
emerged as large manufacturing centres. In 1897, along with other outlying
districts, they were incorporated into the city.

Other towns on the coast, or those well connected with coastal ports, also
emerged as important industrial centres. This was the case of Badalona and of
Mataró, Calella and the smaller centres in the Maresme area (*comarca*)[6] to the
north (the Maresme specialising in hosiery), and of Vilanova i la Geltrú and
Reus to the south. A similar process was to be seen in woollen textiles, with
the towns of Sabadell and Terrassa, followed at some distance by Sant Martí
de Provençals, establishing their dominance.[7]

Yet, Catalonia's drive to industrialise was hindered because it lacked
reserves of both coal and iron ore, which drove up energy costs. This made it
impossible to develop a modern iron and steel industry. Metalworking did
take root, but it was hampered by an unfavourable tariff policy, driven by the
demands of the foreign railway companies and textiles manufacturers for
cheap rails, rolling stock and machinery. Although some larger metal factories, such as La Maquinista Terrestre i Marítima, were set up, they were
unable to compete with machinery imports so tended to specialise in less
profitable areas such as the construction of bridges and other metallic structures. Matters were only to improve from the late 1880s onwards with the
takeoff of Basque iron and steel production (removing the need to rely so
heavily on foreign inputs), the withdrawal of concessions to foreign railway
companies, growing duties on foreign produced coal and metal imports, and
a fall of the value of the peseta on international markets.[8]

The relatively high price of coal also conditioned the industrial strategy of
the cotton textile industrialists, providing a great stimulus, particularly as
transport links improved significantly from the 1870s, for the expansion of
the industry on the banks of the Muntanya rivers in order to take advantage
of cheaper water power. Moreover, industrialists also hoped to escape from
the increasingly militant labour force in the larger towns and save money
through lower labour costs. Two areas stood out: the banks of the rivers Llobregat and Cardener in the *comarques* of the Berguedà, Bages and Baix Llobregat (usually referred to as the Llobregat Valley, with the first two
comarques known as the Alt Llobregat), and of the Ter and Freser further to
the north-east, largely in the Ripollès, Osona and Gironès *comarques*. In the
former area, Manresa was to emerge as a major centre of both spinning and
weaving. There would be no such equivalent in the latter zone, but a very
high concentration of factories were to be found between the towns of Ripoll
and Roda in an area known as the Ter Valley (see figure 1.2.).[9]

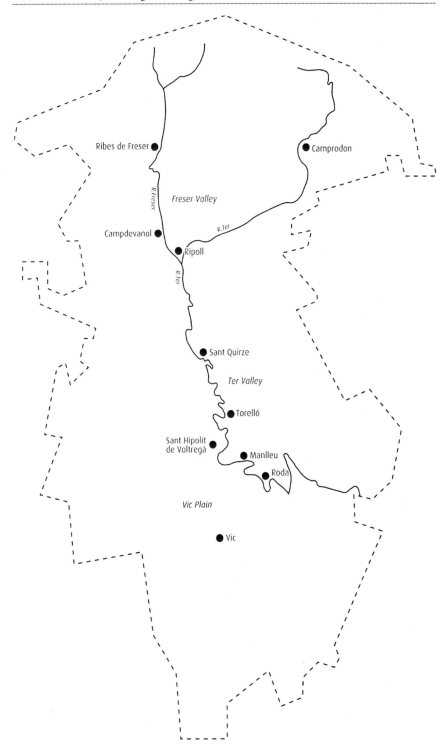

Figure 1.2. The Ter and Freser Valleys

Table 1.1. The Geographical Location of the Catalan Cotton Textile Industry in 1919 (Number and percentage of workers in each area)

	Spinning	Weaving	Finishing
Barcelona, Pla and Coast[1]	7,708 (22.2%)	24,671 (41.8%)	4,951 (68.1%)
River-Bank Areas[2]	24,895 (71.5%)	23,954 (40.6%)	301 (4.1%)
Other	2,199 (6.3%)	10,451 (17.7%)	2,016 (27.7%)
Totals	34,802	59,076	7,268

Notes:
1. Coast includes the city of Reus.
2. The River Bank Areas are the Llobregat, the Ter and Freser valleys, the Garrotxa and the Segrià.

Source: Calculated from, Cámara Oficial de Industria de Barcelona, *Memoria reglamentaria de 1919*, Barcelona, 1920, 139–63 and 220–5.

It was an option which was particularly attractive to the owners of relatively large spinning and integrated spinning and weaving mills for whom energy requirements were an important component of total costs. Thus, a report by the Barcelona Chamber of Industry indicated that in 1913, 66.7 percent of the cotton industry's spindles were located away from Barcelona and the Pla.[10] Detailed statistics compiled by the same body in 1919 confirmed that while around 40 percent of weavers continued working in Barcelona and on the coast just over 70 percent of spinners worked in river-bank factories (see table 1.1.). However, it should be emphasised that costs were only lower in Catalan terms. The rivers on which these factories operated were of the typical Mediterranean variety. They carried little water most of the year round and were liable to dry up in summer and ice up and on occasions flood in winter. By international standards the cost of both steam and water power was high.[11]

Catalan industry was also held back by the backwardness of much of the Spanish economy and, in particular, by her low-productivity agrarian sector. There is considerable debate amongst economic historians on the extent to which Spanish farming modernised in the nineteenth and early twentieth centuries, but there is no doubt that in comparative European terms productivity remained low, with the result that demand for capital and consumer goods was constrained, and, moreover, fluctuated wildly according to the state of the harvest.[12] These weaknesses were brought into stark relief at the end of the 1870s, when falling transport costs and the opening up of virgin land for grain production in Russia and North America led to the European market being flooded by cheap imports of grain. Spain was affected later than most European countries because duties on imported grains were already amongst the highest in Europe, but by the mid-1880s grain prices began sharply to decline thereby hitting purchasing power in the internal market. Hence, the *febre d'or* ended in the economic recession of 1884 to 1886. In response, the country's powerful agrarian elite began ceaselessly to campaign for an increase in tariff levels. Their demand was answered at the end of 1890, and in the following years the tariff was raised still further.[13]

Perhaps the government had to take some action. All European governments with the exception of Britain took measures to stem imports of foreign grain. And despite the towering tariff wall there were improvements in the productivity of Spanish agriculture, and an increase in the purchasing power of the rural population was visible, especially after 1910. However, these improvements were largely limited to newer, export-oriented sectors, such as fruit and garden produce, in which Spain enjoyed comparative advantages. The main effect of the new prohibitive duties was to consolidate the inefficient structure of most of Spanish agriculture.[14] Furthermore, the decline in grain prices was halted at the end of the decade, and from 1895 the depreciation of the Spanish peseta on international markets, together with the impact of a growing budget deficit, provoked an increase in the price of foodstuffs. As a result, at the end of the century Spanish grain prices were the highest in western Europe. The high cost of living acted as a further break on demand for manufactures and helped keep real wages low.[15] This fact has obvious social implications which will be discussed in more detail in subsequent chapters.

Despite the fact that Catalan manufacturers, in general, also enjoyed substantial protection, like their agrarian counterparts they reacted to the crisis by arguing that tariffs of industrial imports should be raised. They also met with success, achieving a sharp increase in tariffs on industrial goods in 1891, with duties on imported iron, steel and textiles set at a particularly high level (although the metal industry was still considerably more exposed). Much of Spanish industry and agriculture was now heavily protected. Moreover, the general European climate of nationalist ambition and inter-imperialist rivalry, coupled with the weakness of the Spanish economy, stimulated successive governments to go further, with the result that by 1906 Spain had the highest nominal tariff barriers in western Europe.[16] This was not the only concession to manufacturing interests. In 1882 cotton textile industrialists were granted progressively reduced duties on their exports to the major remaining colonies (Cuba, Puerto Rico and the Philippines) and in 1891 tariffs on manufactured imports from outside Spain were also applied to the colonies.

These measures helped the cotton textile industry weather the economic storm. Thus, during the 1890s Catalan industrialists, further aided by the fall in the value of the peseta, were able to substitute part of cotton thread and higher quality fabrics still imported. In addition, the colonies provided a ready market for the industry's surplus production. Between 1885 and the peak year of 1897 exports as a proportion of total Spanish cotton textile production grew from 3 to 20 percent.[17] However, the fact that much of Catalan industry was now sheltering behind high tariff barriers was hardly likely to encourage it to compete on the international market. In addition, the attempt to build the industry on the base of export-led growth to the colonies was soon to be shown a chimera.

The unequal trading relations with the remaining colonies encouraged rebellion against Spanish rule and, after a brief and disastrous war with the United States, Spain lost her last colonies in Asia and the Americas in 1898.

The cotton textile industry was seriously affected. It could not now compete with the United States in the Antilles and, consequently, by 1902 exports had fallen to only 6.6 percent of total production. Nevertheless, it was able to fend off total disaster. Between 1899 and 1901 it benefited from good harvests and from orders to clothe the repatriated Spanish troops. Then, during the first decade of the twentieth century, costs were further cut, and there were productivity gains in some sectors of Spanish agriculture, increasing demand for cotton textile garments.

The industry also benefited from the continued fall in the value of the peseta. Moreover, desperate efforts were made to find alternative foreign markets. Some success was achieved in South America and between 1905 and 1912 exports again rose to over 10 percent of total production (although this was to require hefty export subsidies, financed by the cotton industrialists themselves). This did not, however, suffice to lift the cloud of gloom which hung over the industry. Growth decelerated from 1898, with poor harvests in the middle of the decade combined with increases in the price of raw cotton producing serious over-production crises between 1902 and 1905, and between 1907 and 1910, which fierce competition between manufacturers only served to exacerbate.[18] Particularly hard hit by the need to cut back production were the river-bank industrialists, who usually rented water at a fixed price. The more they used, therefore, the cheaper it became. They always had the problem that they were forced to limit output for part of the year due to lack of water, but between 1900 and 1914 they found that often they could not work at full capacity even when water was abundant.[19]

Woollen textile industrialists also reacted glumly to the new post-colonial economic environment. They had never had much success in exporting their produce, perhaps because the climate in the American colonies was never much suited to heavy woollen fabrics, but those gains they had made were more than undone. At their high point in the 1890s, exports to the colonies represented 10 percent of total production, but by 1907 the figure had fallen to 3 percent.[20]

Yet not all Catalan industry was thrown into disarray. Textiles may have represented the most dynamic industrial sector up until the 1880s, but other industries also experienced a process of capitalist modernisation during the nineteenth century and contributed significantly to the overall process of economic growth. The food processing industry was of key economic importance and other consumer-based industries, from construction to printing and clothing, developed apace.[21] Moreover, from the 1890s a growing diversification of Catalan industry could be discerned. The textile industries were not alone in being badly hit by the loss of the Cuban market, but the return of Spaniards resident in the colonies also brought in its wake a large repatriation of capital. And this, together with the other favourable factors outlined above, combined with the growing use of poor-gas motors and electric dynamos by small-scale concerns, made it possible for the Catalan economy to grow at a moderate pace during the first decade and a half of the century. The metal industry, in particular, also benefited from the 1906 tariffs, which considerably raised import duties on imported machinery, and from the 1907

Law of National Protection, by which the state favoured Spanish companies in all public works' projects. Overall, the economic climate improved markedly between 1898 and 1902. The years between 1904 and 1909 were depressed, but economic development again accelerated from 1910.[22]

Much of the territory's industry was then given an enormous boost by the very specific factors associated with the First World War. Spain remained neutral, allowing her to export to the warring nations and substitute their products both in internal and foreign markets. The bonanza was not to last. The end of the war to an important degree saw a return to the status quo ante, as Catalan industry was faced by renewed foreign competition. There was a drastic fall in exports in 1920, followed swiftly by a contraction of the economy. It then became clear that much of the euphoria had its roots in short-term speculation rather than long-term capital investment. Nevertheless, the manufacturing sector did grow substantially, with figures elaborated by Albert Carreras indicating that industrial production in 1923 was over 37 percent higher than in 1913. This reflected the impact of the substitution of steam power by electricity, import substitution and technological innovation, accompanied by further industrial diversification. Indeed, after the post-war recession a significant recovery took place between 1922 and 1923.[23]

Industrial Structure and Factory Size: Hierarchies within Catalan Industry

The considerable heterogeneity and diversity of Catalan industry was above all evident in Barcelona itself. Table 1.2., which outlines the number of industrial workers in the city's principal industries in 1905 and 1920, serves rather to undermine the stereotypical view of the Catalan capital as dominated by King Cotton. As Spain's premier industrial centre its industry supplied the needs of much of the Spanish market, but it was also a great urban conurbation and centre of consumption, and, after Bilbao, Spain's second largest port. Its dominance of the internal Spanish market was reflected not only in the importance of textiles, but also in the weight of such industries as clothing and food processing. As a port and urban metropolis the city also had large transport and construction industries, while, outside the industrial sector, there were probably over 30,000 shop workers and clerks, about 20,000 domestic servants, and several thousand waiters and cooks.[24] The growing diversification could also be seen in the growth, between 1905 and 1920, of the number of workers in electricity generation by 338 percent, in the metal industry by 320 percent,[25] in chemicals by 230 percent, and in the construction and woodworking industries by 167 percent.

Table 1.2. Number of Industrial Workers in the Principal Barcelona Industries in 1905 and 1920[1]

Industry	1905 Number	%	1920 Number	%
Textiles	26,989	18.6		
			} 47,872	24.9
Textile finishing Trades	7,678	5.3		
Sailors, dockers and transport workers	22,327	15.4	14,317	7.4
Clothing	20,479	14.1	14,402	7.5
Construction[1]	15,229	10.5	20,727	10.8
Metal	8,943	6.2	27,131	14.1
Food Processing	8,129	5.6	7,268	3.8
Printing	7,495	5.2	8,191	4.3
Woodworking	3,858	2.7	11,116	5.8
Chemical industries	3,399	2.3	7,662	4.0
Glass and ceramics	3,069	2.1	5,112	2.7
Paper industries	2,784	1.9	3,120	1.6
Furniture trades	2,686	1.8	4,571	2.4
Leather trades	1,628	1.1	4,132	2.1
Electricity generation	1,070	0.7	4,279	2.2
Others	9,520	6.6	12,376	6.4
Total	145,283	100.1	192,276	100

Note:

1. Carpenters working on building sites have been included under construction. Given that between 1905 and 1920 the population of Barcelona increased by 148,580 it is difficult to believe that the active industrial working class grew by only 45,778. One of the problems is that the 1905 census was, in general, more accurate than any subsequent studies. It is no doubt also the case that the 1920 census missed large numbers of outworkers and labourers. In 1918 the Catalan demographer, Josep María Tallada, suggested that there could be up to 50,000 unskilled, casual workers in the city who did not appear on the census returns. See, J.M. Tallada, *Demografía de Catalunya*, 55.

Sources: 'Censo obrero de 1905', in *Anuario Estadístico de la Ciudad de Barcelona, 1905,* Barcelona, 1907, 599–606; Ministerio de Trabajo y Previsión, *Censo de población de 1920,* vol. 5, Madrid, 1929, 250–1.

Yet this should not hide the weaknesses of Catalan industry. In the first place, the limited size and instability of the Spanish market made it difficult to build large factories that sold a mass-produced standardised product. Indeed, rather than grow in size, in several branches of Catalan industry, manufacturers adopted the strategy of putting out part of their production at periods of peak demand in order not to have capital lie idle when the market contracted. Furthermore, this combination of small size, inability to mass produce and relative market inelasticity meant that in many branches of industry replacement of man by machine proceeded at a slower pace than in the major western European economies. This trend was reinforced by the individualism of the industrialists and the dearth of qualified technicians to oversee the introduction of new technologies in smaller workshops, together with the availability of a skilled and relatively cheap labour force.[26] Consequently, at the turn of the century, with the exception of some quite large concerns, throughout the economy the normal unit of production remained the family firm, whose capital formation was dependent on the reinvestment of profits, rather than the joint stock company. It was only after 1914 that the formation of joint stock companies became more common, especially in the newer branches of industrial activity, such as chemicals, the hydro-electric and incipient steel industries.[27]

This pattern was reflected in the low ratio of workers per factory. In overall terms, during the first two decades of the century the average number of industrial workers per unit of production was, according to the sources available, approximately 13.6:1 in Barcelona in 1907, and 16.7:1 in Barcelona and 13.6:1 in the rest of the province in 1923, and even these figures no doubt significantly underestimated the number of marginal workshops (see table 1.3.).

Table 1.3. Number of Industrial Workers per Unit of Production in Barcelona City and Province in 1907 and 1923[1]

	1907	1923	
	A[2]	A[2]	B[2]
Textiles and Finishing Trades	52.0	59.0	65.0
Transport and Public Services	42.1	53.8	59.9
Clothing	7.8	6.7	2.5
Construction	32.3	19.4	10.0
Metal	7.7	14.2	6.2
Food Industry	7.5	4.9	2.0
Printing	14.9	12.8	5.2
Furniture trades	7.4	n/a	n/a
Paper and Chemicals	16.3	15.9	16.5
Woodworking[3]	4.3	4.9	2.7
Glass and ceramics	13.2	56.3	19.2
Leather trades	5.3	8.0	11.2
Others	13.6	4.1	9.3
Totals	13.6	16.7	13.6

Notes:
1. Figures for 1907 have been elaborated by dividing data for the number of units of production indicated in the 1907 *Memoria* by the 1905 AECB census of the number of workers. It should be stressed that they offer only a very rough guide. Thus, for example, while the figures for 1907 refer to units of production those of 1923 give us the number of employers. Moreover, it may well be the case that the greater numbers of workers per employer in the 1923 figures has more to do with an underestimation of the total number of workers in the city than with any growth in factory size.
2. A refers to Barcelona city (for 1923, 'Barcelona First Zone'), B to the rest of Barcelona province.
3. The 1923 figures include the usage of cork.

Sources: 'Censo obrero de 1905', in *Anuario Estadístico de la Ciudad de Barcelona, 1905*, Barcelona, 1907, 599–606; Ministerio de Fomento, *Memoria acerca del estado de la industria en la provincia de Barcelona en el año 1907*, Madrid, 1910, p. viii; Ministerio de Trabajo, Comercio e Industria, Dirección General de Estadística, *Anuario Estadístico de España*, año IX, *1922–23*, Madrid, 1924, 342–3.

Such estimates should, however, be treated with caution. They do not indicate that most of Barcelona and Catalan industry was lilliputian in scale and technologically stagnant. They are averages, and the industrial structure was subject to a clear hierarchy. A capitalist sector had grown up with, at its apex, powerful families running a number of relatively large companies. Below this level were to be found a large group of medium-sized concerns. They proliferated most in Barcelona, where there were several hundred work-shops employing between about thirty and sixty workers. The syndicalist, Emili Salut, in his evocation of the early twentieth-century Fifth District in the centre of Barcelona, describes them as being like prisons or barracks, with iron bars on the windows.[28] These enterprises were very much integrated into the system of capitalist manufacture, using small steam engines, poor-gas motors or dynamos to power machinery in at least part of the production process. Yet further down the manufacturing tree were to be found a plethora of small-scale employers, who worked alone or with an assistant or two, and either provided a specialist service or simply engaged in repair work.

Each industry and each sub-sector was of course different. Enterprises in transport, textiles and chemicals tended to be big by Catalan standards. In the first case this was down to the presence of the railway and tram companies. In textiles I have stressed the growth of a factory-based industry and in the city itself there were no marginal concerns. Yet even here specialisation had not gone as far as in Britain, with Catalan spinning factories producing a broader range of thread counts.[29] Average factory size was also much smaller. In Barcelona at the turn of the century several relatively large factories with between 500 and 1,500 workers stand out, the largest of which were La España Industrial in the neighbourhood of Sants; Fabra i Coats, which had two factories close by in El Clot and Sant Andreu (along with a industrial work town in Torelló); Sert Germans, which spun and wove textile 'mixes' in El Clot; Godó Germans, which spun jute in Poble Nou; and Caralt i Cia, based in L'Hospitalet, which specialised in hemp. On the Llobregat and Ter river banks relatively large factories also emerged. The largest were on the Llobregat where Colònia Sedó had nearly 2,000 workers between 1900 and 1910, followed by the Güell and Rosal company towns with around 1,000. Yet, their development was also stymied by the small volume of water in Catalan rivers.[30]

Below the level of these enterprises was to be found a large number of weaving establishments in both Barcelona and the medium-sized industrial towns, which employed between 25 and 250 workers. Finally, in smaller towns and villages there were lots of diminutive workshops, some of which still employed hand-loom weavers. These different levels of industrial activity were not independent. Textiles was a prime example of how in Catalonia industrialists reacted to the nature of the Spanish market by putting out part of their work to smaller subordinate enterprises in order to limit risk. This was very clearly the case in the Sabadell woollen textile industry. The use of steam power required important capital outlays, and a number of steam-powered factories (*vapors*) were built during the nineteenth century. However, in order to save costs more than one industrialist often shared the same premises.

Moreover, it was common for industrialists to rent out unused rooms to independent weavers known as *drepaires*. The idea behind the arrangement was to meet peak demand, but not to have to invest in equipment which would lie idle for much of the time.[31] As cotton textile manufacturers had a broader market they never had to go so far, but when trade was brisk weaving establishments in Barcelona and the larger textile towns subcontracted work out to dependent weaving workshops generally located in smaller towns within the major textile producing areas. In addition, looms were rented out by the factories to petty manufacturers, who then employed peasant women (who combined factory labour with agricultural work) in small workshops.[32]

This further exacerbated the atomisation of the industry. According to statistics collected by the Catalan industrialists themselves, in 1919 the average factory-worker ratio in Catalan cotton textiles was 1:87 with an average of 73 workers per weaving shop and 130 per spinning factory, and these statistics seem not to have taken into account the small-town marginal workshops.[33] And, in the first decade of the century, while the average English spinning factory had between 60 and 80,000 spindles its Catalan equivalent had less than 6,000. The drawbacks were summed up by a commission of leading industrialists, who stated in 1906: 'A greater industrial concentration is necessary. Small factories are expensive and uneconomic because they have to distribute general costs over small production runs, and because of the greater costs of production.'[34]

Similar hierarchies could be seen in other sectors of the economy. Like much of textiles the chemicals industry required relatively heavy capital outlays. Thus in Barcelona during the first decade of the century there were over a dozen large factories producing heavy chemicals, a couple of large soap factories, and below this level large numbers of industrial workshops engaged in the manufacture of such products as fertilisers, perfumes and paints. In other industries, unit size varied even more. In food processing during the same period Barcelona had over 650 bakers' shops and nearly 200 patisseries, but an important factory-based industry had grown up in the distillation of spirits and manufacture of beer, sweets, biscuits and chocolates, pastas, and in flour milling.[35]

In the metal industry there were also a number of relatively large factories, which employed between about 500 and 1,000 workers, of which the names of La Maquinista, Alexandre Germans, El Vulcano, and Societat Material per a Construccions i Ferrocarrils (Fundició Girona) in the Barceloneta and Poble Nou neighbourhoods (close to the port and train station) stand out. But well over 50 percent of the workforce was employed in plants of about forty to sixty workers each. On the margins of the industry were to be found a sea of tiny concerns. Of the 1,000 metalworking establishments which operated in Barcelona, 600 consisted of locksmiths, tinsmiths, plumbers and blacksmiths, who largely worked alone or with a worker and apprentice or two. In comparative terms the industry's inability to take advantage of economies of scale was particularly acute. As the economist, José Playá, pointed out, 'the machine-building firms can rarely specialise owing to the lack of a market', and consequently, 'to survive it is absolutely necessary that they undertake a wide variety of tasks, producing in each case only a limited number of copies'. This could be seen in La Maquinista, which received such a varied demand for castings that for each order it had to make a new mould. Moreover, a technological time lag with the major European producers was also apparent. In La Maquinista, for example, management recognised in 1910 that the factory's machine tools were obsolescent, but no action was taken until the years 1917 to 1923.[36]

The importance of medium-sized enterprises could also be seen on the city's building sites. The second half of the nineteenth century had seen the rise of the figure of the contractor, who put together all the elements required in the building process. The most important of these was Foment d'Obres i Construccions (FOCSA), which was formed in 1900 and subsequently grew rapidly on the back of local authority and state contracts. Many building sites, if one adds the bricklayers and their labourers to workers in the trades subcontracted, could easily employ above forty workers. But there were also large numbers of independent master builders, stonecutters, painters, and carpenters 'dedicated to repairs' and 'botched jobs'.[37]

The clothing industry was also fully integrated into the capitalist economy and like textiles could mass produce a relatively cheap product. This meant that there were strong similarities with the industrial structure of the major European powers. The manufacture of suits and shoes took place partly in workshops, but was to an increasing extent put out to home workers. This growth in putting out was even more pronounced in the production of underwear, bedlinen, shirts and the like. There were several factories – the largest of which was L'Aguila, which employed 300 workers in 1916, and which also set up a chain of shops throughout Spain – which undertook key parts of the production process but put out most of the work. This practice was made possible by the development of the sewing machine, and had the great advantage that manufacturers did not have to maintain expensive fixed capital in an industry which was seasonal.[38]

In Barcelona medium-sized mechanically-powered workshops extended beyond the major branches of industry thus far considered to take in a whole range of trades, from the manufacture of confetti and artificial flowers to cardboard boxes. One area in which an extreme division did, however, remain was that of commerce. In Catalonia, unlike in Britain and France, larger department stores had hardly made their appearance. In the first decade of the century in Barcelona there were two or three such stores along with several important wine and spirits merchants, but they were surrounded by a sea of diminutive concerns. As late as 1922 the average number of workers per commercial enterprise was only just over two.[39]

Outside the Catalan capital the situation was somewhat different. In the medium-sized industrial towns textiles was frequently complemented by a significant metal industry and a whole host of smaller trades. Areas on occasion specialised in a particular product and in some cases production was mechanised. For example, the large cork-producing industry, centred on the Empordà on the northern Catalan coast, was slowly mechanised from the turn of the century. Some large industries extracted raw materials from the locality. An example is cement manufacture in Sant Joan de les Abadesses. From the turn of the century several large factories were established in well-connected areas outside Barcelona because of the cheapness of the land. This could be seen in the rapidly expanding electricity industry, with a large Pirelli factory located in Vilanova i la Geltrú. Water power also provided opportunities for industrial development. The cotton textile industry has already been dealt with, but much of the paper industry, concentrated on the Anoia and Llobregat rivers to the east of Barcelona, also used water power. Yet these factories were the exception. Outside the major towns were to be found thousands of builders, locksmiths and blacksmiths, who often plied their trade in tandem with work in the fields.[40]

The Labour Process

Despite the small scale of plant and the technological time lag in some sectors of industry, as elsewhere, attempts by industrialists to restructure the labour process, impose more direct control on the shop floor, and reduce costs, were very much a feature of Catalan industry. This would profoundly affect divisions of labour and, as we shall see in the following chapter, have a key impact on the development of labour organisation and culture.

The most radical transformations probably took place within cotton textiles, for which, given the existence of a number of local studies, we can give a relatively full picture. In the nineteenth century there were two key moments in which technological renewal was accompanied by a wide-ranging recasting of the labour process. When the industry mechanised between the 1780s and 1870s the introduction of mule jennies in spinning and then power looms in weaving, combined with the consolidation of a factory-based system, was accompanied by the construction of sexual divisions of labour which to an important degree gave men primacy in the production process. They worked as foremen, undertook the more highly skilled and well-paid tasks of spinning and finishing the cloth (stamping, dying and bleaching), and monopolised auxiliary posts (carpenters, electricians and the like). In areas in which work on the land, which men preferred, was scarce, they also took on the less well remunerated task of power-loom weaving. Meanwhile, the worst paid jobs, which were concentrated in the processes preparatory to spinning and weaving, were reserved for women. Power-loom weavers and spinners also often took on a supervisory role, employing assistants who would one day become weavers and spinners themselves. Hence they built up informal systems of apprenticeship, acting in many respects like skilled journeymen. Most power was given to the spinners, who paid the assistants – young lads known as piecers – out of their own wages.

This division of labour was congenial to male workers, who while recognising that it was necessary for their wives and daughters to engage in paid labour, viewed this as supplementary to rearing the children and undertaking household chores. This is a subject which I shall discuss at more length in the next chapter. For industrialists the divisions of labour adopted also provided stability and, no doubt, chimed with middle-class conceptions of the man as the bread winner. But they were also relatively expensive and compromised the industrialists' control over their labour force. Male workers used systems of apprenticeship to control both entry to the trade and also to ensure the employment of members of their own families. They enjoyed considerable autonomy of the factory floor, expected respect, and disciplined and even sacked assistants when they deemed it necessary. Male spinners in particular became a highly-paid elite, who, in the late nineteenth and early twentieth centuries, earned an average of 40 percent more than the male weavers.[41]

As a result, industrialists became increasingly critical. For example, Josep Ferrer Vidal complained in the 1870s that the industry could not compete with foreign producers because despite low nominal wages labour productivity was much lower than abroad. The solution, he maintained, would be to intensify production and employ lower-paid women, subjecting them to more detailed supervision by foremen and overseers.[42] Already in 1854 in the spinning branch of the industry, in Barcelona, when self-acting mules began to replace the mule jennies – which were more physically strenuous – industrialists pushed for women to take over. They defeated a strike in the industry but in subsequent years, for reasons yet to be studied, did not push home their advantage. In Barcelona and its surrounds in the early 1880s the only factory to use female spinners – on some small self-acting mules it had – was La España Industrial.[43]

The issue again came to the fore in the 1880s when, on the one hand, the growth in river-bank factories led to increasing competition in the industry, and, on the other, the economy was hit by a deep economic recession. In spinning, in order to intensify production industrialists attempted to increase the number of machines minded by spinners from one to two ('Trabajo a la inglesa' or the 'English-style system' as they called it) and to recast the labour process through the introduction of the ring frame, which was developed in the United States during the 1870s. A much smaller and less imposing machine than the mule, it was more productive at lower thread counts and required little skill. This made it especially attractive to Catalan manufacturers given that they tended to specialise in the production of relatively low counts of thread. Furthermore, industrialists and their representatives argued that, given 'the simplicity of its mechanism and the economy of its use', it allowed 'with all the more reason than on the self-acting mule the employment of women and girls'.[44]

Thereafter, over the next two decades, first in Barcelona and then in much of the Muntanya, employers combined the introduction of the ring frame with the employment of women as spinners. At the same time, these women lost the men's right to subcontract piecers and were much more closely supervised. By 1907 60 percent of the industry's spindles were ring-frame, the highest percentage in any European country with the exception of Italy. By 1929 it had reached almost 80 percent.[45] In this sector the relatively inexpensive nature of the machinery and the breadth of the market meant that despite small factory size manufacturers had kept abreast of technological modernisation.

On the weaving side of the industry there were no such spectacular technological developments, but the changes which did take place were no less significant. In response to the 1880s crisis, industrialists began substituting men for women on the power looms, with the result that by the first decade of the century in most industrial centres men were only working on the largest of power looms and on jacquard looms. Weavers in Barcelona were also adamant that from this period there was constant downward pressure on wages.[46] As in the case of spinning, this substitution also allowed employers more direct control over the workforce, for instead of truculent men who regarded themselves as journeymen, they found it easier to impose a closer and more direct supervision over the female labour force. Furthermore, employer attempts to cut wages by lengthening the pieces woven, and to raise productivity by increasing the number of power-looms each weaver had to mind from two or three to four (an approach which, as in spinning, was defended by industrialists because it was the system that operated in Britain), were a source of constant tension in the industry.

The overall impact on male employment in the industry was significant. In 1856 in his detailed study the Catalan architect, Ildefons Cerdà, indicated that in cotton textiles, excluding the finishing trades, 30 percent of workers were men (as against 43 percent women and 27 percent children).[47] All the indications are that the percentage of male workers increased over the next two decades. However, the tide turned from the mid-1880s. By 1905, according to a census prepared by the local authorities, men made up only 19 percent of the industry in the city. Similarly, figures in 1923 (again excluding the finishing trades, which remained in the hands of skilled, male workers) indicated 23 percent of all textile workers in Barcelona were men. In a similar vein, evidence from other industrial towns in which weaving predominated also suggests that men formed under 20 percent of the labour force.[48]

Technological modernisation and the reorganisation of work structures was by no means limited to cotton textiles but could be seen across much of Catalan industry. For example, a dramatic transformation in working practices took place on the port of Barcelona, which underwent a comprehensive modernisation programme in the early-twentieth century. One of the main results was the greater use of steam-powered loading and unloading equipment, and the construction of new wharfs which allowed ships to dock sideways and thereby did away with the need for lighter boats. This not only increased productivity, but also made it possible for employers to bear down on labour costs by greatly cutting the demand for coal unloaders.[49]

No less profound if less spectacular changes were occurring within a whole host of trades in the more important urban centres. Frequently, these focused on what historians have referred to as artisanal trades, in which workers undertook a formal apprenticeship before becoming journeymen (*fadrins* in Catalan). Until the early-nineteenth century these trades had been overseen by the guilds, with, typically, a whole series of regulations in place in order to limit entry into the trade and ensure the quality of the final product. The archetypal artisanal worker enjoyed a high degree of autonomy on the shop floor and had some control over the pace of work and over the tasks undertaken by the apprentices. This mentality could still be seen in operation in late nineteenth and early twentieth-century Catalonia. In Barcelona industrialists complained that the lack of discipline by men, who sang and smoked at work, was hampering productivity. In Sabadell the anarchist 'rationalist teacher', Albà Rosell, recalled that when he was aged ten in 1891, he began work as an assistant to his brother and uncle in a woollen weaving shed, and that they often went for a chat or to the local café and left him weaving.[50]

Very little work has been done on the labour process within the craft trades and so one must be cautious. It is impossible for one person to carry out an exhaustive study of the myriad branches of Barcelona industry. Nevertheless, a twofold process appears to have taken place. On the one hand, as in other western European countries, industrial expansion actually led to an increase in the absolute number of journeymen.[51] On the other, in the face of increased competition, and in order to cut costs and expand market share, within the more capitalist sector of the economy, industrialists undertook a whole series of reforms which were leading to the erosion of the position of the journeymen on the shop floor. To be sure this was not a unilinear process. Industrialisation threw up new skills and provided new opportunities for workers. Nevertheless, by the 1900s, in a whole series of trades, manufacturers were looking to reduce the autonomy of skilled workers within the labour process by such means as introducing more detailed divisions of labour, attempting to wrest control of apprentices out of their hands, increasing supervision at the point of production, introducing piece rates and adopting new technological advances where feasible. This was commented on in 1897 by the labour publication, the *Revista del Ateneo Obrero de Barcelona*, which noted with alarm:[52]

> For thirty years the fatal consequences of the present industrial regime have been felt. The division of labour, on the one hand, which transforms the worker into a simple machine destined to do only part of the work of his trade, and the excessive number of apprentices on the other, are a real danger for the future of our industry.
>
> When a master pays an apprentice he thinks that he has the right to employ him on all sorts of tasks, and makes little effort to teach him the trade. The result is that the majority of apprentices will inevitably add to the number of vagrants or have to apply for jobs which do not require any particular skill, like those of sweepers, porters, carriers, and others.

On occasion, as in the case of cotton textiles, there were threats to break the position of skilled men and replace them with semi-skilled workers who could quickly be trained on the job, or by women or children. However, in comparison with the major western powers the slow pace of technological change meant that divisions of labour were not usually totally recast by the introduction of semi-automatic and automatic machine tools and the employment of large numbers of semi-skilled workers operating within a factory setting. The result would be important for our understanding of the Catalan working class and labour movement. What some historians have referred to as the 'artisanal phase' of the labour movement was extended well into the twentieth century, with problems faced by journeymen workers remaining a key issue in labour relations.[53]

As might be expected, as in the case of industrial structure, each industry was rather different. In some sectors an elite 'aristocracy of labour' could survive. This was the case of workers such as hatters, glove makers, goldsmiths and silversmiths. Other groups of workers did not maintain such a privileged position, but faced no concerted attempt by employers to redivide the labour process in their favour. This was, for example, the case of the glassworkers up until 1914. The average glassworks was considerably larger than that of most workshops, with two large bottlemaking plants, in Badalona and Poble Nou, employing about 700 workers between them in 1907. By this time the larger factories had installed Seimens furnaces, which produced a continuous supply of molten glass, and employed a large number of unskilled labourers. It was also, according to the factory inspectors, the industry which most regularly flouted the laws relating to the use of female and child labour.[54]

Yet at the heart of these capitalist enterprises was to be found an artisanal work team or *placa*. The strength of this team on the shop floor rested on the inability of the employers to mechanise production. Thus a report noted in 1916 that in the glassmaking factory of Joan Girall Laporte in Cornellà, 'from the fusion of the igneous mass ... through to the packaging, a long and complicated series of processes are carried out in which the hand of the worker is of primary importance. This is unlike most industries, in which the machine is the principal factor'. At the centre of the bottlemaking team was the glassblower who had to combine great skill with physical stamina. Blowing the glass 'requires a special skill and certain operations can only be learnt by youngsters of fourteen to sixteen years of age after eight to ten years of practice'. Glassblowers were thereby in a strong position drastically to limit entry into the trade, and this they did by 'not teaching nor tolerating that anyone outside their own family should be taught the profession'.[55] Yet their status would by no means be maintained indefinitely. During the First World War, in the face of 'the rise in the price of raw materials' and 'continuous strikes and wage rises' new glassblowing machinery was introduced throughout the industry, thereby making the glassblowers' skills redundant.[56]

Another group of workers which could to a certain extent be considered in a similar position were Barcelona's 400 coopers. Within Catalonia important nuclei of coopers were to be found in Poble Nou and in the towns around Reus, Tarragona, and Vilafranca del Penadés. From the 1880s they had, in fact, encountered considerable difficulties. They faced two basic problems. The first derived from the import of second hand casks through the port of Tarragona, which led to unemployment in the region. The second was a result of the severe competition coopers faced from a large number of tiny workshops which operated in rural areas around the town of Vilafranca. Employers in these workshops took on journeymen for part of the year on very low rates, surviving the rest of the time through self-exploitation. Merchant capitalists who bought the final product nevertheless encouraged them to remain in business.[57]

The Sant Martí coopers put pressure on the Barcelona merchants not to buy these cheap casks. In this they appear to have had considerable success. The coopers maintained a strict apprenticeship system, remaining a 'group apart', who 'passed on the trade from father to son and only slowly admitted new faces into their union'. As a result, it seems that they enjoyed the best working conditions in Spain. From the late-nineteenth century onwards they were faced by another concern, when news came from abroad that machinery had been developed to assist in the making of the casks. The Spanish coopers' federation stated that the introduction of any such machinery would be a 'terrible blow to our trade' and, at least until the years of the First World War, worker opposition seems to have ensured that the new technology was kept at bay.[58]

However, in a number of key industries, capitalist transformations, which were greatly to impact on workers' lives, were, from the nineteenth century, readily apparent. This was the case in the construction industry. Within this industry some groups of workers retained a relatively privileged position. This was the case of the plasterers, wallpaperers and, to an extent, marblers and brickmakers. In the second decade of the century, for example, plasterers worked only a seven-hour day and regulated apprenticeship extremely tightly.[59] Yet these formed only a small minority of workers in the industry. In most trades the transformation of the industry from the mid-nineteenth century had fundamentally changed the way they worked. Until this date the industry had been run by master builders, but they were thereafter increasingly replaced by the figure of the contractor. The old master builders had, on being employed, contracted workers from the various specialities (bricklayers, carpenters, painters and the like), and then charged for the job once the work was complete. However, the contractors competed for building contracts by attempting to put in the lowest bid before commencing the work, and then employed the bricklayers and bricklayers' labourers directly, and, at the same time, subcontracted work out to the other trades in the industry.

As a result the contractor had a vested interest in driving down costs, and trades so subcontracted lost their autonomy and were drawn into fierce competition for work. This was reflected in the proliferation of piece rates in the sector. In addition, the need to control costs led contractors to tighten their supervision of the workforce, and to employ large numbers of labourers to undertake the heavier, unskilled, tasks. This was combined with attempts to increase the quantity of cheap apprentice labour and employ apprentices on more complex work as quickly as possible. In carpentry, moreover, the introduction of mechanical saws led to rapid increases in productivity and, the carpenters claimed, to unemployment.[60]

In printing, at the turn of the century compositors also complained at the growing number of apprentices, who, as the division of labour was extended, after a year or two undertook tasks which the journeymen felt should be reserved for them. Furthermore, the journeyman bookbinders railed at the extensive employment of women in the trade. Most serious of all, in the late nineteenth century the position of the hand compositors appeared to be in grave danger as in Europe a technological revolution hit the industry. In the

1880s, two new type-setting machines, the linotype and monotype, were developed in the United States. They were rapidly introduced into newspaper and book printing in Britain in the following decade.[61] These machines allowed massive gains in productivity, and could, at least theoretically, be operated by workers after only a limited period of training. Again in Catalonia there was a time lag, but, from the middle of the first decade of the new century, newspaper offices and large book publishers began to deploy them.[62]

The situation in the metal industry was in some respects similar. This may at first sight seem surprising. Throughout Europe the industry evolved out of artisan-dominated workshops, but in both France and Germany, with the introduction of semi-automatic and automatic machine tools, artisanal workers were, to an important degree, replaced by semi-skilled workers, who undertook a short period of training on the job.[63] In Barcelona this also seems to have occurred in the large, new plants which manufactured electrical equipment, where a detailed division of labour operated. However, in the key areas of machine-building and repair work apprenticeship systems remained in place, with the new apprentices trained either by journeymen or by foremen (*mestres de taller*). Their survival was based on the lack of specialisation and up-to-date machinery, with workers having to turn their hand to a wide variety of tasks. Employers complained that such systems failed to produce a technically competent workforce, while workers accused the employers of diluting the journeymen's controls over apprenticeship in order to reduce costs. A good example of the latter is provided by the mechanics of Sabadell, at the turn of the century, who came out on strike because apprentices, who lived with their employers, were being brought in from rural areas. They were very low paid, their apprenticeship was stretched out from three to four years, and they did work that the journeymen considered to be their preserve. In addition, the journeymen rejected the use of *anyals*, who were employed on low wages for a trial period of one year after having completed their apprenticeship.[64]

Nevertheless, it was the journeymen tailors and shoemakers who found themselves in the most desperate predicament. Here, because mass production was possible, Catalan manufacturers were, like their European counterparts, able to a large extent to undermine the position of the skilled male workers. In the first case, the key factor was the invention of the sewing machine, which allowed industrialists to replace tailors by female workers, who were employed from home in the expanding standardised sector of the industry, while at the same time they moved to impose piece rates on the bespoke tailors.[65] In shoemaking, men were employed as cutters and fitters in the workshops, but women were also taken on, either at home or in the factory, to sew on the soles and polish the shoes. In addition, work was also put out to a large number of male shoemakers. They were particularly badly paid and, therefore, proved a serious competitive threat to the factory-based workers. Finally, from the end of the nineteenth century new mechanised workshops were set up under U.S. patent using new sewing, nailing and fitting machinery, thereby making the skills of the fitter redundant.[66]

Conclusions

The industrialisation process in Catalonia was, therefore, marked by a number of quite specific features. It was dominated by textiles, but this was not incompatible with considerable industrial diversity, particularly marked in Barcelona itself. In addition, the early-twentieth century was also to see a slow process of diversification. Catalan industry was uncompetitive in western European terms, and this had prompted – in alliance with the grain producers of central Spain and iron and steel manufacturers in the Basque Country – a retreat behind protective tariffs. One of the most important consequences was the resultant high internal prices of both basic foodstuffs and manufactures. Moreover, it was relatively small-scale, and in some areas a clear technological time lag could be discerned in comparison with the major western economies. Yet this did not prevent manufacturers from redividing the labour process and introducing new machinery, spurred on by fierce competition within the Spanish market and, in some areas, from abroad. As a result, a complex industrial hierarchy was evident, manifested in the juxtaposition of a capitalist sector with the continuance of petty manufacture. It was the construction of this hierarchy that was at the heart of the paradox of Catalan industrialisation. While at the bottom of the industrial ladder manufacturers were self-employed or at best had an assistant or two, at the same time, capitalist enterprises were springing up and great fortunes being created. It is to the ways in which workers, employers and the state tried to cope with this new world that the following chapters will turn.

Notes

1. Vicente Pérez Moredo, 'La modernización demográfica, 1800–1930', 57.
2. Calculated from, *Nomenclatura de España, 1900,* and *Nomenclatura de las ciudades, villas, lugares, aldeas y demás entidades de la población de España formado por la dirección general de estadística con referencia al 31 de diciembre de 1920,* vol. 1.
3. The term is, for example, used by Havelock Ellis, *The Soul of Spain,* 273.
4. On urban and industrial structure see also, Enriqueta Camps, *La formación del mercado de trabajo en la Cataluña del siglo XIX,* 28–44.
5. Pere Gabriel, 'La població obrera catalana, una població obrera industrial?'.
6. Administratively Catalonia had been divided into four provinces. The *comarques* are smaller units, linked geographically and, or, economically. During the period of this study they had no specific administrative function but attracted strong local loyalties.
7. Jordi Nadal, 'La formació de la indústria moderna', 55–6 and 70; Jordi Nadal and Xavier Tafunell, *Sant Martí de Provencals,* 28–82; Josep María Benaul, 'La industria tèxtil llanera a Catalunya, 1780–1870'.
8. Alberto del Castillo, *La Maquinista Terrestre y Marítima, personaje histórico, 1855–1955;* Jordi Nadal, 'La metalúrgia'.
9. For the Llobregat, see Josep Oliveras Samitier, *Desenvolupament industrial i formació urbana a Manresa, 1800–1870;* and Gràcia Dorel-Ferré, *Les colònies industrials a*

Catalunya; for the Ter, Joaquim Albareda i Salvadó, *La industrialització a la plana de Vic, 1770–1875*.

10. Instituto de Reformas Sociales, *La jornada de trabajo en la industria textil*, 180.

11. Albert Carreras, 'El aprovechamiento de la energía hidráulica en Cataluña'; Dorel-Ferré, *Colònies industrials*, 57–113.

12. For an overview of the debate see Joseph Harrison, 'The Agrarian History of Spain, 1800–1960'.

13. Ramon Garrabou, 'La crisi agrària espanyola de finals del segle XIX: una etapa del desenvolupament del capitalisme'.

14. Gabriel Tortella, 'Producción y productividad agraria, 1830–1930', 67–73; Jordi Nadal, 'Un siglo de industrialización española, 1833–1930', 93–5; James Simpson, *Spanish Agriculture: The Long Siesta, 1765–1965*.

15. José María Serrano Sanz, *El viraje proteccionista en la Restauración*, 96–7 and 160–2.

16. Serrano Sanz, *Viraje Proteccionista*, 164–214; José Luis García Delgado, 'Nacionalismo económico e intervención estatal, 1900–1930', 184–5.

17. Carles Sudrià, 'La exportación en el desarrollo de la industria algodonera española, 1875–1920'.

18. There are a number of contemporary accounts by figures in the business associations: Guillermo Graell, 'La industria catalana'; Joaquín Aguilera, 'Solución a la crisis', and 'La crisis de la industria algodonera'; Eusebio Bertrand i Serra, 'Un estudio sobre la industria algodonera'. See also, R.J. Harrison, 'The Spanish Famine of 1904–1906'; R.J. Harrison, 'Catalan Business and the Loss of Cuba'; Joaquín Romero Maura, *La Rosa del Fuego*, 157–8, 220–1 and 465–6.

19. *El Trabajo Nacional* (hereafter, ETN), 1 July 1904, 16 July 1909; Instituto de Reformas Sociales, *Jornada*, 49–50. This also explains why night work was so common in areas in which water power was used.

20. Esteve Deu i Baigual, 'La indústria llanera de Sabadell en el primer quart del segle XX', 6.69–6.72.

21. Jordi Nadal, 'La industria fabril española en 1900: una aproximación'.

22. Edouard Escarra, *El desarrollo industrial de Cataluña, 1900–1908*, 122–8; Castillo, *Maquinista*, 320–4; *Anuari d'Estadística Social de Catalunya* (hereafter AESC), *1912*, 152–6.

23. Albert Carreras, 'La producción industrial catalana y vasca, 1844–1935', 201–2. On the impact of the war see also Chapter Seven, 225–6.

24. 'Censo obrero de 1905', 599–632; Ministerio de Instrucción Pública y Bellas Artes, *Censo de población, 1900*, vol. 3, 124–5.

25. This was no doubt an exaggeration brought about by an underestimation in the 1905 figures. The Catalan economist, Federico Rahola y Trémols, calculated that there were 12,000 metalworkers in the city in 1907: see Federico Rahola y Trémols, 'Del comerç y de la industria de Catalunya', 426.

26. Escarra, *Desarrollo industrial*, 68–74; Rahola y Trémols, 'Del comerç', 365 and 396; Instituto de Reformas Sociales, *Jornada*, 431–2.

27. Pedro Casals, 'El crecimiento de las sociedades anónimas'.

28. Emili Salut, *Vivers de revolucionaris*, 96.

29. Instituto de Reformas Sociales, *Jornada*, 48.

30. Data for Barcelona is taken from *La Publicidad* (hereafter, LP) during a big strike in 1913. For the Llobregat, see Dorel-Ferré, *Colònies industrials*, 91.

31. Deu i Baigual, 'La indústria llanera de Sabadell', 3.17–3.106.

32. On this structure see Instituto de Reformas Sociales, *Jornada*, 421–37; Ministerio de Fomento, *Memoria acerca del estado de la industria en la provincia de Barcelona en el año 1907*, 188–96; Rahola y Trémols, 'Del comerç', 399.

33. Calculated from, Cámara Oficial de Industria de Barcelona, *Memoria reglamentaria del año 1919*, 137–63.

34. ETN, 16 May 1911; Federación Internacional de Industrias Algodoneras, *Memoria del congreso celebrado en Bremen los días 25 al 29 de julio de 1906*, 195 and 199–200.

35. Ministerio de Fomento, *Memoria*, 1–32 and 161–82; Nadal and Tafunell, *Sant Martí*, 83–100.

36. Nadal and Tafunell, *Sant Martí*, 133–5 and 144–6; José Playá, *Estado y estadística de las industrias mecánicas y eléctricas en la provincia de Barcelona*, 17–21 and 56–9; Castillo, *La Maquinista*, 355–6.

37. Soledad Bengoechea, *Organització patronal i conflictivitat social a Catalunya*, 5–10; Ministerio de Fomento, *Memoria*, 74–82; Rahola y Trémols, 'Del comerç', 341.

38. Ministerio de Fomento, *Memoria*, 229–49; Albert Balcells, 'La mujer obrera en la industria catalana durante el primer cuarto del siglo XX'; *Solidaridad Obrera* (hereafter, SO), 26 Aug. 1916.

39. Escarra, *Desarrollo industrial*, 44–7; Ministerio de Fomento, *Memoria*, 679; Ministerio de Trabajo, Comercio e Industria, *Anuario Estadístico de España, año IX, 1922–23*, 342–3.

40. The best overviews are to be found in the Ministerio de Fomento, *Memoria*, and Rahola y Trémols, 'Del comerç'. On the Empordà cork industry see Hermoso Plaja, 'Mis memorias', 1–3; Escarra, *Desarrollo industrial*, 67; and Cámara Oficial de Industria de Barcelona, *Memoria reglamentaria*, 263. Data on the paper industry can be found in *Memoria reglamentaria*, 251.

41. I have dealt with the period 1820 to 1885 in more depth in my article, 'Industria, oficio y género en la industria textil Catalana, 1833–1923'.

42. Josep Ferrer Vidal, 'La indústria tèxtil d'ahir', 3–5. Ferrer Vidal stated that Catalonia employed 11.93 workers per 1,000 spindles compared to only 3.29 in England. It should, however, be noted that Catalan spinning machines were on average much smaller than their British counterparts, that thread counts in Catalan factories were in general lower and therefore the thread broke more easily, that machines were often old and that there was often a lack of technical expertise. Hence, the same level of productivity as in England would require a higher intensity of labour.

43. Carles Enrech, 'El Llano contra la Montaña', 515.

44. ETN, 1 May 1912, 89–92.

45. Rahola y Trémols, 'Del comerç', 397; Lucas Flórez Beltrán, *La industria algodonera española*, 93.

46. *El Socialista* (hereafter, ES), 27 Jan., 3 Feb. 1899; Instituto de Reformas Sociales, *Jornada*, 59. In Barcelona wage rates declined from around 3.5 pesetas a day in 1873 to 3.16 in 1905: see, Miguel Izard, 'Entre la Impotencia y la Esperanza', 31; 'Censo obrero de 1905', 618.

47. Ildefonso Cerdá, 'Monografía estadística de la clase obrera en Barcelona en 1856'.

48. 'Censo obrero de 1905', 599; Ministerio de Trabajo, Comercio e Industria, *Anuario Estadístico, 1922–23*, 342; Instituto de Reformas Sociales, *Jornada*, 43, 53–4 and 453–9.

49. ETN, 30 March 1903; *La Ilustración Obrera*, 27 Aug. 1904; *Anuario Estadístico de la Ciudad de Barcelona, 1907*, 541–51.

50. Miguel Sastre y Sanna, *Las huelgas en Barcelona y sus resultados durante los años 1910 al 1914 ambos inclusive*, 36; Albano Rosell, '*Recuerdos de educador*', 41. I would like to thank Pere Solà for allowing me to consult this work.

51. For the European context, see Dick Geary, *European Labour Protest, 1849–1939*, 19.

52. *Revista del Ateneo Obrero de Barcelona*, Feb. 1897.

53. See, for example, Roger Magraw, *A History of the French Working Class*, vol. 2, *Workers and the Bourgeois Republic*, 3–20. Magraw argues that in the French case, by the end of the nineteenth century the skilled-apprenticed sector was entering a definitive crisis.

54. Rahola y Trémols, 'Del comerç', 432–5; *La Ilustración Obrera*, 25 May 1905; Instituto de Reformas Sociales, *Memoria de la inspección del trabajo correspondiente al año 1910*, 67.

55. *La Hormiga de Oro. Ilustración Católica*, 1 April 1916; ETN, 30 May 1895.

56. The use of glassblowing machinery was first reported in 1904, but its use did not become generalised until after 1914: see, ETN, 1 May 1904; Manuel María Balaguer, 'La industria química', 115. In her study of the Resseguier bottlemaking factory in Carmaux, France, Joan W. Scott states that the position of the skilled glassblowers was undermined at the beginning of the twentieth century: see Joan W. Scott, *The Glassworkers of Carmaux*. This

backs my assertion that the 'artisanal phase' of labour organisation lasted longer in Catalonia.

57. *El Eco de los Toneleros*, 30 Oct. 1887; Federación de Oficiales Toneleros de la Región Española, *Actas del 15 congreso celebrado en Sans los días 9 al 18 de mayo de 1887*, 111.

58. Alfredo Bueso, *Recuerdos de un cenetista*, 26; Miguel Sastre y Sanna, *Los huelgas en Barcelona y sus resultados durante el año 1905*, 20–33; Federación de Oficiales Toneleros de la Región Española, *Actas de la conferencia verificada en San Martín de Provensals los días 26, 27 y 28 de enero y del congreso XXII celebrado en la misma localidad los días 9 al 16 de abril de 1894*, 22–3; SO, 9 May 1909; Rahola y Trémols, 'Del comerç', 436.

59. Jacques Valdour, *L'ouvrier espagnol*, 325–6; *El Diluvio* (hereafter, ED), 7 Feb. 1923. Although, amongst the marblers there was concern in 1911 at the introduction of stone-cutting machinery, and within brickmaking there was conflict over the use of piece rates.

60. Ministro de Fomento, *Memoria*, 82 and 116; Sastre y Sanna, *La huelgas ...1903*, 42, *Las huelgas ...1906*, 33 and 39–45; LP, 23 Sept. 1901; *El Trabajo*, 4 Jan. 1902; Confederación Regional de Oficiales y Peones de Albañil de Cataluña, *Memoria y actas del primer congreso celebrado en Vilanova y la Geltrú en el local del ateneo vilanovés los días 28 y 29 de julio de 1914*, 15–16.

61. John Child, *Industrial Relations in the British Printing Industry*, 155–82.

62. SO, 28 Oct. 1910, 17 Feb. 1911; *Boletín de la Unión Obrera del Arte de Imprimir*, 2 July 1912.

63. Michael P. Hanagan, *The Logic of Solidarity*, 129–36; David Crew, *Town on the Ruhr*, 183.

64. Playá, *Industrias mecánicas*, ETN, 15 Dec. 1897; José Serrat y Bonastre, 'De la formación del maestro de taller en la industria metalúrgica'; José A. Barret, 'Raquitismo metalúrgico nacional. Sus causas y sus remedios' 139–49; Arxiu Municipal de Sabadell, 11.4., *Conflictes laborals 1899. Huelga de cerrajeros y trabajadores de la fábrica de Harmel Hermanos*. On the more varied tasks undertaken in Catalonia, the workers themselves commented: 'The majority of our employers only do repair work, and this shows us that Spanish metalworkers are not inferior to the rest. Foreign metalworkers, who are employed in large workshops, become specialists in one type of work and have no knowledge of the rest. We, on the contrary, do all types of work, and are therefore trained to be genuine workers, capable of all classes of construction and repair work.' ED, 18 Sept. 1910, *Morning Edition*.

65. Balcells, 'Mujer obrera', 78–9; ED, 3 June 1903, *Morning Edition*.

66. SO, 5 June 1914; ETN, 30 May 1895; ED, 16 June 1903, *Night Edition*; Sastre y Sanna, *Las huelgas ...1903*, 25–6; Salut, *Vivers de revolucionaris*, 85-6; LP, 26 Oct. 1900, *Morning Edition*; 'Censo obrero de 1905', 615; Jordi Nadal, 'La transformación del zapato manual al zapato "mecánico" en España'.

2

GENDER, SKILL AND CLASS
Hierarchy and Solidarity within the Catalan Working-Class Community

In this chapter I shall be looking in some depth at the lives of industrial workers on both the shop floor and within their communities. My concern will be a classical one within labour history: I wish to evaluate the extent to which workers were irredeemably fragmented or, on the contrary, had enough in common to forge joint strategies and fight for broadly held goals in order to right perceived injustices and improve their working conditions. First, I shall contrast the impact of factors which served to stratify workers with those which could *a priori* unite them. Second, I shall discuss in some detail workers' lives within their neighbourhoods: the articulation of family and friendship networks, relations with individuals from other trades, industries and social classes, and patterns of leisure. Finally, I shall focus on workers' de-coding of their lived experiences. As we shall see, much of labour's language hailed from the world of market regulation and the guilds, but it was to take on new meanings as it clashed with the realities of rapid urban growth and capitalist development.

Gender, Skill and Class within the Labour Process

From the outset it becomes clear that there were a number of sharp fractures within the workplace, which would need to be overcome, or at least sublimated, in order for joint action to be possible. Cultural attitudes within society towards women produced a dichotomy between male and female labour. There are few surprises here for the student of gender relations in western Europe. According to patriarchal middle-class mores, there was a clear divide between the public and domestic spheres: the former was the preserve of men, while women should remain in the home undertaking domestic chores and rearing children. As shown briefly in the previous chapter, workers never adopted such a rigid framework. Their values were inherited from the popular moral economy of pre-industrial Europe. Peasants and artisanal workers did not reject female paid labour, but rather saw it as complementary to that of the male, who was viewed as the primary worker outside the home.[1]

This set of male values very much conditioned the type of work men and women performed. In urban Catalonia working-class men were expected to undertake, if possible, a recognised apprenticeship, which would give them access to a trade (*ofici*), and a higher and more stable income than that of a labourer. Such formal apprenticeships were limited to a series of male-dominated trades, which enjoyed a relatively high status and wages, and comparatively short working hours. Moreover, in the textile industries, which were totally transformed by the industrial revolution, men also tried to establish informal apprenticeships and carve out a privileged status for themselves within the factory system.

Women, on the other hand, tended to be employed in low-status factory work when young (the 'factory lice' as they were charmingly referred to in bourgeois circles). The most obvious example was cotton textiles, in which women were above all concentrated in the low-paid preparatory processes, which, as the cotton textile manufacturers correctly pointed out, the male workers regarded as 'improper for the male sex'.[2] Furthermore, when in the late nineteenth-century industrialists put women on spinning and weaving machines, previously run by men, they cut back the autonomy men had previously enjoyed and also cut wage rates. It was not, therefore, that the jobs the women performed were necessarily easy to learn, but that women were not conferred the same status and found it more difficult to limit access to their areas of work. In this sense, terms such as 'artisan' or 'skilled worker' have as much to do with manufacturing cultural barriers as with intrinsic skill. The work undertaken by women was labelled as complementary to that of the primary male bread winner and a female preserve, and, therefore, both poorly paid and subject to low status, leading to the conception, amongst male workers, of 'women's jobs' and a 'woman's wage'.[3]

Upon having children women tended, in their mid-twenties, to retire to the domestic sphere, although here they would continue to earn a small income as seamstresses, dressmakers, and the like, or, in smaller numbers, undertake the harsh but socially more rewarding work of washerwomen. This made paid labour more compatible with raising a family.[4] Thus, during the first decade of the century textile factories were staffed by large numbers of young unmarried women in their twenties, while adult males remained employed well into their thirties and forties.[5] Nevertheless, not all women followed this course given that factory labour was considerably better paid. In Barcelona in the 1900s, the best paid women's factory jobs were in spinning and weaving, in which they could earn over 3 pesetas a day, compared to the miserable sum of between 1 and 2 pesetas for a twelve-hour day paid to female outworkers.[6] Female employ was particularly important because generalised low real wages meant that for all but foremen and workers in the most elite trades it was impossible for men to earn enough to keep their wives and children at home. Hence, after giving birth some women returned to the factory, leaving young children with older relatives if possible, but otherwise entrusting them to the care of elderly neighbours, or with local Church schools, some of which invested in free nursery care in order to attract a working-class clientele. In Barcelona the latter's activities were important, catering for several thousand working-class children (in most cases from the age of three onwards). The problem, as we shall see in Chapter Five, was that in return their mothers had to agree to being drawn into the city's network of religious associations.[7]

This meant that women's work was quantitatively very important. In Barcelona, the scale of female outwork propitiated a certain invisibility of female labour. Official statistics indicated that women and girls made up 30 percent of the industrial labour force between 1905 and 1920, but this was a significant underestimation. In the rest of Catalonia, on the other hand, the sheer importance of textiles within the economy meant that, even according to official statistics, by 1920 over 38 percent of all industrial workers were women and girls.[8] Despite the image of Catholic traditionalist Spain, in which the women's place was in the home, given the relative paucity of male wages, in international terms the incidence of female paid labour was probably high. Certainly I have detected no tendency comparable to that of elite skilled workers in Britain, who in some respects aped bourgeois norms, insisting that their wives only undertake child-rearing and the household chores.[9]

Moreover, as well as industrial workers, in Barcelona there were, according to the 1900 census, 19,172 female domestics (probably close to 50 percent of the number of female factory workers). Yet their world was far removed from that of the factory. They were employed from the age of eight. Girls of working-class Catalan families sometimes worked as domestics before moving on to industrial work, but they were more often sent to Barcelona by peasant families from outside the city, coming from as far away as Valencia, Aragón, or even Castile and Galicia. These workers were both spatially and culturally distant from the industrial working-class communities and labour protest. Serving and living in middle-class neighbourhoods and often from a conservative and Catholic background, their contacts with the native working class could be limited (see table 2.3.). Unfortunately studies of this group of workers are very scarce on the ground. Sometimes, it seems, they only worked in Barcelona for several years before returning to their village. Yet they could also act as a bridgehead, bringing their family to the city after having established themselves. In addition, they on occasion met young Catalan workers in the Sunday afternoon dance (their one entertainment) thereby linking up with the local community.[10]

In Barcelona, the cultural conception of female work as complementary meant that average skilled male workers' wages were about twice as much as female factory workers. Even more discriminatory was the fact that women tended to work longer hours than men. In Barcelona during the first decade of the century male skilled workers generally laboured between forty-eight and sixty hours a week, but in textiles the working week stood at sixty-four hours, including a nine-hour day on Saturdays. This also tended to be the working week in other low-paid factory occupations. Outside Barcelona working hours in textiles varied considerably, but in the worst area, the Alt Llobregat, they averaged between fourteen and sixteen hours a day. The skilled men were often family members of the women and would get up a couple of hours after them in the morning. Their working day was harsh enough and few men, it seems, went out to the café or tavern during week days. But women had an additional burden to bear. Not only were they expected to look after the children but also do the housework. As the syndicalist from Igualada, Joan Ferrer, noted, this 'submerged women in a indignant state of slavery, for on Sunday they needed to do the washing and tidy the home. This was very neglected during the week because of the long periods of time they spent in the factory'.[11]

Such attitudes would also make it difficult for men to consider women as fully constituting part of either the trade and industry or the union movement. This outlook was strengthened by the view, shared in both middle and working-class male circles, that only men could play an active role in the world of public affairs. Hence, as we shall see in subsequent chapters, there were a number of instances in which no effort was made to unionise female workers. This was combined with an overt antagonism towards women workers when they were employed in what were regarded as male jobs, which was seen as undermining the man's status, putting pressure on wages rates, leading to male unemployment, and, on occasions, weakening the union. The most dramatic example of this struggle was in cotton textiles. Here, as I have already shown, from the 1880s in particular, industrialists began to replace men by women in weaving and spinning. This not only led to wage cuts but also propitiated a tightening of labour discipline, with employers using patriarchal values to their advantage. While male skilled workers would be treated with respect, women could be subjected to a much harsher regime. Thus, in Barcelona in the early-twentieth century in textiles and other industries in which female labour predominated it was the norm to work in silence.[12]

In the Ter Valley, where male work centred on high-status spinning, and where there was little alternative employment, recruitment of women onto the new ring frames led to a long-running and violent conflict. Growing use of female labour was seen by the men as a mortal threat which would take away their livelihood and plunge the working-class communities into poverty. The vehemence of their feelings was expressed in 1911, when the Ter Valley unions launched a campaign in support of a government bill to abolish female night work. This, the unions claimed, was necessary 'given the weakness of the female sex', and they made no secret of the hope that:[13]

> With the introduction of the said law hundreds of unemployed men will find work and they will, therefore, cease to be half women (*hombres mujeres*) dedicated to domestic chores, which are a woman's preserve. With this work they will be the family's bread winners, while their women will be able to stay at home and really carry out the sacred duties of a mother and wife. This does not happen at present due to the distribution of work in the factories.

In Barcelona the replacement of male weavers never produced similar strife, but within the textile unions hopes remained that one day male workers would once again dominate the textile industry. As will be shown in subsequent chapters, from the 1900s onwards the attitudes of some male trade unionists became somewhat more open. Yet fear of the impact of women's work could still lead to blanket condemnations. Hence, the National Textile Federation stated in its Second Congress held in March 1915 that: 'The [male] workers should not accept that their womenfolk work in the factories. Those who do should be declared our enemies.'[14] Behind these views was the idea, probably widespread in male working-class circles, that for men paid labour, particularly within skilled trades, was a life-enhancing experience, whereas for women it was a disagreeable necessity. In the words of the anarchist union organiser, Josep Soler Gustenech: 'Work dignifies men whereas it stultifies women.'[15] Hence it was that male skilled labour could be seen as the antithesis of female work, further distancing the two worlds.

Such tensions were replicated in a wide range of Catalan industries. In the first two decades of the century some unions, like the pâtissiers, tried to confine women workers to tasks which were 'proper for their sex'. Both shop-workers and waiters complained that women were increasingly being employed, the latter arguing that this was leading to growing prostitution. In printing, from the turn of the century onwards, the bookbinders' union attempted to prevent women being used as folders and cutters. In 1915 the National Federation of Pasta Makers agreed that women should not be employed in the elaboration of pasta, and, in the same year, cake and pastry-makers came out on strike in part to prevent the extension of female employment in the trade. Similarly, once a male-dominated union was strong enough the attempt could be made to turn back the clock. In 1918 the Barcelona textile dyers' union agreed that when women's posts became vacant they should be replaced by men.[16]

The marginalisation and subordination of women was strengthened by the generalised belief that the male head of household should keep close control over his wife and children (his superior status, for example, indicated by the fact that he would not tell his wife the amount he earned). It was further reinforced by a public discourse – generalised in all sectors of society, including trade-union circles, and current in political debate – which utilised stereotypical attributes of men, women and homosexuals. Thus union members were told that in their struggles against the bourgeoisie they had to 'know how to be MEN' and show their 'masculinity' and 'virility'. Not to do so would be to transgress one's own gender and become 'weak little women (*mujerzuelas*)' or even 'impotent and castrated'. In similar terms, office workers who cosied up to the bourgeoisie 'showed themselves to be effeminate'. Women active in strike action or protest movements became token men, showing 'energy, virility and determination', but within this mindset, although men might not live up to their name and women exceed expectations, the norm was the courageous man and fawning woman.[17]

Within the predominantly male sphere of work there were also important differences in wages and status. Within this sector there were an almost infinite variety of occupations, but one can draw a broad distinction between three major categories: white-collar and shop work; skilled, apprenticed industrial employment; and labouring. The city of Barcelona provides us with the best information to analyse the outlook of and interrelationship between workers in these categories.

Socially and culturally, Barcelona's 30,000-odd clerks and shopworkers (*dependents*) were on the borderline between the working and middle classes. Although often as poorly paid as industrial workers they tended to come from petty bourgeois backgrounds. It seems that they generally stayed on at school until they were fourteen (rather than ten as was generally the case in industrial working-class circles), learnt to read and write, and strongly aspired to improve their social status, either through advancement in the office or by acquiring a small shop. In a context in which 'the form of dress reflected social class'[18] they codified the difference in social background and status by wearing a suit, collar and tie, hat and leather shoes, as against the industrial workers, who wore rope sandals and a cap, and often a blue smock. This indeed led to considerable tensions, with union leaders accusing the 'table jumpers' and 'pen pushers' of aping the middle classes and shunning their industrial brethren. A similar picture was apparent amongst the city's waiters, who, according to one syndicalist critic, were 'slaves with a white tie', who wished to be called employees and not workers, and referred to their centre as a *casino* or club and not as a union. Nevertheless, there was an important difference between the shopworkers and office workers. The former had lower status and no doubt because of this, as we shall see, they were more open to unionisation and sometimes established alliances with industrial workers' unions.[19]

Yet such exclusionary mentalities and practices were not only the prerogative of white-collar workers. Within the industrial sector itself a number of hierarchies were present. Foremen were drawn from the ranks of the workers. In areas such as textiles and the metal industry, they had the prerogative of hiring and firing and in this way networks of dependency were created, which tended to be based on family structures. Foremen, who would earn anything from two to five times as much as the factory-floor workers, almost invariably supported employers during disputes, and for some workers, therefore, to support the strike would mean crossing a powerful family member.[20]

A close relationship with employers could also be found amongst some journeymen. As we saw in Chapter One, apprenticed labour remained a key category in the city of Barcelona. It is impossible to make any kind of accurate estimation of the percentage of Barcelona industrial workers who had undertaken an apprenticeship. According to the urban planner, Ildefons Cerdà, almost 40 percent of adult male industrial workers were journeymen in the mid-nineteenth century (excluding male spinners and weavers, whom he also considered as journeymen, from his figures). There is no reason to believe that numbers had declined by the 1900s. Systems of apprenticeship not only operated in more obviously skilled trades, they were still to be found in a wide range of occupations from, for example, baking to coach driving.[21]

In the large number of small workshops in which the master worked with a few journeymen and apprentices the relationship could be easy-going and cordial. This would particularly be the case in areas such a woodworking, construction and some of the trades classified under the metal industry, like plumbing, where small jobs and repair work predominated, and which were not integrated into the capitalist sector of the economy.[22] The social mobility of industrial workers was, overall, low. Nevertheless, some artisanal workers could, like shopworkers, hope to set up on their own one day. One can, for example, find references to contractors who had started out as stonemasons and bricklayers, and compositors, shoemakers and cabinetmakers becoming small-scale employers. Workers determined to take this road would no doubt also establish a close working relationship with their employers.[23]

Stable, non-conflictive relations were not limited to the small-scale artisanal trades. As we shall see in Chapter Three, in some large factories employers operated a mix of paternalism and social control to keep unions out, and when working conditions were relatively good there could be genuine affection for the boss. Alternatively, in 'strong houses' in which union membership was accepted and collective bargaining agreements in place, relations between master and men were respectful. I have found workshops of this type in, for example, the Sabadell woollen textile industry and Barcelona printing.[24]

The mental universe in which journeymen moved could also encourage them to stay on good terms with their employers. This grew out of the pre-industrial guilds in which masters and men typically worked alongside each other, at least in theory on amicable terms, and held parades on the day of their trade's patron saint and marched together during Corpus Christi. These traditions were in decline by the late-nineteenth century, but they had not disappeared. Some trades still organised religious excursions (*romerías*) on the Saturday before Easter Sunday and on Whitsun. Only one trade, the carters and coachmen, continued to hold a parade, known as the Tres Toms, on its Saint's day, but more modest ceremonies still took place. In 1917 the syndicalist daily, *Solidaridad Obrera*, showed its disgust at the fact that a 'regular number' of bricklayers attended a church service with their employers on the day of their trades' patron saint, Saint Antony.[25]

Workers who were close to their employers were little disposed to participate in broader-based strike and protest movements. Moreover, a sense of aloofness from other groups of workers could also be reinforced by craft workers' conception of their work. Journeymen saw themselves as working in 'honourable' and 'dignified' trades. This idea of the dignified trade was, indeed, oft-repeated in the working-class press during the early-twentieth century, and was linked to the notion that a journeyman should understand all aspects of his work and have a solid education. In the case of printers, for example, this should, it was claimed, include a good knowledge of grammar. Nevertheless, the high levels of illiteracy in working-class circles and harsh reality of much of the work undertaken, with journeymen frequently bullying and beating their apprentices, makes plain that such discourses idealised artisanal work, using as a template a lost and mythical golden age of the guilds.[26]

   This sense of superiority was most notable amongst those trades, analysed in Chapter One, in which workers were relatively highly paid and faced little threat to their position within the process of production. They tended to form separate craft-based unions, refused to integrate into industrial unions and were reluctant to form part of anarchist and Socialist labour confederations. Thus, for example, the president of the Catalan Federation of Glassworkers, Joan Peiró, stated, in 1916, that they had not considered themselves to be ordinary workers 'but ... artists ... labour aristocrats', and that the result was 'the absence of our collective personality ... from the annals of the working-class struggles for its dignity'.[27] Yet elements of this mentality could be found amongst skilled workers whose conditions of work were harsher. For example, syndicalists struggled to convince the poorly paid Barcelona bricklayers to form a single union with their labourers.[28]

   Below this level were to be found some groups of workers who do not seem to have undertaken any kind of apprenticeship, but needed to acquire a significant degree of skill to undertake their job. In such a category could be found the barbers and carters. And at the bottom of the tree we have the unskilled labourers. Unskilled workers were present throughout the city. In the trades they were employed to do both the menial and the most physically demanding tasks. Large numbers of labourers also worked in the construction industry, in the metal industry and on the waterfront. As we have already noted in the case of women workers, this distinction between the skilled and unskilled was never hard and fast, and could have as much to do with self-perception and the ability to raise barriers to entry as any objective measure of difficulty involved. On the port, for example, a group of Barceloneta families of sailors and fishermen, of long standing in the neighbourhood, were largely able to keep loading and unloading work on board ships for their own kin.[29]

   A link can be discerned between skill and geographical origin. Catalonia became a net importer of labour from the 1870s. Henceforth, with death rates higher than birth rates in the city, its growth was predicated upon migration. Between 1890 and 1901 the excess of immigrants over emigrants was 132,394 (an average excess of 11,032 per year). This was to decelerate in the generally more depressed climate of the period 1902 to 1917 (5,613 per year), but took off in the boom conditions of the years 1918 to 1920 (30,779 per year) (see table 2.1.).

Table 2.1. Population Change in Barcelona, 1890–1920[1]

Years	Excess Births over Deaths	Immigration	Emigration	Excess Immigration	Population
1889					420,062
1890–1893	−2,663	n/a	43,146	n/a	460,529
1894–1897	−1,152	n/a	46,423	n/a	505,790
1898–1901	−7,516	n/a	42,825	n/a	542,144
1902–1905	2,387	25,381	8,157	18,289	561,755
1906–1909	−245	29,607	9,241	19,771	581,876
1910–1913	−498	38,432	17,518	23,100	603,421
1914–1917	−4,233	48,342	28,659	28,659	628,144
1918–1920	−10,207	n/a	n/a	92,398	710,335
Totals	−24,127	n/a	n/a	+314,611	+290,273

Note:
1. The table includes those towns integrated into Barcelona from 1897. Figures for total population refer to 31 December. Small discrepancies are the result of inaccuracies in the original figures. For the period 1889 to 1917, columns 2, 4 and 5 are taken from the study in the Instituto de Estadística y Política Social and columns 3 and 4 from the *Anuario Estadístico*. For the years 1918 to 1920 all the information is from the *Anuario Estadístico*.

Sources: *Anuario Estadístico de la Ciudad de Barcelona, 1911–1917*, Barcelona, 1913–1921; Instituto de Estadística y Política Social, *Estadísticas sociales: Monografía estadística de las clases trabajadoras de la ciudad de Barcelona*, Barcelona, 1921, 13.

Claims have been made that from the late-nineteenth century onwards this migration led to a rapid growth in the percentage of non-Catalan southern Spanish workers within the labour force, and, as we saw in the introduction, links have been drawn by historians between this development and growing labour militancy. However, a detailed analysis of the statistics disproves this. In 1900 it was still the case that around 60 percent of the city's population had been born in the province of Barcelona and only 21.7 per cent were non-Catalan Spanish migrants, and most of these came not from southern Spain but rather the contiguous territories of Aragón and Valencia. This pattern was only to change with the economic boom that accompanied the First World War. By 1920 the impact of accelerating migration was making itself felt strongly. According to local government figures, 56.5 percent of the city's population had been born in the province (48.3 percent in Barcelona itself), 12.8 percent in other Catalan provinces and 30.3 percent in the rest of Spain. In total about 210,000 non-Catalan migrants now lived in the city. With respect to their origin, just over 50 percent came from Valencia and Aragón, though the more southerly region of Murcia had also began to make its mark, comprising about 12 percent of the non-Catalan total. Furthermore, the impression is that the statisticians failed to keep pace with the great flood of immigrants who arrived in the city from 1918 and that the real number was significantly higher.[30]

Locals were able to dominate a whole series of areas. Highly skilled and relatively well paid trades, such as coopering and glassblowing, were the preserve of old-established Barcelona families. More generally, workers would frequently ensure that relatives were employed, with the result that within factories there were a series of interlocking family networks. This was the case in the big Barcelona textile mills, which were prized because of the work they could offer to large numbers of family members.[31] Migrants – normally from smaller towns in the province – who already had experience in industry could usually move into a less illustrious skilled trade in the case of men or one of the small and less well-paid textile mills in the case of women. However, adult male migrants who came from peasant areas and had not learnt a trade would inevitably have to take a job labouring.

As figure 2.1. indicates, in the first years of the twentieth century settlement patterns of migrant workers were quite varied.[32] Heavy migration was most apparent in the port neighbourhood of La Barceloneta, where from the 1860s the decline of shipbuilding and fishing was accompanied by a rapid influx of labourers who worked loading and unloading ships.[33] A second magnet was the area behind the army barracks at the bottom of the Rambla, which from the 1920s came to be known as Chinatown, and which comprised the 'most Spanish streets in the Catalan city'. Chinatown was host to the overlapping worlds of petty crime, begging and street prostitution. It was home to a large number of down-at-heal taverns and several cheap cabarets (*cafés concierto* or *cafés de camareras*), outside whose doors gypsy beggars, fortune tellers and petty criminals roamed the streets. But it also housed industrial workers, especially dockers and carters, who worked on the waterfront nearby in Hortes de Sant Bertrán. A high percentage of the former were migrant labourers. It was this mix of *cafés de camareras*, in which archetypal Spanish songs and dances – flamenco, the cuplé and zarzuela – were all the rage, gypsies, and migrant workers, which gave the area an impoverished and decadent 'Spanish' (in reality pastiche Castilian-Andalusian) feel.[34]

Yet in most working-class neighbourhoods natives remained preponderant. In 1900 in those neighbourhoods, indicated in table 2.3., in which industrial workers made up over 70 percent of the active population, non-Catalan Spaniards comprised 25 percent of the total number of inhabitants. This was not much in excess of the Barcelona average. In some of the working-class suburbs the percentage of non-Catalans was lower: in Sants and its surroundings and in the working-class neighbourhoods of Sant Martí it was 16.1 and 18.1 percent respectively.[35] One result of this was that Catalan remained the language of most of working-class Barcelona. Indeed, given the failings of the Spanish education system most workers spoke Castilian-Spanish with difficulty.

Outside the specific areas discussed above there were no large migrant enclaves. Nevertheless, Figure 2.1. does indicate a certain bunching up of migrant workers. This is backed up by qualitative sources. Jacques Valdour, a French integrist Catholic who worked in a number of Barcelona factories between 1912 and 1913, lived for a time in an area between Barcelona and Sants in which workers from the Valencian interior were concentrated, and noted that in general Valencian and Aragonese migrants lived in close proximity within the working-class neighbourhoods, stuck together at work and often frequented the same eating houses and taverns. In some factories in

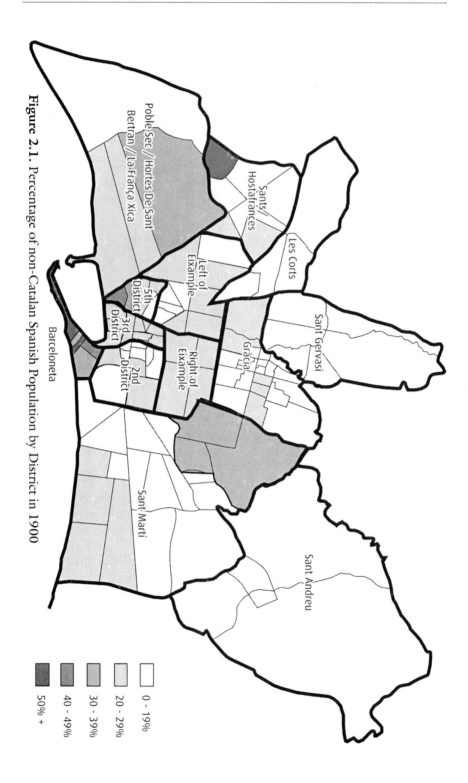

Figure 2.1. Percentage of non-Catalan Spanish Population by District in 1900

Poble Sec /Hortes De Sant
Bertran //la-França Xica

Sants/
Hostafrancès

Les Corts

/left of
Eixample

5th
District

3rd
District

2nd
District

Right of
Eixample

Gràcia

Sant Gervasi

Barceloneta

Sant Martí

Sant Andreu

50% +

40 - 49%

30 - 39%

20 - 29%

0 - 19%

which Valdour worked Catalans tended to be foremen and skilled workers, the Aragonese and Valencians labourers, and he also mentioned cases in which employers only took on cheap Valencian and Aragonese labour.[36] Similarly, the Catalan geographer, Francesc Carreras i Candi, noted that in La Plata in the suburb of Poble Nou, in 1909 there were so many inhabitants from Teruel and Castellón that, 'based on the language of the inhabitants it does not seem that one is on Catalan soil'.[37] This is the pattern one might expect; family networks were established and additional members of the kinship group or acquaintances from the village then settled in the same area.

This tendency would also have been reinforced by the reaction of the host community. It is clear that by the turn of the century a regionalist Catalan identity had developed in working-class circles. It was based on a sense that Catalan workers were more highly skilled and, more generally, that economically, culturally and politically Catalonia was the most 'advanced' part of Spain. I have already indicated that journeymen in Catalonia – as elsewhere – saw themselves as above the labourers, and this sense of superiority would tend to be especially strong when certain cultural stereotypes – such as the boneheaded Aragonese and lazy Castilians – came into play. Such sentiments could be further exacerbated amongst many Catalan workers because once a distinction between Catalans and other Spaniards was drawn 'they' could be accused of acting as strike-breakers, of undercutting wages paid to Catalan workers, and causing unemployment. This attitude would also be reinforced by linguistic differences. The Aragonese spoke Castilian-Spanish. The situation in Valencia was more complicated. Valencian, a dialect of Catalan, was still widely spoken, but many of the migrants came from the poorer Valencian interior where Castilian was the major language.[38]

Yet the fact that migrants were not in general spatially segregated in separate neighbourhoods, and that they were a minority within the larger working-class community, helped limit the growth of ethno-skill cleavages. As Valdour admitted, children of migrants would abandon any hostility their parents may have felt, learn Catalan and be fully assimilated. However, the ethnic mix would begin to change in post-war Barcelona as migration into the city accelerated and, as we shall see, given the shortage of housing stock, slum housing expanded on the working-class periphery.

Problems in Common

Within industrial working-class circles the stratifications discussed above were not incompatible with the development of a sense of problems in common, both at the level of trade and industry and within the wider community. As already stressed, a major concern for almost all industrial workers was the relatively low level of real wages.

Table 2.2. Wages and Expenditure of a Working-Class Family (Husband, Wife and Two Children) in Barcelona, 1905–1917[1]

	Wages (Pesetas per Day)											
Year	Daily Expenditure	% Increase	Skilled Male Workers	% Increase	Male non-apprenticed workers	% Increase	Female Factory Workers	% Increase	Female Outworkers	% Increase	Child Labour	% Increase
1905	4.13		4.25		3.5		2.25		n/a		1.25	
1917	8.05	95	6.4	51	5.2	49	2.82	25	2 (1915)	n/a	n/a	n/a

Note:
1. This table can only be taken as a very rough indication of changes in workers' purchasing power. Data for male skilled workers and female factory workers is most widely available and accurate. Information on labourers' pay is much scantier. I have, unfortunately, been unable to produce statistics for the period 1918 to 1923.

Major Sources: 'Censo obrero de 1905', in *Anuario Estadístico de la Ciudad de Barcelona, 1905*, Barcelona, 1907, 599–632; Instituto de Estadística y Polítical Social, *Estadísticas sociales: Monografía estadística de las clases trabajadoras de la ciudad de Barcelona*, Barcelona, 1921, 74–128; Miguel Sastre y Sanna, *La huelgas en Barcelona y sus resultados durante los años 1903–1909*, Barcelona, 1903–1910.

As table 2.2. indicates, in Barcelona in 1905 a male skilled worker's nominal wage was just enough to cover a small family's needs. However, his actual earnings were significantly lower. They were not paid on Sunday or during holidays, and some trades, such as clothing and construction, were highly seasonal. Moreover, the risk of unemployment in Barcelona was also significant. As indicated in Chapter One, Catalan industry was prone to severe recessions. During the worst downturn, in the middle of the first decade of the century, it was estimated that 35,000 of the city's 150,000-strong industrial workforce was unemployed. In construction, employment was decimated and between three and four thousand textile workers had also been laid off. In 1904 they asked for public subscriptions to be opened on their behalf and women workers staged 'hunger marches' along the Rambla.[39] Even if a worker formed part of a mutual-aid society, sickness and accident benefit only lasted between one and two months. Thus, in times of illness and unemployment working families were quickly forced to pawn their valuables.[40] Manuel Escudé Bartolí, the man in charge of a local census in 1917, calculated that on average workers were employed for 244 days a year (67 percent of the total).[41]

The rise in living standards had been held back by several factors. First, while the long drawn out industrialisation process slowed the transformation of artisanal structures it also made it difficult for the industrial base to support significant increases in real incomes. This, as we shall see, stiffened employers' resolve not to concede improvements in working conditions, a stance which the historical weakness of trade unions had made easier to maintain. In textiles the situation became particularly adverse following the mid-1880s economic crisis and the parallel intensification of competition between the Pla and Muntanya manufacturers.[42] Furthermore, industry's dependence on the unstable Spanish market made workers particularly susceptible to bouts of unemployment. Second, high tariffs and the state's heavy dependency on indirect taxes inflated the price of basic necessities. This was made worse by the onset of an inflationary process from the mid-1890s, which provoked an increase of about 15 percent in the price of basic consumer goods between 1898 and 1914. During the First World War the opportunities to export at a high profit then led manufacturers to neglect the internal market, stoking up an inflationary spiral. The price of basic necessities rose by between 70 and 75 percent between 1912 and 1919, plunging workers into a desperate race just to maintain their purchasing power. This was accompanied by an increase in the price of rented accommodation, with claims that rents had risen as much as 60 percent in the Old Quarter between 1895 and 1915 (see table 2.2.).[43]

Many working-class families no doubt managed on less than the statistics indicate. It was still common to keep chickens, rabbits and the like in cages, and pigeons in the loft, and in smaller industrial towns, like those in the Ter Valley, working-class families frequently rented a plot of land.[44] However, before 1919 (when, as we shall see, real wages were to rise rapidly) it is clear that the vast majority of male workers did not earn a 'family wage' (enough to sustain a family with two children). Only when the wife and children were working would the family be (for a few years at least) in a relatively comfortable position. Hence, unlike the situation in the major industrial powers, the vast majority of Catalan working-class families remained close to subsistence level, spending, in 1917, around 75 percent of their income on food and 10 percent on rent.[45]

Poverty was apparent in the spartan interiors of working-class housing. Matters were made worse by its poor quality. Large numbers of small proprietors owned much of the stock (nearly 24,000 persons lived principally by renting out property in 1920) and invested little in improvements.[46] In addition, investment by the local authorities in urban infrastructure was woefully inadequate. Working-class housing was, in general, still not connected to the drainage network, with septic tanks, located either in a small room or a communal courtyard, an additional health hazard. Conditions were worst in the massively overcrowded popular and working-class areas in central Barcelona, where the workers lived in damp, dark flats, four or five stories high, in narrow, smelly backstreets. In addition, inflationary pressures encouraged the practice of sub-letting, with the result that a flat with three small rooms would frequently house two working-class families.

In the working-class suburbs there was more space, and housing was generally better. Yet in these areas the lack of paving also spread disease; streets were dirty and dusty in summer and muddy with pools of stagnant water in winter. In this environment, throughout the poorer neighbourhoods epidemics were common and tuberculosis endemic; between 1911 and 1920, for example, an average of 544 people died of typhus per year (with a big epidemic in 1914), 309 of the flu, 191 of smallpox and 1,489 of tuberculosis.[47]

Added to this, at the end of the first decade of the century slum dwellings, which had absolutely no urban and sanitary infrastructure, began to appear. On the one hand, they sprang up on the Poble Nou waterfront. The most important nucleus was known as Pekin – so called because it had originally been settled by Chinese in 1870 – located by the seafront around the Old Cemetery. By the first decade of the century there were no Chinese left and it had become a neighbourhood of poor fishermen who lived in 'shacks and huts'. Then, from 1910 the population increased rapidly to around 7,000 by 1918, with the fishermen joined by increasing numbers of migrant industrial workers and down-and-outs. Over the other side of town a similar process could be seen, with slum dwellings growing up on the slopes of Montjuïc above Poble Sec, which by 1914 were inhabited by about 5,000 people.[48]

The overall consequence of inflationary pressures combined with low real incomes and high levels of disease was that Barcelona was not only one of the most expensive cities in western Europe, but, like its Spanish counterparts, it suffered comparatively high death rates, which in the more working-class neighbourhoods easily outstripped births (see table 2.1.).

To this general problem of living standards should be added concerns relating to working conditions. Within the more capitalist sector of the economy technological change, de-skilling, and the recasting of the labour process produced alarm amongst skilled workers, whose representatives maintained that such changes were undermining their position on the shop floor and threatening them with unemployment. Profit was, they argued, being put before high-quality workmanship. Hence, their response was to oppose closer supervision by foremen, further subdivisions of the production process, speed-ups and the use of piece rates, the employment of increasing numbers of apprentices, who were, in the workers' estimation, not properly trained, and any attempts to replace skilled men on new machinery. Such changes were seen as representing both an affront to the men's 'dignity' and the 'degradation' of their trades.

For example, the Barcelona painters lamented that previously many employers had entered the trade for 'love of the art', but, with a few exceptions, their only goal now was to make money. The compositors complained that the employment of an 'excessive' number of apprentices was leading to the formation of 'incomplete workers', and that piece rates had led to a 'lowering' of the trade because 'they have turned men into automatons, taking away their learning'. And their union reacted with fury to an attempt in 1908 by the big publishers, L'Anuari de l'Exportació, to employ young lads rather than trained men on its new linotype machines. In a similar vein the First Congress of the Catalan Confederation of Barcelona Bricklayers and Bricklayers' Labourers, held in July 1914, maintained that bricklaying was an 'honourable profession' and the dream of any boy, but it was rapidly 'degenerating' because the employers had divided them into various categories and were employing large numbers of apprentices without giving them adequate training.[49]

No doubt many workers simply wished to halt threatening technological advances. This was, for example, the attitude of the coopers towards machine-made casks.[50] From this perspective the skilled workers' demands could seem special interest-group pleading. The attempt was made to argue that industrialists were threatening the interests of society as a whole, because cost cutting and the intensification of production was promoting unfair competition and leading to the production of low-quality goods which short-changed the consumer. However, more important in consolidating broader-based working-class support was the fact that the concerns the journeymen raised were felt in wider working-class circles. Most obviously, in cotton textiles the difficulties faced by male weavers and spinners, who saw themselves as skilled workers, were in many respects similar.

In addition, a vague fear of technological innovation, and a linkage between this and unemployment, was widely espoused by working-class spokesmen irrespective of their trade. This would be picked up by the left-wing working-class press and subjected to an egalitarian, solidaristic reading, couched in terms of the supposed causal relationship between the uncontrolled introduction of new machinery and growing unemployment within the working class as a whole. More sophisticated thinkers, like the syndicalist typographer, Joaquín Bueso, maintained that they were not opposed to technological advance per se, which should lighten the burden of work, but to the fact that under the current economic system it only benefited the bourgeoisie.[51] Analyses along these lines were widely expressed by union leaders, along with anarchist-syndicalist journalists and theoreticians.

If we deconstruct this language, again what comes to the fore is an idealised vision of the world of the guilds and of pre-industrial manufacture, combined with a rather stereotypical reading of the impact of capitalist advance. Yet the workers' critique was important precisely because in the context of industrialisation old ideas could come to have a rather different cultural and political impact. I have indicated that in the skilled trades relations between the master and his men were sometimes close, but, at the same time, the language of craft 'dignity', pride, and the 'honourable profession', could serve to drive a wedge between them. Indeed, so common was this stress on the negative impact of untrammelled capitalist development that it could be seen as embodying a 'moral economy' amongst male industrial workers, which rejected liberal free-market economics in favour of some kind of ill-defined system of market regulation. This provided a link between journeymen workers' nostalgia, fears at the new world they faced, and the new ideologies of socialism and communism.[52]

Trade, Industry and Neighbourhood: The Forging of a Working-Class Community?

The coalescence of a sense of interests in common, but also stratification along the lines of gender, craft, regional origin and age, can also be observed at the level of the neighbourhood. Moreover, a focus on neighbourhoods provides the opportunity to analyse the relationship between workers and other social groups in greater detail. As seen in the introduction, in Catalan historiography a conceptual framework, whose subjects are the industrial working class, petty bourgeois and middle classes, has sometimes been replaced by the overarching concept of the 'popular classes', who are deemed to have enjoyed close social, cultural and political ties. A neighbourhood-based analysis will help shed light on the merits of such an approach. Given both the quality of the material available, and its importance for my study overall, I shall continue to focus on Barcelona.

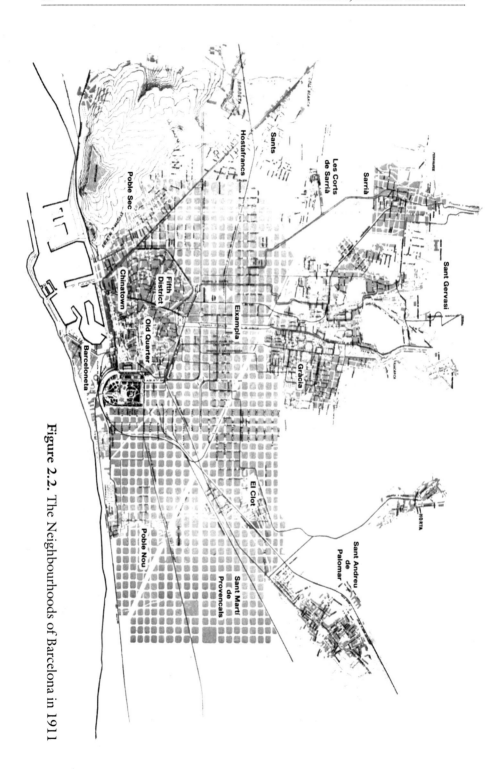

Figure 2.2. The Neighbourhoods of Barcelona in 1911

The physiognomy of the city changed rapidly under the impact of industrialisation. It was in the Old or Gothic Quarter – which from 1897 would be classified as the Second and part of the Third District (see figure 2.2.) – that in medieval Barcelona the nobility had built its palaces and to which from the early-nineteenth century the new class of bourgeois professionals had come to live. The area was crossed by a number of major commercial arteries, behind which were to be found a maze of dark, narrow, streets. The back streets were populated by workers and their families. On the more prosperous avenues, on the other hand, bourgeois, merchants and master artisans often lived in the same building, the more wealthy patrons below and the more modest inhabitants above. It was also in the Second District, around the area of Portal Nou, where high-class artisanal manufacturing had centred, and where, even at the beginning of the twentieth century, luxury trades were still to be found; in the words of Emili Salut: 'Ancient professions in old workshops, which resist the vulgar regime of capitalist exploitation and machinery.'[53]

After the walls were knocked down, in the mid-nineteenth century, work began on the new city outside. Thus slowly, above the city's major square, Plaça Catalunya, the new grid-like Eixample took shape. There was no industry in the central Eixample, and its sunny streets and spacious buildings provided a welcome change from the Old Quarter. Hence, in the late-nineteenth century it quickly established itself as the new elite neighbourhood, with social status measured in terms of proximity to the Passeig de Gràcia (hence the surfeit of *modernista* buildings in this street).

Concomitantly, new largely working-class quarters arose (see table 2.3. and figure 2.3).[54] In the nineteenth century industrial activity centred on a number of extremely densely populated neighbourhoods near the centre of town. The major focus of working-class life was what from 1897 would be known as the Fifth District, on the western side of the old city's main thoroughfare, the Rambla. It was at the bottom of the Fifth District that Chinatown was to grow up, and above and to the west of Chinatown, in the Fifth and lower half of the Sixth Districts (below the Plaça Catalunya, Ronda Universitat and Ronda de Sant Antoni), was located the heart of popular Barcelona nightlife, around Conde del Asalto Street (now Carrer Nou) and the Paral·lel. The area also sustained a large working-class population, including many migrant workers labouring on the docks, but also native workers, congregated around the workshops and small factories which filled its backstreets. In addition, more modern industry began to encroach on other central neighbourhoods to the east of the Rambla.[55]

Yet these areas soon proved too small to accommodate the city's burgeoning economy and more homogeneous working-class suburbs grew up on the periphery. As shown, the La Barceloneta port district to the south-east became heavily proletarianised. Moreover, from central Barcelona manufacturing spilled over into the towns surrounding the city, with tight-knit working-class neighbourhoods emerging. To the east, on the coast, the neighbourhood of Poble Nou grew up, and it was joined by El Clot, Camp de L'Arpa and La Sagrera further north. Administratively, until 1897 these neighbourhoods were located in the municipality of Sant Martí de

Provençals, but in reality Poble Nou and El Clot and its satellites remained two separate communities, each nestling around a nucleus of factories and workshops.[56] Further to the north-east, by the end of the century, Sant Andreu also began to lose its small-town air as increasing numbers of cotton-textile and other plants established themselves. Meanwhile, across the city in the west working-class housing spread from the Fifth District to the slopes of the mountain of Montjuïc, to an area which became known as Poble Sec and La França Xica, and further north the closely connected neighbourhoods of Sants and Hostafrancs also emerged as major industrial centres.

By 1900, therefore, old Barcelona and the Eixample were almost totally surrounded by more proletarian neighbourhoods. The partial exception was Gràcia, which had a strong commercial tradition, and where, like the more working-class neighbourhoods in central Barcelona, industry was superimposed onto a more mixed population. Then, from 1918 in particular, following the economic boom of the war years and accompanying accelerating migration, new working-class neighbourhoods beyond the old periphery were carved out of what previously had been farmland. To the north-east, Poble Nou extended further up the coast and the town of Badalona grew rapidly. To the north the new neighbourhoods of Carmel and Can Dragó materialised, and out to the west, past Sants, within the municipality of L'Hospitalet, Collblanc-La Torrassa sprang up.

As I have indicated, before 1914 the city was faced with the growing problem of slum dwellings. This was subsequently greatly to worsen. The post-war years saw a housing-boom, but this was insufficient to satisfy the needs of the avalanche of migrant workers. Hence the new peripheral neighbourhoods emerged as a mix of poor quality working-class housing and slums. An area known as 'slum city' (*baracòpoli*) expanded rapidly on the slopes of Montjuïc, and slums also grew up on the less urbanised fringes of the Eixample near Sants and Hostafrancs. In all, by 1922 commentators talked of over 15,000 slum dwellers. As might be expected, these slums housed a particularly high percentage of non-Catalan Spanish migrants; 'slum city' and Collblanc-La Torrassa becoming a focus for the new wave of southern *murciano* immigrants.[57]

The inner working-class periphery was administratively incorporated into Barcelona in 1897. Yet in reality not only did the new neighbourhoods retain their own identity, they also remained quite distant from the Barcelona core. Horse-drawn and stream trams connected these areas with Barcelona from the 1870s, but they were noisy, dirty and expensive, and as a result most workers only went 'down to Barcelona' on special occasions. The anarchist-syndicalist activist, Pere Foix, recalls that in turn-of-the-century Poble Nou some of the older inhabitants had only visited Barcelona two or three times in their lives.[58] With the introduction of electric trams in the 1900s, which made travel quicker and easier, and, most particularly, the fall in the real cost of fares between 1910 and 1914, movement became more intense, and some workers began to live further from their place of work. In addition, from the 1900s, as we shall see in later chapters, unions and political organisations made greater efforts to mobilise and organise their clientele on a Barcelona-wide scale. As a result of these changes the city would increasingly be apprehended as a single entity by it inhabitants.[59] Nevertheless, this did not lead to any breakdown of the more working-class neighbourhoods. Generalised poverty meant that workers to a large extent remained in densely populated communities, articulated around the local factories. In textiles, for example, only the most highly paid, such as foremen, office workers and workers in auxiliary trades, lived away from the working-class neighbourhoods and resided in central Barcelona.[60]

Table 2.3. The Social Structure of Barcelona by Neighbourhoods in 1900 (Percentage of Each Category within Each Area)[1]

	Total Active Pop.	A	B	C	D	E	F	G	Total %
Working-Class Neighbourhoods									
Barceloneta	7,026	0.20	80.8	3.3	0.2	0.9	3.5	11.1	100.0
Sant Martí (Poble Nou, Clot, Camp de L'Arpa)	17,615	2.50	74.6	2.6	0.2	0.7	2.2	17.6	100.4
Sants, Hostafrancs and surrounding Areas	11,320	1.90	73.2	3.0	0.4	0.8	2.1	18.6	100.0
Poble Sec/Hortes de La França Xica	7,582	0.50	73.0	4.2	0.7	0.7	3.7	17.4	100.2
Totals	43,543	1.60	75.0	3.1	0.4	0.7	2.7	16.6	100.1
Popular and Working-Class Neighbourhoods									
Sant Andreu	5,805	6.20	66.2	5.4	2.2	0.9	5.3	13.8	100.0
Fifth District	17,343	0.10	65.2	11.5	1.0	1.7	8.9	11.6	100.0
Gràcia	18,089	0.60	64.5	10.2	2.2	2.4	7.1	13.1	100.1
Les Corts	2,030	4.40	64.5	3.3	7.1	0.9	6.6	13.2	100.0
Second District	15,818	3.50	61.6	11.4	1.1	2.5	8.3	11.7	100.1
Total	59,085	1.90	64.1	10.2	1.9	2.0	7.8	12.3	100.2
Middle-Class Neigbourhoods									
Left of Eixample	26,691	0.04	50.4	16.7	2.4	5.0	15.7	9.7	100.0
Cathedral (Third District)	11,509	0.05	48.9	25.1	2.4	7.4	10.7	5.4	100.0
Sant Gervasi	3,762	4.20	45.5	13.7	12.3	3.0	13.8	7.6	100.1
Right of Eixample	11,712	0.07	30.4	24.5	3.7	7.7	28.6	4.9	99.9
Total	53,674	0.3	45.4	20.0	3.3	6.0	17.3	7.6	99.9

A. Agricultural Workers; B. Industrial Workers; C. Commerce; D. Clergy; E. Liberal Professions; F. Domestic Service; G. Other Categories

Note:
1. The original data, based on census returns, divided the city up into its ten administrative districts. However, these cut across socio-economic divisions. Where possible I have restructured the data along the lines of the old neighbourhoods, which had a greater geographic, socio-economic and, indeed, identitarian unity.

Sources: *Anuario Estadístico de la Ciudad de Barcelona, 1902*, Barcelona, 1903, 152–61.

Economic growth and inward migration meant that the industrial working-class (in which I include transport) became an increasingly important component of the city's life. According to the 1900 local government census returns, industrial workers made up 61 percent of the active population. This confirmed the city's status as the premier industrial centre on the European Mediterranean coast. Nevertheless, unlike Paris and London, it was not a great imperial metropolis, with a large administrative hub and several million inhabitants. This, together with its high urban density, had a very important consequence. The periphery remained relatively close to the centre. Workers from Sants and Sant Martí could be in central Barcelona within an hour, and the Fifth District was just five minutes away from the administrative centres on the other side of the Rambla. As a result, as we shall see, workers could quickly and directly intervene in political life.

The urban restructuring led to a hardening of class boundaries. This was most notable in the Barceloneta and the newer working-class neighbourhoods on the periphery, especially Sant Martí and Sants. In these areas industrial workers made up over 70 percent of the active population (table 2.3. and figure 2.3.). Moreover, social segregation could be seen within neighbourhoods themselves. Pere Foix recalls that in Poble Nou the petty bourgeoisie congregated in and around the principal thoroughfare while the rest of the territory was working-class.[61] The so-called 'second periphery', which emerged from 1918, was likely to be even more homogenously proletarian.

In Gràcia and the more working-class areas of central Barcelona the city of capitalist industrialisation was, as already noted, to a greater extent superimposed on and juxtaposed to the city of business and commerce, resulting in a the more diverse occupational mix. Nevertheless, before talking too loosely about inter-class milieux geographical segregation within neighbourhoods has to be taken into account. In the Fifth District and the poorer part of the Sixth District below the Eixample, as in the Old Quarter, streets were socially differentiated. The wider streets, such as Sant Pau, Carme and Tallers, housed quite a heterogeneous population, which included bar staff, white-collar and shop workers, manufacturers, and even lesser members of the liberal professions, but in the poor narrow back streets industrial workers were predominant.[62] In socially mixed neighbourhoods industry was also geographically localised. In the Old Quarter, while the areas around the Cathedral and the church of Santa María del Mar were solidly middle class, industry encroached above all in the back streets near Portal Nou, between Ronda Sant Pere and Princesa Street, superimposing itself onto the high-skilled artisanal trades. Similarly, in Gràcia during the first decade of the century the area around the main thoroughfare, the Carrer Gran de Gràcia, maintained an air of prosperity, but further to the east, in the narrow backstreets beyond Torrent de l'Olla, in an area known as Camp d'en Grassot, and in the barely urbanised upper reaches of the Eixample, industrial activity predominated.

Within more working-class areas friendship ties were no doubt established between workers and the shopkeepers, café and tavern owners, who depended on their custom (although, as we shall see, there would be tensions). Typically, food and other commodities were bought 'on the slate' until pay day,

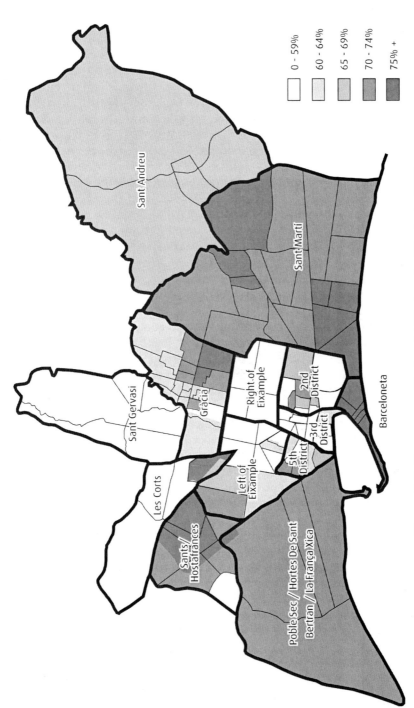

Figure 2.3. Percentage of Industrial Workers by District in 1900

and evidence from both Barcelona and outside confirms that shopkeepers extended credit during strikes. Yet one must be careful not simply to posit a close relation between workers and 'the petty bourgeoisie'. We have already seen that there were tensions between blue and white-collar workers. In addition, relations between workers and the large number of lower-middle class property owners were fraught. Indeed, as we shall see in Part Three, attempts were made by syndicalists in 1918 to organise a tenants' strike. Finally, as might be expected, most commerce was oriented towards middle-class Barcelona. According to the 1900 local government census 60 percent of those employed in commerce lived in those middle-class areas of town, highlighted in table 2.3., which accommodated 34 percent of the city's active population. On the other hand, only 6.5 percent were located in those neighbourhoods with over 70 percent of industrial workers which made up 27.8 percent of the active population.[63] Furthermore, there was a world of difference between shopkeepers who scraped a living in the poorer parts of town and those who owned prestigious establishments in the Old Quarter and Eixample, could afford a domestic and aspired to the same social and cultural position as the upper-middle classes (*gent de bé*).[64]

It was no doubt the case, as I have already indicated, that employers and employees in the numerous small workshops and in elite trades maintained a close relationship on and off the job. But between workers and the more established middle classes relations were much cooler. On the one hand, in middle-class circles there was a keen sense of social hierarchy, on the other, amongst male skilled workers in particular, a strong belief in the value of manual labour and of a worker's worth and independence. Such a mentality was conditioned by a context in which a worker might aspire to becoming a small employer but to cross the bridge to the liberal professions and respectable middle-class Barcelona society was unthinkable.[65] The divide was at its most apparent in the social and cultural distance between more working class and the established middle-class neighbourhoods. Pere Foix commented that in the northern neighbourhoods of Sant Gervasi, Vallcarca and Bonanova, with their 'sumptuous palaces', 'perfumed ladies and well-attired gentlemen', the 'dogs of breeding ... were better fed than the kids of Poble Nou, Sants and La Bordeta'.[66]

More significantly, socio-cultural divisions were also apparent in central Barcelona in the chasm which separated the Fifth District and the middle-class Old Quarter neighbourhoods. Within the Fifth District prostitution was rife in both Chinatown and on a number of well-known streets further north. The Paral·lel and Conde del Asalto Street, in the Fifth and lower half of the Sixth District, were also the focus of 'unrespectable' popular and working-class nightlife, with large numbers of taverns, theatres, cinemas and *cafés de camareras*. As already noted, the most degraded of the latter were to be found in Chinatown, but they were all characterised by risqué singers and dancers and by the close proximity of prostitution. They were denounced by the puritanical Fathers' Association, financed by the ultra-Catholic Second Marquis of Comillas, but were able to stay open because of kick-backs they paid to the corrupt Barcelona police. The more respectable cafés and theatres were, on the other hand, to be found on the Rambla, the Plaça Catalunya and the Passeig de Gràcia in the Eixample.

To be sure, this distinction cannot be seen simply in social terms. The audience in the theatres lining the Paral·lel was largely made up of workers, along with the lower-middle class residents of the poorer neighbourhoods, but the better known cafés, bordellos and *cafés de camareras* drew a more socially heterogeneous male clientele. Men of a higher social standing were able to transgress the cultural boundary. However, one has to be careful when considering the implications. The fact that people were to be found in the same establishment does not mean that they mixed freely or shared the same views. Moreover, in the Fifth District a number of establishments – which revelled in the name of music halls – catered for a more up-market clientele. This differentiation became more pronounced during the First World War, when immense fortunes were made out of exports to the Allies, and, according to some accounts, a new class of nouveau-riche industrialists came to the fore, of looser morals than their predecessors. It was also the years in which the dingy *cafés de camareras* were replaced by glittering cabarets, with their immaculately dressed croupiers and band members, professional singers and dancers, and new sophisticated American sounds: the Argentinian tango and Brazilian machica. In addition, the cabarets themselves became socially divided, with first floor tables reserved for the more substantial patrons.[67]

Other differences between the Fifth District and much of the Old Quarter, whose political impact was much greater, had a closer correspondence to class. Levels of Church attendance were much higher in the Old Quarter, which had a far greater per capita ratio of priests and members of religious communities, and where the overall atmosphere was conservative and puritanical.[68] In addition, as we shall see in subsequent chapters, strikes, riots and rebellions would frequently be ignited in the Fifth District, with the inhabitants of the Old Quarter often being on the receiving end, as demonstrators poured in to protest outside the local government offices in Plaça Sant Jaume, or even to stone the windows of the prosperous shops to force them to close down.

Yet, this should not be taken to mean that the more working-class neighbourhoods were homogenous. Textile workers were relatively evenly spread across the city, but workers from most trades tended to congregate in particular areas. Most remarkable of all was the concentration of sailors and ship loaders in the Barceloneta. According to the 1900 local government census, 80 percent of these workers were to be found in the Barceloneta (as against 6 percent of all Barcelona industrial workers), 56 percent in just two quarters at the bottom of the neighbourhood (Varadero and Concordia). Metalworkers, on the other hand, were much more numerous on the fringes of the Barceloneta, outside the area's grid-based housing plan, and in Poble Nou. Here, it seems, a distinction can be drawn between a migrant, largely unskilled labour force orientated towards the port, and more skilled local workers who laboured in the metal factories.

Trades in which skilled journeymen played a key role also frequently centred on a particular part of town. For example, printers and furniture makers preferred to live in the Fifth District, Gràcia and the most working-class area on the left-hand side of the Eixample (59.9 percent of printers and 62.3 percent of furniture makers, as against 38.5 percent of all the city's industrial workers). Woodworkers, on the other hand, were strongly concentrated in Poble Nou and El Clot within Sant Martí (52.8 percent as against 10.5 of all workers). 43 percent of the men who worked with leather and furs – primarily tanners – were to be found in Sant Andreu and Sant Martí as against 18 percent of the total working-class population. No doubt if the statistics had been further disaggregated by trade even more striking examples could have been found.[69] This propensity for some groups of skilled workers to centre on particular neighbourhoods no doubt reinforced the corporatist tendencies previously discussed. One suspects that this was strongest amongst the most elite crafts, in which workers had a very strong sense of their own superiority. They established close ties on the job, which were further reinforced by close contact within the wider community.

Yet this was not in general incompatible with the establishment of broader ties within the industrial working-class communities. One should not idealise working-class life. In a context of deprivation and lack of education wife-beating was a serious problem, often violent disputes broke out between neighbours, families broke up and children ran away from home, while young lads were quick to steal washing left out to dry and sell it on in Chinatown.[70] Nevertheless, this was accompanied by the establishment of strong friendship networks. In Barcelona a crucial difference between middle-class and working-class life was that whereas middle-class children were kept indoors working-class boys, and to a lesser degree girls, were set free to roam the streets from a very young age. This was frequently a necessity, either because the mother went out to work or because she needed peace and quiet in order to work from home. Moreover, the education system in Spain was highly deficient, and while in the larger industrial towns working-class boys tended to go to school for at least some of the time between the ages of five and ten, it was still very common for girls to stay at home and help their mother. On the other hand, as Emili Salut noted, children in better off households, like the sons of the tavern owner, baker and hardware store keeper, frequently stayed on at school until they were fourteen. These middle-class children went to fee-paying private schools, usually run by the Church (which were themselves socially differentiated, the most prestigious religious orders catering for the elite), while working-class children either went to poorly maintained municipal schools or subsidised private schools (most, in fact, also Church-run).[71]

After leaving school, boys would then begin their apprenticeships, while still, of course, playing together in the evening and at weekends. Later they would frequent cafés, taverns and whorehouses (commonly a working-class boy's first sexual experience would be in a brothel), and Sunday afternoon dances, where matches were made. Once the children grew up social intercourse could remain intense. For married men the primary focus of informal socialisation was the tavern and, especially, the café, which they frequented on Saturday nights (when they had been paid) and Sunday afternoons, dominoes and cards being the favourite pastimes. Indeed, all working-class institutions that had large enough offices, from parties to union headquarters and cooperatives, set aside a room as a café as a matter of course. For an enthusiastic minority bullfighting provided an occasional alternative, while football became increasingly popular in the 1900s.[72]

Women who worked in industrial occupations like textiles also socialised on the job. At the same time, for almost all working-class women, the market, followed by the washhouse, were major gender-specific meeting points. In some areas Church services also remained important. In the larger industrial towns religious observance had by this time declined greatly, but in smaller towns and villages the Church would remain a focal point on Sunday mornings.

Matches tended to be made when workers were in their early twenties. The indications are that pairings within industrial working-class households were totally predominant. The only significant exception was, it appears, domestic servants from peasant families who sometimes married into the industrial working class. Marriage was still the norm but, much to the outrage of the religious authorities, in Barcelona at least, the decline of religious practice had been matched by a growth in cohabitation.[73] Some spaces were filled by the entire family. Given my comments on working-class housing, it will come as no surprise to learn that, weather permitting, families brought their chairs down to the street in the evening and sat outside. Married couples tended to go for a stroll and to the café on Sunday mornings and also, occasionally, families would go on a picnic in the countryside. Now and again, at the weekend, a husband would take his wife and children to a fair, the theatre or (especially from the middle of the first decade of the century) the cinema. In the Barcelona suburbs, indeed, groups of aficionados would put on theatre performances for a predominantly working-class audience.

In addition, religious holidays, saints days and the each town's *festa major* provided an opportunity for the whole community to celebrate. Working hours were long and conditions were harsh but workers did at least enjoy about twenty-three days off a year (including seven – five religious plus two for the *festa major* – which were customary rather than official). These were stoutly defended, not for any religious motives but because in a life of unrelenting toil they provided the one great opportunity for merriment. In Poble Nou, for example, on saints' days stalls were set up which sold fritters (*buñuelos*) and sweets for the children, quacks tried to ply their remedies to the locals, and associations, often based on a particular trade, organised dances. Similarly, during the yearly *festa major* workers enjoyed going to dances and to a small fair.[74]

Conclusions

The analysis undertaken is this chapter has emphasised a number of important points. I have shown that there was a clear stratification along lines of skill and gender, with journeymen having a pronounced sense of their own worth and developing strong bonds not only at work but also within the neighbourhoods in which they lived. This was at its most intense in the case of the elite trades, which were passed on from father to son. Yet this was not necessarily incompatible with the establishment of links to the broader working-class community, based on common problems and concerns, founded upon marriage and cohabitation, wider friendship networks and common leisure pursuits. These links, it has been suggested, were strengthened by the experience of poverty, and by the fact that workers to a degree occupied a distinct cultural space, living in densely-packed neighbourhoods, congregated around workshops and factories. Migrant workers – especially when they came from outside Catalonia – were, to be sure, at first excluded from these networks. Nevertheless, in a context in which they did not live in separate neighbourhoods, to a large extent young non-Catalan migrants and the children of migrant families could and did integrate successfully. This only began to change in the slums and suburbs of the 'second periphery' in the years following the First World War.

A similar ambiguity could also be seen in relations between industrial workers and other social groups. I have demonstrated that a crude reading of the 'popular classes' hypothesis, which posits that the working and lower middle classes intermingled freely, is mistaken. The social distance between industrial workers and the lower-middle to middle class was often wide. In addition, criticism was voiced of white-collar workers for aping the middle classes and there was strong antipathy towards the rentiers who let them property. Yet fluid relations could also sometimes be established. Local tavern owners and shopkeepers could be on close terms with their working-class clientele, dealings with shopworkers were certainly less fraught than they were with office workers, and in some sectors of the economy workers and employers could be on friendly terms. This serves to emphasise the importance of social intercourse at the level of the neighbourhood (*barri*) in created friendship networks. As we shall see in subsequent chapters, such links could also help to build political alliances.

This is as far as a static social and cultural analysis can take us. To further understand relations amongst the various elements within the working class, and between industrial workers and other social groups, it is necessary to take a more dynamic, chronological approach, and study the associations, and industrial and political movements, in which workers participated. In the following chapter I intend to take a first step down this road by analysing the development of Catalan trade unionism within the context of both the state's policies towards labour and strategies developed by the industrialists to cope with 'the social problem'.

Notes

1. Louise Tilly and Joan Scott, 'Women's Work and the Family in Nineteenth-Century Europe'.
2. *Boletín de la Industria y Comercio de Sabadell*, May 1911.
3. Instituto de Reformas Sociales, *Jornada*, 59.
4. On women's work, see also the comments in, Salut, *Vivers de revolucionaris*, 52–3, and Miguel Regàs i Ardèvol, *Confessions, 1880–1936*, 17.
5. For example, in Torelló in 1911 there were large numbers of girls and young women between the ages of fourteen and twenty six employed in the textile factories. The average age of a woman over sixteen was twenty-five but that of a man thirty-six. Of these men, 66 percent were married, but only 10 percent of the women. Arxiu Municipal de Torelló (hereafter, AMT) 'Estadística del trabajo fabril en Torelló, 1911', Carpeta T., Trabajos Varios.
6. 'Censo Obrero de 1905', 607; *Butlletí del Museu Social*, Aug. 1915, 66; *Anuario Estadístico de la Ciudad de Barcelona* (hereafter, AECB), *1902*, 152.
7. Rosell, *Recuerdos de educador*, 8–14; Ramón Albó y Martí, *Barcelona caritativa, benéfica y social*, vol. 1.
8. I have based these statistics on the 1905 'Censo obrero' and Ministro de Trabajo y Previsión, *Censo de Población de 1920*, vol. 5, 102–253. Many middle-class women also secretly sewed or carried out similar activities in order that the family might keep up appearances. AECB, *1902*, 152.
9. E.J. Hobsbawm, 'The Aristocracy of Labour Reconsidered', 239.
10. The figures are taken from, Ministerio de Instrucción Pública y Bellas Artes, *Censo de Población*, 1900, vol. 3, 24–5. I have also used, Cristina Borderías, 'Women Workers in the Barcelona Labour Market, 1856–1936', and information from José Elías de Molins, *La mujer obrera en Cataluña en las ciudades y en el campo*, 17–19; Joan Manent i Pesas, *Records d'un sindicalista llibertari català*, 32; Juan García Oliver, *El eco de los pasos*, 14; and Ricardo Sanz, *El sindicalismo español antes de la guerra civil*, 123–47.
11. Instituto de Reformas Sociales, *Jornada*, 53–4; 'Tejedor sindicalista', *Solidaridad Obrera* (hereafter, SO), 23 June 1911; Pere Foix, *Apòstols i mercaders*, 2nd edn, 212; Juan Ferrer, *Vida sindicalista*, 44. According to 'Tejedor Sindicalista', many men stayed in bed until 7 am, while their wives got up at 4.30 or 5 am.
12. For cotton textiles see Pau Vilà, 'Records d'un treballador', 27. Similarly in the big L'Aguila clothing factory, talking was not permitted. SO, 26 Aug. 1916.
13. 'Gran mitin monstruo en Torelló' in AMT, Carpeta (A), C. 'Asociaciones S, de 1910 a'.
14. *Anuari d'Estadística Social de Catalunya* (hereafter, AESC), *1915*, 57.
15. *El Trabajo*, 10 Dec. 1904.
16. Sastre y Sanna, *Las huelgas ... 1904*, 63; *La Publicidad* (hereafter, LP), 13 July 1910, *Morning Edition*, 21 April 1912; AESC, *1915*, 77; SO, 17 June 1915, 13 July 1918.
17. For example, SO, 4 Aug., 18, 29 Nov., 26 Dec. 1916, 26, 29 Oct. 1917, 11 Aug. 1918.
18. Claudi Ametlla, *Memòries polítiques*, 1890–1917, 108.
19. Salut, *Vivers de revolucionaris*, 42; M. Sans Orenga, *Els treballadores mercantils dins el moviment obrer català*, 45–6; SO, 4 Aug. 1918.
20. Instituto de Reformas Sociales, *Jornada*, 431–2; SO, 4 Feb. 1917; *La Industria Metalúrgica*, Oct. 1922. On the importance and impact of working-class foremen in late nineteenth-century Catalan textiles see also, Angel Duarte i Montserrat, 'Mayordomos y contramaestres: jerarquía fabril en la industria algodonera catalana, 1879–90'.
21. Cerdá, 'Monografía estadística', 617–22 and 645. My comments on the 1900s are based on the 1905 'Censo obrero'.
22. However, where workshops formed the bottom rung of the capitalist chain, working conditions in them were the worst in the industry. Thus, in printing in 1906, conditions were harshest in the small 'coal houses', where workers were not able to unionise, and in cotton textiles in 1917 the Barcelona unions launched a campaign to bring conditions in the smallest factories up to the level of the rest. *Boletín de la Sociedad del Arte de Imprimir* (hereafter *Boletín*), Feb. 1906; SO, 1 March 1917.

23. *Reglamento de la sociedad de obreros canteros de la Montaña de Monjuich*, 6; LP, 8 Oct. 1901, *Morning Edition*; *Boletín de la Unión Obrera del Arte de Imprimir*, 30 June–30 Sept. 1913; SO, 7, 25 Nov. 1917. Although this did not necessarily lead to class harmony once these workers had set up on their own. For example, the compositors claimed after a strike in 1912 that former workers had taken the hardest line. *Boletín*, 30 June–30 Sept. 1912.

24. *El Trabajo*, 16 April 1909.

25. Joaquim M. de Nadal, *Aquella Barcelona*, 69; Joaquim Ferrer, *Simó Piera: Pèrfil d'un sindicalista. II. Simó Piera: Records i experiències d'un dirigent de la CNT*, 25–36; Guia Diamante, *Barcelona*, 72–3; Agustí Riera, *La Semana Trágica*, 216–17; Salut, *Vivers de revolucionaris*, 115; SO, 14 June 1917; Winston, *Workers and the Right*, 27–8.

26. For such discourses see, for example, *Boletín*, Dec. 1904, May, Aug. 1905; Congreso de la Federación de Metalúrgicos y Similares, in *Butlletí del Museu Social*, Aug. 1915, 137. On grass-roots reality, Salut, *Vivers de revolucionaris*, 45.

27. *El Vidrio*, 1 Jan., 1 Aug. 1916.

28. SO, 13 Nov. 1913.

29. Jordi Ibarz Gelabert, 'Sociedades y montepíos', 126–7.

30. AECB, *1902*, 107–9 and 132; *1918–20*, 135–42. On the large number of workers not included in official statistics see Chapter One, 20. It is usual for social scientists to refer to persons who move within a given state as migrants, but Catalans usually refer to non-Catalan Spaniards as immigrants. Here I use both terms indistinctly.

31. On La España Industrial see the comments in SO, 4 Feb. 1917. The assertion made by Joan Connelly Ullman that most of the city's cotton textile workers were migrants is, therefore, mistaken: see Joan Connelly Ullman, *La Semana Trágica*, 115–16.

32. This figure has been elaborated by comparing the data on the total number of Spanish migrant workers in each of the small areas (*barris*) into which Barcelona's ten districts were divided with information on the total population in these areas. This can be found in AECB, *1902*, 99–101, 133–41 and 156–61.

33. Avelino Guitart de Cubas, *Barceloneta*, 186–203.

34. Salut, *Vivers de revolucionaris*, 71–6; Francisco Madrid, *Sangre en Atarazanas*, 7–11, 45–72 and 153–64; Felip Cortiella, *El Morenet*. In this period it was simply known as the Les Drassanes neighbourhood. The first reference to Chinatown I have found is in Madrid, *Sangre*.

35. It has been possible to elaborate these statistics by combining data on the percentage of industrial workers in the active population in each *barri*, with that on the total number of inhabitants and the number of Catalans and non-Catalan migrants, to be found in AECB, *1902*, 99–101, 133–41 and 156–61. The quite high percentage of non-Catalans in wealthier neighbourhoods in central Barcelona is, above all, the result of the large number of domestic servants.

36. Valdour, *Ouvrier espagnol*, 78, 228–52, 289–92 and 321.

37. Francesc Carreras y Candi, 'La ciutat de Barcelona', 1028.

38. Carreras y Candi, 'Barcelona', 229–30 and 347; Ricardo Sanz, *El sindicalismo y la política*, 20; Manuel Lladonosa i Vall-llebrera, *Sindicalistes i llibertaris: l'experiència de Camil Piñón*, 21.

39. *La Ilustración Obrera*, 14, 16 April, 14 May 1904; *Boletín*, Feb. 1906; Sastre y Sanna, *Las huelgas … 1905*, 22; *1906*, 30–4. Although workers in many skilled trades would leave the city, taking up jobs labouring if necessary, when work was scarce.

40. AECB, *1903*, 522; Salvador Vives, 'L'obrer malalt'. Independent mutual-aid societies recruited skilled and white-collar workers and the lower-middle class. In 1901 a city-wide umbrella organisation, the Unió i Defensa de les Germandats, had 25,043 members. AECB, *1904*, 589. As I shall show in the following chapter, employers also organised their own mutual-aid societies. During the first decade of the century both categories grew in importance, and by 1915 there were 703 mutual-aid societies with 146,159 members in the province of Barcelona. *Butlletí del Museu Social*, no. 44, April 1917, 51–2.

41. Instituto de Estadística y Política Social, *Monografía estadística de la clase obrera*, 89. Other sources reached a similar conclusion regarding low real wages. In 1914 the report at the conference of the Catalan Regional Metalworkers' Federation stated that the minimum expenditure of a working-class family with two children was 5.4 pesetas a day. It pointed out

that a metalworker's average pay was 4 pesetas a day, and that if Sundays and holidays were taken into account it was only 3.4 pesetas. If his wife worked, the report stated, she could earn 10 pesetas a week, but this still left a substantial deficit. Federación Regional Catalana de Sindicatos Obreros Metalúrgicos, *Memoria del congreso obrero metalúrgico celebrado en el Palacio de Bellas Artes los días 12 y 13 de abril de 1914*, 16–17.

42. For the situation in Sants see Carles Enrech, *Entre Sans i Sants*, 229–40.

43. Tallada, *Demografía de Catalunya*, 51–66; Jordi Nadal and Carles Sudrià, *Història de la Caixa de Pensions*, 17–24; Pere Gabriel, 'Sous i cost de la vida a Catalunya a l'entorn dels anys de la primera guerra mundial', 62 and 83; Pere Casals, 'L'habitació obrera ahir i avui'.

44. Foix, *Apòstols*, 210; Guitart de Cubas, *Barceloneta*, 167–8; Gonçal de Reparaz (fill), *La Plana de Vich*, 142.

45. Instituto de Estadística y Política Social, *Monografía estadística*, 116.

46. Ministerio de Trabajo y Previsión, *Censo de población de 1920*, vol. 5, 252–3.

47. Elías de Molins, *Mujer obrera*, 32–3 and 42; Foix, *Apòstols*, 209–10; AECB, *1916*, 116; *1918–1920*, 208.

48. Riera, *Semana Trágica*, 193–5; Carreras y Candi, 'Barcelona', 966 and 973–4; Francisco Pons Freixa, with the collaboration of José Mª Martino, *Los aduares de Barcelona*.

49. *El Pintor*, 21 Feb. 1904; *Boletín*, 31 Dec. 1900, 30 June 1901, 30 June, 31 Dec. 1904, May 1908; Confederación Regional de Oficiales y Peones de Albañil de Cataluña, *Memoria de actas*, 15–16.

50. Federación de Oficiales Toneleros de la Región Española, *Actas de la conferencia verificada en San Martín de Provensals*, 22–3.

51. SO, 19 Feb. 1910.

52. The term is taken from E.P. Thompson, 'The Moral Economy of the Crowd in the Eighteenth Century'.

53. Romero Maura, *Rosa del Fuego*, 58–9 and 132–3; Salut, *Vivers de revolucionaris*, 59–60.

54. Figure 2.3, like figure 2.1. and table 2.3., is based on census returns compiled by local officials and reproduced in the 1902 AECB, 152–61. This is the only data I possess that is broken down by neighbourhood. Given that the census returns were far from complete it can only be a rough guide. The 1900 data gives a figure of 94,484 industrial workers (including transport) for Barcelona, but the 1905 'Censo obrero' elevates the total to 146,498. Nevertheless, the fact that, according to the 1900 data, industrial workers made up 60.7 percent of the total active population – a very similar figure to the 61.3 percent indicated by the 1900 Spanish census returns – indicates that it can be used to discuss the overall importance of industrial labour in the city.

55. Emili Salut is an invaluable source for the Fifth District. For a detailed survey of workers and industry in central Barcelona from 1900 see also, Mercè Tatjer Mir, 'Els barris obrers del centre històric de Barcelona'.

56. That these neighbourhoods retained their own separate identities is stressed in José Suñol Gros, *Guia de San Martín de Provensals*, 6; Carreras y Candi, 'Barcelona', 1024.

57. On the growth of slum housing see, Dr E. Mira, 'Barracópolis: La vida de les barraques de Barcelona', and Pons Freixa, *Los aduares*. For the rise of the 'second periphery', see José Luis Oyón and Carme García Soler, 'Las segundas periferias, 1918–1936: una geografía preliminar', and Carles Santacana i Torres, 'La configuració dels municipis periferics: l'impacte cultural i sociopolític'.

58. Foix, *Apòstols*, 212.

59. For an excellent study of this identitarian construction of Barcelona see Pere Gabriel, 'Espacio urbano y articulación política popular en Barcelona, 1890–1920'.

60. Carme Miralles and José Luis Oyón, 'De la casa a la fábrica. Movilidad obrera y transporte en la Barcelona de entreguerras 1914–39'; Carles Enrech, 'la ofensiva contra el oficio en la industria textil catalana (1881–1923)', 578–82.

61. Foix, *Apòstols*, 209–10.

62. Casals, 'Habitació obrera'. Emili Salut's memoirs also indicate that the backstreets of the Fifth District were largely industrial working class.

63. Calculated from the 1902 AECB census, 152–61.

64. For a portrait of the latter see the novel by Santiago Rusiñol, *L'auca del senyor Esteve*.

65. The syndicalist, Joan Ferrer, recalled that as children in his home town of Igualada, the workers never mixed with the sons of the bourgeoisie. From the age of between fifteen and sixteen, 'they went to their business or factory, we passed by, but they didn't even look at us and we treated them in the same way'. Baltasar Porcel, *La revuelta permanente*, 35.

66. Foix, *Apòstols*, 211.

67. Luis Cabañas Guevara, *Biografía del Paralelo, 1894–1934*. For the transition from the *café de camareras* to the cabaret see also, Madrid, *Sangre en Atarazanas*, 155–72. There is a vivid portrait of a cabaret in the 'factional' novel by Francisco Bastos Ansart, *Pistolerismo*.

68. Regàs i Ardèvol, *Confessions*.

69. Data for this section has been elaborated from AECB, *1902*, 152–62.

70. Salut, *Vivers de revolucionaris*, 53–8; Madrid, *Sangre en Atarazanas*, 69–70.

71. Salut, *Vivers de revolucionaris*, 20–6 and 53; SO, 16 Nov. 1917. For more information on schooling see Chapter Five, 146–8.

72. Rosell, *Recuerdos de educador*, 17–20 and 65–6; Valdour, *Ouvrier espagnol*, 250; Foix, *Apòstols*, 210; Coroleu, *Barcelona y sus alrededores*. It was, it seems, frowned upon for married men to visit taverns. Also interesting are the accounts by doctors of popular leisure pursuits in Llorenç Prats, *La Catalunya rancia*.

73. Salut, *Vivers de revolucionaris*, 113.

74. Salut, *Vivers de revolucionaris*, 113–19; Rosell, *Recuerdos de educador*, 35; Valdour, *Ouvrier espagnol*, 57 and 273–4; Instituto de Reformas Sociales, *Memoria de la inspección del trabajo, 1911*, 84–6; Foix, *Apòstols*, 210; Guía Diamante, *Barcelona*; Coroleu, *Barcelona y sus alrededores*, 228; Romero Maura, *Rosa del Fuego*, 150–1.

3

THE STATE, EMPLOYERS AND ORGANISED LABOUR
Political Marginalisation, Social Control and Resistance

In this chapter I will focus on the interplay between state and employer policies towards labour and the workers own attempts to form independent trade unions. Two areas will be subject to particular attention. First, I will investigate whether the state and employers attempted to repress worker dissent, and in the case of the latter, develop systems of social control in the factory based on a fierce labour discipline and paternalism; or whether they promoted social legislation and supported the operation of independent unions and of systems of collective bargaining, which could help integrate workers into the polity. Second, and interrelatedly, I will analyse the structure, policies and practice of the unions themselves. In this section my attention will above all centre on the union revival which followed Spain's military defeat at the hands of the United States in 1898 and reached its crescendo in the summer of 1903. On such questions would turn not only the degree of social and political stability in Catalonia itself, but also, given the territory's economic weight, in Spain as a whole.

The Spanish State and the Catalan Industrialists

At the level of the state, the major feature of the nineteenth century was a reluctance to open the political system up to subaltern political and cultural strata. The dominant political model which emerged from the 1830s was liberal conservative. Voting rights were subjected to severe restrictions and unions pursued. In addition, state security was put in the hands of a militarised police force, the Civil Guard, and the army held in reserve. As a result, workers were only able to organise effectively during brief liberal interludes, with bursts of union organisation between 1841 and 1843, 1854 and 1856, and, above all, 1868 and 1873.[1]

The Cánovas Restoration, inaugurated by a coup d'etat against the First Republic at the end of 1874, to a large extent followed this liberal-conservative model. The political turmoil of the so-called *Sexenio Democrático* between 1868 and 1873, which saw radical liberals for the first time play a key role in national politics, and workers organise national labour confederations, profoundly traumatised Spain's elites and property-owning middle classes. In response, the architect of the new system, Antonio Cánovas del Castillo, was determined that the country should be governed by 'intelligent minorities', with the majority of the population marginalised from political life.[2] This rejection of democracy was codified in the key role reserved for the King in the 1876 Constitution and in the abolition of universal manhood suffrage (introduced in 1868), accompanied, during the first years of the Restoration regime, by a fierce clampdown on unions and the Left.[3]

Nevertheless, the system was not unchanging. In order to ensure political stability Cánovas recognised the need to conciliate moderate liberal opinion. As a result, while organising his own Conservative Party he allowed centrists who accepted the 1876 Constitution to form an 'official' opposition, which became known as the Liberal Party in 1885. On coming to power in the 1880s, on paper at least, the Liberals considerably democratised the new regime, at first easing restrictions on trade unionism, and, subsequently, guaranteeing the freedom of the press and associations, and, finally, in 1890, reintroducing universal manhood suffrage.

These reforms provided a space which civil society and the Left could utilise in order to conquer political and cultural liberties. Yet the new freedoms would by no means be exercised without hindrance. As we shall have ample opportunity to confirm, the Left remained in constant danger of falling foul of the authorities, with the anarchists in particular subject to systematic harassment and, at times, unable to operate openly. Furthermore, universal manhood suffrage remained for many only a theoretical right. Relations between central government and local power-brokers were structured through a system known as *caciquismo*. In essence the Restoration parties were groupings of notables; and while they did elaborate broad political strategies they also functioned as vehicles which offered their followers favours and inducements in return for political support. Hence, at a local level the regime was above all based on patronage and clientalism. Although a democratic facade was maintained, in reality the two 'official' parties rotated in power (the so-called *turno pacífico*), with the Minister of the Interior entrusted with the job of 'making' the parliament. This was done through a process of negotiation between the government's political representative in each province, the civil governor, and the local power brokers, the *caciques* or *fuerzas vivas*.[4]

In Catalonia there was considerable variation in the actual practice of *caciquismo*. In some cases the local elites were relatively weak and the government could parachute in a candidate of its choosing, who had absolutely no links to the locality (a so-called *cunero*). On the other hand, the industrial elite, which had close links above all with the Conservative Party, retained considerable independence, and members of the so-called 'Catalan group' of industrial and financial interests – integrated, from 1888, in the big employers' confederation, the FTN – ensured that they were directly represented in parliament.[5]

This can be seen as part of a process by which the state, to an important degree, privatised power in the hands of local elites. A key result would be low state expenditure and an unwillingness to take on many of the duties which, by the late-nineteenth century, were expected of a liberal-parliamentary regime. For local and regional elites it meant that many aspects of government policy escaped their grasp, but it also had very considerable political advantages. Along with the inducements outlined above, the local *fuerzas vivas* would not have to suffer public officials prying too deeply into their affairs. With respect to the central state, this practice in reality represented an admission of weakness. Rather than build an apolitical, bureaucratic civil service, which operated effectively at a local level, it eschewed responsibility.

As well as putting their weight behind the Restoration regime, which, though not perfect, they saw as at least ensuring order and stability, major industrialists also tried to control labour through their power at factory level. During the nineteenth century, throughout Europe employers were reluctant to accept trade unions and other independent workers organisations. In the wake of economic growth and industrialisation, their first response was to devise new strategies that mixed paternalism and strict labour discipline in order to maintain the smooth functioning of their enterprises. Industrialists came to see themselves as the head of their household and the workers as their children. They provided them with their livelihood and in return they could expect their obedience.

This was the dominant perspective in late nineteenth-century Catalonia and was integrated within an influential conservative current of thought, which, drawing heavily on Catholic anti-liberalism, tried to reconcile tradition with the new world of industry. Liberalism and Jacobinism, it was claimed, had led to the atomisation of society and an overpowerful state. Instead a new synthesis was required in which the 'natural' bodies of society – such as representatives of the Church, economic corporations, reconstituted guilds and heads of family – should play a key social and political role. It was within this context that corporatist ideas, which promoted employer paternalism and joint employer-worker associations, designed to inculcate 'moral' behaviour and educate the workers, and also to foment industrial production, could emerge. Amongst political figures close to the industrial elite variants on such themes were commonplace.[6]

In the major continental European industrial centres such anti-union strategies operated most effectively in large-scale industry. It was in this environment that employers both found it easiest to coordinate their activities and had the resources to put in place paternalist systems and effectively keep unions at bay. Conditions were most propitious in heavy industry, with the archetypal examples often taken to be the iron and steel manufacturers on the German Ruhr and in the French Lorraine, who combined the carrot of housing, sickness pay and even pensions with heavy-handed social control. These industrialists used all means at their disposal to root out union organisers, while, at the same time, rejecting state social legislation and intervention in the regulation of labour relations. Significantly, the big steel-making and ship-building companies in the Basque Country would adopt similar measures.[7]

Nevertheless, between the 1860s and the 1890s in the major industrial states there was a growing tendency for the state and some sectors of indus-try to accept the need to negotiate with independent unions. On the conti-nent this was above all the case in smaller-scale sectors of the economy, oriented towards the production of consumer goods, where industrialists were in a less powerful position vis à vis their workforce.[8] In Catalonia, on the other hand, one is struck by the extent to which, despite the disperse nature of the industrial base, industrialists remained reluctant to bargain with labour unions and tried to put in place their own paternalist-disciplinarian regimes.

Several economic factors encouraged such a stance. First, because of Cat-alonia's sluggish economic development room for economic concessions was limited. Second, in the capitalist sector relatively small firms typically com-peted ferociously against each other for market share. While this might some-times make coordination between industrialists more difficult it also made them little disposed to compromise with labour. Third, despite high tariffs some industries still faced stiff foreign competition, most notably in the case of the metal industry. Nevertheless, one should not undertake too econo-mistic a reading of the reasons behind the industrialists' stance. Just as impor-tantly, as I have stressed, the state had allowed elites to carve out a high degree of autonomy and itself adopted a hostile stance towards organised labour. From the early 1880s onwards, the Liberals took a more equidistant position, but industrialists could still rely on Conservative support. Hence they faced relatively little political pressure to compromise with labour's rep-resentatives.

Furthermore, amongst industrial elites, wealth and power was much more concentrated than the territory's industrial structure would lead us to sup-pose, and this made it easier to put anti-union strategies in place. At the top of the social tree were a number of so-called 'good families', who had diver-sified their investments in industry, banking and the land, and who then, from the late-nineteenth century, began marrying their daughters into old aristocratic blood in order to add social prestige to wealth. The most notable case was that of the Comillas-Güell dynasty, whose foremost representatives during our period were the shy and retiring figure of Eusebi Güell and the abrasive Claudio López Bru, the Second Marquis of Comillas.

Further down the social hierarchy, in urban areas industrialists looked to overcome the limitations of the small size of Catalan enterprise by diversify-ing into more than one concern. They also followed the strategy of inter-marriage, above all strengthening their links with fellow Catalan entrepreneurs. In cotton textiles, indeed, it was common to marry into fellow families within the industry. From the mid-nineteenth century a number of these families, whose wealth was closely associated with textiles, rose to prominence; chief amongst them the Muntadas, who ran La España Industrial, and the families of Godó, Aranó, Juncadella, Rosal, and Llagostera and Sedó.[9]

The most comprehensive attempts to elaborate strategies based on paternalism and social control were undertaken within sectors of the cotton textile industry. This could be seen in two major spheres. First, the industrialists spurned the opportunity to enter collective bargaining with labour. The relatively liberal atmosphere of the *Sexenio Democrático* had seen the rise of a powerful cotton textile labour federation, the TCV, which, although centred on Barcelona, also affiliated workers from the surrounding industrial towns and smaller textile centres in the Alt Llobregat and Ter and Freser. It was undermined with the fall of the First Republic in 1874 but revived when the reforming Liberal Government came to power in 1881, and by 1883 had some 25,000 members, over a quarter of the cotton textile labour force. The federation was in general moderate in tone and attempted to build collective bargaining structures. In the boom conditions of the *febre d'or* this appeared a possibility, with industrialists, who were reluctant to provoke costly disputes, entering into negotiations.

This was to change dramatically from the mid-1880s onwards. As we saw in Chapter One, industrialists faced both intensifying competition and a major recession. Their response was both to force through new more intensive working practices, forge ahead with the employment of lower cost female labour and confront the TCV. Finally, after the Conservatives came to power in July 1890, they launched an all-out assault on the union, which led to its virtual destruction. By the mid-1890s only a few scattered pockets of union organisation remained alive.[10]

At the same time, the larger industrialists looked to further subordinate labour by putting more effective authoritarian-paternalist regimes in place. This process was spearheaded by the owners of the relatively large factories in the Muntanya. By expanding production on the Catalan river banks industrialists were able to take advantage of cheaper water power and, moreover, in a context in which labour agitation escalated from the early 1850s, also hoped to profit from a more subservient and cheaper labour force.[11] Some industrialists were able to realise this second objective by employing workers from the surrounding countryside. Frequently women would enter these factories while male family members continued to work on the land.[12] These workers often had to travel several miles to work and lived in small towns and isolated farmhouses, making it almost impossible to build up the solidarity, both on and off the job, necessary for collective action to be taken. Furthermore, in small towns and rural areas the industrialists acted as local *caciques* and developed a cosy relationship with the local mayor, judge and Civil Guard. In these circumstances recalcitrant workers could expect swift retribution.[13] This, however, also made it difficult to create the kind of disciplined labour force needed for constant industrial production. These so-called 'mixed workers' were still very much attached to the rural peasant economy, and, industrialists complained, were difficult to train and often abandoned their factories when needed on the land.[14]

On both the Ter and Llobregat rivers the influx of industry also brought urban growth. On the Llobregat, Manresa became a major urban centre, with over 23,000 inhabitants in 1900, and a series of populations, from Gironella in the north west to Martorell in the south, grew to the size of small industrial towns, with between about 1,500 and 4,500 inhabitants each. A similar situation could be seen on the Ter. There was no town the size of Manresa, but Ripoll, Torelló, Manlleu and Roda emerged as significant industrial centres. The largest of these towns, Manlleu, had almost 6,000 inhabitants in 1900 and was of 'an essentially industrial appearance, like Sabadell, Terrassa, Mataró, and other towns of the same type'.[15]

Workers in these centres were easier to train but urbanisation also brought in its wake labour agitation. On the Ter there was already a strong tradition of union organisation amongst the hand-loom weavers in the early-nineteenth century, and it seems that this was then transferred onto the new mechanised industry. On the Llobregat, until the 1860s, the labour force had been more quiescent, but union organisation then spread up from big industrial towns of Sadadell, Terrassa and Igualada. It was in order both to ensure a more stable labour force and impose greater social control that employers began to construct company towns. They were also encouraged by legislation approved in 1868, which gave industrial and agrarian work towns fiscal privileges and excused their members from military service.[16]

The first stage in their construction often came in the 1870s, when a number of big factories began to build housing on site along with shops and, occasionally, a school for workers' children. However, the fact that the towns often remained quite open to outside influence and that part of the workforce travelled to work from nearby urban centres meant that the TCV could still pick up much support. In response, following the assault on the unions between 1889 and 1890, larger company towns became more all-encompassing. High stone walls were built around a number of them, management structures became more authoritarian, impressive neo-gothic churches and sumptuous mansions were erected for their owners (emphasising the *loci* of power), the amount of worker housing increased, and facilities such as schools for children, shops and entertainment expanded.[17] Some company towns accompanied this by a policy of promoting stable family structures; a fact that led them not to follow the general tendency to substitute male for female labour.[18] This was made financially viable by the boom in the industry between 1891 and 1896. Indeed, in one rather unique case a major industrialist moved to the Muntanya primarily in order to combat labour activism. The Güell family closed down the Vapor Vell factory in Sants and built a large steam-driven company town in the lower Llobregat Valley at Santa Coloma de Cervelló, which opened in 1891, in order to take advantage of the cheap land and employ 'women, and young girls and boys' of peasant families, who retained 'the spirit of tradition which maintains respect for property'.[19]

In these towns working-class culture was to be rather different than that described in Barcelona in the previous chapter. The workers were typically very isolated from the outside world, left-wing newspapers were prohibited and trade unions banned. The company towns were, at the same time, steeped in conservative Catholicism, with priests and nuns employed both to administer compulsory religious services and to educate the workers' children.

There were, however, important differences between the structure of the industry on the Llobregat and Cardener and the Ter and Freser areas, which would impact on the extent to which employers were able to subordinate the labour force. The Llobregat tended to specialise in lower quality standardised fabrics, and, consequently, for industrialists in this area it made economic sense to spin and weave the product in the same establishment. On the other hand, on the Ter yarn was generally produced for somewhat higher quality garments, which were more subject to variations in taste and hence fluctuations in demand. In this latter branch of the industry it made more economic sense to specialise in spinning and sell on the yarn.[20]

As a result, on the Llobregat relatively large spinning-weaving factories predominated, most of which were turned into company towns. In all, by the 1900s there were twenty-seven such towns, most in the so-called Alt Llobregat. The largest, Sedó, had about 2,000 workers, followed by Rosal and Güell with around 1,000 workers each. The company towns employed an average of between 700 and 800 workers, and about 60 percent of the textile workers in the Llobregat were employed in these towns. Below this level there were some smaller river-based spinning and spinning-weaving establishments and also a large number of weaving factories which wove the surplus yarn. The major centre of this activity was Manresa where there were sixty-three such factories in 1919.

In the Ter and Freser area, on the other hand, on the river banks smaller spinning factories predominated. In 1919 there were fifty-three river-bank factories with an average of 188 workers each. The largest of these concerns had set up company towns. There were at most 17 of these in 1916, with probably about 400 workers each, so they were on average considerably smaller than their Llobregat counterparts. Moreover, they employed about 45 percent of the total textile labour force in the area, a smaller proportion than the company towns on the Llobregat. This was particularly clear in the central area of the Ter Valley between Sant Quirze and Roda. There were also some smaller weaving establishments, but far less than on the Llobregat as most of the yarn was sent down to Barcelona and its surrounds to be woven.[21]

Fragmentary evidence also suggests that on the Ter a smaller number of workers employed in the company towns actually lived on the premises. The most all-inclusive appears to have been the Fabra i Coats' factory, Noves Filatures (referred to by the workers as Els Anglesos or Borgonyà) near Torelló, which by 1915 provided housing for 300 of its 500 workers. The internal regime it adopted was highly benevolent; the paternalist relation between master and men was cemented by a pensions fund, a consumer cooperative, a school, free medical treatment, and a relatively short working week. This ensured the factory would have the best industrial relations record of any on the Ter. Similarly La Mambla, near the town of Orís, provided housing for 45 percent of its workers, but Coromines and Vilaseca, both also to be found near Torelló, housed only 30 and 14 percent respectively.[22] By contrast, in the 1890s, both the great Sedó company town and L'Ametlla de Merola on the

Llobregat seem to have housed over 50 percent of their workers.[23] The differences between the two areas were, indeed, noted (and perhaps exaggerated) by the Socialist union activist, Josep Comaposada, who after visiting the Alt Llobregat in 1913, and the Ter and Freser in 1916, affirmed that while in the former area 'a despicable dictatorial regime' had been established, 'the company towns along the Ter and Freser are no more than factories set up outside the towns. They exploit the workers as do all enterprises of this type, but without the attack on human dignity reaching the incredible extremes it does in the Alt Llobregat.'[24]

This was reflected in working conditions. The Llobregat factories became notorious in the 1890s for their long hours and low rates of pay. A seventy-hours week was the minimum in the early-twentieth century and, it was claimed, a sixteen-hours working day was not uncommon. On the other hand, on the Ter, sixty-six to sixty-eight hours was the norm. Wages were, moreover, between about 20 and 30 percent higher on the Ter. Indeed, there were claims in the 1890s that some Alt Llobregat company towns did not pay wages at all, but gave their workers vouchers which had to be exchanged for goods sold within the town itself.[25]

These differences were important because it was easier to organise worker protest within urban centres and, because of the smaller scale and less all-encompassing nature of the company towns on the Ter and Freser, a much higher percentage of workers in this area lived in such centres. As one observer noted, on the Ter, in 'the small industrial towns the caps (*gorras*) of the workers mix with the Catalan caps (*barretines*) of the peasants; the landscape is more appealing and life somewhat freer than in the company towns'. Consequently, although it would prove difficult for industrialists to maintain effective social control in both areas, workers on the Ter would take the lead in unionisation drives from the turn of the century.

In Barcelona some larger industrialists also adopted paternalist regimes. The most wide-ranging was that set up in the two factories run by Fabra i Coats – which, as we have seen, also had a company town on the Ter – in Sant Martí and Sant Andreu. They included a mutual-aid society, which provided workers with assistance in case of illness and accidents, a one-off payment in case of death, a pensions fund, and, from 1909, a small kindergarten and payment for the treatment of workers with tuberculosis. The factories also gave presents to workers' children at Christmas. Furthermore, aided by economies of scale they were also to operate the shortest working week in the Catalan textile industry.[26] Less impressive was the regime put into practice by Barcelona's largest textile factory, La España Industrial. The factory's owners provided interest-free loans for the workers when necessary and continued to employ them on menial tasks in old age. The sense of belonging was strengthened by the fact that generation after generation of the same family tended to work in the factory. The rapport between master and men could, at least superficially, be seen during the celebrations of the company's fiftieth anniversary in 1897, at which between 5 and 20 pesetas were given to each of the workers, and a raffle was held with sizeable cash prizes for the oldest employees. This prompted a commission of workers to present a message to the director of the factory, Maties Muntadas, eulogising him as their 'affection-ate protector'.[27]

Other large companies adopted similar practices. Once again the key fea-tures were strict social control combined with attempts to ensure the loyalty of the workforce. The big Spanish railway companies, which formed a 'state within a state', sacked any worker caught trying to form a union. On the Barcelona docks, in 1900, employers operated compulsory friendly societies while outlawing independent unions. The gas companies moved in a similar direction somewhat later. Already in the 1900s they operated anti-union poli-cies. Subsequently they introduced new paternalist elements. In 1910 Cata-lana de Gas set up a pensions' fund. The other major gas company, Gas Lebón, followed suit in 1916 and also provided sickness pay (for a limited period) and free medical treatment.[28] Such schemes could also operate in the metal industry. Jacques Valdour recalled that in an establishment in Sants which made electric lights the skilled workers were offered free medical aid and half pay for a maximum of six months in case of sickness. Moreover, all the workers enjoyed a series of small perks such as a bottle of wine and a cigar at Christmas, the chance to arrive half an hour late or work a nine-hours rather than a ten hours' day (with a proportionate reduction in wages) and to smoke at work. The policy was successful, with few unionised workers and no strikes, though he was informed that within the industry this was excep-tional.[29] The Barceloneta and Poble Nou metalworking plants did far less. Nevertheless, as we shall see, strict labour discipline was used to keep the fac-tories union-free, and they did at least adopt a paternalist veneer.

A minority of employers combined such schemes with the promotion of Catholic unions. This strategy was spearheaded by the Second Marquis of Comillas, who was behind the organisation of a National Council of Catholic Workers' Corporations in 1894. At first these were 'mixed unions' to which both industrialists and workers belonged. Given their total failure in Barcelona, from 1907 Comillas funded so-called Unions Professionals, which were set up by the Jesuit priest, Gabriel Palau. They were formally independent but, as might be supposed, did not seriously defend workers' interests.[30] In Comillas' own companies this strategy was combined with the promotion of a paternal-ist apparatus. His shipping company, La Transatlántica, for example, had a mutual-aid society and pensions' fund, a school for workers' children and pro-vided workers with housing and interest-free loans. [31]

Yet the breadth of such paternalist regimes should not be exaggerated. Smaller-scale employers found it more difficult to afford the costs, leading to laments that in Barcelona most cotton textile industrialists had not imitated the plants discussed above.[32] Within much of the cotton textile industry, employers limited themselves to trying to maintain harsh labour discipline over the largely female labour force. It was because of the lack of resources possessed by smaller employers, and because of the need to coordinate activ-ities, that industrialists, as we shall see in the subsequent sections, began to found area-wide mutual-aid societies, which, the Left argued, in effect oper-ated as yellow unions.

The Struggle to Build Independent Unions
I. Textiles and the Muntanya

Catalan conditions, therefore, made it difficult for workers to develop an independent associational sphere. There was little state or employer opposition to the operation of recreational associations, consumer cooperatives and mutual-aid societies, but the organisation of independent unions was a heavily contested terrain. The experience of textiles' trade unionism in the late-nineteenth century indicates that once a town reached the size of about 1,500 to 2,000 inhabitants, its working-class residents could build an associational milieu which could include independent unions. However, as the example of the TCV makes clear, they were vulnerable to devastating employer and, or, state counteroffensives. The climate became particularly adverse from the early 1890s onwards, when the authorities adopted an aggressively anti-union stance. Matters were made worse between 1896 and 1898 because war with Cuba provoked a deep recession.

Matters only improved after Spain's defeat at the hands of the United States in 1898 and the subsequent loss of the colonies of Cuba and Puerto Rico. First, as shown in Chapter One, the aftermath of defeat was to witness an albeit short-lived economic boom. Furthermore, the Restoration parties were to make a more serious attempt to integrate labour into the polity; the result of a perceived need to be seen as 'Europeanising' and 'modernising' Spain in order to head off criticism that they had turned the country over to the *caciques* and overseen her relegation to the ranks of backward, second-rate powers.

The first efforts in this direction were made by the new Conservative Silvela-Dato Government of March 1899, which introduced Spain's first social laws in the area of female and child labour (excepting legislation introduced by the First Republic which was never enforced) and then established the Institute for Social Reforms in 1903, which was charged not only with drawing up draft legislation, but also with undertaking studies of Spain's social reality on which such legislation would be based. Simultaneously, a system of local and provisional committees (Juntas Locales and Provinciales de Reformas Sociales) were established, on which both workers and employers were represented, in order to administer the new legislation. The Institute collaborated with the local and provincial committees, although it did not set up its own factory inspectorate until 1907.[33] This signified an important shift in the authorities' perception of their role. Moreover, they also, for the first time, attempted to incorporate independent unions into collective bargaining. Such a policy was pursued by the Conservative's first post-1898 civil governor in Barcelona, Eduardo Sanz Escartín, who adopted a benevolent stance towards labour. The key question would be, however, whether the authorities could bring employers on board and the extent to which they would maintain such a position over the long term.

The new conditions made possible a rapid revival of union organisation, which was accompanied by a massive surge in the number and duration of strikes. Particularly remarkable was the speed with which new unions sprang up in textiles, and the causes behind their resurgence provides us with a number of insights into labour relations within the industry. The first workers to challenge their employers were male spinners from Manlleu. As indicated in Chapters One and Two, the replacement of male self-acting mule spinners by women on the new ring frames had been a central element in conflict within the industry from the mid-1880s onwards. In most areas the industrialists had been successful, but in Manlleu, and to a degree in the nearby towns of Roda and Sant Hipòlit de Voltregà, the men had been able to defy their employers and ensure that they were employed on the new machines.

In Manlleu a pact had been signed to this effect in 1891. However, industrialists had, throughout the 1890s, looked to chip away at the position of the spinners, provoking the declaration of a strike in February 1899. The fact that the male spinners were central to the production process, maintained a considerable degree of autonomy on the shop floor, and that they were highly respected in their community, made it much easier for them to take on the industrialists than other categories of worker. The strike ended in success and this stimulated a revival of trade unionism on the Ter. New strikes were declared in Torelló, Vic and Roda in March. After an arduous struggle, wage increases were obtained and, just as important, it was agreed that when spinning machines became vacant or new machines were installed they would, in future, be operated by men.[34]

This emphasises that the unions' goal was above all to defend the position of the relatively privileged male workers. But under Catalan conditions simply for them to form a narrow occupational union would have been to invite defeat. Hence, in the 1899 strikes they attempted to mobilise the entire textile workforce – almost the equivalent of the entire working-class community – against their employers. In this they were, in fact, remarkably successful. Particularly important was the attitude of female workers. Although they would benefit from pay rises, if successful the result of the strikes would be to confirm their subordinate position in the factories. Despite this they enthusiastically, and, indeed, aggressively, seconded them.

This would suggest that in a pre-feminist age the women had culturally internalised the concept of the male as the primary breadwinner and their own secondary status within the factory. This was no doubt reinforced by the fact that they were frequently related to the male spinners. In the strikes a strong sense of both family and community solidarity was evident. Moreover, within this environment support for the men was reinforced by the prosaic consideration that once all players, including the industrialists, accepted the cultural ground rule that male wages were primary and female wages supplementary, the substitution of an adult male would lead to a devastating decline in family income. For the men's part, it meant that women were accepted as part of the union movement. Yet the latter's position would, as in the sphere of work, be secondary, with men staffing the union committees and making the policy decisions. Hence, within the unions we see the mix of hierarchy and solidarity which, as I emphasised in Chapter Two, was evident in the working-class neighbourhoods.

The strikes also spread to the area's larger company towns (with the exception of Fabra i Coats), indicating that they were relatively ineffective as tools of social control. This can probably be explained by the fact that they were geographically close to the urban centres, and also that a large percentage of the workforce lived in these centres and came in on a daily basis. Furthermore, the support received by the strikers embraced broader sections of the population. Particularly important in this respect was the attitude of the towns' shopkeepers, who sold the workers food on credit. These tradesmen were almost totally dependent on the workers for business and could, therefore, readily sympathise with their demands. These ties were strengthened because most of the larger-scale industrialists in the area lived in Barcelona and left the running of their factories in the hands of managers. Consequently, the majority did not build up personal contacts with the townsfolk, and could be seen as outsiders who damaged the local community's prosperity through their actions. Finally, during 1900 the strikers were also aided by the benevolent stance adopted by Sanz Escartín. This was perhaps not only the result of the Restoration regime's changed attitude towards union organisation. After the 1898 débâcle, and the loss of the lucrative Cuban market, many industrialists began to distance themselves from the regime. The authorities may have been trying to frighten them back to the fold.[35]

From their base in the major Ter Valley towns, union sympathisers launched a recruitment drive to organise workers in the more outlying areas of the Ter and Freser rivers. Simultaneously, unions staged a come back along the Llobregat and in Manresa. This made it possible to organise a new textile federation in September 1899, the FTE, whose Central Committee was established in Manlleu. At the time of its foundation it had about 7,000 affiliates, but over the following months it organised a series of highly successful recruitment drives. At its Second Congress, held in late June to early July 1900, it claimed between 50,000 and 70,000 members. This was no doubt an exaggeration, but in the short space of a year it had probably managed to affiliate about a third of the industry's workers, and been particularly successful in the Muntanya. This was indicative of a pattern often repeated in Catalan union organisation. Years of enforced silence were followed by feverish attempts to improve working conditions while the economic and, or, political conjuncture was favourable. Nevertheless, Barcelona was a black spot. It was the biggest centre of textile finishing and workers in these trades had begun to organise effectively, but unlike spinning and weaving the finishing trades were dominated by male apprenticed labour, whose demands and actions were more closely attuned to those of workers in other artisanal trades – discussed in a subsequent section – than to the problems facing most textile workers in the city. Hence they did not join the FTE.

The relationship between skill, gender and unionisation helps us to understand the reasons behind this weakness. In the 1870s and 1880s, male weavers and spinners had controlled the TCV from Barcelona, but their position became increasingly endangered. On the one hand, the locus of spinning was shifting to the Muntanya and, on the other, from the 1880s, male power-loom weavers were to a large extent replaced by women. Unlike the spinners on the Ter, the men did not vigorously oppose their substitution, probably because weaving was less highly paid and less 'aristocratic' than spinning and because in Barcelona men had a much more varied range of job opportunities than their counterparts on the Ter, especially given the growing diversification of Barcelona industry from the 1890s. In these circumstances the industrialists were able to tighten their grip and impose a high degree of social control in the female-dominated weaving establishments, with the result that, in the 1890s, union organisation in the industry in Barcelona virtually collapsed. Then, when the general union revival came at the turn of the century, women at first found it impossible to challenge the power of the cotton manufacturers.[36]

The FTE attempted, like the TCV in the 1880s, to negotiate with employers and bring rates of pay up to the level of those in the best paid towns. It also looked to ensure that the new social legislation was enforced and reverse the trend in the industry towards the substitution of male by female labour.[37] Yet it was soon to run into difficulties. As was the case in much of Catalan industry, because workers had not been able to express their discontent for years on end there was great anger and frustration, which boiled over into a large number of wildcat strikes.

The FTE also faced stubborn employer opposition. Within the Catalan employers' federation, the FTN, some leading figures had begun to advocate negotiation with independent unions as necessary to marginalise extremists from the labour movement and put labour relations on a stable footing. Yet this was not a message that had got through to many of the cotton industrialists. As already noted, employers frequently acted as local *caciques* and were loathe to see their control over their workforce compromised.[38] Hostility was sharpened by the pessimistic climate amongst manufacturers following the loss of the Cuban market and intensified further when an economic recession hit the industry in the summer of 1900. The employers' first response was to strengthen their own organisations. They had been taken aback by the initial union surge but they were quickly able to overcome their differences to form a number of local federations.[39]

Industrialists on the Freser then followed up this organisational activity with a lock-out in early 1900. Simultaneously, their rhetoric became increasingly anti-union, while they also accused the Government of exacerbating industrial conflict by favouring the workers' demands.[40] This position needs to be seen in the context of their dismay at the Conservative civil governor not playing his 'traditional' role as guarantor of business interests. Furthermore, they also voiced their opposition to the new social laws introduced by the Government, particularly its decision to limit the working hours of female and child labour, which they saw as an infringement of their 'liberty' to organise their factories as they wished.[41] This emphasised that the Catalan business class, unaccustomed to state interference in its concerns, was ill-disposed to accept any curtailment. As we shall see in the second half of the section, a similar pattern also emerged in Barcelona.

An all-out conflict in the industry was precipitated at the end of October 1900 when in Manresa and on the Llobregat mill owners provoked 3,000 textile workers into taking strike action by sacking their trade-union leadership, and, or, enforcing pay cuts. The employers quickly responded with a lock-out of their own and then tried to impose 'good conduct certificates'. In the future, it was agreed, no worker would be taken on without being recommended by his previous owner. Concomitantly, there were widespread sackings in Ripoll and on the Ter in the Gironés *comarca*. These strikes affected at least some Llobregat company towns and, therefore, indicated that even here there were still difficulties in imposing employer strategies of social control. While workers could be kept non-unionised for most the time, in a context in which they were paid low wages, worked extremely long hours, and lived in poor and overcrowded accommodation, many could still be organised if there was real hope that they could, as a result, improve their conditions of work.[42]

Industrialists in Manlleu then responded to a strike by sacking the town's entire labour force. Accordingly, by the end of November 1900 much of the FTE's membership was either on strike or locked out. The employers benefited from a change in the attitude of the Conservative Government. In Barcelona, from March 1900 onwards, faced by escalating strikes and growing political agitation, the Government had taken an increasingly hard line, responding to agitation by Catalan nationalists by first imposing martial law (which it could declare at will) in the province and then replacing Sanz Escartín. This was the first indication that under pressure the authorities would draw back and revert to previous policies. At the end of October Silvela then stepped down and was replaced by General Manuel Azcárate at the head of a new Conservative Government. In the Muntanya the employers' offensive was launched, perhaps not by coincidence, several days later.

The new authorities rapidly showed themselves favourably disposed to the mill owners. On 1 November the Government reacted to a Carlist uprising by suspending constitutional guarantees throughout Spain.[43] With the press muzzled it then moved against the textile unions. Troops and civil guards were sent to the textile towns, workers were imprisoned – including the Central Committee of the FTE – union headquarters were closed down, the press was censored and working-class papers found it difficult to publish. The FTE's mouthpiece, *Revista Social*, for example, was forced to suspend publication, never to reappear. Not until March 1901 would civilian rule be re-established. As in 1890 to 1891, the chance of putting Catalan labour relations on a more stable footing, with employer and union representatives engaged in collective bargaining, was not taken. The authorities' fear of unions and social strife had resurfaced and they had not been able to maintain the necessary distance from social elites. This, as we shall see, would be typical of the regime over the next twenty years. There were people both within the official parties and close to the centres of power (particularly within the Institute for Social Reforms) who urged the integration of labour into the polity and a firmer attitude towards the industrialists. But all too often, in the heat of battle, they were ignored.

In response, the FTE tried to organise a solidarity strike of the entire Catalan working class. It was followed throughout much of the Muntanya, but in

Barcelona it had no impact and after a short time burned itself out. Consequently, the back of the FTE was broken. Yet the employer onslaught continued unabated. In a meeting of mill owners at the Barcelona headquarters of the FTN it was agreed not to employ those workers most identified with the unions. This decision became known as the 'hunger pact'. The result was that about 800 workers were sacked and in order to find work in a Catalan cotton textile factory they had to hide their true identity. This attack on the unions was combined with moves to intensify production, restructure the labour process and reestablish social control. Such actions quelled labour protest on the Llobregat. In the Ter Valley, however, the workers once again put up a stiffer resistance. The employers were looking to press ahead with their plans to employ women on the ring frames. The refusal of a number of women in Roda to operate the machines escalated into another all-out confrontation, with the Ter and Fresser Valley employers' associations declaring a general lock-out on 11 March 1901.

The anger and frustration felt by the workers now burst into violence. In Torelló a group of workers set fire to the house of the former Mayor and factory owner, Antonio Mercadell. In Ripoll a demonstration of cotton textile workers ended in clashes with the Civil Guard, with one worker killed and two critically injured. The most dramatic events took place in Manlleu, where the workers organised an attack on the local employers' meeting house or *casino*, and injured three of those inside. The crowd then attacked the houses of the Mayor and two more industrialists, setting them all on fire. The size of the crowd made it impossible for the Civil Guard to control. Luckily its commander adopted a conciliatory stance and avoided bloodshed. Order was, nevertheless, only restored when the local authorities promised to do everything in their power to find a solution to the conflict and obtain the reinstatement of the workers subject to the 'hunger pact'.[44]

With these events, class hatred had reached a point difficult to surpass. The situation in the Ter Valley was now extremely explosive and another outbreak of violence was feared. Tempers were, nevertheless, cooled by the replacement of the Conservative civil governor in the run-up to the Liberal victory in the elections held on 19 March 1901. The new man adopted a far more even-handed approach, reaching a compromise solution. On the one hand, the employers agreed to end their lock-out and revoke the hunger pact; on the other hand, their right to employ women on the ring frames was recognised.[45]

The factories finally reopened on 18 March. Amongst the workforce there was considerable discontent at the compromise reached, as it was felt that employers would now have a free hand to employ female labour. The sense of betrayal became more intense when it emerged that few of the workers subject to the 'hunger pact' would actually be re-employed. The workers' fears were, however, in some respects exaggerated. As a result of the employer onslaught, and with no end to the recession in sight, trade-union organisation was greatly weakened throughout the Muntanya. In Manresa and its surrounds, along the Freser and upper Ter, and even in Torelló, the unions were completely destroyed. This meant that unions were restricted to Manlleu,

Roda and Sant Hipòlit. But in these towns the ferocity of the workers' reaction to the March lock-out had made the industrialists draw back from their decision to employ women on the ring frames. They, therefore, became the only areas in the Muntanya which continued to employ large numbers of male spinners on the new machines. In Manlleu this would remain the case until the years of the First World War at least.[46]

From this date the big company towns on the Llobregat also strove to perfect their internal regimes. The model broadly accepted was to maintain a minority of relatively well-paid and well-treated workers in the company towns themselves, and make up the numbers largely though female and child labour who came in on a daily basis from the surrounding towns. This strategy had, it seems, been inaugurated by Güell's new company town from the early 1890s and was successfully pursued in the Sedó company town, amongst others, from the turn of the century. And as a result, in future years the Alt Llobregat manufacturers would more effectively maintain social control in their factories.[47]

Such solutions were more difficult to put into practice on the Ter, where male workers still retained a strong position on the factory floor. This was most evident in Manlleu, and it was here that an attempt was made to establish some form of industrial reconciliation machinery. The project was launched by Albert Rusiñol, the owner of a company town just outside the town, and a leading figure both in the FTN and the major Catalanist party, the Lliga Regionalista. Rusiñol had already reacted to the previous strikes by opening a school in this company town, which he put in the hands of the clergy.[48] He was in touch with more moderate figures with the FTN, two of whom, Federic Rahola and Joaquín Aguilar, drew up its statutes.[49] It was most likely to work in the Rusiñol company town because within the context of the Ter he was considered a responsible employer who paid relatively high wages. It consisted of both a friendly society and an arbitration board of workers and employers to settle disputes. Its members were clearly not Rusiñol's creatures. They participated in the Manlleu Junta Local de Reformas Sociales, supporting social legislation and cuts in working hours.[50]

Joaquín Aguilar hoped that it would serve as a model and create a conservative strata within the working class opposed to industrial militancy. Yet it was never much of a success, only attracting between 150 and 200 members, mostly from Rusiñol's company town.[51] The problem was that affiliates could form part of no other union. Thus, the freedom of workers who participated in it was inevitably curtailed, and consequently supporters of independent trade unions saw the *patronat*, as it was pejoratively called, as an instrument in the hand of the industrialists.[52] Moreover, the position of other Ter and Freser Valley employers was ambivalent. They had published a book in 1902 in which they stated that they favoured 'mixed commissions' formed by 'private initiative' (i.e., by themselves), but given their emphasis on the employer's right to decide wages and working conditions in his factory it is difficult to see what they would discuss.[53] These debates and projects were all part of the discussion taking place within employer circles on the mechanisms needed to stabilise social relations in Catalonia, with the overall stress still on how to subordinate labour to the employers' demands.[54]

Nevertheless, opposition to independent unions was not uniform throughout the textile industries, with the woollen textile industry providing a partial exception. As indicated in Chapter One, the industrial towns of Sabadell and Terrassa specialised in woollen textile manufacture. Industry in Terrassa was concentrated in a relatively small number of concerns and this tended to facilitate the elaboration of authoritarian-paternalist regimes.[55] In Sabadell, on the other hand, the industry was small-scale and retained a familial air. Moreover, in contrast to the cotton textile manufacturers, perhaps because the value of the final product was higher and so the need to cut costs not so urgent, the Sabadell industrialists had made no concerted effort to redivide the labour process and continued employing men in spinning and weaving. As a result, male workers retained a strong position on the shop floor and – unlike the situation in cotton textiles – labour relations in the industry were relatively cordial. Thus, the Sabadell woollen workers had been able to maintain their organisation intact throughout the 1890s. Unions grew in strength from late 1897 and at the end of 1899 2,557 workers formed part of a local labour federation, the FOS. This figure represented about a quarter of the town's industrial working class. The largest union was that of the power-loom weavers, which had 812 members, 'a number of affiliates as great or greater than in its best moments'.[56]

Despite maintaining a mutual-aid society (which, in fact, received very little support), and being at the very least suspicious of union organisation, the woollen-textile industrialists proved willing to negotiate and signed collective agreements in 1898 and 1900. These agreements meant that wages and working hours were a lot better than in the cotton textile towns.[57] There was a dark cloud on the horizon. In the mid-1890s two French firms, Harmel Germans and Seydoux i Cia, had established themselves in Sabadell in order to circumvent Spanish tariff barriers. Their owners were strongly anti-union, production was more intensive in their factories, they undercut local wage rates and, unlike the Sabadell employers, operated piece rates. The workers' unions feared that under threat from the competition Sabadell manufacturers would be forced to follow suit and, therefore, in 1899 launched strikes in the French factories to try and force them into line. The smaller Harmel spinning plant quickly gave way, but Seydoux would be more resilient. The result was a long-drawn-out dispute which, at one point, led to a general strike in the town. However, the owners were able to recruit blackleg labour 'from the countryside and mountains of Catalonia' and, with the factory surrounded by civil guards, continue production.[58]

Yet the rest of Sadadell's industrialists did not follow the same confrontational course. Little affected by the loss of the last colonies the industry did not suffer a major recession until the summer of 1903, when a general downturn hit Catalan industry. And in these circumstances, the woollen weavers were able to gain further increases in wage rates. Only when the recession struck would industrialists begin to nibble away at wages and try to increase working hours. But even then there was no generalised offensive against the woollen industry unions. As noted in the previous chapter, a number of the Sabadell plants became known as 'strong houses' in which unions remained entrenched.[59]

The Struggle to Build Independent Unions
II. Barcelona and the Skilled Trades

In Barcelona both labour organisation and strikes also took off during these years, although, because the economic climate remained buoyant for longer, they did not hit their peak until the summer of 1903. In 1899 there were perhaps around 15,000 workers unionised, but by 1903 the figure had shot up to some 42,000. Even more dramatically, over the same period the number of strikers rose from around 2,500 to 52,000 (see table 3.1.). As in the Muntanya there was a great burst of strike action, with, in most cases, workers able to voice their demands for the first time since the early 1890s.

Table 3.1. Comparison of Strikes, Strikers and Working Days Lost in Barcelona and the Rest of Spain, 1899–1914[1]

	Barcelona			Percentage of Spanish Total		
Year	Strikes	Strikers	Working Days Lost	Strikes	Strikers	Working Days Lost
1899	8	2,403	169,760	n/a	n/a	n/a
1900	21	9,555	149,317	n/a	n/a	n/a
1901	11	16,723	215,931	n/a	n/a	n/a
1902	9	17,689	379,145	n/a	n/a	n/a
1903	74	52,015	1.589,853	n/a	n/a	n/a
1904	25	11,047	358,510	n/a	n/a	n/a
1905	24	1,676	36,042	15.7	8.3	n/a
1906	24	2,491	25,508	16.6	10.2	n/a
1907	21	1,837	54,590	13.8	9.0	n/a
1908	22	2,330	31,517	12.1	5.9	n/a
1909	11	987	3,472	7.5	15.1	n/a
1910	43	15,256	854,692	17.5	67.1	83.8
1911	31	13,065	451,118	10.0	44.2	65.6
1912	47	13,985	266,490	16.8	31.2	23.3
1913	68	43,701	1,886,265	23.9	65.5	67.2
1914	49	18,040	4 69,910	21.7	34.5	42.2

Note

1. Given the lack of any government statistics, data for Barcelona for the years 1899 to 1902 is based on a close examination of the republican and working-class press, above all *La Publicidad*. For the years 1903 to 1913 I have preferred the data elaborated on a yearly basis by the Catalan social-Catholic, Miguel Sastre i Sanna, over data produced (from 1905) by the Institute for Social Reforms. The only change I have made is to reduce the inflated figure of 63,870 strikers he gives for the 1913 textile strike (which was, roughly, the number of strikers in Catalonia as a whole) to a more realistic 27,500. The 1914 figures for Barcelona are taken from Josep Lluís Martín Ramos. For the rest of Spain I have used the data from the Institute for Social Reforms.

Sources: *La Publicidad*, 1899–1902; Miguel Sastre y Sanna, *Las huelgas en Barcelona y sus resultados, 1903–1914*, 8 vols, Barcelona, 1904–1916; Instituto de Reformas Sociales, *Estadística de huelgas. Memoria de 1905–1914*, Madrid, 1906-1917; Josep Lluís Martín Ramos, 'Anàlisi del moviment vaguístic a Barcelona, *1914–1923*', *Reçerques*, no. 20, 1988, 110.

With respect to the workers who unionised, a number of elements stand out. First, unionisation centred on blue-collar workers. There were probably between 230,000 and 250,000 wage earners in Barcelona at the turn of the century, around 150,000 of whom can be classified as working in industry.[60] While around 25 percent of this latter group were unionised at the height of the union revival in 1903, there were only a couple of white-collar unions, the waiters and cooks, and a handful of shopworkers' associations, only one of which, the ADM, actually operated on trade-union lines. During this year a new, and subsequently very important, association of shop and office workers, the CADCI, was founded, but it did not at first function as a trade union, focusing instead on providing mutual aid and education for its members. Only in the second decade of the century did it begin to take a somewhat more militant stance. At its apogee in 1900 the ADM had 800 members, but its numbers had slipped back to 300 by the end of the decade. The impression is that it was able to attract more radical elements (above all shopworkers employed in more working-class areas of town), but that most of the trade stood aloof. The CADCI, on the other hand, enjoyed a steady advance, growing from less than 400 affiliates in 1904 to over 3,000 by 1914; its class-collaborationist stance clearly enjoying greater sympathy. Other groups of employees, from domestic servants to the liberal professions, were even less likely to enter the union orbit. Hence, the cultural divisions within Barcelona society, discussed in Chapter Two, corresponded with those within the world of work.[61]

Yet, as one would expect, there were important variations in the ability to organise of different groups of industrial workers. The pattern was similar to that of the major continental western European countries in the second half of the nineteenth century. Between 1898 and 1900, skilled workers were at the forefront of the growth of labour unions. As emphasised in the previous chapter, they had, through apprenticeship restrictions and shopfloor autonomy, been able to attain a relatively strong position within the process of production, they tended to live in a more stable community environment than the unskilled, and, over time, had developed solidaristic bonds both within the trade and neighbourhood. As a result, they were in a strong position to form trade unions.

Skilled workers were also at the forefront of strike action. During this period strikes were most frequent in metalworking and construction (see table 3.2.), and it was the iron foundrymen, boilermakers and mechanics or engineers (*cerrajeros mecánicos*) in the metal industry, and the bricklayers and their labourers, carpenters and painters in construction, who were involved in the hardest-fought strikes. Other groups of skilled workers, like those in the textile finishing trades, the cabinetmakers, compositors and tanners, also figured heavily.[62] These workers shared some common characteristics; they were under heavy pressure from the advance of capitalism and harboured heart-felt grievances regarding what they perceived as their deteriorating working conditions. Furthermore, the strikes in these industries were above all centred on the medium-sized factories with around thirty to sixty workers. As I have shown, industrialists in the larger establishments could operate authoritarian-paternalist systems more effectively, while the smallest workshops were not normally subject to the same pressures as those in the more capitalistic sector.

Table 3.2. Propensity of Workers in Barcelona to Strike by Industry, 1899–1914[1]

Industry	No. Workers	No. strikers	Length strikes (days)	Days Lost	Strikers as a Percentage of the Workforce
Metal	8,943	26,305	57.1	1,502,016	294.1
Construction	15,229	43,274	33.9	1,466,989	284.2
Sailors and dockers	4,437	9,924	31.9	316,576	224.2
Land transport	17,890	32,000	18.9	604,800	178.9
Leather trades	1,621	1,872	41.9	78,437	115.5
Textiles	26,999	30,431	21.4	651,223	112.7
Textile finishing trades	7,678	8,637	26.1	225,426	112.5
Furniture trades	2,686	2,380	32.0	76,160	88.6
Clothing	20,479	16,290	22.8	371,412	79.5
Woodworking	3,858	2,901	32.4	93,992	75.2
Food processing	8,129	5,551	13.2	73,272	68.3
Glass and ceramics	3,069	1,970	37.7	74,269	64.2
Gas and electricity	2,224	960	8.3	7968	43.2
Book trades	7,495	2,391	26.2	62,644	32.0
Coach and cart makers	2,206	586	93.1	54,557	26.6
Paper and chemicals	6,183	1,063	9.4	9,992	17.2

Note:
1. As in table 3.1. the figures given by Sastre i Sanna for the 1913 textile strike have been reduced to 27,500. The number of workers did not increase massively between 1899 and 1914 so I have taken the 1905 'Censo obrero' as roughly representative of the entire period. Given that most carpenters worked on building sites and that their unions were often more attuned to developments within the construction industry I have included them under this heading rather than in woodworking.

Sources: 'Censo obrero de 1905', in *Anuario Estadístico de la Ciudad de Barcelona, 1905*, Barcelona, 1907, pp. 599–632; *La Publicidad*, 1899–1902; Miguel Sastre y Sanna, *Las Huelgas en Barcelona y sus Resultados, 1903–1914*, Barcelona, 1904–1915.

Nevertheless, once union organisation had taken off, some non-craft workers were to follow suit. As table 3.2. indicates, transport and the waterfront were also high up in the league table of strikes. Between 1900 and 1903 in these sectors it was tram workers, dockers and carters who would most vigorously challenge their employers. This was perhaps related to the fact that they worked in the open air and were not, therefore, subject to such close supervision as factory-based labour. Moreover, many dockers and carters worked on the docks in front of the Fifth District and lived close by. This area, as noted in the previous chapter, also housed many skilled workers, and it would quickly become a hotbed of labour agitation.

Other groups of workers found it much more difficult to follow suit. Indeed, right up until the winter of 1918, when, as we shall see in Chapter Seven, most of the city's labour force flooded into the unions, some groups were barely able to organise at all. This was the case of workers in the paper and chemical industries, in the factory-based sector of food-processing, of workers who laboured in the city's large gas, water and electricity plants, of those employed in female-dominated sweated workshops, and of female out-workers. Moreover, workers in the shipping and on the railways, and to a lesser degree in textiles, found it extremely difficult to unionise effectively.

It is more difficult to assess why workers failed to organise than why they did; silence does not generate information. Nevertheless, several factors were clearly involved. First, the large scale of a number of these industries should be noted. As we saw in the previous section, in shipping, on the railways, and in the gas and electricity plants, paternalist-authoritarian regimes were established, designed to keep unions at bay. The make-up of the labour force was also important. In gas and electricity it was divided between office workers, disdainful of unions, and the lesser skilled, who could be easily hired and fired.[63] In areas such as textiles and the sweated trades, moreover, female labour predominated, and I have already discussed the high degree of social control imposed upon this workforce. In the newly emerging chemical industry, the large factory size and high proportion of unskilled labourers seem to have been key factors. Unskilled workers were often migrants who not only lacked power on the shopfloor but at first would have focused on adapting to their new environment. Nevertheless, it was the female outworkers whose plight was the most desperate. They were isolated and atomised, and received no encouragement from the male-dominated unions.

Once unionised, workers frequently made a number of simultaneous demands. In the inflationary context of the years 1899 to 1914 the call for a wage increase was a key element in many petitions, but, perhaps surprisingly, demands for cuts in working hours were even more common. This related to workers' fears, in the more capitalistic sectors of the economy, that technological change was leading to unemployment. Shorter working hours, union leaders argued, would reduce unemployment and this, in turn, would make it easier to build up a powerful union movement. This was at the root of the increasingly generalised demand for an eight-hours day throughout Catalan industry.

Journeymen also made a series of additional demands to shore up their position against what were seen as the threats of capitalist development. Chief amongst these were the 'regulation' of apprenticeship and, where they operated, the abolition of piece rates. Typically, apprenticeship regulation involved the enforcement of rules regarding the ratio of apprentices to journeymen, the length of an apprenticeship, apprentices' pay, and the tasks apprentices should undertake. There were also attempts, optimistically, to ensure apprentices were fourteen and could read and write. Piece rates, finally, were also opposed as leading to speed-ups, forcing workers to exhaust themselves, compete against each other and produce sub-standard goods. In order to enforce these demands, when they were strong enough workers would try to establish a closed shop.[64]

As with the Muntanya, as the strike wave rose in intensity unions would face growing hostility from both employers and the state. Industrialists, from the outset, began organising their own trade and industrial federations with the express object of striking back. Henceforth a division of labour was established within the employer class; for while the FTN took a more political role (for example, discussing issues of tariff protection with central government), the federations would deal with labour issues. The counteroffensive's overall effectiveness can be gauged from the fact that between 1899 and 1901, with employers caught off-guard by the burst of labour militancy, of thirty-four major strikes sixteen ended in victory and only five in defeat. Yet between 1902 and 1903, with the industrialists now in a much stronger position, only thirteen out of forty-four significant strikes were to end in victory and seventeen in defeat.[65] Within the employer federations, men from middling plants were to the fore. They were, after all, those most frequently affected. The 'good families' of Barcelona, on the other hand, tended to take a back seat. They did not wish to get their hands dirty with the day-to-day business of fighting labour organisation, but they would provide discreet political and financial support.[66]

With respect to the state's response, at first, as already noted, the Silvela-Dato Government adopted a conciliatory stance, but with the rapid growth of strikes in the spring of 1900 it took an increasingly hard line. From May, with martial law in force, large number of union meetings were suspended, the press was banned from commenting on strikes, and at the end of the year the Civil Guard was used to break a strike on the Barcelona docks. Only when the Liberals came to power in March 1901 did matters improve somewhat. Martial law was lifted and constitutional guarantees restored, although the former was briefly reimposed when general strikes were declared in support of the tram workers in May 1901 and metalworkers in February 1902. The latter strike, in particular, also saw large number of workers arrested and union headquarters closed. Unions were soon able to reopen and operate relatively freely. Yet when the Conservatives took office from December 1902 the Government once again toughened up its stance, especially as strikes peaked in the summer of 1903.

Escalating strike action led both workers and employers to try and build broader fronts, with the result that from 1901 the dynamics of industrial relations increasingly took on the appearance of an overarching class confrontation. During 1898 most unions were isolated, small and financially weak. Union committees were, generally, made up of workers who met up after work, often in a local tavern or café. Moreover, separate unions sprang up in each working-class neighbourhood. This reflected the articulation of Barcelona analysed in Chapter Two, with close-knit working-class communities congregated around the local factories and workshops in each suburb. Looked at from the perspective of the city as a whole the result was an enormous proliferation of unions: at the turn of the century there were well over one hundred, including several neighbourhood-based unions of bricklayers, carpenters and the like.[67]

Efforts were, however, quickly put into the construction of trade federations, both at the level of the city and further afield. Such moves made it possible to organise strike action far more effectively and ensure that workers in the same trade would not undercut each other. Thus, in 1898 and 1902 respectively, the Barcelona carpenters and painters founded Catalan federations, while the latter set up a Spanish federation in 1903. These federations brought out their own trade journals in order keep workers abreast of developments and strengthen their sense of craft identity. Moreover, they launched vigorous campaigns and strikes to improve working conditions. In 1899 most workers in construction (including the carpenters) worked nine hours, and an eight-hours day became the centre of their concerns.

In elite crafts, where relations between workers and masters were relatively cordial, union organisation often remained structured along narrow craft lines. A good example of this is the coopers, who, unusually, had managed to operate a Spanish federation from 1872, and who refused to establish ties with other groups of workers in the woodworking industry. However, in more conflict-prone sectors unions felt a need to ally with workers in other trades, in order to confront their employers more effectively. Such a process could, for example, be seen amongst the wood and furniture workers, who founded a Spanish federation in 1899, the National Federation of Woodworking Unions (which did not, however, include the carpenters, a trade that straddled construction and woodworking). In Catalonia this would then provide the springboard for a largely successful campaign to reduce working hours in the industry from ten to nine. Similarly, in printing compositors were behind the organisation of a local printers' federation in 1901, which would then wage a successful industry-wide strike for a nine-hours day in late 1903.[68]

Similar motives were behind the moves by some craft workers to reach out and establish alliances with the unapprenticed. Despite reservations in some quarters, between 1901 and 1903 bricklayers organised joint provincial, Catalan and Spanish federations with their labourers, and in Barcelona, although they operated separate local federations, they launched coordinated strikes for both wage rises and reductions in working hours. Had the bricklayers not adopted such a stance they would have been highly vulnerable to the threat of being replaced by their labourers during strikes. In Barcelona in 1901 they became the first major trade to achieve an eight-hours day (although with the proviso that they would undertake overtime when necessary), leading to much celebration in the working-class press. Moreover, bricklayers in industrial towns throughout Catalonia were quick to try and follow suit.[69]

This need to reach out to the lesser skilled could also be seen in textiles. During 1901 a number of anarchist-influenced unions, with the textile finishing trades' union, the Stampers and Bleachers, to the fore, attempted to organise the mass of female workers by holding a number of pro-union meetings. This once again raises the important question of the relation between male and female workers within the world of work. In Barcelona examples can be found of small craft unions which totally excluded women.[70] However, the weight of textiles in the economy was so great that union activists from the skilled trades overcame the indifference that much of the union movement felt towards the organisation of women, in the belief that to effectively unionise the industry would greatly strengthen the labour movement as a whole. This needs to be seen in a context in which union leaders most closely associated with the anarchist wing of the labour movement argued that, in order to challenge the industrialists successfully, mobilisation of the entire workforce would be necessary.

Their efforts were no doubt aided by the fact that the female weavers were frequently related to the skilled men, with particularly close family connections to workers in the finishing trades. By late 1901 the union activists were starting to enjoy some success, establishing an independent union in El Clot, which by December had about 2,000 affiliates. This revealed the first chink in the textile industrialists' armour. The union probably took root in this part of town because relatively small-scale plants of between forty and sixty workers predominated.[71] On the other side of town, in Sants and its environs, were to be found most of the major factories, like La España Industrial, which could operate anti-union policies more effectively. Unusually, despite the role played by workers from the male finishing trades in the union's formation, it had an all-woman committee, with the fiery anarchist, Teresa Claramunt, its most charismatic figure. Yet this does not mean that it broke free from patriarchal presuppositions. On the contrary, its leadership echoed views voiced in the Muntanya that – to cite one activist – they should organise so that in the future they might 'hand over the machines to our beloved male colleagues'.[72]

The attempt to build industrial fronts could be seen in other sectors in which industrialists were overtly opposed to labour organisation. The carters were able to forge a Local Transport Federation with the dockers in June 1903, which boasted 4,000 members. Metalworkers formed a local industrial federation in November 1901, and, subsequently, a number of Catalan metal unions set up a Spanish federation in the early summer of 1903.[73]

Along with articulating these fronts, faced with employer hostility unions frequently generalised strike action in order to try and bring intolerable pressure to bear. At the same time, fearful of defeat, young activists often resorted to intimidation and violence. During most disputes this was directed at non-unionised workers, although occasionally foremen and industrialists were also targeted. Easy recourse to guns (which were, fortunately, extremely inaccurate) meant that such confrontations would, from time to time, have deadly consequences. In 1903 alone, according to figures by Miguel Sastre i Sanna, 370 workers were arrested and five blacklegs assassinated. The nature of strike action was also affected by the make-up of the security services. The poverty-stricken Spanish state could not afford a large police force. In March 1903, the Barcelona civil governor complained that he only had 207 police and 700 civil guards at his disposal (200 brought in from other centres). Unable to police disputes effectively, the authorities were particularly prone to suspend constitutional guarantees and, or, use mounted civil guards. When matters became particularly serious troops were called out. This precipitated violent clashes between strikers and the forces of order. Furthermore, the inefficiency of both the police and judiciary encouraged activists to use violence because they were so unlikely to get caught. Sastre i Sanna noted that only one person was prosecuted during 1903 and that he was declared innocent.[74]

Nevertheless, labour relations differed notably between industries. In the woodworking and printing industries there was, overall, a grudging acceptance amongst the manufacturers that unions were in Barcelona to stay. In the big construction trades – carpentry, painting and, above all, bricklaying – the employers' reaction was more overtly hostile. Most determined to halt the union advance were the contractors, who were at the apex of industry, whose profits were dependent on keeping down costs, and who directly employed large numbers of bricklayers and bricklayers' labourers. During 1900 they formed a united front with the industry's master bricklayers, and when the bricklayers and their labourers called a trade-wide strike for a wage rise, in 1903, they held firm and forced them back to work empty-handed.[75]

In textiles, transport and the metal industry, employers were determined to break the back of the unions. In the first industry this was a relatively easy task. The women showed in a number of hard-fought strikes at the end of 1901 that they could be every bit as militant as their male colleagues. But at the beginning of 1902 the union still had only a tenuous hold, enabling industrialists to destroy it totally during the heavy repression that followed the general strike in favour of the metalworkers in February 1902.

In transport the two major areas of strife were trams and the waterfront. The tramworkers first unionised in 1900 and there then followed a number of disputes, culminating in a strike aimed at imposing a closed shop on 27 April 1901. The absolute refusal of the tram companies to give way then provided a number of pro-anarchist unions with the opportunity to try to organise a general strike on 7 May. This strike provides us with an important insight into the dynamics of labour relations in Barcelona. When the tram strike began, in working-class areas women and young lads emerged onto the streets and stoned the trams which still operated, then, once the general strike had been declared, they shifted their attention to the windows of factories and shops that refused to close. Within working-class Barcelona the general strike was quite solid for two days, but then quickly petered out. This was indicative of a considerable degree of solidarity. There was a sense within sectors of labour linked to the unions that a defeat for the tramworkers could have negative repercussions for the movement as a whole. This must be seen in a context in which trade unionism in cotton textiles had been undermined by a joint employer-state offensive at the end of 1900, and in which other trades and industries were struggling to unionise against employer hostility.

The role of women is also noteworthy. Union activists sometimes complained that, fearful of losing their partner's income, women had a negative impact during strikes.[76] There is no doubt some truth to this in cases in which strikes affected specific male-dominated trades. When a man came out on strike, a woman's ability to provide for her family was seriously compromised. But in such broader conflicts active participation by at least part of the female community was always a feature. This again emphasises that while women might have seen men as having the primary role in the world of work, this was not incompatible with women giving them active support.

Despite the defeat, the workers were, at first, able to maintain their unions intact, but in late 1903 and 1904, as the union movement was eclipsed, the tram companies were to hit back and destroy the labour unions. Most drastic was the action taken by the Anònima tram company, behind which was to be found British capital. At the beginning of 1904 it appointed a new head, Mariano Foronda, who came from a well-known Conservative family, and who proceeded to sack most of the tram drivers and bring in workers from his native Castile. In subsequent years he would cultivate the typical paternalist-disciplinarian regime to which most Catalan industrialists seemed to aspire, founding a mutual-aid society in 1907, providing free travel for workers and Christmas presents for their children.[77]

The story of the Barcelona waterfront is in many respects comparable. I have already noted that on the docks employers maintained a staunch anti-union stance. In 1900, coal unloaders first made their mark in four strikes in which the right to form an independent union rather than having to belong to the coal merchants' friendly society was a key factor. They followed these up with a new strike at the beginning of 1902 for a wage rise. Because workers were employed on a daily basis and, therefore, vulnerable to being replaced, violence was the hallmark of disputes on the docks. This encouraged the authorities to come down hard in the last two disputes, using mounted civil guards to ride down the strikers milling around the docks and making mass arrests. The result was defeat in early 1902; large numbers of strikebreakers were employed and the workforce was once again forced to join the employer-sponsored friendly society, the Germantat de Sant Joan.

In late 1901 the carters were also involved in a hard-fought but inconclusive strike, in which union activists were victimised. It was this that led them to take the initiative in constructing the Transport Federation in the summer of 1903. With the dockers able to paralyse unloading operations they hoped that this would put them in a stronger position in any future dispute. The coal unloaders also now believed that they could take on the coal merchants more effectively and quickly launched a strike for the recognition of their union. They had overestimated their strength. Despite solidarity strikes by both the carters and other dockers' unions, with the coal merchants enjoying strong state support, and with large numbers of civil guards patrolling the docks, they were totally defeated. 700 strikers were sacked, the coal unloaders' union was destroyed and that of the carters seriously weakened. Once again the coal merchants' mutual-aid society reigned supreme.[78]

Even more important in its implications was an ongoing conflict in the metal industry. At its heart was the employers' refusal to concede the workers' demand for a cut in working hours from ten to nine, with the argument that should they give way they would not be able to compete with foreign manufacturers.[79] Their determination to undermine the labour unions was apparent from 1900, when the Association of Catalan Foundry Owners tried to impose a good conduct certificate on its workforce and the Barcelona Society of Machine Constructors set up a mutual-aid society, open to workers who did not support 'unfounded and inopportune strikes and demands'.[80] This was indicative of the policy the industrialists would subsequently pursue. When the Barcelona Metalworkers' Federation called for a nine-hours day in December 1901 it was rejected out of hand, and, after the declaration of an industry-wide general strike on 16 December, the employers prepared to break the union's back.

Given the importance of this dispute it is worth considering it in some detail. The strike call was widely backed, although not all the workers in the industry came out. As would be expected, a large number of marginal workshops stood aside. Moreover, workers in the large Barceloneta and Poble Nou factories – most notably those of La Maquinista – were also reticent. This does not seem to have been the result of better working conditions.[81] Rather the key factor was the employers' greater ability to put in place anti-union regimes. La Maquinista made its position clear after the defeat of a mechanics' strike in May 1901, when it sacked strikers 'who had been involved in coercions, along with the leaders of the revolt'. Similarly, when the November 1901 strike began, the company threatened to sack any workers who became involved. Significantly, it was after this period of agitation that, in 1903, the factory launched its own mutual-aid society, the Humanitarian Association of the Workers of the Workshops of the Maquinista Terrestre i Marítima.[82]

The metal employers were also helped because, despite the fact that the Barceloneta was the most proletarian neighbourhood in Barcelona, the overall climate was rather hostile to trade unionism. The big shipping companies had successfully blocked unionisation in this part of town. Hence, the metal-working establishments, which were located on the Barceloneta and Poble Nou shoreline, had their southern flank covered. The railway line to France also passed near the shore, creating a barrier against the rest of Barcelona. Finally, the fact that there was such a large concentration of big anti-union shops in itself made union organisation difficult, with metalworkers from the rest of Barcelona having on occasion to storm the Barceloneta to bring production to a halt. Not surprisingly then, union activists were extremely antagonistic towards the Barceloneta concerns, most especially 'that feudal castle' La Maquinista; a limited liability company which had considerable influence in government circles: its director, Josep Cornet i Mas, had been a Conservative member of parliament and it had a number of powerful political figures on its board.[83] This hostility was dramatically demonstrated in February 1902 when a group of strikers armed with clubs and pistols attacked the members of a mutual-aid society, La Fraternal Obrera, many of whom worked in La Maquinista, as they left the premises of the Catalanist association, Catalunya i Avant.[84]

Throughout the strike the employers remained intransigent. Echoing the attitude of the Muntanya industrialists, the Society of Machine Constructors issued a communiqué voicing their dissatisfaction at the Government's response and calling for the civil governor to take a harder line.[85] As a result, the strike drifted and became increasingly embittered, with clashes between strikers, blacklegs and the security forces. It was in this climate that, with the striking metalworkers clearly unable to attain victory by themselves, voices were raised within anarchist circles in favour of a city-wide general strike. This they finally achieved on the morning of 16 February 1902; flying pickets used persuasion (and intimidation if necessary) to prevent workers going in, and, as in the tramworkers' dispute of 1901, groups of workers, including working-class women (some wearing red armbands) and young lads, stoned trams and factories and attacked shops and taverns that refused to close. Even more dramatic, the strike spread to the industrial towns around Barcelona, where workers took advantage of the situation to press for other demands. Furthermore, it also took on elements of a violent insurrection, with street fighting between union activists and the security services.

The use of coercion cannot by itself explain the general strike's success. At one level, as in the case of the tramworkers, it can be seen as rooted in a certain weakness of organised labour. The metalworkers by themselves were not strong enough to achieve victory, and amongst other groups of workers there was a sense that the defeat of what was – along with construction – the major focus of union organisation in the city would seriously weaken the entire labour movement. Sympathy was heightened because many groups of workers faced similar problems, and because of the metalworkers' desperate plight; they had been out for two months and were suffering great hardship. The general mood was captured by the anarchist metalworkers' union leader, Ramon Homades: 'Let no one think that we are defending the metalworkers here, because we are defending all the workers.'[86]

It was not to be, however. Faced with martial law, the deployment of troops, the closure of union headquarters, and the detention of several hundred activists, the solidarity strike crumbled after a week and the metalworkers had to go back. On returning to work the leading figures in the dispute were sacked and the employers took drastic measures to reimpose social control. The two major Barcelona employers' associations formed a new united organisation, the Society of Metallurgists and Machine Constructors. They then agreed that when in future faced by a strike they would subsidise the industrialists affected (as long as they employed less than 20 percent of the workers in the industry), and that all employers affiliated would send a list of the strikers to the Central Committee, who would then be boycotted. It also stimulated industrialists further to coordinate their efforts. In the strike's aftermath, a commission of Barcelona's business associations discussed the need to set up an employment recruitment office and a savings and pensions fund, while industrialists took more interest in the establishment of Catholic unions.[87] Broader middle and upper classes circles were also shocked into action. During the strike a private security force, known as the Sometent, was called onto the streets to maintain order in many industrial towns and in Barcelona's outlying neighbourhoods. It had its origins in medieval times, when it had operated as an ad hoc rural force of local citizens. But it was under ultimate military control and its date-to-day operations were overseen by local elites, and so during the dispute it very much became an instrument in the hands of the propertied classes. This was another example of the way in which the Restoration regime was unable to build an effective administration to which private interests were subordinate. The overall result was the collapse of union organisation in the industry. In May 1903 Catalan metal-workers reacted by founding a Spanish Metalworkers' Federation in Barcelona, but the various Catalan unions had been severely weakened.[88]

Conclusions

There were several major features of labour relations in turn-of-the century Catalonia. First, one is struck by the breathtaking pace at which union organisation and strike action took off. A pressure-cooker effect could be seen in operation; after years of suffering in silence many workers were impatient to have their grievances heard. Second, this points to the limitations of employer strategies for maintaining social control. These years revealed that in periods of economic boom it was extremely hard to hold labour militancy in check. Third, much of business remained extremely hostile to trade unions. Hence, the intensity of industrial conflict in urban Catalonia, with the union resurgence followed by a determined employer counteroffensive. I have noted that there were significant differences between industries, but in a series of key sectors employers marshalled their forces in order specifically to smash union organisation.

There were economic factors involved in stiffening employer opposition to labour organisation. But probably just as important was the inability of the Spanish state to take the lead in helping to incorporate labour and capital into collective bargaining structures. Employers had grown accustomed to running their enterprises as they saw fit and looked askance at any attempt to limit their autonomy. Thus, what they viewed as unwarranted state interference simply served to provoke a series of harsh attacks on the Restoration parties by employer representatives. The reappraisal by both the Conservative and Liberal parties in the aftermath of 1898 was important. At last the regime had come to realise that labour relations and working conditions were a matter of interest to the state. Yet, as strike activity soared the Restoration parties became increasingly hesitant, taking a harder-line against the unions. This boded ill both for the future of labour relations, and, indeed, broader political stability within urban Catalonia.

This pattern of social strife also very much conditioned the development of Catalan unions. The more elite crafts tended to operate exclusionary unions. It was those workers who were unable by themselves to achieve their goals, and, or, were vulnerable to employer counterattacks, who looked for support outside their trade. At first, as in the case of the metal and waterfront workers, this was undertaken at the level of the city. In part, at least, this reflected the fact that union organisation was young and rudimentary, and, therefore, focused on the locality. Yet it represented a significant advance over the small, isolated, neighbourhood unions formed from 1898, and it helped stimulate the identitarian construction of the city as a single entity above the individual suburbs. Furthermore, some groups of workers aimed to go further and develop either Catalan or Spanish industrial federations. In this period it was the cotton textiles' unions which in this respect had most success.

Because of the pressures workers faced, inter-trade federations were set up with relative ease. This can be seen by comparing events in Catalonia with Britain, where powerful craft federations had been built from the mid-nineteenth century onwards. In the latter case, the post-1840s economic boom, combined with growing state tolerance for trade unionism, stimulated the emergence of large trade federations, composed of so-called 'respectable' workers, which distanced themselves from the 'labouring poor'. Their members were both able to earn a 'family wage' and cocooned themselves from sickness and unemployment through union mutual-aid benefits. The unions of craft workers and elite factory workers, such as the mule spinners, had little interest in integrating unskilled and semi-skilled workers and, indeed, on occasion, actively obstructed their organisation.[89]

In a Catalan context, the factors previously outlined would make such developments unthinkable. Not only were many unions vulnerable and unstable, but, as shown in Chapter Two, Catalan working-class communities were relatively close-knit and afflicted by acute poverty and high death rates. These circumstances could engender considerable levels of solidarity. Indeed, the February 1902 strike was the first European city-wide general strike whose origin lay in a demand for improved working conditions.[90] The difficulties faced also conditioned what Charles Tilly has referred to as workers' 'repertories of collective action'. In the trade-union sphere it is notable that industries in which social conflict was fierce were marked by high levels of violence during disputes. Union weakness also frequently led to the generalisation of strike action, and general strikes were accompanied by other forms of violent 'direct action', such as the stoning of trams and factories. This should serve to remind us that in Europe the nineteenth century saw no smooth transition to systems of stable, peaceful collective bargaining. Eric Hobsbawm has noted that in eighteenth-century England workers, unable to form unions, engaged in 'collective bargaining by riot'.[91] Yet, such violent protest was not limited to a 'pre-industrial' age. In a context of state and employer hostility and union instability, in early twentieth-century Catalonia the use of overt, physical coercion would still, frequently, be a complement to strike action. This is an issue which I shall further develop in relation to other forms of worker protest. Furthermore, as we shall see, such factors will be of great importance when looking at the relative success of those political groupings which tried to represent Catalan workers.

Notes

1. For an overview of state building in nineteenth-century Spain see, Adrian Shubert, *A Social History of Modern Spain*, 168–90.
2. See Antonio Cánovas del Castillo, *Discursos parlamentarios*.
3. For a succinct analysis see Pere Gabriel, 'El marginament del republicanisme i l'obrerisme'.
4. For the relationship between the late nineteenth-century Restoration system and the Catalan elite see, Borja de Riquer, 'Burgesos, polítics i caçics a la Catalunya de la Restauració'.
5. On the operation of *caciquismo* in Catalonia see also, Albert Balcells, Joan B. Culla and Conxita Mir, *Les eleccions generals a Catalunya de 1901 a 1923*; and *Actituds polítiques i control social a la Catalunya de la Restauració*, ed. Conxita Mir.
6. Jordi Solé Tura, *Catalanismo y revolución burguesa*, 2nd edn; Gary Wray McDonogh, *Good Families of Barcelona*, 53–7.
7. Crew, *Town on the Ruhr*, 146–8; Magraw, *A History of the French Working Class*, vol. 2, 36–46; Juan Pablo Fusi, *Política obrera en el País Vasco*, 76–8.
8. See, for example, Stefan Berger, 'The British and German Labour Movements before the Second World War', 222–9.
9. Wray McDonogh, *Good Families*; Riquer, 'Burgesos'; Dorel-Ferré, *Colònies industrials*, 91 and 189–95.
10. For a more in-depth analysis of this conflict see, Miguel Izard, *Industrialización y obrerismo*, 167–78; Angel Smith, 'Social conflict and trade union organisation in the Catalan cotton textile industry, 1890–1914', 346–52; Enrech, 'El Llano contra la Montaña', 592–3.
11. The importance of labour disputes in stimulating the shift to the Muntanya is emphasised in Escudé Bartolí, 'Aprovechamiento de la fuerza hidráulica en la provincia de Barcelona'.
12. Elías de Molins, *La obrera en Cataluña*, 74–5; Instituto de Reformas Sociales, *Jornada*, 449.
13. For the 'outlying districts' of the Ter see the comments by the Catalan Socialist Josep Comaposada in, 'La vida del obrero en la comarca del Ter III. Camprodon', *La Justicia Social* (hereafter LJS), 18 Nov. 1916, 2.
14. Instituto de Reformas Sociales, *Jornada*, 49–50 and 224.
15. José Comaposada, 'La vida del obrero en la comarca del Ter. X Manlleu', LJS, 28 Dec. 1916, 1–2.
16. See Ignasi Terrades, *Les colònies industrials. Un estudi entorn del cas de L'Ametlla de Merola*, 15 and 29–31. Although Terrades' claim that costs were not a key factor in the shift of factory production to the Muntanya seems mistaken, his discussion of the relationship between state policies and the growth of the company towns remains important.
17. For the Llobregat see Dorel-Ferré, *Colònies industrials*, 85–100, 182–3, 252–70 and 319–32; Terrades, *L'Ametlla de Merola*, 155–7; and Carles Enrech, 'Les colònies no neixen es construeixen'.
18. This was the case of the big Sedó company town in the 1890s, approximately 35 percent of whose workers were men and 65 percent women. On the other hand, the Ametlla de Merola company town nearby replaced its male by female weavers. Dorel-Ferré, *Colònies industrials*, 305–10; Terrades, *L'Ametlla de Merola*, 155.
19. Colonia Güell y Fábrica de Panos y Veludillos, *Breve reseña escrita con motivo de la visita hecha a dicha colonia por los señores congresistas de la semana social*, 44.
20. Flórez Beltrán, *Industria algodonera*, 110.
21. The major sources I have used are, Cámara Oficial de Industria de Barcelona, *Memoria*, 139–63 and 220–5; Juan Sallarés y Pla, *El trabajo de las mujeres*, 129–30; Escudé Bartolí, 'Aprovechamiento', 44–6; Leopoldo Negre, 'Encuesta sobre las condicions econòmic-socials a les conques del Ter i Fresser'; José Comaposada, 'La vida del obrero en la comarca del Ter. 1 Los rios del Ter y Fresser', LJS, 4 Nov. 1916, 1–2; Reparaz (fill), *Plana de Vic*, 229; Dorel-Ferré, *Colònies industrials*. As always, statistics are often incomplete and somewhat contradictory. The above can only, therefore, be taken as indicative.
22. *Memoria sobre las obras sociales a favor de los trabajadores de la compañía anónima 'Hilatura de Fabra i Coats' de Barcelona;* Arxiu Municipal de Torelló, Lligall T, Trabajos Varios, 'Reg-

istro de lo obreros de ambos sexos que trabajan en esta localidad'; Negre, 'Enquesta', 124–5; Joaquim Albareda i Salvadó, 'Les colònies industrials a la conca del riu Ter'.

23. Dorel-Ferré, *Colònies industrials*, 332; Terrades, *L'Ametlla de Merola*, 138.
24. José Comaposada, 'La vida...I', LJS, 4 Nov. 1916, 1–2.
25. José Comaposada, 'El movimiento fabril'; Miguel Renté, *La abolición del salario por la participación en los beneficios*, 23; Izard, *Industrialización*, 85–6.
26. *Memoria sobre las obras sociales*, Albó y Martí, *Barcelona caritativa benéfica y social*, vol. 1, 12. Similarly, in 1897 Sert Germans in Barcelona operated a mutual-aid society and invalidity benefit fund, and Vidua de Tolrà in Sant Martí a invalidity benefit fund. Renté, *Abolición*, 75–6.
27. *La España Industrial en su 82 Aniversario, 1847–1929*, 94: see also, *El Trabajo Nacional* (hereafter, ETN), 30 May 1897; *Revista del Ateneo Obrero de Barcelona*, June 1897.
28. Amaro del Rosal, *Historia de la UGT en España, 1901–1939*, vol. 1, 97–8; Angel Marvaud, *La cuestión social en España*, 211–2; LP, 26 May 1910, *Morning Edition*; SO, 20, 25 Oct., 3 Nov. 1916.
29. Valdour, *Ouvrier español*, 259–65.
30. Frances Lannon, *Privilege, Persecution and Prophecy*, 146–69; Winston, *Workers and the Right*, 38–64.
31. Marvaud, *Cuestión social*, 211–12.
32. Renté, *Abolición*, 76.
33. For a general overview see, *La legislación social en la historia de España*.
34. For these conflicts I have used, above all, *El Socialista* (hereafter, ES) and *La Publicidad*, the local papers from the Ter, *El Ter* and *La Plana de Vich* (hereafter, LPV) and the mouthpiece of the new textile federation, *Revista Fabril* (hereafter, RF), complemented by the account by the leading Socialist activist, Juan de Catalunya [pseudonym of Joan Codina], 'Los obreros de la industria textil IV. Continua el relato', *Justicia*, 22 Feb. 1930, 2.
35. This was the claim made by Juan de Catalunya in 'Los obreros en la industria textil IV'.
36. For the growth of the FTE, along with information in LP see RF, 7 June, 5 July 1900, and LPV, 1 Aug. 1900. The importance of job alternatives in Barcelona is stressed by Borderías in 'Women's Work', 161–3.
37. RF, 5 July 1900.
38. For example, before the union revival in Ripoll factory supervisors had ensured workers voted for the candidate of the employer's choice. In Anglés, on the banks on the Ter near Girona, the parish priest excommunicated any workers who unionised. LP, 19, 22 Feb. 1899. Many more illustrations could be given.
39. LP, 2 Sept, 6 Oct 1900, *Morning Editions*; LPV, 8 Aug. 1900.
40. See for example the comments by the president of the Alt Ter i Freser employers' association in LP, 18 Oct., *Morning Edition*, 1900.
41. See the discussion in the FTN in ETN, 10 Feb. 1900.
42. Jaume Serra i Carné, ' La vaga de 1900 a Manresa', 109–31; Dorel-Ferré, *Colònies industrials*, 377–92. Good conduct certificates were still required in 1913: see Instituto de Reformas Sociales, *Jornada*, 53–4.
43. For information on periods in which martial law was in place and, or, constitutional guarantees suspended see Archivo Histórico Nacional, Governación, Serie A (hereafter, AHN), 44/20 and 60/8.
44. On these riots see LPV, 14, 21 March 1901.
45. LPV, 28 March 1901.
46. *La Guerra Social*, 18 July 1903; LJS, 16 Feb., 4 March 1916.
47. Colonia Güell, *Breve reseña*, 44; Dorel-Ferré, *Colònies industrials*, 404–12.
48. ETN, 17 June 1897; *El Ter*, 19 May 1900.
49. Alberto Rusiñol, *Bases para la creación y el funcionamiento de los jurados mixtos en Manlleu*.
50. Arxiu Municipal de Manlleu, Governació, S.149, A.395.
51. Arxiu Municipal de Manlleu, Governació, S.149, A.395.
52. *El Productor* (hereafter, EP), 26 Oct. 1901, *La Guerra Social*, 4 July 1903.
53. Asociaciones de Fabricantes del Ter y del Freser, *Los jurados mixtos en España*.

54. See the comments in Romero Maura, *Rosa del Fuego*, 160–1 and 429–32; Borja de Riquer, 238–9.
55. Josep M. Benaul i Berenguer, 'Dues ciutats i dues polítiques. Sabadell i Terrassa, 1900–1923'.
56. Rosell, *Recuerdos de educador*, 72–3; *El Trabajo* (herafter, ET), 23 Dec. 1899, 6 Jan. 1900. *El Trabajo*, which first appeared in late 1898, was the mouthpiece of the Sabadell local workers' federation.
57. Deu i Baigual, 'Indústria llanera', 4.16. In 1900, the working week in Sabadell woollen textiles was sixty hours and male power loom weavers earned about 30 percent more than the Barcelona female power loom weavers.
58. Arxiu Municipal de Sabadell (hereafter, AMS), 11.4., Conflictes laborals 1899, 'Huelgas de cerrajeros y trabajadores de la fábrica Harmel Hermanos', and, 'Huelgas de los trabajadores de la fábricas de tejidos e hilados Seydoux y Ca'. The quotation is from SO, 19 Aug. 1910.
59. AMS, 11.4. 'Conflictos laborales 1902. Huelga general de los obreros e incidentes posteriores'; ET, 18 Jan., 1 Feb. 1902, 16 May 1903.
60. This is simply an approximation. As already noted, until 1920 Spanish census data does not distinguish between wage earners and employers. According to the 1920 census, there were 317,595 wage earners in the city, 125,319 outside the industrial sector: see Ministerio de Trabajo y Previsión, *Censo de población, 1920*, vol. 5, 250–3.
61. On the CADCI see Manuel Lladonosa i Vall-llebrera, *Catalanisme i moviment obrer*. The data for the ADM's membership is taken from LP, 3 Sept 1900 and Xavier Cuadrat, *Sindicalismo y anarquismo en Cataluña*, 325.
62. Based on data from Miguel Sastre i Sanna, I have calculated that between 1903 and 1914 over 70 percent of strikes that affected 20 workers or over were carried out by journeymen.
63. When the workers from Gas Lebón, came out on strike in 1903, 350 out of 550 of them were sacked: see Sastre y Sanna, *Las huelgas ...1903*, 52–5.
64. Data from Sastre i Sanna indicates that between 1903 and 1914 the workers' principal demand (included in 36 percent of strikes) was a reduction in working hours (or in a few cases the petition that they should not be raised), followed by calls for wage increases (30 percent of cases). Furthermore, in approximately 20 percent of strikes, demands were made relating to the labour process, in 16 percent of strikes an objective was the readmission of sacked colleagues, the demand for a closed shop was made in 9 percent of strikes, and union recognition was an aim in 7 percent of cases. However, the first two demands predominated in strikes which affected a whole trade or industry, while strikes for readmission tended to be much more localised. The 'regulation' of apprenticeship was an explicit demand in 9 percent of strikes, but it was implicit in many more.
65. The data for 1899 to 1902 is based on press reports. For 1903 I have used Sastre y Sanna.
66. For construction see Bengoechea, *Organització patronal*, 113, 160–4, 316–17.
67. 'Sociedades obreras', in AECB, *1903*, 481–6; Pere Gabriel, 'Sindicats i classe obrera a Catalunya, 1900–1923', 381.
68. For the period 1899 to 1903 I have read *La Publicidad*, which has provided me with much of the information for union organisation and strikes. Some copies of the journal of the carpenters' federation, *La Cuña*, have also been preserved. For strikes in construction and woodworking during 1903 see also Sastre y Sanna, *Las huelgas ...1903*, 15–18 and 33–5. I have dealt with industrial relations in the printing industry in more detail in my article, 'Los tipógrafos de Barcelona (1899–1914). Relaciones laborales, desarrollo sindical y práxis política'. The Catalan and Spanish federations I have mentioned were loose organisations dominated by Catalan unions, whose membership was still small. In 1903 the painters had 425 members and the carpenters 3,650: see Sastre y Sanna, *Las huelgas ... 1903*, 56–60 and 87–8. I have only dealt with federations operating in the key trades, but many others functioned elsewhere. A wealth of information is to be found in Gabriel, 'Sindicats', 485–591.
69. For these federations, see *Suplemento de la Revista Blanca*, 11 May 1900; EP, 21 March 1903.
70. For example, in 1907 in the clothing trades and amongst umbrella makers workshop-based men were unionised and women, whether employed in the workshops or from home, were not. Sastre y Sanna, *Las huelgas ...1907*, 24–8 and 34–8.

71. Nadal and Tafunell, *Sant Martí*, 74–5.
72. EP, 23 Nov. 1901.
73. EP, 6 June 1903.
74. Sastre y Sanna, *La huelgas …1903*, 73–5; AHN, 441/1.
75. For the role of the employers see Bengoechea, *Organització patronal*, 39–101.
76. See, for example, the pamphlet by the leading anarchist José Prat, *A las mujeres*, 21–2.
77. On the general strike see LP, 7, 8 May 1901, *Night Editions*. For Foronda's reforms, Sastre y Sanna, *Las huelgas …1904*, 101, *1909*, 29–32, and Albó y Martí, *Barcelona caritativa*, vol. 1, 351–2.
78. For the 1903 strike and the coal merchants' reaction see Sastre y Sanna, *Las huelgas …1903*, 28–9.
79. In the field of machine tools, despite high tariffs the major foreign producers had a cost advantage. Nevertheless, the fact that some big factories, like La Maquinista, focused more on building metallic structures indicates that they may have exaggerated the importance of foreign competition: see Casimiro Lerulot, *La gran jornada obrera (huelga general de Barcelona, 1902)*.
80. LP, 18 April 1900, *Morning Edition*; 14 Aug. 1900, *Morning Edition*.
81. A comparison of wages in La Maquinista and general wage levels in the industry does not reveal any dramatic differences: see, Arxiu Nacional de Catalunya, Fons de la Maquinista Terrestre i Marítima, carpeta 17, salarios, 13 de septiembre a 10 de octubre de 1914; *Anuari d'Estadística Social de Catalunya, 1912*, 50–2.
82. Castillo, *La Maquinista*, 292–3; LP, 6 Nov. 1901; 'Sociedades obreras', in AECB, *1903*, 520.
83. Lerulot, *La gran jornada*; Bengoechea, *Organització patronal*, 334.
84. LP, 17 Feb. 1902, *Morning Edition*.
85. LP, 13 Jan. 1902, *Night Edition*.
86. ED, 17 Feb. 1902. *Morning Edition*.
87. Sastre y Sanna, *Las huelgas …1905*, 16–17; Romero Maura, *Rosa del Fuego*, 217–18; Nadal and Sudrià, *Caixa de pensions*, 42–5; Gemma Ramos and Soledad Bengoechea, 'La patronal catalana y la huelga de 1902', 89–92.
88. AMS, Treball 22c, 1900–1918, Afers Socials, 1903. The Barcelona Metalworkers' Federation would, indeed, be wound up during 1903. For the Sometent see also, Eduardo González Galleja and Fernando del Rey Reguillo, *La defensa armada contra la revolución*.
89. See, for example, Gordon Phillips, 'The British Labour Movement before 1914'; H.A. Turner, *Trade Union Growth Structure and Spread*, 144–9; and Keith Burges, 'New Unionism for Old?', 169–81.
90. Connelly Ullman, *La Semana Trágica*, 132.
91. E.J. Hobsbawm, 'The Machine Breakers'.

Part II

Building the Anarchist-Syndicalist Movement, 1898 to 1914

ANARCHISM, SOCIALISM AND THE GENERAL STRIKE, 1898 TO 1909

In this chapter I aim to explore the linkages between trade unionism and the working-class Left. Unions were the major building blocks of both the anarchist-syndicalist and Socialist movements, as they struggled, on occasions fiercely, to monopolise labour representation. This was not a easy task. Within individual unions there was tension between the view that they needed to maintain their independence in order to recruit as many workers as possible, and perhaps avoid state repression, and the idea that they should be grouped in more politicised organisations which would ensure inter-trade solidarity and fight for their emancipation. My first task will, therefore, be to assess the level of support attained by anarchist-syndicalists and Socialists within the unions and their ability to mobilise workers effectively. Their success or otherwise was closely related to their respective labour strategies and practices. Hence I will go on to discuss this question, with particular reference to the extent to which such strategies were suited to Catalan conditions. Finally, I shall analyse in some detail the anarchist and Socialist milieu; their members, the relationship between the various core groups, and ideological tensions and divisions. Only by such means can one begin to construct a picture of their motivations, strengths and weakness, and their broader impact on society.

The Articulation of an Independent Labour Movement, 1868 to 1898

Both anarchism and Marxist Socialism made their appearance in Spain during the late-nineteenth century. In order to understand the movements' future direction several developments during this first phase need to be taken into account. When unions first gained a foothold in the mid-nineteenth century the political language most widely espoused amongst the leadership hailed from left-liberalism and republicanism. It stressed the need to fight for a democratic secular state but did not directly challenge private property. At most, union activists argued that producer and consumer cooperatives could be a possible vehicle for worker emancipation.

This was to change when, on a visit to Spain in 1868, Mikhail Bakunin's close friend, Giuseppi Fanelli, was able to interest two groups of union leaders in Barcelona and Madrid in anarchist ideas and introduce the International Working Men's Association or First International into Spain along with Bakunin's clandestine Social Democratic Alliance. This proved a crucial moment in Spain's labour history. When Fanelli arrived the Bourbon dynasty had just been overthrown, and the next four years were to witness both unprecedented political upheaval and a rapid growth of labour organisation. It was in this context that, in a congress held in Barcelona in 1870, trade unionists influenced by Fanelli integrated much of the Spanish union movement into the Spanish branch of the International, the FRE. The resolutions passed would be crucial for the future evolution of organised labour, introducing key elements of the anarchist creed into the labour movement. The leadership adopted the idea, so beloved in anarchist circles, of the key role of the politically educated minority (*minoría consciente*) in sparking the revolution. Henceforth this *minoría consciente* would be ensconced in both the anarchist 'affinity groups' and the trade unions. In addition, they embraced the belief that the labour movement should act independently of any political party and that its goal was the economic emancipation of the working class and the establishment of some form of collectivist society.

As a result, anarchists would strongly influence the country's major labour confederation. This had two key results, both for the evolution of anarchist doctrines and for labour organisation in Spain. First, grafting anarchism onto the labour unions meant that the union activists had to balance the movement's radical doctrines with practical day-to-day activities and compromise with sceptical 'pure' trade unionists and supporters of republicanism. This could be seen in the 1870 congress in which, although the decision was taken that the FRE would remain separate from political parties, it was tacitly agreed that individuals within it could be politically active. This need to compromise with other political tendencies would be an important feature of Catalan anarchism throughout our period.

Second, while anarchists influenced the labour unions their own doctrines were also moulded by the conditions in which they worked. This was apparent in a number of respects. Within the anarchist creed the subject of the revolution was less clearly defined than Marx's industrial proletariat. Mikhail Bakunin, in many respects the movement's founder, showed faith in the revolutionary potential of the poorest and most marginalised sectors of society, amongst whom the peasantry were a key component. Other anarchists believed that the shackles of authoritarianism would be broken by a broader interclass alliance.

Yet in urban Catalonia the strong link with the unions meant that the bulk of anarchists – like their Marxist counterparts – saw industrial workers as the key emancipatory force. It was not for nothing that when Anselmo Lorenzo, one of the key figures of late nineteenth-century Spanish anarchism, published his history of the period in 1901, he entitled it *El proletariado militante*.[1] There were attempts by some anarchists to reach out to 'intellectual workers', although this was combined with a degree of suspicion directed at comrades who did not undertake manual labour.[2] Nevertheless, the Bakunist heritage was apparent in their sensitivity towards the most downtrodden sectors of urban society; the unemployed, beggars, prostitutes and the like (theirs was, after all, a fate which could easily befall industrial workers), and in the anarchists' stress on the need to prevent any divisions emerging between better-off, skilled sectors of labour and a miserable 'fifth estate'.

Furthermore, while Catalan anarchists saw the unions as both the harbingers of revolution and the building block of the future post-capitalist society, during the 1870s and 1880s the revolutionary elan of many Catalan anarchists was open to question. For Bakunin the revolution would be the product of an insurrection by the working masses led by a revolutionary elite. He himself had little time for union bargaining and strikes for concrete gains. On the contrary, many Catalan anarchists became very much involved in union negotiations. And, in the 1870s, despite anarchist claims regarding the revolutionary potential of the unions, in reality the FRE was rather centralised, with union leaders following quite a moderate strategy, setting up strike funds and calling on the rank-and-file to be careful not to declare over-precipitous strikes (only to support 'scientific strikes', to use the language of the day).[3]

The confederation had to go underground when the Bourbon monarchy was restored at the end of 1874, but its relatively moderate stance was confirmed when a new pro-anarchist labour confederation, the FTRE, was set up in the more open climate which followed the Liberals' accession to power in 1881. Other sectors of the organised labour movement took an even more reformist line. A large number of textile unions broke with the anarchists, preferring to affiliate to the cotton textile federation, the TCV, which from the 1880s onwards operated independently. The federation was republican in outlook and aimed to create a stable organisation that could do business with the employers; modelling itself, in this respect, on the British New Model Unions.[4] As a result, between 30,000 and 40,000 Catalan workers had affiliated to the FRE at its highpoint in 1873, but the FTRE had only just over 13,000 Catalan members in 1882. Its leadership was based in Barcelona but its centre of gravity had shifted to Andalusia.[5]

The anarchists had gained a head start over potential Marxist rivals in Catalonia. Nevertheless, Marxists were to make an impact within the cotton textile industry in the 1880s. From 1873, the group of Madrid trade unionists, converted by Fanelli, evolved in a Marxist direction. They began to gain a foothold within a number of Madrid artisanal trades and clandestinely founded the Spanish Socialist Party, the PSOE, in the city in 1879. Madrid would remain the party's headquarters for many years to come. Nevertheless, over the subsequent decade the power of the Socialists began to grow in Catalonia. This was based on the collaboration between Socialist union leaders and the TCV, made possible by a number of similarities in their political and trade-union outlook. Unlike the anarchists, both believed in the key role of political parties, and while the Socialists wished to establish an independent party of the working class, and the TCV largely championed republicanism, there were sufficient ambiguities in their respective positions for a dialogue to be possible. Moreover, against the anarchist stress on the revolutionary potential of the unions, they both saw their role as simply to improve working conditions. As a result of this alliance, by the mid-1880s, Socialist prospects in Catalonia looked relatively bright. In 1888 they decided to set up their own labour confederation, the UGT, whose headquarters was based in Barcelona. In the following year 71 percent of the confederation's 3,355 affiliates were Catalan.[6]

More broadly, despite the influence of anarchism within sectors of Catalan labour, in the boom conditions of the *febre d'or* in the early 1880s, for a brief instant labour appeared to be in the process of establishing stable collective bargaining relations with employers. This benefited the TCV and Socialists, because they had operated a very cautious union practice, emphasising the need to work effectively with the industrialists and build up their own labour organisations. It was soon to prove a mirage. The years between 1883 and 1893 witnessed an offensive against labour, by both employers and the state, which would produce a break in the continuity of the union movement. In 1883, frightened by the spread of the FTRE, the Liberal Government cracked down. Then, as the economic climate worsened, employers confirmed their anti-union credentials. Most dramatic, as shown in the previous chapter, was the all-out offensive against the TCV between 1889 and 1891, which led to its almost total destruction.

The implications were wide-ranging. In Catalonia the TCV had been the fulcrum around which reformist labour politics revolved. Its fall meant that the possibility that business trade unions, which operated within the parameters of the Restoration regime, might dominate the Catalan labour movement was effectively undercut. This point is worth stressing. Some historians have argued that in the early-twentieth century the state was bound to adopt a hard line in response to the rise of anarchism and syndicalism. This ignores the fact that in the late-nineteenth century – and again, as we shall see, between 1900 and 1901 – it helped undermine more malleable alternatives.

The virtual destruction of trade unionism within cotton textiles badly affected the Socialists. On the one hand, as the leading Catalan Socialist, Josep Comaposada, was later to comment, this offensive made it impossible to operate the 'strong and stable bodies' which they, like the TCV, favoured.[7] Furthermore, it occurred in a context in which relations between the Socialists and the TCV were breaking down as a result of the former's attempt to build its own independent party-union organisation along social-democratic lines. The foundation of the UGT in 1888 was a symptom of these tensions.[8] The split cost the Catalan Socialists part of their union base, although in some Muntanya towns, above all in Manresa and in the Ter Valley, their staunch defence of union organisation and established working practices against the employers' onslaught earned them a good deal of sympathy. This was to become clear when unions revived at the turn of the century.

The break in Catalan labour organisation also profoundly affected Catalan anarchism. As we shall see, the policies of the FRE and FTRE would in many respects anticipate the new revolutionary-syndicalist doctrines elaborated in France during the 1890s and after. However, in Spain in the 1880s, under the impact of growing state repression and the worsening economic climate, voices were raised, particularly in Andalusia, against what was seen as the FTRE's over-centralisation and lack of revolutionary spirit. There were antecedents. When the FRE operated clandestinely between 1874 and 1880 a current emerged which advocated violent, insurrectionary acts ('propaganda by the deed') in order to kindle rebellion by the masses. Under the impact of this criticism, and with the FTRE in crisis, younger figures within the Catalan organisation took on board the complaints and, in 1888, replaced the FTRE by a much more decentralised Pact of Union and Solidarity between the unions. Later in the year they then set up an Anarchist Organisation of the Spanish Region (OARE) to maintain relations between the various anarchist groups.

This brought Spanish anarchism much more into line with the dominant European anarchist current usually referred to by historians as anarcho-communism, which echoed the insurrectionary stance advocated by Bakunin. The OARE was seen as a ginger group, which would spearhead the revolution. The new union movement, it was believed, was much better suited to follow its lead. In place of 'scientific strikes', it was now argued, unions should act aggressively, and strikes be generalised through solidarity movements, which could produce a revolutionary conjuncture. In order to carry out this function unions and union confederations should not operate large strike funds, nor have mutual-aid societies or cooperatives attached, which, they maintained, would result in the creation of a privileged conservative elite alongside a downtrodden underclass who would not be able to afford union dues. Even this was not sufficient for some anarchists, who rejected all committees and conferences, claiming that the revolution would only be sparked by spontaneous acts. It was in this latter milieu that groups emerged that rejected all unions as inevitably reformist.[9]

The new outlook was put to the test when union organisation briefly revived during the economic upturn of the early 1890s. This occurred when, within anarchist circles, increased interest was being shown in the concept of the general strike. It had already been suggested by Bakunin that capitalism might be overthrown by such a strike. French anarchists again took this idea up in the late 1880s and it was subsequently adopted by a number of trade-union associations and socialist groupings.[10] In Catalonia, such ideas chimed with the new radicalism of the anarchist activists and were enthusiastically extolled by the founders of the OARE.

At this point, at an international conference held in 1889, the European Socialist parties agreed that from 1890, on 1 May of each year, the working class in each country would take action in support of an eight-hours day. Spanish anarchists quickly seconded the call. In Barcelona, however, this by no means implied that they would work together. Between 1890 and 1893, in consonance with their respective trade-union strategies, Socialists called one-day stoppages and the anarchists launched indefinite general strikes. This would henceforth constitute one of the key battle grounds between them.

While for the anarchists the general strike was a revolutionary tool, for the Socialists it served only to exhaust the workers and invite state repression. This dispute was part of a wider gulf in their respective union strategies. In contrast to the anarchists, the PSOE-UGT maintained that powerful unions, staffed by paid officials, should build up strike funds and make every effort to reach a negotiated solution to industrial disputes before undertaking strike action. Moreover, in order to tie workers more effectively to the unions, these should where possible operate mutual-aid societies and consumer cooperatives. Socialists referred to this practice as *sindicalismo a base múltiple.*[11]

The May day strikes launched between 1890 and 1893 demonstrated the pros and cons of the new anarchist strategy. They would generate great enthusiasm and allow workers to mobilise, but also made them vulnerable to state repression. These are themes that I shall examine in greater detail for the early-twentieth century. Suffice it to note that the strikes were accompanied by large numbers of arrests and the closure of union headquarters. The climate became particularly difficult from 1892 onwards, when the authorities once again clamped down after an uprising of landless labourers in the Andalusian town of Jerez.

It was in this climate that anarchist terrorism first made itself felt in the city of Barcelona. The belief that 'propaganda by the deed' could encompass individual acts of terror emerged in France in the 1880s. In Catalonia it took hold amongst anarchist groups who rejected union organisation and extolled spontaneous acts of defiance. The first assassination attempt in Barcelona in September 1893 – a bomb attack on General Arsensio Martínez Campos in response to the execution of a number of Jerez peasants – was followed by blanket repression. The subsequent five years were to witness a spiral of action and repression, which culminated in June 1896 with the round-up of hundreds of anarchists, labour leaders and even left-wing sympathisers. They were imprisoned in the military castle of Montjuïc overlooking Barcelona, where torture was used to extract false confessions of guilt. Five of those arrested were executed and leading anarchist activists were subsequently forced into exile. The bloody epilogue was the assassination of the Spanish Prime Minister, Antonio Cánovas del Castillo, by the Italian anarchist, Michele Angiolillo, in August 1897.

By no means all anarchists supported terrorist acts. Nevertheless, a climate was created in which attacks on leading politicians or military figures were received with broad sympathy in anarchist and even wider working-class circles.[12] It was a legacy which would pervade the whole period of this study. The anarchists were driven underground and formal links with labour were broken, but the figure of the anarchist martyr to the cause was also created. Nor was the movement totally undermined. In Barcelona in 1896, according to a conservative critic, there remained 500 anarchist activists who operated within informal groups, and who retained a much broader diffuse sympathy.[13]

The Trade-Union Revival in Cotton Textiles, 1898 to 1900

The working-class Left was further hit by the economic crisis that engulfed Catalan industry between 1896 and 1898. The economic revival and political liberalisation that followed provided anarchists and Socialists with a new lease of life, but also served to highlight the difficulties they faced in subordinating unions to their respective causes. This could be seen in the Catalan cotton textile industry, with the formation of the new Catalan-based cotton textile federation, the FTE, in September 1899. In the mid-1890s, union organisation in the industry was at a low ebb. The TCV retained the support of only a few pockets of male spinners. Disgusted by its leadership's collaborationist policies, other political groupings founded their own textile federations. The anarchists organised a Free Pact in the early 1890s, which gained some backing in Barcelona and the Ter Valley, but was soon to founder. The Socialists had rather more success. They set up their alternative, the Unión Fabril Algodonera, in 1894, and affiliated a number of cotton textile workers' groups on the Ter, in Manresa, Sant Martí, and Vilanova and Vilassar in southern Catalonia. The Mataró hosiery workers also joined and the town became something of a Socialist bastion in subsequent years.[14]

Given the crisis of the Catalan labour movement in general, and within cotton textiles in particular, the Unión Fabril Algodonera remained weak, but it was the only organisational nexus between the individual unions. Yet when trade unionism began to revive, from 1898, it became clear that the Socialists were in no position to lead the textile unions. Unlike the situation in Madrid and Bilbao, where they had been behind the organisation of the first unions and could, therefore, be identified with the entire organised working class, in Catalonia they represented one tendency amongst several. Hence the need for political compromises in order to achieve unity. This became possible during 1899. Within the Ter, as unions grew, a district federation was formed, under the presidency of the 'well-known anarchist' Gaspar Viñolas. This federation played a prominent role in the formation of the FTE, reaching an agreement with the Socialists to call a congress open to all the industry's workers.[15] Unification was probably made easier because, following the débâcle of 1890 to 1891, no one had any significant organisational structures to defend. In addition, the Catalan Socialists had become used to collaborating with other political forces within the TCV. However, this meant sacrificing their own federation, which was integrated within the UGT, a fact that may well have led to tensions with the Madrid-based PSOE leadership.

The new federation's base was very diverse. Most workers joined not because they sympathised with any particular ideology but because they sought union representation. As the anarchist weekly, *El Productor*, put it, at the FTE's Founding Congress, 'there were delegates of various political persuasions (*tendencias sociológicas*), although the vast majority maintained a purely trade-unionist perspective'.[16] Hence its leadership maintained that it was only concerned with trade-union affairs. This stance would be *de rigueur* within Catalan trade and industrial federations over the next decade and a half, reflecting the political diversity within Catalan labour and the need to recruit as widely as possible.

This did not, of course, stop the various political tendencies from vying for influence. The remnants of the TCV had affiliated and exercised considerable influence through its president, Ramon Fontanals. Within the FTE he held the important post of president of the First District, which encompassed Barcelona and the surrounding towns, and played a key role in the recruitment drives which the FTE launched during the year. The Socialists, however, were in the strongest position. They maintained the support of textile unions in the towns of Manresa, Mataró, Sant Martí and Roda, and were also dominant within the FTE's mouthpiece, *Revista Social*, whose editor was the leading Socialist Toribio Reoyo. Moreover, another key figure in the FTE, Josep Genollà, was a Socialist. He was president of the Fourth District (the Ter) when the federation was founded. He moved on to preside over the Sant Martí textile union, then the Sixth District (Manresa and its surroundings), finally replacing the independent Manlleu union activist, Angel Aguilar, as the FTE's president in August 1900. The anarchists were, in fact, the poor relations in the FTE. Their influence was almost entirely limited to the Ter, and depended on such figures as Gaspar Viñolas and Jaume Romà, the latter the president of the Torelló textile union.[17]

The anarchists' subordinate position within the FTE becomes even clearer if its policies are examined. The federation never condoned the class collaborationism of the old Catalan-wide TCV. On the contrary, in response to the mill owners' attacks on working conditions and established working practices, it bitterly criticised their greed and selfishness. Nevertheless, its leadership counselled prudence in taking strike action. In addition, much of the old organisational structure of the TCV was resurrected, including the employment of paid officials. Both these decisions flew in the face of anarchist union strategy. Moreover, the FTE's General Secretary, Josep Guiteras, who himself had links to the Socialists, argued that unions should provide mutual aid and operate strike funds. The FTE's leaders also supported the implementation of the Government's social legislation. Indeed, in February 1900, Guiteras and Fontanals visited Madrid to offer the Government its backing in the face of a campaign by textile industrialists against the proposed legislation covering female labour and night work. This led to strong criticism from a number of anarchists, who accused them of reformism and of collaborating with the bourgeoisie.[18]

The Socialists' hope was to fashion the federation along European social-democratic lines. It is important to stress that this held out the possibility of Catalan trade unionism and working-class politics developing along a very different path to that along which it would subsequently travel. Historians have often stated that by the turn of the century the Socialists had 'failed' in Catalonia. This is based on hindsight. In other circumstances the Socialists could have gone on to build a strong position in what was, in terms of the size of the workforce, numerically the biggest industrial sector in Catalonia, and, after construction and transport and communications, the third largest in Spain.[19]

Yet, despite their strong position, most of the Catalan Socialist leadership wished to maintain their distance from the UGT. This became clear at the federation's Second Congress, when the Mataró branch proposed that it should join the Socialist confederation. The proposal was not finally voted upon and it was Toribio Reoyo who opposed its discussion. He maintained that before the FTE could affiliate it needed to consolidate its strength and that in the present circumstances such a move would lead to disunity. Furthermore, he argued that there were 'special circumstances', especially the 'endless number of strikes' in the industry, which counselled against such a move.[20] The argument put forward by Reoyo that the FTE was not yet strong enough to join the UGT is difficult to accept. In September 1900 the UGT had little more than 26,000 members throughout Spain. This meant that, on paper at least, the FTE, had at least twice as many affiliates. For Reoyo the question of preserving unity was important. Moreover, he was clearly concerned that the FTE would not integrate well into an organisation which attempted to impose a high degree of discipline on its membership and which only supported strike action as a last resort. His hope was probably that labour relations with the textile employers might at some future date be stabilised and collective bargaining institutionalised, thereby bringing the FTE into line with UGT practice.

Instead, relations within the industry headed in the opposite direction. From the end of the year the employers launched their offensive against the textile unions and this led to a marked shift in the balance of political forces within, and union practice adopted by, the FTE. At the root of this change was the fact that there seemed no alternative but to take drastic action to halt the employer onslaught. Already, at the beginning of 1900, the FTE leadership had threatened the Ripoll employers with a general strike if they did not lift the lock-out that they had imposed along the Freser. This was the first time that, in exasperation, it had contradicted its conciliatory approach to industrial disputes. The Freser lock-out, nevertheless, proved just a warning. The employers' offensive began in earnest at the end of the year and left the majority of FTE members either locked-out or on strike. In such circumstances to attempt to negotiate was hardly an option and amongst the rank and file the belief grew that only a general strike could halt the industrialists in their tracks. Once the offensive was underway a number of Barcelona trade unions went further and called for a solidarity strike of the entire Catalan working class, whose aim would be to put pressure on the Government to restore constitutional guarantees and to force the employers to reopen their factories.

This initiative was apparently supported by the FTE's Central Committee despite the majority not being identified with the anarchists. Moreover, both the Federation of Cork Workers, based on the northern Catalan coast, and a Ter confederation of artisanal workers, both under anarchist influence, gave their backing.[21] This, however, immediately had the effect of alienating the Socialists, as became apparent when an FTE delegate, Joan Matamala, visited Madrid to ask the PSOE's general secretary, Pablo Iglesias, to sign a letter supporting the workers and protesting at the attitude of the authorities and the Catalan industrialists. The letter had already been signed by the Madrid-based anarchist, Federico Urales, and the left-wing republican, Alejandro Lerroux. Nevertheless, a meeting of the PSOE's National Committee refused to give its consent because, they argued, the effect would be to favour the declaration of a general strike to which they – unlike Lerroux and the anarchists – were opposed. The Socialists then accused the anarchists of being behind the general strike, and, once it was clear by the middle of December 1900 that it had failed, their mouthpiece, *El Socialista*, triumphantly announced that their cautious approach had been vindicated. This attitude was endorsed by the leading Barcelona Socialist, Josep Comaposada, a figure close to Pablo Iglesias, who chided the 'dreamers who took it seriously'.[22]

This was probably not the most sensible course to have pursued. The Socialists' phobia of the concept of the general strike had led them radically to oppose the FTE's strategy, leaving them open to the charge that they were abandoning the textile workers.[23] Matters were made worse because of the wounding language they employed. Moreover, it was not clear exactly what their alternative was. Nevertheless, the political consequences of the destruction of the FTE were ambiguous. The anarchists had not shown that a general strike had any talismanic qualities, and at a local level, in the Ter and Maresme in particular, Socialists (who may not have liked the stance taken by the leadership) continued to play an important role.

Anarchism, Socialism and the General Strike in Barcelona, 1898 to 1903

In Barcelona, between 1899 and 1903, events took a not altogether dissimilar turn. In 1899, as unions began to stir, with the anarchists still subject to heavy repression it was the Socialists who emerged as the standard bearers of organised labour. They operated the only two union centres in the city, the Centre de Societats Obreres, run by the UGT leadership, and the Grup de Corporacions Obreres, under the auspices of the local branch of the PSOE, and played a key role in organising new unions. Furthermore, these centres were open to all unions that wished to join and several took advantage of this fact to establish a base without affiliating to the UGT. The UGT headquarters even included, from 1899, the remnants of the TCV. More surprisingly, even the UGT's leadership was not all Socialist, with both republicans and leading TCV representatives playing an active role. Hence the UGT operated very much as an umbrella organisation, allowing it considerable influence outside the limited circle of its paid-up unions.[24]

This continued Socialist presence in Barcelona, which has hitherto been overlooked, casts in a rather different light the decision to move the headquarters of the UGT to Madrid, taken in its Sixth Congress in September 1899. The argument usually put forward is that this was a response both to the crisis in Catalan recruitment and to the consolidation of Madrid as the strongest nucleus of Socialist organisation. It is true that while there were only 759 UGT affiliates in Barcelona province in September 1899, the

Madrid UGT had 6,535 members. Yet this does not tell the whole story. It has, in the first place, to be remembered that, unlike Madrid, labour organisation in Catalonia had suffered a wholesale crisis during the 1890s. In 1899 only one Barcelona union, the tanners, had over 1,000 affiliates, as against three of the unions affiliated to the Madrid UGT. Furthermore, as already stressed, the Socialists had considerable influence within the Catalan labour unions. Nine unions attended the Unión Fabril Algodonera's Sixth Congress, before it integrated into the FTE. And thirty unions were affiliated to the Barcelona Socialist centres in the autumn of 1899 (twenty to the UGT's Centre and ten to the PSOE's Grup). This does not compare unfavourably to the twenty-eight unions linked to the UGT's Madrid union centre in October and represented the core of organised labour in Barcelona. The big difference was in the number of unions affiliated to the UGT, which stood at twelve in Madrid and four in Barcelona.[25]

However, from the mid-1890s a damaging split had developed between the UGT leadership and the local branch of the PSOE. It became particularly serious when, at the end of 1898, the Barcelona PSOE broke with the Centre de Societats Obreres and set up its own labour confederation, the Grup de Corporacions Obreres, leading them to celebrate 1 May 1899 separately.[26] In these circumstances the UGT (which had unions' affiliated in both centres) could not operate effectively. The veteran Socialist, Juan José Morato, stated later that the schism was the result of 'internal personal rivalries', but there were also clear policy differences within Spanish Socialism.[27] Under Pablo Iglesias the Madrid-based PSOE leadership – which also controlled the Madrid UGT – wanted to structure the Socialist movement along the lines advocated by the French Socialist, Jules Guesde, who argued that the party should operate independently of all other left-wing organisations, and forge a homogeneous Socialist movement, in which the union was *de facto* subordinate to party interests. However, the Catalan UGT wanted to operate a more open and independent labour organisation, which for those grouped around the leading figure in the Centre de Societats Obreres, Basilio Martín Rodgríguez, meant once again linking up with the TCV. Two other Catalan heavyweights, Josep Comaposada and Toribio Reoyo, broke with Martín Rodríguez, but their views cannot be regarded as Guesdist either. As already seen, Reoyo opposed the FTE integrating within the UGT. Moreover, seemingly all Catalan Socialists wanted closer ties with republicanism.[28]

I seems, then, that while the move to Madrid was in part motivated by the need to overcome the Catalan split and anchor the organisation in the locality in which the UGT had most affiliates, Pablo Iglesias's backers were also mindful of the fact that this would make it easier to impose Guesdist orthodoxy. Spanish labour leaders always had one eye on events in France and it may well be that the party leadership feared that if they failed to act they would be marginalised from an autonomous union movement. This is the fate that befell Guesde's Fédération des Syndicates in 1895. In this respect it is worth noting that the decision to move to Madrid was taken several days after the Catalan Socialists had sacrificed the Unión Fabril Algodonera in the name of working-class unity. From Madrid the Socialists would henceforth talk with a more united voice (the overlap between Socialist party and union leaders was unprecedented within European social democracy). The problem was that Spain's major industrial centre was Barcelona.

Despite losing the UGT headquarters, in Barcelona during 1900 the Socialist centres continued to play a key coordinating role; they further expanded their membership and were finally to unify in 1901. Yet by the beginning of this year their overall profile was lower; their growth failing to keep pace with the rapid union revival. Evidence suggests that there was a connection between their partial eclipse and the rise of industrial conflict in the Catalan capital. As has been pointed out, they had adopted a moderate trade-union practice, with the result that they were not to be found leading the unions into battle against the industrialists, but rather trying to rein them in. Hence they played practically no part in the major strikes of these years. This very much put them in the shade, particularly because, unlike the situation in the Muntanya, in Barcelona the economic climate remained buoyant and employers were often forced to capitulate.

Two examples illustrate this situation particularly well. The largest strike called in 1900 affected 1,300 mechanics and attracted widespread working-class sympathy. Yet, the Socialists vehemently attacked the 'hastiness' of the union, arguing that it did not have the 'necessary consistency' to launch the strike, and criticised its 'rejection of the efficacy of strike funds'.[29] At least on this occasion they could argue that the strike was lost. But in the construction industry they criticised a strike which ended in a partial victory. In 1899, the only painters' union in Barcelona, La Defensa, formed part of the UGT Centre. In 1900 a new union called La Fraternal was founded, which from the outset adopted a more aggressive stance. This proved popular and its membership rapidly outstripped that of La Defensa. Then in June 1900 it made a series of demands, including an eight-hours day, provoking a trade-wide lock-out. The Socialists responded by accusing La Fraternal of provoking the lock-out though its violent language and excessive demands. Such behaviour, they argued, threatened the existence of the unions.[30] Yet La Fraternal was able to achieve a 50 céntimos wage increase. Subsequently, in 1903, the two unions fused on terms unfavourable to the Socialists.

In the increasingly febrile atmosphere of 1900 the Socialists lost influence in the main branches of Barcelona industry. From the start they made little headway in construction. In the metal industry they enjoyed more success, but during the year the big iron foundrymen and boilermakers' unions left the Centre. In printing the Socialists experienced a similar haemorrhage of support. The compositors' union, L'Art d'Imprimir, had actually been founded in the PSOE's headquarters in 1899, but left soon afterwards. It was followed in 1900 by the bookbinders, thereby leaving the Socialists with no influence in the printing industry.[31]

In this context a number of characteristics which identified pro-Socialist unions became apparent. It should immediately be emphasised that one cannot be too dogmatic in this respect. There would be overlap between the unions under Socialist and anarchist influence. Clearly, in a small neighbourhood union an influential personality or two could be of crucial importance.

Nevertheless, there can be no doubt that from 1900 the Socialists did well amongst groups of workers who enjoyed relatively cordial relations with employers and hence remained somewhat aloof from the major industrial conflicts in their respective industry. This was apparent in construction, where in 1900 the only union affiliated to the UGT was the 'aristocratic' marblers. It could also be observed in the metal industry, where by the end of the year only the moderate copper boilermakers and locksmiths' unions continued to give their support. Indeed, the latter's union flag consisted of two arms intertwined, representing harmony between labour and capital.[32] Both the marblers and the copper boilermakers maintained ties with the Socialists from 1889 or 1890 right through to 1914. It was, finally, visible in the Socialists' ability (unlike the anarchists) to make an impact amongst shopworkers, with the ADM closely associated, especially between 1904 and 1909.

Some similarities could also be discerned outside Barcelona. From the 1890s onwards, the Catalan Socialists built up support amongst artisanal workers in the towns of Tarragona, Sitges, Reus and Tortosa, to the south of Barcelona. A common denominator of the labour relations in the artisanal trades in these areas appears to have been a lower level of industrial conflict than was the case in the Catalan capital itself. The Socialists also has some success in mobilising shop workers outside Barcelona. In particular, in October 1903 the ADM was behind the formation of a national federation, in which Socialist influence was felt.[33]

There are parallels here with the situation in Madrid, which became the UGT's bulwark between 1890 and 1910. Santos Juliá has argued that in Madrid the UGT's cautious trade-union practice was pursued effectively because capitalist development had had only a limited impact on the major artisanal trades, and, consequently, relations between masters and men were still close.[34] Evidently the equation between the Socialist movement and factory proletarians, which some historians have made, does not bear scrutiny. On the contrary, an important feature of the UGT's practice was its link with less radicalised artisanal workers. It was an odd situation for what was meant to be a revolutionary Marxist organisation dedicated to the overthrow of capitalism. It was, moreover, a practice which could only translate effectively into the factory age if modernisation was accompanied by an institutionalisation of labour relations. Herein lay the great difficulty in Barcelona.

These problems represented an opportunity for the anarchists. In late 1897 only one Madrid-based anarchist weekly, *La Idea Libre*, edited by Ernesto Alvarez, an ex-colleague of Pablo Iglesias who had converted to anarchism, operated in the whole of Spain. In subsequent years, as labour organisation revived and repression eased, a number of anarchist groups would take up the cudgel. In Madrid, in July 1898, a much more important anarchist publication, entitled *La Revista Blanca*, came out edited by Federico Urales (pseudonym of Joan Montseny). A cooper by trade, he had been active in the Catalan union movement in his home town of Reus in the 1880s. Like so many prominent anarchists he was totally self-taught, and by dint of perseverance was able to open his own lay school. He was subsequently caught up in the Montjuïc repression and after a period of exile in London moved to

Madrid. Here, in 1897, he contacted the left-wing republican, Alejandro Lerroux, and convinced him to launch a campaign for a judicial review of the Montjuïc trial through his daily, *El Progreso*. As shown in the next chapter, the campaign could be of crucial importance in mobilising popular anger and allowing the left-wing opposition to get their anti-regime message across.

Vociferous campaigns for the release of their prisoners (*presos sociales*) would be a key feature of the anarchist movement in subsequent years. Urales and Lerroux were to become heroes in anarchist circles, and it was this prestige which made it possible for Urales to bring out *La Revista Blanca*. It was focused above all on anarchist theory and on developing libertarian perspectives in science and the arts, but, in May 1899, the editorial team also brought out a weekly *Suplemento de la Revista Blanca* (renamed *Tierra y Libertad* in January 1902), which linked up with Catalan anarchists and reported widely on strikes and union affairs.

This was crucial because it provided a nexus for anarchists who were beginning to work within the unions. The first specifically anarchist weekly to appear in Catalonia was *La Protesta*, published by Ernesto Alvarez, who had established ties with several anarchist groups located in Barcelona and in the surrounding industrial towns. It first appeared in Valladolid in 1899, but then moved to Sabadell in June 1900. Alvarez's stay was not to be a happy one. This may at first seem surprising. Anarchists had in the past attained some influence in Sabadell and from 1899 the city rapidly emerged as the strongest centre of union organisation in Catalonia. However, the Sadadell Labour Federation (FOS) adopted a union strategy at odds with that advocated in most anarchist circles. The woollen weaver, Carles Piazza, the director of its mouthpiece, *El Trabajo*, stressed the need for the unions to be well organised. In practical terms this meant that the woollen workers backed the formation of an arbitration board, that unions affiliated to the FOS paid relatively high dues and that Piazza became a paid official in 1901. Piazza did not regard this as contradicting anarchist doctrine. *El Trabajo* argued that only a powerful labour movement would be able to carry out a revolutionary general strike.[35]

This position can be read at several levels. The woollen weavers were at the heart of the FOS. As seen in the previous chapter, they were able to establish relatively stable relations with employers. And, as in cotton textiles, the size and complexity of the woollen workers' organisation had led them to employ paid officials. In ideological terms, this conditioned them to remain wedded to the outlook of the old FTRE. As we shall see, it also meant that they were particularly disposed to adopt a moderate reading of the new syndicalist doctrines being elaborated in France.

On the other hand, the tone of the anarchists linked to *La Protesta* was shrill and violent; they openly called for anarchist groups to exercise control over the unions and demanded that they adopt an overtly revolutionary strategy. Hence, already in 1899, while based in Valladolid, they accused the FOS of being too cautious, bureaucratic and centralised. After the publication moved to Sabadell matters did not improve. The anarchists linked to it picked up some support in the woodworkers', printers' and bricklayers' unions, but had no weight in the woollen textile industry or within the FOS itself. *La Protesta* would, in these circumstances, return to Valladolid in October 1900.[36]

The gap left by *La Protesta* was filled on 7 and 8 April 1901, when twenty-five representatives of thirteen anarchist groups met in Barcelona and agreed to name a commission, which would organise meetings, actively operate within the trade unions, 'destroying the tutelage exercised by the authoritarian Socialist party', and publish a weekly newspaper entitled *El Productor*.[37] Behind this publication were a group of anarchists linked to the shoemaker Leopoldo Bonafulla (pseudonym of Joan Baptista Esteve), who had been actively involved in the anarchist movement since the 1880s (bringing out the first *El Productor* between 1888 and 1893), and who, like most of his contemporaries, had been caught up in the Montjuïc process and spent some time in exile. His foremost confidant was the remarkable figure of Teresa Claramunt, who, although originally from Sabadell, was now based in Barcelona where she worked hard to organise the female textile workers. They were supported by a number of young activists, closely involved in the resurgence of the unions. The publication combined some theoretical pieces with detailed information on labour organisation, and soon achieved a significant circulation in trade-union circles.

It was joined by a more theoretical anarchist weekly, entitled *La Huelga General*, from the end of the year. Its backer was Francesc Ferrer, an ex-republican who, while based in Paris between 1885 and 1901, had become increasingly interested in anarchism and the lay education movement, and who had inherited a small fortune from a Parisian spinster to whom he had given Spanish lessons. Ferrer's wealth and drive would make him a highly influential, if rather distant and enigmatic figure, within the anarchist movement. Unlike almost all Catalan anarchists, he did not come from an industrial working-class background, took great care over his attire and enjoyed the life of a man of independent means. This, along with his continued contacts with republicans, would produce suspicion and even hostility within some anarchist circles. Yet his dedication to the revolutionary cause was sincere. As we shall see in the next chapter, he would attain international fame through the Modern School, an attempt to establish a network of 'rationalist' educational establishments throughout Catalonia.[38]

His foremost collaborator was the veteran, Anselmo Lorenzo, who met Ferrer in Paris after briefly being exiled to France after the Montjuïc trial. Lorenzo did not speak in meetings but enjoyed a high standing in anarchist circles, and his prolific output during the 1900s would gain him a reputation as the movement's most eminent theoretician. By the end of the decade he had become 'the old man' or 'grandfather', a figure whom all promising young activists would, in reverential tones, be invited to meet.[39] Other members of the group were connected more directly with the union movement and spoke at meetings with the Bonafulla group; most notably José López Montenegro, a septuagenarian ex-army colonel who had made a name for himself as a 'rationalist' school teacher, and Marià Castellote, the president of the Barcelona Bricklayers' Labourers Federation during 1901.[40]

The ideology and strategy adopted by these groups was little different from that of the years 1887 to 1893. They believed that anarchists should direct the unions. Nevertheless some, like Bonafulla, emphasised the need for unity above ideology at union meetings.[41] This did not mean that they abjured their anarchist ideals while engaged in union work. Rather, they advanced the rather sophistic argument that because 'economic emancipation' was in the interest of all workers, as 'conscious workers' all that they were doing was embodying the workers' real interests.[42]

Anarchists working within the unions had a clear idea of the shape that the union movement should take. As in the late 1880s, they argued that it should be totally decentralised. Dues should be low in order to encourage membership and not create privileged strata within the working class. Local or national federations should perhaps not charge dues at all, but simply operate as centres for exchange of information. This emphasis on decentralisation mirrored their vision of the future libertarian society, which was to be based on a system of communes, as set out in Pyotr Kropotkin's *The Conquest of Bread*, 'the gospel of the new society' according to Lorenzo.[43]

At the same time workers, they argued, should be mobilised against employers and the state. In this respect great emphasis was laid on the general strike as the key weapon in the workers' armoury. This reflected the debate over the issue which had taken place in France during the 1890s, where individualist doctrines had had more impact than in Spain and the bridge between labour and anarchism needed to be rebuilt. Some French anarchists, led by Fernand Pelloutier, began to develop a new doctrine known as syndicalism (or revolutionary syndicalism as it is now usually referred to), arguing that anarchists should become totally immersed in the unions, forming a 'conscious minority' who would lead them down the revolutionary road. The revolutionary weapon par excellence would be the general strike, which would be followed by the expropriation of the means of production by the unions, who would then run the new communist society. Others, like the highly influential anarchist propagandist Jean Grave (a personal friend of Ferrer's), whose articles and pamphlets were frequently translated into Spanish, continued to refer to themselves as an anarcho-communists, but strongly backed the idea of a general strike.

In Spain debates regarding syndicalism hardly registered between 1899 and 1903. The reason, I think, as a comparison of Pelloutier's ideas and practice and that of pro-union Spanish anarchists makes clear, is that there seemed little in syndicalist ideology to which they could object. At this point it appeared very much to belong to the anarchist mainstream. Only later would issues such as the role of the anarchist groups in organising the revolution, the place of workers who rejected anarchism within a syndicalist labour confederations, and the make-up of the new communist society, lead to polemic.[44] On the contrary, the idea of the general strike was taken up with gusto. There was some debate amongst anarchists on the ease with which capitalism could be overthrown, but their catastrophist analysis of present-day state and society – which was viewed as both profoundly unjust and unnatural – encouraged the belief that it could be done in short shrift.[45] It was a view given further currency by the weakening of the Restoration regime after the crisis of 1898. The way was led by José López Montenegro in the *Suplemento de la Revista Blanca* between 1899 and 1900, and the theme was then developed above all by Francesc Ferrer, in his aptly named publication, *La Huelga General.*

These authors put forward the argument that strikes limited to individual trades or factories (*huelgas parciales* as they were called) would achieve little long-term benefit, although they should be supported because they helped build the union movement and create a sense of solidarity amongst workers. Only the general strike would be the handmaiden of the new society. In line with Pelloutier, Montenegro envisaged the strike as both short and peaceful. The capitalist state, he maintained, would capitulate with little struggle. This position was, however, increasingly criticised in France in the late 1890s, where it was argued that a general strike would provoke an inevitably violent confrontation with state power. It was a view picked up by Ferrer, who to the question 'Will blood be spilt?' answered, 'yes, plenty.'[46] This fitted in with the generally held belief amongst Spanish anarchists, that a 'terrible, devastating revolution' by armed workers would sweep away the old order away. Rather than contradicting such a stance the idea of the General Strike now provided a plausible trigger for a workers' uprising.[47] It was quickly popularised by books and pamphlets. Of key importance were *La Revista Blanca, El Productor* and *La Huelga General,* which all set up their own small publishing houses and brought out works on the general strike.[48] It was in this atmosphere that Ferrer's publication was given its name. Nor was this merely a theoretical concern. As we shall see, the organisation of general strikes would become an obsession in anarchist circles during these years.

Anarchist sympathisers gained an increasingly high profile within the Barcelona labour movement from 1901. In this year they played a leading role in the big strikes in the metal industry and construction, while Leopoldo Bonafulla and his collaborators launched a series of meetings in support of striking workers and two major protest campaigns against the Government. This was typical of anarchist strategy, which centred on mobilising street-level agitation. The first big meeting was held at the end of March to protest at the conduct of the authorities and support a tanners' strike in Igualada. During the rest of the year a number of meetings of this type were organised. They proved very popular, attracting two or three thousand workers at a time. In July and August the anarchists also launched their first campaign, against government repression of a strike in La Coruña. The strike had been anarchist-led and the Socialists refused to participate, but in Barcelona the meetings were well attended.

They followed this up in November with a campaign against the Government's proposed strike legislation. A bill had recently been introduced into parliament which specified the lapse of several days between the calling of a strike and the actual withdrawal of labour power in order for it to be declared legal. Both anarchists and Socialists argued that the bill represented an attack on the right to strike. Yet in Barcelona it was the anarchists who seized the initiative, forming a commission which then called a series of meetings, the largest of which received the support of forty-nine unions and was attended by a crowd of several thousand. In all at least sixty-eight Barcelona unions affiliated to one or more of the protest meetings organised by the anarchists during the year.[49]

In these meetings Bonafulla's flexibility was also on show in that he was happy for non-anarchists to participate. Most active was the left-wing republican, Lluís Zurdo Olivares, who argued both in favour of an independent party of the working class and the revolutionary general strike.[50] What, however, all these speakers had in common was that they demanded a more combative union strategy, and a more forceful opposition to government policy, than that offered by the Socialists. This was not only a question of rhetoric. Anarchist union activists often took the lead in strikes and street demonstrations, beating up and firing on blacklegs, intimidating employers, and confronting the police. Indeed, one could draw a profile of the typical anarchist trade unionist. He was the type of man who would not take an insult from an employer or a foreman lying down, was quick to resist any attack on working conditions, would rally support for strike action and then take the lead 'on the street '. He and his comrades would also be very active in the mass union and protest meetings; a crucial factor in getting radical resolutions approved. As a result, militant anarchism was a young man's game, with many dropping out after a strike defeat, a sacking and, possibly, imprisonment. For those that remained, as the following chapters will show, support within the family and neighbourhood, and the camaraderie within the movement itself, could provide significant compensation for the hardships suffered.

As a result of the escalation of social conflict and political tensions, then, the anarchists' confrontationalist style had attracted quite widespread working-class sympathy. Support was strongest amongst workers in trades in which labour relations were especially poor. The bricklayers and bricklayers labourers' unions had a high profile in the anarchist camp. The same can be said of the major painters and carpenters' unions. The anarchists also received backing from the mechanics and iron foundrymens' unions, and through them from the Barcelona Metalworkers' Federation. By 1901 anarchist sympathisers also dominated the compositors' union, L'Art d'Imprimir, and the tanners, cabinetmakers, carters, and textile-finishing trades' unions.

Anarchists' class-based ideology and grass-roots activism meant that throughout this period they would be at the forefront of attempts to challenge exclusivist attitudes amongst formally apprenticed male workers and overcome skill and, to a degree, gender divisions within the workforce. Hence, they acted as a bridge between the skilled and unskilled and campaigned for unified unions. They had some success in construction and metalworking, industries in which, as shown in the previous chapter, much of the workforce needed to look outside the narrow confines of the trade and mobilise more widely in order to take on their employers. Anarchists played a key role in the formation of the provincial and Spanish federations of bricklayers and bricklayers' labourers, and were instrumental in forging local and national federations of metal unions.

These federations, it should be stressed, did not declare themselves specifically anarchist, which, they feared, would lead to disunity, but anarchists were highly active within them. Moreover, they were organised in direct competition with the UGT, which from 1902 began a push to set up Spanish trade federations of its own. The latter had little impact in Catalonia. In 1903 the Socialist bricklayers' and metalworkers' federations had one Catalan union between them.[51] It was a similar story in woodworking. The Carpenters' Federation of the Catalan Region, which had been founded in 1898, stated that it represented all workers and centred only on 'economic matters', but a considerable anarchist influence was apparent. Subsequently, when the Socialists set up their own National Federation of Carpenters and Similar Workers in 1903 no Catalan unions joined.[52]

The anarchists' interest in mobilising the unskilled also led them to play a key role in the reorganisation of the female cotton textile workers in late 1901. Not surprisingly, then, the new union represented a total ideological break with the TCV. Dues were very low and there was no strike fund for, in the words of its leading activist, Teresa Claramunt, 'to fight the bourgeoisie and defeat it what is needed is energy'.[53] The brief resurgence of unionism in cotton textiles helped alter the perception of female workers amongst the men. Women were not only encouraged to organise but also to speak on union platforms. The very fact that Claramunt played such an active role in the anarchist movement helped break down stereotypes. This trend was further stimulated by anarchist theorists, who attacked the discrimination which women suffered, championed the intellectual equality of women and affirmed that they should have equal rights.[54]

Yet, this did not mean that anarchist activists saw men and women in the same light. Like workers in general, they viewed women as 'the weaker sex'. This comes through, for example, in the large number of anarchist sketches and stories in which chaste working-class women fell victims to the lascivious advances of industrialists and foremen.[55] Furthermore, they saw the woman's natural sphere of action as located in the home, both giving their children a revolutionary education and encouraging their menfolk.[56] Hence, they also argued that men should have primacy within the workplace; even Teresa Claramunt called on the female textile workers 'not to play the bourgeois's game, who makes her take the place of a man because she is easier to exploit'. Such attitudes explain why the Second Congress of the anarchist labour confederation, the FRESR, held in October 1901, agreed to 'get our poor companions and dear children out of the workshops and factories'.[57] Thus, while anarchists vehemently rejected conservative arguments that women were naturally inferior, they failed to question the dominant paradigms regarding a woman's nature, her place in the world of work and public sphere. This no doubt made it easier for them to link up with the male-dominated unions, but meant that women would play only a limited role in the movement.[58]

The growing level of support allowed the anarchists finally to form a local federation in opposition to the Socialists at the end of 1901. *La Huelga General* stated that in line with anarchist principles it would have no strike fund. Subscriptions would, moreover, be voluntary, and the federation's funds would – once administrative costs had been dealt with – be dedicated to 'acts of solidarity'.[59] This growth was not limited to Catalonia. As the labour movement revived, anarchists also made headway in Galicia, Asturias, Valencia and, especially, Andalusia, where social conflict grew dramatically from 1901. These developments encouraged them to set up their own labour confederation (or 'free pact' to use the language of the time), the FRESR, whose Founding Congress was held in Madrid in October 1900.

It made ambitious membership claims. Federico Urales stated in his memoirs that 52,000 workers were represented at its Founding Congress and that in October 1901 it had 73,000 affiliates.[60] This meant that on paper it easily outstripped the UGT. Yet this is, to a large extent, what it remained; a paper tiger, which failed to establish any organic link with its union base. The problem was the organisational model. Like previous anarchist confederations it was structured along the lines of local federations, which linked all workers in a particular area, and Spanish trade federations, which united all workers in the same trade. But the degree of autonomy which the anarchists believed should be given to the individual unions meant that it could not function effectively. The Founding Congress took the decision that, rather than pay fixed dues, affiliated unions should simply cover expenses at the end of the year, and the Second Congress, held in October 1901, went further, making dues voluntary. The result was that very few unions ever actually contributed to running costs, leaving the so-called Regional Office facing a perpetual funding crisis.[61]

In terms of its policies, it responded to the concrete concerns of its working-class base, with, for example, resolutions in favour of the abolition of piece rates, and, as noted, measures to prevent the employment of female and child labour. Simultaneously, it elaborated a typically anarchist union strategy, which emphasised mobilisation over negotiation and, above all, championed the general strike, both as a means to achieve specific ends and to overthrow capitalism.[62] In Barcelona the organisation of such strikes became an obsession. The pro-anarchist meetings held during 1901 were punctuated by continuous calls for a general strike, which came to be seen by many of the speakers as a panacea for all the workers' ills. It was recommended to force employers to recognise the workers' right to form trade unions; to show solidarity with striking workers; to put pressure on the government to release political prisoners or to withdraw its strike legislation; and, finally, as the only means of overthrowing capitalism.

Nor were these calls merely hot air. On 1 May 1901 the anarchists were able to organise a one-day stoppage in much of working-class Barcelona. Flushed by this relative success, on 7 May nineteen Barcelona unions, linked to the FRESR, voted to launch a general strike in support of the tram drivers. It was only to last two days. However, they were more successful in February 1902 when they engineered a week-long stoppage in favour of the metalworkers. As I stressed in the previous chapter, solidarity at the level of the working-class community was a crucial element in the strike's relative success. However, in order to understand why the February 1902 stoppage in particular took off, one also has to look at the institutional and political context. Anarchists were influential within the Barcelona Metalworkers' Federation, and its first president, Ramon Homades, was a committed activist. Given the industrialists' intransigence the strike committee concluded that only a solidarity strike by the entire working class could bring them victory. But a first attempt to call such a strike, on 3 January, failed to materialise.[63]

The Metalworkers' Federation reacted by adopting a more conciliatory tone. It agreed to the formation of a commission of republican and Catalanist local councillors, in order to try to find a solution. This commission suggested that a committee of worker and employer representatives be formed, along with two engineers, to see if it was feasible to reduce working hours. These discussions did not finally bear fruit. However, the fact that they were taking place at all provoked harsh criticism from the anarchist press. The metalworkers, they maintained, had not pursued an energetic line of action and had let the strike drag on interminably. Leopoldo Bonafulla went so far as to say that it was now lost.[64] Within the Metalworkers' Federation, then, there were elements in favour of a negotiated settlement. Had they been successful the anarchist activists would, no doubt, have been marginalised, but the refusal of the industrialists to make concessions made their position untenable. After the negotiations had failed it again became clear that action would have to be taken by the rest of the working class if the metalworkers were not to be defeated. The anarchists also reassessed their position. They still criticised the handling of the dispute but once again stressed the need for the working class to take decisive action on the metalworkers' behalf. It was in these circumstances that a mass meeting, attended by 5,000 workers on 15 February, supported the general strike call.

The 1902 general strike represented the high point of anarchist influence within the Barcelona labour movement.[65] As has been emphasised, the anarchists' growth over the past two years had been made possible by the escalation of industrial conflict and social tension. It was against this background that their confrontationalist tactics seemed to make sense. Yet the general strike ended in failure and the metalworkers were forced back defeated. As we saw in the previous chapter, repression was severe. In April there were still ninety-two prisoners in the Modelo prison including many anarchist activists. One did not have to be actively involved to be imprisoned; Anselmo Lorenzo, for example, was locked up for several months, accused of being a 'moral author'.[66] This highlighted the extent to which the regime's post-1898 reforming intentions had been derailed. Faced with anarchist agitation both parties were quick to declare martial law and come down hard. Yet, after several months, the authorities had to restore constitutional guarantees and release those not actually charged. Hence, a sense of grievance and a point around which anarchists and the broader union movement could rally was created, and neither the stability of the regime nor the social climate in Barcelona was enhanced.

In this instance, the anarchists were again free to agitate from late January 1903 onwards. Despite their defeat they continued to enjoy considerable support. Twenty-four unions were affiliated to the local anarchist labour federation, and through campaigns and protest meetings they were once again able to extend their influence further afield. They were favoured because the level of industrial conflict remained high with strike rates peaking in June and

July. Pro-anarchist trade unionists were involved in many of these disputes, leading Leopoldo Bonafulla at one point to predict that another general strike was shortly to be declared. It was not, however, to be. The anarchists attempted to declare two further general strikes during the year, but neither had much impact.

The first, called in solidarity with a general strike in Reus in early February, was a total flop. The second was rather better prepared. The escalation of strikes in much of Spain encouraged the Barcelona-based Regional Office of the FRESR to launch a campaign for the release of workers (generally from anarchist unions) held in prison. This was an emotive issue which could galvanise the anarchist core and also, given the ease with which imprisonment could befall union activists, draw sympathy from wider working-class circles. It proved a considerable success, with a large number of simultaneous meetings held on 14 June. The Regional Office kept up the pressure, declaring that if the political prisoners had not been released by the beginning of August a three-day general strike would be called throughout Spain. The strike was finally restricted to 3 August, but in Barcelona, despite the fact that sixty-five unions had published a fly-sheet giving their backing, its repercussions were limited.[67] The most dramatic events would, in fact, occur near Valencia, in the small town of Alcalá del Valle on 1 August, where there was a bloody clash between workers and the Civil Guard. Three workers were subsequently given life sentences and another three sentenced to twenty years. Over subsequent years their release was an issue around which anarchists would try and rally support.

The anarchists' effectiveness was also being sapped by intensifying repression. In the spring the Conservative Government issued instructions to the Barcelona civil governor to keep a strict eye on anarchist meetings and the anarchist press, and take action against any article which attacked state institutions or the monarchy. Simultaneously, it issued instructions that, in line with the 1887 Associations Law, more than one union could not occupy the same premises. This serves to emphasise the double standards applied by the authorities to Socialists and anarchists. No action was taken against the UGT headquarters in Madrid, despite the fact that the Associations Law should presumably also have applied. Socialists were tolerated as a more responsible opposition, while most Restoration politicians saw the anarchists as beyond the pale.[68]

These failures also point to the ambiguous relationship between the anarchist activists and the broader union and working-class base. The anarchists had been able to generate support for a general strike in circumstances in which there appeared to be no other option. Yet after the defeat of the metalworkers there was resistance to a repeat performance, especially for causes which seemed less vital. This tension was particularly evident in the relationship between the anarchist vanguard and the Sabadell labour movement. The poor relations between the anarchists of *La Protesta* and the FOS have already been noted. During 1901 the FOS was to develop closer ties with the Barcelona anarchists. The Sabadell woollen power-loom weavers joined the FRESR in January 1901. In the same month Carles Piazza died, and publication of *El Trabajo* was suspended until October. When it reappeared it took a more overtly anarchist line, and the FOS actively campaigned for the FRESR.[69] This period of open cooperation culminated in February 1902, when the Sabadell labour movement enthusiastically seconded the Barcelona general strike.

In 1903, however, tensions began to resurface. Thus, no Sabadell delegate attended the FRESR's Third Congress, held in Madrid in May 1903. Moreover, at the beginning of August *El Trabajo* declared that it was not sorry that the general strike to secure the release of Spain's political prisoners had failed, because badly organised stoppages always ended in bloody repression. Later in the month the woollen power-loom weavers attended a congress held by the Socialists in Badalona in order to set up a new textile federation.[70] It failed to take off, but the uneasy relationship between the anarchists and Sabadell weavers was again exposed.

This highlighted the problem at the heart of anarchist strategy. They had been able to harness rank-and-file militancy, but often seemed unable to channel it in a positive direction. Between 1901 and 1903 they had tried constantly to declare general strikes, often without it being clear what exactly they wished to achieve: whether to win a specific battle or provoke a revolutionary general strike. Indeed the answer to this question – as comments in the run-up to the February 1902 general strike indicate – seems to have been unclear to many anarchists, and their line of reasoning was probably that a general strike was the best means to achieve a concrete goal, and that with any luck the stoppage might take a revolutionary turn. By the summer of 1903, however, a reappraisal was obviously needed. It would be difficult for anarchists to question the validity of the whole concept, but the FOS was gaining some backing in anarchist circles for its argument that general strikes were a doubled-edged sword and should be used with care.[71]

This distance between the anarchist core and the working-class base was also apparent in the anarchists' relations with the Barcelona unions. Although sixty-odd Barcelona unions had been in some way linked to the anarchists they did not accept all aspects of anarchist ideology. Many were clearly not very committed supporters at all. Thus, relatively few unions actually sent delegates to the FRESR's national congresses and less than thirty affiliated to the pro-anarchist local federation formed at the end of 1901. Indeed, as has been stressed, not all the speakers at the 1901 rallies organised by Leopoldo Bonafulla and his colleagues were unambiguously anarchist. In fact, once one descends from the level of the leadership to that of the trade-union rank and file it becomes increasingly difficult to fit workers into such neat categories as anarchist, Socialist or republican.

This ambiguity was present at a number of levels. The anarchists, of course, rejected parliament and elections. Yet, as we shall see in the next chapter, many workers could quite happily go to anarchist trade-union meetings and then vote republican at election time. On the trade-union front, anarchists combated strike funds and argued that mutual-aid societies should operate separately, but few union statutes had such impeccably anarchist credentials as those of the Barcelona textile workers' union. Despite anarchist claims that 'energy' rather than money was needed to win industrial disputes, most Barcelona unions tried to build up some kind of strike fund, and a few paid accident benefits. This last category included the Barcelona bricklayers.[72] Similar discrepancies could be seen over the question of the role of the state. Anarchists theoretically opposed all forms of state intervention. Yet many workers close to the anarchist camp believed the acts limiting the use female and child labour would lead to an improvement in working conditions. This is a subject which I shall further develop later in the chapter. Moreover, the anarchists' claim that outside agencies should not be brought into negotiations over working conditions was not taken very seriously. In fact, Barcelona civil governors were constantly involved in discussions aimed at solving industrial disputes.

Workers took little notice of anarchists in other fields. For example, there were a large number of small consumer cooperatives in Catalonia. Anarchists were generally hostile. In part this was ideologically driven: they claimed that cooperatives led to the embourgeoisement of those who affiliated and obstructed the workers' emancipation. In addition, it reflected frustration that the cooperatives often remained inward looking and failed to reach out beyond their base in the skilled working class.[73] But the cooperatives' involvement in union affairs was far greater than statements by anarchist theoreticians would leave one to believe. The larger cooperatives, in which republicans were often influential, allowed union meetings to take place on their premises and frequently supported workers' families during strikes. Not surprisingly then, many workers formed part of the neighbourhood consumer cooperative and their local union.[74]

Workers' motivations explain how this was possible. They might trust a well-known anarchist trade unionist, but this did not mean that they would forgo the opportunity to purchase cheaper basic necessities or reject social legislation. I am unaware of any Barcelona unions that had a consumer cooperative attached and very few provided mutual-aid, but the main reason was probably the embryonic nature of the Barcelona union movement. Moreover, given the state of Catalan labour relations, there was a distinct advantage to be gained from differentiating unions from other working-class associations; workers could enter into hard fought conflicts in the knowledge that their cooperative or mutual-aid society was safe. The overall result would be a high degree of organisational diversity, although, as I shall show in the next chapter, this hid a greater ideological and cultural convergence between the different organisations and tendencies linked to labour than might at first glance be expected.

It was worker disaffection with the anarchists' constant calls for a general strike that, in 1903, the Socialists hoped to tap into in order to win back support. Despite fading from centre stage in the context of escalating social conflict they maintained their complete opposition to the anarchists' trade-union practice. This could be seen in the aftermath of the 1902 general strike. From the first the Madrid Socialists did their utmost to prevent the extension of the strike outside Catalonia, arguing that to have seconded it would have invited a bloody repression and the formation of an authoritarian government, and that if the workers had been in a stronger position than the bourgeoisie then they should have attempted a social revolution.[75]

By adopting this line of argument the PSOE-UGT was reaffirming its *de facto* reformist trade-union and political policy, while at the same time trying to maintain intact its ultimate goal of social revolution. The line taken by the Madrid party leadership was strongly backed by the Catalan Socialists.[76] As in the case of their condemnation of the general strike called by the FTE in January 1901, this stance probably lost them support. They could point to the ineffectiveness of anarchist tactics, but, in a context in which the metalworkers' plight attracted overwhelming sympathy and little alternative appeared on the horizon, the anarchists could again portray the Socialists as having betrayed the workers. Indeed, the claim that the UGT general secretary, Antonio García Quejido, had sent a letter to the British Trades Union Congress advising them not to support the metalworkers, was oft-repeated in anarchist publications. Josep Comaposada was later to admit that such attacks were very effective.[77] He was able to experience this reaction at first hand. In the aftermath of the defeat anarchists pushed for the expulsion of the Socialist leaders from the city's unions. Toribio Reoyo was thrown out of the printers' union after the general strike, and Comaposada was expelled from the shoemakers' union after he opposed a general strike in the trade in 1903.[78]

Despite this experience, the Catalan Socialists maintained the same stance in 1903, and took advantage of the failure of the general strike in favour of the Reus workers to form an anti-general strike front. Under Socialist guidance a number of unions held two meetings in February in which they rejected the use of the general strike. They also decided to form a new local federation and published a manifesto in which, in an exercise designed to salvage their revolutionary credentials, they argued that a general strike could only be put into practice when bourgeois society was ripe to be overthrown. At present, it was claimed, the working class's lack of culture and of political awareness made this impossible.[79]

The manifesto was signed by nineteen unions, including the TCV. Yet the Socialists were unable significantly to increase their support in union circles. In February they formed a Catalan Socialist Federation and began publishing a Socialist weekly entitled *La Guerra Social*.[80] However, their impact in Barcelona remained limited. The Centre de Societats Obreres was closed down after the February 1902 general strike and subsequently failed to reopen. The one bright spot was that they began to recruit sailors and stokers at the port as part of a push by the UGT to create a national federation of sailors and port workers. However, the unions were destroyed following the failure of a strike in 1904. In the summer of 1903 *La Guerra Social* was forced to admit that it was the anarchists who had the greatest influence within the Barcelona unions.[81] This was of considerable importance for the future development of the Spanish labour movement. It was the failure of the Catalan UGT to grow strongly between 1899 and 1903, at a time when the confederation as a whole tripled its membership, that turned Barcelona into the UGT's weak link.[82]

The Formation of Solidaritat Obrera, 1904 to 1909

Debates over the general strike became redundant from the autumn of 1903, when a deep recession hit Catalan industry. By the middle of the decade the overall number of workers unionised in Barcelona had declined to about 20,000. Almost all the city's unions were greatly weakened and some totally destroyed. Furthermore, the Government maintained its repressive stance, with unions in Barcelona still prevented from sharing the same headquarters.

As a result, as in the 1890s, some anarchist activists became increasingly disconnected from the working class, moved in déclassé bohemian circles, became influenced by Nietzsche and Stirner, and, as we shall see in the next chapter, a small minority probably became involved in terrorist activities. Other groups tried to maintain links with organised labour but found this difficult. Leopoldo Bonafulla's credibility was shaken when it transpired that, imprisoned after the 1902 general strike, he had accepted financial help from the Liberal politician, José Canalejas. He was fiercely criticised in *Tierra y Libertad* and denounced by thirteen anarchist groups in Barcelona.[83] From the end of the year he moved *El Productor*'s headquarters from central Barcelona to Gràcia, and would henceforth be a much more peripheral figure.

This left those anarchists closest to Ferrer and Lorenzo to play the central role. They were in charge of the Regional Office of the FRESR while it was in Barcelona (between early 1901 and February 1902 and again between early 1903 and May 1904). In this latter year they also formed a group known as '4 de Maig' (after five anarchists executed in the fortress of Montjuïc on 4 May 1897), and, with financial backing from Ferrer, were able to set up a Centre for Social Studies, which held talks and debates on anarchist theory and practice. Simultaneously they brought out a number of anarchist publications. Most significantly, in November 1906 they took over *Tierra y Libertad* and transferred its editorial committee to Barcelona. Unlike almost all anarchist weeklies it would achieve a high degree of stability, rising to become the archetypal early twentieth-century anarchist mouthpiece.[84]

They tried to maintained the anarchists' mobilising tradition, launching a campaign for the release of the Alcalá del Valle prisoners from the end of 1903, with support from French anarchist circles close to Ferrer, but it proved a pale shadow of the Montjuïc protest movement. The cause was not as immediately relevant and the weak Barcelona unions were unable to bring together large numbers of workers. In March 1904 they also revived the local federation, which had ceased to function several months previously. Yet in the aftermath of the failures of 1903, and in the face of economic recession and heavy-handed government repression, there was growing scepticism at the revolutionary potential of the unions and criticism of the effectiveness of strike action. This could be seen at a congress of unions from Catalonia and the Balearic Islands, organised by the Barcelona local federation in Sabadell between 30 October and 1 November 1904, during which criticisms were voiced at the way unions were presently constituted. What they meant was made clear in the 4 de Maig press, which argued that repression by the civil governor had led the workers to abandon the unions, 'believing them to be too legalistic', and take 'a new direction in their struggle against capital', and stressed the importance of the anarchist affinity group in sparking the revolution.[85]

This brought out the extent to which in Spain the idea of the general strike had been fused with Bakuninist insurrectionism, which was, on an international plane, strongly advocated by anarchists such as the Italian Erico Malatesta (whose pamphlets were a firm favourite amongst Spanish anarchists). A clandestine number of *La Huelga General* affirmed in late 1904 that the general strike should be used by the anarchist elite to launch an assault on state power. In similar terms the printer Tomás Herreros, who was close to the 4 de Maig group, stated that rather than spend their time on producing newspapers and on educational initiatives, they should form revolutionary anarchist groups, whose job it would be to 'forge men capable of taking the lead at the right time'. Moreover, this stance was combined with sympathy for 'propaganda by the deed'. The clandestine issue of *La Huelga General* included a list of 'criminals' (including Alfonso XIII) who should be assassinated. In a similar vein, Teresa Claramunt affirmed that only violent acts (she gave the example of the supposed assassination of a number of employers in her home town) would frighten the industrialists into making concessions.[86]

However, not all anarchist unionists backed the stance taken by the leadership of the Barcelona federation. A more positive assessment of the unions' potential was encouraged by the growing success of the French labour confederation, the CGT, which took up the baton of syndicalism. Its major theorists, Emile Pouget and Georges Yvetot, built on the inheritance of Pelloutier, making his ideas more compatible with the actual operation of a labour confederation. Like Pelloutier they stressed that nothing could be expected of parties and parliament. Workers should confront industrialists on the economic terrain without intermediaries (through their own 'direct action'). Strikes for concrete goals were now seen in a more favourable light. It was argued that they would make workers more combative and class-conscious, strengthen the unions, and, finally, escalate into a revolutionary general strike. 1902 to 1908 were the confederation's 'heroic years', during which it launched a number of spectacular and lengthy strikes.[87]

Given this backdrop, many Catalan anarchists enthusiastically welcomed syndicalist ideas, which they continued to view as a form of anarchism. For Anselmo Lorenzo, for example, 'they have returned to us, amplified, corrected and perfectly systematised, ideas with which the Spanish anarchists inspired the French'.[88] Hence, between 1904 and 1909, in anarchist circles an important effort was made to publicise syndicalist doctrine. Anselmo Lorenzo himself played an importance role in this process, translating two pamphlets by Pouget in 1904. The most widely read of all syndicalist works, Yvetot's *ABC syndicaliste*, followed in 1908.[89] Morever, Spanish anarchists themselves began disseminating syndicalist doctrine. Important in this respect was *El Trabajo*, under the leadership of the veteran anarchist, Josep Miguel, who had imbibed syndicalist ideas while in exile in France in the 1890s. And, from 1906, easily the most talented Catalan anarchist writer, Josep Prat, a shy, retiring figure who never spoke at meetings, also began translating works on syndicalism and elegantly outlined the key components of syndicalist theory.[90]

Nevertheless, there were elements within syndicalism which could trouble some anarchists. First, though the syndicalists emphasised the decentralised nature of the CGT, in order to function effectively it was rather more centralised than the anarchist 'free pacts'. Thus, all unions affiliated paid dues regularly, the need for some paid officials was accepted and industrial federations promoted. Second, in many respects like the Spanish FTE and FTRE in the 1870s and 1880s, the CGT represented an amalgam of syndicalist ideologues and workers of other or no particular political persuasion. This led to fierce internal debates over syndicalist doctrine. As against the emphasis by syndicalists, who hailed from the anarchist camp, on the importance of the 'conscious minority', others argued that workers would be radicalised by the practice of the class struggle. This served to downplay the role any revolutionary elite might have in the confederation. For their part 'apolitical' unions or unions under Socialist influence maintained that syndicalism meant simply that the CGT should operate independently of any political doctrine (including anarchism). A compromise was worked out in the 1906 Chartre d'Amiens, which, on the one hand confirmed the CGT's revolutionary goals but, on the other, affirmed that it was apolitical but not specifically antiparliamentary. Workers of all persuasions could form part of the organisation, and pursue whatever political agenda they wished outside its doors, as long as they did not bring these views into the unions. It was exactly the same compromise as the Spanish FRE had reached in 1870, and would provoke fierce debates between the revolutionary syndicalists and their opponents in subsequent years.

Similar debates would rage in Catalonia. First off the mark was the Sabadell FOS, which celebrated the fact that the CGT's practice offered a higher degree of stability than the Spanish 'free pacts'. Hence, *El Trabajo* combined syndicalist rhetoric with continued stress on the need for unions to build up their strength and not be carried away by 'impetuous' general strikes, which would endanger their existence. At the same time, the FOS played a leading role in establishing contacts with the CGT and launched the only significant campaign that Catalan unions would undertake between 1904 and 1906. This followed the CGT's decision to declare a general strike in favour of the establishment of an eight-hours day on 1 May 1906. The FOS seconded the initiative, explaining that it was not to be achieved by legal, reformist, means. On the contrary, workers would attain it though their own 'direct action' by simply walking out after eight hours.[91]

This was a point around which unions could unite without inviting government repression. The importance attached by Barcelona unions to reducing working hours meant that the proposal generated considerable enthusiasm. Led by figures close to the anarchist camp the campaign began in earnest in January 1906. Articles supporting the stoppage were published in all the working-class press, a pamphlet was printed, and a large number of fly sheets distributed. Furthermore between 15 and 16 April a meeting was held in Valls to discuss action to be taken on 1 May. In all, fifty delegates from one-hundred unions attended. They represented the core of the Catalan labour movement. The meeting declared itself in favour of direct action but, taking count of the realities of the times, asked only that those unions and localities that were in a strong enough position second the movement.[92] Its objective was, as might be expected, not to be achieved. In Barcelona and several other towns there were big stoppages on 1 May, but they could not be sustained. The reasons were clear. The economic recession was still very deep and union organisation far too weak for such a revolutionary demand to have any chance of success. Yet, it did bring a large number of Catalan unions into closer contact and also confirmed that pro-anarchist workers still played an important role within the labour movement.

The campaign also stimulated discussion of the possibility of regrouping the individual Catalan unions into a new confederation. The FRESR had moved to La Coruña in August 1905 and was henceforth completely inoperative. It would be officially wound up by the local unions in March 1907.[93] This emphasised the extent to which anarchist 'free pacts' were unable to achieve any lasting union. The idea was encouraged because in Barcelona there was an increase in union activity from the end of 1906 and the economic recession eased somewhat in the following year. Anarchist activists were also extremely concerned that the decline in trade unionism had been matched by an unprecedented political mobilisation. The April 1907 general elections witnessed a vibrant and passionate campaign between Catalanists and anti-Catalanist republicans in which many workers enthusiastically participated. Anarchists tried to counteract this through 'antipolitical' meetings and propaganda, but, as Anselmo Lorenzo recognised, faced by the 'bourgeois Solidarity'(Catalanists) and the 'bourgeois anti-Solidarity' (anti-Catalanist republicans), they had to construct 'worker solidarity'. He was backed by the rest of the *Tierra y Libertad* editorial team, who, despite their previous scepticism, from the end of 1906 also began to take an interest in French syndicalism and stress the need for workers to re-enter the unions.[94]

Within the anarchist camp discussions of the need to set up a Spanish confederation on the lines of the CGT took place from the end of 1906, but the general view was that individual unions first had to be strengthened.[95] This allowed the Catalan Socialists to take the initiative and play a leading role in the creation of a new union confederation, albeit at the more modest level of Barcelona city. This may at first sight seem surprising, but there were several factors in their favour. They had experience of operating 'open' union federations. In addition, in the economically depressed climate of these years few unions would sympathise with the anarchists' militant strike policy. In a manner similar to the years 1898 to 1900, the Socialists might, therefore, given their stress on the need for solid trade-union federations, be able to play an important role in reorganising the labour movement.

None the less, they faced a number of difficulties. By themselves they were not strong enough to spearhead a union revival and would have to collaborate with union activists close to the anarchist camp. Yet, their reaction to the 1902 general strike had earned them the title of enemies of the working class, and between 1904 and 1906 they remained locked in bitter conflict with the anarchists. It was, therefore, clear that in order once again to play a leading role within the Barcelona labour movement they would have seriously to reconsider their policies. Such a reappraisal took place between 1904 and

1908, when the Catalan Socialists appeared to break with the moderate trade-union practice of the past and adopted a syndicalist veneer. This change was a response to conditions in Catalonia, but cannot be understood without reference to events in the rest of Europe. In the years after 1900 syndicalist ideas had made considerable headway. Furthermore, in Socialist circles a left-wing opposition had grown up against the *de facto* reformism of the Second International. These leftists did not, in general, advocate the use of the general strike to overthrow capitalism, but they called for a move away from what they viewed as an excessive concentration on elections, and supported the use of mass strikes for political ends.[96]

In Barcelona, Socialists linked to the shopworkers' unions provided the stimulus for change. The theoretician behind the new strategy was Antoni Fabra Ribas. University educated, he had first entered labour politics in 1898 when he helped to organise the shopworkers in his home town of Reus. He spent much of the period between 1901 and 1908 abroad, especially in France, where he made contacts with left-wing Socialists and became influenced by syndicalism. Thus, like the French Socialist Left, he rejected the subordination of the union confederation to the party. Furthermore, he became sceptical as to the value of electoral politics and instead stressed the need for militant rank-and-file action by a united working class. In France a united Socialist party (the SFIO), founded in 1906, took on board many of the Left Socialists' ideological postulates. Unlike the PSOE it did not try and build its own labour confederation, but instead worked through the CGT. In view of the UGT's weakness Fabra Ribas hoped to apply a similar formula, first to Catalonia, and perhaps eventually to the whole of Spain.[97]

The victory of the tendency captained by Fabra Ribas was assured at the Catalan Socialist congress held on 27 and 28 September 1908 to reorganise the by then defunct Catalan Socialist Federation. Fabra Ribas, who had recently returned from abroad, became the federation's secretary, and he was also elected to the post of editor of its new mouthpiece, *La Internacional*.[98] In practical terms, the man who did most to put the new strategy into effect was Antoni Badia Matamala, who was president of the Barcelona shopworkers' union, the ADM, almost continuously between 1902 and 1908. In the summer of 1907 it suggested that a meeting be held to discuss the reconstruction of a local federation. The anarchists own federation had once again ceased to function and so the formation of some kind of coordinating body was an obvious necessity. It was for this reason that an important number of pro-anarchist, republican and independent unions agreed to the plan. The new confederation, known as Worker Solidarity (SO) (following the phrase coined by Lorenzo), was, accordingly, founded on 3 August 1907, with the support of over fifty Barcelona unions. Two months later the first number of its weekly newspaper, under the same name, also appeared (written in Castilian-Spanish, *Solidaridad Obrera*).[99] The drawing on the front page emphasised the concerns of the confederation's leaders. Catalan workers had been drugged by the siren calls of the bourgeois republicans and Catalanists. Only the workers' solidarity movement could bring them to their senses (see figure 4.1.).

Figure 4.1. Front Page of the First Number of *Solidaridad Obrera*

At first SO gained wide-ranging support, including all those anarchists who rejected individualist Nietzchien doctrines. From August 1907 Anselmo Lorenzo called on workers to join and Francesc Ferrer subsequently provided funding for the publication and a down payment to rent new larger headquarters, which was referred to as the Barcelona Workers' Centre, in September 1908. Barcelona Socialists grouped around Fabra Ribas also strongly defended the new body and even advised unions under their influence to leave the UGT in order to join. Finally, the major Barcelona republican organisation, the Republican Union, which hoped to attract SO into its circle of influence, adopted a benevolent stance.[100]

During the first month of SO's existence the idea which emerged most forcefully was the need for working-class unity in order to build up a strong labour federation which would effectively stand up for workers' rights. Hence it was portrayed as defending workers' true class interests against 'bourgeois' politicians. At the same time, it tried to balance the different tendencies within its midst.[101] The Socialists, because of their continued weakness in Barcelona, relied on moderate independent unions to ward off anarchist dominance. As in the case of the French CGT, the ideological glue which held the organisation together was syndicalism. And in line with French syndicalist thought, there was a move away from the revolutionary voluntarism of earlier years. Josep Prat in particular stressed that before carrying though the revolutionary general strike it would first be necessary to build the strength of the labour unions. This perspective was combined with criticism of the 'unfertile enthusiasms' of the period 1901 to 1903.[102]

The unitary nature of SO allowed it to gain widespread backing. At its peak in July 1908, although its mouthpiece only managed to sell an average of 3,000 copies a week, seventy-one unions were affiliated, representing between 10,000 and 15,000 workers.[103] Because of the fragile state of union organisation in the city they only represented at most 10 percent of the city's industrial workforce, but included the bulk of the city's union movement. Not only did the more militant unions join; unions representing more moderate groups of workers, who usually maintained an independent existence, and certainly had no sympathy for the anarchists' trade union strategy, also became members. Thus a number of shopworkers' unions affiliated, along with a significant number of elitist craft unions, such as the coopers, stonemasons, marblers and plasterers. SO's ability to obtain such wide-ranging support needs relating not only to its broad political base but also to the economic depression of these years. The high level of unemployment and continued weakness of union organisation kept even the most militant union activists in check. This made it possible to form a labour federation which, although committed to revolutionary goals, put the need to build the unions before any other consideration, and this in turn encouraged more moderate unions to come on board.[104]

Nevertheless, it adopted the campaigning style of its turn-of-the-century counterparts. Its first big protest movement came in early 1908 in response to the threat of renewed state repression under the auspices of the Conservative Prime Minister, Antonio Maura. Constitutional guarantees were suspended and a large number of anarchists rounded up in Barcelona on 2 January following the explosion of several bombs. Then, at the end of the month, new anti-terrorist legislation was introduced into parliament, which would have given the police sweeping new powers to close down anarchist centres and newspapers and detain anarchist suspects without a court order. SO had totally repudiated terrorism, but rightly feared that if approved the law would be used against them. Maura (who had been stabbed and wounded by a lone anarchist activist during a visit to Barcelona in April 1904) believed that drastic action had to be taken against the anarchists because they imposed their ideas 'through daring, criminal, means'. The anarchists from *Tierra y Libertad* held a big protest meeting on 16 January and SO followed this up with meetings in Barcelona and other industrial towns from the end of May. Faced with a broad alliance against his proposed legislation Maura was finally forced to back down.[105]

From the outset SO aspired to be more than just a local federation and it was soon to correspond with unions in other parts of Catalonia and even in the rest of Spain. 'Propaganda tours' to different parts of Catalonia were also launched by leading figures in SO, strengthening contacts. As a result, SO's Second Congress, held between 6 and 8 September 1908, which aimed to create a Catalan confederation, was a considerable success, with fifty-five Barcelona unions, sixty unions from outside the Catalan capital, and five local labour federations, present.[106] As might have been expected, the delegates were mostly from the industrial towns clustered around Barcelona, followed by the Maresme, the Ter Valley, and Reus and Tarragona in the south. However, SO's quantitative impact should not be exaggerated. Outside Barcelona, more unions sympathised than actually joined: over the next year probably no more than twenty unions, representing at most 5,000 affiliates; little more than a drop in the ocean. Nevertheless, SO's leadership could, with some justice, claim that up to September 1908 the confederation had enjoyed considerable success. The statutes elaborated after the congress reflected the compromise between the different schools. On the one hand, individual unions would have great autonomy and there would be no paid officials; on the other, local unions that wanted to declare a general strike had first to consult with the leadership.[107]

At the congress, in order to reach out further, the decision was taken to take up an old initiative from the 4 de Maig group and re-launch the campaign for the release of the Alcalá del Valle prisoners. The movement helped further develop ties with anarchist-inspired unions outside Catalonia, but it was not able to attract the interest achieved by the campaign for the repeal of the anti-terrorist law. As at the turn of the century, it was concrete issues, based on local problems that impacted seriously on the base, that galvanised most support.

This was not the only setback the organisation faced. Rather than moving forward, during the second half of 1908 and 1909 a series of disputes surfaced which called SO's future into question. First, the confederation came into conflict with Barcelona's leading republican grouping, led by the flamboyant figure of Alejandro Lerroux. This is an issue which will be examined in the next chapter. In addition, conflict also broke out within the confederation itself. When SO was formed great effort was made to construct a solid, united, front. Figures like the anarchist, Jaume Bisbe, and the Socialist, Antoni Badia Matamala, played a key role in this respect, recognising the need to 'sacrifice part of our own beliefs' in order to 'work in unison for our common emancipation'.[108] The problem was that there were still very real ideological differences between the two groupings, which could not simply be swept under the carpet. All agreed that syndicalism was the guiding principle behind SO, but, as in the case of the CGT, there was no unanimity as to what exactly this meant. While anarchists pointed to the role of the 'conscious minority and the unions' revolutionary mission, Socialists emphasised the supposedly apolitical and therefore 'neutral' nature of the organisation. The antiparlimentary current was particularly strong in SO's mouthpiece, *Solidaridad Obrera*, under the editorship of Jaume Bisbe.[109] During 1908 and 1909 it particularly upset the Socialists by running a series of articles by Josep Prat on syndicalism and parliamentary socialism. His position was in line with that of the French revolutionary syndicalist theoreticians, but included a sharp and wounding critique of Second International Socialism, which, he maintained, had become increasingly bourgeois and reformist.[110]

Questions related to union strategy and labour's response to social legislation also caused controversy. With respect to the first question, while anarchists continued to advocate aggressive, generalised 'direct action', Socialists remained wedded to the UGT's union practice. This could be seen in SO's September 1908 regional congress, in which the Socialists were able to muster an important degree of support. Only a small minority of Barcelona delegates were pro-Socialist, but they were backed by delegates representing unions from Mataró, Manresa, Roda, Tarragona and Reus, allowing them, in some instances, to gain the upper hand. This became clear when the question of union tactics was discussed. A commission, the majority of whose members were Socialists, presented a motion which stated that before striking a union should take into account the state of the industry, possible repercussions in other branches of the trade, the percentage of workers unionised, and whether there were sufficient funds to finance its first stages. Most importantly, it underlined that if a union wanted financial support for a strike it would need the agreement of the leadership (the Federal Commission). This was, not surprisingly, strongly opposed by the anarchists, and after much debate a compromise was finally reached. The original motion was passed along with the addition that 'our main weapon will be direct action', though 'other tactics can be used when the circumstances so require'.[111] The debate showed, despite the views expressed by Fabra Ribas, how little syndicalist ideological baggage the Socialists had in reality taken on board, for the whole point of revolutionary syndicalism was that the general strike should be the result of a massive build-up of industrial conflict. Hence the final resolution was totally contradictory, indicating the extent to which SO was a fragile compromise.

Controversy also raged over the role that SO should play in the Barcelona Junta Local de Reformas Sociales. As noted, these Juntas were set up at the beginning of the century to oversee the implementation of social legislation. Anarchists and Socialists held totally contrary views on this issue. For the former they were simply a bourgeois deception, for the latter a tool which workers could utilise to improve their living conditions. Evidence from Catalonia during the first years of the century could give encouragement to both camps. In some towns outside Barcelona, with a large industrial workforce and independent unions, workers had been able to get sympathetic – on occasion

Socialist – councillors elected, and operated the Junta Local to some effect. This was the case in the larger Ter Valley towns, in Mataró, Sabadell, Taragona and Reus. On the Ter, for example, through a Junta Provincial which covered the whole *comarca*, workers' representatives were able to use legislation limiting women's working hours to eleven a day to push for the establishment of a sixty-six hour week throughout the area (it had been sixty-eight hours in 1901).[112]

Furthermore, on occasion these juntas provided a useful forum for the resolution of disputes. This fact no doubt helps explain why Socialism was influential in a number of these towns. This was certainly the case in Mataró, where Socialists operated effectively in local government, and in Reus, where, according to a leading local Socialist, Josep Recasens i Mercadé, by taking over the Junta Local in the middle of the decade Socialists were able to wrest leadership of the local union movement from the anarchists.[113] This was important because Reus – followed by Mataró and the Maresme – would subsequently become the most important Socialist centre in Catalonia. In contrast, in Sabadell the Socialists had very little weight. But here the FOS backed the election of worker candidates onto the local Junta, despite the complaints of the anarchist-syndicalist writers of *El Trabajo*.[114]

In much of the territory, however, social legislation was to a large degree ignored. This was particularly the case in smaller towns and in rural areas where the industrialists acted as *caciques* and controlled local affairs. A factory inspectorate operated from 1907, but it lacked funds, and this, combined with the opposition from industrialists and local authorities, and also, in the case of child labour, the connivance in evading the law of many workers who needed the additional income, meant that it faced an uphill struggle.[115] In Barcelona matters were not helped by the fact that the republicans, although influential in local government from 1905, did little, while the Junta Local, which was manipulated by a number of Catholic unions, hardly functioned.[116] Hence, in the city, legislation was ineffectively enforced. In textiles an eleven-hours day operated, but in the sweated clothing trades during high season women still frequently worked longer. Enforcement of legislation passed in 1904, outlawing Sunday working, was similarly lax. Subsequent years were to witness the unedifying spectacle of shopworkers stoning shop windows and being dispersed by the police for trying to enforce the law. As the factory inspectors were to comment, the reaction of workers to social legislation was, as a result, ambiguous. Union representatives often worked hard for legislation to be enforced, but the problems they faced led to scepticism.[117]

From the outset SO adopted an ambiguous position on the issue. Badia Matamala as usual tried to reconcile the different points of view, maintaining that as the affiliated unions were autonomous they could hold the most diverse opinions on the subject.[118] Nevertheless, divisions came out into the open at the end of 1908. The September regional congress accepted the need to fight for the implementation of laws relating to the Sunday rest day and the employment of minors, but there was also a vote of protest against the Barcelona Junta Local, 'because of its connivance with the bourgeoisie'. Another anarchist-inspired motion, which stated that the workers should never have anything to do with organisations of this type, was discussed but not finally approved. Notwithstanding, the anarchists were in future to argue that the decision had been taken not to cooperate with the Barcelona Junta Local. The situation became more tense in November when a number of Barcelona unions affiliated to SO participated in elections held to renew it, while other unions stood aloof and accused those that had done so of breaking the resolution passed at the last congress.[119]

Divisions of this kind naturally weakened the confederation. The Socialists claimed during 1908 that the anarchists were using the non-political nature of SO to try and impose their own dominance. They were particularly critical of the association's mouthpiece, maintaining that the pro-anarchist stance of some of its writers was discouraging some unions from joining and making others think of leaving.[120] Squabbling continued into 1909, with pro-anarchists removing Badia Matamala from the Federal Commission sometime in the early summer, thereby leaving the Socialists without representation.[121] Then in June a delegate meeting decided that, at its next congress in September SO should become a national confederation. This would, of course, bring it into direct conflict with the UGT. Indeed, internal strife, combined with the dispute with the republicans, had the effect of weakening the confederation from mid-1908 onwards. Thus, the September 1908 congress was attended by only fifty-five Barcelona unions even through seventy-two had been affiliated a few months previously. This decline in membership continued during the following year, with perhaps only forty-three unions remaining affiliated in July 1909.[122]

Moreover, divisions within SO were not wholly limited to anarchists and Socialists. The moderate course which SO pursued in practice led some anarchists to take an increasingly critical view of the confederation. Most radical were the anarchists grouped around Leopoldo Bonafulla, who accused its leadership of being authoritarian and reformist, and now argued (contrary to the group's practice between 1901 and 1903) that each political tendency should operate separately.[123] *Tierra y Libertad* remained more supportive, but it criticised Socialist influence following the 1908 Catalan congress. Indicative of these anarchists' thinking was the comment by Josep Prat – who wrote regularly for the publication from 1908 onwards – that SO had to decide whether to 'fuse with the official leadership of the Socialist parties ... or take a determinedly autonomous, libertarian stance, and use the revolutionary method of direct action and the class struggle'.[124]

By 1909, then, SO had a very uncertain future. In fact, over the following year, in a context of heightened industrial conflict and confrontation with the state, the coalition of forces it represented was to break up. The first indications of the probable consequences of intensified conflict with the authorities and employers came between 1908 and 1909. During 1908 SO's language became more radicalised. In July 1908 it published a manifesto warning that with the passage of the anti-terrorist bill any possibility of a peaceful evolution of society would be lost and that the proletariat would have no choice but to take the revolutionary road.[125] The Restoration regime's continued difficulty in distinguishing between delinquents and union activists was making the task of building unions, which would enter into dialogue with the state, extremely difficult. The radical language SO adopted in response no doubt made its more moderate backers uncomfortable.

Several months later, cotton textiles topped the Catalan workers' agenda for the first time since 1901, in the context of growing unrest within the industry. In 1908 SO began to make efforts to revive unions in the textile towns, and by the spring of 1909 a new textile federation was being forged. But this took place against a backdrop in which the economic climate remained gloomy, industrialists were looking to further cut costs and would fight tooth and nail against a new federation. As a result a number of disputes blew up from the second half of 1908. In Sant Feliu de Codinas, a dispute with the largest factory owner and village *cacique* ended in a brief general strike in May 1909.[126] On the Ter tensions also resurfaced. Faced with high wage costs and declining profit margins, the Rusiñol company town closed in May 1908 and when it reopened offered lower wages. Most seriously affected were men working on the ring frames, who would have to take a 20 percent cut. The workers refused to enter and a long strike ensued. It was to be the death knell of the friendly society, the Patronat, centred on the Rusiñol factory; its members joining the town's independent union, 'convinced at last', according to the local Manlleu union, 'of the wickedness of the employer class'.[127] SO responded by calling a delegate meeting, followed by an assembly open to all union members, in Granollers on 10 and 11 July. The assembly's conclusions were significant because for the first time since the foundation of SO the question of a possible general strike was once again put on the table.[128] It is doubtful, given the weakness of union organisation in much of Catalan industry, whether this would have been possible. Yet, once again employer hostility to union organisation was pushing Catalan labour down the path of violent protest.

Conclusions

The period between 1899 and 1909 highlights the complex relationship between the union base and the Socialist and anarchist core. On the one hand, unions wished to recruit as many workers as possible and this often made them wary of linking up with anarchist or Socialist-inspired confederations. Nevertheless, they could prove attractive to some. In a context in which similar pressures were afflicting many industrial workers they allowed them to share their concerns and provided solidarity and support outside the limits of the trade. Furthermore, their ideologies gave more politically active workers a means to understand a world in which, it appeared to them, they were the victims of capitalist development, and in which their quest to improve their working conditions was being blocked by state and employer hostility.

An analysis of the groups of workers drawn to the anarchists and Socialists provides little succour for the view, sometimes expressed, that in western Europe Socialists recruited more effectively amongst factory proletarians while anarchists were above all supported by artisans. There can never be a simple relationship between industrial relations and ideology. Nevertheless, the evidence does suggest that the anarchists did better amongst workers within the more conflict-ridden trades and industries. At a trade-union level their practice of mobilising against industrialists and the state could, particularly during economic upswings, enthuse workers desperate to challenge their employers' authority.

They were also helped by the fact that most Catalan workers had been unable to structure professionally-run craft or industrial labour federations. On the contrary, outside the textile industries paid officials were not employed, union committees were highly democratic and were made up of workers who dealt with union business in their spare time. Hence, because there were no union bureaucracies to hold back rank-and-file activists, in the heated atmosphere of the mass meetings it was easy for the most radical propositions to win the day.

The Socialists, on the other hand, tended to take root more effectively where at least one of the following factors operated: there was some tradition of more bureaucratic union organisation, unions had some influence over the local authorities, and industrialists at least grudgingly negotiated with the unions. This made life particularly difficult for them in Barcelona. That is not to say that there was any inevitability about their eclipse. Had they adapted more effectively to the climate of Barcelona, and taken a leftist stance at the turn of the century, then they could no doubt have offered a more serious challenge. It is interesting to note that this was precisely the position taken by the Vizcayan Socialists, whose organisation before 1914 was centred on the open-cast iron-ore mining field. Social conflict in the mines was raw and frequently violent, and under Fecundo Perezagua the local UGT frequently ignored official UGT strategy during disputes.[129] The Catalan Socialists never took such a route because of the links they had established with the TCV in the 1880s and the fact that they came into sharp conflict with the anarchists over union practice between 1890 and 1893. Nevertheless, all was not lost. As the experience of SO indicated, a reappraisal of Socialist strategy would bring results. The question was whether this could be maintained when industrial strife once again reached dramatic levels from 1910 onwards.

Notes

1. Anselmo Lorenzo, *El proletariado militante*.
2. Palmiro de Lidia (pseudonym of Adrián del Valle), 'Evocando el pasado (1886–1891)', 212.
3. Still of crucial importance for the 1870s and 1880s are Max Nettlau, *La Première Internationale en Espagne, 1868–1888*; and Josep Termes i Ardévol, *Anarquismo y sindicalismo en Cataluña*.
4. Termes i Ardévol, *Anarquismo y sindicalismo*, 255–6; Ramón Casterás, *Actitudes de los sectores catalanes en la coyuntura de los años 1880*, 43–101.

5. The 1882 figures are to be found in *Congreso de la Federación de Trabajadores de la Región Española celebrado en Sevilla los días 24, 25 y 26 de setiembre de 1882*, 79–93.

6. Santiago Castillo, 'La implantación del PSOE hasta su cuarto congreso (1884–1994)'; Gabriel, 'Sindicats', 328–31.

7. *La Justicia Social*, 2 July 1910.

8. Casteras, *Actitudes*, 98; Santiago Castillo, 'Los orígenes de la organización obrera en España', 101–2 and 155–63.

9. Alvarez Junco, *Ideología política*, 548–52; Jordi Piqué i Padró, *Anarco-col·lectivisme i anarco-comunisme*, 75–111; George Essenwein, '*Anarchist ideology and the Spanish working class movement (1880–1900); with special reference to Ricardo Mella*', 185–93; Francisco Madrid Santos, 'Los grupos anarquistas en España: un estudio sobre la organización'.

10. F.F. Ridley, *Revolutionary Syndicalism in France*, 141–2.

11. For the Socialists' union strategy see, Manuel Pérez Ledesma, 'La primera etapa de la UGT (1888–1897): planteamiento sindical y formas de organización'.

12. See, for example, the reminiscences of the anarchists Joan Ferrer and Emili Salut in Porcel, *Revuelta*, 22–30, and Salut, *Vivers de revolucionaris*, 50–2.

13. Manuel Gil Mestre, 'El anarquismo en España y en especial en Cataluña', 370–1. Emili Salut recalled that when he was a young apprentice at the turn of the century: 'The repeated preachings of our journeymen in the workshops and construction sites [served] to pass on to us the sad legacy of the Montjuïc anarchists, for in addition to the constant oral propaganda, crusading weekly newspapers and small fascicles, they even reminded us of the wretched castle by singing the various songs they practised in choral societies.' *Vivers de revolucionaris*, 151.

14. Juan de Cataluña, 'Los obreros de la industria textil III', *Justicia*, 8 Feb. 1930, 3–4; Castillo, 'Orígenes', 102–4; *La República Social*, 3 March 1897, 12 Jan., 20 April 1898. *La República Social* was a weekly Socialist newspaper published in Mataró between 1897 and 1898.

15. Juan de Cataluña, 'Los obreros en la industrial textil IV. Continúa el relato', *Justicia*, 22 Feb. 1930, 2; *La Publicidad* (hereafter, LP), 9 Aug. 1899, *Morning Edition*.

16. *El Productor* (hereafter EP), 27 July 1901.

17. For Genollà's Socialist credentials see *El Socialista* (hereafter, ES), 27 Dec. 1901. The FTE – like the TCV – was divided up into a number of districts.

18. Santiago Castillo refers to Guiteras as an 'old Socialist militant' in 'Orígenes', 104. For the FRE's attitude to social legislation see Juan de Cataluña, 'Los obreros...IV', and *Revista Fabril*, 5, 12 June, 19 July 1900.

19. Tuñón de Lara, *Movimiento obrero*, vol. 2, 11–12.

20. *Revista Fabril*, 19 July 1900.

21. *Suplemento de la Revista Blanca*, 1, 8 Dec. 1900. The secretary of the Ter confederation was the anarchist, Francesc Abayà.

22. ES, 14 Dec. 1900, 8 Feb. 1901.

23. *Suplemento de la Revista Blanca*, 1, 8 Dec. 1900.

24. Castillo, 'Orígenes', 239; *La República Social*, 22 Sept. 1897; LP, 30 May 1899, *Night Edition*.

25. For the Madrid figures see, Santiago Castillo, *Historia del socialismo español*, vol.1, *1870–1909*, 230–7. Data from Barcelona has been gleaned from a close reading of the republican daily, *La Publicidad*, and the Socialist weekly, *El Socialista*: see in particular, LP, 22 Oct. 1899, *Morning Edition*, and ES, 24 Nov. 1899. The division within Socialist ranks, but also their relative strength, was brought out in the comments by the anarchist weekly, *La Protesta*: 'Last Tuesday thirty-two unions from Barcelona and its surrounding areas met to try and organise a federation. However, as soon as the two bands of Socialists came face to face there was no holding back the storm. Poor working class in the hands of the Socialists!' *La Protesta*, 27 Aug. 1899.

26. ES, 30 Dec. 1898.

27. Juan José Morato, *El Partido Socialista Obrero*, 139.

28. On relations between Socialists and republicans see, Antonio Robles Egea, 'La conjunción republicano-socialista'. For the views of Martín Rodríguez, Reoyo and Comaposada regard-

ing links with the republicans see LP, 30 April, *Morning Edition*, 2 July, *Night Edition*, 21 Sept., *Morning Edition* 1899, and the debates in the PSOE's Fifth Congress in ES, 21 Sept 1899. Of the three, Comaposada was closest to Pablo Iglesias; he wrote on Catalan affairs in *El Socialista* and regularly corresponded with him: see their 'Epistolario inédito'.

29. ES, 23 Nov. 1900.
30. ES, 15 June 1900.
31. *Boletín del Arte de Imprimir*, 31 Dec. 1899; LP, 12 Aug. 1900, *Morning Edition*.
32. LP, 24 April 1900, *Morning Edition*.
33. For a quantitative survey of Socialist groups in Catalonia see Cuadrat, *Socialismo y Anarquismo*, 17–37 and 131–56. For the shopworkers see Mª Dolors Capdevila, 'Aportació a la història del socialisme català II'.
34. Santos Juliá, *Madrid, 1931–1934*.
35. *El Trabajo* (hereafter, ET), 12 Jan. 1901. Piazza was regularly criticised in the *Suplemento de La Revista Blanca* and *La Protesta*. For the FOS's statutes see, ET, 18 April 1903.
36. *La Protesta*, 9 Sept. 1899, 19 Jan. 1901; Rosell, *Recuerdos*, 78. The veteran Sabadell anarchist, Jaume Sallent, subsequently claimed that, 'the woollen workers are to blame for all that has gone on, because they are the most numerous and reactionary branch [of the FOS].' *La Protesta*, 19 Jan. 1901.
37. LP, 12 April 1901, *Morning Edition*; *La Protesta*, 18 April 1901.
38. Some references to Ferrer's character are to be found in, *Ferrer y la Huelga General*, and Luis Bertrán, '*Yo acuso*'.
39. Porcel, *Revuelta*, 50–1; Plaja, 'Mis memorias', 12. There is a short biography of Lorenzo by Federica Montseny, *Anselmo Lorenzo*.
40. On Montenegro see Federico Urales, *Mi vida*, vol. 2, 68–71, and Lorenzo's forward to José López Montenegro, *El botón de fuego*.
41. LP, 7 July 1901, *Morning Edition*, 22 Sept. 1901, *Night Edition*.
42. See, for example, Antonio Apolo in *Suplemento de la Revista Blanca*, 7 Sept. 1901; and José Prat, *Necesidad de asociación*.
43. *La Revista Blanca*, 15 Sept. 1899. However, echoes of the FRE and FTRE's belief that the union confederation would form the basis of the new society were still to be heard. Antonio Cruz, for example, believed that craft federations could 'provide something' for the society of the future. *La Huelga General* (hereafter, LHG), 5 Jan. 1902.
44. For example in 1904 the Barcelona-based anarchist journal, *Natura*, commented that the translation of a pamphlet on syndicalism by Pouget dealt with questions 'well known here' and showed that 'the spirit of free syndicalism, common in Spain, is making strides in France'. *Natura*, 1 June 1904. On Pelloutier and the origins of French syndicalism see, for example, Jeremy Jennings, *Syndicalism in France*, 11–55.
45. In Bonafulla's words, 'present-day society is based on lies and falsehoods, was founded through robbery and violence and is sustained through criminal acts'. EP, 5 Sept 1903.
46. LHG, 5 Jan. 1902.
47. I have based this section on a reading of the *Suplemento de la Revista Blanca*, *El Productor* and *La Huelga General*. The quote is by Antonio Apolo, a close ally of Bonafulla, from EP, 27 June 1903. For the anarchists' portrayal of the revolution see also Litvak, *Musa Libertaria*, 371–81.
48. An article by Montenegro was published in *El Congreso Revolucionario Internacional de París*, (which, though published in Argentina, was distributed in Spain by the anarchist press), and as a separate pamphlet, *La huelga general*. In 1902 *La Revista Blanca* published *El trabajador y la huelga general*, which was written by the editorial team of *La Huelga General*. *El Productor* followed in 1903 with *La Huelga General (6 postales)*, while in the same year *La Huelga General* published *Por qué de la Huelga General*, by a Paris-based Committee for the General Strike. For the impact of syndicalism in Spain see also Pere Gabriel, 'Sindicalismo y huelga'.
49. For these campaigns I have used above all data gleaned from *La Publicidad*.
50. LP, 31 March, *Morning Edition*; 14 July, *Night Edition*, 1901.
51. EP, 20 Dec. 1902, 21 Feb., 21, 28 March, 6 June 1903; *La Guerra Social*, 28 March 1903; ET, 12 Sept. 1903; Gabriel, 'Sindicats', 504–5.

52. *La Cuña*, 1 Jan, 1 March, 1 April 1898; Sastre y Sanna , *Las huelgas ... 1903*, 87–8.
53. EP, 30 Nov., 7 Dec. 1901.
54. See, for example, Prat, *A las mujeres.*
55. Lily Litvak, *Musa Libertaria*, 80–92.
56. This was the position taken by Soledad Gustavo (pseudonym of Teresa Mañé), the wife of Federico Urales and co-director of *La Revista Blanca*: see, for example, *La Revista Blanca* 1 July 1899.
57. EP, 2, 30 Nov. 1901.
58. For a stimulating overview of male anarchist attitudes towards women see, Temma Kaplan, 'Other Scenarios: Women and Spanish Anarchism'. Kaplan argues that male anarchists' attacks on the Church and family structures, to which women felt strongly attached, were key factors in retarding their incorporation into the movement. However, in urban Catalonia during this period the Church was already losing support amongst working-class women and the issue of 'free love' only concerned the most committed core of anarchists. For which see Chapter Five, 237–58. Kaplan's data, it should be noted, is largely drawn from Andalusia.
59. *La Huelga General*, 15, 25 Dec. 1901.
60. Urales, *Mi Vida*. vol. 1, 72. *El Socialista*, on the other hand, maintained that at most 34,000 workers were represented at the Founding Congress. ES, 26 Oct. 1900.
61. *Suplemento de la Revista Blanca*, 27 Oct. 1900; *La Protesta*, 19 April 1901; EP, 14 Dec. 1901, 10 Jan., 10 Oct. 1903. For more details on the FRESR see, Francisco Madrid Santos, 'Racionalismo pedagógico y movimiento obrero en España: Ferrer Guardia y "La Huelga General"'.
62. EP, 2, 23 Nov., 7, 14, 28 Dec. 1901; Urales, *Mi vida*, vol. 1, 72–3.
63. LP, 2 Jan. 1902, *Morning Edition.*
64. EP, 25 Jan., 1 Feb. 1902; LHG, 25 Jan., 5 Feb. 1902.
65. This was recognised by *La Publicidad* when it stated that anarchists and Socialists, 'have for some time now competed for the leadership and organisation of the Barcelona and Catalan working class. The libertarians have prevailed, perhaps because there are more of them and they are more active'. LP, 25 Feb. 1902, *Morning Edition.*
66. *La Protesta*, 5 April 1903; Montseny, *Anselmo Lorenzo*, 34–5; Salut, *Vivers de revolucionaris*, 48–9.
67. The account of these campaigns is based on *El Productor*. For the attempted one-day strike, see 4, 11, 18, 25 July, 1, 8 Aug. 1903.
68. Archivo Histórico Nacional, Gobernación Serie A (hereafter, AHN), 44/21 and 24. In 1908 Antonio Maura's civil governor in Barcelona, Angel Ossorio y Gallardo, lamented that 'there is no clearer and more effective way [than the suspension of constitutional guarantees] to kill off anarchist publications'. AHN, 60/10. Some historians who focus on 'high politics' underestimate the level of repression at grass-roots level. Guilty of this, I think, is Javier Tusell in *Antonio Maura*, 104.
69. ET, 26 Jan., 12 Dec. 1901, 1 Feb. 1902.
70. ET, 15, 29 Aug. 1903; *La Guerra Social*, 12 Sept. 1903.
71. For example, the Barcelona correspondent of the Mahón (Menorca) anarchist weekly *El Porvenir del Obrero*, argued that they should not be declared for purely economic goals: quoted in ES, 13 May 1903.
72. LP, 18 Aug. 1900.
73. See, for example, the comments by Lorenzo and Bonafulla in EP, 20 May 1904.
74. For example, when a certain Vicente Arpa died in 1918 it was reported that, 'the union of tinsmiths and the cooperative El Adelanto Obrero, of whom Arper was the founder, have lost one of their best comrades'. *Solidaridad Obrera* (hereafter, SO), 15 Oct. 1918.
75. ES, 27 Feb., 7 March 1902.
76. ES, 18 April, 14 Oct. 1902.
77. *La Justicia Social*, 16 June 1910. On Quejido and the Trades Union Congress see, for example, Anselmo Lorenzo, *El obrero moderno*, 27.
78. *La Guerra Social*, 4 April 1903; EP, 8 Aug. 1903; Salut, *Vivers de revolucionaris*, 83.
79. ES, 27 Feb. 1903.

80. ES, 14 Feb. 1903.
81. *La Guerra Social*, 27 June, 4 July 1903.
82. In Barcelona UGT membership actually declined from 759 in 1899 to 552 in 1902. In Catalonia as a whole the UGT had around 2,500 members in 1901 and 3,500 in 1903. In September 1903 total UGT membership stood at 46,574. For the Catalan figures see Cuadrat, *Anarquismo y socialismo*, 108–9 and 230–1; ES, 14 May, 16 Oct. 1901; Gabriel 'Sindicats', 331.
83. *Tierra y Libertad*, 25 Dec. 1902: see also Romero Maura, *Rosa del Fuego*, 231–3.
84. Enric Olivé Serret, 'El moviment anarquista català i l'obrerisme, 1900–1909', 57–60.
85. On the local federation and Catalano-Balear Congress see *La Ilustración Obrera*, 12 March, 2 April, 14 May, 11 June, 16 Aug. 1904; ET, 25 Oct., 12 Nov. 1905. For anarchist insurrectionism, *Espartaco*, 18, 25 Nov. 1904. This section is also based on a reading of *El Productor*.
86. Juan Avilés, 'Republicanismo librepensamiento y revolución: la ideología de Francisco Ferrer y Guardia', 268; *La Tramontana*, 2 Jan. 1908; *El Rebelde*, 9 Nov. 1907.
87. *Le syndicalisme révolutionnaire*, ed. H. Dubief; Ridley, *Revolutionary Syndicalism*.
88. Anselmo Lorenzo, forward to José Prat, *La burguesía y el proletariado*, p. xiii.
89. E. Pouget, *Bases del sindicalismo*; E. Pouget, *El sindicato*; George Yvetot, *ABC sindicalista*.
90. For Josep Miguel see Rosell, *Recuerdos*, 84–6. Prat translated Enrique Leone, *El sindicalismo*, and Luis Fabbri, *Anarquismo y socialismo*, and explained syndicalist ideas in *La burguesía*.
91. ET, 25, 28 Jan. 1905, 30 June, 7 Sept., 26 Dec. 1906, 12 Jan. 1907.
92. *La Cuña*, 16 Jan., 26 April 1906; ET, 21 April 1906; Cuadrat, *Anarquismo y socialismo*, 165–6.
93. *Tierra y Libertad*, 13 June 1907.
94. *Tierra y Libertad*, 26 Nov. 1906, 3 Jan., 2, 9 May, 25 July 1907.
95. *La Cuña*, 21 Feb. 1907; ET, 29 Dec. 1906; *Tierra y Libertad*, 13 Dec. 1906.
96. Geary, *European Labour Protest*, 123–5.
97. *Nuestro Programa*, 30 June 1903; *Revista Socialista*, 16 May, 1, 16 June, 1, 16 Nov., 1 Dec. 1904, 1 Jan., 16 Feb. 1905; *La Internacional*, 6, 20 Nov. 1908; Antonio Fabra Ribas, *La Semana Trágica*, 15–17 and 214; Cuadrat, *Anarquismo y socialismo*, 288–9. For the left-wing French Socialists see, Roger Magraw, 'Socialism, Syndicalism and French Labour', 74–86.
98. *La Internacional*, 30 Nov. 1908.
99. José Negre, *Recuerdos de un viejo militante*, 7–8; Angel Pestaña, 'Historia de las ideas y luchas sociales en España VI', *Orto*, Nov 1932, 31–4; Porcel, *Revuelta*, 50–1.
100. Negre, *Recuerdos, 9; Boletín del Arte de Imprimir*, Aug. 1907; SO, 13 Feb. 1908; Cuadrat, *Anarquismo y socialismo*, 179–209; Joan B. Culla i Clarà, *El republicanisme lerrouxista a Catalunya, 1901–1923*, 180.
101. Thus the first so-called Federal Commission included Antoni Colomer, of no known political persuasion, as General Secretary, with Antoni Badia Matamala and Jaume Bisbe, representatives of the federation's Socialist and anarchist wings respectively, as secretaries. The General Secretary was – with the exception of several months in 1908 – a neutral figure through to July 1909.
102. SO, 3 Sept. 1908, 26 Oct. 1907.
103. SO, 12 July 1908; Negre, *Recuerdos*, 12.
104. SO, 13 Feb., 5, 12 June 1908, ET, 17 Jan., 15 Feb., 6 June 1908.
105. For Maura's position see, Javier Tusell and Juan Avilés, *La derecha española contemporánea*, 31. Data on the meetings is to be found in *Solidaridad Obrera* and *Tierra y Libertad*.
106. SO, 13 Feb., 14 March, 5 July, 18 Sept. 1908.
107. Confederación Regional de Sociedades de Resistencia Solidaridad Obrera, *Estatutos*.
108. SO, 9 Nov. 1907, 5 June 1908.
109. Bueso, *Recuerdos*, 25; Constant Leroy (pseudonym of José Sánchez González), *Los secretos del anarquismo*, 234.
110. All these articles are reproduced in Prat, *Burguesía*.
111. SO, 18 Sept. 1908.

112. Arxiu Municipal de Vic, Junta de Reformas Sociales, 1900–1912; Arxiu Municipal de Torelló, Lligall T, Trabajos Varios; Arxiu Municipal de Manlleu (hereafter, AMM), Governació, S.149.395, Reformas Sociales, Actas.
113. Mª Dolors Capdevila and Roser Masgrau. *La Justicia Social*, 4; Josep Recasens i Mercadé, *Vida inquieta*, 62. Scattered press reports indicate that between 1896 and 1909 Socialist councillors were elected in Manlleu, Montesquiu and Roda on the Ter, in Manresa on the Llobregat, in Mataró and Calella in the Maresma, and in Sitges in the south.
114. ET, 30 July, 12 Nov. 1904, 26 Feb. 1906.
115. Marvaud, *Cuestión social*, 290. The inspectors expressed their concerns in their annual reports: see, for example, Instituto de Reformas Sociales, *Memoria general ... 1910*, 54 and 65.
116. José Comaposada in Instituto de Reformas Sociales, *Jornada*, 125–6.
117. Instituto de Reformas Sociales, *Memoria general de la inspección del trabajo, 1912*, 65–8.
118. SO, 14 March 1908.
119. SO, 18 Sept., 18, 25 Dec. 1908; *La Internacional*, 11 Dec. 1908. Similar disputes could be seen in other Catalan towns.
120. SO, 14 March 1908; *La Internacional*, 11 Dec. 1908.
121. On the fall of Badia Matamala see the letter from Anselmo Lorenzo to Francesc Ferrer in Salvador Canals, *Los sucesos en España en 1909*, vol. 1, 246.
122. Cuadrat, *Anarquismo y socialismo*, 350.
123. *El Rebelde*, 2, 18 May 1908. They were in particular very critical of the fact that Marià Castellote – a member of the 4 de Maig group – had appeared before a parliamentary commission. This needs to be understood within the context of the break between Bonafulla and the Anselmo and Ferrer group in 1902. For which, see also Chapter Five, 152–3.
124. *Tierra y Libertad*, 17 Dec. 1908.
125. SO, 12 July 1908.
126. The roots of this dispute are explained in, LP, 12 July 1909, *Night Edition*.
127. *La Internacional*, 28 May 1908; SO, 4 June 1909; LP, 2–12 June 1909; AMM, Governació, S.149.395.
128. LP, 27 June 1909, *Morning Edition*, 14 July, *Night Edition*.
129. See Fusi, *Política obrera*.

5

WORKERS AGAINST THE STATE
Anarchism, Republicanism, Popular and Working-Class Protest, 1898 to 1909

Union organisation and strikes formed only one aspect of workers' intervention in the public realm. As I have already indicated, the Restoration regime aimed to marginalise the country's subaltern classes from political life. This chapter will be looking at the extent to which the state was able to achieve this, at counter-strategies elaborated within working-class circles, and at the role played by anarchists in the elaboration and implementation of anti-statist protest. Moreover, I will discuss the impact of such resistance on the political system as a whole. In particular, I shall focus attention on the role played by labour agitation in weakening the regime and at the political reaction this provoked.

The Political Challenge to the Restoration Regime

As seen in Chapter Three, the Restoration regime was based on *caciquista* foundations, it kow-towed to powerful interests and was quick to privatise power in local hands. This made it impossible for it to effectively play a socially integrative role and build up public legitimacy. This was apparent in several areas. First, in comparative European terms the country's tax base was low and a large percentage of taxes were drawn from basic consumer goods (the so-called *consumos*). When combined with Spain's relatively slow and uneven economic development this meant that the state offered little in the way of public services.[1] One important consequence was an underdeveloped state education system. The inhabitants of Barcelona were amongst the best educated in Spain, but between 1900 and 1903 little more than 14 percent of children between the ages of five and twelve were educated in state schools, about 20 percent received no education at all, and 43 percent of persons over the age of five were illiterate (34.5 percent of men and 50.3 percent of women). As can be imagined, in rural areas the situation was far worse.[2]

Second, unlike the more dynamic nineteenth-century liberal regimes, the Restoration regime did little to generate a sense of national pride amongst the civil population, and forge a reciprocal sense of rights granted and duties owed to the motherland. Rather, patronage and clientelism fostered a climate in which the law was seen as a burden which should, if possible, be shifted onto the shoulders of others. This was apparent in the military sphere where obligatory state conscription was not introduced. Between 1850 and 1912 it was possible to avoid military service (the *quinta*) by paying between 1,500 and 2,000 pesetas to the treasury or by finding a substitute (and from 1868 members of company towns were also excused). In 1912 the law was reformed, but middle-and upper-class youths only had to do between five and ten months training after which they were released in exchange of a payment.[3] It was hardly a system designed to inculcate a sense of service to a state that regarded all its citizens as equal.

Finally, the regime made little attempt to use its institutions to try and create a broad support base. Rather, this was a task largely left in the hands of the Catholic Church. The regime was steeped in religious imagery and, moreover, gave the Church a central role in the areas of education and welfare. It was a shared hope amongst conservative liberals that it would act as a bulwark against dangerous and radical doctrines. Yet it was singularly ill-equipped to undertake this task. The Church hierarchy was dominated by ultra conservatives whose rigid Scholastic doctrines were incompatible with liberalism and democracy. Thus, although the Church hierarchy reached a modus vivendi with the Restoration regime, its goal remained some kind of idealised ancien-regime society in which it would be the dominant force within the state.

Simultaneously, it vigorously defended the social status quo. Church leaders justified inequality as divinely ordained and preached acquiescence, in the knowledge that such sacrifice would be rewarded in the afterlife. They saw it as their job to work with the elite in order to moralise the working classes, while also providing Christian charity. Hence the Church establishment moved in the cultural world of the upper class. By the 1900s, it dominated education in Spain. Children of the middle and upper classes were almost exclusively educated by the Church. In Barcelona during the first decade of the century, around 60 percent of children in education went to non-subsidised private fee-paying schools, the great majority of which were run by the religious orders. As in the trade-union sphere, the Church also attempted to attract workers, offering schooling to their children either for free or at much reduced rates. Given its wealth, its efforts in this field were important; statistics are contradictory, but between 1909 and 1914 it seems that in Barcelona between 11,500 and 14,000 children (between about 13.5 and 16.5 percent of the school population, not much less than numbers attending state schools) were taught in free or heavily subsidised Catholic schools. Moreover, it operated its own orphanages, poorhouses, and the like, and also ran those under local government control. It also put on evening classes, probably attended by around 3,000 young adults, predominantly drawn from working-class circles, while perhaps 4,000 poor children attended Sunday school and catechism. Workers who attended assiduously would receive other forms of Church charity (such as, for example, the distribution of free food vouchers and children's clothing). Similar efforts to reach out could be seen in other areas, especially in the provision of free medical and hospital treatment.[4]

Catholic spokesmen were proud of the provision they provided. Yet their outlook meant that their work was suffused with a condescending paternalism. The class component was reflected in the central role that the upper-classes played in the institutions' financing and the importance of committees of well-to-do 'ladies' in their administration. The Church's identification with reaction and its links to the social elite had the effect of slowly but surely alienating working-class opinion. Catholic traditions were kept alive by the migration of peasants from the conservative interior, but amongst established working-class families a period of transition was underway in which the maintenance of a vague religiosity was accompanied by a growing hostility towards the Church establishment. In smaller industrial towns regular Church attendance remained common, but in Barcelona it was increasingly limited to the major events of the Catholic calendar, baptism, marriage, and a Christian burial. Thus, the French Catholic writer, Jacques Valdour, contrasted the bustling churches in the bourgeois centre of the city, and 'the churches in the industrial suburbs, deserted during the week and half-empty on Sunday'.[5] Valdour also noted that Church attendance remained stronger amongst working-class women, who were above all targeted by the Church and played the major role in their children's schooling. However, in some cases this was probably because of the benefits their families could obtain. As we shall see, women would be at the forefront of anticlerical protests. It was in this atmosphere that the hard-line anticlerical and frequently atheist anarchist and republican core could readily recruit adepts.

Until the mid-1890s, the regime faced little in the way of a serious challenge, but the political context was totally transformed by the impact of the Cuban uprising of 1895, Spain's military defeat at the hands of the United States of America in 1898, and the subsequent loss of her colonies in the Americas and Pacific. In working-class circles the high death toll produced by the fighting in Cuba, and the fact that the middle classes could buy their way out of military service, produced growing anger. In all around 60,000 Spaniards died between 1895 and 1898, the vast majority coming from peasant and working-class backgrounds. This regime's lack of concern for its troops was rammed home in the aftermath of the defeat when penniless soldiers, often sick and disabled, were simply dumped at ports and left to find their own way home.[6] On the working-class Left, protest against the war was articulated by anarchists and Socialists, whilst republicans also mobilised against what they saw as the regime's disastrous failure to pursue the war effectively. This was of key importance for the history of the first third of the twentieth century. Henceforth, no regime could use 'social imperialism' as a tool to mobilise support: anticolonialism would be a widely shared sentiment within the urban lower classes.

In addition, in the aftermath of defeat the middle classes were dismayed by rises in taxes, designed to counter the ballooning deficit, and at the loss of valuable export markets, especially in Cuba. This dovetailed with fierce criticism of the Restoration regime from within the Spanish intelligentsia. The protestors adopted what was known as a 'regenerationist' language. *Caciquismo*, inefficiency and corruption, it was argued, had turned Spain into the sick man of Europe. This rotten edifice had to be swept away in order for Spain to modernise.

Nowhere was this opposition greater than in Barcelona. Between 1899 and 1903 the city not only witnessed a burst of strike activity; in general and local elections the official parties were ousted by the new Catalanist and republican organisations. Catalan nationalists or Catalanists were first off the mark, mobilising above all amongst the discontented middle classes and sectors of the petty bourgeoisie. Their central claim was that Catalonia was being exploited and ruined by an inefficient central state and they demanded wide-ranging home rule to put things right. In the spring of 1901 a new party, the Lliga Regionalista, was founded and a candidature linked to the Catalanist camp won the general elections in Barcelona.

On the Left, they were contested by the republicans, most of whom rejected Catalan nationalism. From the 1860s in urban areas republicanism had been the main vehicle for popular and working-class opposition to the regime, picking up support amongst an amalgam of the professional middle classes, the petty bourgeoisie and industrial workers. The republicans' ideological roots were liberal rationalist. They saw themselves as representing the interests of the 'people' (*pueblo*) against a reactionary elite, who stood in the way of democratic change and social reform. Yet, as in the case of the Catalanists, it was only in the aftermath of 1898 that they were to mount a serious challenge in urban Spain, founding a new unified party, the Republican Union, in 1903. Their bulwark became Barcelona. In the May 1903 elections the party attained around 35,000 votes (almost 68 percent of the voters and 31 percent of the electoral roll), at a time when there were about 60,000 industrial workers with the right to vote in the city.[7]

They key figure in this revival would be the Andalusian-born son of a military surgeon, Alejandro Lerroux. Based in Madrid, in the 1890s he came to the forefront of left-wing republican politics. He and his colleagues had little hope that the regime could be transformed at the ballot box. Rather, they looked to some combination of a military coup (*pronunciamiento*) and urban insurrection. He also believed that the movement had become staid and dated and that in order to prosper republicanism had to radicalise its politics and appeal to a broader working-class clientele. This attitude was dramatically illustrated when, at the end of 1897, as we saw in the previous chapter, he agreed to launch a campaign for a judicial review of the Montjuïc trial.

The campaign reached its climax in the summer of 1899, when large crowds were drawn to meetings throughout urban Catalonia. The largest, on 2 July in Barcelona, attracted 7,000. The image of republicanism as the main political opposition to the Restoration regime was enhanced by the high profile of republican speakers at these meetings. Ironically, given the campaign's objective, the repression to which the anarchists had been subject meant that they played virtually no part. As in the trade-union sphere, on the working-class Left it was the Catalan Socialists who made an important showing; the popular mobilisation strengthening their belief – as against the position of the Madrid PSOE leadership – that an alliance with the republicans represented the way forward. The campaign did not, as many had hoped it would, loosen the regime's grip on power. But at least the sentences of the remaining prisoners were commuted in the spring of 1900.[8]

The campaign also made Lerroux's name in Catalonia and, as a result, he took the decision to rebuild republicanism from the industrial rather than the political capital of Spain. Central to this whole process was his proletarianised language, which was calculated to appeal to working-class and anarchist milieux. There had, since the 1870s, been a degree of fluidity in relations between anarchists and the republican Left, and Lerroux aimed to rework the republican movement by moving onto anarchist terrain, blurring the distance between their aims and objectives. Hence, in anarchist circles he maintained that they were all fighting for a social revolution, for 'economic equality', and that the struggle would continue 'until men do not need laws, nor government, nor God nor bosses'.[9] At the same time, he stepped up collaboration with the anarchists, allowing his new weekly newspaper, *Progreso*, to publish their writings. Then, in Barcelona, from early 1901 he worked with Francesc Ferrer's Modern School movement and gave at least verbal support to their aggressive strike actions.[10]

He accompanied this with efforts to build up a worker-dominated sub-culture in the proliferating republican centres, known as Fraternidades, which provided cafés and weekend entertainment, offered schooling, and opened mutual-aid societies and consumer cooperatives, in order to tie sympathisers to the movement.[11] By this means Catalan republicanism was becoming 'classed'; a process often repeated in western countries during the nineteenth century as progressive liberals came under pressure from the working-class Left. In one other respect the new class realities impinged on Barcelona's political landscape. With the rise of the Lliga Regionalista and the Republican Union, while middle and upper-class neighbourhoods largely voted for the former, popular and working-class areas generally opted for the latter.

The Anarchist Alternative:
The Culture of Protest

This climate, together with the rebirth of union organisation, gave the anarchists' furious critique of the social order an increasingly broad audience. The economic and political system, they maintained, was operated in the interests of three intertwined forces: capital, the political class and the Roman Catholic Church (sometimes lumped together as 'the bourgeoisie'). Taken as a whole they were viewed as an unproductive and parasitic outgrowth that fed off the workers, the only truly productive class in society.

In each sphere their critique was relentless. I have already examined the anarchists' virulent attacks on the industrial elite. Their antipathy towards the political system of the Restoration was accentuated by the practice of *caciquismo*, which helped justify their absolute rejection of the parliamentary political process (their 'antipoliticism' in the language of the day). 'Politics' was seen as a den of vice, which would contaminate anyone who came into contact with it. They viewed the Church as both giving capital and the regime ideological cover and exploiting society for its own ends. For Teresa Claramunt, for example, 'Monkish Spain' was under the thrall of a 'Jesuit bourgeoisie'. Similarly, Francesc Ferrer sustained that under the malign influence of the mother of Alfonso XIII, María Cristina, 'the Jesuits are the rulers of Spain'.[12]

The ideological roots of anarchism help us understand why anticlericalism was such an important component of its political language. The anarchists fused socialism with liberal rationalism and positivism. Like republicans, they saw history as an 'eternal struggle between [the forces of] reaction and progress, tyranny and liberty, darkness and light',[13] and viewed the Church as the central ideological component in this reactionary coalition. Hence their constant assertions that official Spain still lived in the Middle Ages and that its repressive practices were redolent of Torquemada and the Inquisition. It was a message which would play very well amongst the western European Left, where the view was prevalent that Spain – like Tsarist Russia – was a bastion of reaction. The Church's antiliberal ideology and the close relationship between it, social elites and the state meant this vision was not altogether unrealistic, though the anarchists clearly exaggerated its influence over all aspects of policy.

The state, they believed, was defended both culturally and by force. State and Church education, the anarchists argued, was used to 'poison children's young minds' through religious and patriotic dogmas.[14] The Hounds of Hades who protected this rotten edifice were the security forces and military. Antimilitarism would be a central feature of anarchist propaganda during the first decade of the century. On the one hand, they focused on the operation of military service, claiming that poor soldiers were forced to massacre their brothers at home and abroad to the exclusive benefit of the bourgeoisie.[15] Tension was exacerbated by the army's intervention in strikes and also by the frequent use of military tribunals to punish criticism. The anarchists combined this critique with an uncompromising anticolonial stance. The aim of colonial ventures, they maintained, was to exploit the natives and rob them of their land and mineral resources, exclusively to the benefit of local elites.[16] Given the experience of Cuba, and the new unpopular adventure in Morocco, this stance elicited much sympathy in working-class circles.

Yet, while all anarchists subscribed to the broad picture outlined above, the anarchist milieu would be much more disperse than that of its Socialist counterparts, who, particularly from the 1900s, tried to maintain a significant degree of internal party discipline. In large measure this can be traced to the anarchists' stress on bottom-up federalism and libertarian defence of individual freedom. They operated through loose 'affinity groups'; the most important published their own newspaper and, or, pamphlets, the rest simply functioned as debating societies. We have a fair idea of how many groups we are talking about. The conservative critic, Gustavo La Iglesia, claimed in 1907 that there were fifteen in Barcelona and eighteen in other Catalan towns. And at the end of the year, twenty-two anarchist groups, nineteen of which were from Barcelona, signed a manifesto in favour of the release of political prisoners.[17]

There were a large number of issues on which for them to focus. Anarchists adopted a holistic critique of 'bourgeois' society and this spawned a variegated set of interests. A first key area of concern was the natural and social sciences. Anarchists believed that private property and the state had undermined the harmony of the natural and human worlds and led society to develop in an unnatural direction. Hence the idealisation of nature and the appearance in the anarchist press of articles eulogising the animal kingdom. However, for the anarchists, the advance of human reason was revealing this error. In positivistic terms they envisaged nature and human society as operating in parallel. While science was uncovering the laws of natural evolution, sociology would carry out the same task within the sphere of social development. Both, they believed, were aligned with 'liberty' and 'justice' and served to undermine the world view of the Church and bourgeoisie. The most inquisitive turned to new spheres of inquiry, such as criminology and psychology, in their quest to explain the workings of capitalism and the roots of dissent. The anarchists' emphasis on ideas in promoting social change also meant that, for many, education was a major concern. Simultaneously, the importance of scientific advance was reflected in pieces, above all in more theoretical anarchist journals, on great scientific thinkers and new scientific discoveries.

In addition, the anarchists placed great emphasis on individual freedom against stifling 'bourgeois' morality and social norms, encouraging a wide-ranging critique of bourgeois cultural practices and the exploration of alternatives. This was apparent, for example, in their rejection of Church and state intervention in all areas of human life, which they regarded as an authoritarian imposition; their interest in vegetarianism, which was embraced because of what was viewed as the natural solidarity which should operate within the animal kingdom and also because of savagery inherent in the slaughter and consumption of meat; and in the links between the worlds of anarchism and of iconoclastic artistic production.

The overall result was that in the first years of the century there were an array of associations whose activities would overlap but remain to a degree separate (a fact which, when combined with petty rivalries and jealousies, would provide ample room for frequent disputes). We have already stressed the importance of those anarchists grouped around Leopoldo Bonafulla, on the one hand, and Francesc Ferrer and Anselmo Lorenzo, on the other, who not only made the greatest effort to mobilise labour but also sustained the most popular Catalan anarchist weeklies. Following the scandal which erupted over financial payments from Canalejas in 1902, and his retreat to Gràcia, Bonafulla was to a large degree marginalised. Denounced by anarchists close to Lorenzo, he became their implacable enemy. He continued to work closely with Teresa Claramunt and brought out a number of publications which laid particular emphasis on 'antipoliticism' and antimilitarism, coming to view himself as the self-appointed guardian of anarcho-communist orthodoxy.

From the outset the interests of the Lorenzo and Ferrer (4 de Maig) group were more eclectic, spanning trade unionism, education and cultural work. By the middle of the decade they had consolidated their position as the key figures within the anarchist camp. Ferrer himself was, from 1904 onwards, to take a totally backseat role, not appearing at all in the group's press. Lorenzo was to remain important ideologically but was racked by poor health. This left a number of younger activists, the best known of whom were Lorenzo's stepson, Francesc Miranda, and Marià Castellote, in charge of day-to-day events.

On friendly terms with these men were the Galician, Ricardo Mella, and his Catalan disciple, Josep Prat, along with Federico Urales the most sophisticated anarchist thinkers of their generation. Between October 1903 and September 1905 they managed to sustain a high-quality bi-monthly journal, entitled *Natura*, which included articles by leading European anarchists, and ranged across the entire gamut of anarchist philosophical and cultural concerns.[18] Other figures cultivated a more specific field. Between 1902 and 1905, the Avenir group focused on theatre and the arts, while at a political level trying to make anarchism compatible with Catalan identity. This latter aim was also taken up by another anarchist group from 1903, La Tramontana, which also joined the 4 de Maig group's Centre for Social Studies. Simultaneously, a number of anarchists linked to Lluís Bulffi championed Neo-Malthusianism, and published a series of journals in which they argued that birth control was a key factor in raising working-class living standards. Outside Barcelona such specialisation was not possible, but between 1900 and 1909 on the Costa Brava (Palamós and then Sant Feliu de Guíxols), and in Reus, Tarragona, Lleida, Sabadell, Terrassa and Mataró, a series of small anarchist groups were able – normally very briefly – to sustain weekly or bi-weekly newspapers and, or, edit pamphlets.[19]

Some anarchists were drawn to the individualism of Nietzsche and Stirner, forming small groups with names such as 'The Individual Against Society', 'State Power and I', 'Voluntarism and I' and 'The Sons of Whores'. It was this milieu above all that spawned anarchist bohemians, who railed against the stifling conformity of bourgeois culture and paraded their own radical lifestyle. Examples from the anarchist-dominated *tertulia* in the café of the Teatro Lírico Español on the Paral·lel, founded around the middle of the decade by the future leader of Catalan syndicalism, Salvador Seguí, were the 'failed artist' Martí, who travelled throughout Spain and Europe without a penny; Muntanyà, who devoured works of philosophy, was quick to corner anyone who would listen to his theories, and who committed suicide; and 'Gambetta the orator', who was 'dirty as a dog'.[20]

It was also within individualist circles that anarchist bombers were probably drawn. There is ample evidence from the anarchist press of continuing sympathy for 'propaganda by the deed'.[21] Despite the adoption of the general strike as a revolutionary tool, some still hoped that a spectacular assassination could fatally wound the regime and precipitate a revolutionary conjuncture. Most notably, as we shall see in the next section, Ferrer was probably involved in two attempts to assassinate the King in 1905 and 1906.

Yet this does not mean that the more mainstream anarchist currents were behind all the terrorist outrages of these years. In the period between 1904 and 1909 there were a large number of mysterious bombings in Barcelona. Around sixty-six bombs were planted, most of which were simply left in the street, killing at least eleven people and wounded seventy-one. They were to provoke a terrorist psychosis in middle-and upper-class society and within official circles. In January 1907, in a twist of black comedy, no doubt spurred on by the exploits of Sherlock Homes, a series of respectable institutions paid for a member of Scotland Yard, Charles Arrow, to investigate the crimes. Yet Arrow's adventure did have a serious side. He set up his own Office of Criminal Investigation together with a private 'special' police force. This was a first intimation that, when faced with what was regarded as official incompetence, local elites were willing to take matters into their own hands and that the authorities lacked the will to oppose them.[22] There was feverish speculation as to the culprits. All the major anarchist groups categorically, and, it seems sincerely, rejected the bombings. There was general stupor that anyone could regard simply leaving bombs in the street as a revolutionary act.[23] Indeed, the importation of syndicalist doctrine and the appearance of SO in 1907 was to mark a sea change in the attitude of the libertarian camp towards terrorism. It was widely accepted that the union movement would spark the revolution, while 'propaganda by the deed' would only lead to renewed government repression of the unions. Unfortunately some elements would, from 1910 onwards, import terrorism into the unions themselves.

In left-wing circles it was claimed that agents provocateurs or even the religious orders were behind the bombs. One cannot rule out the intervention of the former, but the suspicion is that most of the bombers hailed from the most extreme, individualist fringe of anarchism. Poorly educated and with little to lose, their understanding of the world was shaped by fevered debates in cafés and taverns. In addition, it is probably not a coincidence that they became active after the hopes for a revolutionary general strike dissipated after 1903 and anarchists became increasingly cut off from working-class circles. The growing unlikelihood of a revolution spearheaded by the unions could have stimulated the search for desperate alternatives.

We know that the first attacks were carried out by a group under the leadership of Joan Rull, who came from such a background. Seguí had actually formed part of the same affinity group, The Sons of Whores, when they met up in a tavern in Chinatown at the turn of the century, although he seems to have broken with them before the bombings began.[24] The most incredible aspect of the whole affair was that after Rull was tried and acquitted in 1905 he actually started to work as an informer with the support of the city's civil governors. He claimed to be able to stop the bombs being planted in exchange for a fee, and he was in a position to maintain his part of the bargain because his gang was still planting them. He was finally arrested in June 1907 and, one suspects to hide the authority's blushes, after a quick trial was executed with indecent haste on 8 August 1908. Yet his was not the only gang responsible. After a lull, bombs were once again planted from December 1907.[25]

At the heart of the anarchist movement there was a small core of committed activists passionately wedded to the cause, their enthusiasm fired by its promise of a total economic, social and cultural reordering of the world. For self-taught workers it must have provided an inspirational release from the daily grind and their penny-pinching efforts to make ends meet. Through their own example and actions, they believed, they would provide an ethical and cultural alternative to present-day society. This dedication could be seen in their refusal to conform to church-state rituals. They held 'intimate events' to celebrate 'free unions', at which Church ceremonies invariably came in for vigorous criticism. Similarly, they would give their children a civil baptism, inscribing them with names drawn from the anarchist cannon. Finally, they would be seen off with a civil burial, friends and colleagues accompanying the coffin to the 'free cemetery'.

Their commitment also comes through in the remarkable efforts made by anarchist groups to sustain newspapers on a financial shoestring, set up a little publishing house, and read and collect as many publications as was materially possible. These newspapers were not simply produced by the editorial team. The anarchists' belief in the self-worth of every individual, and fierce rejection of any innate intellectual superiority on the part of 'the bourgeoisie', encouraged anarchist activists throughout Spain to send in their own contributions. Although this did little for the literary quality of the papers it no doubt created a strong sense of participation and belonging. Indeed, complaints voiced suggest that people frequently bought a particular paper in anticipation of seeing their own contribution appear.

Such contributions were not limited to doctrine. As has often been remarked, anarchists also used drawings, poems and short stories to get their message across. As they correctly anticipated, it was often easier to make converts by establishing an emotional connection than through abstract doctrine. Hence, the anarchist press was populated by drawings of greedy industrialists, fat priests and generals, by stories of altruistic anarchist 'apostles', and poems which sung the praises of the future anarchist paradise. This was supplemented by longer novels and plays by the most able anarchist writers, often themselves then serialised in the anarchist press. They also served as a welcome foil to the endless doctrinal tracts, which repeated basic anarchist tenets *ad nauseam*.[26]

The press's heath mirrored that of the movement as a whole. By the end of 1902 *El Productor* was able to recommend nine Spanish anarchist papers to its readers.[27] However, from the summer of 1903, with the authorities taking an increasingly tough stance, it became impossible to sustain 'combat' papers for any length of time. Most damagingly, at the end of the year a number of anarchists received long prison sentences for antimilitarist propaganda.[28] Indeed, leading figures were under constant surveillance from the Barcelona police's rather unsubtly named Special Brigade for the Persecution of Anarchism, and would spend frequent spells in prison.[29] The situation was only to improve from mid-1906 when repression eased somewhat. Subsequently, the birth of SO in the autumn of 1907 signified an important shift in the movement's centre of gravity, with syndicalist papers produced by local labour federations rather than anarchist groups gaining a higher profile. The Sabadell-based *El Trabajo* was unique in this respect for the years 1898 to 1906. In August-September 1907 it was joined by *Solidaridad Obrera* and the bi-weekly from Terrassa, *La Voz del Pueblo*, and over the next two years papers supported by the local federations of Vilafranca del Penadés and Igualada would follow.

Catalan workers also exchanged and read works from much further afield. Hermoso Plaja recalled that in his native Palamós as a young activist at the beginning of the century he most enjoyed *Tierra y Libertad*, then published in Madrid, *El Corsario*, based in La Coruña, *Los Templarios* from Morón de la Frontera, and *El Cosmopolita* from Jerez, along with other freethinking and anticlerical publications.[30] There was even a significant two way flow of papers and pamphlets between Spain and Latin America (above all Argentina and Cuba), encouraged by the migration of workers, including anarchists, fleeing from a 'hunger pact' or political persecution.

The press sold in considerable numbers. The bestseller up until June 1905, when it ceased publication, was *La Revista Blanca*, which sold 8,000 copies. Catalan-based publications managed between 3,000 and 4,000 copies, but their impact was more widely felt as they were read aloud by enthusiastic activists at the place of work, café or tavern, and passed on to try and gain new disciples.[31] This was a not infrequent means of recruitment. Angel Pestaña, a leading anarchist figure in the second decade of the century, was acquainted with anarchist ideas by reading *El Obrero Moderno*, published in Murcia, which he regularly found in a carpentry workshop while working on the railways in Vizcaya.[32]

They were supplemented by dozens of pamphlets and books from the press's publishing houses and from popular publishers who included anarchist authors amongst their works, most notably Sampere based in Valencia and Los Pequeños Grandes Libros in Barcelona. A stern conservative critic admitted that they sold well in working-class circles, both because of their low price and because of the anarchists' enthusiastic proselytisation.[33] In 1904 much of this material could be bought through *El Productor*, which offered 181 works in its 'sociological section', nineteen in its 'pedagogical section' and another nineteen in its 'drama section', giving sympathisers access not only to the main Spanish and European anarchist thinkers but also making available those scientific tracts and literary works seen as most effectively undermining Christian dogma.[34]

It is impossible to know the number of anarchist core activists who regularly attended meetings and produced the press and pamphlets. Only fragmentary figures are available. When the Centre for Social Studies was set up it had eighty-four affiliates. In the small town of Palamós on the Empordà coast there were thirty activists committed to the cause.[35] My overall impression is that in Catalonia as a whole in the middle of the decade there were no more than several hundred dedicated activists. Many of the smaller groups (ironically, given their strong opposition to the consumption of alcohol) simply met up in local taverns. A wider forum for anarchists was provided by the Teatro Español *tertulia* already mentioned. At first it was a bohemian-philosophical debating society, but from 1907 onwards, as Seguí became more focused on union work, syndicalists made their presence felt. Frequently anarchist groups would be found operating in the cafés of larger working-class associations. This was the case of a group of anarchists in Igualada, who from about 1910 met at a 'science table' in the local café-cum-choral-society, the Chor Vell.[36]

Yet in such forums anarchists were largely preaching to the converted. Hence the need to build an autonomous cultural base in order to recruit more extensively. Because of the anarchists' vociferous anti-statism they saw this as a top priority, but given both their own lack of resources and state hostility it proved an extremely difficult task. A Centre Fraternal de Cultura, founded by the anarchists close to the Avenir group in Barcelona in August 1903, held talks by leading anarchist figures, and organised the odd 'drama' and, or, 'literary soirée' in popular theatres. Under the direction of the anarchist playwright, Felip Cortiella, Avenir also put on a number of plays between 1902 and 1905. The Centre for Social Studies followed a similar pattern, combining talks with occasional Sunday morning 'artistic soirées'. More modest variants on this same theme were the 'sociological soirées' – like the one organised by the Bonafulla group in the La Zorrilla theatre in Gràcia in April 1904 – which included talks, poetry reading and revolutionary songs.[37]

They were able to reach out further by connecting with the unions. Yet even here their organisational achievements were modest. The local federation they set up at the end of 1901 had no union headquarters. By 1903 four leading pro-anarchist unions had come together in a centre in the Fifth District.[38] This was important because it provided a space for members of different trades to develop strategies in common, and also to build up off-the-job friendship networks, but any attempt to develop it further was blocked by the authorities' opposition to unions setting up in the same headquarters. In these circumstances, they were limited to giving talks and holding soirées in the headquarters of sympathetic unions. Between 1903 and 1905 the headquarters of the Gràcia bricklayers, where Bonafulla was influential, played an important role in this respect. It operated a small school, held frequent talks and weekly musical events, and an occasional 'family soirée', put on by the school teacher and children. In central Barcelona, the headquarters of the tramworkers' union had no school but played quite a similar role until it was destroyed by the tram company's new director in 1904.

The soirée (*velada*) was the favourite means of bringing in larger numbers of workers – including family members – than could be attracted to a political or philosophical talk. The format was borrowed from the liberal tradition. Larger soirées would typically include an introduction by a significant anarchist figure, music by a choral band and, frequently, two plays, one of which would have a social and political message while the content of the other was rather lighter. These plays were usually put on by small theatre groups formed by the anarchists themselves. Yet limited resources meant that, with the exception of theatre performances, dozens rather than hundreds of workers were drawn to these events.

Matters became particularly difficult in the middle of the decade given the level of state repression, with anarchists hardly able to hold any meetings between mid-1905 and mid-1906.[39] They were hit by a new bout of heavy repression at the beginning of 1908 following the declaration of martial law in response to a series of bomb blasts. The Centre for Social Studies was closed down and a large number of activists arrested. It was never to reopen. This marked a shift in the structure of the anarchist movement under the influence of the new syndicalist doctrines. As in the case of the press, the labour confederation rather than the anarchist group would now take a more central role. Later in the year, with financial aid from Ferrer, SO was able to buy a new, more spacious, headquarters, complete with a large function room and a café, in which workers could play cards and dominoes.[40] This was indicative of the hopes Ferrer and his fellow anarchists were now placing in syndicalism. Over the next few months it was to hold frequent meetings. Furthermore, it founded a theatre group, which put on a series of plays in local theatres, and in July 1909 it opened a Syndicalist Athenaeum, which would hold frequent talks and debates. Nevertheless, the anarchist groups still maintained their own cultural spaces and, indeed, in the more tolerant climate from mid-1906 set up a couple of cultural associations in the Barcelona suburbs, in Poble Nou and El Clot.[41]

In the field of educational work the anarchists faced a similar set of problems. From the 1870s, anarchists had tried to build their own network of schools, but they had been held back by lack of funds and state repression. In early 1901 only one anarchist school operated in Barcelona, run by José López Montenegro in Poble Nou. Much more common were lay workers' schools linked to the republican movement. This was to change with the foundation of Ferrer's Modern School later in the year. According to Ferrer, the lay schools did not go far enough. He envisaged his schools as being overtly atheist and antistatist and, at the same time, both coeducational and interclass. Coeducation was meant to recognise women's intellectual equality, although, as was the norm in anarchist circles, Ferrer laid stress on the educational role that women who had attended 'rationalist' schools could play within the home.[42] Ferrer also backed interclass education because of what he saw as the natural solidarity between children and the key role that he believed 'intellectual workers' would play in the forthcoming revolution. This distanced Ferrer from most Catalan anarchists, who, as has been noted, were from a working-class background and were suspicious of middle-class revolutionaries.[43]

The original Modern School opened in Bailèn Street in central Barcelona in September 1901 with thirty students. It was, in fact, rather an elitist institution, with the emphasis on training 'rationalist' teachers. This again pointed to the distance between Ferrer and the union activists. Talks were given in the school on a Sunday. These were respectable affairs, supported by the city's liberal Left, which largely dealt with matters of a scientific nature. This indicates Ferrer's desire to reach out beyond a working-class audience and again points to the significance anarchists attached to science as an antidote to clericalism. The school also established a publishing house, in order to produce suitable educational material, which Ferrer put in the hands of Anselmo Lorenzo. Despite their very different lifestyles they would cooperate closely until Ferrer's execution in July 1909, with Lorenzo translating a number of French works for publication. From October there followed a well-produced bulletin, which included articles from European pedagogical reformers.

This was not the end of the story. Over the next four years a large number of schools, which used material provided by the Modern School, and sometimes employed 'rationalist' teachers close to Ferrer, were set up in the Barcelona suburbs and in industrial towns throughout Catalonia and beyond. At the movement's highpoint in 1906 there were about forty-nine schools in Catalonia, which taught well over 1,000 students, who, with the exception of the Bailèn Street school, were to a large extent drawn from working-class families.[44]

Its overall impact was still limited. In Barcelona there were around 6,000 children being educated in private lay schools.[45] Yet while not numerically preponderant the Modern School's teachings certainly represented the most radical and determined ideological assault on the establishment to be found in Spain. Evidence is fragmentary but it may also have played a significant role in training anarchist cadres. For example, the future syndicalist activist and gunman, Joan Manent, went to the Barcelona Modern School. In Igualada a group of youngsters, amongst whom Joan Ferrer stood out, attended the local rationalist school and then went on to form the anarchist vanguard in the town. Between 1907 and 1909 Hermoso Plaja, who was later to become the key anarchist activist in Tarragona, was at a rationalist school in Palamós, run by the leading Barcelona anarchist, Ernest Cardenal.[46]

Occasionally its branches had the support of local unions. More often, as in the case of the schools in the Barcelona suburbs, they were backed by local republican associations.[47] This, along with Ferrer's resources, was the key to the Modern School's success, for it gave them access to republican cultural centres and, where republicans were strong on the town council, they could receive subsidies. These links between Ferrer and the republicans need to be understood with the context, already outlined, of similarities in some aspects of their cosmographies, with both believing in 'progressive' anticlerical education. Moreover, Ferrer and Lerroux had other connections. They both hailed from the left-wing insurrectionary republican tradition and, indeed, when they first met in 1892, Lerroux had shown interest in a revolutionary scheme hatched by Ferrer, which included the assassination of the royal family.[48] Furthermore, although Ferrer subsequently evolved towards anarchism his ideology retained eclectic elements. Thus, while he supported the general strike he believed the revolutionary process could pass through a republican phase, and although he financed the anarchists he would, until 1908, also provide Lerroux with funds and remain on close terms with his followers.[49]

As far as the actual publications of the Modern School's publishing house were concerned, they reflected the compromise between anarchism and left-liberalism, comprising a mixture of works by committed anarchist theorists and positivist and evolutionist popularisers of history, sociology and science. Underlining much of the work was a strong anticlerical and antireligious tone. The fourteen works published between 1901 and the spring of 1905 (forty-seven by 1914) were important in that they helped disseminate an alternative world view to that of the Church and conservative elites. A number of the books had print runs of several thousand and went through a number of editions, although their eclecticism meant that only in part did they provide a specifically anarchist perspective.[50]

Much more problematic was the utilisation of works by the Modern School in the educational field, the reason for which they had ostensibly been produced. They aimed at a wide market: schoolchildren and adult evening classes, together with a more general readership. It was in the first area in particular that the problems lay. No doubt in a context in which a diet of rote learning and severe physical punishment was the norm, the classes of the Modern School could represent some kind of liberation. But the stated intention of taking dogma out of the classroom by allowing the children to question received wisdom and think for themselves was never met. Rather, they were subjected to textbooks which were either overtly propagandistic, and, or, far too complex for readers who were mastering basic reading skills. This was a criticism laid at Ferrer's door by several 'rationalist' teachers, who broke with him. The problem was his determination directly to challenge Church and state combined with his simplistic understanding of the concepts of truth and falsehood. The teachings of the Church were, he argued, false and in order to dispel superstition, dogmas and conventionalisms, it was necessary to propagate the new gospel of science, reason and truth, which was embodied by anarchism.[51]

Yet even taking into account the Modern School, the numbers that anarchists could reach through their educational and cultural associations was relatively limited. Their efforts to integrate workers may indeed have been hampered by the extent to which their concerns distanced them from most workers' everyday lives. It required enormous self-sacrifice to learn to read and write and acquire a degree of culture, a fact which helps explain the disdain with which they viewed the 'ignorant masses' and 'slavish workers', who failed to stand up to their exploiters.[52] Anarchists emphasised the need for workers to engage in serious study and not succumb to vices such as alcohol, tobacco, prostitution and gambling. Leisure should have an educational purpose. Hence, their disgust at what they saw as the degrading entertainments around the Paral·lel and the barbarous pursuit of bullfighting.[53] Such attitudes were behind the heroic efforts of anarchist centres to build up small libraries and their decision to prohibit the consumption of alcoholic beverages in their cafés. Hence, no anarchist-syndicalist union centre would be complete without paintings and slogans daubed on the walls warning at the evils of drink (and on occasion promoting vegetarianism) alongside images of, or quotations from, the pantheon of anarchist heroes.[54]

This emphasis on sobriety, study and sacrifice, pervaded the committed core who ran the early twentieth-century working-class parties and organisations in western Europe. In early twentieth-century Spain it would be epitomised by the austere figures of Pablo Iglesias and Anselmo Lorenzo. As already noted, anarchists believed that it was crucial to lead by example. On a practical level it was also necessary for people to be literate and reliable. Yet it was a culture which regarded what was, in fact, the typical night out of the working-class man, which included a game of cards or dominoes, a coffee or a glass of wine, and might well end up with a visit to the brothel, as reprehensible. Lorenzo went so far as to criticise unions for renting large headquarters where 'there is gambling, alcohol is consumed and there is even dancing'.[55]

In anarchist circles this sense of distance with most workers was probably intensified by cultural practices such 'free love' and vegetarianism. Joan Ferrer admitted that his 'science table' was at first viewed with suspicion, but that its members leading role in labour disputes then gained them sympathy. This may provide the key to the relationship between the anarchist purists and the more diffuse working-class base. Workers in anarchist unions might look up to the activists at the time of a strike or campaign, but they would be little inclined to break with ingrained attitudes and leisure pursuits that committed anarchists would find offensive. Indeed, from 1910 onwards, within the CNT tensions developed between the anarchists and workers affiliated to what they considered as above all a union organisation. Hence, though the anarchists might ban alcohol from their centres they had to accept gambling, and even well-known syndicalist activists were sceptical of at least some of the attitudes of the 'men with beards and moustaches'.[56] For example, as a young man the leading Badalona activist, Joan Peiró, loved bullfighting, and Salvador Seguí enjoyed – on the rare occasions that he could sample it – a good meal followed by a cigar.

Yet despite these difficulties anarchists were able, on occasion, to reach out and mobilise large numbers of industrial workers. The key, as indicated in the previous chapter, was the leading role they played in labour agitation and protest campaigns, above all through their aggressive 'direct action' tactics, which included mass meetings, street demonstrations and violent industry-wide strikes.

Leaving aside for a moment the trade-union sphere, anarchists used meetings for a number of functions. Big meetings in local theatres were held to promote specifically anarchist causes. No year would go by, for example, without a meeting commemorating the Paris Commune and the so-called 'martyrs of Chicago'. They were combined with more generic pro-anarchist and 'antipolitical' meetings, the latter usually held at election time. The fact that the political system was sustained through *caciquismo* and nepotism without doubt favoured the spread of anarchist ideas. All the indications are that, within Catalan working-class circles, cynical attitudes towards politicians were widespread.[57] This would help both sustain the anarchist core in their beliefs and help with recruitment, although, as we shall see, total separation from the field of 'politics' would be difficult to achieve.

Nevertheless, such actions did not mobilise large numbers of workers. More important in this respect were meetings they organised through supportive unions. The First of May was an important yearly event. Anarchist (and, indeed, republican and Socialist) workers made great efforts to bring industrial Catalonia to standstill, and, from 1901, the anarchists held well-attended meetings in which they were able effectively to put across their message. Nevertheless, their uncompromising moral stance also brought problems. Their affirmation that it should be a day for reflection and not a simple holiday did not prevent large numbers of workers holding picnics – the more important sponsored by Lerrouxists and Socialists – in the afternoon.

Also effective in mobilising mass support were protest movements, which frequently focused on government repression and backing for strikers from other parts of the country. These gave the anarchists a chance to attract sympathy and make their presence felt, not only through the meetings themselves but also through debates in the unions, through the press, pamphlets and flysheets (frequently stuck on walls at night). As in the case of 1 May, these campaigns were very much bound up with labour organisation, for it was only via sympathetic unions that workers could be integrated. As shown in the previous chapter, thousands could be drawn in. The anarchists' critique of the state clearly connected with the experience of many, who, for reasons already outlined, viewed it as serving the interests of social elites and little disposed effectively to pursue policies which were in the interests of the workers.

Most emotive were the campaigns aimed at freeing what were viewed as political prisoners (*presos sociales*). Such campaigns were particularly important for the anarchist activists in that they created bonds of friendship and a sense of common purpose. Subscriptions were constantly being raised for prisoners in the press, while the prisoners themselves would frequently write letters lamenting their fate. Demands for the release of colleagues, along with prison visits by friends and family and the articulation of support networks for destitute prisoners' families, also helped create a sense of unity. Frequent imprisonment meant that many fell by the wayside. But for those that remained the sense of injustice and moral outrage could also be a source of strength, providing proof of the state's reactionary nature. Accordingly, the events of the Mano Negra, Jerez, Montjuïc and Alcalá del Valle were known by heart and continuously recited in the press and on public platforms. Moreover, anarchists would play a key role in more generic protest movements which could attract mass support. As will be shown in a subsequent section, the key issues were anticlericalism and colonialism in Morocco.

Finally, anarchists were keen to extend protests to other aspects of workers' lives. Throughout this period they were above all concerned with workers as producers, but they also gave some attention to the problems they faced as consumers. One of the key areas in this respect was the cost of rented accommodation, which had been on the increase from the end of the nineteenth century. In its 1903 congress, the FRESR recommended the formation of tenants' associations. From September onwards an anarchist group, Els Desheretats, began to agitate for the creation of such as organisation. In the spring of 1904 the idea was taken up by the 4 de Maig group, big meetings were held and a rent strike threatened. The movement subsequently petered out but the issue would come up again during the First World War.[58]

Anarchism, Republicanism and Catalan Nationalism

Throughout this period a key issue for the anarchists would be their relations with Alejandro Lerroux's left-wing republicans. Orthodox anarchists poured scorn on the notion that the republic would bring greater freedom and improved living conditions, but there was, as already noted, a significant degree of overlap in their political languages. Both groupings viewed the country as gripped by a titanic struggle between the forces of 'reaction' and 'progress'. This is of fundamental importance in understanding the growth of anarchism from the late-nineteenth century onwards. It meant that converts from republicanism (which many well-known anarchists were) did not have to undergo any traumatic paradigmatic shift in their world view: on the one hand, the subject of the revolution became more specific, with the industrial working class rather than the *pueblo* now taking centre stage; on the other hand, the ultimate endpoint of historical 'progress' was extended to libertarian communism.

It was because of these similarities that anarchists and republicans consumed the same literary genres. Realist novels with a social content were the preferred option. It was a tradition which was continued in the plays of Fola Igurbide, social melodramas often with an overtly political message, and a must for working-class families on the Paral·lel during the second decade of the century.[59] This would have its counterpart in cooperation at a cultural and political level. This was, as I have already stressed, encouraged because, from the late 1890s onwards, Lerroux radicalised his discourse. On the anarchist side, between 1899 and 1900, *La Revista Blanca* and its *Suplemento* were supportive of Lerroux and *El Productor* was tolerant. In addition, anarchists contributed regularly to Lerroux's weekly, *Progreso*, praising, to quote Leopoldo Bonafulla, his 'noble aims'.[60] Further elements drew them together. They shared a common predisposition to use force. Hence, while the young anarchist activists would frequently lead attacks on blacklegs, Lerroux's youth wing, the Young Barbarians, fought pitched battles with clerical Carlists. More broadly, both groups believed that only through a violent insurrection would the old order be swept away and would be at the forefront of all the antigovernment revolts of this period.

Indeed, there are indications that Ferrer and Lerroux were involved in two conspiracies to assassinate King Alfonso XIII in 1905 and 1906. On the first occasion, two bombs were thrown at the King's cortège during an official visit to Paris on 31 May 1905. The indications are that while the mastermind was the Parisian-based anarchist Pedro Vallina, Ferrer had supplied funds and Lerroux was kept informed. The second attack was perpetrated by Mateo Morral (a teacher at the Modern School) exactly one year after, when he threw a bomb at the King's wedding procession. It was a bloody affair; twenty-three people were killed and over one-hundred injured, although the King was himself unharmed. Again it seems that Ferrer provided funding and that Lerroux was kept in the picture. The hope was that the assassination of the monarch would destabilise the entire political system.[61] On this occasion Ferrer was imprisoned and put on trial but acquitted; a fact that did not prevent the authorities from permanently closing the Barcelona headquarters of the Modern School.

In areas where theoretical divisions were significant, points of contact could still be found. I have already emphasised differences with respect to the subject of the revolution. Yet, as Lerroux's ideology became increasingly 'classed', he narrowed his definition of the *pueblo*, stating in a letter to Ferrer in 1899 that it represented 'those who earn a wage, do not have enough bread to eat or sufficient education'.[62] At the same time, anarchists were not untouched by the left-liberal language, continuously expounded in the republican, freethinking and anticlerical press, which was widely read by workers close to the anarchist cause. Hence, for example, Bonafulla himself on occasion referred vaguely to the '*pueblo*' and 'the disinherited' as the agents of the future revolution.[63]

Even where they were in theory separated by an ideological gulf, when one looks beyond the core to the broader mass of sympathisers there are discernible coincidences. There were overlaps between the cultural spaces in which the radical Left moved. In some small towns all the local 'progressives' met in the same social and cultural centre. This meant that at grass-roots level neat ideological divisions tended to become blurred. Thus, in the case of 'antipoliticism', while anarchist theorists tended to see all bourgeois regimes as equally nefarious, for many workers the republic still held out the promise of a major shift in the balance of power and great improvements in living conditions. Furthermore, when push came to shove, it would be difficult for the anarchists themselves to remain neutral when faced with the choice between a monarchy or a republic. The Restoration regime was widely viewed in republican and anarchists circles as the common enemy, and, while they might not have the same ultimate goals, many no doubt felt that they could at least travel part of the road together. Indeed, one suspects that, especially given Lerroux's radicalised discourse, differences in anarchist and republican objectives were themselves unclear to a large number of workers, who frequently belonged to unions close to the anarchist camp, but voted republican at election time. Significantly in this respect, there was a ready transfer of working-class activists from one movement to the other. Between 1901 and 1906 a number of quite well-known anarchists joined the Lerrouxists, and between 1914 and 1919, with syndicalism in the ascendancy, significant numbers of the Radical youth became CNT activists.

At the turn of the century the Socialists argued that there was a republican-anarchist alliance in the city, which despite anarchist denials operated at election time.[64] This was an exaggeration. Nevertheless, it was the case that, while there was a considerable degree of understanding between the two, the Socialists were left out in the cold. It has been argued that this needs to be seen in ideological terms: while republicans and anarchists saw history as forged by the battle of ideas between reaction and progress, as historical materialists the PSOE-UGT focused on the economic sphere and the class struggle.[65] A careful study of turn-of-the-century Barcelona calls this into question. On the one hand, while a class-based analysis of society might theoretically be more central to Marxist Socialism, in reality in a Catalan context both Socialists and the great majority of anarchists saw industrial workers as the agents of revolution. Furthermore, although some orthodox Socialists, like Pablo Iglesias, viewed attacks on the clergy as a 'distraction' from the 'real' struggle against the industrial bourgeoisie, Catalan Socialists participated alongside anarchists and republicans in anticlerical agitation and, as noted, pushed for closer ties with the republicans. In the Montjuïc campaign of 1899 they were indistinguishable from the other speakers; Toribio Reoyo, their key figure, emphasising the 'struggle between liberty and justice' and claiming that 'the Jesuits have seized all the money in Barcelona'. Liberal rationalism had greatly influenced the whole of the Spanish and European Left.[66]

Rather, it was the Socialists' political strategy that separated them from the anarchists and Lerrouxist republicans. They followed a moderate trade-union practice and also, increasingly, focused on making political gains through the ballot box. Hence they were vehemently opposed to what they saw as irresponsible anarchist-Lerrouxist attempts to spark revolution. It is significant in this respect that moderate republicans, including the Catalan nationalist Left, sympathised more with the Socialists than the anarchists, believing that they would more effectively be able to work with them to modernise Spain. In addition, hostilities between Socialists and anarchists-Lerrouxists had an institutional dimension. Anarchists and Socialists directly competed for trade-union support while the Lerrouxists never attempted seriously to build a union base. On the other hand, Socialists and republicans went head-to-head in elections, with the anarchists looking on. Between 1900 and 1903, in both these spheres the Socialists lost out. They were out of step with the radical temper of labour in Barcelona, failed to build a strong union organisation and without this would find it impossible to compete at a political level; all the more so because Lerroux was able to offer such a seductive alternative.[67]

Nevertheless, from the spring of 1901 the understanding between Lerroux and the anarchists ran into growing difficulties. Lerroux's decision to participate in elections, along with the realisation that he was re-building the republican party, led to a break, with Federico Urales and the anarchists writing for *La Revista Blanca* and its *Suplemento* leading the way.[68] At heart was the basic incompatibility between anarchist ideology and party politics. In addition, there was a growing realisation that Lerroux was a demagogue, whose rhetoric would not necessarily be matched by his actions. This was brought home by the 1902 general strike, during which he stayed in Madrid and made no public comment, only to make a strong, well-publicised defence of the strikers in parliament once the danger had passed.[69] This no doubt helped shore up his working-class base, but leading anarchists increasingly saw him as a sham.

Accordingly, 'antipolitical' orthodoxy was reasserted with scathing criticisms of the notion that Lerroux might be considered a 'republican anarchist' who would carry through a 'revolution in parliament'. This was combined with renewed anti-electoral agitation, which, on occasion, led to violent clashes with young Lerrouxists. Notwithstanding, Francesc Ferrer and a group of anarchists based in Paris and Madrid, most notably Pedro Vallina and his mentor, Fermín Salvochea, remained close. As indicated, it was within this milieu that the attempted regicides of 1905 and 1906 were planned. José Alvarez Junco has pointed out that unlike most Spanish anarchists they came from a middle-class family background. Culturally they felt at home with the republican Left and readily took to conspiracy.[70] It was within working-class circles, above all, that Lerroux was viewed with growing hostility.

The 4 de Maig group also maintained a somewhat ambiguous position. From 1904 *Tierra y Libertad* was overtly anti-Lerrouxist, but republicans close to Lerroux participated in the anarchists' Alcalá del Valle campaign between 1903 and 1904, and, after the arrest of a large number of anarchists in the spring of 1905, a League in Defence of the Rights of Man was formed by Lerrouxists and members of the Centre for Social Studies, which then held a number of meetings. At the same time, republican lawyers were hired to help those detained. Subsequently, in a new campaign against prison conditions in late 1906 and early 1907, the Centre invited left-wing politicians to participate, and complained that only the Lerrouxist labour lawyer, Josep Puig d'Asprer – who had played a key role in defending anarchist prisoners – consented.[71]

Important in maintaining these ties was the continued belief in some anarchist circles that when fighting reaction all liberals should unite. The links are also explained by the unequal nature of the relationship between the Republican Union and the anarchists between 1904 and 1906. While the republicans could expect between 20,000 and 25,000 votes in general and municipal elections, the anarchist union base had been totally undercut. This left the latter in a weak and exposed position. In addition, anarchists were dependent on the Lerrouxists for maintaining the branches of the Modern School. The Lerrouxists themselves were happy to throw a paternalist cloak around the anarchists in return for the muting of any criticism. Given the anarchists' reputation as fearless defenders of workers' rights this was useful in providing them with popular credibility. It was not, however, a situation that all anarchists would tolerate. With the war cry of 'out with the dirt', Bonafulla and *El Productor* saw the opportunity to wound their foes in the 4 de Maig group and launched an all-out attack on what he saw as the collaborators.[72]

While the anarchists remained divided and the labour movement weak, such attacks did not bother Lerroux very much. Matters changed with the foundation of SO in 1907. As already emphasised, the objective of the organisation's syndicalist leadership was to build a self-sufficient union confederation with its own independent cultural and educational base. It viewed Lerrouxism as a major obstacle in its path. This propitiated a realignment within the Left, with Socialists and anarchists, under the syndicalist banner, rounding on the republicans. They now had the wholehearted support of the 4 de Maig group which, as seen in the previous chapter, integrated into the confederation. This left Ferrer in an awkward position. Hopeful that a general strike might precipitate the revolution, he discreetly allied with the syndicalists, leaving his relations with the republican camp to become increasingly strained.

Lerrouxists were vulnerable to the syndicalist challenge because they made no attempt to structure a working-class party. The republican elite was largely made-up of middle-class professionals. Furthermore, although Lerroux was the major figure in Barcelona, the Republican Union's leader was the moderate Nicolás Salmerón, and within Barcelona itself many of the leading republicans came from a solidly middle-class background and viewed Lerroux's perceived anarchistic rabble-rousing with distaste. Lerroux was to break with the Republican Union in 1908 and found his own Radical [Republican] Party, but by then he was moderating his tone with the hope of building a new Spain-wide organisation. The party's attempt to be with the workers but not of the workers was emphasised by the fact that rather than establish links with labour through the sphere of production, and build a trade-union base, it did so through the realm of consumption; that is via its republican centres, cooperatives and mutual-aid societies. Its reaction to the formation of SO and to subsequent criticism was cautious. At first it tried to maintain a paternalist relationship with the confederation, but alarmed by the new, aggressive, syndicalist vocabulary it responded by publishing a number of articles in its daily, *El Progreso*, dismissing anarchist doctrines.[73]

A first confrontation came in August 1907, when *El Progreso* implicated the young Salvador Seguí in the Rull gang's bombings. Seguí had becoming increasingly involved in trade-union work – he was on the organising committee of SO – and was keen to clear his name. The crisis came when he turned up to a big Lerrouxist meeting against Inspector Arrow's new police force, with a friend, to answer the accusations. A fight broke out, a pistol was drawn and a man shot dead. Seguí was not the author but he spent nine months in prison before being acquitted. On the other hand, it certainly helped forge his reputation in anarchist-syndicalist circles.[74]

From the summer of 1908 onwards, conflict became continuous. The conduct of two former anarchists who had gone over to the Lerrouxist camp, Ignaci Clarià and Josep Maria Dalmau, provided SO with the opportunity to attack. They ran what was meant to be a 'communist' print shop called La Niotipia, but in fact enjoyed a privileged position and in 1908 dismissed a number of workers, including Tomás Herreros, a leading figure in SO.[75] In response the print workers' union, L'Art d'Imprimir, which was close to SO, argued this showed that La Niotipia was in fact a capitalist enterprise and expelled them from the union. The decision was supported by SO, which now called for *El Progreso* to remove the two from its own print shop, where they also worked. Its failure to comply gave SO the opportunity to launch an all-out assault on the paper, declaring a boycott at the beginning of 1909 and simultaneously conducting a campaign of union meetings – leading, on occasion, to physical confrontations with Lerrouxist activists. It culminated in an assembly of the 'organised working class' called in order to judge the paper. The assembly, which was held in SO's headquarters on 21 March, was attended by representatives from forty-seven Barcelona unions, six local federations, two craft federations and forty-five unions from outside the Catalan capital: the bulk of the Catalan trade-union movement. It approved a motion stating that the paper would be declared an 'enemy of the organised working class' if within eight days it had not accepted L'Art d'Imprimir's demands.

Despite the Lerrouxists' electoral strength the leadership of SO had, therefore, obtained the support of the majority of Catalan unions. This brought home the Lerrouxists' vulnerability to a challenge from organised labour. SO had chosen its terrain well. Rather than launch a direct assault on Lerroux and the party – which would lay them open to the charge of involvement in 'politics' – its spokesmen argued that their quarrel was with the three administrators of El Progreso and that they had been provoked by the fact that the paper had supported the 'bourgeois' owners of La Niotipia. Thus it maintained that the conflict 'is simply a dispute between a bourgeois company and a union'. However, the implication was that El Progreso and, by extension, the Radicals supported the bourgeoisie and were, therefore, the enemies of the working class. It was a charge openly and repeatedly voiced by the confederation from the beginning of 1909. Only independent action by the working class would bring about the revolution, 'nothing is to be hoped from the bourgeoisie WHATEVER CLOTHES THEY WEAR'.[76]

Yet, despite the support that SO garnered from the Catalan unions it made little impression on the Radicals' working-class base. This was brought home by the results of the December 1908 by-election and the May 1909 municipal elections in Barcelona, at which the Lerrouxists obtained 30,000 and 34,000 votes respectively. There are perhaps two main explanations of SO's inability to influence significant numbers of republican workers. First, the confederation offered no direct political challenge to the Lerrouxists, who therefore remained the only unambiguously left-wing party strongly rooted in the city's history. Second, union organisation in Barcelona still remained weak; only when the syndicalists mobilised a large percentage of the city's workers within their unions would they be able to put Lerroux's position in jeopardy.

Indeed, the Lerrouxists' continuing strength allowed them to strike back at SO to some effect. 'Many workers formed part of the [Lerrouxist] Casa del Pueblo and Solidaridad at the same time',[77] and they had considerable influence in a number of Barcelona unions. As the dispute became increasingly bitter, the Lerrouxists looked both to discredit SO's leading figures and pursuade those unions under their influence to leave. In this they had some success. By the spring of 1909 a total of eight unions had followed the republicans' advice and Lerrouxist sympathisers resigned from other affiliated unions.[78] This put Ferrer's relations with the republicans under further strain. He personally remained on good terms with Lerroux (who had been forced into exile in Argentina in early 1908 after losing his seat in parliament and would not return until October 1909), but his support of SO led to growing hostility towards Ferrer's rationalist schools at a local level. This, together with government repression, provoked a crisis, with, the indications are, only two or three small schools remaining directly linked to the Modern School in Barcelona in 1909.[79]

Yet this did not put a total end to cooperation between anarchists and republicans. The advent of syndicalism exacerbated a clear contradiction in anarchist thought. When focusing their attention on unions and the class struggle, anarchists and syndicalists linked to SO emphasised that Lerrouxists represented the class enemy. But at a political and cultural level they still saw the need for all 'honourable men' to support 'noble causes' in the fight against reaction.[80] Hence in the autumn of 1907 the La Tramontana group gave backing to a Lerrouxist campaign against Inspector Arrow's new police force, and in early 1909 Catalanist and Lerrouxist republicans were involved in the new anarchist campaign for the release of the Alcalá del Valle prisoners. Such ambiguities would continue into the second decade of the century.

At the beginning of this period, amongst broad sectors of labour, the reaction to the rise of Catalanism was much more hostile than towards the growth of Lerrouxist republicanism. This was influenced by events that had taken place over the previous twenty years. In the early 1880s there had been a degree of fluidity in relations between republicans, Catalanists and anarchists. Catalanist ideology had appeared liberal democratic and 'progressive'. Moreover, Catalanists benefited from the fact that the defence of Catalan liberties against a hostile central state was present in the most influential republican tradition, known as Federalism. Finally, in protectionist campaigns launched from the late 1880s, they gained some sympathy not only from industrialists but from more reformist sectors of labour, represented at a trade-union level by the TCV and in the cultural sphere by workers' cultural centres known as Ateneus Obrers (Workers' Athenaeums).[81]

Yet from the end of the decade, as social strife intensified, it proved increasingly difficult to hold the political middle ground, and Catalanism's locus moved rightwards as it strove to broaden its middle-class appeal. This shift was confirmed when many industrialists gave their support to the Lliga Regionalista in 1901. The party brought together a group of conservative Catalan intellectuals and representatives of the industrial elite, both heavily influenced by antiliberal Catholic thought.[82]

The overall result was that within much of the Left there was a growing identification between Catalan nationalism and 'reaction'. Criticism was encouraged by the antiregionalist current present within much European left-wing thought. From the French Revolution onwards liberals frequently identified 'progress' with the construction of the nation state, which, they believed, fomented material and cultural advance. On the other hand, they equated regionalism with the forces of reactionary clericalism and feudalism. This perspective was taken up by Marxism and also incorporated into the world-view of many anarchists. Marx and Lenin declared themselves to be internationalists but also argued that the large Western nation states would lay the economic foundations for the transition to communism. For collectivists and communists this phase of human society tended to be identified with the disappearance of nation states as humanity merged into a single world federation. This provoked hostility towards what Engels described as 'remnants of nations', which objectively served to hold up this process, with the result that a degree of nation-state patriotism could lurk behind their internationalism.[83]

Anti-Catalanism was an important component in Lerrouxist ideology. Heirs of nineteenth-century liberal Spanish nationalism, Lerrouxists attacked the Lliga as an amalgam of reactionary 'Vaticanists' and 'plutocrats', whose 'separatist' ideas were a backward-looking anachronism.[84] Similar views could also be seen amongst Catalan Socialists and many anarchists. In 1899, for example, the Socialists celebrated the lack of working-class participation in a tax-payers' strike fomented by the Catalanists (the Tancament de Caixes).[85] Anselmo Lorenzo's hostility was well known. Francesc Ferrer 'hated Catalanism' and reacted furiously to a suggestion that the Modern School's classes should be in Catalan.[86] Most anarchist union activists, like Teresa Claramunt, took the same line. Hence, they accused Catalanists of 'wanting a free Catalonia and the Catalans to be slaves', stated that they were against 'all particularisms' and proclaimed that the future anarchist society would be 'a great region, a single motherland'.[87] The right-wing bias of the Lliga Regionalista sharpened this critique. It was this attitude that helps explain why, from the turn of the century onwards, the great majority of the Catalan anarchist and syndicalist press would be written in Castilian-Spanish. Similarly, language classes in anarchist cultural centres usually ignored Catalan. Rather (along with the teaching of French), Esperanto was promoted as the potential single world language. Indeed, this critique of Catalanism was even taken up by the remnants of the TCV, keen to dispel their class-collaborationist image.[88]

However, there was an alternative left-wing perspective, which would provide a connection with Catalanism. It was rooted in another facet of liberal-rationalist thought; support for the struggles of the 'oppressed peoples' of Europe and the Americas from tyrannical multinational empires and oppressive colonial rule. Such views would also penetrate the working-class Left. Mikhail Bakunin himself had started his political life as a pan-Slav nationalist and after his conversion to anarchism still believed that 'natural nationalities' should be integrated in the future world collectivist confederation.[89] Furthermore, at the end of the nineteenth century, although there were divisions, many Spanish anarchists came to sympathise with the Cuban separatists, both because workers and peasants were to the fore, and because they were viewed as struggling for freedom against colonial oppression.[90] Should Spain be viewed as a reactionary state machine, rather than a nation, and, or, the relation between Spain and Catalonia be regarded as colonial, then liberals and the Left could rally to the Catalanist cause. It was this mindset which made it possible for some republicans to turn to Catalanism from the 1880s. In 1904 they broke away from the Lliga and subsequently operated their own political organisations.

Within the Catalan anarchist movement there were two inter-linked groups which maintained a dialogue with the world of Catalanism. First, there were those who wished specifically to build bridges with Catalan nationalism. Of central importance here were a group of playwrights and artists who emerged within the literary *modernista* movement in the early 1890s, at a time when a number of young Spanish intellectuals briefly flirted with anarchism. In this respect, similarities could be seen with the libertarianism expounded by a new wave of painters and literary figures in Paris in the 1890s. In both contexts, anarchist aesthetics, with its emphasis on individual liberty and critique of bourgeois values, found an echo amongst sectors of the intelligentsia exasperated by 'bourgeois' conservatism and philistinism. In Catalonia, moreover, such figures could also sympathise with Catalanism – and therefore wish to build a bridge between both movements – because of their concern that Spanish backwardness was holding back Catalonia's cultural and social modernisation.[91]

The key figures were the writers Pere Coromines and Jaume Brossa, who briefly linked up with mainstream anarchists in the weekly newspaper, *Ciencia Social*, between 1895 and 1896. Corominas maintained that in areas like Catalonia there existed a 'love for the motherland', which anarcho-communists should channel. Brossa took a more overtly political stance, arguing that the struggle for Catalan autonomy and independence was positive in that it would weaken the forces of Spanish reaction.[92] At the same time, within the anarchist camp a small group led by Felip Cortiella, a typographer who came from a downwardly mobile middle-class family, formed a theatre group and also promoted avant-garde European art. Both groups were particularly taken by the plays of Henrik Ibsen, because of their focus on the individual's revolt against claustrophobic bourgeois norms. At the turn of the century, Cortiella formed the Avenir group, which in 1905 briefly brought out a weekly newspaper of the same name written in Catalan. Amongst its writers, Jaume Bausà took the most overtly Catalanist line, arguing that the Castilians were the dominant Spanish race, and linking the struggle for social emancipation with the fight by the oppressed Catalan race for liberation. More circumspect was Cortiella, who accused the Spanish anarchist movement of focusing too much on class. Such views tacitly favoured the construction of interclass alliances.[93]

However, the importance of these figures in Catalan literary circles should not be exaggerated. The stark repression of the anarchist movement after 1896 had, in fact, frightened most *modernistes* away. Then, from the turn of the century onwards, the rise of political Catalanism provided a rather safer outlet for their dissatisfaction with the state of Spain. Most notably, in the 1900s Pere Coromines (who was almost executed during the Montjuïc trial) re-emerged as a moderate republican Catalanist. At the same time, leading *modernistes*, such as Santiago Rusiñol (who though never close to the anarchists was still an admired figure), increasingly connected with a bourgeois clientele, accentuating their elitism. Many young artists of a new generation, such as Pablo Picasso, had little interest in politics.[94] This led to a growing criticism of *modernista* artists by leading anarchists, such as Urales, Lorenzo and Prat, along with Cortiella. Furthermore, the influence of the literary anarchists who stayed on board should not be exaggerated. Brossa – who married a daughter of Ferrer – had contacts with the Modern School, but seems to have played no active role in its development, and in the second decade of the century drifted towards the Catalanist Left, while Cortiella remained a respected but distant figure.[95] Their big problem was that, as distinct from the Cuban case, Catalan nationalism was not a movement of the downtrodden against overt economic and political discrimination.

Nevertheless, a number of anarchists more closely linked to working-class circles also collaborated with *Avenir* and focused on the need to make anarchism compatible with Catalan identity. These included the anarcho-communist theoretician, Josep Mas Gomeri (who was to be on the Federal Commission of SO in 1908), and well-known anarchist activists like Josep Grau (an important figure in the 4 de Maig group, who would write for *Solidaridad Obrera*) and Joan Usón. Their basic argument was that Catalan workers needed to be addressed in their own language if they were to be won over. This was a more promising terrain because, as stressed in Chapter Two, industrial workers continued to speak in Catalan and retained a sense of regional Catalan identity. Nevertheless, they remained orthodox anarchists; perhaps the only difference between their writings and those of figures like Lorenzo was that they implicitly rejected the notion that 'progress' was linked with Castilian-Spanish cultural homogenisation. They formed an anarchist group called La Tramontana, which in late 1903, and again from August 1907, brought out a paper by the same name written in Catalan (harking back to a publication which had appeared in the late-nineteenth century and attained a wide readership). It is difficult to gauge their overall appeal within anarchist circles. All the indications are, however, that they remained a minority wing, with most publications, from *El Productor* to *Tierra y Libertad*, maintaining a cosmopolitan, overtly anti-Catalanist stance.

During the first decade of the century, Catalan nationalism itself continued to find difficulty in making its mark in industrial working-class circles. Along with the Lliga's right-wing policies, the problem was that most republican Catalanists hailed from solid middle-class families and remained socially rather moderate. Hence, they above all attracted support from those on the fringes of the great industrial conflicts and close to the world of the middle class. This explains why many white-collar workers flocked to the cause, with the biggest office-workers' association, the CADCI, becoming a bastion of radical Catalanist politics.[96]

Yet they found difficulty further extending their base amongst industrial workers. At an institutional level they were only able to garner some support from the Ateneus Obrers. By the 1900s these Ateneus had attained considerable importance, educating around 2,000 children in Barcelona and also holding adult evening classes. However, their political standpoint was a very specific one. They were set up by figures close to the TCV and received financial support from the local authorities and, on occasion, the industrialists themselves.[97] So although one can agree with Josep Termes that the Ateneus showed clear Catalanist sympathies, he is mistaken in the claim that they were representative working-class institutions and that their Catalanism was shared in wider working-class circles. This is indicated by the criticisms to which they were subject by both anarchists and Left republicans.[98]

There could, on the other hand, be more fluidity in relations between Catalanists and the non-Catalanist Left in some areas outside the Catalan capital, where local republican groups often remained independent of Lerroux. Sabadell is a good example. Here the dominant tendency, the Federal Republicans, remained on quite good terms with labour while showing some sympathy for Catalanism. The fact that the woollen textile industrialists remained loyal to the Restoration regime and, hence, that there was no compromise between Catalanism and local elites probably helps explain this. Nevertheless, even here, workers did not mobilise behind an overtly Catalanist party.[99]

In Barcelona, matters improved somewhat in 1906, when a broad alliance called Solidaritat Catalana was forged. It grew in response to an attack by army officers on the offices of two Lliga newspapers in November 1905 and the subsequent decision by the Liberal Government, under severe military pressure, to make all criticism of the army in future subject to military jurisdiction. Its significance was that Catalanism could now be seen as a civic protest movement in defence of individual liberty against the reactionary Spanish state. The indications are that in these circumstances greater numbers of workers became interested in Catalanism and drawn into its cultural networks. This was emphasised in the April 1907 general elections, when the coalition gained around 51,000 votes in Barcelona, as against the 22,000 given to the Lerrouxists, and was victorious in many of the more working-class neighbourhoods.[100]

However, in subsequent years much of this goodwill was frittered away as the coalition fell apart. The main problem was that Catalanist identity remained rooted in the world of the middle class and in a divided society it failed to reach down and mobilise labour along Catalan nationalist lines. The Lliga once again moved rightwards and developed contacts with the Conservative Government of Antonio Maura, while the Catalanist Left still found it hard fully to identify with the demands of industrial workers. Particularly revealing in this respect was the fact that its leaders initially appeared to give their approval to the repression unleashed after anticlerical riots in July 1909. In the May 1910 general elections, they would be eclipsed by the Lerrouxists in those parts of town with the highest percentage of industrial workers. This failure to nationalise Catalan industrial workers meant that while these workers maintained a Catalan regional identity this tended not to be incompatible with an over-arching Spanish identity.[101]

Workers against the State: From the 1902 General Strike to the 'Tragic Week' of 1909

The problems of leftwards learning Catalanists also stemmed from the fact that they aimed to topple the Restoration regime through parliamentary means, at a time when, given its *caciquista* foundations, a peaceful democratic transition was extremely unlikely. The Restoration's lack of popular legitimacy, its limited attempts to reach a broad consensus for its policies, and the perceived need to use force to remove it, meant that protests against the state and its allies were – like many industrial disputes – raw and violent. The non-institutionalised nature of protest was reflected in the repertoires of collective dissent. Workers above all struck at what were perceived as the major symbols of oppression, and used the three major weapons at their disposal: industrial muscle, insurrection and pressure on consumption.

This was evident in both the 1902 general strike and in the anticlerical riots of July 1909, generally referred to as Tragic Week. Despite the fact that the

1902 strike was called in solidarity with the metalworkers it soon became clear that many workers also hoped that the regime might be brought down. In Barcelona large numbers came onto the streets to protest and, in the more popular and working-class quarters, smaller groups became involved in street fighting with the security forces. This was a hazardous undertaking. Press records and an eyewitness account indicate that in the city about thirty-one workers were killed (including one strike breaker), along with a civil guard, a member of the Sometent, and, possibly, a soldier. There were also clashes outside the capital. In the most serious incident, in Terrassa, the Sometent shot two workers dead.

Street fighting was combined with attempts to starve middle-class Barcelona and hence, presumably, force the authorities to compromise. Groups of workers turned back carts laden with food before they reached town, and domestic servants who came in to market, and delivery boys, had food and money taken off them. On occasion this food was then distributed amongst working-class women and children. Furthermore, strikers tried to prevent meat being taken out of the main slaughterhouse, leading to violent clashes with troops and the Civil Guard. Simultaneously, in Barcelona and other industrial towns, booths located on the outskirts, which levied a tax on food entering the town (the so-called *consumos*), were burnt to the ground. This was an accompaniment to all protest movements in the territory. They were seen as the most visible element of an unjust tax regime, which, above all, hit the poor. Women and young lads were to play an important role in these actions. These were the same people who, at the beginning of the strike, were involved in stoning trams and factory windows. As contemporary commentators made clear, they came from the same milieu as the male strikers and street fighters; often they would be family members.

Yet while these tactics certainly put pressure on the authorities they also widened the gap between industrial workers and their families and other social groups. Petty bourgeois sympathisers would have been alienated by attacks on their property. Growing fear of disorder was intensified by the wild language employed. A widely distributed fly-sheet, 'Burgeses: leed y meditad!', no doubt written by the anarchist leadership, informed the authorities that Angiolillo's heroic act (the murder of Cánovas) was not sufficient revenge for the repression they had unleashed since Montjuïc, and that should they continue down the repressive road their motto would be 'an eye for an eye, a tooth for a tooth'.[102] As shown in Chapter Three, elites responded by strengthening the Sometent and looking for new means to re-impose social control.

Despite the fact that the catalyst for the events of Tragic Week was very different, there were many similarities in the way events unfolded. The revolt took place after two years of rising tension following the appointment of Antonio Maura as Conservative Prime Minister in January 1907. There were concerns at the antiliberal implications of a numbers of his policies. As seen in the previous chapter, in 1908 SO launched campaigns against both the suspension of constitutional guarantees and Maura's proposed anti-terrorist law. Criticism was not limited to working-class organisations. Outside Catalonia, the Left formed an alliance against the proposed law, in which the 'official' Liberal Party participated, indicating that in the face of growing social and political strife the cosy Restoration *turno* was starting to break down.[103] Under intense pressure Antonio Maura finally dropped the bill at the end of June 1908. The respite would, however, prove only temporary. The spark that ignited Tragic Week was a flare up of the war in Morocco. From the turn of the century Spain had sought to control the north of the country. The response on the Left was unanimously hostile. Memories of the débâcle of 1898 were fresh in workers' minds and with redemption payments still in operation the country's poorer classes would clearly bear the brunt of the fighting. A crisis situation then developed in early June 1909, when Maura reacted to an attack on a Moroccan railway line by local tribesmen by calling up army reservists. This was a grossly insensitive act. These were men who had been selected for military service but had not yet served; many now had wives and children and their call-up would, therefore, throw their families into poverty.[104]

Protests were held in many Spanish cities, but the greatest repercussions were to be felt in Catalonia, from where most of the reservists were drawn. The first troops began to leave for Morocco from the port of Barcelona on 12 July. As a result, it became the focus for noisy demonstrations against the war. The culmination of this phase of protest came on Sunday 18 July. The soldiers who had to embark were accompanied through the centre of town by a great multitude. Women, especially soldiers' wives, were in the forefront. When the men finally embarked in the midst of a tumultuous throng they were accompanied by cries such as 'Down with the war!', 'Down with Maura, Güell and Comillas!', 'Let the rich, let the mine owners and let the friars go!', and 'you're going to defend a company not Spain!'. This was a reference to the fact that the Comillas-Güell dynasty had invested in mining operations in the colony (along with, it was claimed in left-wing circles, the Jesuits). There was a particularly angry response to the presence of ladies from upper-class families on the quay, giving out religious scapulars, to be worn around the neck. Accompanied by cheering, a number of soldiers threw them into the sea.[105]

The elite, it should be noted, in this and other protest campaigns, was very much personalised in the figures of Maura and the Comillas-Güell dynasty, who were seen as being at the heart of a clerico-business conspiracy to attack Morocco for their own interests. The fact that they had invested in the Moroccan mines and that – as in 1898 – ships from Comillas's shipping line, La Transatlántica, were used for transport, served to further intensify criticism. This was, indeed, the dominant representation of power relations amongst the entire working-class Left and within Lerrouxist republicanism. The high profile of working-class women in these demonstrations was particularly notable. This is explained by Temma Kaplan's argument that women saw their role as above all to be that of 'life providers' within the family and community, and that it was in contexts in which this was put in jeopardy that they took to the streets.[106] Hence also, their central role in the burning of tax booths and, as we shall see in Chapter Eight, street protests against rising prices during the First World War.

Matters became further radicalised on 19 July, when news came through of a bloody confrontation with heavy Spanish casualties. In response there were street protests and clashes between demonstrators and the security forces on the Rambla. The left-Catalanist daily, *El Poble Català*, came out in opposition to the war, but of the Catalan political parties only the Lerroux-ists launched a vigorous protest campaign in Barcelona. They were followed by SO, which planned a series of antiwar meetings throughout Catalonia. The most dramatic took place in Terrassa on Wednesday 21 July, attended by about 6,000 people. There were fiery speeches from the anarchist, Marià Castellote, and by Antoni Fabra Ribas. The public responded with continu-ous ovations, women cried out and there were calls for the war to end. Josep Comaposada was later to state that he had never witnessed anything like it. The final motion, which was unanimously approved, threatened a general strike.[107] Popular outrage had now reached a critical point, and the Govern-ment had to take some action. It chose repression. On Thursday morning, the Minister of the Interior, Juan de la Cierva, prohibited antiwar meetings and ordered the arrest of anyone heard shouting antiwar slogans. The fol-lowing day the Barcelona civil governor, Angel Osorio y Gallardo, suspended telegraphic and telephonic communications with Madrid. Barcelona was now isolated and, as Joan Connelly Ullman has stated, consequent upon the Gov-ernment's action, 'the antiwar protest had either to die or take a revolution-ary turn'.[108]

This again pointed to the difficulties inherent in pursuing a parliamentary route to reform. The Spanish Socialists were put in a particularly uncomfort-able position. They were nervous that any radical resolution would drew an energetic response from the authorities. However, the scale of the protest movement finally made action unavoidable, leading them to call a peaceful general strike from 2 August.[109] This delay meant that the initiative quickly passed to SO. In a secret meeting held on Thursday 22 July, the Federal Commission decided to declare an indefinite general strike on the following Monday. Its ostensible aim was to protest against the war but from the out-set it was hoped that it might spark a Spanish-wide protest movement, which could topple the monarchy. The Catalan Socialists at first argued that SO should wait, given that the PSOE-UGT was to call a nationwide stoppage, but fearful that if they opposed the strike they would, as in 1902, be branded enemies of the working class, they joined in. A strike committee was then formed, made up of the 'rationalist' teacher, Miguel V. Moreno (pseudonym of José Sánchez González), the anarchist activist, Francesc Miranda, and Antoni Fabra Ribas.[110]

Events proceeded in quite a similar fashion to those of 1902. The strike committee informed union leaders from outside the capital of their plans on the Sunday. On the morning of Monday 26 July pickets came out in force. As in 1902, women and young lads played a leading role, with many women wearing a white ribbon to show their opposition to the war. They were to maintain a high profile throughout the week. At first a lot of shopkeepers and businessmen sympathised with the workers' aims and so offered no resis-tance. Those who did risked their shop and factory windows being smashed.

At the same time a ferocious assault was launched on the trams, which left two tram workers dead and eleven wounded. Women – according to Coma-posada, above all factory workers – were again heavily involved.[111] It should not be forgotten that the old tramworkers' union had been pro-anarchist and that from 1904 the trams were operated by blacklegs. Revenge was in the air. By the time they were withdrawn from service in the afternoon the city was at a standstill. Moreover, over the next day or two the strike call was seconded throughout urban Catalonia, including the smaller textile towns.

Martial law was quickly declared, but the forces at the captain-general's orders were inadequate for the task at hand. There were only a limited num-bers of troops and they would not be used until reinforcements began arriv-ing on the Wednesday. This encouraged the insurrectionaries, who, on the Tuesday morning, began putting up barricades in the more working-class quarters. The revolt's base was politically heterogeneous, with young activists close to the Lerrouxists probably predominating. The SO leadership set up its headquarters in a tavern in a back street in the Fifth District, well protected by a sturdy barricade. As in 1902 the revolt was accompanied by attempts to empty the city of food supplies, heavy fighting again taking place around the slaughterhouse. Outside Barcelona, telegraph and telephone lines were cut and train lines blocked, and throughout the territory, inevitably, consumer tax booths were burnt to the ground.

The fact that the protest movement had received wide-ranging left-wing support and that it was aimed directly at the Government explains why the fighting was considerably more intense than in 1902. In an attempt to prise the recruits away from their officers, strikers applauded the soldiers to cries of 'Up with the army, down with the war!' and 'Long live the army, long live Spain!'. They may have had some impact – until the Wednesday fighting was left to civil and security guards – but when reinforcements arrived they quickly proved themselves loyal and entered the fray. Wednesday and Thurs-day, in particular, would see bitter fighting on the barricades. In Catalonia over 100 workers died (about four-fifths of them in Barcelona) along with about seven members of the security forces.[112]

Within the strike committee a considerable degree of consensus on their ultimate goal was achieved. Its members might dream of a social revolution but they soon realised that the one possible option was, in fact, a republic.[113] This once again highlights the ambiguity of the working-class Left's ideology. While anarchists and left-wing Socialists might theoretically disdain a repub-lic, in what looked like a revolutionary conjuncture most saw it as an improve-ment on the Restoration monarchy. In addition, it was clear from the outset that only republicans could provide a wide enough social base to give the movement any chance of success.

Outside Barcelona, revolutionary committees were set up in several towns. Most dramatically, in Sabadell, a revolutionary junta declared a social federal republic on the Tuesday, while troops and civil guards were pinned back in their barracks and at the train station until the following Sunday.[114] Never-theless, Barcelona was the key to future events. On a trip down from his farm-house near the town of Montgat, on Monday 26 July, Francesc Ferrer tried to convince the Radicals to take the lead. The strike committee made efforts along the same lines. Yet, as already noted, the Radical leadership had begun to distance itself from its riotous past. Moreover, with Lerroux out of the country his deputy, Emiliano Iglesias, had no wish to become involved in a movement that he believed had no chance of success. In desperation Fabra Ribas and the Socialists called on the Catalanist republicans to lead the movement, but received the same response. Consequently, the revolt had no clear leadership or sense of direction. When, therefore, large numbers of troop reinforcements arrived in Catalonia on Thursday, and it became clear that the strike had had no repercussions outside Catalonia, it quickly petered out.

By this time dozens of religious institutions had been gutted by fire throughout much of urban Catalonia. In Barcelona, the centre of the destruction, according to the Catholic journalist, Agustí Riera, fifty-nine such buildings were attacked. This was the most shocking of the events of Tragic Week. The first building was actually set alight at Monday lunchtime in Badalona and similar acts were carried out in the neighbourhood of Poble Nou that night. Then on the Tuesday, in the Fifth District, as the barricades went up, more buildings were attacked. That evening families gazed out from their balconies at the great plumes of smoke which rose above the city. Very specific reasons have been adduced for these events. Joan Connelly Ullman points to the role of the Radical Party, arguing that it wished to divert the workers from revolutionary action and took the opportunity to rid itself of competition from Catholic private schools. Lester Golden, on the other hand, maintains that women took the lead in attacking the Church infrastructure and that the key factor was the competition female outworkers faced from convents and religious schools.[115]

These were probably significant factors. A particularly large number of religious schools that taught the poor were put to the torch. Nevertheless, attacks were by no means confined to them. All types of buildings, including neighbourhood churches and convents in which no schooling took place, suffered. Furthermore, although well-known activists in the Radical Party no doubt played a significant role, contemporary sources pointed to the spontaneous nature of the attacks.[116]

I would argue that a more holistic approach is necessary. José Alvarez Junco points to the key importance of left-wing anticlerical propaganda in heightening hatred of the Church.[117] The politicisation of urban Catalan society following the 'Disaster' and the growing strength of the Left meant that it could mobilise against the Church much more effectively. Strong anticlerical sentiment was expressed during the Montjuïc campaign. It was further whipped up between 1899 and 1900 when republicans – with anarchist and Socialist support – launched a campaign against the policies of the 'clerical' Francisco Silvela Government.[118] Indignation was maintained at boiling point by 'clergy-eating' republicans in the popular anticlerical and freethinking press, with José Naken's *El Motín* particularly popular in working-class circles. In addition, the Church was villified in left-wing plays and novels. Most widely read were cheap anticlerical melodramas, which included such offerings as the play, *La monja enterrada en vida o el secret d'aquell convent (The*

Nun Buried Alive or the Secret of that Convent), a great hit in the Odeón Theatre on the Paral·lel.[119] The denigration of the Church reached paranoid proportions. In 1900, for example, Teresa Claramunt claimed to have noted down over 200 reports of attacks by members of religious orders, almost all on children, including rapes and murders.[120]

Yet by focusing on anticlerical propaganda there is the danger of taking too top-down an approach. The liberal-rationalist mirror may have produced a distorted reflection of the place of the Church in Spanish life, but what is remarkable is the enthusiasm with which anticlerical propaganda was received. The reasons for this hostility have already been discussed. Central, I think, was the Church's backward-looking antidemocratic rhetoric and the fact that conservative Spanish liberalism employed it as its first line of ideological defence rather than the secular apparatus of the state. The belief that the Church was the keystone holding the Restoration arch together meant that rather than a 'diversion' many saw the attack on it as a central component in the struggle for a republic. Hence the cries heard from arsonists and from approving bystanders of: 'Out, out ... burn it all. We want the republic', and 'Out with the nuns. Long live the republic!'[121]

The lack of institutional outlets for discontent encouraged the use of violence. This was not a new phenomenon. In July 1899 there were serious anticlerical riots in Barcelona following inflammatory attacks on the clergy in a meeting in favour of the revision of the Montjuïc judicial process. During the rioting an attempt was made to storm the Jesuit convent in Caspe Street and a Catholic girls' school was almost burnt down. There would be nothing else on this scale until 1909. Nevertheless, a large pro-anarchist meeting on 31 March 1901 was followed by another march on Caspe Street and on 1 May a convent belonging to the Maristas' order was broken into and vandalised. Then, in Barcelona during the 1902 general strike, there was an attempt to set the Santa Clara convent alight.[122]

These incidents point to the depth of anticlerical sentiment. No specific organisation was behind it. This can be seen in the run-up to Tragic Week, when the whole of the Left railed against the Church. Then, once the general strike was called, the authorities took such a long time to take control of events that arson attacks could be carried out with virtual impunity. Thus, groups were able to set buildings ablaze without opposition and would often return to finish the job. The arsonists were drawn very largely, if not almost exclusively, from the industrial working class. A well-informed contemporary believed that there could have been up to 10,000 involved in all, although this figure does sound very high.[123] In Barcelona, from the Tuesday onwards, a number of groups, some of which reached over 100 strong, prowled the streets and carried out the attacks; their numbers swelled as they rolled from one institution to the next, working themselves up into an anticlerical frenzy. They were made up of large numbers of women and youths (between about fifteen and eighteen years old) with some older men also involved. The former were no doubt the same people who had come out to stone the trams and enforce the shut-down. Indeed, women were, at least on occasion, the most fanatical, scolding the men if they showed any hesitancy.[124]

The aim of the arsonists was to destroy the wealth of the Church. The religious themselves were not usually harmed. In the cheap novels and newspapers of the day, wild stories had circulated of girls being kidnapped and of nuns kept against their will. Some, no doubt to their bemusement, were informed as they were escorted away that they were being liberated. Male religious were sometimes treated more harshly, with two shot dead, two wounded and one suffocated.

Assaults on buildings were accompanied by few robberies. Indeed, along with a red flag, some barricades had signs with 'the death penalty for thieves' written on them, and there were apparently instances when the arsonists prevented robberies taking place. They wished to make clear that their motives were of a different order. There was, above all, a consuming passion to destroy everything in sight. In convents this even included the orchards and vegetable plots, with vegetables pulled out of the ground and trees uprooted. Within the churches stone images were smashed and the interiors set ablaze, while everything that could burn was thrown onto great bonfires. Barcelona, one of the rioters commented, was being 'purified' by fire.[125] There were outrages. Most notably, fired by anticlerical stories of nuns being tortured and buried alive, in the Jerónimos' convent in the Fifth District the multitude, on finding some mummified corpses bound head and foot, decided to parade them round the streets as proof they had been tortured. One young man was later executed for macabrely dancing with one that he found outside his shop upon leaving work.[126]

As far as the reaction of the locals was concerned, in working-class areas there was a good deal of approval. Crowds gathered, chanted and clapped. A young sacristan from the Jerónimos' convent was later to comment: 'What most disheartened me was seeing that many of the balconies in front were full of people who frenetically applauded the barbaric acts.'[127] Indeed, during this assault onlookers prevented firefighters from reaching the scene. In addition, in a number of instances, members of the religious orders remembered that members of the families, or even persons who had or were attending a religious school, participated in the violence.[128]

In more middle-class areas there were instances of men driving back the arsonists by firing at them from their balcony and shots were fired from within the Jesuits' convent in Caspe Street to ward off an attack (as had been the case in 1899). This was not, however, common. On the other hand, in some towns outside Barcelona the insurrection took on elements of a class war. In Manresa, after three convents had been burnt down, the mayor organised the Sometent to defend the town hall. In the ensuing gun battle one revolutionary and one member of the Sometent were killed. Similarly, in the nearby town of Monistrol, and in Igualada, there were shoot-outs pitching Catholics, the Sometent, Mossos d'Esquadra – county police employed by the Diputacions – and civil guards against the insurrectionaries.[129]

Middle and upper-class Barcelona was traumatised by these events. Claims were made that the insurrectionaries were not real Catalans but a migrant rabble that had fallen prey to anarchist and Lerrouxist propaganda. The attempt by most Catalan nationalists and industrialists to 'ethnicise' social and cultural conflict and therefore avoid addressing real social grievances was, indeed, apparent throughout this period. In addition, the mix of fear and impotency which accompanied the uprising was thereafter transformed into demands for a thoroughgoing retribution. Lluís Muntadas, the president of the FTN and brother of the director of La España Industrial, in a letter to Maura, a personal friend of his, maintained that an 'iron fist' was needed.

Such a state of mind was even shared by the moderate figures on the Catalanist Left. As they did after the 1902 general strike, the business corporations also looked for longer-term solutions, combining demands that the security forces be strengthened with proposals for the formation of 'professional unions', which were seen as a means of establishing employer control.[130] Their deep concern was shared by military circles. The military had very much been turned into an instrument of public order by the Cánovas Restoration, and amongst the officer corps there was fear that it alone stood in the way of social disintegration.[131]

Those who demanded drastic action were not disappointed. The events of Tragic Week strengthened the resolve of what was to became known as the Maurista Right of the Conservative Party to deal with subversion harshly. It was aimed most particularly at those close to SO. Perhaps reacting to information from Catalan elites, the authorities put forward the theory that the uprising had been led by Francesc Ferrer, who, they claimed, led SO. Over 2,000 people were arrested of whom more than 200 would be sentenced by military tribunals. Of these five were executed and fifty-nine given life sentences. Arrests included not only people directly involved but also those whom, the authorities believed, sympathised with or could have provoked the riots. Hence, a climate of fear pervaded working-class Barcelona; one could easily end up in prison as the result of a simple tip-off. Known anarchists and syndicalists were targeted above all. While constitutional guarantees were suspended the Government was empowered to send them into internal exile, even if they were not accused of any specific crime. One hundred and seventy-eight persons suffered this fate, including seventy-eight suspected anarchists (the opportunity also being taken to cleanse Barcelona of 'foreigners' and 'thieves, vagabonds and the like').[132] It was a gruelling ordeal. They were forced to walk between mounted civil guards to their destination, usually small towns and villages in the centre of Spain, and then left to their own devices. Ferrer's family and several associates, including an asthmatic Anselmo Lorenzo, were packed off to Teruel. Teresa Claramunt ended up in Huesca. Many survived because more liberal elements within the towns gave them support.[133] Those who could rapidly packed their bags. The best known fled to France (until the First World War there were no border controls), others changed address or moved town.

Yet the Government went further than this. Not only did it shut down trade-union and Radical centres, it also closed 120 non-Catholic schools, including the moderate Ateneus Obrers, in Barcelona province.[134] This reflected the view on the Conservative Right that the whole radical liberal and socialist milieux operating in urban Catalonia was a threat to order and needed to be eliminated. This did not bode well for the consolidation of democratic institutions. Unless accompanied by a permanent shift to more authoritarian rule it was also counterproductive; sooner or later these establishments would have to be reopened. Ferrer hid in his home but was caught and executed after a military trial. In reality his participation had been limited. He had, as noted, come down to Barcelona on the Monday and tried to convince the Radicals to take the lead. Then, excited by news that the revolt had taken off, on the Wednesday he had attempted to get republicans in Masnou and Premià de Mar, near his farmhouse, to join in. But in fact he was being tried more generically as a dangerous revolutionary, whom the Government and military believed to be behind the attempted assassination of the King in 1906.

It was to be the Government's undoing. There followed an international outcry led by the French Left (which had the effect of deterring any further executions). It was then taken up by the Spanish republicans and Socialists, who, as in the case of the campaign against Maura's antiterrorist bill, were supported by the Liberal Party. In this climate Alfonso XIII concluded that it would be best to sacrifice his Prime Minister. The Maura Government fell on 21 October 1909 and constitutional guarantees were restored soon after. This was a blow to the whole Restoration system. Disgusted by the Liberals' attitude, Maura henceforth refused to cooperate with them, leading his own party to split in 1913. Faced with the chill wind of real politics the official parties were having to appeal to public opinion and take stances on matters on which Spaniards were passionately divided. The outcome temporarily favoured the Left. Storm clouds were, however, gathering. Within upper-class Catalan circles the feeling was growing that the Restoration regime was not protecting their interests sufficiently. Ominously it was a view shared by many army officers. They had identified with Maura's policies and were disgusted by his fall.[135] It was this growing distance from the Restoration regime that was to be at the root of an alliance between officers and industrialists in Catalonia between 1919 and 1923, thereby opening the road to dictatorship.

Conclusions

The period after 1898 saw rapidly escalating protest against the Spanish state. It has been argued that this can be seen in terms of a struggle between the authorities and the left-wing opposition to attain 'hegemony' over civil society.[136] However, the extent to which the state aimed and worked to establish cultural domination is open to doubt. Certainly, one of Cánovas's objectives was to tie elites and the wealthy middle classes to the polity. In this, until 1898 at least, he had considerable success. Yet his intentions with regard to the 'lower orders' were rather different. As noted, the state's exertions in the cultural field were limited. The task of integrating labour was to a large extent left to the Church, which actually proved more rigid than the 'official' parties themselves. Moreover, the reforming impetus of the regime proved weak. Talk of the need to cut the *caciques* down to size and provide new social benefits meant little in practice, while the regime's undemocratic foundations, the country's regressive taxation system, the lack of social spending, the use of the military to quell protests, and the desperately unpopular colonial war, fomented unrest.

It was this failure to instigate any wide-ranging projects of reform that explains why opposition to the Restoration regime was so broadly based in urban Catalonia. On the Left, at a political level it was captained by the republicans, but a key feature of this period was the growing weight of industrial labour within political life. This manifested itself in the 1902 general strike and, above all, during the Tragic Week of 1909. This revolt enjoyed the sympathy of sectors of the liberal petty bourgeoisie, but on the ground was to a large extent a proletarian movement. It was this sense of industrial workers' potential power and destiny that led SO's leading figures to round on Lerrouxism.

These new realities created a complex layering of cosmographies, political identities and class relations. I have stressed that liberal rationalism was taken up on the working-class Left and penetrated deeply into urban popular and working-class culture. This could provide the basis for an interclass reform project, as indicated by the continued widespread equivalence between 'progress' and the republic. Yet bitter social and political conflict would give these ideas a harder, class-based edge. The writing of anticlerical tracts was not the same as workers actually burning down churches. When the latter occurred in 1909, the clerical versus anticlerical divide took on elements of a class war.

Of key importance in the construction of political identities was the neighbourhood. The revolts which accompanied the 1902 general strike and the Tragic Week centred predominantly on the more popular and working-class quarters. They were led by industrial workers but probably enjoyed some sympathy from shopworkers, tradesmen and the like, who lived in close proximity. On the other hand, within middle-class Barcelona the protests were, by and large, denounced. Many middle-class republicans sympathised with goals such as downgrading the role of the Church, but they recoiled from insurrectionary violence.

Such violence was at the heart of workers 'repertoires of collective protest'. In Chapter Three we saw how, in a context in which labour relations remained non-institutionalised, mass mobilisation was used as a tool in industrial disputes. Such considerations also applied within the broader political sphere. Unable to work effectively through the channels of parliamentary government, workers used what syndicalists came to describe as 'direct action' in order to make their voice heard. Anarchism – and, indeed, Lerrouxism – were both dependent on and fed into this environment. Forty years ago, in a study of rural Andalusia, Eric Hobsbawm argued that anarchism was an ideology appropriate to millenarian peasants rather than industrial workers.[137] Whether one agrees with Hobsbawm's depiction of rural Andalusian anarchism or not, his thesis ignores the extent to which anarchism could adapt to city-based movements. This could occur, as in the case of Barcelona, in a context in which street-level protest was the only effective means of applying pressure on industrialists and the state.

The overall political consequences were, however, problematic. Such strategies had the effect of alienating middle-class opinion and gave industrialists ammunition to back up their calls for the state to take tough action. The anarchist-syndicalists could respond in two ways; push ahead with plans for proletarian revolution or link up with other sectors of the Left in an anti-regime alliance. The path they took would be crucial, for, threatened by the working-class Left, the Right would in future prove willing to take drastic steps to preserve, as they saw it, order and stability.

Notes

1. Towards the end of the nineteenth century, state expenditure had not yet reached 10 percent of national income, while between 1850 and 1890 about 27 percent of that income was used to service the public debt and another 25 percent was eaten up by the Ministry of War: see, Gabriel Tortella, *El desarrollo de la España contemporánea*, 350–9.
2. *Anuario Estadístico de la Ciudad de Barcelona* (hereafter, AECB), *1907*, 312–13; 'Resum d'estadístiques', *Gaseta Municipal de Barcelona*, no.23, 10 June 1935, 31–2. However, it should be noted that the situation thereafter improved considerably: by 1915 those not attending school had been cut to probably not much more than 5 percent and in 1920 illiteracy rates in the city were down to 19.6 percent.
3. Nuria Sales, 'Servicio militar y sociedad en el siglo XIX'; Carolyn P. Boyd, *Praetorian Politics in Liberal Spain*, 30.
4. For this section I have used above all, AECB, *1907*, 312–13, *1909*, 206–9, and *1910*, 245–77, along with Albó y Martí, *Barcelona caritativa*, vol.1. For a good overview of Spanish Catholicism see Lannon, *Privilege, Persecution and Prophecy*.
5. Valdour, *Ouvrier espagnol*, 28. For the Ter Valley see, Joaquim Albareda i Salvadó, 'L'escola laica a la Plana de Vic a principis del segle XX'. On working-class religious customs see also, Rosell, *Recuerdos*, 8–16 and 60–1.
6. This is stressed in working-class memoirs: see, Salut, *Vivers de revolucionaris*, 14–19; Montserrat Roig, *Rafael Vidiella, l'aventura de la revolució*, 22.
7. For Catalan electoral data see, Balcells, et al., *Les eleccions generals*, 498. The calculation of the number of working-class electors comes from Romero Maura, *Rosa del Fuego*, 128. For the republicans' political discourse see also, Duarte i Montserrat, *Republicanisme català*.
8. This section is based on a reading of *La Publicidad* (hereafter, LP) during 1899: see also, José Alvarez Junco, *El Emperador del Paralelo*, 133–76.
9. The quotations are taken from a letter to Ferrer in 1899, reproduced in *Causa contra Francisco Ferrer y Guardia instruida y fallada por la jurisdicción de guerra de Barcelona, año 1909*, 399.
10. LP, 8 Sept. 1901.
11. See Culla i Clarà, *Republicanisme lerrouxista*, 40–78; Romero Maura, *Rosa del Fuego*, 125–8 and 326–8.
12. The quotations by Claramunt are from *El Productor* (hereafter, EP), 6 July 1901, 15 April 1905. Ferrers's comments are to be found in V. Muñoz, 'Correspondencia selecta de Francisco Ferrer Guardia', 9.
13. *Tierra y Libertad*, 2 April 1908.
14. *Espartaco*, 11 Nov. 1904.
15. EP, 14 Feb., 4 July 1903, 6 Feb. 1904.
16. José López Montenegro expresses such views in EP, 27 July 1901.

17. Gustavo La Iglesia, *Caracteres del anarquismo en la actualidad*, 292; *La Tramontana*, 4 Dec. 1907.
18. See the reprint, *Natura. Revista Quincenal de Ciencia Sociológica, Literatura y Arte*.
19. Francisco Madrid Santos, 'La prensa anarquista y anarcosindicalista en España desde la I Internacional hasta el final de la guerra civil', vol. 2, 135–245.
20. Salut, *Vivers del revolucionaris*, 81–2 and 153–63.
21. This included figures like Leopoldo Bonafulla, Teresa Claramunt and Francesc Ferrer: see, for example, *Suplemento de La Revista Blanca*, 5 Oct. 1900; EP, 19 Oct. 1901, 9 March 1903, 20 Feb. 1904.
22. Archivo del Conde de Romanones, 96/58; Joaquín Romero Maura, 'Terrorism in Barcelona and its impact on Spanish politics, 1904–1909'.
23. This was the case of all the significant anarchist publications, including *El Productor* and *Tierra y Libertad*.
24. Porcel, *Revuelta*, 54.
25. Before his death Rull accused anarchists and Lerrouxists of being behind the bombings. He gave his 'memoirs' to the Carlist lawyer, Dalmasio Iglesias, and they were read out in parliament: see Connelly Ullman, *Semana Trágica*, 184–6. Yet they are not trustworthy. On two more occasions during this period former anarchists – Miguel V. Moreno and Inocencio Feced – would be turned and then induced to write books or pamphlets accusing their former colleagues. A police informer, Joan Tosas, also operated in the anarchists' midst, and they claimed that he acted as an agent provocateur.
26. For the use of drawings, poems and stories see Clara E. Lida, 'Literatura anarquista y anarquismo literario'; Litvak, *Musa libertaria*.
27. EP, 20 Dec. 1902, 12 Sept. 1903. Francisco Madrid's exhaustive catalogue indicates that at the end of 1902 there were an additional five or six anarchist newspapers: see 'Prensa anarquista', vol. 2, 135–77.
28. EP, 10 Oct., 12 Dec. 1903, 23 Jan. 1904; Cuadrat, *Socialismo y anarquismo*, 92–5.
29. The detailed nature of the surveillance is made plain in *Causa por el delito de rebelión militar, 1909–1910*, vol. 1, 257–9.
30. Plaja, 'Memorias', 4–5.
31. For *La Revista Blanca* see Litvak, *Musa libertaria*, 268. In 1904 the print-run of *Espartaco* (produced by the 4 de Maig group) was about 4,500, and its successor, *El Mismo*, by the same group, sold 1,950 copies in January 1905. In October 1908 *Tierra y Libertad* sold close to 3,000 and *La Tramontana* had to stop publishing in Catalan in late 1907 because it could sell no more than 2,500. *Espartaco*, 2 March 1905; *El Mismo*, 26 Jan. 1905; *Tierra y Libertad*, 29 Oct. 1908; *La Tramontana*, 19 Sept. 1907. This needs to be put in perspective. In Barcelona in 1900 the daily press sold well over 50,000 copies and by 1913 it sold about 200,000: see Borja de Riquer, 'Los límites de la modernización política: el caso de Barcelona, 1890–1923', 29.
32. Angel Pestaña, *Lo que aprendí en la vida*, vol. 2, 17.
33. La Iglesia, *Caracteres del anarquismo*.
34. *Boletín Trimestral de la Biblioteca de El Productor*, in EP, 24 April 1904.
35. *La Ilustración Obrera*, 23 April 1904; Plaja, 'Memorias', 5.
36. Porcel, *Revuelta*, 37–8.
37. I have built up this picture from a reading of *El Productor* and *La Ilustración Obrera*.
38. Salut, *Vivers de revolucionaris*, 80–2.
39. *Anarquía*, 1 Aug. 1906.
40. Fabra Ribas, *Semana Trágica*, 37–9.
41. *Anarquía*, 15 June 1906; *Solidaridad Obrera* (hereafter, SO), 2 Jan. 1908.
42. Francisco Ferrer Guardia, *La Escuela Moderna*, 48–53. This is Ferrer's own account of the school's operation.
43. See the article by Ferrer in *La Huelga General*, 15 Nov. 1901. For Ferrer's educational ideas see also Pere Solà i Gussinyer, *Las escuelas racionalistas en Cataluña, 1909–1939*, 23–7, and Sol Ferrer, *Vida y obra de Ferrer*, 85–6.
44. Ullman, *Semana Trágica*, 162–76; *Juicio ordinario ante los tribunales militares en la plaza de Barcelona contra Francisco Ferrer Guardia*, 10.

45. Culla i Clarà, *Republicanisme lerrouxista*, 109–11; AECB, *1909*, 182–204.
46. Manent i Pesas, *Records*, 15–18; Porcel, *Revuelta*, 37–8; Plaja, 'Memorias', 12–13.
47. Bueso, *Recuerdos*, 20; *La Ilustración Obrera*, 3, 17 Dec. 1904; Porcel, *Revuelta*, 23.
48. Alvarez Junco, *Emperador del Paralelo*, 106–7.
49. Ferrer retained the populist heritage of republicanism and modified his discourse according to the audience. In *La Huelga General* he ('Cero') maintained that the 'republicans aren't revolutionaries, only the general strike will bring the revolution'. Yet in 1906 in a letter to the anticlerical journalist, José Nakens, he stated: 'If we want a revolution and for someone to personify it, that someone is Lerroux.' *La Huelga General*, 15 Feb. 1902; Alvarez Junco, *Emperador del Paralelo*, note 104, 307. Between 1901 and 1903, while union militancy was at its highpoint, he seems to have envisaged a simultaneous anarchist-inspired general strike and a republican uprising precipitating a social revolution.
50. *Publicaciones del la Escuela Moderna*, 1 May 1908, cited in *Boletín de La Escuela Moderna*, ed. A. Mayol, 279; E. Pataud and E. Pouget, *Como haremos la revolución*, 217–22.
51. See the note on the publishing house's aims, probably written by Ferrer himself, in Nicolás Estévanez, *Resumen de la historia de España*, 201–5.
52. These phrases were used by Teresa Claramunt and Francesc Miranda in EP, 13 July 1901, *Tierra y Libertad*, 28 Feb. 1908.
53. Porcel, *Revuelta*, 37–8; Salut, *Vivers de revolucionaris*, 149–64.
54. García Oliver, *Eco*, 120–1; Albert Pérez Baró, *Els Feliços anys vint*, 21.
55. EP, 20 May 1904.
56. Bueso, *Recuerdos*, 52.
57. Valdour, *Ouvrier espagnol*, 304–6.
58. EP, 12 Sept., 12 Dec. 1903, 9 Jan., 4 March, 11 June 1904; *La Ilustración Obrera*, 16 April, 18 June, 23 July, 20 Aug. 1904.
59. Federica Montseny, *Mis primer cuarenta años*, 20–1.
60. *Progreso*, 23 April 1899.
61. See in particular, Romero Maura, 'Terrorism', 143–6; Alvarez Junco, *Emperador del Paralelo*, 288–313.
62. *Causa contra Francisco Ferrer*, 399.
63. *La Revista Blanca*, 15 April 1899.
64. *La Guerra Social*, cited in *El Socialista* (hereafter, ES), 5 July 1901.
65. Alvarez Junco, *Ideología política*, 515–27.
66. The quotations from Reoyo are in LP, 2 July 1899, *Night Edition*. In an anticlerical meeting earlier in the year Comaposada, who was closer to Iglesias, also attacked the 'exploiters supported by Catholic education'. LP, 23 April 1899, *Night Edition*. For the European context see, E.J. Hobsbawm, 'Religion and the Rise of Socialism'.
67. In 1890 Catalonia accounted for 47 percent of the Socialists' 3,782 votes, but in the April 1903 elections Catalans made up only 2 percent of their 14,500 electors. In Barcelona itself they did not even bother to present a candidate. Balcells, et al, *Eleccions generals*, 57–86; Castillo, 'Orígenes', 144–5; ES, 12 July 1903.
68. For the break see, *Suplemento de La Revista Blanca*, 4, 11 May 1901.
69. Culla i Clarà, *Republicanisme lerrouxista*, 53–7.
70. Alvarez Junco, *Emperador del Paralelo*, 310–12.
71. For this campaign see, *Tierra y Libertad*, 22 Nov. 1906; 3, 10 Jan. 1907.
72. EP, 10, 24 June, 1, 29 July, 9 Sept., 14 Oct. 1905.
73. Culla i Clarà, *Republicanisme lerrouxista*, 80.
74. Manuel Cruells, *Salvador Seguí, el Noi del Sucre*, 65–72. However, not all anarchists were supportive of Seguí. *La Tramontana* had backed the Lerrouxists' campaign and was, therefore, angered by his actions. *La Tramontana*, 14 Aug. 1907.
75. Herreros had already produced a pamphlet attacking Lerroux, *Lerroux tal cual es*. He had distanced himself from the 4 de Maig group between 1905–7, perhaps because of their continued links with the republicans.
76. SO, 9 Jan., 26 March 1909. For this campaign I have used SO and the *Boletín del Arte de Imprimir*.
77. Marvaud, *Cuestión social*, 185.

78. LP, 19 April 1909, *Night Edition*.
79. In 1909 the headquarters of the movement was the Laplace school, headed by Ferrer's close associate, José Casasola, and small schools were run by Manuel Villalobos Moreno in Hostafrancs and José Robles in Poble Nou: see Connelly Ullman, *Semana Trágica*, 382; Canals, *Sucesos en España*, 153.
80. *Tierra y Libertad*, 18 June 1908; *La Tramontana*, 14 Aug. 1907.
81. Izard, *Industrialización y obrerismo*, 143–4; Fèlix Cucurull, 'De la revolució monàrquica al "tancament de caixes", *1875–1900*', 246.
82. Solé Tura, *Catalanismo*, 171–94; Riquer, *Lliga Regionalista*, 155–211.
83. See Stefan Berger and Angel Smith, 'Between Scylla and Charybis: Nationalism, Labour and Ethnicity Across Five Continents'.
84. Ametlla, *Memòries*, 240–1; Culla i Clarà, *Republicanisme lerrouxista*, 50–3; Alvarez Junco, *Emperador del Paralelo*, 347–50.
85. ES, 20 Oct. 1899; *Revista Fabril*, 20 April 1900.
86. Foix, *Apòstols*, 264–5; Rosell, *Recuerdos*, 26; Ferrer, *Escuela Moderna*, 36.
87. EP, 13 July 1901; LP, 21 July 1901, *Night Edition*.
88. See the speeches by Ramon Fontanals and Joan Vidal in LP, 8 May 1900, *Night Edition*.
89. *Bakunin on Anarchism*, ed. Sam Dolgoff, 29 and 401–2.
90. Carlos Serrano, 'Anarquismo fin de siglo', 125–76.
91. For anarchism and *modernisme* see Jordi Castellanos, 'Aspectes de les relacions entre intel·lecuals i anarquistes a Catalunya al segle XIX', 7–28; Joan Lluís Marfany, *Aspectes del modernisme*; Xavier Fàbregas, 'El teatre anarquista a Catalunya'; Angel Duarte i Montserrat, *Pere Coromines: del republicanisme als cercles llibertaris, 1888–1896*.
92. *La Revista Blanca*, 1 Dec. 1899.
93. *Avenir*, 4 March, 25 May 1905. On this group see also Foix, *Apòstols*, 264; Porcel, *Revuelta*, 58; Litvak, *Musa Libertaria*, 220–7. Foix mistakenly includes Leopoldo Bonafulla in this group. *El Productor* very much supported the anti-Catalanist line.
94. J. Richardson, *A Life of Picasso*, vol. 1, 153.
95. For Brossa and the Modern School see Pere Solà i Gussinyer, *Francesc Ferrer i Guardia i L'Escola Moderna*, 28.
96. Lladonosa i Vall-llebrera, *Catalanisme i moviment obrer*.
97. See, for example, *Revista del Ateneo Obrero de Barcelona*, 1886–1908.
98. Josep Termes i Ardévol, 'Els Ateneus Populars: un intent de cultura obrera'. For anarchist attacks see, for example, EP, 2 April 1904; *Espartaco*, 25 Nov. 1904.
99. See Esteve Deu Baygual, 'Republicanisme i obrerisme a Sabadell, de 1900 a 1914'; Riquer, *Lliga Regionalista*, 65; Castells, *Informe de L'oposició*, vol. 2, 12.24. Esteve Deu claims that the difference between Barcelona and Sabadell is explained by the higher level of non-Catalan migrant workers in Barcelona. This is not sustainable. As I have already indicated, a high percentage of Barcelona workers were native Catalans: see Chapter Two, 43–7.
100. Porcel, *Revuelta*, 50–1; Balcells, et al, *Eleccions generals*, 468.
101. Comments by labour activists tend to bear this out. For example, in a speech attacking Spanish colonialism in Morocco in 1911, the printer, Joaquín Bueso, affirmed that, 'those who for centuries and centuries fought for their independence have no right to usurp the independence of other peoples. If in the past the Spanish threw the Moors out of Spain, then the Moors have the right to throw out of Africa whomsoever should want to seize it'. SO, 11 Aug. 1911.
102. This section is based on a reading of *El Diluvio*, *El Liberal* and *Las Noticias*, along with, *La huelga general de Barcelona: Verdadera relación de los sucesos desarrollados con motivo del paro general de Barcelona durante la octava semana este año por un testigo ocular*; Larulot, *La gran jornada obrera*; and Ignacio Clarià 'Mi asesinato'. The fly-sheet is reproduced in Riquer, *Lliga Regionalista*, 343–4.
103. For an overview see, Connelly Ullman, *Semana Trágica*, 88–96.
104. Salut, *Vivers de revolucionaris*, 105; Bueso, *Recuerdos*, 29.
105. José Brissa, *La revolución de julio en Barcelona*, 32; Salut, *Vivers de revolucionaris*, 113; José Comaposada, 'Los sucesos de Barcelona I', ES, 29 Oct. 1910, 2–3; *El Poble Català*, 19 July 1909; *El Progreso*, 19 July 1909.

106. Temma Kaplan, 'Female Consciousness and Collective Action: The Case of Barcelona, 1900–1918'.
107. Fabra Ribas, *Semaua Trágica*, 31–2; Comaposada, 'Sucesos de Barcelona I'.
108. Connelly Ullman, *Semana Trágica*, 315.
109. Cuadrat, *Socialismo y anarquismo*, 367–72.
110. Slightly different accounts by participants are to be found in Leopoldo Bonafulla, *La revolución de julio*, 14; Fabra Ribas, *Semaua Trágica*, 35–6; Bueso, *Recuerdos*, 31; José Comaposada, 'Los sucesos de Barcelona, I–IX'.
111. Sastre y Sanna, *Las huelgas …1909*, 29–32; José Comaposada, *La Revolución de Cataluña*, 9.
112. Salut, *Vivers de revolucionaris*, 107; Canals, *Sucesos en España*, 158; Connelly Ullman, *Semana Trágica*, 512–13.
113. Comaposada, 'Los sucesos de Barcelona III', ES, 12 Nov. 1909, 2.
114. Castells, *Informe de l'oposició*, vol. 3, 13.61–74.
115. Connelly Ullman, *Semana Trágica*, 343–505; Lester Golden, 'Barcelona 1909: las dones contra la quinta i l'església'.
116. See, for example, Bonafulla, *Revolución de julio*, 68; Ametlla, *Memòries*, 268; ES, 20 Aug. 1909. This is also the position taken by Romero Maura, *Rosa del Fuego*, 519–20, and Culla i Clarà, *Republicanisme lerrouxista*, 212.
117. Alvarez Junco, *Emperador del Paralelo*, 386–97.
118. Connelly Ullman, *Semana Trágica*, 48–57.
119. Plaja, 'Memorias', 2; Bueso, *Recuerdos*, 36; Salut, *Vivers de revolucionaris*, 101; Comaposada, 'Los Sucesos de Barcelona VI', ES, 3 Dec. 1909, 1–2.
120. *Suplemento de la Revista Blanca*, 5 Oct. 1900.
121. Riera, *Semana Trágica*, 169–71.
122. LP, 3–6 July 1899, 31 March 1901, *Night Edition*; 2 May, *Morning Edition*; ED, 19 Feb. 1902.
123. Riera, *Semana Trágica*, 33.
124. Riera, *Semana Trágica*, 189 and 202–4.
125. Bueso, *Recuerdos*, 40.
126. Valuable inside information is to be found in Salut, *Vivers de revolucionaris*, 97–108; Bueso, *Recuerdos*, 29–47.
127. Riera, *Semana Trágica*, 127.
128. Riera, *Semana Trágica*, 167–71 and 192–3.
129. Riera, *Semana Trágica*, 252–7.
130. There are first-hand testimonies of the reaction in middle-class Barcelona in Ametlla, *Memòries*, 271–2; Amadeu Hurtado *Quaranta anys d'advocat*, vol. 1, 159–63; Pere Coromines, *Diaris i records*, vol. 2, 105. Soledad Bengoechea deals with the industrialists' reaction in 'Els dirigents patronals i la Setmana Tràgica'.
131. Boyd, *Praetorian Politics*, 21; Sebastian Balfour, *The End of Spanish Empire, 1898–1923*, 164–87.
132. The most detailed statistics are in Canals, *Sucesos*, 206–86. See also Riera, *Semana Trágica*, 279–82.
133. Bonafulla, *Revolución de julio*, 101–12.
134. Connelly Ullman, *Semana Trágica*, 507.
135. Boyd, *Praetorian Politics*, 21.
136. Radcliffe, *From Mobilization to Civil War*, 1–15.
137. Hobsbawm, *Primitive Rebels*, 74–92.

6

THE FOUNDATION OF THE CNT, 1910 TO 1914

The years between 1910 and 1914 represent a little known chapter in the history of Catalan trade unionism and the anarchist-syndicalist movement. The one element that is always stressed is that 1910 saw the formation in Barcelona of a new Spanish anarchist-syndicalist union confederation, the CNT, which, from 1916 onwards, would compete both aggressively and effectively with the Socialist UGT for working-class support throughout Spain. The period is usually portrayed as representing a significant degree of continuity with the first decade of the century, before the sharp break provoked by the economic boom and escalating 'labour wars' that accompanied the First World War. In this chapter I shall analyse whether this was in fact the case, or whether, on the contrary, many of the key elements of the intense labour strife of the period between 1917 and 1923 were already gestating within Catalan society. As part of this endeavour, I shall examine the new Catalan-based labour confederation in rather more depth than has hitherto been the case, focusing on both its ideology and strength within the labour movement.

Union Organisation and Social Strife, 1910 to 1911

The months following the fall of Maura saw a great mobilisation in favour of an amnesty. It was initiated by the anarchist-syndicalists, but gained the support of Socialists and republicans, most particularly the Radicals. The Lerrouxist leadership was especially keen to adopt a high profile in order to draw a veil over their less than heroic actions during Tragic Week itself. The strength of grass-roots feeling quickly became apparent, with the protests culminating in a massive demonstration of 90,000 in the streets of Barcelona on 16 January 1910. The demonstrators' silence, broken only by the occasional clapping of hands, and the order in which it was conducted, left a lasting impression. The young syndicalist, Adolfo Bueso, was later to comment that 'it was so big that nothing like it was ever to be seen again, even during the [Second] Republic'.[1] Later in the month the new Liberal Government responded by conceding a partial amnesty. It left out many prisoners and exiles, but took the wind out of the campaign's sails. With a much broader amnesty in November many of the most prominent anarchist-syndicalist activists could once again operate openly.

The campaign brought out a number of important features of Barcelona left-wing politics. It again emphasised that when 'progress' and 'liberty' were at stake cooperation between the different sectors of the Left was possible. Indeed, as was the case in the run up to Tragic Week, their analysis of the state and its evils was indistinguishable. Both anarchist-syndicalists and Radicals saw the enemy as 'clericalism, the bourgeoisie in its most abominable manifestation, the plutocracy and its dynastic interests', and maintained that the Maura government had been 'engendered by the Vatican and [was] led by Jesuits'.[2] The meetings and demonstrations also indicate the social base of radical anticlerical and insurrectionary politics. Newspaper sources agreed that most of those present were industrial workers, but that there were also others, who 'belonged to all the social classes'.[3] This reflects the fact that while workers were most receptive, the tradition of free thought and anticlericalism attracted a sector of lower-middle and middle-class opinion.

The experience of Tragic Week no doubt served to sharpen antidynastic and antimilitarist feeling in working-class circles, but the resurgence of anarchist-syndicalism in the following months was based on a rapidly improving economic climate. This made possible, from the spring of 1910 onwards, a union reorganisation combined with a great surge in strike action (see table 3.1.). To a large extent it affected workers from the same trades and industries as at the turn of the century, who began re-articulating their local, Catalan and Spanish federations, many of which had ceased to function. There was, however, an important new player on the scene. Since the early 1900s, when an attempt to unionise the railway workers had been broken, they had remained very much under the thumb of the big companies. But, from 1909 onwards, the UGT began to make inroads and in the spring of 1910 was the driving force behind the formation of a Catalan Section, which first penetrated the workshops and warehouses of the stations of El Clot and Poble Nou and then began to recruit in other parts of Catalonia. By early 1911 it had over 1,000 members.[4]

Yet the most dramatic conflicts once again affected metalworkers and dockers. A Metalworkers' Union, founded in 1905, had only 300 members in 1909, but from the spring of 1910 it launched a recruitment drive and by August had seen its membership rise to 2,200. On the docks, the coal unloaders were, from the first time since 1903, able to challenge their employers and form an independent union, which by the end of July 1910 had 1,305 affiliates. As in 1903, they received strong support from the carters, who had already rebuilt their union, and together with a number of smaller port unions they set up a new Federation of Waterfront Unions in December, with about 7,000 members.[5] From the spring onwards they began testing the waters. The carters were largely successful in a series of disputes in which they demanded union recognition, job security and limitations on the tasks they had to perform. Then, in July, the coal unloaders launched a strike in which they also achieved union recognition, preference for the employment of unionised men, and the agreement of the coal merchants to enter into collective bargaining.

During this year the growth of union organisation, to a degree at least, caught industrialists by surprise. Of the thirty-two strikes which involved more than twenty workers, twelve ended in victory, nine with a compromise and eleven in defeat. Nevertheless, the relatively high number of defeats indicates that employers were now rather better prepared than they had been in 1900. Moreover, they were quickly able to marshall their forces and counter-attack; in 1911 (not including a number of solidarity strikes which had no impact on the workers concerned) only two strikes involving more than twenty workers produced victory, while three ended in compromise and fourteen were lost. Most painful of all, violent industry-wide stoppages in metal-working and on the waterfront were broken and the unions totally undermined, thereby to an important degree putting into reverse the union revival.

The first big defeat, in the autumn of 1910, looked in many respects like a re-run of the metalworkers' strike of 1901 to 1902. The workers demanded a nine-hours day, union recognition, and that all disputes in progress should be resolved on terms favourable to the workers. Faced by a number of employer provocations, the union then brought out over 8,000 workers on 12 September. The progress of the dispute once again serves to illustrate the relationship between industrial structure, employer strategy and the workers' ability and willingness to unionise. On the one hand, as in 1901, it proved very hard to mobilise the big factories in the Barceloneta and Poble Nou areas. They seconded the strike when 1,500 strikers marched into the area on 13 September, but after the intervention of the police most returned to work over the following week. On the other hand, the strike brought out the distance between the worlds of capitalist and petty manufacture. Figures produced by the civil governor's office indicated that the strike had affected 180 of the city's 326 metalworking establishments and that at its highpoint 9,000 of the city's 11,600 metalworkers had downed tools. Thus, the average number of workers per factory in those factories in which there was a strike was fifty, while in the workshops in which the strike had no impact the average number of workers was little over five. The republican daily, *El Diluvio*, described the latter as 'small workshops in which the owner works with a few apprentices'. The owners of these premises in general refused to join the employers' association and most of the workers were not unionised. Many of the former granted a nine-hours day, according to the employers' association because they only did repair work and did not face foreign competition, but, dramatically, their workers refused to support the men out on strike. They clearly inhabited a separate social and cultural space.[6]

As in 1901 and 1902, the employers' association – with the support of the FTN – remained totally intransigent and encouraged the authorities to put the strike down, stating that it had been provoked by 'a commission with no relation to the workshops and factories' and that it was, therefore, a 'problem of public order'. Simultaneously, faced with growing worker protest, employers looked further to strengthen their organisations. Crucially, in early September a new Barcelona Employers' Federation was founded, based on the metal, construction and woodworking industries. The union, on the other hand, was willing to negotiate. At the end of October, to the chagrin of SO, it agreed that the Institute for Social Reforms should look into the viability of a nine-hours day if the industrialists would, in the meantime, agree to a fifty-six hours week, but the proposal was turned down.[7]

As a result, the metalworkers faced an uphill struggle. From October there was a slow drift back to work and by the end of November they were in a desperate situation. In was then that violence flared. There were clashes with non-strikers and the security forces, in which firearms were frequently used. Some of these confrontations were spontaneous, but anarchist-syndicalist gunmen also began specifically targeting strikebreakers. At least eleven workers suffered gunshot wounds and two died (one an anarchist-syndicalist, the other a strikebreaker). Moreover, attacks were launched on foremen, employers and members of the security forces. A security guard was shot dead, two foremen were killed, one shot and the other stabbed, an employer was shot and wounded, and a director was injured in a stabbing. As a result of the attacks and clashes over sixty arrests were made. La Maquinista, viewed as the union's foremost foe, was in the front line, with its director, Ernesto Tous, badly hurt in the above mentioned knife attack.[8] The man responsible for this assault was the secretary of the Metalworkers' Union, Ramon Archs, the son of an anarchist executed in 1894. Archs was imprisoned, but acquitted before fleeing to France. As we shall see, he would return to play a leading role in the Barcelona labour wars between 1919 and 1922.

These attacks can in part be explained in terms of the harshness of labour relations in Barcelona. In addition, as already noted, some anarchists justified assassinations. The employer associations reacted by criticising the 'impunity enjoyed by those who incite assassinations in meetings'.[9] They were furious that they were being targeted, but also used the attacks to demand more wide-ranging repression. In subsequent years this would be an oft-repeated scenario. This was why the attacks were strategically so counterproductive, making it much more difficult for the authorities to maintain an even-handed approach.

Anarchists were later to claim that they were encouraged because employers reacted by giving way. On this occasion at least this was not the case. As in 1902, with defeat looming, there were calls by anarchist-syndicalists for a general solidarity strike, but they were resisted, perhaps because the consequences of the 1902 strike were still vivid in people's minds. Matters were made worse because the Government took an increasingly hard line. The Liberal Prime Minister, José Canalejas, saw himself very much as a reformer. Between 1910 and 1912 he would try (unsuccessfully) to limit the power of the religious orders, he modified the *quinta* system, forcing middle-class youngsters to do a period of military training, and he abolished the *consumos*.

However, he combined this with a staunch defence of the political system, distinguishing between legitimate 'economic' and illegitimate 'political' strikes, and was quick to come down hard on what he perceived as subversive threats.[10]

At first he viewed the strike as an economic dispute and, much to the chagrin of the employers, instructed the civil governor to take an equidistant stance. This led the industrialists to contact the captain-general of Barcelona, Valeriano Weyler, who sympathised with their position and at one point promised to declare martial law.[11] This reflected the army's view of itself as the guarantor of public order against subversion and was a first intimation of what would, over the following ten years, become a key aspect of Barcelona's political life: the establishment of an alliance between business and the military to crush the labour movement in defiance – if necessary – of civilian authority. On this occasion, matters were resolved when at the beginning of November, one suspects buckling under pressure from the military and industrialists, the Government changed its position. It brought in a new civil governor, Manuel Portela Valladares, who took a much tougher stance, having the union's central and strike committees prosecuted following a reference made at a meeting to the need to rob jewels from churches in order to feed the workers. As a result, by December 1910 the union was left with no alternative but to call the strike off. There followed the routine sackings of union activists, with over 1,000 workers losing their jobs.

Defeat on the waterfront quickly followed. On the docks, tension was high because the coal unloaders had broken the monopoly of the coal merchants' friendly society, the Germandat de Sant Pere Pescador, to which, until the July 1910 strike, the workers had to belong. A major dispute was precipitated when the new union overplayed its hand and called for a number of changes to working practices. Underlying its demands was the impact of the modernisation of the port of Barcelona in recent years. An oversupply of hands had already been a problem at the beginning of the century, but it was exacerbated by the construction of larger wharfs that allowed ships to dock sideways and the greater use of unloading equipment. In negotiations the union had already called for an eight-hours day, and for unloading equipment only to be used when six or more ships were in dock. Faced with the coal merchants refusal to budge, on 9 December it then gave the order that ships not moored 'correctly' and ships unloaded with the use of equipment be boycotted. There then followed a rapid escalation of hostilities which culminated in a strike.

Despite solidarity strikes by carters and other dockers' unions it was defeated. As in 1903, its Achilles Heel proved to be the ease with which blackleg labour could be recruited, a fact which also led the dispute to become increasingly violent. The union made a last desperate attempt to reach a settlement by putting negotiations in the hands of a number of prestigious 'neutral' figures, but the coal merchants scented victory. When the strike was finally called off on 19 January 1911 most of the strikers were unable to find work. As a result, the unloaders' union was shattered. Moreover, the carters also found that when they wished to return to work many of their places had been taken. They stayed out for a further month – during which time violence also flared and a number of employers were shot at – before being forced back; not only was their union almost totally destroyed but their employers followed the lead of the coal merchants and set up their own friendly society.[12]

Events on the waterfront once again showed how difficult it was for unskilled workers to unionise effectively when faced with tenacious employer resistance. The combined result of this string of defeats was that, in early 1911, union membership in Barcelona was overall probably little higher than it had been in 1909. Outside Barcelona the situation was no better. In cotton textiles, unions represented small pockets in a large sea.[13] The situation in Sabadell woollen textiles was better. In 1910, in the context of a growth in sales of woollen garments, the industry's unions recruited new members, including affiliates from the big Seydoux plant, which – as seen in Chapter Three – had already been at the centre of a general strike in 1899.[14] However, as in Barcelona, a heavy strike defeat would soon follow. Union encroachment on the Seydoux factory produced the spark. In response, the Seydoux factory sacked several union activists. The Sabadell labour federation, the FOS, then called an all-out strike in the factory and demanded that it come into line with working practices in the rest of the town. The problem was that the workers recruited in 1899 refused to come out, leaving the dispute to become increasingly radicalised. Under the committed anarchist-syndicalist, Bru Lladó, the FOS launched a boycott of industrialists who had dealings with the Seydoux factory. This was very much in line with tactics propounded by the French revolutionary syndicalists, but had the disadvantage that it brought the rest of the town's industrialists – who did not sympathise with the French factory – into the front line. Despite the fact that many woollen workers, who worked in well-unionised 'strong houses', were opposed to Lladó's strategy, he responded to an employer lock-out with a general strike and suggested that the CNT call a revolutionary general strike during its Founding Congress at the beginning of November.[15]

He did not receive a positive reply, but in any case the issue was made academic when, at the same time as it took action against the metalworkers, the Government launched a full-scale assault on the Sabadell union leadership. Leading activists were arrested for their utterances in favour of a general strike and the FOS headquarters closed, precipitating a return to work. Not everyone was readmitted; with, according *El Trabajo*, 500 families subject to a 'hunger pact'. Several days later, in the Spanish parliament, José Canalejas defended the use of force, stating that he had to intervene when 'those people [i.e., the anarchists], who are not workers ... but exploiters of the working class' tried to take the movement over. The Lliga MP, Josep Bertran i Musitu, for his part lamented that the authorities had been too soft on the metalworkers.[16] The attitude of the person who was regarded as the regime's major reforming figure, and of the principal party of the Catalan Right, boded ill for the future stability of Catalan labour relations.

The Foundation of the CNT, 1910 to 1911

After the repression which followed Tragic Week, SO was able to hold its first meeting on 18 December 1909 and its newspaper reappeared the following February. Then, in the spring, thanks to the union reorganisation, it began to grow quite rapidly. While it probably had only around 4,500 members in Barcelona in November 1909, by March 1910 the figure had reached between 11,000 and 11,500. Just as important, this growth produced a strong sense of dynamism and optimism amongst its leading figures.[17] As in the years 1899 to 1903, the intensification of social strife also thrust SO to the forefront of labour protest.

This no doubt emboldened the anarchist-syndicalist leadership. It did not allow Socialists back onto the organisation's Federal Commission and this, together with growing labour militancy, explains why the organisation took a more radical line than during 1907 to 1909. First, it decided to push ahead with a scheme to form a national confederation. A national Founding Congress was quickly organised and held in SO's headquarters, the Barcelona Workers' Centre, between 31 October and 1 November 1910. It was open to all unions that wished to attend but was not, in fact, a very impressive affair, with one hundred and eight unions and six local federations directly represented, of which seventy-six unions and five local federations were Catalan (forty-two unions from Barcelona). Only a handful of delegates from outside the territory were actually present. Given this balance of strength it was, understandably, agreed that the headquarters of the CNT should be based in Barcelona and that its unions should elect the leadership.

Many similarities could be discerned with the turn-of-the-century anarchist movement. Once again the anarchist-syndicalists' fierce egalitarianism came through. They laid great emphasis on the need to integrate all sectors of labour, including the most marginalised and downtrodden, and created an invalids' union (an important number of whom were workers injured in industrial accidents) during 1910.[18] The basic structure of the new confederation was also similar to that of its predecessors, with the Founding Congress agreeing to set up Spanish 'federations of crafts and similar crafts', to which the CNT's First Congress, held the following year, added local, *comarcal* and regional confederations, which would integrate all the affiliated unions within a particular area. Nevertheless, the emphasis on federations of similar trades probably indicated the influence of French syndicalist thinking on the need to form industrial unions. Such influence could also be seen in the decision to follow the lead of SO and charge membership dues, which were set at a similar level to those of the UGT.[19]

In addition, the Federal Commission hardened its ideological stance, exacerbating tensions within the Catalan organisation. As in 1907 to 1909 these continued to focus on the interpretation of syndicalism. Two opposing views were debated within the Syndicalist Athenaeum and in the pages of the anarchist-syndicalist press. The clearest exponent of a more moderate reading was Joaquín Bueso, a compositor by trade and an ex-Lerrouxist, who was put in charge of *Solidaridad Obrera* (as the confederation's newspaper was still called) in December 1910. In line with the resolutions approved at the CGT's Chartre d'Amiens, he argued that Socialists and anarchists should work together within the unions, and that these should remain politically neutral so as to group together the greatest number of workers possible. He also felt that workers who defended *el sindicalismo a base múltiple* should be allowed into the CNT. This might, he admitted, at first reduce revolutionary enthusiasm, but it would serve to integrate workers who might otherwise fall by the wayside, and who would, in any case, be radicalised by daily experience of the class struggle. Bueso, then, wished to maintain the broad trade-union front represented by SO. His stance also implied that the CNT should continue to place emphasis on the need to strengthen the unions and not be carried away by revolutionary adventures.[20]

Bueso was opposed by the anarchist-syndicalist revolutionaries. In the pages of *Solidaridad Obrera* the case against was taken up by the 'rationalist' teacher, Félix Monteagudo, who maintained that, on the contrary, within the unions it was the role of the 'anarchist-socialist' to 'lead the workers to direct, revolutionary, action'.[21] The corollary of this was the argument put forward by Manuel Andreu, an electrician who wrote regularly for *Tierra y Libertad*, that syndicalism was simply anarchist doctrine applied to the economic sphere.[22] Monteagudo's position was, as would be expected, backed by the movement's theoretical heavyweights. For example, in several pamphlets published between 1910 and 1913, Anselmo Lorenzo stressed that it was the role of the politically-aware workers (*obreros conscientes*) to inspire the 'apathetic mass'.[23] Similar statements were made in the works of CGT activists translated into Spanish, who hailed from the more pro-anarchist wing of the French confederation.[24] It was a stance underwritten by *Tierra y Libertad*, under the directorship of Tomás Herreros from 1910 to 1911. This was important because as Spain's premier anarchist publication, whose circulation had grown to around 10,000 (a significant percentage of which was sent abroad), it reached a wider audience than *Solidaridad Obrera* itself.[25]

Within broader union circles opinion was more mixed. As we shall see, there would be widespread concern at the leadership's impulsive actions. Yet its stance could find favour amongst union activists in the more conflict-ridden trades, whose experience was generally that a committed minority of workers carried the burdens of organising the unions and carrying strikes. Hence the carpenter, Joan Pey – a leading figure in the Catalan CNT from about 1916 – claimed in 1911 that there was no need to wait until the trade was strongly unionised before taking strike action, because the *obreros conscientes* would bring the rest out.[26] Such attitudes explain why anarchist-syndicalist activists linked to the CNT continued to belong to anarchist affinity groups, which they saw as playing an important coordinating role. In 1913 they formed a Catalan Federation of Anarchist Groups, which, in February 1914, comprised at least ten affinity groups.[27] These disputes were not just a matter of theory. They also revolved around the location of power within the confederation – with anarchist-syndicalist activists claiming the right to lead the movement – and also its future direction. The hard-liners' victory would mean that, as against Bueso's stress on the need to build an all-inclusive union, they would construct a narrower, more overtly revolutionary movement.

The position taken by the Federal Commission over this question was therefore of the utmost importance. In the first months of 1910 its composition was very unsettled. A degree of continuity was only achieved when, in July, José Negre, a typographer from Valencia, took charge. Nevertheless, its ideology remained constant. With no Socialist input, it unrestrainedly extolled the virtues of direct action, but, in terms of which Bueso would approve, it maintained the myth that the organisation was ideologically neutral because it simply defended workers' interests. Hence, it stated that it was made up of workers of diverse political viewpoints, even those who practised *la base múltiple*, who, it hoped, would be convinced of the superiority of direct action tactics.[28] Yet, it also argued that it was the task of the *obreros conscientes* to guide the unions towards revolution. This clearly put it on the side of the anarchist-syndicalist theoreticians, like Prat and Lorenzo. Moreover, in classical syndicalist terms, it was agreed at the CNT's Founding Congress that the revolution would be ignited by a revolutionary general strike; an inevitably violent confrontation between the workers and the bourgeois state.[29] This marriage of the anarchist concept of the revolutionary elite and the syndicalist doctrine of the leading role of the unions in the destruction of capitalism, which would, in the 1920s, become known as anarcho-syndicalism, remained dominant within the CNT throughout the rest of the period under study.

The radicalisation of SO's ideology and the decision to found the CNT, which would inevitably compete with the UGT for working-class support, led relations with the Catalan Socialists to become increasingly tense. After Tragic Week the Socialist weekly, *La Internacional*, was closed down, and Fabra Ribas forced into exile. They were not to be without a publication for long. Reus was becoming an increasingly important branch within the regional party and from November 1909 the Reus Socialists brought out their own publication entitled *La Justicia Social*. The significance of Reus was confirmed in December of the following year when a congress held to reform the Catalan Socialist Federation decided that its headquarters should be located in the town, with *La Justicia Social* as its mouthpiece.

The reaction of the supporters of Fabra Ribas – who included most of the Socialists from his home town of Reus – to the anarchist-syndicalists' plans to set up the CNT was, at first, to try and engineer a compromise. Thus, in the spring of 1910, *La Justicia Social* argued that while SO was more active than the UGT, and did not suffer from the latter's excessive centralism, it was more sectarian and lacked the UGT's practical organisational spirit. In such circumstances a fusion would bring out the best of both.[30] Yet such a possibility was remote. The Madrid-based Socialist leadership had no intention of losing control of the UGT and the Catalan anarchist-syndicalists confirmed in June that they were committed to setting up an alternative national body. At the CNT's Founding Congress they stated that they did not want to cross the UGT and that they envisaged a possible future unification, but this sat uneasily with their commitment to direct action and the general strike.[31]

La Justicia Social subsequently fell silent on the issue, while arguments over whether unions should adopt direct action or *la base múltiple* raged in the anarchist-syndicalist and Socialist press. From his French exile Fabra Ribas, backed by the leader of the French Socialist party, Jean Jaurés, called on the Catalan Socialists to stay on board.[32] This advice was not taken. The heterodox supporters of Fabra Ribas stayed away from the CNT's Founding Congress, leaving it to a group of Catalan 'Pablista' Socialists – that is supporters of the strategy advocated by the PSOE-UGT's leader, Pablo Iglesias – to fight a rearguard action to try and abort its birth. Shortly afterwards, at the Catalan Socialists' 1910 regional conference, the decision was taken to leave the newly formed CNT.[33] One suspects that Fabra Ribas's sympathisers were loathe to consummate an inevitable break with the PSOE-UGT and felt distinctly uncomfortable at the prospect of forming the minority wing of an increasingly radicalised pro-anarchist confederation. This decision would be of key importance in the future development of Catalan Socialism. They would be saved an uphill battle over the future direction of the CNT, but would also be isolated from Catalonia's largest labour organisation.

The Catalan Socialists were not only worried by the radicalisation of SO's discourse during 1910. The biggest difference with the years 1907 to 1909 was that the new social climate encouraged the anarchist-syndicalist leadership to put its ideas into practice and organise solidarity strikes. Once again the vista of the revolutionary general strike swung into view. The first two such strikes were called on 27 July and 5 September 1910 in support of the Vizcayan mineworkers. The first attempt had a very limited echo. In September the atmosphere was somewhat more favourable, but only about 5,000 workers downed tools in Barcelona, and the strike had no impact in the rest of Catalonia. Yet, undeterred by these failures, the Barcelona CNT continued down the same path. In October it offered to declare a general strike in support of the Barcelona metalworkers. Then, in January 1911, it called another general strike, this time in favour of the coal unloaders, which yet again had little impact. Indeed, only the Sabadell FOS was rebuffed when it called for a general strike in support of the woollen textile workers during the CNT's Founding Congress, perhaps because the delegates feared that the confederation would be declared illegal.[34]

Strong parallels could be seen with the situation at the turn of the century, with the leadership trying to declare general strikes at each and every possible opportunity. The idea propagated increasingly widely in French syndicalist circles, that the CGT had to build up its strength before any revolutionary movement could be launched, and that they could only reach this point by first winning a whole series of localised disputes, had clearly not found wide-ranging favour. Josep Prat – in the tradition of the Sabadell FOS during the first decade of the century – put this argument forward. He also pointed out that in Spain the peasantry had to be incorporated into the union movement before a revolutionary general strike could be successful, but both Tomás Herreros and Anselmo Lorenzo continued to look down upon mere 'economic' disputes and believed that a vociferous protest movement could ignite the revolution. The latter argument was put most effectively by Antonio

Loredo, a Galician barber, who had spent a number of years in Latin America. On his return, around 1905 or 1906, he had joined the 4 de Maig group and was now making a considerable impact in anarchist circles. The economy was now in crisis, he argued, and workers were no longer in a position to make short-term gains. In these circumstances it was the job of the syndicalists to go on the offensive, generalise strikes and carry through the revolution.[35] These different attitudes between the CGT and CNT sprang from the diverse trajectories of the two confederations. The CGT had grown very considerably, but its revolutionary impetus had been knocked by a series of defeats between 1905 and 1909. In response, some leading figures, fearing for the confederation's survival, took a more cautious approach and began to see revolution as a rather more long-term affair.[36] On the other hand, within Catalonia there had been little opportunity for the emergence of a more stable leadership, who might feel that they had a stake in the organisation and wished to build it up.

There were a number of reasons behind the failures of the attempted general strikes. First, the overall strength of Barcelona trade unionism should not be exaggerated. In September 1910 there were still only between 25,000 and 30,000 workers unionised in the city, and numbers declined thereafter. Second, on his return from Argentina in October 1909, Lerroux set about trying to build a Spanish party of the centre left, which would appeal to a greater degree to the middle classes. Hence, he further moderated his tone and the Radicals actively opposed the strikes. This had, as the anarchist-syndicalists admitted, a considerable impact within working-class circles.[37] Last but by no means least, there was dissention within CNT ranks. The moderate republican daily, *La Publicidad*, maintained that the July 1910 general strike was launched by anarchists, and opposed by, 'the healthy elements within Solidaridad Obrera'. It returned to the same theme in October, when it commented on the 'mutual distrust between the anarchists and the trade-union elements, who are in dispute over control of the centre'.[38]

Such concern was widespread within the organisation. *La Justicia Social* affirmed that the September 1910 general strike failed because the confederation's largest unions, 'opposed an idea which could not succeed because the atmosphere was inappropriate'.[39] Moreover, in October the striking metalworkers rejected the proposal that a general strike be declared on their behalf because of the possible repressive consequences. Lerrouxists had considerable influence within the union and it seems that they orchestrated the opposition. Then, in January 1911, the CNT' Federal Committee (as it was now called) decided to go ahead with its general strike on the waterfront despite objections from the carters. Tensions were reflected in criticism within *Solidaridad Obrera* of the metalworker and waterfront strikes, which, it claimed, had been lost because the unions had sought the help of 'mediators' and had not, therefore, employed direct action.[40] As the sections on these strikes make clear, these comments were extremely short-sighted and indicate that the leadership's ideology was blinkering their view of grass-roots reality. A divide was opening up between men like Negre, who took a voluntarist, short-term revolutionary stance, and important sections of the membership.

Discontent over the direction the CNT was taking impacted on membership figures. In the rest of Spain, between 1910 and 1911, it had made some strides, affiliating small but not insignificant groups, above all in Andalusia, Aragón, Asturias and Valencia. Yet in Catalonia itself, during 1911, it was forced on the back foot as opposition to the leadership's strategy, and, most probably, fear of being ensnared in a government backlash, led a number of unions to break away.[41] In Barcelona, between 1910 and 1911 between forty-two and forty-five unions were affiliated, no more than were affiliated to SO in July 1909. In 1911 meetings of the local federation mustered an average of only around thirty delegates. Until the end of 1910 the total membership rose, but the defeats of the big strikes in the metal industry and on the waterfront threw this into reverse; in September 1911 the Barcelona CNT had just 7,666 affiliates, less than SO had had during 1909 and comprising well under half the city's unionised workforce.[42] This narrowing of support could also be seen in terms of personnel; not only did the Socialists leave, but a disillusioned Joaquín Bueso also resigned to form part of the Catalan PSOE at the end of 1911. Somewhat more impressive were sales of the CNT's newspaper, which stood at 7,000 in September 1911 (up from 4,500 a few months previously, no doubt because once SO became a national confederation the number sent outside Catalonia greatly increased), but this hardly made it a mass circulation weekly.[43]

Furthermore, the instability of these years meant that the confederation was not in a position to build a strong cultural base. The Syndicalist Athenaeum, located in the CNT's headquarters in central Barcelona (until May 1911, a smaller centre than Ferrer's funds had allowed them to rent during 1908 and 1909), and a Sant Martí Workers' Centre, based in El Clot, in which anarchist-syndicalists were dominant, organised regular talks, but, as previously, these would have largely been preaching to the converted. This was also the case of the Teatro Español *tertulia*, which was still going strong. The Syndicalist Athenaeum also managed to put on a series of plays in local theatres and carry out a few meetings outside the city, but the impact was probably not very great. Moreover, following the collapse of the Modern School, unions did not have sufficient resources to sustain any 'rationalist' schools. There was an attempt to re-build specifically anarchist cultural associations – groupings or centres of rationalist culture as they were now referred to – but only two, one in Sant Andreu and the other in Poble Nou, actually operated, the first without its own headquarters.[44]

In the rest of Catalonia the situation was worse. In September 1911 the CNT had only 4,159 Catalan affiliates from outside Barcelona. In particular, it had lost the backing of unions from Manresa, Vic and the Ter, Mataró and the Maresme, Reus and Sitges, where the Socialists and independent trade unionists were influential. Hence, support was now limited to workers from several industrial towns in Barcelona province, most notably Terrassa and Sabadell (although it temporarily lost its union base in Sabadell after the strike defeat of 1910), followed by Badalona, Igualada, Vilanova and Villafranca.[45] This would be a key feature of the Catalan CNT through to 1923:

its heart was Barcelona and it found it much more difficult to mobilise workers from further afield.

In Barcelona, a number of similarities could be discerned amongst the unions who broke away. First, white-collar workers were heavily represented. With one small exception, all the shopworkers' unions, which had previously affiliated, left. The last to do so was the ADM (the union which had done most to set up SO in 1907), with the result that the white-collar trade-union and associational sphere would become an increasingly important locus of opposition.[46] Second, unions which disaffiliated often represented workers who enjoyed a relatively stable position within the labour process and who could be on quite cordial terms with employers. Such, for example, was the case of the stonemasons, stonecutters, plasterers and Sants brickmakers in construction, and the coopers in woodworking. As in the years 1899 to 1903, the radicalisation of social conflict was leading divisions to open up within the organised working class. While the CNT picked up support amongst industrial workers in conflict-prone sectors of the economy, white-collar and shopworkers and workers in the more elite crafts disaffiliated. In addition, the CNT was not able to bring on board the railway workers' Catalan Section, which had over 1,000 members in 1910. At the same time, craft and industrial federations maintained their independence, not wishing to become overtly linked to a particular ideological current in case they lost membership. This was, for example, the case of the National Federation of Woodworking Unions, which, despite having over one-third of its 1,500 members within the CNT in September 1911, kept its 'traditional autonomy'.[47]

Nevertheless, amongst broad sectors of the industrial working class a sense of shared interests could, at least in part, transcend political and ideological differences. For example, unions frequently stayed within the CNT despite the fact that they were out of step with the leadership.[48] Moreover, unions that did not belong to the CNT could often still be relied upon to provide monetary support for striking workers. Thus, over sixty Barcelona unions contributed funds to the metalworkers in 1910 and the third largest contributor was the Barcelona coopers' union, despite the fact that it had already withdrawn from SO.[49] To understand this it is necessary to relate back to comments made in Chapter Three on solidarity within the working-class communities. There was a recognition, at least amongst industrial workers employed within the more capitalistic sectors of the economy, that fellow men should be supported whatever organisation they belonged to. Hence, institutional divisions did not necessarily lead to a schism at the level of the grass-roots.

The syndicalists' difficulties did not give the Socialists any great boost. Outside Barcelona they experienced some growth during these years. This is an issue with which I shall deal in a subsequent section. Yet in Barcelona their recovery was very limited. In 1911 they enjoyed the sympathy of at most fifteen unions in the city (five of which belonged to the UGT). On the waterfront and amongst railway workers they benefited from the fact that the UGT had been busy trying to construct national federations. However, in 1911 the Catalan Section broke away from the UGT's Railwayworkers' Federation. Down at the port there was a small cadre of sympathetic union activists, but little in the way of unions. This only changed in 1913 when the sailors and stokers' union, El Naval, reformed and joined the UGT. They also almost totally lost their influence within the shopworkers' trade unions. Overall, those unions within which they were influential probably had little more than 1,000 members. This compares unfavourably with the years 1902 to 1903 when, as we saw in Chapter Four, the Socialists were able to mobilise a significant force behind an 'anti-general strike front'.[50]

In part, the Socialists suffered from the same difficulties as the syndicalists. As the case of the Catalan Section showed, union federations put unity above all else. Yet years of anarchist-syndicalist and Lerrouxist attacks, the 1899 decision to relocate the headquarters of the UGT to Madrid, and, subsequently, its growing identification Socialist party policy, no doubt had a damaging impact. The Catalan 'Pablista' Socialist, Jacinto Puig, admitted that many 'legalist' unions refused to join the UGT because they considered it 'political'. In a similar vein, Joaquín Bueso, although increasingly alienated from the CNT, remained critical of the UGT because, he felt, it had failed to maintain a necessary distance from the PSOE. *La Justicia Social* also attacked the UGT's centralism, a stance echoed by the Catalan railway workers' leadership, who, additionally, objected to its overt links to the PSOE.[51] These criticisms of centralisation were not without substance. It should not be forgotten that both the PSOE and UGT committees were elected by the Madrid branch and that the president of both organisations was Pablo Iglesias. The key political decisions were obviously all taken by this small group of leaders. With respect to the actual operation of the UGT there was considerably more leeway. The big Asturian and Vizcayan branches operated with a good deal of autonomy, and when, in the 1910s, they began to build industrial federations of miners and steel and metalworkers, their headquarters were located in these areas. Had the Socialists dominated Catalan textiles the situation would, one imagines, have been similar. However, the stronghold of the Socialist craft unions was Madrid and it was from here that most of the UGT trade federations operated. The problem was that, from a Catalan perspective, this gave the impression that to join a UGT federation was to lose control of one's destiny.[52]

Other aspects of the UGT operation could also put workers off. Given the emphasis of mutual-aid benefits and the need to build up a strike fund, individual UGT unions tended to charge relatively high dues.[53] Moreover, until a large fund had been built up a strike would not get official UGT support. A railway workers' delegate from Reus, whose local union was affiliated to the UGT, declared in 1914 that in reality this meant that they would never be able to come out with official support.[54] This indicates the extent to which the UGT had originally been conceived of as a union geared to the needs of relatively privileged journeymen and had some difficulty adapting to workers in industries in which labour relations were highly volatile.

The difficulties faced by the Socialists meant that the CNT remained the only serious labour confederation in Barcelona. Despite the setbacks of previous months it was not daunted when events in August and September 1911, in the run-up to its First Congress, provided it with its best opportunity to carry though the dreamed-of general strike. As in 1909, it was the colonial war in Morocco which aroused discontent. In response two parallel protest movements were launched. The first followed the decision of the Spanish Socialists to sign a pact (*Conjunción*) with a number of republican groups in November 1909, whose ultimate aim was to overthrow the Restoration regime. It was forged in the heat of the anti-Maura campaign, but can be seen as a logical consequence of the PSOE-UGT's increasingly pragmatic stance. Leading Socialists subsequently argued that because of the country's backward social and economic structure it would be necessary to go through a 'bourgeois democratic' stage before the goal of communism could be achieved. The republicans were taken to be representatives of the more progressive sectors of the bourgeoisie, with whom they should ally in order to bury the Restoration and put in its place a full-blown democracy. Its first major offensive was a campaign against the Moroccan war from the spring of 1910, during which a large number of meetings were held in Catalonia in July, with both left-wing Catalanists and Socialists participating.[55]

The second campaign was initiated by the French CGT following the Agadir Incident of May 1911, a clash between France and Germany over influence in Morocco, which raised fears of a European war. The CGT gained support from unions in a number of countries including, in Spain, both the CNT and UGT, and organised meetings in Berlin, Paris, Madrid and Barcelona at the end of July and beginning of August. The Barcelona meeting, the largest indoor gathering seen in the city for a number of years, was an enormous success.

This showed that despite intense rivalry, common opposition to the Restoration regime could provide the basis for an understanding between anarchist-syndicalists and Socialists. It even seemed that there might be some common ground over tactics. It was official CGT policy to declare a general strike in response to a European war and in both Madrid and Paris this was echoed by both CNT and UGT representatives.[56] This may seem surprising given the Socialists generally moderate union and political strategies. However, the fact that the Restoration regime was based on undemocratic foundations meant that – unlike, say, the British Labour Party – the PSOE-UGT could not fully travel down the gradualist, parliamentary, path. Rather, revolution was contemplated – albeit with some trepidation – as a means to overthrow the regime, and – despite their general opposition to the anarchists' tactics – some Socialists at least recognised that in order to both put pressure on it, and, or, engineer its removal, a general strike (or threat of a general strike) was the only real weapon at their disposal. Yet joint participation in this campaign represented, at most, a fragile compromise. No Catalan anarchist-syndicalists travelled to the Madrid meeting (despite the fact that two members of the CGT were present), and in Barcelona the UGT was represented by the Madrid-based figure of Adrián García, with the Catalan Socialists staying away.

Divisions once again came to the fore at the end of August, when a strike wave broke out in several parts of the country, allowing the political atmosphere to become increasingly heated. Most notably, a strike on the port of

Bilbao became generalised between 11 and 12 September. It was a situation almost designed to prompt the CNT to take precipitate action. It held what it referred to as its First Congress in Barcelona between 8 and 11 September 1911 and followed it up with a secret session, which elected a strike committee, charged with the task of organising a general strike, ostensibly in support of the workers of Bilbao. The strike was planned for the following Monday, 18 September. On Friday 15 September a new strike committee was formed, made up of the caretaker of the CNT's Barcelona headquarters, Miguel Sánchez González, Salvador Seguí, and Jaume Coll, an *enragé* who worked in textile finishing. They pushed ahead with preparations, sending a circular out to anarchist-syndicalist workers' centres throughout Spain and producing a revolutionary manifesto. Then, on the Saturday night, they tried to stop the city's daily newspapers from coming out. Two leaders of the Lerrouxist youth also integrated into the committee and tried unsuccessfully to bring the party on board. This needs to be read in the context of divisions between the Lerrouxist youth movement and the party leadership, with much of the youth wishing to maintain the old radical heritage. As in July 1909, it also points to the ambiguity in the strike's aims. Some anarchist-syndicalist activists were no doubt contemplating a social revolution, but the hope that the Restoration regime might be overthrown and replaced by a republic was probably not far from the thoughts of many.[57]

It was not, however, to prosper. To understand why it is necessary to take a trip down into Barcelona's demi-monde of informers and police spies. The police had, probably in the aftermath of Tragic Week, managed to recruit one of SO's most significant anarchist revolutionaries, Miguel Villalobos Moreno (pseudonym of José Sánchez González). One suspects that he was turned after being captured – he had been on the strike committee during Tragic Week and might have faced the death sentence.[58] Miguel Sánchez González, who, as noted, was on the 1911 strike committee, was his brother; Moreno presumably introducing him into the movement. He was also an informer and an agent provocateur, producing, it appears, a 'revolutionary plan' which included the dynamiting of the army's Montcada barracks and the assassination of Valeriano Weyler, the captain-general of Barcelona. With information he provided, between Saturday 16 and Sunday 17 September the police were able to move decisively against the CNT. Hence, on the Monday the strike failed to take off to any significant degree. The infiltration of the movement by informers was a problem to which the syndicalists were particularly vulnerable; operating in semi-legality with no permanent bureaucracy, it was easy for the police to either plant spies or to turn anarchist-syndicalists. These events also shed light on the activities of the Special Brigade of the Barcelona police. Between 1910 and 1911, it had continually harassed CNT activists, following and temporarily arresting them, opening correspondence and putting pressure on landlords to dismiss them, while using informers-cum-agent-provocateurs to undermine the movement.[59]

Despite the police's success in stifling the strike in Catalonia, the crisis was not at an end. It had a considerable impact in several Spanish regions in which there was a significant anarchist-syndicalist presence. The most serious events occurred in a number of Valencian towns where the strike, led by anarchists and left-republicans, took on an insurrectionary character. In Cullera insurgents assassinated a judge and a town clerk. As a result, death sentences were handed out to six men (which would eventually be commuted), who quickly joined the pantheon of anarchist martyrs. Canalejas responded by declaring martial law throughout Spain, and only regained total control of the situation at the end of the week.

The CNT, then, did everything in its power to radicalise the crisis. On the other hand, as in July 1909, the PSOE-UGT leadership proved reluctant to take action. The UGT was finally pressurised into declaring a 48-hours national protest strike for Wednesday 20 September, but the Government, forewarned, had no difficulty in taking preventative action. It was, in fact, a face-saving gesture. The differences between the UGT and CNT should be put down to both ideology and organisational structure. While the Socialists might theoretically contemplate using violent action against the regime they were loathe to make such a move when the odds on any tangible result were very slim. No doubt the UGT hierarchy feared the impact any such move would have on the organisation, while the PSOE leadership did not wish to frighten away more moderate republican leaders and throw the *Conjunción* into crisis. On the contrary, as already stressed, the anarchist-syndicalists had no professional leadership, little in the way of an organisation to preserve, and professed to disdain the views of 'bourgeois republicans' . It was a situation which encouraged an all-or-nothing mentality amongst the anarchist-syndicalist hardliners. Hence, while the temper of many of the CNT's leading figures was impatient, the watchword for the Socialists was still caution.

The latter were, in fact, no doubt correct in their assessment that there was still no opportunity of overthrowing the monarchy. Despite the growth in union activity over the past two years, labour agitation was limited to only a few provinces. In particular, the agrarian south remained quiescent, and the state was well placed to crush any attempted revolution. Nevertheless, their stance did not go down well amongst many union activists. Not only were the anarchist-syndicalists able to repeat their charge that the Socialists were traitors and *adormideras* (sleepers), there was also considerable discontent within the PSOE-UGT itself. In particular, a younger generation of activists, and intransigent trade unionists like the Basque miners' leader Facundo Perezagua, were unhappy at the line the party had taken.[60] This discontent was, as shall be seen, particularly notable in Catalonia.

Here repression was vigorous. One hundred and sixty-two workers were detained, including most the CNT's leading figures, of whom ninety-two were prosecuted for involvement in a revolutionary conspiracy. Seven were to be held until the following June when the charges were dropped (according to Emiliano Iglesias because the authorities wished to protect their informers).[61] Furthermore, the CNT was declared illegal and its headquarters shut down. In the following month the authorities also began to close the headquarters of all those Barcelona unions affiliated to it. It would not be possible to begin reconstructing any kind of a Spanish-wide movement until 1915. Government repression also affected the PSOE-UGT. Several leading Socialists were arrested and the organisation was also temporarily declared illegal. Nonetheless, both the party and union were soon able to function normally once again. Clearly, the Government regarded the Socialists as a more moderate and responsible opposition than the anarchists and acted accordingly. Canalejas also fell victim to these events. He was assassinated by an anarchist outside a Madrid bookshop in November 1912. The killer appears to have acted alone, but it could only have accentuated the view in official circles of the anarchists as a bunch of criminal desperados.

Union Organisation and Strikes, 1912 to 1914

Yet despite this defeat the situation would in no way parallel that of the years 1904 to 1909, for the economic climate remained relatively buoyant and, in a number of trades and industries, unions would strengthen from 1912. This was reflected in strike statistics, with the number of working days lost in 1913 greater than in any other year between 1899 and 1918 (see tables 3.1. and 7.1.). Strike levels were once again high in the metal and construction industries, and in a whole host of trades in which craft workers still played a key role. On the waterfront, employers maintained control, but Catalan railway workers came out on strike in 1912, while in 1913 female textile workers carried out what would be the most dramatic strike in Catalonia before the famous La Canadenca dispute of 1919. Growing union power is indicated by the fact that in a number of sectors, especially in construction and woodworking, demands were made for a closed shop. Nevertheless, many disputes would still prove an uphill struggle. Overall, between 1912 and 1914, just over 50 percent of strikes, which involved over twenty workers, were lost.[62]

In construction and woodworking, as in the metal industry in 1910, these disputes served to highlight the relationship between capitalist manufacture and social conflict. In construction, the big limited liability company, Foment d'Obres i Construccions, emerged as the workers' most powerful foe. In previous years it had taken the lead in re-imposing a nine-hours day on bricklayers, with other contractors following suit. Hence, during 1912, the key battleground became the bricklayers' unions effort to reconquer the eight-hours day, first established in 1901. From 1913 other trades within construction and woodworking were then able to go on the offensive. Faced with rising prices wage rises became a priority, although the workers' growing strength also meant that they could put forward demands for the 'regulation' of apprenticeship, the abolition of piece rates and the closed shop. During strikes by painters in 1913, and power sawyers in 1914, the smaller employers quickly accepted the workers' demands. In the former case, the larger employers then boycotted the 'master craftsmen', who responded by setting up their own separate federation. Throughout these years unions claimed that the larger-scale employers were the most intransigent.[63]

There was once again a tendency for disputes to become generalised, and, in the heat of battle, both workers and employers where necessary re-formed and tried to build up their trade and industrial federations. This was most notable in the metal, construction and textile industries. In the metal industry, the Metalworkers' Union collapsed soon after the 1910 defeat, but a new Barcelona federation was formed at the end of 1913. During the year workers from a number of metal trades once again struck for a nine-hours day. The largest strike, undertaken by the iron foundrymen, ended in defeat, but workers were more successful in some of the industries' smaller trades. Strife also spread outside Barcelona and closer contacts were established between a number of Catalan unions. The Catalan metal employers then organised a national conference in April 1913 in which the need to build greater unity and foment Catholic unions was discussed, and a National Association of Metallurgists was established. In response, at the beginning of 1914, the Sabadell metalworkers' union took the lead in forming a new Catalan Regional Metalworkers' Federation, which in April had 1,500 members. The affiliated Catalan unions were also the driving force behind the organisation of a National Confederation of Spanish Metalworkers in Alicante in July.[64]

In construction, the impetus to establish links between the unions sprung from the 1913 strike by the Barcelona painters' federation, which for the majority ended in defeat. While the industrialists had been given support by the Barcelona Employers' Federation, which was led by the hard-line building contractors, most of the city's construction workers' unions also strongly backed the painters, with the result that an industry-wide general strike was only narrowly averted. Furthermore, the strike stimulated the foundation of Barcelona's first Construction Workers' Federation on the last day of the year. Importantly, the carpentry unions, who had until then formed their own separate organisations, joined, and only the most elite crafts – the plasterers, marblers and tile makers – stood aloof. The fact that there were now industrial federations in both the metal and construction industries was crucial for the future of industrial relations in the city.

In the following year, in construction, an industry-wide conflict again loomed. The origin of the dispute was to be found in carpentry. Strife within the trade over the unions' demands for a minimum wage, the 'regulation' of apprenticeship and a closed shop culminated, at the end of 1913, with a city-wide lock-out followed by a general strike. The dispute then further escalated. The master carpenters appealed to the Barcelona Employers' Federation, which threatened a lock-out throughout the construction industry if the carpenters did not return under their old conditions by 10 February 1914. The civil governor managed to cool tempers and set up an arbitration board, which finally accorded a wage increase. Nevertheless, the employers' willingness to counterattack and use the weapon of the industry-wide lock-out was a sign of things to come. As we shall see in subsequent chapters, it was to be a key feature of the 'labour wars' in the city after the First World War.[65]

However, the most dramatic events were to occur within textiles. After Tragic Week the bulk of the industry remained quiescent. The CNT's Founding Congress had once again stressed the importance of unionising female workers. The resolution passed, which affirmed that only through paid labour and equal working conditions could women achieve equality, is the first example I have found of modern feminist doctrines entering syndicalist discourse.[66]

But on the ground it had little impact. This was to change in 1912 and, unusually, it was Barcelona that was to take the lead. A new union, called La Constància, was founded in May 1912 and grew rapidly from the spring of 1913, reaching 8,000 affiliates by July. This was the first time since 1901 that female weavers and preparatory workers had been unionised in any numbers. The genesis of the union was also similar. The industry had remained rather depressed between 1910 and 1911, but 1912 saw a flood of new orders leading to labour shortages. Male-dominated unions, especially workers in the textile finishing trades, whose own unions grew rapidly between 1910 and 1911, would play a key role in its foundation. The union at first took off in Sant Martí and then started to make headway in other areas.

Male workers, as in the past, took a leading role. Nevertheless, some changes were afoot. Women did have a minority of posts on the union committee and, as in 1901, they began to take part in anarchist-syndicalist union meetings. The experience of working together within the union also changed attitudes. Joan Ferrer recalled that when female textile workers were first unionised in Igualada in 1913, in union meetings they sat at the front while the men sat at the back (thereby replicating the spatial segregation of the church service), but they then began to mix. At the same time, women got involved in the libertarian Ateneu Porvenir's theatre group, danced with the men and went on excursions.[67]

In the spring of 1913, La Constància established contacts with the woollen textile unions of Sabadell and Terrassa, with the objective of forging a new Catalan textile federation. It held its first conference in Barcelona between 11 and 22 May, calling itself the Catalan Regional Textile Federation (Federació Regional Fabril de Catalunya). Importantly, workers in the textile finishing trades were, unlike the situation in 1900, fully integrated into the federation. This was another example of the way in which employer hostility encouraged the construction of broad fronts. The formation of the federation also stimulated a renaissance of union organisation in the industry. Unions in the Muntanya remained extremely weak, but new life was breathed into those in the medium-sized industrial towns on the Pla nearer Barcelona.

As at the turn of the century, the newly-organised workers demanded a rapid improvement in their working conditions. The federation responded at the beginning of July by calling for a fifty-hours week (down from sixty-four hours in Barcelona and, with the exception of woollen textiles, longer hours elsewhere) and threatened strike action should the employers resist. One of the key finishing trades, the calenders and sizers, had already achieved this demand in Barcelona in 1912, and the hope was to extend it throughout the entire industry. Events would now move very quickly. Afraid of a major dispute, the authorities tried to appease the union and for the first time made serious efforts to ensure that industrialists complied with social legislation limiting night work for women to forty-eight hours. However, in Sants a number of factories reacted by simply cutting the night shift, catalysing labour militancy in a neighbourhood in which the union had previously been very weak. In response, the federation's union delegates met on 27 July, agreeing that La Constància should elect the strike committee and that it should call a strike when it saw fit. This committee's room for manoeuvre was highly restricted. On 29 July, solidarity strikes were declared in a number of Sants factories, and under pressure from the rank and file, and afraid that if it failed to act enthusiasm would wane, it declared a general strike that very night.

Once declared the strike spread rapidly. By 30 July in Barcelona most of the industry was at a standstill. Outside the city, in the Muntanya, factories stayed open but workers in the towns around Barcelona also came out. At the end of the first week it was estimated that around 50,000 workers were affected. These events again served to explode the myth that female workers were somehow particularly passive. They found it difficult to organise but when they did so they acted very much like their male counterparts. The size of the strike and the possibility that it could spread to other sectors of the economy led the Liberal Government, now under the Count of Romanones, to seek a compromise. At this time the textile manufacturers did not have their own federation. Hence the Government contacted the head of the FTN, Eduard Calvet (himself a cotton textile industrialist), and asked him to enquire as to the maximum the employers would concede. He replied that they would go no lower than a sixty-hours week. The Government still faced the problem that, given the authorities' chequered history in the enforcement of social legislation, there was a great deal of scepticism amongst the labour force. To counter this it agreed immediately to publish a Royal Decree limiting hours in the industry to sixty per week or 3,000 a year (the latter addition, as we shall see, a concession to the industrialists) in return for the immediate end of the strike.

Many of the female textile workers argued passionately in union meetings against the compromise. As the discussion of working conditions for female textile workers in Chapter Two makes clear, a fifty-hours week (including a half-day on Saturday) would have made an enormous difference to their lives.[68] Nevertheless, with unions outside Barcelona in favour and cracks beginning to appear in the strike, a return to work was finally agreed on Sunday 24 August. Because of disputes over the new working week it would be a slow process, but most factories were operating normally by Monday 1 September. In reality the gains made would be limited. Amongst the industrialists the following weeks saw a revolt against Calvet and the compromise reached, led by Josep Muntadas, a relative of the director of La España Industrial, who, in an open letter to the Home Secretary, bitterly criticised the Government and accused it of unleashing a 'civil war' in the factories.[69] A minority of industrialists went so far as to call for an industry-wide lock-out. This process culminated in the formation of a new hard-line Federation of Textile Industrialists of the Pla and Muntanya. At first it was at odds with the FTN, but once Calvet had resigned they closed ranks. At the same time, the Barcelona employers informed the authorities that they would only cut working hours to sixty-two per week. This, in fact, added up to the 3,000 hours per year specified in the Royal Decree, once the workers' 'traditional' holidays were taken into account. Industrialists in the Muntanya went further, stating that as there had been no dispute they saw no reason to modify working conditions at all. Furthermore, when the decree was published the authorities did not vigorously enforce it. This would produce much resentment in working-class circles but there was little that could be done. La Constància in particular was seriously weakened both by internal divisions and because disillusioned women withdrew their support.[70]

The Mataró hosiery workers were behind the decision to hold a new congress in Barcelona between 25 and 27 December 1913, in which it was decided to turn the federation into a Spanish-wide National Textile Federation (Federación Nacional del Arte Fabril y Textil). In reality this made little difference to its make-up. More important, the congress vented its frustration at the result of the strike, declaring the Institute for Social Reforms a 'useless body' and threatening another general strike if the industrialists did not implement the sixty-hours week.[71] Yet before the First World War only the cotton textile workers in the Ter and Freser were able to take any action. Within the Muntanya, workers in the Alt Llobregat remained unorganised. The new policies introduced by industrialists at the turn of the century, designed to tighten social control, had clearly borne fruit.[72] On the Ter, on the other hand, they once again showed their capacity to mobilise. The publication of the Royal Decree had galvanised them into action. At the beginning of 1914 they felt strong enough to demand a reduction in working hours from sixty-six to sixty-two (that is, if we accept the industrialists' argument regarding 'traditional' holidays, the maximum legal working week in the industry) and a 10 percent wage increase, and, faced with the employers' refusal to budge, declared a strike on 2 March. It was not to be a success. The industrialists, their profit margins still under pressure, were determined to resist. Furthermore, the textile federation, greatly weakened after the events of the previous year, could give little assistance. On 23 March La Constància declared a general strike in support, but it was a failure. The only consolation was that they were able to ensure an orderly return to work and prevent any sackings, thereby, according to *La Justicia Social*, thwarting any attempt to 'impose a regime of terror, like the one that operates in the Alt Llobregat'.[73] It should be emphasised that the Government – now under the Conservative Prime Minister, Eduardo Dato – had proved itself incapable of enforcing its own legislation.

During these disputes violence escalated futher. Most notably, in 1912 during strikes in textile finishing four employers were fired at before a fifth, Carles Bargalló, was assassinated on 29 April. Violence was also directed at what were considered yellow or employer friendly unions. As we have seen, from 1910 onwards, industrialists took more interest in Catholic unions, and, in Barcelona, in 1912 Catholic Unions Professionals (Professional Unions) began to proliferate. In 1913 the only such Unió Professional to have recruited widely represented white-collar workers, with over 1,000 members, but thirteen other such unions had been founded. This began to trouble the anarchist-syndicalists. In construction, for example, at least one of the reasons behind the demand for a closed shop was to block their growth. Within the textile finishing trades more drastic action was taken: a leading figure with the Unió Professional, Camil Piqué, was assassinated on 4 December 1913. These assassinations represented a departure from past practice, with, the indications are, a team of gunmen operating within the textile finishing unions.[74]

It was not only the anarchist-syndicalists who turned to violence. During the 1913 textile strike four important figures within the union were, the anarchist-syndicalists later affirmed, working as informers for the Special Brigade. It would be a frequent claim in subsequent years that they planted a bomb in the Sant Martí Workers' Centre in order to get the strike's leading figures arrested and undermine it. After the strike, syndicalist sources maintain that they formed part of a gang, whose activities were financed by 'Muntadas', working for the head of the Brigade, the chief of police, Francisco Martorell. In early 1914, the syndicalists affirmed, they assassinated one CNT activist, Sendra, and wounded another, Jaume Sabanés.[75] The important point to note is that many of the elements of the 'labour wars', which shook Barcelona between 1918 and 1923, were making their presence felt. An anarchist-syndicalist squad was targeting employers and members of the Catholic unions, and the police were for the first time, it seems, willing to countenance counter-terrorism and accept funding from employers.

Anarchism, Syndicalism and Labour, 1913 to 1914

From 1912 the anarchist-syndicalists began to reorganise. No amnesty was proclaimed until April 1913, but by June 1912 all the activists apprehended in September 1911 had been released. The Sant Martí Workers' Centre (from where La Constància was organised), which from October published its own newspaper, aptly named *El Sindicalista*, provided an important point of contact. The main Barcelona Workers' Centre was allowed to reopen in July 1912 and the local federation operated from January 1913. *Solidaridad Obrera* then reappeared on 1 May 1913, and, following the legalisation of the CNT's Catalan regional confederation, the CRT, a regional committee was elected in July. However, this return to open activities would quickly prove precarious. After an attempted general strike in August, in support of the textile workers, the CRT was illegalised and its leading figures arrested. It would not function again until the following August.[76]

Operating underground for much of the time, the organisation was not able significantly to rebuild its membership. The only figures that I have found for these years refer to October 1913, when, despite being suspended, thirty Barcelona unions were affiliated, representing 5,155 members, along with 2,000 members from the local labour federations of Vilanova, Vilafranca, Igualada and Sabadell.[77] In addition, the anarchist-syndicalists' cultural institutions remained relatively weak. Following the example of Poble Nou, 'centres of rationalist culture' were set up in Sants and La Barceloneta. Most importantly, the Sants centre was able to rent a large headquarters in August 1912 and began holding large numbers of talks. Then, in early 1914 it set up a consumer cooperative and a school, which in April taught 120 children.[78]

Yet these statistics by themselves do not accurately reflect the anarchist-syndicalists' impact. In 1912 they actively agitated for the release of their political prisoners and followed this up in 1913 with a vigorous campaign to convert *Solidaridad Obrera* into a daily. Their illegalisation in August prevented this, but they were able to keep it afloat as a weekly. Their morale was, moreover, boosted by the fact that the years 1910 to 1914 saw a great escalation of industrial strife throughout much of central and western Europe, accompanied by a surge in support for syndicalism.[79] As in the past, they also mobilised far more widely than their paper membership would suggest and they were able to play a leading role in labour organisation in several key sectors of the economy.

A number of trade and industrial federations, though remaining independent, came under strong anarchist-syndicalist influence. In the metal industry the new Barcelona Metalworkers' Federation was controlled by the anarchist-syndicalists. Moreover, they attained a leading position in the Catalan Regional Metalworkers' Federation set up in January 1914. This became clear at its First Congress, held in April, when a motion presented by the Central Committee rejecting state intervention in industrial disputes and supporting direct action was approved by a majority of ten to four. The Catalan Regional Metalworkers' Federation, together with the Alicante metalworkers' union, were then responsible for the organisation of the Confederation of Spanish Metalworkers, which subsequently rivalled the UGT's National Metalworkers' Federation. At the founding congress the decision was taken to press ahead despite the UGT sending two delegates to try and reach a settlement. The tone was set by the president of the Catalan Federation, the well-known anarchist-syndicalist, Josep Climent, who launched a virulent diatribe against UGT union strategy.[80]

The anarchist-syndicalists were also to enjoy an increasingly dominant position in construction. They were strong in the Barcelona painters and woodworkers' federations (refounded in October 1910 and March 1911 respectively). The leadership of the National Federation of Woodworking Unions, 60 percent of whose 2,938 members were Catalan at the end of 1914, was more distant. Nevertheless, there was a strong anarchist-syndicalist presence, with the result that it refused to link up with the UGT's own National Woodworkers' Federation, which had no Catalan members between 1911 and 1913.[81]

In bricklaying, a new Catalan federation was set up in 1910, whose headquarters was in Reus. Under the captaincy of the Reus union it became increasingly pro-Socialist, and established close contacts with the UGT's National Bricklayers' Federation. In response, in June 1913 a number of Barcelona unions broke away and formed their own Catalan Confederation of Bricklayers and Bricklayers' Labourers. There was no doubt as to the new organisation's political leanings, its first communiqué rejecting the policies of the 'state reformists' and championing direct action. As in the case of the metalworkers, the very use of the term *confederation* was significant: it indicated sympathy for the CNT and opposition to what were viewed as over-centralised UGT *federations*. So was the fact that in typically syndicalist terms it aimed to cut across divisions of skill and integrated labourers, that its dues were low (at 2 céntimos a month) and that it did not establish a strike fund. The new confederation proved more successful than its rival. It gained the support of most of the towns around Barcelona and soon had over 2,500 members. Not satisfied, in 1914 it began to work towards the foundation of a Spanish bricklayers and bricklayers' labourers confederation to rival the UGT organisation. Its ultimate aim was to set up a national confederation of Spanish construction workers. For the time being this came to nothing, but when the local Barcelona Construction Workers' Federation was set up at the end of 1913 the anarchist-syndicalists were in control.[82]

In textiles the situation was rather more complex. Anarchist-syndicalists were dominant within the Barcelona textile finishing trades and played a leading role in organising La Constància. Outside Barcelona they retained the sympathy of the Sabadell and Terrassa woollen textile unions and were able to extend their support to other textile towns on the Pla (most notably Igualada and Vilanova). On the other hand, Socialists remained influential within the textile unions of Mataró, the Maresme and the Ter Valley, and also controlled the newly-organised cotton textile workers' union in Reus. Moreover, from towns such as Reus and Tortosa in Tarragona Province, from 1911 they were also to organise tenant farmers and land workers in the surrounding countryside. They still had the problem, particularly in Tarragona, that although unions might be under Socialist influence they would not join the UGT. Nevertheless, they did enjoy significant if modest growth: between 1910 and 1916 UGT affiliation in Catalonia rose from the derisory figure of 652 affiliates (1.6 percent of the Spanish total) to the small but somewhat more respectable figure of 5,652 (7.4 percent of the Spanish total).[83]

Within the Catalan textile federation there was a balance of political forces. This was reflected in the deliberations at the federation's December 1913 congress. Socialist influence could be seen in the decision to set dues at a relatively high level (20 céntimos a month, on top of dues paid to the local unions), and in the call on unions to exercise caution before coming out on strike. However, the anarchists were, it seems, instrumental in the agreements not to appoint paid officials, recommend affiliated unions reject the intervention of outside bodies during industrial disputes, and to strongly criticise the Institute for Social Reforms. In this respect, the tardiness of the Government in enforcing its Royal Decree played into their hands, making it much easier for them to dismiss social legislation as a bourgeois fraud. Furthermore, the decision to declare a general strike for a nine-hours day should the Government fail to enforce it also had an anarchist ring to it. The aggressive stance championed by the anarchists could also, finally, be seen in the agreement to declare the remnants of the old textile federation, the TCV, 'yellow and bourgeois'.[84]

Over the next four years anarchist-syndicalists and Socialists would continue to vie for power. At first it seemed that the syndicalists would come out on top. The congress's decision to leave it to the Barcelona textile unions to elect the federation's Central Committee allowed the president of La Constància, Joan Martí, a hard-line anarchist weaver, to become its general secretary. However, with the failure of the Barcelona unions actually to set up a committee and the defeat of the 1914 strike on the Ter the Socialists launched a counteroffensive. In May 1914 Mataró was charged with organising the Central Committee under the well-known Socialist, Constantí Perlasio.

There was also an unstable balance of power on the railways. In June 1912 the UGT launched a Federation of Spanish Railwayworkers. The Catalan Section participated but retained an independent stance. Over the following months, under the presidency of Pere Ribalta, the Lerroxists would emerge as the most powerful force within the Catalan union, although there was also an influential anarchist-syndicalist current. This was a perfect recipe for conflict with the Socialist leadership. The federation's founding congress had voted a series of improvements in the industry but had not agreed when they should be presented to the companies. In subsequent months the largest of the Catalan companies, Madrid-Zaragoza-Alicante (MZA), had taken a provocative stance, transfering union activists and introducing a new unpopular shift system. In response, in September 1912 the Catalan Section agreed to present the federation's demands to the companies that operated in Catalonia and declare an immediate general strike if they were not met. As so often, it was a mix of rank-and-file indignation and pressure from anarchist-syndicalists within the union that produced this result. The Socialist leadership at first opposed the call, but it was forced to hold a ballot in which a majority supported the Catalan Section.

A nationwide strike was declared on 9 October 1912, but it quickly ran into trouble. Canalejas promised to introduce a bill into parliament which would meet the railway workers' main demands, but he also militarised those strikers who were army reservists, forcing a return to work. As it was, the bill did nothing of the sort, setting up arbitration procedures within the industry but also taking away the right to strike. The companies introduced some improvements in working conditions, but this was accompanied by reprisals against the activists. In subsequent months this was enough to undermine union organisation in the industry. In large measure, they were able to take advantage of the divisions which already existed amongst workers within the myriad trades and grades and the recriminations which followed the strike defeat. Hence, by mid-1913 there was little left for Lerrouxists, anarchist-syndicalists and Socialists to squabble over.[85]

As in 1910 and 1911, the CNT leadership remained convinced that syndicalism gave them the blueprint to both mobilise the working class and harness rank-and-file militancy for revolution. The result was a high degree of sectarianism. Following the decision of the CNT's First Congress, in September 1911, to recommend that the CNT unions adopt direct action, it became increasingly insistent that affiliated unions put its tenets into practice. During 1913, with José Negre the most influential figure in the organisation, they also maintained a hard 'antipolitical' line and remained highly critical of the Socialists, who were accused of collaborating with the bourgeoisie and using union dues not to fight the industrialists but to pay for UGT officials, electoral expenses and worker deputies.[86]

The Catalan Socialists' response was much more flexible. Under the leadership of the Reus Socialists the Catalan Socialist Federation once again distanced itself from the Madrid leadership, accusing it of being insufficiently focused on union work and denying that the *Conjunción* would produce any tangible results. Simultaneously, they made overtures to the anarchist-syndicalists, with the hope that they might build a united proletarian front. It was such a front, rather than the Socialist-republican alliance, which, Antoni Fabra Ribas believed, could launch a Spanish revolution. Hence, in many respects the Catalan Socialists reasserted the policies of the period 1907 to 1909, when they had formed part of Solidaritat Obrera. Indeed, Fabra Ribas and *La Justicia Social* very much became the standard bearers of a leftist current within the PSOE-UGT, which was also strong in the Basque Country and Asturias.[87] In response, the CRT's newspaper began to warm to the Catalan Socialists, but rather than any possible fusion it look forward to the 'decomposition' of the UGT and to its 'healthy elements' joining them.[88]

Simultaneously, the anarchist-syndicalists remained bitterly critical of the Radicals, celebrating the fact that Lerroux's increasingly moderate position, combined with corruption scandals and divisions within the party, was leading to a loss of support, most particularly within the more popular and working-class areas of Barcelona. With only 17,000 votes in the November 1913 elections, the party was by no means the force it had been three years previously. Similarly, they maintained their distance from Catalanism, opposing the foundation of the Mancomunitat, an administrative body which the Restoration elites had conceded to the Lliga and which Catalan nationalists saw as a first step towards political autonomy. It covered the whole of Catalonia and took over many of the responsibilities of the four Catalan Diputacions Provincials (County Councils). Dismissively, *Solidaridad Obrera* stated that 'the autonomy of the bourgeoisie' would only benefit a minority at the cost of the majority. The only autonomy they wished for was the workers' 'economic independence'.[89]

Yet, despite the critique of the Radicals, there was still a degree of cooperation with the republican parties. CNT unions continued to use the Lerrouxists' centres and labour lawyers. In 1912 the League in Defence of the Rights of Man – first founded in 1905 – was also resuscitated by a number of Barcelona unions and meetings held by both anarchist-syndicalist activists and republican labour lawyers for the release of 'social prisoners'. At the end of the year, a campaign was also launched by the Syndicalist Athaeneum, with republican support, in favour Dr Queraltó, a republican Catalanist who had been put on trial for claiming that the Anti-Tuberculosis Foundation (which was supported by the city's elite) did not care about the poor. Furthermore, when another campaign against the war in Morocco was launched by the *Conjunción* in the summer, although anarchist-syndicalists did not actively participate, *Solidaridad Obrera* gave its support.[90] Again there was a dichotomy between two aspects of anarchist-syndicalist thought: the exaltation of the class struggle and dismissal of all 'bourgeois' parties, and the recognition of the need for at least some cooperation in the fight for 'liberty' and 'progress'.

These links between the unions and republican 'politicians' led to disquiet in some anarchist circles. Despite the ideological victory of the anarchist-syndicalists, strike defeats, the rise in the number of industry-wide disputes, plus growing employer unity and use of the lock-out, also provoked renewed debate over union strategy. One area of discussion centred on the question of industrial unionism. The anarchist heritage was in this respect contradictory; on the one hand anarchists had stressed union autonomy, but, on the other, they had emphasised the need to cut across divisions of skill, ethnicity and gender. This implied the need to build bigger unions. It was this latter point which was taken up by the French syndicalists, who, from the first decade of the century, championed industrial unions. Within Catalonia, opinion was divided. Adolfo Bueso, the younger brother of Joaquín, recalled that the anarchist veterans, the 'men with beards and moustaches', were opposed. Uppermost in his mind must have been Anselmo Lorenzo, who even rejected trade federations because of what he saw as their bureaucratic implications.[91]

But the tide was flowing in the other direction. The CNT's founding congress passed a resolution in favour of 'unions of trades and similar trades'. Over the next four years, in the face of employer hostility and the use of the lock-out, in the pages of *Solidaridad Obrera* it was argued that 'federations of similar trades', in reality industrial federations, would make the organisation as a whole both stronger and easier to run. Others maintained that the key lay in the construction of industrial unions at a local level. This was the opinion of Manuel Andreu, who over the next four years would play a key role in the Catalan organisation. Nothing had been achieved by the end of 1914 but, as we shall see in the next chapter, the need to form local industrial unions, or what were called Sindicats Unics, would subsequently become central to CRT union strategy.[92]

More heated were exchanges over the use of the general strike. Discord bubbled to the surface following the decision to declare a general strike in support of the textile workers on 10 August 1913. It was taken in a meeting of the local federation on 3 August, but was opposed by most of the executive of both La Constància and the Catalan Regional Textile Federation. Those opposed included the well-known activist, Josep Roca. Bitter infighting ensued. On 9 August an attempt was made by a number of CRT hardliners, led by the CRT's treasurer, the ex-railwayworker Emili Polo, to storm the Sant Martí Workers' Centre and take over the running of the strike, leading the authorities to carry out large numbers of arrests and outlaw the CRT. Over the following month the struggle to control La Constància continued, culminating in the hardliner, Joan Martí, finally taking over as president on 9 September 1913 after a stormy meeting in which shots were fired.[93] Once again, as in the strikes of the metalworkers and dockers in 1911, the leadership was taking a more voluntarist line than part of its membership.

This new period of illegality provoked a reappraisal of strategy within sections of the confederation. In November, a new committee elected to reorganise the CRT stressed the need to avoid 'epileptic reactions which tire the members and result in disorganisation'. The new line was reiterated in the following year in a number of articles published by *Solidaridad Obrera*, which affirmed that general strikes should only be declared when it was clear that a majority of workers would second them. In March 1914, in a surprising move, it actually criticised the Barcelona railwayworkers' union for voting in favour of a general strike in support of the tramworkers because, it maintained, 'the general atmosphere' was not appropriate. In October it admitted that the 'energy used up, the blood generously spilt, has made us cautious and prudent'.[94]

It is difficult to know exactly who championed this new line. In particular, I have not been able to ascertain who formed part of the 1913 Reorganisation Committee. On the one hand, it appears that (rather as happened in the CGT between 1904 and 1909) leading anarchist-syndicalist hardliners, faced with repression and loss of legal status, drew back. Central in this respect was José Negre, who, although in Paris between June 1912 (when he was released from prison) and the end of 1913, quickly re-established himself as a key figure. After his return he joined a commission running the movement until the various committees could be re-formed and was elected general secretary of the CNT's new Federal Committee in August 1914. Closely allied was Francesc Miranda, Anselmo Lorenzo's stepson, a bookbinder by trade, who was also on the organisation's steering commission during 1914 and who became the general secretary of the newly formed local Barcelona federation in October. A distinctive figure, dressing, like Francesc Ferrer, 'in the Parisian style', with a straw-coloured suit, he was known as a fiery revolutionary and had played a very active role on the barricades during Tragic Week.[95]

On the other, a number of younger activists, who from 1907 onwards had taken up leading positions within the local unions, were also probably pushing for a more cautious approach. As we shall see, from 1916 onwards they would clash with the anarchist-syndicalist revolutionaries over the future direction of the organisation. Salvador Seguí was to emerge as their leading figure. During these years, although he had no official position within the CRT-CNT he became a leading speaker and the general secretary of the Barcelona Construction Workers' Federation in January 1915. Behind the scenes he was probably already very influential. There was tension between him and Negre and he was mistrusted by orthodox theoreticians like Ernest Cardenal.[96] Seguí's supporters were men like Josep Roca, who opposed the CRT's attempt to hijack the La Constància strike.

Conclusions

The years 1910 to 1914 witnessed a significant growth in organised labour. Over Spain as a whole it was the Socialists who most benefited. The number of UGT affiliates rose from about 41,000 in mid-1910, to 147,128 in January 1913, though it subsequently fell back to 119,000 members by August 1914.[97] Acting illegally for much of this period, the anarchist-syndicalists could not boast any such growth in membership within the CRT-CNT. Nevertheless, a careful examination of the role they played within Catalan organised labour provides a more positive evaluation of their strength than paper statistics on affiliates. Crucially, their focal point of support was Barcelona and the CNT still remained, despite its trials and tribulations, the only serious blue-collar labour confederation in Catalonia. Furthermore, in the key sectors of metalworking, construction and woodworking, Catalan-based trade and industrial federations, which showed sympathy for the syndicalists, rivalled

Socialist federations which operated outside Catalonia. Even when the federations were politically more divided – as in the case of textiles – they still refused to join the UGT. Hence, as in the period 1899 to 1903, an autonomous Catalan sphere of labour organisation was being consolidated. Nevertheless, the fact that the Catalan CRT was unable to integrate white-collar workers and that even amongst many industrial trades there was considerable opposition was an indication of potential weakness. Its difficulties revolved around a union strategy which, as previously, could both mobilise and enthuse, but could also bring both devastating defeat and heavy repression. This was to further weaken the organisation by producing serious dissension within its own ranks.

These years also saw a pronounced rise in industrial conflict. Within Barcelona, disputes took an increasingly industry-wide character and both workers and employers adapted to new times and increasingly championed industrial unionism. At the same time, Restoration governments had little success in mediating disputes between labour and capital. They were distrusted in working-class circles, whilst amongst the business class attempts to take the lead in establishing collective bargaining and forcing compromise were viewed with resentment. It was a view no doubt strengthened by the attacks by CNT gunmen on employers and foremen. On one occasion, during the 1911 metalworkers' strike, contacts were established between business representatives and the Barcelona captain-general. This was a taste of things to come. Key sectors of the Barcelona garrison and Barcelona business would subsequently emerge at the head of a conservative reaction against what they perceived as a misconceived strategy of weak Restoration politicians of placating and thereby encouraging the forces of revolution. Moreover, these years, the indications are, saw some industrialists side-stepping the law to back a parapolice force aimed at undermining the CNT. In these circumstances it is no exaggeration to state that major features of the post-war 'labour wars' were already taking shape within Catalan society.

Notes

1. Bueso, *Recuerdos*, 31.
2. The quotations are taken from *El Progreso*, 11 Nov. 1909, and from the pro-amnesty committee in *El Poble Català*, 25 Dec. 1909. Leopoldo Bonafulla also believed that the executions which followed Tragic Week took place because 'the ... clergy imposed them'. *Revolución de julio*, 99–100.
3. The quotation is from *La Publicidad* (hereafter, LP), 3 Jan., *Morning Edition*.
4. Instituto de Reformas Sociales (Sección Tercera), *Conflicto de obreros y empleados en la compañía de ferrocarriles, Septiembre-octubre 1912*, 7–8; *Solidaridad Obrera* (hereafter, SO), 26 Feb., 26 March 1910; LP, 24 May, 2 June 1910, *Morning Editions*; *La Justicia Social* (hereafter LJS), 2 July 1910.

5. *La Internacional*, 5 Feb. 1909; SO, 19 Aug. 1910; *El Diluvio* (hereafter, ED), 21 July 1910, *Evening Edition*; LP, 14 Dec 1910, *Evening Edition*, 31 Dec. 1910, *Morning Edition*.
6. LP, 14, 16 Sept., *Evening Editions*; ED, 15 Sept., *Morning Edition*. As seen in Chapter One, according to official statistics 10,000 establishments were classified as working in the metal industry, but the remaining 8,000 were tinsmiths, plumbers, locksmiths, and the like. In reality, there were probably closer to 14,000 metalworkers in Barcelona at the time, but this does not affect the basic argument.
7. This account of the strike is based on LP, ED and SO, along with Sastre y Sanna, *Las huelgas, 1910–1914*, 23–62, and Bengoechea, *Organització patronal*, 103–19.
8. For these attacks, along with press reports I have used Miguel Sastre y Sanna, *La esclavitud moderna*, 95–101. For Archs see Lladonosa i Vall-llebrera, *Sindicalistes i libertaris*, 15–16, and Porcel, *Revuelta*, 121–2. For Archs' trial *Tierra y Libertad*, 15 Nov. 1911.
9. Diario de las Sesiones de las Cortes (hereafter, DSC), 29 Oct. 1910, 1631.
10. Raymond Carr, *Spain, 1808–1936*, 492–6; Lannon, *Privilege, Persecution and Prophecy*, 136–9; Boyd, *Praetorian Politics*, 30.
11. Bengoechea, *Organització patronal*, 106–9.
12. I have used the local press, indicated above, and the account by Sastre y Sanna in *Huelgas ... 1910–1914*, 93–105.
13. José Comaposada, *La organización obrera en Cataluña*, 38.
14. Chapter Three, 83.
15. For the Sabadell strike, along with the newspapers cited I have used *El Trabajo, Boletín de la Cámara de Industria y Comercio de Sabadell*, Oct. 1910 and Sept. 1912, and Castells, *Informe de l'oposició*, vol. 3, 14.2. It should, however, be noted that, as in the past, labour relations in Sabadell subsequently stabilised.
16. DSC, 29 Oct. 1910, 1629–1633, 11 Nov. 1910, 1897.
17. José Prat, *Orientaciones*, 7; SO, 12 March, 2 April 1910.
18. Such concerns came through very strongly in Lorenzo's writings: see, for example, *El proletariado emancipador*. The need to operate an invalids' union was discussed at length in the Founding Congress, *Congreso de Constitución de la Confederación Nacional del Trabajo*, 238–42 and 340–1.
19. 'Primer congreso de la CNT (8, 9 y 10 de septiembre de 1911)', in Cuadrat, *Socialismo y anarquismo*, 640–2. As in the case of SO, dues were set at 3 céntimos a month for Catalan unions (2 for the newspaper), with other Spanish unions paying 1 céntimo a month. In contrast, in 1907 affiliates to the UGT paid 5 céntimos a quarter, but an extra 10 céntimos a week during an official 'reglamentary' strike. For the UGT see Carlos Forcadell, *Parlamentarismo y bolshevización*, 327.
20. *El Trabajo*, 24 July 1910.
21. SO, 29 July 1910.
22. *Tierra y Libertad*, 14 Feb. 1912.
23. The quotation is taken from Lorenzo's pamphlet, *La masa popular*, 27–30.
24. Pataud and Pouget, *Cómo haremos la revolución*; Emile Pouget, *La Confederación General del Trabajo en Francia*.
25. Ferrer, *Simó Piera*, 39; Madrid Santos,'Prensa anarquista', vol. 2, 397–403; *Tierra y Libertad*, 3, 31 May 1911. By August 1914 the circulation of *Tierra y Libertad* was up to 13,000: see *Tierra y Libertad* 14 Oct. 1914.
26. *La Cuña*, 1 May 1911.
27. *Tierra y Libertad*, 18 Feb. 1914.
28. *Congreso de Constitución*, 59.
29. SO, 13 May 1910; *Congreso de Constitución*, 56 and 75–8. There was dissention in other areas. While the French syndicalists argued that the unions would build the classless society of the future, for some Spanish anarchists, brought up on the writings of Pyotr Kropotkin, this smacked of centralisation. This no doubt explains why the CNT's Founding Congress agreed that syndicalism was a 'means' to destroy capitalism, not an 'end' or an 'ideal'.
30. LJS, 2 April 1910.
31. SO, 24, 29 June, 2 Dec. 1910; *Congreso de Constitución*, 56.

32. Tuñón de Lara, *Movimiento obrero*, vol. 2, 126.
33. LJS, 31 Dec. 1910.
34. LP, 28 July 1910, *Morning Edition*; LJS, 17 Sept. 1910; *Congreso de constitución*, 88–9 and 94–5. For events in Vizcaya see Fusi, *Política obrera*, 298–312.
35. José Prat, *Sindicalismo y Socialismo* and Ricardo Mella, *Sindicalismo y anarquismo*; Tomás Herreros, *El obrero moderno*. For Loredo see, above all, *Tierra y Libertad*, 9, 16, 30 Nov. 1910.
36. Ridley, *Revolutionary Syndicalism*, 84–7; Nicolas Papayanis, *Alphonse Merheim*, 59–70.
37. ED, 6 Sept. 1910, *Morning Edition*. On Lerroux's strategy see, Culla i Clarà, *Republicanisme lerrouxista*, 221–34.
38. LP, 28 July, 8 Oct., *Morning Editions*.
39. LJS, 17 Sept 1910. According to ED, on the other hand, two of the largest unions, the carters and coal unloaders, abstained and stated that they would join in if the strike had taken off by breakfast time. ED, 6 Sept. 1910, *Morning Edition*.
40. SO, 17 Feb. 1911.
41. Nevertheless, in its First Congress, held in September 1911, non-Catalan unions represented the modest total of 14,485 affiliates: see 'Primer congreso', in Cuadrat, *Socialismo y anarquismo*, 625–9.
42. SO, 8 Sep. 1911.
43. See above all, SO, 18 Nov. 1910, 8, 15 Sept. 1911. Pere Gabriel has elaborated a list of over forty trade unions which had participated in SO at some point during 1907 and 1908, but which had broken away by 1910: see 'Sindicats', 416–17.
44. We have put this section together from scraps of information in the local press. On the failure to sustain rationalist schools see 'Primer congreso' in Cuadrat, *Socialismo y anarquismo*, 659–60.
45. *Congreso de Constitución*, 99–104; SO, 8 Sept. 1911.
46. By 1910 the CADCI had 1,600 members and a number of cooks and waiters' unions, which kept their distance from the CNT, had about 1,000 affiliates between them. Membership figures for a large number of Barcelona unions are to be found in LP, 16 Nov. 1910, *Morning Edition*.
47. *La Cuña*, 1 May, 1 Dec. 1911.
48. The bakers' union La Espiga and the marblers remained affiliated, even though they were close to the Socialists, as did the cabinetmakers and locksmiths, despite declaring themselves in favour of *La base múltiple*. More generally, many unions – including the carters and Barcelona bricklayers – continued to participate in the elections of representatives onto the committee of the Junta Local de Reformas Sociales: see, LP, 16, 24 Nov. 1910, *Morning Editions*. The Barcelona Socialist, Jacinto Puig, declared it inexplicable that unions should present themselves to these elections 'and therefore declare themselves in favour of action within the bounds of legality, while forming part of the confederation, Solidaridad Obrera, which takes an anti-legalist stance'. LJS, 11 March 1911.
49. Calculated from data in ED, Sept. 1910–Jan. 1911.
50. For the period 1910 and 1911 I have found membership figures for eight of the unions under Socialist influence. They had around 800 affiliates. None of those whose membership is unknown seem to have been particularly strong.
51. LJS, 11 March 1911; SO, 1 May, 16 July 1911. On the growing subordination of the UGT to the PSOE see Manuel Pérez Ledesma, 'Partido y sindicato: unas relaciones no siempre fáciles'.
52. For the UGT trade federations see Santiago Castillo, *Historia de la Unión General de Trabajadores*, vol. 1, *Hacia la mayoría de edad*, 120–31.
53. In 1907 UGT unions generally paid their local union 1 peseta a month. It was here where the real difference with the CNT unions lay. In the CNT, unions were able to charge what they wanted, but the activists emphasised the need for fighting spirit and not large sums of money. In Barcelona around 1910 to 1914 dues tended to vary between 15 and 80 céntimos a month, towards the lower end where the anarchist-syndicalists were particularly influential.
54. *La Unión Ferroviaria, Sección Reus Norte*, May, Aug. 1914.

55. For Socialist ideology see Paul Preston, *The Coming of the Spanish Civil War*, 7–37. For the campaign, Cuadrat, *Socialismo y anarquismo*, 525–42. The Lerrouxists at first joined the *Conjunción* but left at the end of 1910 following a series of corruption scandals in the Barcelona Town Hall.

56. *El Socialista*, 11 Aug. 1911; LP, 9 Aug. 1911, *Morning Edition*; SO, 14 July, 11 Aug. 1911; *Tierra y Libertad*, 8, 16 Aug. 1911. Tomás Herreros was imprisoned as a result of comments made in the Barcelona meeting and not released until an amnesty in 1913.

57. Regarding the strike committee, the best information is to be found in a turgid polemic between Emiliano Iglesias and an anonymous syndicalist in SO, 5–15 Jan. 1917. For divisions within the Radical Party see, Culla i Clarà, *Republicanisme lerrouxista*, 258–9.

58. In July 1910 a group of anarchist exiles published a fly-sheet warning their Catalan colleagues that in Paris – to where he had supposedly fled – Moreno enjoyed a lavish lifestyle with no visible means of support: see, 'A los lectores de la prensa española. A los anarquistas', Internationaal Instituut voor Sociale Geschiedenis, *Max Nettlau Archive*, File 535. He was then paid to write a supposed exposé of Ferrer and the anarchists, under the pseudonym Constant Leroy, entitled *Los secretos de anarquismo*.

59. On the Brigade's activities see the comments by Joaquín Bueso in, SO, 3 March 1911. This offensive against the CNT activists was subsequently confirmed by the civil governor: see, Manuel Portela Valladares, *Memorias*, 90.

60. Pablo Fusi, *Política obrera*, 323–4.

61. LP, 14 Oct. 1911, *Night Edition*, 1 Dec. 1911; *Tierra y Libertad*, 29 May, 5 June 1912.

62. As for previous years I have based this on data from the Institute for Social Reforms and from Miguel Sastre i Sanna.

63. I have used LP, SO and the *Anuari d'Estadística Social de Catalunya, 1913* and *1914*. For union complaints that large-scale employers took the hardest line see, for example, SO, 13 March 1914.

64. I have used SO and LP along with, Primer Congreso Nacional de Industrias Metalúrgicas, *Exposición del cuestionario*, and Federación Regional Catalana de Obreros Metalúrgicos, *Memoria del congreso*.

65. For this section, along with SO, LP and LJS I have used Sastre y Sanna, *Las huelgas ... 1910–1914*, 48–53, 227–302 and 275–83, and *Anuari d'Estadística Social de Catalunya, 1913*, 109–11 and 115–23.

66. *Congreso de constitución*, 81–91.

67. Porcel, *Revuelta*, 60–3.

68. See Chapter Two, 38–9.

69. Instituto de Reformas Sociales, *Jornada*, 566–70.

70. For the 1913 strike I have used, above all, LP and Instituto de Reformas Sociales, *Jornada*. For the industrialists' stance see also Bengoechea, *Organització patronal*, 120–53.

71. LP, 27 and 28 Dec. 1913; SO, 1 Jan. 1914; LJS, 3 and 10 Jan., 7 Feb. 1914.

72. For which see Chapter Three, 82.

73. On the Ter Valley strike the major newspaper source is LJS. The quotation is from LJS, 4 April 1914.

74. On the shootings in textile finishing, see F. Baratech Alfaro, *Los Sindicatos Libres en España*, 42–3. The Unions Professionals and the assassination of Piqué are discussed in Winston, *Workers and the Right*, 49–59. According to Winston, at their high-point in 1915–16 they had between 6,000 and 7,000 members.

75. The four 'traitors' were Lluís Mas, Amadeu Camprubí, Federic Roigé and Marià Sanz: see, above all, La Confederación Nacional del Trabajo a La Opinión Pública de España, *A toda conciencia honrada, manifestaciones y orígen del terrorismo en las luchas sociales; quienes somos y adonde vamos*, 12–16. Their source, they maintained, was Epifaneo Casas, who also worked for the gang. Baratech, who joined the virulently anti-CNT Sindicatos Libres, also states that these workers betrayed the strike and planted the bomb. Strangely, however, I have found no reference to this bomb in the press during the strike. Sastre i Sanna mistakenly indicates that Sabanés was assassinated: see *Esclavitud moderna*, 109. In fact, he played an active role in the anarchist-syndicalist terrorist apparatus during the First World War years. He was employed in textile finishing and, one suspects, targeted because he had been

active in the shootings of 1912. I have found no independent confirmation of the murder of Sendra.

76. *Tierra y Libertad*, 10 July 1912; LP, 7 Jan. 1913; SO, 17 May, 15 July 1913, 26 March, 6 Aug., 20 Nov. 1914.

77. SO, 20 Nov. 1913.

78. I have used *Tierra y Libertad* and *Solidaridad Obrera*. For the Sants school see *Tierra y Libertad*, 22 April 1914.

79. Geary, *European Labour Protest*, 121–5. *Solidaridad Obrera* carried regular features on these developments. Moreover, between 27 September and 2 October 1913 an International Syndicalist Congress was held in London. José Negre, who was in France, represented the CNT. *Solidaridad Obrera* hoped that it would lead to the foundation of a new syndicalist international.

80. Federación Regional Catalana de Obreros Metalúrgicos, *Memoria del congreso*, 26; SO, 4, 11 June, 9 July 1914. In April 1914 the Catalan Regional Metalworkers' Federation had 1,500 members.

81. Along with the left-wing press one can also consult the federation's mouthpiece, *La Cuña*, for 1912–14. It should, however, be remembered that the ambiguities of previous years remained. For example, the president of the Barcelona Woodworkers' Federation, Francesc Subirà, was an anarchist-syndicalist, but in 1911 the federation itself wanted to build up a strike fund and operate a cooperative. This former pretension, at least, was dropped in its 1913 statutes: see Arxiu del Govern Civil de Barcelona, Negociat 1ᵉʳ, Foli 137, núm. 6856.

82. One can follow these events in SO and LJS. For the confederation's statutes see, Confederación Regional de Oficiales y Peones Albañiles de Cataluña, *Reglamento*.

83. Cuadrat, *Socialismo y anarquismo*, 494–5; Gabriel, 'Sindicats', 432–52; Capdevila and Masgrau, *La Justicia Social*, 17. Even less impressive were the number of Catalan members of the PSOE: 252 in 1907 and 304 in October 1915 (in this latter year 2.1 percent of the Spanish total): see Forcadell, *Parlamentarismo y bolshevización*, 112 and 320–1.

84. LP, 27, 28 Dec. 1913; SO, 1 Jan. 1914; LJS, 3 Jan., 7 Feb. 1914.

85. For this section, along with the Catalan press I have used, Instituto de Reformas Sociales, *Conflicto de obreros y empleados*.

86. For Negre see SO, 1 March, 12 June 1913.

87. The key source is still LJS. Overviews of the Catalan Socialists' position are to be found in Capdevila and Masgrau, *La Justica Social*, and Gabriel, 'Sindicats', 423–52.

88. SO, 30 Oct., 6, 13, 27 Nov., 4 Dec. 1913, 9 April, 2 July, 6 Aug. 1914.

89. The quotation is taken from SO, 30 Oct. 1913. On the Radical Republicans see, Culla i Clarà, *Republicanisme lerrouxista*, 258–73.

90. I have gleaned this information from LP and *Tierra y Libertad*.

91. Bueso, *Recuerdos*, 52. For Lorenzo's views, SO, 11 Aug. 1911.

92. SO, 16 Dec. 1910, 13 Jan. 1911, 17 March, 26 June 1913, 26 March, 8 Oct. 1914. Jaume Bisbe had already called for the formation of industrial unions in 1907: see SO, 9 Nov. 1907.

93. I have followed these events above all in LP, 3 Aug.–10 Sept. 1913. For membership of the CRT Regional Committee see, SO, 3 July 1913. *Tierra y Libertad* was later to claim that Polo was an agent provocateur. *Tierra y Libertad*, 15 Dec. 1915.

94. SO, 27 Nov. 1913, 19, 26 March, 29 Oct. 1914. The tramworkers' strike was part of an attempt by the anarchist-syndicalists to challenge the dominance of Foronda, but it was quickly snuffed out.

95. There is a brief portrait in Porcel, *Revuelta*, 43.

96. For which see, Manuel Buenacasa, 'Figuras ejemplares que yo conocí [1957–64]', in his, *El movimiento obrero español*, 190; Hermoso Plaja, 'Salvador Seguí, hombre de la CNT', in *Salvador Seguí*, 60. I give a portrait of Seguí in the next chapter, 235–7.

97. Ministerio de Trabajo, Comercio e Industria, *Anuario Estadístico de España, 1922–23*, 344.

Part III

The Gun and the Sword:
The Catalan CNT from
Revolution to Repression,
1915 to 1923

THE WAR-TIME ECONOMY AND THE RISE OF THE SINDICATS UNICS, 1915 TO 1918

The aim of this chapter is threefold. First, to look at the causes behind the rapid growth of strike action and union organisation between 1916 and 1918. Second, to analyse the rise of the Catalan CNT and the reforms undertaken in its organisation, practice and ideology. Finally, to study the impact these developments had on Catalan social relations and the reaction of the business community. There has been controversy regarding these issues. As noted in the previous chapter, despite the fact that Spain remained neutral, some authors have seen the impact of the First World War as provoking a sharp break in Catalan and Spanish history. Not only have they pointed to the influence of rapid economic growth and high inflation in underpinning the increased strength of organised labour and providing a strong sense of grievance, they also maintain that the rise of a new *nouveau riche* class of businessmen, who were more intransigent than their predecessors, and an influx of 'unassimilated peasants' from southern Spain, served enormously to exacerbate social tensions.[1] It is my intention to test these hypotheses in the context of this chapter.

The Growth of Organised Labour, January 1915 to June 1918

Without doubt the First World War was to have a substantial impact on labour relations. The outbreak of war initially provoked the dislocation of Spanish markets, a financial panic, and a sharp rise in unemployment, but from the late spring of 1915 the economic climate rapidly improved and there followed an unprecedented economic boom. It was favoured by a rapid expansion in the use of electricity, which freed Catalonia from the constraints of high-cost steam power, making it easier for industry to take advantage of the country's neutrality both to export to the warring nations and substitute their products in internal and foreign markets. The textile industries were able greatly to increase both the volume and value of exports between 1915 and 1917, in particular supplying French troops and then penetrating markets previously dominated by the warring powers. Import substitution also benefited the chemical and metal industries. The latter was further stimulated by the need to produce electrical generating equipment and by the growth in the car industry. House building also accelerated from 1910 to cope with a rapid influx of migrant workers. This in turn was to have a powerful knock-on effect on the cement, metal, ceramics and furniture industries. Outside Barcelona, in the foothills of the Pyrenees, these years were also to see the construction, at breakneck speed, of hydroelectric infrastructure.

However, the boom also led to intense inflationary pressures. In part this was because many manufacturers concentrated on export markets, where both the lack of competition and the demands of the warring powers provided rich pickings, and tended to leave the internal market undersupplied. To make matters worse, the opportunities to charge high prices for exports meant that manufacturers of both capital and consumer goods increased their prices on the home market. These difficulties were exacerbated by the inability of the antiquated Spanish rail system to cope with the increase in freight, resulting in shortages and forcing costs still higher.[2] Overall, the cost of living index in Barcelona rose by between 70 and 75 percent from 1912 and 1918, and, moreover, accelerated from 1916.[3] Consequently, as can be seen from table 2.2., workers were plunged into a desperate race to boost their pay packets in order simply to maintain their purchasing power.

The favourable economic conjuncture and spiralling inflation gave many workers both the opportunity and also a pressing reason to unionise. Nevertheless, the position of organised labour was only slowly transformed. Although greater stress was placed on wage increases, the push to cut working hours, abolish piece rates and 'regulate' the labour process remained major concerns. Furthermore, the number of strikes only grew slowly. The economic crisis, provoked by the onset of hostilities, meant that labour conflict was at first subdued.

Nor did the success rate of strikes immediately improve. According to figures by the Institute for Social Reforms, in Barcelona during 1915 almost 60 percent of strikes affecting over twenty workers ended in defeat. The big increase in strike activity came in the following year, as the economic climate rapidly improved. Between 1916 and 1918 the number of working hours lost in Barcelona averaged well over one million. Labour's strengthening position was also reflected in the success rate of strikes. In 1916, 43 percent of strikes with over twenty workers were lost, but in 1917 only 25 percent of such strikes ended in defeat.[4] Nevertheless, the 1917 to 1918 strike rate was still in line with previous highs in 1903 and 1913 (see tables 3.1. and 7.1.).[5]

With respect to union organisation, a similar pattern presented itself. Thus, at the highpoint of the previous decade, in the spring of 1903, up to 42,000 workers had been unionised, while between late 1917 and early 1918 around

62,500 industrial workers were organised, with perhaps about 12,500 shop and white-collar workers integrated into a variety of associations.[6] This means that around 28.5 percent of industrial workers were unionised in 1903 and (using the 1920 figures for the number of industrial workers in the city) about 32.5 per cent in late 1917 and early 1918.[7] Between late January and early April 1918 a temporary lull fell on the city when the Government reacted to food riots by suspending constitutional guarantees – a subject to be examined in the following chapter – but the union offensive was to be resumed thereafter. From late 1918 what may be described as a historically new conjuncture could be discerned, with the strength of organised labour increasing massively.

Table 7.1. Comparison of Strikes, Strikers and Working Days Lost in Barcelona and the Rest of Spain, 1915–1923[1]

	Barcelona			Percentage of Spanish Total		
Year	Strikes	Strikers	Working Days Lost	Strikes	Strikers	Working Days Lost
1915	36	14,191	191,125	20.4	43.8	42.1
1916	51	61,058	1,976,920	20.6	59.6	80.4
1917	55	12,912	941,380	17.2	17.2	47.0
1918	84	55,002	1,197,850	17.0	33.5	37.4
1919	70	156,000	3,250,000	7.4	46.8	45.5
1920	166	73,563	1,251,090	14.3	28.6	16.2
1921	26	3,589	101,950	7.0	4.2	3.6
1922	82	18,388	192,650	16.3	14.7	7.2
1923	62	23,587	981,480	14.4	18.6	29.3

Note:
1. For Barcelona I have used the detailed data elaborated by Josep Lluis Martín Ramos. In undertaking the comparison with the rest of Spain I have used the official data from the Institute for Social Reforms . Given the greater accuracy of the Barcelona figures, the table no doubt exaggerates the relative importance of strike activity in the city.

Sources: Instituto de Reformas Sociales, *Estadística de huelgas, 1915-1923*, Madrid, 1923-1926; Josep Lluís Martín Ramos, 'Anàlisi del moviment vaguístic a Barcelona, 1914-1923', in *Reçerques*, no. 20, 1988, 110.

With respect to the trades and industries in which workers were unionised, there was also a significant degree of continuity. At first, in Barcelona, unions strengthened in industries in which they had already made a mark, but they then started to challenge the industrialists in new areas. In the craft-based sector of the economy, in some trades such as tanning, glassmaking, wood-working and furniture-making, skilled, apprenticed workers took advantage of the new situation to establish virtual closed shops within many workplaces by 1918. Crucial with respect to the two latter trades was the organisation of a unified Union of Carpenters, Cabinetmakers and Similar Workers in August 1916, which was able to establish an eight-hours day throughout the wood-working industry. A key moment was a general cabinetmakers' strike, called in September 1916, which affected almost 1,000 workers. The new union supported the strikers through the levy of 'extraordinary dues', of first 1 and then 2 pesetas a month, on the remaining affiliates. Under pressure the employers capitulated in February 1917, despite the fact that the authorities had closed down the union's headquarters. Jaume Roca, an anarchist-syndicalist union leader from the textile finishing branch, declared it the greatest victory for many a year. Thereafter, the union grew rapidly. With almost 6,500 affiliates at the end of 1917, it had unionised about one-third of the total workforce.[8]

Unions faced a more difficult task in the construction industry. Bricklayers and their labourers were the only group of workers who were able to undertake major strikes in 1915. The unions' demands focused on ensuring that the eight-hours day and wage agreements were respected. This brought the construction unions into a long-running dispute with Aixerit, the contractor building the Barcelona Bull Ring. It culminated in the decision of the Construction Workers' Federation, in August, following the sacking of union activists, to declare a general strike throughout the industry and boycott the bullring. The results were mixed, with some non-unionised men, already working on the bullring, staying in, while the stonecutters, marblers and Sant Martí carpenters' unions refused to second the strike, leading the federation to declare them 'yellow'. This brought out the fact that while a loose industrial federation might be an improvement on isolated individual unions, united action could still not be guaranteed. The federation finally had to accept a compensation package for the men who had been fired.

In 1916, bricklayers turned their attention to achieving wage increases, but they were still dogged by disunity. January to April was to see a long four-months strike by over 5,000 bricklayers and their labourers, which also spread to other industrial towns. Again, in order to support the strikers, the Construction Workers' Federation, which now had 4,000 members, declared a general strike from the end of January. Yet this again provoked dissension within its ranks, with some twelve local unions refusing to second it. Over the next three months the contractors' association, the Mutua de Contratistes, refused to give way. It was helped by the decision by the Government, in early March, to shut down centres which harboured more than one union. Finally, in mid-April the federation acknowledged defeat. It reached an agreement with smaller non-unionised employers, who had broken with the Mutua, but the city's major contractors refused to recognise it. It was a blow from which the workers would take some time to recover.[9] Only from the spring of 1918 would a new Barcelona-wide Bricklayers and Bricklayers' Labourers Union be able to launch a new recruitment drive in the city's construction sites, enrolling 5,500 workers, about 40 percent of the industry's workforce, by the summer.[10] Yet the big contractors would remain powerful foes.

In the metal industry it was a similar story. The Barcelona Metalworkers' Federation came out on strike for a nine-hours day, between January and March 1916, and this was followed by strikes in other Catalan towns. The results were not altogether encouraging. Again, the workers' efforts were dogged by discrepancies between the neighbourhood unions. They were finally conceded a nine-hours day by some smaller employers, but the larger factories held out and sacked large numbers of union activists. Not until the spring and summer of 1918 was a new united union able to put sustained and increasingly successful pressure of employers to accept the unionisation of their plants and the nine-hours day. As in many other industries, it pursued the policy of calling strikes in single plants and supported them by raising the dues paid by the rest of the unionised workforce. In September 1918, 5,130 workers, a little over 25 percent of the city's metalworkers, were unionised, but the big factories, like La Maquinista, El Vulcano, and the Girona Foundry were still resisting.[11]

The big employers on the waterfront and in transport also proved a difficult nut to crack. A new sailors and stokers' union, El Naval, was formed in 1915, but suffered a big setback in the summer of 1916 when a strike called by the UGT's National Maritime Transport Federation was lost, provoking bitter divisions. Simultaneously the UGT launched a strike against one of the country's biggest railway companies, the Compañía del Norte, which, by contrast, was a great success, serving both to strengthen the Socialist Railwayworkers' Federation and revitalise railway workers' unionism in the city. Carters and coach drivers were also to consolidate their position, but Mariano Foronda put up fierce resistance to attempts to unionise tramworkers. Moreover, on the port, dockers to a large extent remained under strict social control. Along with El Naval, only a small port workers' union and a union of ships' cooks operated.[12]

In textiles the unions also had to battle hard, but had considerable success in consolidating their presence. As in 1913, the textile union La Constància led the way. Under the leadership of one of the industry's finishing trades, the calenders and sizers, it began to recover from the 1913 stoppage in 1916, calling an unsuccessful strike for a wage increase between July and September. Despite this setback, the calenders' policy of holding large neighbourhood meetings and encouraging men from the finishing trades to affiliate female family members bore fruit, with the result that by the end of 1917 it had over 10,000 affiliates. This new found strength allowed the union successfully to pursue a policy of declaring strikes in those – largely small – companies, which paid below generally agreed rates, with, once again, the strikers supported by 'extraordinary dues' from the rest of the membership. Most importantly, it was able to break out of its bulwark in El Clot and unionise considerable numbers in areas like Sants and Gràcia.[13]

In the new climate, union organisation in the industry was, once again, to grow throughout much of urban and small-town Catalonia. Industrialists in the Alt Llobregat managed to keep their company towns union-free, but by the summer of 1918, with over 20,000 workers unionised in Barcelona, around 10,000 affiliated in the medium-sized textile towns, and unions once again established in the Ter and Fresser Valleys, the total membership of the National Textile Federation was well in excess of 30,000.[14]

As in previous years, the cotton textile unions had to fight for acceptance every inch of the way and were vulnerable to counterattacks. The most dramatic example would be a lock-out in Reus during 1915. Over the previous five years the local union federation had built up an independent textile union, but the intransigence of the local industrialists made it very difficult to settle disputes. Matters came to a head when a strike for better conditions in the town's largest textile plant, La Fabril Cotonera, produced an increasingly radicalised conflict. Encouraged by support from the various Catalan employers' associations, the local textile industrialists launched a city-wide lock-out. Like their Barcelona colleagues in 1913, the female cotton textile workers threw themselves body and soul into the dispute and refused to accept any compromise, but were finally defeated, leading to the virtual collapse of the union.[15]

In Barcelona during 1916 and 1917 equally bitter conflicts focused on the warpdressers in weaving (*contramaestres*) and the textile finishing trades. Until the war years the warpdressers – skilled workers, from whom the foremen were usually drawn, who repaired the machinery and changed the pieces on the looms – had remained non-unionised, but from 1915 they set up their own union called El Radium. This alarmed the textile employers, who feared losing control of their plants. The most radical action was taken by four large Sants and L'Hospitalet factories – Joan Batlló, Balet i Vendrell, La España Industrial and Trinxet – who simply sacked the unionised men and recruited new staff, leading to a long, tense and frequently violent standoff. Tension in the industry further escalated in March 1917, when employers reacted to a work-to-rule by calenders and sizers, who were demanding a pay rise, by locking out the entire workforce. Members of this union formed the committee of La Constància, and there were fears that the employers were attempting to destroy union organisation throughout the industry. The workers received strong support, with female textile workers patrolling the streets to ensure no calenders went back. Important in this respect were family and friendship networks within the textile industry; calenders who did break ranks must have faced ostracism. The calenders were finally forced to accept a poor compromise; they gained a small wage rise but 140 workers lost their jobs. Nevertheless, La Constància did not buckle, and, at the end of 1917, the textile finishing trades' unions had around 4,000 affiliates each, the bulk of the workforce.[16]

In other industries significant attempts were also made, often for the first time, to affiliate low-skilled, often female workers. In clothing, tailors were at the forefront of a unionisation drive, but by 1918, trade unionism had also begun to penetrate the sweat shops, employing female seamstresses. This was brought home when a strike of tailors and garment workers for an nine-hours day in the summer of 1918 spread to the major factories, L'Aguila and El Segle, which largely employed migrant female labour. Finally, El Segle capitulated and L'Aguila was forced to reach a compromise.[17]

In the food industry, on the other hand, while bakers, waiters and cooks made big strides, the food-processing factories, which employed large numbers of low-skilled female workers, remained non-unionised. In the big gas, water and electricity plants the situation was worse. A union covering all three industries was set up in the autumn of 1916 but, under employer pressure, quickly collapsed. Big firms like the electricity suppliers, Ebro Power and Irrigation, Gas Lebón and Catalana de Gas were, for the time being, to stay union-free zones.[18] Much more success was enjoyed by shop and white-collar workers, who would, during these years, attain a substantial weight in the city's social and political life. The CADCI had over 4,000 members by 1917, and overall, at the end of the year, around 10,000 shop and office workers, and 2,500 cooks and waiters, were affiliated to various types of associations.[19]

As in previous years, strikes were often hard-fought, violent affairs. Those launched by the bricklayers in early 1916 and the cabinetmakers in late 1916 and early 1917 were especially tumultuous. There were also frequent attacks on strike-breakers and, occasionally, employers and foremen, during strikes involving workers in the textile finishing trades, metalworkers, carters and tanners. Moreover, in a number of trades and industries attacks on property were commonplace. Thus groups of bakers and women textile workers smashed shop and factory windows respectively. This strategy was also adopted by cabinetmakers, who went further, overturning carts laden with furniture and penetrating establishments to destroy the contents. Attacks on blacklegs were, as we have seen, nothing new; in the harsh world of Barcelona industry, beatings, stabbings and shootings were relatively common. Female textile workers, for their part, cut off strike-breakers' hair; it acted as a public humiliation which would mark the woman out within her community. Nevertheless, if we compare the figures for 1910 to 1914 and 1915 to 1918 some differences can be observed. While there was actually a fall in the overall number of attacks (341 as against 104), there was an increase in the number of workers shot, indicating increased targeting of blacklegs.[20] Furthermore, this was matched by a steep rise in shootings of employers and foremen. This is an issue which I shall examine in some depth when discussing the rise of Catalan anarchism-syndicalism.

Between 1915 and 1918, then, union organisation grew substantially, but one could hardly talk of a stabilisation of labour relations and the spread of systems of collective bargaining. While unions were increasingly central to the life of both Barcelona and the Catalan industrial towns some employers were still holding out, above all in larger plants and within sectors of the economy where workers were less skilled. It was not, therefore, the rise of any *nouveau riche* type of entrepreneur which was leading to increased industrial conflict, but rather the extent to which organised labour was now unionising more effectively and starting to break into new industrial sectors.

Nevertheless, faced by the rise of unions and strikes, the Barcelona employers began to shift their stance. While they wished to have no truck with the anarchist-syndicalists, they came to recognise that unions would not simply disappear and hence some kind of negotiating machinery needed to be set up. This explains why, after the big August 1917 general strike – dealt with in the next chapter – they began to talk of the need for what they called 'compulsory trade unionism' (*sindicalización forzosa*). All the workers and employers in particular trades and industries would elect representatives, who would establish wages and working conditions. The scheme had its origins in Catholic corporatist thought. The abolition of the guilds in the early-nineteenth century had led to the dissolution of the links between labour and capital, which these new bodies would supposedly restore. It had the advantage, employers felt, that they would not have to deal with an independent labour confederation, that bargaining would take place at a local level, and that strikes could only be declared after negotiations had broken down. They also optimistically believed that once the anarchist-syndicalist 'tyranny' had been broken, a new moderate stratum of union leaders would emerge. However, it also meant that they would have to concede state intervention in their affairs, for government bodies would both organise the elections and underwrite the agreements. As will be seen in Chapter Nine, as the social crisis worsened during 1919, the employers vigorously pushed the authorities to adopt such a system.[21]

Salvador Seguí and the Reorganisation of the Catalan CNT

A significant degree of continuity could also be seen in the Catalan anarchist-syndicalist movement. This was visible with regard to its leadership. Much more information is available on the organisation's personnel for the post-1914 period and this makes it possible to give a more rounded picture. José Negre and Francesc Miranda took a leading role in the organisation's reconstruction from the autumn of 1914 and were to remain key figures during 1915. Tomás Herreros, for his part, remained influential in *Tierra y Libertad* and in the anarchist affinity groups. Other figures also began to make their mark. An important independent personality was Manuel Andreu, who became general secretary of the CRT in August 1914 and took over the editorship of *Solidaridad Obrera* in 1915. He led a somewhat disordered lifestyle but was highly intelligent and emerged as the most eloquent and incisive voice in favour of the organisation's reform.[22] Increasingly important was also the firebrand, Eusebi Carbó, a cork worker who had been born and bred in Palamós in northern Catalonia. He had settled in Barcelona in 1910 and subsequently established himself as a frequent contributor to the anarchist press.[23] Also influential was Antonio Loredo, who from 1910 had been joined by several other so-called 'Americans' (often of Spanish origin), including the flamboyant bohemian, José Borobio, who edited *Solidaridad Obrera* between 1916 and 1917, and at night did a hypnosis act in local cabarets. The Americans role reflected the interconnection between Spanish and Latin American anarchism that had developed from the late-nineteenth century.[24]

A couple of migrants from other parts of Spain also rose quickly within the organisation. Very important in subsequent years would be the Aragonese carpenter, Manuel Buenacasa, who arrived in Barcelona in late 1914, having, it seems, been boycotted by local industrialists. He was already a well-known activist in Zaragoza, and had entered into contact with Catalan anarchist-syndicalists through the National Federation of Woodworking Unions.[25] He would only be outshone by Angel Pestaña, who settled in Barcelona just after the outbreak of the First World War in August 1914, and would over the next two years rise to become the organisation's second most prominent figure. Until this time he had led a nomadic lifestyle. He was born in the province of León in 1886 and experienced a harsh and uncertain childhood, working with his father in mining and railway tunnelling in northern Spain after they had been abandoned by his mother. Following the death of his father in Vizcaya, when he was fourteen years old, he became involved in union and anarchist agitation in Bilbao. From 1907, harassed by the authorities, he then spent some time in France before settling in French Algeria (where he learnt the craft of watchmaking) and marrying. But with the outbreak of the First World War, fearful of the consequences, he decided to move to Barcelona.

In Barcelona, within anarchist-syndicalist circles, there was some knowledge of his activities in Bilbao and he had already written an article for *Tierra y Libertad*. But his rapid rise was based on the close contacts he established with the anarchists linked to *Tierra y Libertad* and his effective intervention in debates on the relationship between anarchism and syndicalism in the Syndicalist Athenaeum. By the end of 1914 he was on the paper's editorial board and also threw himself into trade-union work. Tall and slim, he was a melancholy aesthete; soft spoken in informal conversation but also an eloquent speaker, adept in the use of jokes and anecdotes. Salvador Seguí's nickname 'the gentleman of the sad countenance' very much summed up his appearance, a fact he took advantage of by, on occasion, disguising himself as a priest in order to elude the authorities.[26]

Although from a working-class background, all these men devoted much of their attention to writing and proselytising and were active in the anarchist groups. This meant that they would be much exercised with matters of anarchist theory. They were joined by other figures whose power base was located within the unions and who were much more focused on discussions with employers and managing demands and strikes. Some of these men, as we shall see, were highly pragmatic with respect to ideology and strategy, focusing above all on union building. The best known of these labour activists was soon to become Salvador Seguí, the greatest leader the Catalan CNT was to produce, but there were hundreds of men who, in their spare time, would dedicate themselves to union work. With the trade-union revival of 1916 their voices would become increasingly powerful.

One of the features which characterised the leadership cadres of the wartime CNT was their diverse geographical origin. This can in part be related to the fact that Barcelona was highly dependent on migrant labour. It was further encouraged by the anarchists' egalitarian, internationalist, ideology, and by their stress on the need to affiliate the lesser skilled. This meant that both non-Catalan youngsters seeking an apprenticeship and older migrants were welcomed into the fold. Moreover, the embryonic state of the organisation, and the lack of hierarchical, bureaucratised structures, meant that the leadership was very fluid and, in these circumstances, those ambitious and quick-witted enough, or who had a magnetic personality, could quickly make their mark. Only from this perspective can one explain the meteoric rise of Angel Pestaña.

This diversity also had its reflection in language usage. As in the years 1898 to 1914, Catalan continued to be the major vehicle of oral communication and Castilian-Spanish was predominantly used within the press. This caused few problems. Youngsters born outside the Catalan-speaking area, as was the case of the metalworker of Andalusian origin, Enrique Rueda, learnt the language while young. Adults, such as Pestaña, after a period of time, had no problem understanding Catalan, but continued to speak in Castilian.[27] The lack of strongly held nationalist beliefs limited tensions, although, as we shall see in Chapter Eight, disagreements regarding relations with the Catalanist Left were to have linguistic and cultural undertones.

As previously, almost all of the organisation's leading figures remained working-class autodidacts who plied a trade. There were a few men from middle-class families, but in order to be fully accepted as CRT leaders they had to work in industry. A good example of this is Seguí's close friend, Josep Viadiu. His father was an employer in the tanning industry, but he earned his spurs as an organiser in the National Tanners' Federation.[28] On the other hand, middle-class labour lawyers, who were to play a key role defending CRT members in court, were viewed with some ambiguity. Their help was much appreciated, but many saw them as a breed apart, who could never be fully assimilated.

After 1914 in particular, this fact would accentuate the differences between the CNT and the Socialists. The years after 1910 were to see an influx of middle-class professionals and intellectuals into the PSOE-UGT, who, as in other European countries, sensed that social-democracy could provide the most effective vehicle for the reform of what were class-ridden societies in which old aristocratic values still predominated.[29] They were able to play an important role because of the existence of a separate party political sphere, and because the shop floor and the union leadership was increasingly mediated by a professional bureaucracy. It was this that made it possible for Julián Besteiro, Professor of Logic at Madrid University, to become a member of the UGT and PSOE national committees during the war. In Catalonia a similar trend could be seen, with a number of middle-class professionals, such as Rafael Campalans and Dr Ramon Pla i Armengol, joining the party. Such a development was inconceivable within the CRT, in which only in 1918 would the first tentative steps towards professionalisation be made. This growing divergence between the CNT and UGT may, indeed, have sharpened syndicalist criticisms of Socialist 'politicians', who were seen as exploiting the workers for their own ends. It was, no doubt, because of the very different milieux in which they operated that, following CNT criticisms over the UGT's lack of preparations for a jointly organised general strike in August 1917, Pablo Iglesias sniffily retorted, 'you manual workers see it like that, but we intellectuals see things differently'.[30]

The organisation was caught on the back foot by the outbreak of the war. It was evicted from its headquarters and until the end of 1915 had to put up with a totally inadequate centre, which was not large enough serve as a focus for union and cultural work. Moreover, *Solidaridad Obrera* was thrown into crisis because it could no longer send the 1,000 copies it had been supplying abroad.[31] The economic crisis also meant that at first it made little progress on the trade-union front. During 1915 there was a group of around twenty-seven Barcelona unions close to the organisation but many did not pay their dues regularly, while contacts with other Catalan unions appear to have been sporadic. Overall it had no more than 15,000 members.[32]

It was also slow to rebuild after the heavy repression of the previous years. Between 1915 and 1916 the CNT National Committee (as it was increasingly referred to) functioned irregularly, and it was not until the Andalusian Regional Federation was set up at the spring of 1918 that it could begin to reconstruct any kind of Spanish-wide confederation.[33] Even in Barcelona itself, until 1918 the organisation remained on a far from solid footing. Various local committees came and went without having any effective presence. Hence the entire Catalan organisation would be run on a day-to-day basis by a Barcelona-based CRT Regional Committee. Yet this does not mean it was inactive. As in the past, an undernourished organisational structure did not prevent it from galvanising working-class protest. As we shall see in the next chapter, it was at the forefront of agitation against rising prices. It was also in the thick of the big Barcelona strikes in the textile, construction and metal industries during 1915 and 1916. As already noted, they did not go according to plan. Once again, faced with the defeat of both the metalworkers and bricklayers, on 7 March 1916 the CRT turned to the well-worn recourse of a general strike. It had a considerable impact in the major industries in which the anarchist-syndicalists had been relatively strong, lasting for several days, but did not alter the course of the strikes.

As in the aftermath of the 1913 general strike, these defeats led to renewed calls for a rethink of union strategy. In addition, there was deep disquiet at the divisions which had opened up between the neighbourhood construction unions during 1916, and at the leadership's inability to carry part of the workforce with them, and this produced calls for organisational reform. The key figures behind these demands were a group of men whose primary sphere of operations was the labour unions. They were above all trade unionists, who had become involved in labour agitation during the first decade of the century and who, by the First World War, were in their thirties and taking up positions of responsibility.[34] The key point is that, immersed in the realities of trade-union life and keen to take advantage of the more favourable conditions to build their unions and turn the CRT into a powerful labour confederation, they were to willing to take a more pragmatic position than many of those linked to the anarchist groups and *Tierra y Libertad*. Underlying these demands was the fear that highly radicalised anarchists, operating within the affinity groups, endangered the organisation's existence, and the belief that that it was the union leaders who should be in control of the organisation's destiny.

The major personality was without doubt Salvador Seguí. He was born in Lleida in 1887 but when he was only one or two years old his family moved to the Barcelona Fifth District. A rebellious youth, he had attended school infrequently. At the age of ten he began to work as an apprentice painter but was never to settle, moving from job to job, either to earn a little extra to support his impoverished parents or because he had fallen out with his employer. In this sense Seguí was quite typical of the anarchist-syndicalist activists. He was a Catalan native who became a journeyman, but was not apprenticed into an elite craft and was habituated to poverty and even hunger. Indeed, when there was no alternative he was not adverse to having a meal in a cheap guesthouse (*fonda de sisos*), refusing to pay, then fighting his way out. As in the case of many of the more intelligent workers in a similar position, he was highly receptive to emancipatory literature and, in typically anarchist fashion, did not shy away from trying to help organise the most marginal and destitute groups in society. As a young man he led marches of the unemployed to the town hall to demand work in the 'municipal brigades' and even attempted to 'emancipate' the prostitutes in Chinatown by plying them with anarchist pamphlets.

From the turn of the century he became involved in trade-union and anarchist agitation. He worked within the painters' union but also affiliated to a Barcelona Federation of Anarchist Groups and went through a Nietzschean phase, forming part of a group called The Sons of Whores. It was around this time, in 1904 or 1905, that he started the *tertulia* in the Teatro Español.[35] From the foundation of Solidaritat Obrera in 1907 he increasingly focused on trade-union work. As we saw in Chapter Six, his violent intervention in a Lerrouxist meeting in August of that year and subsequent imprisonment, gained him considerable notoriety. But his growing reputation from around 1910 was based on a number of qualities. He had a good memory and proved an effective administrator. Probably more important in an atmosphere in which personal prestige was all important, a big man with a robust frame, he was self-assured, decisive and, above all, an excellent orator, with a booming, baritone voice. In addition, he enjoyed debate, was generous and known for his bonhomie. (This occasionally got him into trouble for giving away CNT funds to those in need.) Indeed, he loved to be the centre of attention and rarely seems to have spent a night indoors. Between 1913 and 1915 he became a key figure in the construction industry, but he emerged as the CNT's 'number one ... by right' in 1916 when he took over from Manuel Andreu as secretary of the CRT and also became the secretary of the Committee of the Valencia Assembly.[36] The first post effectively put the entire Catalan organisation in his hands, while the second, as we shall see in the following chapter, made it possible for him to take charge of establishing an alliance with the UGT.[37]

I have no information on the exact circumstances in which Seguí was elected secretary of the CRT. As seen in the previous chapter, there was already some suspicion of him in harder-line anarchist-syndicalist circles. He was perhaps helped by the fact that Anselmo Lorenzo had died at the end of 1914, for he would surely have protested vigorously at the direction in which Seguí was to take the organisation. More importantly, he was backed up by 'a team of men who held him in high esteem and appreciated his great leadership qualities',[38] and these men had attained, by 1916, a strong position within the CRT unions. Major labour organisers close to Seguí included friends within the Barcelona Construction Workers' Federation, the bricklayers Simó Piera and Josep Molins, the plasterer Enric Valero, and the carpenter Joan Pey, along with the metalworker, Francesc Botella, and the tanner, Josep Viadiu. Seguí, though a masterful orator, was little taken to writing and so Viadiu, along with the printer, Salvador Quemades, began to act as his secretaries. Both of these men would emerge as talented propagandists in their own right. Quemades, it seems, helped Seguí with his articles and pamphlets.

He was also supported by other colleagues, more focused from the outset on writing in the anarchist-syndicalist press, in particular Agustí Castellà (who was the brother of his partner and lived in the same house as Seguí until early 1919), and Antoni Amador.[39] In addition, a large number of labour leaders, although personally more distant, were behind reform. They included the glassworker from Badalona, Joan Peiró, who emerged as a major figure in the organisation in 1917, and activists within the Barcelona textile unions, like the brothers Jaume and Josep Roca.

Seguí did not overtly challenge the CNT's anarchist-syndicalist ideology. Between 1916 and 1919 most of the Catalan CRT's leading figures, from Seguí to Negre, took up the idea that syndicalism was anarchist doctrine applied to the trade-union sphere. During 1917 it was, in fact, Negre, who had now studied French revolutionary syndicalism in more depth, who took the lead in explaining the CRT's ideology. He now seemingly took a more flexible position, maintaining that through the experience of the class struggle workers would understand their true interests and the strategy which best suited their needs. This would inevitably lead them to practise the ideals outlined by the *obreros conscientes* within the organisation. At the same time, he stressed working-class unity and was highly critical of anarchists within the Argentinian labour confederation, the FORA, who had divided the movement because they had tried to 'impose' anarchism.[40]

There was nothing in this with which Seguí and his supporters would disagree, but they did lay particular stress on two points. First, they maintained that it was above all the work of the trade-union leaders to guide their less politically aware colleagues. Seguí totally rejected any suggestion that the anarchist groups might play any kind of directing role. This was highly controversial because it would sideline a whole swathe of the movement. A crucial theoretical corollary of this was Seguí's insistence that the economic underpinnings of the communist society of the future would be built by the union movement. Second, Seguí and his supporters argued that while they were anarchists outside the unions, within them they had to be syndicalists. This meant that as union leaders they should focus on purely economic issues. Discussion of questions such as religion and politics would only serve to divide the workers. Like Joaquín Bueso before them, they realised that this was necessary in order to bring less committed trade unions on board.[41] This directly contradicted the tenets of more hard-line anarchists and anarchist-syndicalists, who stressed the need to politicise the workers.

There were two major areas in which Seguí's 'team' instituted reform. First, rather than violently chastise the Socialists they allied themselves with them and even considered the possibility of unification in order to strengthen the position of organised labour within the polity. Second, they pushed for the establishment of larger city-wide unions and for the reform of the statutes of the CRT in order both to encourage more workers to join and put it on a more financially viable footing.

The reform of union structures would be the first major campaign. In response to the divisions that had opened up during the 1915 and 1916, *Solidaridad Obrera*, under the editorship of Manuel Andreu, a supporter of

Seguí, stressed that in order to defeat the industrialists they had to build broader-based local unions with a single central committee, thereby ensuring unity. It was in this context that the term Sindicat Unic (SU, a 'Single Union') was born during the summer of 1916. At first it did not necessarily mean an industry-wide union, but this was the logical endpoint, and, by 1917, leading figures in the organisation, such as Angel Pestaña, were arguing that SUs should be local industrial unions.[42]

This differed from the UGT's union strategy, which consisted of trying to build up Spanish craft and industrial federations. Within the CRT there was debate on whether these SUs should be the building blocks of national federations. Some anarchist-syndicalists, such as Peiró and Viadiu, who had key posts in the glassworkers' and tanners' trade federations respectively, were of this opinion. It was, moreover, a position with which Seguí sympathised. However, the majority argued that the establishment of the SUs should go hand in hand with the abolition of such federations. This focus on locality can in part be explained because the CNT was no more than a confederation in embryo. It was still to a large extent based on Barcelona and the need to build city-wide industrial unions was the major concern for most activists. But active hostility to the Catalan and Spanish trade and industrial federations also had a political dimension. The anarchist heritage was rooted in opposition to bureaucratic union organisation. Seguí and his supporters were starting to question the anarchist stress on spontaneity, but there was a lot of suspicion of what were seen as over-arching union structures, distant from the membership. Perhaps more important, trade and industrial federations retained an autonomous existence and were wary of explicitly affiliating to the CNT. Moreover, as Manuel Buenacasa pointed out, some of their unions did not even feel it necessary to affiliate to local CNT federations. Disbanding trade and industrial federations would, therefore, help to subordinate the local unions to the anarchist-syndicalist movement.[43]

The support for SUs was linked to a push for a thorough overhaul of the way in which the Catalan CNT was managed. Manuel Andreu set the tone, arguing that in the past the organisation had only operated effectively during major strike waves, and had been otherwise ineffective because, on the one hand, it had given support to workers from unaffiliated unions, and, on the other, many of those theoretically affiliated did not pay their dues. If it wanted to build a 'real local federation and ... a powerful regional confederation' it would have to make sure that all unions paid their dues along with any further contributions required, while boycotting recalcitrant unions.[44]

A major focus of the proposals was, therefore, the need to integrate as many workers as possible into the CRT and to resolve its constant cash crises. Its ability to build the organisation, launch campaigns and operate a daily paper were seriously hampered both by the lack of funds, the disperse means by which they were collected and the dearth of reliable leaders. Hence, the proposals, endorsed by Salvador Seguí, that dues should be set at a somewhat higher rate and that they should employ a paid secretary. In addition, a committee set up in late 1917 to look into the running of *Solidaridad Obrera*, in which Joan Peiró was a leading figure, called for the paper's editorial team to be paid, and, reflecting this group's wish to ensure that the labour leadership actually controlled the organisation, argued for the formation of an 'executive and consultative committee', made up of union representatives, to oversee the running of the paper. Moreover, Peiró demanded an overhaul of the statutes of the CRT to ensure that it genuinely represented all Catalan unions rather than being run by representatives of the Barcelona trades.[45]

These reforms were difficult to justify in anarchist terms. In reality, whatever the new leadership might claim, they was diluting traditional anarchist practice in the name of union building. This was in fact intimated by those close to Seguí. Thus, Ricard Fornells, the secretary of the Barcelona local federation from December 1917 onwards, stated that in the past an 'excessive radicalism' had prevented the organisation from 'operating in a broad sense', and a lead article in *Solidaridad Obrera* claimed that one of the advantages of the SUs was that the unions would be stronger and, hence, would not have to undertake so many inconvenient strikes, 'for unions, in order to reorganise ... like peoples need peace'.[46] It was on this question in particular that opposition reared its head, with claims that the anarchist emphasis on direct action was being lost and that the new focus on supporting strikes through supplementary dues contravened the principles of direct action, copying the tactics of the UGT.[47]

In order to head off this criticism, contain damaging splits and push through their agenda Seguí's supporters needed to reach compromises with more 'orthodox' colleagues, including the previous leadership. Between 1916 and 1918 it proved possible, to a significant degree, to achieve this objective. It was important, in this respect, that Seguí did not explicitly break with anarchist-syndicalist doctrine. Furthermore, the organisation began to grow significantly from 1917 onwards. This in itself seemed an endorsement of the new union practice. Finally, the argument that his 'team' was imitating the UGT was only partially valid. It was true that their reforms would, in structural terms, reduce the distance between the two confederations, but, despite the note of caution, the CRT retained its mobilising tradition. What the reformers aimed to build was a body which would remain more decentralised than the UGT and, to a degree at least, continue to take on industrialists 'in the street', but which had sufficient organisational weight to function effectively. And few could object to the construction of big local unions, which incorporated the unskilled and took on the industrialists much more successfully.

From the outset they could count on Manuel Andreu. He was the principal writer on *Solidaridad Obrera* until November 1917, from where he remained an eloquent champion of reform. José Negre and Francesc Miranda accepted less high profile positions and did not rock the boat too much (in the case of the former, until the events of July and August 1917, discussed in the next chapter). Negre was on the editorial board of *Solidaridad Obrera*, and Miranda remained an important figure on both the CRT and CNT committees. Also generally supportive was Buenacasa, who was an active and influential presence, secretly replacing Francesc Miranda as the general secretary of the CNT in August 1917. This would be a key post because it would be from then on that the CNT would in reality begin to build a Spanish-wide organisation.[48]

Nevertheless, the key figure would be Pestaña. He was admired as a combative anarchist 'purist' in early 1915, but over the next three years, in the words of Joan Ferrer, 'from being an intransigent anarcho he became a revolutionary syndicalist',[49] and allied with Seguí. Simultaneously, he asserted his position as number two in the organisation. From March 1916 he was a member of the Valencia Committee. Then he took over the running of the CRT in March 1917 when Seguí and the old committee resigned, lamenting that they had been unable effectively to reorganise the organisation. Finally, he would replace José Borobio as director of *Solidaridad Obrera* in November of the same year. He was able to take on so many roles because he worked from home as a watch repairer and, therefore, spent much of his time in the organisation's headquarters. From 1916 the Seguí and Pestaña double act would be crucial to the CNT. While the former could appeal to less committed trade unionists, Pestaña retained his links with anarchist hardliners and acted as a guarantor of ideological integrity.

In order to cement the reform process, a Catalan congress was held in the Sants Rationalist Athenaeum (as the Sants Rationalist Centre was called from 1915 onwards) between 28 June and 1 July 1918. Seemingly frustrated at the slow pace of change, as already noted Seguí resigned as CRT general secretary in March 1917. This in no way signified his eclipse. Rather, it gave him a free hand to concentrate on relations with the UGT and the celebration of the congress. The 'Organisational Committee' was headed by Seguí, and made up of a number of figures who broadly shared his priorities.[50] Their first goal, to integrate as many workers as possible into the organisation, was reflected in the decision to invite non-affiliates. The fact that 73,860 workers were represented was, in this respect, a considerable achievement. These included a group of Socialist unions from outside Barcelona, led by Miguel Mestre from Reus, who continued to pursue an understanding with syndicalism.[51]

Nevertheless, Seguí's supporters were able to set the agenda. CRT dues were set at 10 céntimos a month. It was agreed that *Solidaridad Obrera*'s editorial team should be paid, and that the CRT Regional Committee should also have a paid secretary to help with its work. In addition, the decision was taken that all affiliated unions would have, in future, to form part of the SUs and local federations. However, in order to head off opposition, it was decided that individual unions would be given some time to join and that the sections would have more powers than had originally been envisaged. They would have their own committee, hold assemblies and call strikes. Only if the issue concerned the whole industry would it be dealt with at the level of the SU.[52] Similar compromises were reached in other areas. Regional and national trade and industrial federations were rejected a priori, but it was agreed that this was an issue that the next CNT congress should address. Furthermore, in a move that no doubt disturbed the 'purists', after Miguel Mestre and others had voiced their opposition to a resolution which required affiliated unions to adopt direct action, with the support of Joan Peiró it was toned down. Unions, it was agreed, should 'preferentially' use direct action, but it would not be imposed because this could divide the workers. There was a similar compromise with respect to links with political centres. It was decided that unions affiliated should 'try not to' set up in such centres, but there was no absolute prohibition. This was criticised by Pestaña; an example of the way in which, although cooperating with Seguí, he also played to a more radical gallery.[53]

These accords emphasised that while Seguí considered himself an anarchist, the new union practice was much closer to that advocated by the French CGT's Chartre d'Amiens, backed at SO's regional assembly in 1908. Working-class unity was, to an important degree, to take precedence over doctrine. The term, 'syndicalist realist', used by the Socialist, Joan Codina, to describe the leadership of the Barcelona textile unions from 1916 onwards, is an accurate portrayal of the practice Seguí wished the Catalan CRT to pursue.[54] The congress reinstated Seguí as CRT general secretary, putting him in charge of the actual implementation of reform.

The Rise of the Catalan CNT, January 1916 to January 1919

Throughout the war years the anarchist-syndicalists continued to operate in an uncertain legal framework. They were still subject to frequent imprisonment and along with other attributes an adeptness at jumping out of windows and climbing over rooftops and down drainpipes remained extremely valuable. During major disputes, the police's Special Brigade routinely rounded up anarchist-syndicalist activists, only for them to be released without charge.[55] Moreover, they also continued to fall foul of the Jurisdictions Law and legislation penalising attacks on the regime and incitement to violence and revolution. To be the director of *Tierra y Libertad*, for example, virtually guaranteed regular prison stretches.

To make matters worse, the growing threat posed by the labour movement to the Restoration regime would in itself encourage governments to suspend constitutional guarantees more frequently, making it possible to hold prisoners without charge (the so-called *presos gubernamentales*) and difficult for unions to operate openly. The longest such suspension during these years was between 25 January and 14 April 1918, following several days of protest by women over the rising price of coal and food. The atmosphere of confrontation was heightened because civil guards surrounded CNT premises when important meetings were held. Furthermore, the state's unwillingness to forge a civilian police could still lead to tragedy. The worst incident occurred in Badalona on 26 August 1918 when civil guards opened fire on 1,000 workers protesting in the town square at the arrest of three of their colleagues. Four were killed and over fifty wounded. Yet the only person detained and put on trial was Joan Peiró, for an article deemed to insult the armed forces.[56] Nevertheless, as we shall see, the CNT also gratuitously provoked the authorities. Between 1915 and 1918, shootings, particularly of employers and foremen, rose rapidly, bringing further retribution upon the heads of the activists.

This, together with employer hostility, meant that the world of the CRT labour leaders remained that of frequent sackings, periods spent in prison and in hiding from the authorities. Hence they were unable to follow any set routine. Seguí, for example, had periodically to work in southern Catalonia out of sight of the authorities.[57] But despite the danger, a life spent in the factory in which one, in any case, earned barely enough to pay the bills and would, most likely, end up in poverty in old age, could seem, to the most restless or daring, little compensation in comparison with the whirlwind of union meetings, revolutionary preparations, escapes from the police, and the evening *tertulias* with anarchist-syndicalist colleagues.

As in the past, in a favourable economic climate haphazard state repression was not sufficient to prevent the organisation's growth. Between January 1916 and January 1919 there were two phases in the development of the CRT. The first, which lasted until the summer of 1918, saw the organisation, for the first time, attain a substantial weight in the city's social and political life. Once again, anarchist-syndicalists would be at the forefront of the strikes in the metal and construction industries, and would again enjoy substantial backing amongst skilled unions from the more conflict-ridden trades. An important addition to these groups would be the glassworkers. Until this date the journeymen glassblowers had considered themselves an 'aristocratic' elite and had remained rather aloof from syndicalist organisation. But under Joan Peiró their stance changed dramatically. Peiró made his name in 1908 at the age of twenty-one, when he defended the right of journeymen assistants and other inferior categories to form part of the glassworkers' union. It was his rejection of craft-based, elitist, trade unionism which would from 1916 draw him towards anarchism-syndicalism.[58] In subsequent years he would show himself to be both a practical and tenacious union activist. But his rise as a major figure within the National Federation of Glassworkers in 1916 must also be seen in the context of the changing structure of the industry. During the war years, as was noted in Chapter One, the glassworkers faced a serious threat to their position with the introduction of glassblowing machinery, combined with attempts by the major employers to institute a much higher degree of industrial discipline and social control in their factories. In Catalonia, the result would be bitter industrial conflict in the major factories in the trade, such as Costa in Badalona and Vilella in Poble Nou, and it was in this context that the glassworkers' unions became less elitist, formed a single Barcelona and Badalona-wide union, and integrated into the CRT. This reorientation strengthens my argument that there was a link between threats posed by capitalist development to craft workers and growing labour militancy.

During the war years, the anarchist-syndicalists also made some progress outside the craft-based sectors of the economy. In transport, union organisation revived amongst the carters, who remained affiliated. On the port they were not able to rebuild organisation amongst the coal unloaders, but set up a union of port workers and, importantly, in late 1916 wrested control of El Naval, the union of sailors and stokers, from the Socialists, after the loss of the nationwide strike. They also began to challenge the employers in some areas in which there had been little tradition of union organisation. Most remarkably, they set up a union, La Efusió, specifically aimed at labourers, which had 7,000 members by September 1918. In addition, their Union of Gas, Water and Electricity Workers managed to recruit 800 members in 1917, before falling to an employer counterattack. Similarly, they started recruiting women engaged in the manufacture of cardboard boxes, only for the employers to hit back and undermine the union.

However, amongst lesser skilled workers it was once again in textiles that the anarchist-syndicalists most effectively made their presence felt. Most important in this respect was the rise of La Constància, which remained under their influence. Moreover, the growth of textile unionism in Barcelona helped them retake control of the National Textile Federation. The way in which this occurred further illustrates the link, discussed in previous chapters, between severe industrial strife and anarchist-syndicalist penetration. From the spring of 1914 onwards, the federation's Mataró-based committee was to a large degree in Socialist hands, but over the following two years the escalating number of disputes threw it on the defensive.

Events in Reus during 1915 represented the first big blow. The reaction of the Socialists, who led the local union, to the strike and lock-out was contradictory. A more moderate wing, captained by Josep Recasens i Mercadé, followed what may be referred to as classic UGT tactics, opposing any escalation of the dispute and criticising the strikers for not reaching a negotiated settlement. Another group within the local party, led by Miguel Mestre, backed the decision taken by the workers first to ask the other Reus unions to come out in support and then, as the situation became increasingly desperate, for the Nacional Textile Federation to call a general strike. The Socialists were put under increasing pressure by a group of anarchist-syndicalists who, as the dispute became radicalised, garnered support amongst the female textile workers. The federation's Mataró leadership was, however, unenthusiastic at the prospect of calling a general strike. Furthermore, La Constància stated that it would only respond if the Reus workers adopted the aggressive union tactics associated with direct action, with the result that the general strike failed to materialise and the Reus textile workers went down to defeat.[59]

This outcome once again indicates how difficult it was to operate a moderate trade-union strategy in Catalan cotton textiles. The loss of the strike was a serious blow to the prestige of the Reus Socialists, both dividing the local party and allowing the anarchist-syndicalists to make inroads. In the following year leadership of the National Textile Federation passed out of Socialist hands for similar reasons. When the Barcelona cotton textile workers once again flooded into La Constància in 1916 they immediately called for a wage increase and came out on strike. The federation's committee officially supported the strike, but considered the demand ill-timed. As a result, once the strike had been defeated, it faced a barrage of criticism and in September had to resign. Leadership of the federation then passed into the hands of the Barcelona union of sizers and calenders, which was close to the anarchist-syndicalists and was running La Constància.[60]

With the growth in textiles' trade unionism the profile of female orators grew. Several women then shot to prominence after having played a leading role in the riots and demonstrations organised by working-class women against rising prices during January 1918; most notably the textile workers Roser Dolcet and Lola Ferrer, and Libertad Ródenas, a member of the well-known Valencian anarchist family. After constitutional guarantees were reestablished in April, they were to participate actively in meetings organised by both the National Textile Federation, La Constància, the CRT and CNT, and also set up a lively Women's Anarchist Group in the Sants Racionalist Athenaeum.[61]

Yet the ambiguity apparent in previous years with respect to a woman's place in the world of work and within the labour movement remained. Some activists did take a positive approach. Angel Pestaña argued explicitly that the clock could not be turned back and that women should be welcomed onto the shopfloor. Others continued to view paid labour as primarily a male activity. Hence, 'Juan Fuentes' (Joan Peiró) could state in 1916 that the economic crisis was motivated by 'the intervention of women in jobs which should only be carried out by men'. Such views were not limited to trade unionists. In a talk to the Women's Anarchist Group in 1918 the rationalist teacher, Abelardo Saavedra, informed his audience that, 'one shouldn't repeat the mistake made by some modern freethinkers, who attempt to liberate women by exploiting them both in the home and at work'. Most extreme was 'Montegualdo' (probably Félix Monteagudo), who railed against the 'macho-feminists', who, in the countries at war, had supported the influx of women into sectors of industry previously dominated by men, thereby doing, he claimed, the bidding of the bourgeoisie.[62] At the same time, both male and female syndicalists complained that many men were not doing enough to unionise their womenfolk.

This contradictory attitude to women could also be seen in men's dominance of textile union committees (which represented a regressive step in comparison to earlier years). As noted, La Constància was run by men from the calenders and sizers' union, and similar practices were common in other parts of Catalonia. Lola Ferrer specifically complained at this. This led the CRT, in its 1918 Sants Congress, not only to reiterate that women should be unionised, but also to declare that when women formed part of a trade they should have their own union representatives.[63] Yet there is no evidence that this was acted upon. Moreover, like their predecessors, this new generation of female anarchist activists did not themselves embrace equality within the world of work. Libertad Ródenas, for example, believed that women might one day abandon factory work, and argued that a woman should not compete with men in the workplace because 'she relinquishes her own personality'.[64] But activist women were the minority. Even within anarchist-syndicalist circles – at least according to Joan Peiró's son – there were many apolitical women, who had internalised their exclusion from the public and political spheres and sacrificed their health and happiness 'for an idea which generally was not their own and which they didn't understand'.[65]

It was no doubt the case that committed anarchist-syndicalist activists tended to treat their 'companions' and wives better than many other workers. There was, as already seen, great emphasis in anarchist circles on the evils of drink and the tavern, and there was also, in the press, the occasional attack on men who mistreated their wives. In addition, a CRT manifesto, published in June 1917, called for a hypothetical future republican government to introduce a divorce law.[66] Nevertheless, they remained unable to offer a full-blown critique of patriarchy. Indicative of this was their suspicion of feminism, which was dismissed as a bourgeois preoccupation of only secondary importance, limited to asking for the 'poor, small and restricted rights that men have'. Feminists were urged to struggle for the emancipation of both men and women.[67] In this way the question of gender inequalities was to a significant degree put on hold until after the revolution.

Given the increasingly buoyant state of the labour movement, from the summer of 1916 Seguí and his supporters put into practice their policy of seeking unity amongst neighbourhood unions and then constructing the SUs. Throughout they faced considerable opposition from neighbourhood and elite craft unions, who wished to maintain a high degree of independence, and, in a number of cases, were in Radical or Socialist hands. Several also operated accident and sickness benefits and feared that they would be swept away. In construction, some unions still refused to form part of the local federation, and, when in October 1916 the Barcelona Federation of Bricklayers and Bricklayers' Labourers met to consider a motion advocating the formation of an SU, it was defeated.[68]

The anarchist-syndicalists were, however, aided by the fact that the CRT operated as the only coordinating body in the city. Furthermore, as the organisation grew in strength, their position became more prominent and, if all else failed, union activists were not adverse to coercing workers into joining. This is an issue to which I shall return. Their first major success was the formation of a wood and furniture workers' SU, the Union of Carpenters, Cabinetmakers and Similar Workers – subsequently renamed the Union of the Woodworking Industry – in August 1916. As noted, its effectiveness was demonstrated in the cabinetmakers' strike, launched in September of the same year, during which activists close to Seguí put in place a highly effective strategy of raising 'extraordinary dues' to raise funds. Then, at the end of the year, the anarchist-syndicalists formed a new united Metalworkers' Union, the embryo of a future SU. A unified Barcelona Bricklayers and Bricklayers Labourers' Union followed in 1917. Again, a number of neighbourhood unions refused to join, but most were integrated in the spring of 1918. In January and May 1918 respectively the decision was then taken to wind up the Catalan Confederation of Bricklayers and Bricklayers' Labourers and Barcelona Construction Workers' Federation in anticipation of the formation of an industry-wide construction workers' SU following the Sants congress.[69]

By the summer of 1918, then, in Barcelona the anarchist-syndicalists had begun, for the first time, to build a powerful union confederation. At its heart were the thirty-three unions that sent representatives to two or more CRT Regional Committee meetings during 1918 and whose membership totalled a little over 46,000 workers; that is, between one quarter and one fifth of the city's industrial working class.[70] Yet non-affiliated unions also grew in strength during these years, with, during 1918, upwards of 100 often small unions with over 25,000 affiliates remaining independent. As in previous years, their core would be white-collar workers and shopworkers, and more elite craft and other unions distant from the world of the major industry-wide conflicts, to which can be added a number of neighbourhood unions who refused to join the new unified structures.[71] In the case of the former, of key importance was the CADCI which, although increasingly involved in union work, looked, at a political level, to build an interclass Catalanist alliance and remained culturally and ideological distant from the world of industrial labour and the CRT.[72] A new recruit to the latter was the warpdressers' union, El Radium, which worked closely with the other textile unions, but, no doubt because of these workers' relatively high status, failed to join the CRT.

This balance of power was to change dramatically during the second phase of union growth, after the Sants Congress, when, until January 1919, the organisation was to grow at astonishing speed. This was helped because, until early 1920, the economic climate remained generally buoyant. In addition, in the aftermath of Sants, the CRT pushed on and established SUs in most of the major industries, first in Barcelona and then in other significant industrial towns. In the late autumn, the strength of labour was to reach a critical mass; unions were increasingly able to paralyse entire trades and industries, keep the workers out for a considerable length of time if necessary, and put immense pressure to bear on the industrialists.

This created its own dynamic, with activists engaged in a feverish push to unionise entire industries. To convince the sceptics 'gangs' (*colles*) were set up, who beat non-unionised workers and forced them to pay fines. Threats of violence were also extended to workers in independent and even Socialists unions who refused to join the SUs.[73] The most reticent were specifically targeted by anarchist gunmen. In order to understand why this happened one has to remember that from the turn of the century, at grass-roots level, anarchist-syndicalist activists had been engaged in a continuous war to establish the unions, win strikes, and keep blacklegs at bay. The fact that they were now on top was hardly likely to turn them into pacifists. The overall result was that power relations in the economy were seriously disturbed, with what seemed like a procession of union victories between October 1918 and January 1919. This had a key knock-on effect on wealth distribution within Catalan society. From late 1918 until early 1920, probably for the first time since the *febre d'or* between 1875 and 1883, with the rate of inflation in decline, workers were able to achieve very substantial improvements in real wages, more than making up for the losses of the war years.[74]

The push to establish SUs throughout the city at first sharpened opposition. Thus, in construction, unions such as the brickmakers of Horta, stonecutters, marblers and stucco plasterers opposed the move, while in carpentry dissidents tried to set up an anti-syndicalist union, and in the book trades at first only a minority of the city's unions integrated into the new SU.[75] But even unions identified with the anarchist-syndicalist cause had their reservations.

For example, in metalworking it proved difficult to convince the iron foundrymen and tinsmiths that they should affiliate. Opposition was broader in the textile industry. Here trade unionists had from 1916 operated at a distance from the group which surrounded Seguí – with Lerrouxists maintaining a degree of influence – and showed themselves opposed to the disbanding of their textile federation. Particularly damaging was criticism by Josep Roca, its influential former general secretary.[76]

The anarchist-syndicalist leadership was not to be deterred. SUs were established in the construction and metal industries in early November and the decision taken to insist that all unions join their SUs by the beginning of January 1919. Simultaneously, the big construction, woodworkers and metalworkers' SUs imposed closed shops. These were made much easier to operate by the issuing of a single CRT union card. Moreover, the consolidation of the SUs was accompanied by the election of shop stewards, who were to play an effective role in unionising the shop floor. Within heavily unionised industries they became powerful figures, and the focus for the industrialists' ire. In January, among the major industries, only textiles had yet to set up an SU, but even here the various unions (with the exception of El Radium) had agreed in principal to its formation (albeit after all the union committees had stepped down).[77]

The new structures, combined with rapid union growth, meant that the anarchist-syndicalists were able to break into new areas from which they had hitherto been excluded and make much more progress in recruiting the unskilled, including growing numbers of new migrants from the south of Spain. This was the case, for example, of the unskilled male cardboard box and paper makers, who formed part of the SU of Printers, Cardboard, Paper and Similar Workers. The CRT was also able to further increase unionisation rates amongst women workers. For example, in glassworking, where women were employed in electric lamp factories, they were integrated into the SU of Glass, Electric Lamp and Similar Workers. Most remarkably, in 1919 the CRT's Food Workers' SU set up a domestic service section, and began to have some success in recruiting maids, waitresses and female cooks.[78]

The way in which the lesser skilled and migrant workers were incorporated into the CRT has important implications for the analysis of the wellsprings of labour militancy during these years. It has been argued by Gerald Meaker that the high levels of industrial conflict can be put down to an influx of peasant migrants from the south and east of Spain who 'carried within themselves ... the seeds of hatred and rebellion'.[79] Yet the evidence so far amassed does not support the view that these newly arrived workers were the catalyst of industrial strife. On the contrary, as the experience of other European labour movements might lead us to expect, at first they proved difficult to unionise. As an anarchist-syndicalist activist was later to admit, when they arrived, 'they were eager to please the boss in order to stabilise the precarious situation that they suspected they were in. These ignorant and fearful people supposed that the native workers were harassing them in order to wreck their efforts to settle in a "modern" land'.[80] It was in the context of the tightening labour market that the CRT was increasingly able to recruit them to its unions. But there is noth-

ing to suggest that there was any particular predisposition of these workers to
join the unions because of their previous peasant status. Rather it was once
they had settled in Catalonia that they became pulled into the world of strikes
and class confrontation. Then, once unionised, rather like the female textile
workers, often miserably exploited, they proved hungry for redemption.

As it grew, the CRT set its sights on those powerful industrialists who had
until then kept their enterprises union free. This could be seen in the construction industry, in which from May 1918 the bricklayers and bricklayers'
labourers backed a strike by the Montjuïc quarrymen, who worked for the
'powerful and invincible' Foment d'Obres i Construccions. The company
finally capitulated in mid-November. More significant was the boycott
launched against the wealthy and influential owner of Construccions y Pavi-
ments, SA., Joan Miró i Trepat (who would subsequently play a key role in
the Employers' Federation), after he sacked a number of unionised men
engaged in building the Ritz Hotel in August. Not only was he forced to back
down but he also had to pay a fine of 4,000 pesetas.[81]

In the metal industry and in textiles similar tendencies could be observed.
In August 1918, El Naval launched a boycott of the major shipping company,
La Transmediterránea (which was in the hands of the Comillas-Güell
dynasty), which was trying to force its workers to join its company-run
friendly society. In September, the workers from the big metalworking plant,
El Vulcano, which was owned by La Transmediterránea, seconded the boycott and also came out on strike. They were defeated and the position of the
Barceloneta and Poble Nou metal industrialists, therefore, remained strong.
Nevertheless, the Metalworkers' Union was able to bring out the workers of
the Girona Foundry in the same month, following a number of sackings,
despite their being non-unionised. This led to a bitter dispute, which was still
unresolved when constitutional guarantees were suspended in January 1919.
Similarly, in textiles, trade unionism made headway amongst the big Sants factories. This could be seen in the dispute with the warpdressers of El Radium,
which, as shown, blew up in 1916. Although La España Industrial remained
firm, both Trinxet and Balet i Vendrell gave way.[82]

By the end of the year, therefore, anti-union enterprises increasingly
looked like islands within a unionised sea. Growing union power produced a
succession of victories, the Construction SU alone claiming that it had
brought ninety-six disputes to a successful conclusion between November
and December 1918. This encouraged the CRT to launch a campaign for an
eight-hours day throughout Catalonia from the end of the year.[83] Simultaneously, it strengthened outside the Catalan capital, holding frequent union
meetings at weekends, at which leading Barcelona figures would speak. During 1918 the CRT began to take root in southern Catalonia. In Tarragona
province it was able to undermine the power of the Socialists and build its
own federation.[84] This, together with the rising price of paper, probably
explains why *La Justicia Social* ceased publication in late 1916, leaving the
Catalan Socialists without a voice. Headway was also made in Lleida province,
where the anarchist-syndicalists' determination to reach out to the most marginalised and exploited led them into an explosive confrontation with the

country's leading electricity supply company, Ebro Power and Irrigation. It was a British and Canadian owned business, which had invested heavily in the provision of hydroelectric power from the Pyrenees.

Following the formation of the Lleida local federation, the CRT began to unionise the workforce building a new reservoir for the company near Camarasa on the Noguera Pallaresa river north of Lleida. It was the type of company that the CRT was itching to challenge. The workers lived on site, wages were low, they paid over the odds in the company shop and were guarded by armed civil guards. Furthermore, the company's key role in the economy meant that the mobilisation of these workers would be strategically important. When, therefore, the workers of La Camarasa came out on strike in early December, the Lleida Federation called a general strike and the CRT announced its intention to force a shut-down of the company's plants throughout Catalonia. It was clearly seen as a trial of strength in which the CRT would consolidate its new-found power. As we shall see in Chapter Nine, it was this conflict that would be at the root of an all-out confrontation with the Catalan industrial elite during 1919.[85]

By January 1919, then, the CRT almost totally dominated labour organisation in Barcelona. Only a few unions in the industrial sector of the economy, such as El Radium and the Sant Martí coopers, explicitly refused to join. Moreover, non-industrial and white-collar workers also started to come under pressure. This was reflected in the massive rise in CRT membership. At the end of September 1918 it stated that it had 67,000 affiliates in Barcelona, and Manuel Buenacasa was later to claim that it reached the, seemingly exaggerated, figure of 345,000 Catalan members by the end of the year.[86] On the contrary, under pressure, in Barcelona the Socialist base almost totally collapsed. When, during the war years, trade unionism revived amongst the railway workers, they once again linked up with the UGT federation, but by 1919 in Barcelona itself, the local party, which occupied three small centres, was supported by 'half a dozen miserable craft unions'.[87]

In addition, the CNT National Committee was beginning to build a truly national organisation. In September 1918, 90 percent of the membership was still Catalan, but labour protest had taken off in Andalusia in the spring and there followed a huge growth of union activity. In organisational terms, a great boost was the decision taken by the 25,000-strong National Federation of Agricultural Workers, at a congress in Valencia on 25 December 1918, to join the CNT.[88] This engendered a climate of euphoria in CRT circles and encouraged the belief that almost anything was possible. Joan Peiró later recalled that, by 1919, only about 3 percent of workers in Badalona were non-unionised, and that the union headquarters was 'absolutely packed with workers every night'.[89] Clearly, many had benefited greatly from the union victories of the previous months. Nevertheless, below the surface there were tensions. There may well have been a current of resentment amongst at least some of those forced to join, exacerbated by the need to pay high dues during long-drawn-out strikes. Moreover, skilled workers could also feel uneasy at having to work alongside the unskilled within the SUs. A good example of this is provided by printing, where, following a big strike defeat in 1914, most skilled workers had joined two anti-syndicalist unions, one independent and the other Socialist, whereas the SU mobilised lesser skilled workers engaged in the manufacture of paper and carboard boxes. When on 30 December 1918 the SU came out for an eight-hours day and the abolition of piece rates, and then used flying pickets to try and bring out the whole industry, there was at first considerable hostility. The Socialist sympathiser, Adolfo Bueso, remarked contemptuously that when the non-SU unions met to discuss the issue, the majority of SU supporters, who congregated outside, 'were outsiders (*forasteros*), labourers from the paper factories, who despite knowing nothing about printing shouted like morons'.[90]

In fact, the strike was totally successful, and most workers subsequently joined the SU. Yet in Bueso's remarks one could see the origin of ethno-skill divisions within the labour force. In middle-class circles the integration of southern migrants would be presented as evidence that the CNT was an organisation of feckless outsiders, who were undermining the harmony of Catalan society. This theme would be appropriated by non-syndicalist union leaders and no doubt reflected real tensions within the unions and on the shopfloor. Within this discourse the semi-mythical figure of the anarchist *murciano* would be of central importance, epitomising bourgeois fears of the threat of organised labour and most particularly the CNT.[91]

The Catalan CNT and the Terrorist Apparatus

These fears were heightened because the growth of the Catalan CNT was accompanied by the consolidation of a stratum of gunmen within its ranks, who, the indications are, began to operate autonomously. Overall, between 1916 and 1918, twenty-seven employers and members of employers' families were attacked, of whom eight were murdered and fourteen injured. Eighteen foremen and overseers suffered the same fate, four of whom were killed and twelve wounded. Furthermore, the number of attacks accelerated between 1916 and 1918, with eight murders between August and December 1918. The great majority of these incidents were shootings. With respect to their occupation, of those for whom we have details, twelve worked in textiles, ten in woodworking, five in the metal industry, and four in construction. This escalation was accompanied by a growth in the shootings of workers. Whereas eight workers had been assassinated between 1910 and 1914, over the next four years the figure rose to fourteen. In 1918 alone, eighteen workers were wounded in shootings and six killed. Moreover, during the same year thirty-five bombs were placed either on the city streets or outside factories (and on one occasion thrown into a factory injuring one of the employers' sons mentioned above).[92]

At the time *Solidaridad Obrera* strenuously denied any CNT involvement, but the language employed by the paper was both aggressive and threatening. For example, during the calenders and sizers' strike of 1917 'Anelka' called for an 'implacable, cruel and inhuman war' against the employers, and an editorial reacted to the murder of Josep Barret, the president of the Society of

Metallurgical and Mechanical Industrialists, in January 1918, with the comment: 'The day of Saint Martin arrives for all pigs.'[93]

Pestaña was later to admit that figures within the organisation were behind most of the attacks. He revealed that young activists began to form 'action groups' within the textile industry in 1916 and that they received the support of a small group within the leadership of the National Textile Federation. In fact, as indicated in the previous chapter, this was a process that was already underway in 1912. The gunmen were young hotheads at the sharp end of labour disputes, some of whom probably had links with anarchist groups. There must have been a good deal of overlap between these men and the *colles* who beat and fined workers. What was, however, new about these years is that they began to be financed by the unions, thereby opening the way for the formation of a professionalised group of gunmen.[94] Furthermore, the indications are that these gunmen began coordinating their activities. The authorities were later to claim that a group of gunmen met up in Paris in 1918 to discuss 'the way in which the social question should be dealt with'.[95] One suspects that Ramon Archs, who would lead the CRT's terrorist apparatus when he returned from France the following year, was heavily involved. Simultaneously, although I have no definite evidence, a group within the organisation must have specialised in bombmaking. The CNT was rapidly developing a terrorist wing.

As in previous years, these terrorist groups grew in strength in the context of the bitter conflicts of this period. Between 1916 and 1917 this was most dramatically illustrated in the case of textiles. As already seen, two hard-fought disputes erupted, which affected the warpdressers of El Radium and the calenders and sizers. It was then that shootings, focused on foremen and warpdressers who had remained loyal to their employers, began. The first foreman to be gunned down and murdered was Llorenç Cases on 3 August 1916. There followed a spate of attacks between March 1917 and January 1918 in which five foremen and warpdressers, the son of a foreman, the director of a factory and two factory owners, were shot. Three were killed in all, along with the coachman of one of the employers. A similar situation could be seen in 1918 in the Girona Foundry, one of the big metalworking plants still holding out against the CNT. In this case non-unionised workers were targeted, with two killed and four wounded during October and November.

These gunmen were given succour by the circles in which they moved. Pestaña maintained that most anarchist-syndicalists were both uninvolved and critical. However, until 1919 the attitude of the CRT leadership was ambiguous. They continued to support strong-arm tactics, as reflected in the decision taken at the Sants Congress to set up 'propaganda and action committees' within each major union. One of their roles was to plan tactics during strikes, with the result that they inevitably became involved in shootings.[96] In this climate the distinction between union activists and gunmen became ambiguous and fluid, with the latter regarded as comrades even by those who disapproved of their actions. Very significant in this regard is the admission by the printer, Rafael Vidiella, a personal friend of Seguí, that on one occasion, despite totally repudiating his action, Seguí hid a gunman in his house,

'because', in his own words, 'I won't deny shelter to a fugitive'.[97] This attitude was no doubt further encouraged by the fact that there seems to have
been no revulsion at the assassination of intransigent employers amongst
union activists, nor indeed in wider working-class circles.

The most notorious murder of these years, that of Josep Barret, a leading
figure in business circles, in January 1918, provoked a police offensive against
the gunmen. The police maintained that there was one 'action group' operating whose members were from rather diverse occupations, but which had
links to the metal industry, and at least three other groups active in textiles,
and that finance had been provided by the textile and foundrymen's unions.[98]
This was probably quite accurate. Yet elements of the police themselves were
also involved in criminal activities and this was to muddy the waters even further. During the first years of the century the Barcelona police force was
underpaid, inefficient and corrupt. A serious attempt at reform was undertaken between 1907 and 1909, but its long-term consequences were negligi-
ble.[99] Indeed, police corruption became more flagrant from 1914. As shown
in Chapter Two, in war-time Barcelona the area around the Paral·lel witnessed the rise of glitzy cabarets and music halls, which engaged in illicit
gambling and as a matter of course paid bribes to the police.

The war itself also provided new opportunities for unscrupulous public servants. Because large numbers of industrialists supplied the Allies with clothing, blankets and armaments, Barcelona became a centre of German
counterintelligence operations in Spain, which aimed both to influence public opinion towards the war through bribes and subsidies and disrupt the
Allies' supply networks. Inevitably, contacts developed between the Barcelona
police and the German spy ring. The key figure was Manuel Bravo Portillo,
chief of the Barcelona Special Brigade from August 1917. Tall and slim,
always immaculately attired, sporting his trade-mark Kaiser-style moustache
and cane, he was a regular on the music-hall scene. He earned kick-backs
from prostitution and gambling and so it is no surprise that he was also taken
onto the payroll of the German Embassy.[100] One of Bravo Portillo's main
functions was, through contacts he had in the port of Barcelona, to warn the
Germans when ships with supplies for the Allies were leaving port so that they
could be sunk on the high seas. This was revealed by *Solidaridad Obrera* on
9 June 1918, when, in a dashing coup, it published two secret documents
which showed that in January he had provided information which had
allowed the German navy to sink the Spanish merchant ship, the *Joaquín
Mumbrú*, provoking Bravo Portillo's arrest soon afterwards.

Bravo Portillo's control over the Special Brigade also brought its network
of informers and agent provocateurs under his wing. Catalan syndicalists
accused them of taking money off industrialists with the promise they would
end strikes and then bribing union leaders.[101] More dramatically, the war
between former trade unionists, now in the pay of the police, and syndicalist
gunmen escalated. The 'action groups' launched an offensive against the 'traitors' of 1913, assassinating Federic Roigé on 31 May 1917 and wounding
Lluís Mas in late April 1918. This led to reprisals against CNT activists. On 3
May 1918 Maurici Puig, a leading figure in La Constància, was fired on, and

the warpdresser, Jaume Sabanés, was (for a second time) wounded on the following day.[102]

In addition, Bravo Portillo's access to informers allowed him to carry out another, vital, service for the Germans. Josep Barret, whom the police maintained had been killed by the syndicalists, was producing mortars for the French army. Hence the decision was taken by German counterintelligence first to try and organise a strike in order to disrupt production in his factory and, once this failed, to eliminate him. The instrument chosen was Eduard Ferrer, the secretary of the Metalworkers' Union. Ferrer was coerced and bribed into working for Bravo Portillo and organised the assassination. He managed to convince two members of the union's committee that the assassination was necessary because Barret was a hardliner who was standing in the way of any concessions. He then recruited and paid five activists to carry the attack out.[103]

Thus, the police round-up began after a crime that a high-ranking police official had masterminded. This does not, however, mean that those accused by the police were not involved. The arrests began after a tip-off from Ferrer himself, who might have given up the perpetrators with the hope that, not knowing he was an informer, they would not implicate him. Yet he was not able to stay out of the limelight for long. The suspicion that Bravo Portillo was behind the murder surfaced in the press and was soon picked up by *Solidaridad Obrera*. Soon after, the name of Ferrer emerged. This meant that he was a marked man; he was murdered by CNT gunmen a little over a year later in September 1919.[104]

Conclusions

The rise of labour protest was, therefore, closely connected to the war. The economic boom had made it easier to organise workers and the rapid inflation had certainly sharpened discontent. Nevertheless, it is clear that the agitation sprang from within Catalan society itself. To a large extent previous demands and grievances were amplified in the context of the war. Furthermore, the catalyst was strikes and protests led by indigenous industrial workers rather than peasant migrants, and the challenge was posed to established business interests rather than to any class of *nouveau riche* interlopers.

As a result, by January 1919 a sea change in the balance of power between Catalonia's social classes had taken place. Not only had the Catalan CNT risen to a position of unparalleled strength, under men like Salvador Seguí it now had a much clearer and more realistic strategy. Industrialists in particular, and the more conservative sectors of Catalan society in general, had been badly shaken by the growth of unions and strikes, and most particularly by the fact that the CNT was becoming increasingly hegemonic. In addition, as we shall see in the following chapters, revolution in Russia and the subsequent turmoil in central Europe, also encouraged talk of social upheaval in Spain itself. Finally, their sense of fear and foreboding was further exacerbated by the rise of the anarchist gunmen.

Faced with these challenges, the major employers' federations had little inclination to negotiate with the anarchist-syndicalists. This was to produce what in terms of social and political stability was the worst of all possible worlds. Despite calls for 'compulsory unionisation', in practice major industrialists tried maintain their anti-union strategies. Yet, outside very specific areas, most notably the Alt Llobregat, they were increasingly unable to hold back the union tide. In this climate their minds were concentrated on ways of striking back and destroying the Catalan CNT. The degree of hatred and loathing were demonstrated in an astounding note published by the Barcelona Employers' Federation – which since 1914 had declined in strength and by now only represented the employers in the construction industry – in September 1918, in which it called for a 'holy crusade' against the CRT 'without remorse nor weakness'. As for the CRT leadership: 'The most humane thing to have done would have been to exterminate them by such rapid and efficient methods as are used on wild animals.'[105] As I shall show, it was a procedure that would be put into effect from the following year.

Notes

1. For the supposed rise of the *nouveau riche* businessmen see, for example, Juan Antonio Lacomba, *La crisis española de 1917*, 34–5. Gerald Meaker has laid particular emphasis on the radicalising role of migration from the rural south in *Revolutionary Left*.

2. Overviews on the Catalan economy during the war are to be found in, Josep Lluís Martín Ramos, 'L'expansió industrial'; Joseph Harrison, 'The failure of economic reconstruction in Spain, 1916–1923'; Angel Calvo, 'Estructura industrial i sistema productiu a Catalunya durant la Primera Guerra Mundial'; Carles Sudrià i Triay, 'Una societat plenament industrial'.

3. Gabriel, 'Sous i cost de vida', 61–7.

4. Instituto de Reformas Sociales, *Estadística de huelgas, 1915–1917*. It should, however, be noted that the 1917 statistics for Barcelona are poor. In 1918 the Institute fails to report on strikes in the city at all, and its data remains very incomplete through to 1923.

5. Looking back from 1918, Joan Ferrer later recalled: 'We would have to go back to the first years of the century to find a similar level of influence.' Porcel, *Revuelta*, 96. Brief accounts of labour conflict over this period are also to be found in two articles by Josep Lluís Martín Ramos, 'De la tregua a la expansión reivindicativa', and, 'Anàlisi del moviment vaguístic a Barcelona (1914–1923)'. A great deal of information on both union organisation and strikes is also to be found in Gabriel, 'Sindicats', 542–714.

6. For data on union membership from 1917 to 1918 see, above all, 'Las sociedades', in *Anuario Estadístico de la Ciudad de Barcelona* (hereafter, AECB), *1917*, 479–90, and Confederación Regional del Trabajo de Cataluña, *Memoria del congreso celebrado en Barcelona los días 28, 29, 30 de junio y 1 de julio del año 1918*, pp. xxix–xxxv. The AECB data refers to late 1917. I have not included the 1,420 workers it reports as forming part of the Catholic Unions Professionals or those integrated within a variety of friendly societies.

7. The data for the number of industrial workers is to be found in table 1.2. However, it must not be forgotten that the 1920 figures in particular seriously underestimated the number of migrant workers.

8. *Solidaridad Obrera* (hereafter, SO), 31 Oct., 3, 4, 13, 30 Nov. 1916, 12, 17, 20 Feb. 1917; AECB, *1917*, 484.

9. I have pieced events in construction during 1915 to 1916 together from reading SO, *La Justicia Social* (hereafter, LJS) and *La Publicidad* (hereafter, LP). For the spread of brick-layers and bricklayers labourers' strikes to other industrial towns see, Instituto de Reformas Sociales, *Estadística de huelgas, 1916*, 231–5.

10. SO, 10 Jan., 15 May 1918, 14 Jan. 1919.

11. I have used SO along with the *Anuari d'Estadística Social de Catalunya, 1915*, 65–93; Confederación Regional del Trabajo de Cataluña, *Memoria*, pp. xxix–xxxv; and Martín Ramos, 'De la tregua', 122.

12. Again, SO is my key source. On the impact of railway workers' strike in Spain see also, Francisco J. Romero Salvadó, *Spain 1914–1918*, 36–7.

13. SO, 30 Oct., 17 Nov., 1916, 1 March, 16 April, 1 June 1917; AECB, *1917*, 483.

14. The most important source on Catalan union membership is the report of the CRT's Sants conference, Confederación Regional del Trabajo de Cataluña, *Memoria*, pp. xxix–xxxv. However, not all the unions affiliated to the textile federation attended.

15. Albert Arnavat, *Classe contra classe*; Capdevila i Masgrau, *La Justica Social*, 24–5; Bengoechea, *Organització patronal*, 148–9. One can also follow the dispute in *La Justicia Social*.

16. For these textile strikes I have used SO along with Jaume Marquès i Mir, *Història de l'organització sindical tèxtil 'Radium'*, 27–42.

17. SO, 4, 5, 9, 14, 25 June 1918.

18. SO, 16 Nov. 1916, 24 Dec. 1917.

19. The CADCI figures are taken from, Lladonosa i Vall-llebrera, *Catalanisme i moviment obrer*, 286.

20. For beatings and shootings I have used, above all, Sastre y Sanna, *Esclavitud moderna*, and José María Farré Morego, *Los atentados sociales en España*, supplemented by data from the press.

21. For a stimulating overview of the industrialists' thinking and strategy see, Soledad Bengoechea, 'The Barcelona Bourgeoisie, the Labour Movement and the Origins of Francoist Corporatism'.

22. Porcel, *Revuelta*, 64.

23. In the Biblioteca Arús in Barcelona there are portraits by his boyhood friend Hermoso Plaja 'Eusebi Carbó Carbó. Bibliografia', and by his partner, Margarita Gironella, 'Eusebio Carbó y Carbó (Datos biográficos)'.

24. The links between Spanish and Latin American anarchists are stressed in, Diego Abad de Santillán, *Memorias, 1897–1936*, 52–6.

25. See Buenacasa's *Movimiento obrero*, along with Meaker, *Revolutionary Left*, 152.

26. Pestaña's own autobiographical account is, *Lo que aprendí*. See also, in particular, Carlos Arbón, 'Angel Pestaña', in *Siluetas*, August 1923; Foix, *Apòstols*, 121–203; Adolfo Bueso, 'Angel Pestaña: "Caballero de la triste figura" del anarcosindicalismo'; Porcel, *Revuelta*, 100. The *Tierra y Libertad* article is 'Crónica de Algier', 22 June 1910.

27. Lladonosa i Vall-llebrera, *Sindicalistas i llibertaris*, 21.

28. Porcel, *Revuelta*, 76–80. With enormous generosity, between 1922 and 1923 he used his inheritance to help companions escape from the police and the anti-CNT gunmen of the Sindicatos Libres.

29. Arno J. Mayer, *The Persistence of the Old Regime*.

30. Pestaña, *Lo que aprendí*, vol. 2, 64–5.

31. SO, 31 Dec. 1914, 1 April 1915; LJS, 1 April 1915.

32. SO, 13 May 1915; Meaker, *Revolutionary Left*, 41.

33. Buenacasa, *Movimiento obrero*, 42; Díaz del Moral, *Agitaciones campesinas*, 304–5. Mistakenly, Buenacasa states that the Andalusian Regional Confederation was formed at the end of 1917.

34. Sanz, *El sindicalismo y la política*, 108–9. For the importance of Seguí and his team in promoting this reforming strategy see also, Pere Gabriel, 'Red Barcelona in the Europe of War and Revolution, 1914–30'.
35. For which, see Chapter Five, 153 and 157.
36. The expression is by Bueso in 'Angel Pestaña', 53.
37. For this section I have used, above all, Salut, *Vivers de revolucionaris*, the chapters by José Viadiu, Hemoso Plaja and Manuel Buenacasa in *Salvador Seguí*; Foix, *Apòstols*, 53–120; and Madrid, *Sangre en Atarazanas*, 45–8.
38. The quotation is by his close friend Simó Piera, in Ferrer, *Simó Piera*, 67.
39. See the comments by Buenacasa and Angel Samblancat in *Salvador Seguí*, 98 and 109–110; Ferrer, *Simó Piera*, 45; Foix, *Apòstols*, 97; Ferrer, *Vida sindicalista*, 60; and Roig, *Rafael Vidella*, 42.
40. Negre wrote two sets of articles on syndicalism in *Solidaridad Obrera* between 25 April and 3 June 1917, and the pamphlet *¿Qué es el sindicalismo?*
41. On Seguí's views see in particular, Hermoso Plaja, 'Salvador Seguí, hombre de la CNT' 66; Foix, *Apòstols*, 89; Salut, *Vivers de revolucionaris*, 41. Seguí outlined his position in several speeches made in Madrid during 1919, which have been edited by Antonio Elorza, and in the posthumously published pamphlet, *Anarquismo y sindicalismo*.
42. SO, 4, 8, 12, 14, 15 Aug., 2 Sept. 1916; 8 March 1917.
43. See the comments by Buenacasa in SO, 20 Sept., 18 Dec. 1918, and his pamphlet, *¿Qué es el Sindicato Unico?*
44. SO, 8, 9 March, 13 June 1917.
45. SO, 19 Nov. 1917, 18, 29 April, 19 May, 27 June 1918.
46. SO, 14 April, 5 June 1918.
47. SO, 22 May 1917, 16 Sept. 1918.
48. Buenacasa, *Movimiento obrero*, 195.
49. Porcel, *Revuelta*, 100.
50. SO, 5, 16 March 1917; Buenacasa, *Movimiento obrero*, 165.
51. Socialist representation centred on Reus and Sitges. The Barcelona Socialists, who continued to pursue a more orthodox 'Pablista' line, stayed away. For the debates see Confederación Regional del Trabajo de Cataluña, *Memoria*.
52. On these concessions see Ferrer, *Simó Piera*, 69–74.
53. SO, 30 June 1918.
54. Juan de Catalunya (pseudonym of Joan Codina), 'La federación fabril y textil VII', *Justicia*, 22 March 1930, 3.
55. SO claimed that 167 workers were arrested in 1916 and that only one was actually put on trial. SO, 30 Sept. 1918.
56. Manent i Pesas, *Records*, 44.
57. Porcel, *Revuelta*, 76–80.
58. Manent i Pesas, *Records*, 327–8. There is a biographical outline of Peiró and a selection of his writings in Pere Gabriel, *Joan Peiró*.
59. Our key source for the CRT is again SO. For the Reus strike see, Arnavat, *Classe contra classe*; and Capdevila i Masgrau, *La Justica Social*, 24–5.
60. Juan de Cataluña, 'La federación fabril y textil VII'; Gabriel, 'Sindicats', 544–51; Balcells, 'Mujer obrera', 68–72; SO, 14, 30 Aug. 1916.
61. Lola Iturbe, *La mujer en la lucha social y en la guerra de España*, 60–70.
62. SO, 6 Sept. 1918, 22 Oct. 1916, 15 July 1918; *Tierra y Libertad*, 18 April 1917.
63. SO, 26 June 1918; Confederación Regional del Trabajo de Cataluña, *Memoria*, 19–20.
64. SO, 29 July 1918.
65. José Peiró, *Juan Peiró: teórico y militante del anarco-sindicalismo español*, 19.
66. The CRT's minimum programme is reproduced in Lacomba, *Crisis española*, 472–5.
67. See, in particular, the article by 'R' in SO, 29 Dec. 1917.
68. SO, 31 Oct., 1 Nov. 1916. The plasterers, Horta bricklayers and locksmiths refused to form part of the Barcelona Construction Workers' Federation.
69. SO, 6 Nov. 1917, 15 May, 25 June 1918.

70. Other unions maintained more distant links. Representatives of a further fourteen unions went along to just one CRT meeting during the year, and, overall, fifty-three Barcelona unions representing 51,992 workers attended the Sants Congress. Twenty eight of the thirty-three unions mentioned above were present as the congress and represented 44,300 workers. These included all the major CRT unions: see, SO, 2, 6, 19, 23 Jan., 22, 29 April, 19, 22, 31 May 1918. There were, however, still problems with unions supposedly affiliated not paying their dues.

71. We do not have totally accurate figures. The best sources are the 1917 AECB and the 1918 Sants Congress. Pere Gabriel has estimated that about 34,000 unionised Barcelona workers never attended this congress. 'Sindicats', 684–5.

72. Lladonosa i Vall-llebrera, *Catalanisme*, 284–363; Pérez Baró, *Els 'feliços' anys vint*, 24–5.

73. F. Viladomat, 'Els anarquistes i els sindicats 1', in *Justicia Social*, 19 April 1924, 3; Pérez Baró, *Els 'feliços' anys vint*, 24–5.

74. See, for example, Gabriel, 'Sous i cost'; Raimon Soler i Becerro, 'La evolución del salario en una empresa textil algodonera'; Carles Enrech, 'L'ofensiva patronal contra l'ofici', vol. 2, 647 and 673.

75. SO, 25 July, 11 Sept. 1918, 3 Jan. 1919; Bueso, *Recuerdos*, 105.

76. Culla i Clarà, *Republicanisme lerrouxista*, 307–8; SO, 28 Aug. 1918.

77. SO, 4 Nov., 17 Dec. 1918, 3 Jan 1919; Bueso, *Recuerdos*, 109; Pérez Baró, *Els 'feliços' anys vint*, 66.

78. Iturbe, *La mujer en la lucha social*, 40.

79. Meaker, *Revolutionary Left*, 147. Meaker also makes the claim that the majority of CNT gunmen were *murcianos*. This is totally unsubstantiated. I have not been able to identify a single gunman who came from Murcia.

80. Juan Ferrer, 'Leyendo "Els Altres Catalans"', 13. Significantly between 1915 and 1918 *Solidaridad Obrera* did not bring up the issue of migrant labour on a single occasion.

81. SO, 15 July, 25, 30 Aug., 5, 7, 15 Oct. 1918, 4 Jan. 1919.

82. SO, 19 Oct., 26 Oct. 1918, 5, 11 Jan. 1919.

83. SO, 3, 14 Jan. 1919.

84. Plaja, 'Memorias', 26–7.

85. SO, 11, 12, 20 Nov., 2, 3, 5, 11, 14, 17, 19, 20, 21 Dec. 1918, 3 Jan. 1919.

86. SO, 30 Sept. 1918; Buenacasa, *Movimiento obrero*, 165. In January 1919 the Barcelona Woodworkers' SU claimed a membership of 13,000, the Construction Workers' SU stated that between 75 and 80 percent of bricklayers and bricklayers' labourers were unionised (close on 10,000 men), and the National Textile Federation stated that it had 40,000 members. SO, 4, 11 Jan. 1919.

87. Pérez Baró, *Els 'feliços' anys vint*, 65.

88. SO, 30 Sept. 1918; Buenacasa, *Movimiento obrero*, 52 and 99. On the revival of labour organisation in Andalusia see Díaz del Moral, *Agitaciones campesinas*, 265 ff.

89. Juan Peiró, *Trayectoria de la Confederación Nacional del Trabajo*, 71–2.

90. Bueso, *Recuerdos*, 105.

91. Joan Ferrer noted that 'the Catalanists felt annoyed if a CNT activist was called Roig, Pagès or Ferrer. They wanted them to be called Martínez, Pérez or Fernández'. Porcel, *Revuelta*, 97.

92. For this section I have used Sastre y Sanna, *Martirología social,* and Farré Morego, *Los atentados*, supplemented by information from the press and anarchist-syndicalist sources.

93. SO, 6 June 1917, 9 Jan. 1918. The feast of Saint Martin is the day that pigs are traditionally slaughtered in Spain.

94. Pestaña's revelations are to be found in, *Lo que aprendí*, vol. 2, 64–5 and 74–105. Also interesting is Madrid, *Sangre*, 30, and for 1919–23, Sanz, *El sindicalismo y la política*, 55–60 and 85–7.

95. Barcelona civil governor to the Minister of the Interior, 20 May 1923, in Archivo Histórico Nacional, Gobernación Serie A (hereafter, AHN), 58/13.

96. Confederación Regional del Trabajo de Cataluña, *Memoria*, 111.

97. Rafael Vidiella, 'Salvador Seguí'.

98. SO, 14, 16, 18, 21, 25 April 1918.

99. For the Barcelona police during the first decade of the century see Romero Maura, 'Terrorism in Barcelona', 169–76. For a devastating critique of their operation see the telegram by the civil governor of Barcelona, Manuel Portela Valladares, to the Minister of the Interior on 1 July 1923, in AHN, 58/13.

100. See Madrid, *Sangre*, 155–64; Rafael Vidiella, *Los de ayer*, Salut, *Vivers de revolucionaris*, 114. On the German spy network in Spain see Romero Salvadó, *Spain 1914–1918*, 17–19 and 67–73.

101. SO, 11, 22 Dec. 1916, 14, 20 Jan. 1917.

102. SO, 18, 22 April, 7, 8, 11 May 1918. Sabanés was accused by the police of forming part of an 'action group'. Presumably Puig was suspected of making payments to the gunmen.

103. Manent i Pesas, *Records*, 53–4; Leopoldo Martínez, *Los mártires de la CNT*, 61; Pestaña, *Lo que aprendí*, vol. 2, 69–70, and *Terrorismo en Barcelona*, 86–97. Barret was, indeed, a staunch anti-unionist. In a meeting between the Barcelona civil governor and the employers on 20 January 1916 to discuss a metalworkers' strike, his view was that 'the workers should be starved back'. Archivo del Conde de Romanones, 96/38 (4).

104. SO, 23, 28 July 1918.

105. SO, 16 Sept. 1918. The authenticity of this note is confirmed in Bengoechea, *Organització patronal*, 284.

8

BETWEEN REFORM AND REVOLUTION
The Catalan CNT and the Left-Wing Challenge to the Restoration Regime, 1915 to 1918

Trade unions were the major building blocks on which the CRT was erected. Nevertheless, during these years the organisation attempted to fortify its network of cultural institutions. More spectacularly, it was able to take advantage of growing working class and popular disturbances, triggered by rapid prices rises, to step up its campaigns against the government and state. This is the first area on which I shall focus. The increasing strength and assertiveness of the labour opposition was part of a process through which the regime was challenged from a number of quarters. As a result, 1917 saw a revolutionary conjuncture unfold during which the Restoration regime was in danger of being toppled. In these circumstances, for the first time the CRT-CNT became a significant player on the Catalan and Spanish political stage. This provided the organisation with new opportunities, but also brought uncertainty and difficult choices. It opened the doors to an alliance with other forces on the Left in order to overthrow the Restoration regime and lay the groundwork for a more fully democratic political system. Yet any such *entente* would question anarchist-syndicalist orthodoxy and produce dissension. It is with these issues that the second part of the chapter will deal. Above all, I will centre my attention on the role that the CRT would play in the assault on the Restoration regime, the impact this would have on both its own internal development and, more broadly, on Catalan society and the Spanish polity.

Building the Catalan CNT: The Culture of Protest

In 1915 the CRT's cultural base remained small, with, in Barcelona, only three centres linked to the confederation: those in Sants and Poble Nou, along with the CRT's own headquarters, the Barcelona Workers' Centre (located in relatively spacious premises from the end of the year). The latter housed several affiliated unions, the weekly paper, *Solidaridad Obrera*, the Syndicalist Athenaeum, and the Barceloneta Rationalist Centre. Of these, the Sants Rationalist Athenaeum and the Barcelona Workers' Centre would provide the springboard for a modest expansion over the next three years. They both operated cafés, thereby giving activists a space to meet informally. The Workers' Centre organised frequent talks and set up a theatre group which put on weekend soirées, while its Syndicalist Athenaeum continued to offer a forum for theoretical debates. It was matched by the Sants centre, which, under the dynamic stewardship of the rationalist teacher, Joan Roigé, also held talks and soirées and, with the support of local unions, it was able to keep its school, called La Llum, open. In 1918, seventy children attended its daytime classes and it also held evening classes for adults. During 1916 there were also new additions to the movement's cultural infrastructure. Late in the year La Constància opened a school in its headquarters in El Clot, which by 1918 was functioning effectively, and the pro-syndicalist Gràcia union headquarters opened its own cultural athenaeum, which held night classes.

From the spring of 1918 this cultural base became significantly more dynamic. A new Barcelona Centre of Rationalist Education founded the League of Rationalist Education in June, organised a hiking club and started evening classes in French and Esperanto. In addition, a cultural centre was set up in Sant Andreu and a libertarian choir founded. This was combined with a growth in the number of soirées and meetings.[1] Yet, economic penury still remained a pressing problem. Thus, the Barcelona Centre for Rationalist Education admitted that it was in crisis in the summer of 1918 because on average only between ten and thirty of its 103 members paid their monthly dues.[2] The centres were only able to operate with union support, but the unions themselves had limited funds and were often reluctant to sink a substantial percentage of them into teaching. As a result, as the anarchists were the first to lament, while La Llum was a significant success, they were unable to develop any significant network of rationalist schools.[3]

More important in terms of articulating an anarchist-syndicalist subculture were the soirées, along with meetings and the occasional play in local theatres. As during the first decade of the century, it is very difficult to put a figure on attendance. Those held in the workers' centres may perhaps have attracted between fifty and one hundred people, while ticket sales indicate that a benefit performance for Felip Cortiella in the Apollo Theatre pulled in a crowd of 536.[4] Overall, perhaps several thousand workers occasionally attended anarchist-syndicalist cultural events, with, at most, a few hundred very closely involved. Nevertheless, by the end of 1918, with two or three soirées and lectures to choose from each weekend, a relatively dynamic cultural milieu was finally being forged.

Similar problems were also to beset the press. Tomás Herreros set up an anarchist printers, called Germinal, and this made the diffusion of the anarchist press and pamphlets much easier. Yet it proved impossible to build a high-circulation press. This could be seen in the case of the CNT's flagship, *Solidaridad Obrera*. Efforts to bring it out as a daily finally bore fruit in March 1916, during the first major post-war strikes in construction and the metal industry.[5] This step was enormously important, allowing the anarchist-syndicalists to discuss the development of their movement in greater depth. Evidence suggests that during strikes this helped maintain morale and gave workers a sense of the significance of their actions, but in January 1917 it sold only 6,000 copies, the great majority in Barcelona itself.[6] Since becoming a daily it had made an effort to report on international events, especially the war, but given the preponderant diet of syndicalist theory and practice, unions and strikes, it could not attract a large readership.

Consequently, even though CRT affiliates were asked to pay 2 céntimos a month to support the paper it remained in dire financial trouble, with the situation deteriorating at the end of 1917. In November it was revealed that to ward off the constant threat of closure, the director, José Borobio – who had taken over from Manuel Andreu in May 1916 – had accepted money from the German embassy in return for running a series of articles provided by German counter-intelligence, criticising Spanish emigration to France. This almost certainly had no bearing on the paper's stance on the war, but Borobio was forced to step down and the entire editorial team (including Andreu, who would henceforth drift away from the movement) followed him. His replacement. Angel Pestaña, claimed that when he took over sales were no more than 3,500.[7]

In the following year the quality of the paper cannot be said to have improved. Indeed, Andreu's punchy leads advocating reform probably achieved more resonance than Pestaña's often opaque disquisitions on anarchist and syndicalist theory. It was able to double its sales in January 1918 when it covered the women's protest movement against the rising price of basic necessities in some detail, but had to stop publication when constitutional guarantees were suspended on 24 January and was not to reappear until mid-April. Hence, the general secretary of the local federation, Ricard Fornells, could still 'lament that the workers do not buy *Solidaridad Obrera*', and the rising cost of paper meant it was in constant danger of having to suspend publication. Its fortunes were to revive spectacularly on 9 June, when in a dashing coup Angel Pestaña published the secret documents showing that Bravo Portillo was in the pay of the German embassy. Despite having doubled its print run it sold out at eight in the morning, and later in the day, Pestaña remarked, 'extraordinarily, in the elite cafés and restaurants copies of *Solidaridad Obrera* were passed from hand to hand'.

By this time, it seems, sales had risen to about 32,000. Yet the rocketing cost of paper meant that the more copies sold the more money it lost, with the result that in May it had to reduce its size from four to two pages. In October a new attempt was made to broaden its appeal. The CRT agreed to establish a telegraphic service, open the paper up to leading intellectual figures 'whether or not from our camp', who would be paid to write articles, and once again publish four pages, but they had to double its price from 5 to 10 céntimos.[8] Despite these difficulties, between 1915 and 1918 *Solidaridad Obrera* had passed from being a paper read by a small minority of Barcelona workers to one which was beginning to attain a quite significant influence. As in the case of the cultural associations, this was indicative of a cultural base which though still limited in size was broadening its appeal.

More dramatic in their impact would be the CRT's campaigns. As in previous years, meetings to protest at the closure of a union and, or, repression of a strike, in support of a particular group of strikers, plus the continuous struggle to free 'social prisoners', would help galvanise the movement. Calls for amnesty were also given pathos and a personal touch by concentrating on individuals. During 1915 and 1916 the CRT devoted much attention to José Castellví, who had spent twenty-two years in the Barcelona La Modelo prison for having kidnapped a *cacique* from his village in Huesca.[9] Its first big campaign was to protest at the trial of an 'American' anarchist, Jesús Vega, who had shot and slightly wounded the chief of police, Francisco Martorell, after – so he claimed – he had tried to turn him into an informer. It demonstrated the anarchist-syndicalists' ability to mobilise. In the two weeks before his trial on 21 May 1915, at least two soirées and fifteen meetings were held (the biggest in a local cinema), posters went up and cinema and theatre-goers were showered with fly-sheets. Finally a large, hostile crowd gathered outside the law court on the day of his trial, a fact that did not stop him from getting six years.[10] *Tierra y Libertad* then launched its own campaign in the summer of 1915. In February of that year a group of peasants had clashed with the Civil Guard in the town of Cenicero near Logroño and killed one of them. They now faced trial by a military tribunal and quickly became martyrs to the cause. A prisoners' committee was elected, funds raised and meetings held throughout Spain in August and September 1915, and, again, in Catalonia, in the following May and September.[11] Subsequently, between December 1916 and January 1917, the calenders' and sizers' union, with the support of the CRT, held protest meetings against the Barcelona police, during which labour leaders voiced their anger at arbitrary arrests, the close vigilance to which they were subject and brutality in police cells. Furthermore, in order to strengthen the campaign's impact, tales of police bribery and corruption were freely aired in *Solidaridad Obrera*.[12]

However, these protests were handicapped by a lack of funds and tended to peter out after a month or two. It was only the intense discontent provoked first by the economic dislocation caused by the war, and then by the rising cost of living, which could provide the focus for more sustained action. The wide-ranging sense of anger felt across much of urban Spain also stimulated calls for united action by the Left. It was a challenge which less sectarian anarchist-syndicalists, like Seguí, who emphasised the need for working-class unity, were willing to take up.

In late August 1914 the CRT set up a commission to decide what action to take over the economic crisis, which Socialists, republicans, and representatives of other working-class associations were quick to join. Over the next two months unemployment rose rapidly, leading to clashes between unemployed protestors and the security forces. Once again the anarchist Left called for revolutionary action, while 'Socialists and pure trade unionists' were more cautious. Angel Pestaña, who had only just arrived in Barcelona, took an intermediate position – indicative of the role he would play within the organisation in subsequent years – arguing for the 'organisation of revolts', which would frighten the authorities into making concessions. The CRT's first big meeting was held in the Palau de Belles Arts theatre on 8 October, attended by 4,000 workers. A resolution passed threatened a general strike if no action were taken within fifteen days, and a large demonstration following the meeting ended in serious clashes with the Civil Guard.[13]

Yet, in the following days it was the Catalan Socialists who briefly took the lead. This demonstrated the strength that they still retained within Catalan organised labour, especially through their influence in the textile industry. Because they continued to pursue the strategy inspired by Jaurés and Fabra Ribas, of uniting the Catalan unions, they were particularly predisposed to building broad fronts. The Socialist-dominated Mataró leadership of the National Textile Federation organised an assembly of Spanish unions on 18 October, attended by both independent unions and those close to the anarchist-syndicalist camp, to decide what action to take. It was a considerable success, with fifty-nine delegates, representing around eighty unions, together with the Catalan Regional Metalworkers' Federation, and the local workers' federations of Barcelona, Manresa, Sabadell and Igualada present. From outside Catalonia only delegates from Alcoy made the trip, but a large number of unions gave their support (including the National Committee of the UGT).

It was decided to hold meetings throughout the country by 25 October, and then, if the authorities did not then take action within seventy-two hours of the last meetings, to 'act radically'. This was clearly a threat to call a general strike. Yet unlike the years 1910 to 1913, with both Manuel Andreu and Salvador Seguí now key figures, the CRT showed that it could step back when necessary. A large number of meetings were held in Catalonia, but it soon became clear that strike action would not be widely supported. The Socialists were never enthusiastic and the anarchist-syndicalists back-tracked. *Solidaridad Obrera* demanded restraint: 'When it is the right moment to act we will act. We must be neither impatient nor weak: energy and calm.' A further large meeting was held in Barcelona on 25 January 1915, which called for a general strike on 15 February, but once again no action was finally taken.[14] Overall, the campaign had served to galvanise protest, but in the following months the CRT found it impossible to sustain the impetus. In part this reflected the improved economic climate, in part the continued weakness of the Catalan labour movement and of the CRT itself.

Yet, from the spring of 1916, accelerating inflation produced strong grass-roots pressure from the trade unions for action to be taken, with calls for a joint UGT and CNT campaign by a number of independent labour federations and UGT unions. In Catalonia such action was again strongly supported by the Socialists, who remained keen to build bridges with the CRT. The anarchist-syndicalists responded positively. This was not to everyone's liking. In *enragé* anarchist circles alliances with Socialist 'politicians' did not go down well, and for this reason that the CRT leadership always referred to the UGT and never mentioned the Socialist party. Nevertheless, it realised that in order to pressurise the regime it was necessary to build links with the

Socialist unions, who could mobilise large numbers of workers outside Catalonia. In February 1916 the UGT's membership totalled over 76,000, while that of the CRT was still probably not much more than 15,000. Moreover, for people like Seguí, who were trying to get away from the hardliners' short-term insurrectionary agenda, the Socialists more measured approach would, no doubt, have its attractions.

It was in this atmosphere that the CNT held an assembly in Valencia on 14 May 1916, attended by seventy delegates, at which it was agreed to launch a campaign to reduce the price of basic necessities, demand a broad new amnesty, and try and coordinate its actions with the UGT. Once again, a general strike was threatened if the authorities took no action. A Barcelona-based committee, composed of Seguí, Pestaña and Miranda, was appointed to plan the campaign. Seguí was its secretary and, as a result, would be the key figure in future negotiations with the Socialists. Shortly afterwards, between 17 and 24 May, the UGT held its Twelfth Congress in Madrid. Here, despite the moderation of the Socialist leadership, under rank-and-file pressure, a resolution was approved, which called for a day of demonstrations and meetings to be held throughout Spain, a one-day stoppage and, if no action were taken by the Government, the organisation of an assembly to decide what further action to take. Furthermore, it was agreed to support an alliance with the CNT. Such a stance was vigorously promoted by a left-wing current – whose demands were to a large extent articulated by *La Justicia Social* – which was emerging within the Socialist movement and pushed the organisation to adopt a more aggressive class line. The spirit of understanding was reflected in the presence of Andrés Ovejero, representing the UGT, in the Valencia Assembly (who embraced Miranda in the closing meeting), and the leading Madrid anarchist, Mauro Bajatierra, along with Eusebi Carbó, at the UGT congress.[15]

The political repercussions of this alliance will be analysed later in this chapter. Suffice it to note for now that over the following months it would provide a focus for the mobilisation of working-class discontent. On 9 and 10 July, the Valencia Committee held a series of protest meetings. Simultaneously, on 8 July, the alliance between the UGT and CNT was formalised in the so-called 'Pact of Zaragoza', signed by Seguí, Pestaña and the Zaragoza union leader, Angel Lacort, on the part of the anarchist-syndicalists, and Francisco Largo Caballero, Julián Besteiro and Vicente Barrio, for the Socialists. It was agreed to campaign for price controls and a broad amnesty, hold a one-day general strike and, if this were not effective, to 'continue the action in ways in which the circumstances impose'. The CRT leadership had, therefore, largely deferred to the UGT, no doubt because the latter were in a stronger position, but the threat of more radical action should the one-day strike have no impact was more in keeping with the anarchist-syndicalist heritage and enough to sell the agreement to most activists.[16]

A first round of meetings was planned for 16 July. They had to be put on hold when the Prime Minister, the Count of Romanones, responded to a general railway workers' strike by declaring martial law. But the campaign was launched on 15 October, with big protest meetings in Barcelona and Madrid, followed by further meetings in a large number of towns over the next two weeks. With 5,000 present, *Tierra y Libertad* declared the Barcelona meeting 'perhaps the most important in the annals of the Barcelona proletariat'.[17] The focus was on the state's supposed subordination to 'hoarders', and 'plutocratic interests', who were, the speakers claimed, speculating with and profiting from the war, and its lack of concern with the plight of workers. Notable was the presence of large numbers of women. They were finding it increasingly difficult to make ends meet and this brought them to the forefront of the agitation. The UGT and CNT subsequently issued a joint communiqué giving the Government an ultimatum. It responded by pushing a new (but limited) amnesty bill through parliament, and approving legislation aimed at controlling price rises. Its centrepiece was the creation of a Madrid-based committee (Junta de Subsistencias) with branches in the provinces, which would oversee measures designed to ensure an adequate supply of basic foodstuffs at regulated prices.

Understandably the labour opposition was sceptical. A new round of protest meetings was held from 12 November onwards. Then on 19 November, in the Madrid Casa del Pueblo, after some hesitation, the CNT endorsed the Socialist strategy of calling a twenty-four hours general strike on 18 December.[18] In industrial Spain it was a considerable success. In Barcelona itself it proved difficult to bring workers out in areas in which industrialists had instituted powerful systems of social control, but in the major industrial sectors (with the exception of the waterfront) it was widely supported, and, moreover, spread to the medium-sized industrial towns. Notable was the large number of women and young lads on the streets, stoning trams and exhorting workers not to go in.[19] Again, the stoppage emphasised the CRT's ability to mobilise far more widely than its paid-up union base. It was also Spain's first political general strike and as such represented an unprecedented challenge to the ruling order. This is a theme I shall develop in the second half of the chapter.

Yet the movement was significant from another perspective. Amongst the activists it heightened awareness of the importance of the sphere of consumption as an arena of exploitation and struggle. One way in which this was manifested was in the growth of a CRT-inspired tenants' association. The anarchist-syndicalists were in a particularly strong position to promote such organisations. Their emphasis on direct action and lack of bureaucratic controls spawned grass-roots initiatives and militancy. As noted in Chapter Five, there had already been talk of the need to form a tenants' union in the first decade of the century, but only in March 1917, stimulated by steep increases in the price of rented accommodation, was a committee set up. The key aim was to put pressure on landlords to reduce rents, return tenants' deposits and improve the standard of accommodation. From January 1918, under the hard-line anarchists, Pere Jul and 'E. Mateo Soriano' (pseudonym of Estanislao Maqueda Mateo), the committee began actively to enrol tenants – several hundred had joined by the end of the month – and in June called a series of well-attended neighbourhood meetings. Its goal was to set up neighbourhood committees as a prelude to some form of active protest movement.

Success was, however, mixed. It ran into problems staffing the committees and from the summer began to run out of steam. In October 1918 it focused protest on the leading Radical figure in the town hall, Emiliano Iglesias, for introducing a new tax on rents, leading to a noisy protest in the Plaça Sant Jaume. But despite talk of a rent strike none was ever attempted. Funding may have been a problem, and it was also no doubt difficult to mobilise enough workers for what was a totally unprecedented initiative. As in other areas, discussion over strategy also brought out tensions within the CRT. Seguí's close friend, Josep Viadiu, hoped that it would help broaden the organisation to take in other social classes, including shopkeepers, who also, to a large extent, rented accommodation. This is important because it shows how Seguí's men were thinking in terms of reaching outside the industrial working class. On the contrary, for E. Mateo Soriano, one of Seguí's harshest critics, it was a new means to attack the state. Viadiu's hopes were not, in fact, necessarily well founded. Such a movement held the risk that it would bring the CRT into confrontation with sectors of the petty bourgeoisie. As noted in Chapter Three, Barcelona's property structures were highly atomised and the small landlords would inevitably become its enemies. However, this would as yet remain only a potential source of strife. It was not until the Second Republic that the Catalan CNT would be strong enough to organise actual tenants' strikes.[20]

Not all protest movements against rising prices were led by the CRT. January 1918 was to see spontaneous action orchestrated by women. The backdrop was the continuing escalation of prices. The winter of 1917 to 1918 was the worst of the war. Statistics for Barcelona indicate that the prices of basic necessities rose 21 percent between 1914 and 1916, but 39 percent between 1916 and 1918. In Spain as a whole, between March 1917 and March 1918, they rose by 17.6 percent.[21] January 1918 witnessed a new twist to the inflationary spiral, with a particularly steep rise in the price of coal along with significant increases in the price of bread. *Solidaridad Obrera* renewed its attack on 'hoarders' and, in typically anarchist-syndicalist terms, suggested that bread and coal sold at extortionate prices should simply be taken.[22]

Yet the paper in no way instigated the protests that followed. Clashes between women and coal suppliers began on 9 January. The next day, a large commission of women first visited the mayor and then the civil governor to protest at the rise in prices. Then, on 11 January, groups of women, who were engaged in heated discussions, came together in Olmo Street in the heart of the Fifth District and began to demonstrate. They forced factories in which women worked and shops to close in the morning, and cafés and cabarets to shut down in the evening. Those who resisted had their windows stoned. The women's intention was twofold. On the one hand, they wished to produce a crisis situation and, thereby, force the authorities to take action; on the other, by shutting commercial establishments they aimed to bring their predicament home to all social classes.

A similar pattern was repeated the following day, when women met up in the Plaça Reial in the morning, before heading off to forcibly close down shops and factories. Matters further escalated on Monday 14 January, when groups of women set off to close down factories in Poble Nou and Sants, and commissions were sent to the other more outlying neighbourhoods. The impact was dramatically apparent in the afternoon. Until then 1,000 women at most had been involved in the demonstrations, but they were now joined by large groups from the suburbs, helping to swell the number of protestors to up to 12,000. It was on this day that the most serious incident of the protests occurred. At one point large numbers of women tried to force their way in to see the civil governor. When they were on the stairs of his official headquarters they were charged by civil guards and several were badly injured when the banisters gave way.

Henceforth, demonstrations were prohibited, the security forces guarded the city's markets, patrolled the streets and broke up any large gatherings of women. Bravo Portillo in particular excelled himself in leading police charges on the demonstrators. But the women had successfully brought much of the industry in which female labour predominated to a halt. Even according to official figures, on 19 January, 273 factories, which employed 20,500 women and 500 men, had closed. They had been particularly successful in the textile industry, especially in those factories in which La Constància was strong. Moreover, from 24 January onwards, protests began to spread to urban areas outside Barcelona.[23]

During the protest movement there were also numerous smaller-scale incidents in which women took action on the ground. In the early days of the dispute they forced coal merchants to sell at the price set by the provincial price-control board. Carts containing coal and foodstuffs were overturned by protestors, who either stole the merchandise or, on one occasion at least, forced the carter to sell it off cheaply. Similar scenes were seen in the major markets where women tried to set what they saw as a just price. From the first the authorities began intervening and tried to force shop owners to sell basic necessities at the stipulated price. Moreover, on 20 January, the Radicals, who were influential within local government, got the price-control board to set new, lower rates. This led to further incidents when some shopkeepers refused to sell their goods and had their shops stormed. This agitation may be seen as a representing a further prong in the protestors' strategy. They tried to use their muscle on the ground to force prices down. Simultaneously, in order to heighten pressure on the middle and upper classes they began sending domestic servants home before they reached the market.

These events can be analysed at a number of levels. First, they once again brought to the fore the key role that women played in movements linked to the defence of the family. Women clearly saw it as their responsibility to ensure that family members were provided for, going so far as to prevent men from participating in demonstrations. Pamela B. Radcliffe has recently argued that in Gijón during this period consumer-based protests against rising prices were interclass movements of the 'popular classes' against social elites.[24] There are several problems with this approach, at least if one attempts to apply it to Barcelona. There was, it is true, some scope for protests over prices to attract a broad social base. *Solidaridad Obrera* qualified its usual class-based rhetoric and adopted a more populist discourse, arguing that 'everyone,

the workers and the middle classes' suffered at the hands of the 'big companies, plutocrats and hoarders' who had the Government in their pockets.[25]

However, there is overwhelming evidence that in Barcelona the women
were very much drawn from an industrial working-class background. I have
already analysed in Chapter Two how friendship networks amongst working-
class women were built up within the community. These were to form the
springboard for the protest movement. Furthermore, the women's participation in previous working-class disturbances was of fundamental importance in
providing them with an iconography of protest that they could now apply. As
in the 1902 and 1909 general strikes, they both stoned windows and
attempted to denude the city of consumer staples in order to put maximum
pressure to bear on the state and make life as uncomfortable as possible for
the middle and upper classes. Amongst the protestors there was an expecta-
tion of gender solidarity. Hence, women of any social class caught on the
streets were (no doubt vigorously) invited to join the protestors, but it is very
much to be doubted that they enjoyed the experience. The only other women
they had significant success in mobilising were the waitresses of the Paral·lel,
because they themselves often came from the popular and working-class quarters of town.[26]

Nor would it be true to say that the protests were directed exclusively at
social elites. While it was the Asturian coal owners and Castilian cereal producers who were making a large profit, it was the (frequently modest) shop-
keeper who suffered a broken window or had his merchandise stolen.
Moreover, attempts to broaden the movement sat uneasily with comments in
union meetings and in the press that 'small shopkeepers ... steal, the same as
the rest', that shopkeepers who were hoarding should be forced to sell
cheaply, and those who refused should have their establishments sacked. The
shopkeepers' discontent was voiced by a deputation of their association, the
Unió de Ultramarins, to the civil governor. The requirement to sell at the
price set by the price-control board was, they argued, leading to their ruin.[27]

The protests were not, in my view, as Lester Golden has claimed, undertaken in opposition to male factory-based labour. In the labour press the
women's actions were applauded and it was in this atmosphere that they
became increasingly assimilated by the major left-wing organisations.[28] It was
women close to the Radical camp who were, from the outset, behind the frequent visits to the civil governor. In response to the elaboration of a new,
lower, tariff of prices by the Radical majority on the local price-control board,
on 19 January the Radical-dominated women's commission accepted the new
list and advised the women to return to work on Monday 21 January. However, the anarchist-syndicalists then mobilised against the accord, accusing the
commission members of selling out. They were able to do this effectively
because, as seen in the previous chapter, over the past four years they had produced a group of female leaders, who, from 21 January onwards, put their
weight behind a new strategy of linking female protest to the CRT by holding not only illegal meetings of women in the open air (difficult for the
authorities to break up by force), but also joint male and female meetings
addressed by leading CRT activists.

Through grass-roots pressure they then hoped to enforce a 'people's price list' (*tasa del pueblo*) which was, helpfully, printed out and distributed to shoppers. It was also, at least in part, under CRT auspices that the movement began to spread outside Barcelona. Faced by this dangerous escalation, on 25 January 1918 the Government declared martial law, closed down union headquarters and arrested a number of anarchist-syndicalist activists. Constitutional guarantees would not be restored until 14 April. These events highlighted the strengths and weaknesses of syndicalist strategy. As I have emphasised, the anarchist-syndicalists derived their strength from their use of mass activism. Yet, by rejecting compromise they risked provoking intense state repression. As far as the relation between the CRT and female protest is concerned, what once again comes through is that most activists wanted to harness female discontent to intensify and broaden working-class agitation. But, as stressed in the previous chapter, the women were seen as auxiliaries, who were subordinate to the male CRT leadership.

The movement can, finally, also provide additional insights into the nature of working-class protest in Barcelona. Behind the women's actions could be seen a rejection of market forces in favour of some form of regulated 'just price'(a term which was actually used). In this respect the opposition of many male workers to unfettered capitalist development and their attempts to 'regulate' apprenticeship, and women's efforts to fix prices below market rates, reflect the same cultural outlook. As was the case throughout Europe, workers and their families retained a 'moral economy', which rejected liberal political economy in favour of some form of regulation by the state and community.[29] Furthermore, the strategies adopted point to the continuing importance of the riot within workers' 'repertoires of collective action'. As in the case of unions and strikes, with only limited means of influencing state policy through political interlocutors, protest 'in the street' was the only real means by which workers – whether male or female – could make their voice heard. It was, as has already been stressed, a situation which fitted the anarchist-syndicalist tenet of 'direct action' like a glove.

The Crisis of the Restoration Regime, the CNT-UGT Alliance and the Rise of Organised Labour, 1916 to 1917

From 1916, rising working-class protest would feed into an escalating political crisis, precipitated by a series of increasingly powerful challenges to the regime. The upshot would be that in the summer of 1917 it briefly seemed that a coalition of forces might bring it down and put in its place some form of democratic political system.

At the heart of the growing problems faced by the Restoration regime was its *caciquista* foundations and the difficulty it had in channelling and integrating political agitation and labour protest. This could be seen on a number of fronts. First, the war was to have an important ideological and political impact in Spain. When it broke out, Eduardo Dato's Conservative administration immediately proclaimed Spain's strict neutrality, but from the outset a fierce dialectical battle sprang up between the so-called *Aliadófilos* and *Germanófilos*, respectively supporters of the Allied and German causes. While republicans and most Socialists fervently supported the Allies, believing that they represented the values of democracy, liberty and progress, on the other side of the political divide, conservative opinion sided with the Central European Powers, who were viewed as guarantors of order and stability. For a system dependent on depoliticisation, the polemic was damaging. It inflamed political debate and, moreover, provoked tensions and divisions within the ruling parties themselves. This was most dramatically demonstrated when the Count of Romanones was brought down in March 1917, with the connivance of King Alfonso XIII, after trying to take Spain closer to the Allied camp.[30]

Second, rapid industrial growth and the increasing weight of urban middle class and business interests encouraged Catalanist protest, led by the Lliga Regionalista. The party had strong anti-liberal Catholic roots, but the need to build an interclass coalition to take on the Restoration regime led it in a democratic direction. From 1916 onwards, under the dynamic leadership of Francesc Cambó, it attempted to gain support from other parts of the country through its 'Catalunya i La Espanya Gran' programme, which promoted a vision of a decentralised and industrially dynamic Spain.[31] Simultaneously, labour's capacity to intervene in the political process was growing. This was not just a question of its expanding trade-union base. Until the war years the working-class Left had, in terms of its influence over the country's political development, very much played second fiddle to republicanism. The tables were now beginning to turn. In much of Spain, while the Socialists were busy building up party and union structures, republicans proved unable to forge mass, professionalised political parties, or effectively enthuse the working class. In Catalonia, on the other hand, the republicans could not break out of the crisis into which they had entered between 1911 and 1914. This was particularly clear in Barcelona where, between 1910 and 1916, electoral participation fell from 58 to 37.3 percent, and the republican (Lerrouxist and Left Catalanist) vote plummeted from about 56,000 to 30,000, allowing the Lliga to emerge as the most voted party.[32]

Both the Catalanist and Radical republican camps were afflicted. Like its predecessors, the Left-Catalanist UNFR, founded in 1910, remained an ineffective force. It failed to appeal to most of the working class, lost middle-class votes to the Lliga, and finally disintegrated in the spring of 1916. In the previous year radical Leftists had broken away, and in April 1917 set up the PRC. Encouraged by the rise of working-class politics in Spain and Europe, it was led by a group of men who rejected the cosy middle-class world of the UNFR leadership and wished to link up with labour. This can be seen as part of a broader process of radicalisation of sectors of the Spanish intelligentsia. Thus, it stated that its aim was to create a socialist party based on the working class, and that it looked to work closely with the CRT, encouraging the latter's leadership to ally with it and enter the world of electoral politics. Men like the party's new president, Marcel·lí Domingo, Lluís Companys, and the handicapped doctor, Francesc Layret, established close contacts with the CRT leadership, Companys and Layret acting as labour lawyers for the organisation.[33]

They were helped by the fact that the war years had seen growing sympathy for Catalanism on the Left. The struggle by the 'small nations' in southeastern Europe against the Central Powers encouraged increasing numbers of left-wing journalists and intellectuals to champion the cause of anti-state nationalisms, which were seen as battering rams against reactionary centralised states and multinational empires. Such a process took place within the Catalan branch of the PSOE, which became much more receptive to Catalanist demands. This was echoed within the Catalan CRT. Most importantly, Manuel Andreu came out in support, arguing, in two articles published in *Solidaridad Obrera* in March 1917, that Catalonia was one of the 'natural nationalities' which was being held back by reactionary centralism. The articles caused quite a stir in syndicalist and anarchist circles, producing, it seems, a generally negative reaction. José Borobio, the current editor of *Solidaridad Obrera*, took up the cudgel and restated what might be referred to as anarchist-syndicalist orthodoxy: workers are all equally exploited, and in any case improved communications were breaking down national barriers and leading the world to become increasingly cosmopolitan.[34]

However, amongst the majority who rejected any overt Catalanisation of the CRT one cannot talk of total homogeneity. Figures such as Angel Pestaña, Francesc Miranda and Eusebi Carbó had inherited the outlook of the likes of Anselmo Lorenzo and Francesc Ferrer. They not only rejected Catalanism but also had little time for Catalan identity or the usage (particularly in written form) of the Catalan language. Esperanto might one day become the one world language, but in the meantime Castilian-Spanish would conveniently function as its surrogate. In addition, they generally took a hard class line, ruling out any compromises with 'bourgeois' movements.

The position of Seguí, on the other hand, was closer to that of the La Tramontana Group during the first decade of the century. He was a libertarian federalist and regarded Catalan nationalism, especially while under the hegemony of the Lliga, as a divisive and destructive force, but his pragmatism meant that he was much more receptive to working with republican and democratic politicians. He was a sworn enemy of Lerrouxism, but regarded the leaders of the PRC as sincere revolutionaries, and, in particular, struck up a friendship with Layret. Moreover, he cultivated his Catalan, attended talks at the left-Catalanist educational institution, the Ateneu Enciclopèdic Popular, and participated in *tertulias* in which Catalanist intellectuals were present. He was no doubt encouraged in this respect by the fact that during the first and second decades of the twentieth century the prestige of Catalan as a cultural and literary vehicle grew.[35] One may, therefore, conclude that he and his supporters respected Catalan identity and were willing to enter into a dialogue with the world of Catalanism. Yet Seguí remained a committed anarchist-syndicalist, who believed that acting independently the CRT would be at the heart of the revolutionary process in Spain. This very much limited the PRC's room for maneouvre. It was a party led by middle-class professionals, with a social base made up largely of the petty bourgeoisie and white-collar workers, and without an organic link to the labour movement its impact was limited.

More significant in terms of Catalan politics was the continued decline of the Radicals' working-class and popular base, as Lerroux pressed on with his plans to forge a Spanish-wide party of the centre Left. In November 1918 he went so far as to state that his aim was a peaceful transition to 'an orderly republic', and that this regime would deal more energetically than the monarchy with 'the Bolshevik threat' and 'anarchist outrages'. Such comments were seized on by the anarchist-syndicalists, who remained intent on severing links between the Radicals and their working-class base. A good opportunity was provided when Pere Jul was shot and wounded at a meeting organised by the Radicals in favour of intervention in support of the Allies on 1 May 1917. A campaign was launched against the 'act of Lerrouxist barbarity'. It was not, however, totally successful, with the Radicals again showing that they still had influence in the labour movement and could counterattack to some effect.[36]

Yet the balance of forces was shifting very markedly towards the anarchist-syndicalists. From 1914 the decline in working-class electoral support for the Radicals was accompanied by a loss of young activists, some of whom transferred across to the CRT.[37] In response, *Solidaridad Obrera* argued that both the regime and the 'advanced political parties' were entering into crisis and that this gave the proletariat the opportunity to organise independently and confront the state on its own.[38] This was, in fact, quickly to prove an exaggeration. Working-class organisations had become an important component on the Left, but to take on the Restoration regime effectively they would need to form part of a broader coalition.

This became increasingly apparent as the political crisis of the regime deepened. This would present enormous opportunities but also great dangers to Salvador Seguí and the anarchist-syndicalists, who, on the one hand, saw their role as preparing a working-class communist revolution, but, on the other, would find it difficult not to become involved in a broader movement aimed at burying the hated Restoration regime. At first there seemed little reason to suppose that the Catalan CNT would stray off an orthodox path. During 1914 to 1915, it continued to promote a hard, class-based, revolutionary line. With the outbreak of the First World War the Socialist leadership supported the Allies because, it argued, they were on the side of democracy. A minority of anarchists and syndicalists took a similar stance. On the international plane their foremost representative was Kropotkin. Anarchist-syndicalist groups in Gijon, Zaragoza and Mahón backed this position, as did Federico Urales. Most, however, railed against what they saw as an inter-imperialist war, in which the workers were being sacrificed on the alter of the national bourgeoisies' lust for new colonies and markets.[39] Horror at the war was genuine, but the fact that they saw both sides as equally at fault emphasised their profound alienation from the institutions of western European, and by extension Spanish, state and society.

This attitude had clear repercussions in the Spanish political arena. Both Socialists and anarchist-syndicalists saw parallels between events in Europe and Spain. For the Socialist leadership, by democratising the continent the more progressive national bourgeoisies of France and Britain were, like it or not, opening the door to Socialism. In Spain, they believed, the Socialist-republican alliance, the *Conjunción*, could play a similar role. The anarchist-syndicalists' analysis, on the other hand, seemingly ruled out participation in a reforming, interclass, coalition. They continued to view the domain of 'politics' as unclean and poured scorn on the notion that some bourgeois regimes might be preferable to others. This was accompanied by a rather abstract working-class internationalism. They declared themselves to be antipatriots and antimilitarists, affirming, in the words of Francisco Jordán, that the European bourgeoisies were using patriotism as a tool to divide the working class. Yet below the surface there was more sympathy for the Allies than was readily apparent. Even Anselmo Lorenzo admitted that they were 'the least bad alternative', and Seguí, though he did not wish to rock the boat, hoped for an Allied victory.[40]

Opposition to the war stimulated them to organise the first Spanish conference since the ill-fated CNT congress of 1911. Following the call by the French anarchist, Sebastian Faure, for an international campaign against the war, the Syndicalist Athenaeum of El Ferrol in Galicia decided to hold an international peace conference in the city between 30 April and 2 May 1915. The Catalan CRT responded enthusiastically, sending Andreu, Pestaña, Miranda, Loredo and Carbó, with Tomás Herreros also present, representing *Tierra y Libertad*. In the weeks leading up to the conference the delegates held a number of meetings in Barcelona in order to raise awareness and mobilise support. Representatives of both anarchist groups and trades unions were present. Resolutions were passed in favour of the reorganisation of the CNT (with its National Committee to be located in Barcelona), for a new international syndicalist confederation to be established, and for workers to organise 'a general strike of protest and revolutionary affirmation' against the war where possible.

Given the weakness of the Spanish movement in 1915 the conference in reality achieved little, although it no doubt served to strengthen personal contacts between a number of the country's leading anarchist-syndicalist figures. It was also interesting in that it highlighted differences in tactics between the Barcelona representatives. In the first session the original resolution, calling for an international general strike against the war, was backed by Carbó and Herreros, but subsequently watered down. At the end of this session, several Portuguese delegates – the only non-Spaniards present – were expelled. Carbó, with the support of Pestaña, Loredo and Herreros, called for a spontaneous revolutionary general strike in response, but the majority voted simply for protest meetings to be held. There was clearly a division between the hotheads, Carbó and Herreros, who seemingly wished to call a general strike at every possible occasion, and Andreu and Miranda (who now clearly adopted a more moderate position), who refused to endorse precipitate action. It was the latter who, along with Seguí and his 'team', and a reformed Pestaña, would subsequently prevail within the Catalan CRT.[41]

This became clear when the alliance was forged with the UGT between May and July 1916. It signalled the victory of Seguí's strategy of pursuing broader alliances and not taking precipitate action. This attracted the opposition of some anarchists, who were becoming increasingly critical of syndicalism. Their fears were sharpened because, on the international plane, under Léon Jouhaux, the French CGT had broken with its anti-militarist heritage and entered the war-time coalition Government, the Union Sacrée. The anti-syndicalist cudgel was first taken up by Federico Urales, who in 1914 returned to Barcelona from Madrid and began writing for the leftist daily, *El Liberal*. From March 1916 criticisms also began to appear in the pages of *Tierra y Libertad*. Over the next year a number of anarchists attacked the CRT for supposedly losing its revolutionary impetus and becoming increasingly centred on union-building. They remained insurrectionaries in the mould of Bakunin and Errico Malatesta, and emphasised the need for anarchists to spearhead the revolution and inject revolutionary spirit into the unions. The first serious confrontation took place between Mas Gomeri and 'Fray León de Alma Fuerte' (Manuel Andreu) in April 1916, but the feud was quickly patched up. Andreu was replaced as editor of *Solidaridad Obrera* by Borobio, and Pestaña moved across onto the editorial board of *Tierra y Libertad*, which, in the following weeks, would swing around and support Seguí. Yet relations would remain tense, with criticism resurfacing from September. Not surprisingly, the Catalan Federation of Anarchist Groups took a similar anti-Seguí line.[42]

A division was therefore opening up between anarchists and anarchist-syndicalists. The former were stronger within the movement's cultural institutions, but were also to receive support from young, radicalised, labour activists within the CRT. Discontent raised its head in October 1916, centred on the issue of the alliance with the UGT and the rather gradualist strategy adopted. It coalesced around the metalworker of Andalusian origin, Francisco Jordán, who had taken over as general secretary of the CNT, and who was closely linked to the anarchist groups. Rather than a one-day stoppage Jordán proposed an indefinite general strike. This was vehemently opposed by the Socialists, who appealed to Seguí over Jordán's head, and in a meeting in Madrid on 19 October, at which Jordán along with anarchist-syndicalist representatives of the National Textile Federation and the Zaragoza workers' movement were present, the Socialist position was ratified.[43] This was not, however, the end of the story. When the one-day general strike was declared on 18 December Jordán tried to precipitate a violent confrontation by sending a telegram to Madrid stating blood had been spilt on the streets of Barcelona. Reaction to the strike also indicated that hopes of revolutionary upheaval remained very much alive. On 28 December *Solidaridad Obrera*, which under the directorship of Borobio took a more radical line than Seguí, affirmed that the strike could have taken a revolutionary turn, as could future general strikes.[44]

Nevertheless, Seguí's position was not seriously challenged. It was difficult to argue that he and his supporters had strayed far from anarchist-syndicalist orthodoxy. They were having some success in building a unified labour movement whose ultimate goal was, everyone agreed, a social revolution which would result from an inevitably violent confrontation with state power.[45] From early 1917 matters became more complex, when developments on the international plane, and their impact on Spain, began to seriously weaken the regime. March 1917 saw the Tsar overthrown in the first Russian Revolution and early in the following month the United States of America entered the war. By sharpening the perception that the war represented a transcendental clash between democratic and autocratic values, these events further intensified the division between *Aliadófilos* and *Germanófilos*, with street fights breaking out between the most radicalised sectors of each current. Furthermore, the Russian Revolution raised hopes within the republican-Socialist *Conjunción* that anti-monarchist, democratic change would sweep through Europe. Equally, the Right became increasingly fearful of the consequences of an Allied victory. Thus, it seems, it was the events in Russia which tipped Alfonso XIII towards the German cause. Indeed, the March Revolution would spark a trend which over the next twenty years would have highly destabilising consequences: the tendency for both Left and Right to draw parallels between Russia and Spain.

Both the Catalan CNT and the PSOE-UGT saw these developments as opening the way for a possible overthrow of the Restoration regime, and so were happy to maintain their pact. Nevertheless, their analyses of the consequences of the regime's fall were very different. The CRT maintained its neutralist, anti-imperialist stance, and argued that the war was precipitating a revolutionary crisis in Europe.[46] For the Socialist leadership, on the other hand, the hope was intensifying that the way might be open to a liberal-democratic republic. In January 1917, an assembly of Catalan CNT unions upped the ante, threatening an indefinite general strike should the authorities fail to take action to curb inflation.[47] For many, no doubt, the hope was that this would provoke a revolutionary conjuncture. Then, in the early spring, the Socialists began to devise a strategy to engineer the regime's demise. They adopted a two-pronged approach. First, the labour unions would act as a battering ram to bring down the regime. Second, the political Left would ally, support the strike and provide the ministers for the new government. In March they consolidated their alliance with the republicans and then held a meeting with Seguí, Pestaña and Lacort in the Madrid Casa del Pueblo. Here, after discussions, Besteiro drew up a manifesto whose key provision was that they would prepare a general strike 'for an indefinite period of time', in order to 'force the ruling class to undertake those fundamental changes in the system, which will guarantee a minimum, decent, living standard'. Furthermore, either at this meeting or shortly after, it was agreed that the central Spanish strike committee should be run by the UGT and based in Madrid. In Barcelona a local strike committee was also set up, on which both anarchist-syndicalists and Socialists were represented.[48]

Given the Socialists' generally cautious approach, the decision to call an open-ended general strike was a bold one. In large measure it was precipitated by the sense that now was the time to strike, along with the well-founded belief that the Restoration regime would not peacefully democratise. Furthermore, it was necessary in order to bring the CRT on board. Seguí and Pestaña could present the accord as in line with the agreement reached in January. On the surface at least their strategy remained rather different from that of the Socialists. They did not renounce the right to take independent action, and, while republicans and Socialists might be aiming for a liberal-democratic republic, they continued to argue that they could push revolutionary change further. At the same time, *Solidaridad Obrera* kept its distance from the republican-Socialist alliance, warning of the dangers of falling prey to those sectors of the bourgeoisie, who, it maintained, wished to use the workers for their own ends.

In addition, the anarchist-syndicalists' reading of the Russian Revolution provided them with a more sophisticated analysis of the revolutionary process in Spain, allowing them to argue that they could take advantage of a liberal-democratic regime to undertake more sweeping social change. In Russia, it was argued, there was now a situation of dual power. The 'capitalist elements' were attempting, through the Duma and the Provisional Government, to 'implant the same democratic system that in Europe has given power to the capitalist class'. But they were opposed by 'committees of workers and soldiers', who really represented the people, were watching over the Government's actions, and would eventually take over. This was the strategy the CRT would also try and implement in Spain. In line with this position, on 25 May, Seguí, Miranda (who had taken over as CNT general secretary when Jordán was arrested in March) and Pestaña, respectively representing the Valencia Committee, the CNT and the CRT, produced a manifesto 'to the Spanish people' in which they re-affirmed that the CNT-UGT pact would bring in the social revolution.[49]

Nevertheless, in recognition of their relative strength, Seguí had again allowed the Socialists to take the initiative, and he was vulnerable to the accusation of dealing with 'politicians'. An attempt was made by Seguí's critics to break the pact with the Socialists in May, following a declaration by the UGT's general secretary, Martínez Barrio, that the Spanish workers would sympathise if diplomatic relations were broken off with Germany. In response an 'assembly of unions, anarchist groups and athenaeums' was called on 10 May in Barcelona. The fact that the anarchist groups were represented would put the radicals in a stronger position, and it was agreed to send the editor of *Solidaridad Obrera*, José Borobio, to Madrid to warn the Socialists that if they continued to support intervention in the war the pact would be rescinded. Borobio met with the UGT's National Committee on 17 May. Largo Caballero refused to budge and Seguí, Pestaña and Miranda felt the need to publish their manifesto on 25 May precisely to defend the pact. In it they reaffirmed the need for proletarian unity, stated that Borobio had confirmed that there was no official Socialist position on the war and that the Socialists still supported an indefinite general strike.[50] Seguí's position was still very strong. Not only did he retain the backing of the labour leaders close to him, but, to a degree at least, the support of more orthodox anarchist-syndicalists like Negre and Miranda.

The CRT and the Crisis of 1917

June was to see a new, dramatic, twist to the revolutionary spiral, which would, for the first time, allow the CNT to play an important role within Spanish political life. The crisis was precipitated by the Spanish army, which maintained a high degree of institutional autonomy and retained the ability to intervene in the political process as it saw fit. This was dramatically demonstrated from early 1916 onwards, when medium-ranking officers based in Spain, hit by high inflation, began to form Juntas de Defensa to press for improved working conditions. The focus of the movement was Barcelona, where the central committee, the Junta Superior, was to be found. The King, by ordering the arrest of its members, exacerbated the crisis. On 1 June the *junteros* reacted by publishing a manifesto, couched in reforming, 'regenerationist' language, which gave the authorities twelve hours to release the officers and approve the Juntas' statutes. As Manuel de Burgos y Mazo, Minister of Justice from 11 June commented, it produced, 'a commotion the like of which the country had not seen for many years'.[51] Alfonso XIII quickly backtracked and the Liberal Government of the Marquis of Alhucemas resigned on 9 June. Still intent on maintaining the *turno*, the King invited the Conservative, Eduardo Dato, to form a new government two days later.

The possibility that the army might support reform galvanised the opposition into action. In meetings on 5 and 16 June, Socialists, republicans and Reformists agreed to work together to establish a provisional government which would pave the way for general elections to a constituent parliament. Shortly after the Lliga threw its hat into the ring and tried to integrate the centre-right into the anti-Restoration front, by bringing on board the representatives of manufacturing interests throughout Spain, along with the supporters of Antonio Maura, who despite his authoritarian tendencies, also employed an anti-*caciquista*, regenerationist language. This was combined with attempts by both Cambó and Lerroux to gain the Juntas' backing. With regard to strategy, Cambó had no desire to provoke violence or to strengthen the working-class Left. Accordingly, rather than rely on strike action, the Lliga tried to put together a parliamentary alliance to demand reform. The idea was to pile unbearable pressure on the King to form a new provisional government, made up of all the opposition forces, which would then call elections to a constituent parliamentary assembly.

The republicans and Socialists temporarily fell into line behind this position. A first assembly of Catalan deputies and senators was held in Barcelona on 5 July, with a second Spanish-wide assembly in the same city on 19 July. This was indicative of where the heart of the protest movement was located. The assemblies supported regional autonomy and made the key demand that the Spanish parliament, the Cortes, reopen as a constituent Cortes and prepare free and fair elections. Dato responded to the threat by suspending constitutional guarantees on 26 June, but, biding his time, allowed the meetings to take place. The second assembly was awaited with great anticipation and clearly enjoyed wide-ranging sympathy in Barcelona. However, Cambó was not able to get Maura's backing. Despite the fact that the grand old man of

Spanish Conservatism had spent the last decade attacking the non-representative nature of the Restoration regime, he refused to become involved in an unconstitutional movement, which could call the monarchy into question. Furthermore, without the involvement of more conservative Spanish forces the Juntas would not give their support. They continued to employ an anti-Restoration rhetoric, but most of the officers were, at heart, right-wing centralists, and would not contemplate an alliance with Catalanists and the Left. After July 19 this left open the question of how to proceed. The assembly movement had shaken the regime, but it was hard to see how it could now despose it.[52]

The CRT reacted to the crisis by subtly shifting its position. Already, from April, in *Solidaridad Obrera*, there were an increasing number of attacks on the Restoration regime per se, rather than on capitalism in the abstract. Also indicative of the organisation's changing stance was the fact that in the manifesto published on 25 May, Seguí, Pestaña and Miranda for the first time admitted publicly that they favoured the Allies. From June the critique of the Restoration regime was intensified. Thus, *Solidaridad Obrera* maintained that: 'We sympathise with no government, but the one we have is particularly hateful to us.' In addition, it recognised that they were embarked on a revolution with 'the healthy elements', 'the majority of the people', or, more specifically, 'republicans and Socialists, men of heart and will' against the 'tiny number of money men and politicians'. Support for the republicans, the paper also admitted, was necessary 'because they have more influence over the mass of the people than the working-class unions'.[53] At a practical level this rhetoric was matched by growing contacts with the Socialists and the PRC.

This re-evaluation can be explained by the ambiguities of anarchist-syndicalist thought. Within the movement the language of class was primary. Emphasis centred on the need to launch an anti-capitalist proletarian revolution, which would sweep away all the miseries of the present-day society. Yet, as I have also stressed, within anarchist-syndicalist ideology there was a second, albeit rather contradictory component; the struggle between the forces of 'reaction', on the one hand, and 'liberty' and 'progress' on the other. This second strand could briefly come to the fore in the summer of 1917 for several reasons. First, Salvador Seguí and his supporters were pragmatists, and had themselves discussed the need for industrial workers to reach out to other social groups. This stance was not theoretically elaborated, but at a political level it could imply the construction of a broad anti-regime front. Second, for the first time it actually seemed that the Restoration regime might be overthrown, and, whatever some harder-line activists might say, within broader left-wing circles (including no doubt the majority of CNT workers) the republic was an enticing prospect. Once the possibility of putting together an alliance to overthrow the Restoration regime became a reality, then the inter-class component of the movement's vocabulary became further accentuated.

Yet, the continued primacy of class-based, revolutionary discourse came through in the anarchist-syndicalists' continued claim that the ultimate consequence of the crisis would be some form of social revolution. As Seguí stated in a discussion with the Catalan Socialist, Manuel Escorza: 'If as a result of the revolution we do not get all that we want, there being no other way, we will accept the liberties, material improvements and other advantages that the new situation gives us. But we will not call a halt to our onward struggle.' An attempt was made to resolve the tension between support for democratisation and social transformation by once again appealing to the experience of the Russian Revolution, and in particular to the role of the peasants and workers' committees or soviets, which were seen as controlling the bourgeois Duma. This was expressed in a manifesto published in July, in which they backed the establishment of a liberal-democratic state in Spain, with advanced social legislation, but stated that they expected it to introduce what were seen as transitional reforms (such as the abolition of the standing army and its replacement by a militia) and that it would be bound by a high degree of union control. Most significantly, they argued, unions would be able to 'veto laws approved by the constituent Cortes'.[54]

Seguí was, therefore, showing a willingness to replace the all-or-nothing revolutionary general strike for a longer term strategy of social transformation. Nevertheless, the CRT's revolutionary heritage still came through in its determination that an indefinite general strike accompanied by an armed uprising be declared. It was this which no doubt helped keep on board many radicals sceptical of the Socialist pact. It also quickly led to tension with the Socialists, who wished to explore all other channels before calling the strike. The distance which separated both movements, both strategically and psychologically, was brought home when the CRT began arming and manufacturing bombs while the UGT took no action. This led to a number of angry exchanges. Most dramatically, on 20 June, Largo Caballero, president of the UGT, had to travel hastily to Barcelona to save the pact. The very different context in which they operated was dramatically apparent. In Madrid he was able to work openly from his office in the Casa del Pueblo, but when he arrived in Barcelona he was led by his Socialist contact, Joaquín Bueso, to Les Planes, a secret location in the hills outside Barcelona. When he arrived he was confronted by 100 angry activists, many of them armed. Francesc Miranda now denounced the links between the Socialists and 'bourgeois politicians' and called for the general strike to be declared as soon as possible. This was indicative of growing tensions between Seguí's supporters and more orthodox anarchist-syndicalists. Only the influence of Seguí and Pestaña saved the pact. Then, fearing for his safety, in order to avoid the police, Largo Caballero was led by Seguí and Pestaña back across the hillside until they reached the Sarrià tram stop.[55]

The CRT's first reaction to the Assembly movement was hostile. The Lliga was seen as the reactionary representative of the Catalan bourgeoisie and the Assembly described as 'the anchor the bourgeoisie has grabbed hold of ... in order to contain the popular avalanche'.[56] Its leadership may have felt some sympathy for the movement, which had strong popular support and was, after all, aimed at overthrowing the Restoration regime. However, they could not (even if they wished) be seen as collaborating with their putative class enemies. Accordingly, while Seguí was in close touch with leading figures within the PRC in order to organise the general strike (who, indeed, supplied the

CRT with some arms), there were only 'small contacts' with representatives of the Assembly movement, and an attempt by Cambó to establish a dialogue was brushed aside.[57]

The upshot was that on the eve of the Spanish Assembly of 19 July 1917 the CRT's attitude was one of expectancy. Although – on the request of the Assembly participants – no general strike was proclaimed, most shops closed in the afternoon. Clearly the CRT hoped that the Restoration edifice would crack and, as Seguí's comments make clear, was determined that its voice be heard if it did. It seems that the CRT had agreed, presumably with members of the PRC and the Socialists, to be ready if required. *Solidaridad Obrera* later stated that it had suspended publication on 17 July to 'take action'. Seguí, it appears, secretly met up with the president of the PRC, Marcel·lí Domingo, to discuss the direction of the movement during 19 July, while activists congregated in a hall in Conde del Asalto Street in the Fifth District only to be dispersed by the Civil Guard. The hope may have been that the Assembly delegates would make some kind of antidynastic declaration, which they could then back up with a general strike. The anarchist-syndicalists' position is indicated in a fly-sheet distributed the day before, which called for a 'republican government which respects workers' rights', and in their advice to local workers' committees to participate in the movement in a 'concrete, affirmative and constructive way', and then impose their 'minimum programme'. They could join left-wing revolutionary committees as long as they maintained their autonomy. However, tension within the movement was demonstrated by the fact that *Tierra y Libertad* openly called for workers to take advantage of the strike to initiate revolutionary action.[58]

In the aftermath of the Assembly a number of activists were briefly arrested and, lacking funds, *Solidaridad Obrera* did not reappear until 1 August. From the first, under the editorship of Borobio, it showed itself totally disillusioned with any interclass reform project. The Catalan bourgeoisie, it claimed, had been frightened by the growing strength of 'the proletariat' and had therefore side-tracked the movement through the assemblies. Hence they had 'assassinated the revolution' and converted the left-wing parties into 'their instruments' in order to attract the 'popular elements'. This was combined with criticisms of the ineffectiveness of the political Left and of the Socialists for seemingly being more interested in the Assembly movement than in organising the general strike. Simultaneously, it reaffirmed its class-based analysis; it was now up to the workers to strengthen their organisation and carry through their own revolution. This was a position backed up by *Tierra y Libertad*, which overtly criticised the CRT leaders for effectively allying with the Lliga and republican 'politicians', and not elaborating a clear revolutionary programme.[59]

Clearly there was great disappointment that the 19 July Assembly had come to nothing. Moreover, the attacks on the republicans indicated the extent to which the attempts to draw closer to middle-class left-wing politicians had been fitful and fearful, with many concerned that basic anarchist-syndicalist tenets were in danger. Hence, the first setback was seen, by some at least, as sufficient reason for all ties to be severed. Such analyses also reflected the fact that although Seguí may have tried to introduce a sense of long-term strategy, hardliners still saw the revolution at every turn. This was particularly the case because expectations had built up enormously since 1 June.

It was in the aftermath of the events of July that criticism of Seguí became increasingly vitriolic and personal. He was suspect, in more hard-line anarchist-syndicalist circles, not only because of his policies but also because of his interests outside the anarchist camp. He had established friendships with some non-Lerrouxist republicans and also joined an intellectual *tertulia* in the Café Suizo on the Rambla, most of whose figures were not anarchists. And in contrast to the puritanical lifestyle of the 'men with long beards' he smoked, enjoyed good food, regularly attended the theatre and cinema, and was Catholic in his tastes. These attacks reflected a divide in the movement between the anarchist cultural core and the anarchist-syndicalist trade unionists, who while committed to the CNT as a labour organisation did not necessarily take that seriously all the former's preachings. It was in these circumstances that anarchists propagated rumours that Seguí wanted to be the 'Spanish Jouhaux' and use the confederation as a political platform.[60] Such claims were not entirely without foundation. Had circumstances been more favourable, as in France, then no doubt under Seguí the Catalan CRT, and perhaps the CNT as a whole, could have moved in a more accommodating direction.

Given their reading of the July Assembly, the anarchist-syndicalists were more determined than ever to push for a general strike. When Pablo Iglesias had arrived in Barcelona for the Assembly on 19 July, he, like Largo Caballero before him, was berated for doing nothing to prepare for the movement. Several days later, on 24 July, Largo Caballero had, once again, to rush to Barcelona to save the pact, assuring the CRT that a general strike was in the offing. It seems that Francesc Miranda once again tried to break it off but was outvoted.[61] Yet a general strike was to be precipitated more quickly than anyone could have foreseen. In July a transport strike, centred on the railway workers of the Compañía del Norte (in which the Second Marquis of Comillas was an important figure), broke out in Valencia. The company reacted by sacking a number of the workers and refusing even to discuss their readmittance. The general view by contemporaries and historians is that this was a result of pressure put on it by the Dato administration in order to provoke the UGT-CNT general strike. The Government had made big concessions to the army and was confident that it would remain loyal. Moreover, a general strike was bound to drive a wedge between the various opposition groups.[62] In this Dato had calculated correctly. Despite the opposition of the PSOE-UGT leadership the Sindicato del Norte, the UGT's biggest union, called a general strike for 10 August. The Socialists, although nervous, believed the regime to be on its last legs and so in order to maintain the unity of the organisation declared what they intended to be a peaceful general strike on 13 August.

It was accompanied by a manifesto which called for a republic, but in all other respects echoed the demands of the Assembly movement. The CRT, on the other hand, took a much more radical line. The 13 August edition of *Solidaridad Obrera* was violent in tone: 'shake with fear, bourgeois' it proclaimed; it was now their turn to seek 'revenge and justice'. At the same time, the CRT distributed fly-sheets, both violently denouncing the Lliga and calling on the soldiers to back the people.[63] Nevertheless, the ambiguity of the previous months remained. The CRT leadership was still in contact with the Left-Catalanists and hopeful that joint action by the working-class Left and republicans could precipitate the fall of the Restoration regime.

The strike took off in the major industrial centres in which anarchist-syndicalist and Socialist influence was strong. In Barcelona, by mid-morning, with the exception of dockers and tramworkers, the city was at a standstill. The choreography of the strike was similar to the disturbances of 1902 and 1909. The CRT activists and part of the republican (especially Lerrouxist) base tried to turn it into an insurrection, with workers smashing tram windows to force them back to the depot on the first morning. But the authorities were to act much more quickly than in 1909. Martial law was declared in the early afternoon. The captain-general, José Marina, had 12,000 troops at his disposal and immediately brought them out onto the streets, setting up artillery batteries at key points. There were to be no attacks on church property. This was probably because the movement had a more definite objective, though the rapid mobilisation of the army – which, despite the hopes of the opposition, soon showed it would defend the regime – would also have put off would-be arsonists.

As in previous insurrections, anarchist-syndicalist activists put up barricades in the heart of the Fifth District. It was even the case that their headquarters, the Cafe Mirallets in Sant Rafael Street, was the same as in Tragic Week. Barricades were also built in other more popular and working-class areas, and there were exchanges of gunfire between the insurgents and the troops and security forces. One of the key battle grounds of the week, in which there were a number of casualties, was between gunmen and armed soldiers trying to ensure that the trams continued running. There was also heavy fighting around the tram depot near Sants and two attacks on police stations. The insurrectionaries were easily beaten back, but there was no systematic attempt to take the barricades until they were abandoned on Friday 17 August. The insurrection quickly spread to the industrial towns. Most spectacular were events in Sabadell, where the union headquarters was destroyed by artillery fire. Nevertheless, unlike Tragic Week, the movement was very much limited to the activist core. Without a burning issue like the war in Morocco to galvanise them, most workers did not risk confrontation with the army and security services.

Once the army had intervened, their actions could represent little more than a holding operation. In Madrid the Socialist strike committee was captured on Tuesday 14 August. This was indicative of the fact that they were hoping that the strike would precipitate a peaceful transfer of power and had made no preparations for a violent revolution. Meanwhile, in Barcelona, Lerroux had been delegated by Socialists and republicans to take charge of the movement, but was, not entirely surprisingly, rapidly to disappear. On Monday 13 August, he met with Catalan deputies and senators involved in the Assembly movement, and also saw Marcel·lí Domingo and Joaquim Bueso, but could not thereafter be contacted. In fact, he had suborned Francisco Martorell, the Chief of Police, to get him out of the city safely. Pestaña was the link man between the CRT and the republicans. He had met the Left-Catalanists, Francesc Macià, Angel Semblancat, and Jaume Brossa, on Monday, where it was agreed that the anarchist-syndicalist leadership should meet with Marcel·lí Domingo and Lerroux on the following evening to decide what action to take.

In this meeting, with Lerroux unavailable, it was agreed to send an envoy to Madrid to find out what was happening, and that in the meantime the anarchist-syndicalists would keep the strike alive, while Domingo and Macià would try and raise armed support in their respective power bases of Tortosa and Les Borges Blanques. They met again the following morning when, outraged by a note written by the committee of the Assembly of Parliamentarians (and signed by Cambó and Lerroux), which stated that they would neither support nor accept responsibility for the general strike, they agreed to publish a 'vibrant manifesto', written by Domingo, calling for a republic. But Marcel·lí Domingo was arrested that very evening, and despite being an MP was very nearly executed by the Juntas in revenge for an article he had written in June calling on the troops to disobey their officers. The participation of the PRC, along with a group of separatists close to Macià, was important in that it confirmed that a far-Left current had emerged within Catalanism, which would collaborate with the CNT, but they could do little to propagate the revolt. At the end of the week, Seguí and his colleagues on the strike committee persuaded hardliners of the need to recommend a return to work on the following Monday. According to Miguel Sastre i Sanna, thirty-two people had been killed in Barcelona (including four members of the security services) and sixty-four had been wounded. Official sources gave the figure of seventy-one deaths in Spain as a whole.[64]

As in the case of Tragic Week, middle-class Barcelona at first greeted the movement with a mixture of fear and sympathy. There was much hope that it would result in the regime's demise. But news that troops were firing on the protestors was met with consternation. After the end of the fighting it quickly became clear where the elite's sympathies lay. The key business, cultural and artistic associations opened subscriptions for the members of the armed services killed and wounded while 'carrying out their duty'. In all, over 200,000 pesetas were raised, with business as the foremost contributor. Here, it seems, are to be found the origins of a tacit alliance between the captain-general and the city's business leaders in the face of what was perceived as a revolutionary threat.[65] It was also in the aftermath of this strike that employers' representatives started to talk of the need for the state to integrate workers and employers into 'compulsory trade unions', thereby undercutting the CNT. Simultaneously the Marquis of Comillas, who was close to the Conservatives, in a letter to the Prime Minister, specifically called for a thoroughgoing repression.[66]

The CRT in 1918: Ideology and Praxis

Despite the revolutionary character of the strike, the CRT was able to operate openly rather more quickly than it might have expected. The strike had been followed by mass arrests and the closing down of union headquarters, but in October the Juntas, smarting at the position that the Dato Government had placed them in, forced it to reestablish constitutional guarantees and then to resign.[67] Moreover, in order to compensate in some measure for their role during the general strike, the Juntas stopped prisoners being tried through the military courts.

The events of July and August had important repercussions for the CRT's future practice. First, they created tensions between Seguí's men and more rigid anarchist-syndicalists. José Negre, for example, who in any case hated Seguí, withdrew. This weakened the position of Seguí because anarchist-syndicalists had until then, to an important degree, maintained a united front against anarchist criticism.[68] They also made it more difficult for the CRT leadership to back any interclass alliance in the future. Hostility to any such policy was further amplified by the impact of the Bolshevik Revolution in November 1917 and then by the revolutionary climate in Germany in late 1918, in the aftermath of the defeat of the Central Powers. The Bolshevik Revolution, in particular, both enthused and radicalised the anarchist-syndicalists, sharpening their perceptions that the end of the war would trigger revolutions throughout Europe. As a result, the CRT-CNT, ironically, gave greater support to the Russian Revolution than did the Socialists, who were concerned at the impact it would have on the Allied war effort. Above all, they were pleased that it challenged social-democratic electoralism, and showed the viability of a radical social transformation. The new general secretary of the CNT, Manuel Buenacasa, became the organisation's major commentator on the events in Russia, and gave the revolution an anarchist twist, claiming that the Bolsheviks had defacto taken an 'antipolitical' stance, because they had refused to become ensnared in the 'bourgeois' electoral game.[69]

Nevertheless, Seguí and his 'team' wished to maintain their links with the Socialists, even going so far as to suggest unification, and did not want to launch any premature revolutionary movement which would undermine the organisation. This provoked further criticism by hardliners, who vehemently opposed any suggestion that they should link up with 'deputies' and 'politicians'. Anarchists were able to raise their profile in late 1918, when the Catalan Anarchist Federation held a clandestine conference in Barcelona, which called on anarchists throughout the country to join the CNT. Yet Seguí's position was still safe. Of key importance was the support he still received from most union leaders, who refused to be lectured to by anarchists who lacked a strong base in organised labour.[70]

The first attempt to reestablish ties with the UGT came in November 1917 when the CNT called for a unity congress. Behind this was probably the belief, in Seguí's circles, that a single Spanish-wide union would have much more chance of overthrowing the regime. Then, in a well-attended Catalan assembly on 13 January 1918, it was agreed to call on the CNT to carry out another joint campaign with the UGT for a wide-ranging amnesty and to threaten a further general strike if their demands were not met. What the CRT leadership envisaged was some kind of a re-run of the 1917 campaign, except that, without republican involvement, the next general strike would, presumably, be explicitly geared to a social revolution.[71]

Yet, relations with the Socialists would be even more fraught than in the previous year. The Socialist leadership, their fingers burnt by the events of the previous August, quickly rebuffed the proposal. This led to renewed criticisms of the Socialists from the pages of *Solidaridad Obrera*. However, the CRT leadership continued to push their case. Rank-and-file pressure in favour of unity was probably still a factor. In addition, they no doubt hoped that in any new organisation, once the UGT had been de-coupled from the 'politicians', they would emerge dominant. In this respect they were further encouraged because, with the international climate appearing increasingly revolutionary, the left-wing current within the PSOE-UGT, which wished to forge a revolutionary alliance with the CNT, was gaining ground.

This was the background to the acceptance of a motion in the CRT's Sants Congress in favour of CNT-UGT unity. It stated that while there were 'defects' in the organisation of the UGT, the CNT also showed 'a lack of practical sense', and that, in these circumstances, they should merge. This was the position that had been adopted by the Reus-based Socialist publication, *La Justicia Social*, which, between 1915 and 1916, had been at the forefront of the Leftist critique of the Socialist leadership. The key figure behind the resolution was probably the Reus Socialist Miguel Mestre.[72] In the subsequent debate it was agreed that there should be an assembly of the entire Spanish labour movement.

However, in the following months, little more was heard of the issue. The Socialist high command, it seems, was able to stifle any such assembly. Relations were further soured when in July the Socialists refused to participate in joint meetings for the release of 'social prisoners', along with reinstatement of railway workers sacked in August 1917. The alliance was then broken off by the CNT, formally because the UGT sent a letter to CRT-affiliate unions inviting them to join. Moreover, the anarchist-syndicalist leadership itself was becoming less enthusiastic towards unity. As shown in the previous chapter, from the summer of 1918 the CRT grew massively, while the CNT sprang to life in other parts of Spain. This occurred at a time when affiliation to the UGT remained rather stagnant; while in June 1918 the UGT had 89,601 affiliates, by the end of the year CNT membership totalled over 100,000. This generated a climate of euphoria in anarchist-syndicalist circles. Both the CNT National Committee and also Seguí's close collaborator, Salvador Quemades, expressed the view that they might be able simply to bypass the Socialist leadership and create a new revolutionary confederation in which syndicalist ideology would predominate.

This conditioned the response to the decision by the UGT's Thirteenth Congress, held between 3 and 10 October 1918, to authorise the National Committee to seek unity with the CNT. This represented a compromise between the old leadership, under figures such as Largo Caballero and Besteiro, and the union's leftist current, now led by a number of Madrid-based figures, who established their own newspaper, *Nuestra Palabra*, in the same month. However, the anarchist-syndicalists were not quickly drawn. Manuel Buenacasa, the general secretary of the CNT, stated that the organisation was in principle favourable, but would need to call a national congress. Quemades went much further and argued that fusion would only be acceptable if members of the Socialist party did not influence the decisions taken. Given that the PSOE and UGT leaderships were virtually the same, an alliance under these conditions was, of course, unrealisable. Nevertheless, contacts had, it appears, been established between the UGT Left and the CNT, and Quemades might have been thinking along with lines of a merger between the two. Yet, at least in 1918, this was an illusion, with no indication that the writers of *Nuestra Palabra* wished to divide the PSOE-UGT.[73]

Conclusions

From 1915 to 1917 the Catalan CRT had, despite reservations, participated in a broad-based movement aimed at overthrowing the Restoration regime. Had it been successful and had a liberal democracy been established, there was the potential for the CRT-CNT to evolve in a more pragmatic direction. Such potential was certainly present in the ideology of Seguí and his followers. As in the case of many French syndicalists, union building could have become an end in itself and the revolution could have slipped into the distance.[74] It was not, however, to be. The stance adopted by the army ensured that the Restoration regime was to stagger on for five more years. At first it seemed to the CRT-CNT that the failure of the 1917 general strike would not be of major significance. By the end of 1918, the organisation's hopes for social revolution in Spain and, indeed, the whole of Europe were riding high, but at that precise moment it would become embroiled in an increasingly radicalised confrontation with industrialists and the military in which not only would its revolutionary dream be dashed, but it would also be faced with destruction. It is on this dramatic conflict that the final two chapters will focus.

Notes

1. For the Sants Athenaeum see, Hermoso Plaja, 'Salvador Seguí', 62; Foix, *Apòstols*, 25–6; Solà i Gussinyer, *Escuelas racionalistas en Cataluña*, 72. Our principal sources of information are *Solidaridad Obrera* (hereafter SO) and *Tierra y Libertad*. There were other minor cultural associations, such as a pro-Esperanto association, which operated from 1916, and a school called Galileo set up in 1918.

2. The Syndicalist Athenaeum admitted similar problems. SO, 27, 30 July, 3 Aug 1918.

3. See the comments by Félix Monteagudo in the Sants Congress, in Confederación Regional del Trabajo de Cataluña, *Memoria*, 35.

4. SO, 15 Nov. 1918.

5. Pestaña, *Lo que aprendí*, vol. 1, 54–5; Porcel, *Revuelta*, 68; SO, 28 Jan. 1917.

6. SO, 8 Jan., 6 Feb. 1917, 28 May 1918.

7. SO, 9, 12 Nov. 1917; Pestaña, *Lo que aprendí*, vol. 1, 74–5.

8. SO, 6, 18 Jan., 14, 18, 28 April, 18 May, 9, 10 June, 12 Nov. 1918; Porcel, *Revuelta*, 95. Some additional information is to be found in Susanna Tavera, *Solidaridad Obrera*.

9. Comité Pro Castellví, *La verdad en marcha*.

10. See SO, February–May 1915. It is again impossible to estimate overall numbers who attended the meetings, but a soirée organised by the tinsmiths was a great success, with over 300 present. SO, 4 Feb. 1915.

11. *Tierra y Libertad*, 28 July, 8, 15 Sept. 1915; 17 May, 16 Sept. 1916.

12. SO, 23 Dec. 1916, 5 Jan. 1917.

13. Bueso, *Recuerdos*, 59; *La Justicia Social* (hereafter LJS), 5 Sept., 17 Oct. 1914; *El Diluvio*, 9, 10 Oct. 1914.

14. My major source is LJS along with Bueso, *Recuerdos*, 59–60.

15. For these congresses see *Renovación*, May, June 1916; *Tierra y Libertad*, 17, 24 May 1916; Gabriel, 'Sindicats', 431–6; Romero Salvadó, *Spain 1914–1918*, 32–7; Viadiu, 'Nuestro "Noi del Sucre"', 8–11; Buenacasa, *Movimiento obrero*, 122. On the Socialist Left see, Forcadell, *Parlamentarismo y bolshevización*, 40–4, 103–36 and 172–205.

16. For the pact see, *El Socialista*, 14 July 1916.

17. *Tierra y Libertad*, 18 Oct. 1916.

18. For the campaign I have used, above all, SO, *Tierra y Libertad* and *El Socialista*. For the Socialists see also Romero Salvadó, *Spain 1914–1918*, 32–42.

19. On the strike in Catalonia see, *La Publicidad* and *El Diluvio*, 18, 19 Dec. 1916; Ferrer, *Simó Piera*, 44.

20. For this section I have used SO. For the articles by Viadiu, Mateo Soriano and Víctor Grazuela see 12 Jan., 14 June 1918, 9 Jan. 1919.

21. Instituto de Reformas Sociales, *Movimientos de precios al por menor en España durante la guerra y la post-guerra, 1914–1922*, 34; Instituto de Reformas Sociales, *Encarecimiento de la vida durante la guerra: precios de las subsistencias en España y en el extranjero, 1914–1918*, 82.

22. SO, 8, 9 Jan. 1918.

23. For these events I have used SO from 10–25 January. See also, Lester Golden, 'Les dones com avantguarda: El rebombori de pa del gener de 1918'.

24. Radcliffe, *From Mobilization to Civil War*.

25. SO, 12 Jan. 1918.

26. Madrid, *Sangre*, 101–17.

27. SO, 11, 22 Jan., 13 Dec. 1918.

28. For example, the syndicalist metalworker, Enrique Rueda, stated at the closing meeting of the CRT's Sants Congress: 'The Catalan woman is able, because of her political beliefs (*orientación social*) and her energy, to play an important role in our struggle for emancipation .... Today she is asking us to defend liberty, she encourages us in our struggles.' Confederación Regional del Trabajo de Cataluña, *Memoria*, 82.

29. For the 'moral economy' of male skilled workers see Chapter Two, 50–1.

30. Gerald Meaker, 'A civil war of words'; Romero Salvadó, *Spain, 1914–1918*, 60–84.

31. Jesús Pabón, *Cambó, 1876–1918*, 439–93.

32. For the malaise of Spanish republicanism see in particular, Manuel Suárez Cortina, *El reformismo en España*. The electoral data is taken from Balcells, et al., *Eleccions generals*, 530 and 555.

33. Joaquim Ferrer, *Layret, 1880–1920*. For contacts between Seguí and the left-wing Catalanists see also Salut, *Vivers de revolucionaris*, 140–2.

34. SO, 14, 15, 22, 24, 25, 28 March 1917. Pere Foix – who incorrectly dated these articles by Andreu to 1916 – states that as a result of the fuss he was forced to step down as editor

of SO and replaced by Borobio. This is, however, mistaken. Borobio took over as editor from Andreu in May 1916, before the articles were published. Foix also maintains that Felip Cortiella was offered the editorship of *Solidaridad Obrera* in 1917 (but no doubt, in reality, in 1915 or early 1916 before Borobio was appointed), but insisted it be published in Catalan. Both Pestaña and Miranda refused to countenance the idea. *Apòstols*, 266.

35. For this section I have found particularly useful, Ferrer, *Simó Piera*, 75–8; Lladonosa i Vall-llebrera, *Sindicalistes i llibertaris*, 20; Foix, *Apòstols*, 53–120; Porcel, *Revuelta*, 76–80 and 97–106; Salut, *Vivers de revolucionaris*, 140–74; Hermoso Plaja, 'Salvador Seguí', 68. Language usage could led to tension within the different sectors of the movement. Thus, for example, the school operated by La Constància taught in Catalan, leading to criticism by Fortunato Barthe, a cultural anarchist in the Lorenzo mould.

36. SO, 3–13 May 1917. On the continuing Radical shift to the centre see Culla i Clarà, *Republicanisme lerrouxista*, 274–330.

37. Buenacasa, *Movimiento obrero*, 200.

38. SO, 3 Jan. 1917.

39. SO, 4 Feb 1915, 22, 26 Oct 1916; *Tierra y Libertad*, 23 June 1915. For divisions over this issue see also, Lladonosa i Vall-llebrera, *Sindicalistes i llibertaris*, 24; Bueso, *Recuerdos*, 74; Montseny, *Mis Primeros Cuarenta Años*, 22–4.

40. SO, 22, 26 Oct. 1916.

41. SO, 18 March, 1, 22 April, 13 May 1915. Loredo was to die in Logroño in 1916, helping organise the campaign for the Cenicero prisoners. *Tierra y Libertad*, 26 March 1916.

42. *Tierra y Libertad*, 22, 29 March, 5 April, 3, 17, 24, 31 May, 9 Aug., 6 Sept. 1916, 7, 28 March 1917.

43. Romero Salvadó, *Spain, 1914–1918*, 39; SO, 26 Aug., 9 Dec. 1916. It should be noted that the post of CNT general secretary was not yet an important one. The CNT had not built any sort of organisation outside Catalonia and the National Committee had not functioned for some time.

44. SO, 11, 25 Nov., 28 Dec. 1916. Simó Piera maintains that Jordán lost his post as CNT general secretary as a result of the telegram. This does not appear to be accurate. On 5 February 1917 *Solidaridad Obrera* referred to Jordán stepping down after being arrested: see Ferrer, *Simó Piera*, 24 and 47; SO, 5 Feb. 1917.

45. SO, 8, 9 Dec. 1918.

46. SO, 3, 22 Jan., 15 April 1917.

47. *Tierra y Libertad*, 10 Jan. 1917.

48. Pestaña, *Lo que aprendí*, vol. 1, 57–9; Bueso, *Recuerdos*, 78.

49. SO, 30 April, 9, 25 May, 13 June 1917.

50. SO, 11, 18, 25 May 1917. The fact that Borobio agreed to go also needs to be viewed at another level. As would later be revealed, *Solidaridad Obrera* was receiving funds from the German spy ring, and for its editor to play such an active role in trying to dissuade the Socialists from taking an actively pro-Allied stance was probably worth a significant sum. On the Madrid meeting see also, Romero Salvadó, *Spain, 1914–1918*, 90–1.

51. Manuel de Burgos y Mazo, *Vida política española*, 22.

52. For Cambó's strategy see Pabón, *Cambó, 1876–1918*, 495–582.

53. SO, 11, 12, 14, 21 June, 1, 13 August 1917.

54. Hermoso Plaja, 'Salvador Seguí', 66; SO, 11 June 1917. The manifesto is reproduced in Lacomba, *La crisis*, 472–5. The Belgian-French revolutionary, Victor Serge (known as Alexandre Kibaltchiche), who was in Barcelona from early 1917 until August and struck up a friendship with Seguí, confirms the attempt to draw on Russian experience: see his *Memoirs of a Revolutionary, 1901–1941*, 56.

55. On the Les Planes meeting see, Largo Caballero, *Mis recuerdos*; Pestaña, *Lo que aprendí*, vol. 1, 59–62; Plaja, 'Salvador Seguí', 70–1; Ferrer, *Simó Piera*, 149.

56. SO, 6 July 1917.

57. Samblancat, 'A los 37 años del asesinato de Salvador Seguí', 107; Lladonosa i Vall-llebrera, *Sindicalistes i llibertaris*, 25; Rafael Vidiella, 'La lluita de classes i la repressió a Barcelona del 1917 al 1923', 14.

58. SO, 1 Aug. 1917; Burgos y Mazo, *Vida política españoia*, 65 and 75–6; Victor Serge, *Birth of our Power*, 42–93. *Birth of our Power* is a 'factional' novel based on Serge's experiences in Barcelona during the summer of 1917. It provides much insight but needs to be treated with caution. For example, the clashes which accompanied the holding of the Assembly are much exaggerated.

59. SO, 1, 2, 3 Aug. 1917; *Tierra y Libertad*, 8 Aug., 7, 14 Nov. 1917.

60. See Hermoso Plaja, 'Salvador Seguí', 66; Foix, *Apòstols*, 89; Salut, *Vivers de revolucionaris*, 141. On one occasion, a heated debate in the Syndicalist Athenaeum between the 'American', Joaquín Cortés, and Seguí's close friend, Agustí Castella, ended in a fight: see, Bueso, *Recuerdos*, 78.

61. An article in *Tierra y Libertad* maintains that the CNT National Committee wished to break off the pact but was outvoted by delegates from outside Barcelona. *Tierra y Libertad*, 7 Nov. 1917.

62. This is, for example, the view taken by Romero Salvadó, *Spain, 1914–1918*, 123–30.

63. For the 13 August edition of SO and the fly-sheet calling for military support see Archivo de Eduardo Dato, 76/12. For the other fly-sheet see, *Anuari de Catalunya, 1917*, 155.

64. For these events I have used in particular, Ferrer, *Simó Piera*, 52–8 and 144–5; Pestaña, *Lo que aprendí*, vol. 1, 64–5; Bueso, *Recuerdos*, 78–93; Roig, *Rafael Vidiella*, 43–9; Marcelino Domingo, *En la calle y en la carcel*, 77–99; Ferrer, *Revuelta*, 84–9; Culla i Clarà, *Republicanisme lerrouxista*, 319; *La huelga sangrienta de Barcelona*; Sastre y Sanna, *Martirología*, 126; Meaker, *Revolutionary Left*, 79–93. *Solidaridad Obrera* stated that they had suffered twenty-two dead and forty-three wounded, while nine soldiers were killed and thirty-seven injured. SO, 25 Oct. 1917.

65. On middle-class attitudes see, Hurtado, *Quaranta anys*, vol. 1, 310–13, and Ametlla, *Memòries*, 381. Information on the subscriptions in, Arxiu Històric de la Cambra de Comerç, Indústria y Navegació de Barcelona, 657/12.

66. Bengoechea, *Organització patronal*, 293; Fidel Gómez Ochoa, 'El partido conservador y el problema social durante la crisis final de la Restauración: la sindicación profesional y obligatoria', 273.

67. Romero Salvadó, *Spain, 1914–1918*, 140–9.

68. For Negre see Porcel, *Revuelta*, 147; Buenacasa, *Movimiento obrero*, 39.

69. SO, 22 Aug., 25 Sept., 3, 9, 15 Oct., 12, 17, 19 Nov. 1918.

70. Buenacasa, *Movimiento obrero*, 51–2; Plaja, 'Memorias', 39. Illustrative of this issue was the fact that during the amnesty campaign a number of union activists refused to support a prisoners' committee because it was not made up entirely of union delegates: see SO, 1, 10 Nov., 3, 20 Dec. 1917.

71. SO, 11 Nov. 1917, 14 Jan. 1918; *Tierra y Libertad*, 16 Jan. 1918.

72. Confederación Regional del Trabajo de Cataluña, *Memoria*, 57–8.

73. SO, 20, 26 July, 2, 13 Aug., 11 Oct. 1918; Tuñón de Lara, *Movimiento obrero*, vol. 2, 241–2; Meaker, *Revolutionary Left*, 111–28. However, Quemades' outspoken opposition to unity with the UGT did not necessarily reflect the views of all of Seguí's supporters.

74. On this process within French syndicalism see Papayanis, *Alphonse Merrhiem*.

9

1919
The Apogee of the Catalan CNT and the Employer-Military Counteroffensive

Following the rise of the Catalan CNT during 1918, between 1919 and 1923, in the final years of the Restoration regime, it would have a major impact on the Spanish polity. In the aftermath of the August 1917 general strike, the growth of labour agitation and the revolutionary threat it was seen to pose greatly concerned conservative interests, the army and the King. This was to be dramatically illustrated during 1919, when, in a context in which the regime vacillated between conciliation and repression, an increasingly powerful and confident CNT would enter into a cataclysmic conflict with the forces of reaction. It is on this conflict and its consequences, both for the CNT itself, and more broadly for Catalan society and the Spanish political system, that this chapter will focus.

The La Canadenca Strike

The first clash took place between December 1918 and April 1919. By early 1919 most of the Barcelona industrial working class had been enrolled within the CRT. Furthermore, over the previous months it had extended its organisation throughout much of industrial Catalonia. In the process, as already stressed, for the first time it seriously challenged much of the territory's social elite. Their fear was, moreover, heightened by the growing number of shootings in late 1918 and by the impunity with which they were carried out.

This coincided with a radicalisation of Catalanist agitation. Following the August 1917 general strike and the fall of the Dato Government, the King and the political elite of the Restoration regime realised the need to integrate the Lliga into government. When, however, a coalition Government presided over by Antonio Maura fell in November 1918, Cambó had attained few concessions. In addition, the Allies' support for the rights of the small central and eastern European nations in the wake of the Central Powers' defeat encouraged left-wing Catalanists to launch a campaign for an autonomy statute. The Lliga then voiced similar demands and, after it had been rebuffed in a parliamentary debate in early December, took the lead. Over the following weeks the situation in Barcelona became increasingly radicalised, with clashes between young Catalanist radicals and Spanish nationalist (*españolista*) civilians and military personnel.

Overt displays of anti-Spanish sentiment incensed the Juntas de Defensa, who demanded that action be taken. Moreover, the officer corps was shocked by the growth of anarchism-syndicalism, which it saw as a grave threat to order. The latter was the major concern of the employers, with the city's leading business and cultural institutions lobbying the Prime Minister, the Count of Romanones, to respond forcefully to the assassinations. Simultaneously, the Chamber of Industry, with the support of both the FTN and Lliga, elaborated a detailed plan for the introduction, by the authorities, of 'compulsory unionisation'. The captain-general of Barcelona, Joaquín Milans del Bosch, was highly attuned to the demands of both these groups. He was acutely aware of unrest within the Barcelona garrison and also, as a Catalan from an upper-class family, sympathised with opinion in elite Barcelona circles. Hence, on more than one occasion between December 1918 and January 1919, he called for martial law to deal with Catalanist agitation and the 'syndicalist threat'.[1]

He was backed up by the civil governor, González Rothwos, who had become a specialist in dealing with anarchist subversion. He was close to Antonio Maura, had been appointed by him in early 1918, and, unusually, was then kept on when the Liberals came to power. The authorities were obsessed with foreign revolutionaries. Rothwos believed that the syndicalists were receiving funds from abroad, 'to organise a movement similar to the Russian Soviet'.[2]

The fear and hatred engendered by this dual 'red' and 'separatist' challenge was to foster a conservative Spanish nationalist reaction in Catalonia. On 19 January 1919 middle and working-class populists founded the Liga Patriótica Española, which had around 4,000 affiliates.[3] Within this movement young Carlists played a leading role, while it also enjoyed the sympathy of the officer corps. Carlism was the most intransigent anti-liberal movement in Spain with links to the Catholic Church, and had taken up arms in order to install an *ancien-regime* monarchy during the nineteenth century. In Barcelona, the radical Carlist youth was to an important degree drawn from families who had migrated from the peasant interior and maintained the Catholic faith. They retained the movement's violent, militaristic traditions, and were not afraid to take the fight to 'separatists' and leftists. Hence, during January 1919, the Liga Patriótica's members (seemingly with the support of army officers) took to the streets, beating up young Catalanist radicals in order to 'drive the separatist beast back into its lair'.[4]

The new Romanones Government did not wish to go as far as Milans del Bosch demanded, but it was anxious not to upset the military, wanted to maintain the benevolence of the Catalan business community, and was concerned by the growth of the CNT and its spread to other parts of Spain. This was heightened by the fact that two anarchist-syndicalist teams were at that very time proselytising in Aragón, Valencia and Andalusia. The Government's desire to assuage business interests could be seen in its decision to refer their increasingly insistent calls for the implementation of a system of 'compulsory unionisation' and state-run conciliation machinery to the Institute for Social Reforms to see if it could be implemented. Throughout the year the industrialists obsession was to do away with the CNT, which its leaders argued was an unrepresentative organisation, whose leaders had imposed themselves through terror. Within the new unions, business leaders hopefully proclaimed, the genuine and moderate working class would step forward.[5]

The Government finally suspended constitutional guarantees in Barcelona province on 16 January following a riotous meeting by the Juntas de Defensa, after which they informed the captain-general that they would no longer tolerate Catalanist demonstrations.[6] Few would have guessed that they would not be restored until 30 March 1922. The Government then took advantage of the situation to arrest seventy-three leading anarchist-syndicalist leaders, including Seguí, close down union headquarters and suspend publication of *Solidaridad Obrera*. Rothwos was crystal clear that the aim was to 'kill off the present-day unions', which were an 'obstacle to the implementation of reforms'. He even hoped that their action would provoke a general strike, which would 'give us the means to deal with a situation that cannot continue'. This was echoed by Romanones himself, who reasoned that 'given the battle cannot be avoided, we should take the lead and provoke it'.[7]

However, events over the next month would show that the authorities had greatly underestimated the CRT's strength. It was able to demonstrate its new-found power in a dispute which began in the Barcelona offices of the Anglo-Canadian electricity-generating company, Ebro Power and Irrigation, popularly known as La Canadenca, at the beginning of February 1919. As we saw in Chapter Seven, in December the CRT had organised a strike of workers employed at the company's Camarasa dam. By January it was languishing, but at the end of the month, in the company's Barcelona offices, a number of workers in the billing section tried to unionise and were accordingly fired. Their colleagues in the section responded by declaring a go-slow and were also dismissed, leading the dispute to spread to other parts of the company. The workers then turned to the CRT for support and it decided to take up their case, naming a strike committee headed by Simó Piera, a figure close to Seguí, which included representatives from the Wood and Construction Workers' SUs and two delegates from La Canadenca.

The workers of La Canadenca were not unionised, but in typical syndicalist style the strike committee was able to take advantage of the company's intransigence to rally them. On 15 February they made a series of demands, which included both substantial wage increases and the re-instatement of all those sacked. The CRT had two objectives in undertaking this action. On the one hand, it wished to extend its organisation to a key sector of the economy, which had so far been beyond its reach; on the other, it intended to make a show of strength, to demonstrate that it was now a force to be reckoned with, whose activists could not simply be sacked and leaders locked away when it pleased the authorities. For the most militant, once again the spectre of revolution beckoned.[8]

As always, the strategy pursued was one of mass mobilisation, aimed at putting intolerable pressure to bear on the company and the authorities. At first the strike was limited to the office workers, but faced with the company's refusal to concede, the CRT was able to bring out the workers in the electricity generating plant on 21 February, dramatically plunging Barcelona into darkness. Unable to get back to their depot, about fifty trams were stranded in the street. Over the following days the dispute continued to escalate. The Government sent in the military to restore power supplies and, in response, on 26 February, the Gas, Water and Electricity SU called out most of the workers in the city's other electricity, gas and water companies, and solidarity strikes in Sabadell, Vilafranca and Badalona soon followed. In Barcelona, the civil governor and captain-general, egged on by La Canadenca's director, Fraser Lawton, recommended that the Government should take a hard line and militarise army reservists. It was a position tacitly backed by the British Ambassador, who in a note to the subsecretary of the Ministry of the Interior complained that the local authorities had not taken a tough enough stance.[9] This Romanones reluctantly agreed to do on 8 March. At first gas, water and electricity workers were targeted, although they were given the choice of working or being confined to barracks. By 13 March almost all had chosen the latter alternative and were being held in the fortress of Montjuïc. Shockingly for conservative middle-class opinion, the printers responded by imposing 'red censorship', preventing edicts by the captain-general and press reports deemed detrimental to the strikers' interests from being published, and imposing fines (which were paid) on those papers which defied them.

Simultaneously, the CRT further escalated the dispute. Carters struck, thereby hitting supplies of coal, and, on 12 March, it managed to bring out the tramworkers, who were also promptly militarised. On this occasion they were ordered to stay at their posts, but most still refused to work. This was another coup for the CRT. Under Foronda these workers had been subject to a high degree of social control and a new union was only just being organised. The organisation maintained cohesion through underground meetings of union delegates and strikers were kept abreast of events by the clandestine publication of *Solidaridad Obrera* and fly-sheets pasted on walls. Meanwhile, youngsters kept up the pressure on the company by sabotaging its transformers and power cables.

Milans del Bosch, in close contact with Fraser Lawton, now insisted that the Government break the strike by declaring martial law. It was Lawton's opinion that the La Canadenca workers had stayed out because they were being intimidated and that this could only be remedied through the use of military force. Again Romanones reluctantly agreed to the measure on the night of 12 March. Yet it quickly became clear the strike was not about to crumble, despite the fact that about eighty activists had been arrested and about 800 militarised strikers were being held in Montjuïc. It was, in fact, remarkably disciplined and surprisingly peaceful, although a wages clerk who refused to come out was assassinated and several bombs were planted in the bourgeois Eixample. Simultaneously, the vendetta against government informers continued, with the assassination of Lluís Mas on 12 February.[10]

The CRT's resistance was to provoke growing divisions between the Government and employers. This is of central importance for our understanding of these years. Barcelona was to be at the forefront of the process, echoed in other parts of Spain, in which social conflict was intense: the determination of employers to take drastic action to break the back of organised labour, if necessary in the teeth of Government opposition. Fear of social upheaval and even revolution was certainly an important factor in mobilising industrialists, and this was exacerbated by the shootings. These were used to bring pressure to bear on the Government, with the FTN, for example, writing to Romanones in March to complain at the supposed 'complete defencelessness' in which the people of Barcelona found themselves. Yet it should be remembered, as shown in previous chapters, that Catalan employers had called on governments to repress strikes *before* the emergence of a serious revolutionary and terrorist threat. Equally important was the more prosaic consideration that they were faced by a powerful, independent labour association, which had showed an astonishing capacity to mobilise.[11]

Faced by the La Canadenca strike, industrialists in the construction industry reacted by re-organising the moribund Barcelona Employers' Federation and revitalising the Spanish Employers' Confederation. Simultaneously, in textiles industrialists forged a new, unified, Federation of Catalan Weaving and Spinning Industrialists. Henceforth Barcelona employers would captain a movement of Spanish industrialists against organised labour. The Barcelona Employers' Federation and its Spanish extension, whose headquarters was based in Madrid, would engage in industrial warfare, while other older, more august employer associations, with the FTN at the fore, would lobby politicians and the King. Furthermore, powerful industrialists, who enjoyed an astonishingly easy access to ministers, would make use of their own individual contacts.[12]

The industrialists enjoyed considerable sympathy in the more middle-class quarters of Barcelona, where church attendance was high and conservative social and cultural values predominated. Hence, not only business but also elite cultural associations would back the Employers' Federation's demands that the authorities take a tougher stance. Crucially, they also retained the support of the Barcelona garrison.

Fear of subversion widened the political space for authoritarian Spanish nationalist political options. Hence, February 1919 would see the formation of a Unión Monárquica Nacional, made up of a coalition of Catalan monarchist forces, which enjoyed the support of Milans del Bosch and was designed to take on both the Lliga and the Left. Its members argued that Catalanism had opened the flood gates to the revolutionary tide and that only a hard-line government (possibly a military dictatorship) could reimpose order and stability. It gained the support of a number of monarchist *caciques*, aristocrats and also some high-profile businessmen, including the president of the FTN, Jaume Cussó. This highlighted the danger the Lliga faced of losing its conservative base. In response, it would put its demands for autonomy on the back burner and, after some vacillation, from the end of 1919 lent its support to the employer-military counteroffensive.[13]

It was the refusal of the Restoration parties to fully back the employer-military demands that set them on a collision course. This would magnify and intensify pre-existing prejudices in both ambits against what they viewed as a corrupt and out-of-touch political class. During the La Canadenca dispute, while Romanones had at first largely backed military and employer demands, fearful of the situation spiralling out of control, he subsequently backtracked. Thus, from late February he allowed the Lerrouxist labour lawyer and local councillor, Rafael Guerra del Río, to act as an intermediary between the strike committee, the company and the Barcelona town hall, while the interim mayor, Emiliano Iglesias, kept the Prime Minister's sub-secretary, Luis Morote, abreast of developments. Moreover, he put pressure on La Canadenca by warning it that if the strike continued the authorities would have no choice but to take it over temporarily.[14]

In early March, with La Canadenca making concessions, Romanones took further steps to reach an agreement. On 12 March a new civil governor, Carlos Montañés, and a new chief of police, Gerardo Doval, were appointed. The former was a Catalan engineer who had helped set up La Canadenca and was known for his Catalanist sympathies. They were joined in Barcelona by Luis Morote, who had already been civil governor of Barcelona on one occasion and was remembered for the even-handedness of his period in office. His brief was to directly negotiate with the syndicalist leadership, while Doval was charged with cleaning up the Barcelona police and bringing it under civilian control. Such face-to-face negotiations represented a new departure for the Restoration regime and were indicative of the growing power of the CRT. Romanones hoped to cap this initiative off by organising a General Labour Conference in which, presumably, worker and employer representatives could hammer out systems of collective bargaining. It was supported by Seguí, who would have seen it as a way to legitimise the organisation's power. The FTN, however, both opposed these negotiations and rejected any such conference until 'compulsory unionisation' had been instituted.[15]

On the anarchist-syndicalist side, the key figure in the discussions was Seguí, with whom Morote had to hold negotiations from prison. From the first Seguí saw the need to reach an agreement which would leave the strength of the organisation intact. In order to do this he had to face down the hardliners, who wanted to maintain the strike and force a total capitulation of the authorities. For the most militant, the breadth of the movement had convinced them that the opportunity was there to organise a full-blown revolution, and they began a campaign for the declaration of a general strike throughout Catalonia. He responded, in the tradition of the more moderate French syndicalists, by arguing that the organisation was not yet strong enough to carry out the revolution. No doubt he foresaw that to hold out would undermine the Government and help put power in the hands of the authoritarian Right. Under his influence, the strike committee therefore agreed to call the dispute off in exchange for improved working conditions for the La Canadenca workers, a prisoner release and the readmission of all the workers who had been out on strike. For its part, the La Canadenca management agreed to pay part of the workers' wages from mid-February, to wage increases and to an eight-hours day. Moreover, Morote no doubt informed Seguí that Romanones intended to decree an eight-hours day throughout Spanish industry. In reality, the company had to a large extent given way to the strikers.

In compensation, to ally middle-class fears Romanones allowed the Sometent to operate in central Barcelona, with the ultra-conservative Lliga politician, Josep Bertran i Musitu, in charge of operations. This concession was, however, by no means sufficient for the employers. Not only were they opposed to the accord, they also reacted with dismay to the news, in early April, that the Government intended to introduce an eight-hours day from 1 October. They were further incensed when Romanones informed the FTN that he would not support 'compulsory unionisation' because of what he saw as the anti-liberal implications of taking bargaining rights away from independent unions. Over the next three years these issues would further distance the industrialists and the Restoration regime. It quickly became apparent that the Restoration political elite intended to introduce a whole raft of reforms, including pensions and state-backed labour contracts, in order to placate labour militancy, and that the only people willing to support 'compulsory unionisation' were Antonio Maura and his followers.[16]

In their hostility to the accord the industrialists could rely on Milan del Bosch's sympathy. He had already tacitly threatened Romanones with direct army intervention, stating that the officer class was unhappy that Morote's mission had led to 'a loss of respect for martial law'. His initial response to the agreement was to tender his resignation, because, he argued, any further syndicalist agitation would leave him no choice but to 'take measures which are at odds with government policy'.[17] This, he knew, if not rescinded, would provoke a virulent reaction in the Barcelona garrison and hence strike fear in government circles. Employers and the military were thereafter able to take advantage of Seguí's growing difficulties with the revolutionary Left to bury both the agreement and the Romanones Government alongside it.

Seguí had only been able to sell the accord to radical CRT activists with the proviso that 'the people have the last word'. This was the background to a meeting held by the strike committee in the El Bosc theatre on the night of the 18 March and the famous meeting which took place in the Las Arenas bullring on the following day. At the first meeting hardliners had mobilised their supporters and there were calls to clarify that all prisoners would be released. This was difficult for the strike committee because although Morote had stated that the Government would release its detainees, those had been prosecuted were in the hands of Milans del Bosch. Morote had tried to get the captain-general to take similar action but had no power to force him. Given this background, much of the audience was not satisfied with the answers given from the platform.[18]

In response the CRT leadership asked for permission to hold the Las Arenas meeting. Martial law was lifted in order to allow the prisoners out of jail, making it possible for Seguí to address the crowd. Accounts indicate that between 12,000 and 35,000 were present. The atmosphere was at first quite hostile, with fly-sheets distributed at the entrances calling for a general strike. Seguí's oratorical powers were crucial in convincing the audience that they should return to work the following day. Nevertheless, also important was the fact that he retained wide-ranging support within the CRT. Amongst the speakers who supported his stance were not only unionists close to Seguí, but also Francesc Miranda, who represented the prisoners' association. Yet in order to carry the audience he had to affirm that if the strikers who had been militarised were not released, 'an extensive syndicalist movement will be declared throughout Catalonia'.[19]

The General Strike and the Repression of the Catalan CNT, April to August 1919

It is on this question that the pact was to fall apart. Despite efforts to convince Milans del Bosch (including, it seems, a visit to him by Morote and a commission of workers the night before the Las Arenas meeting) he refused to free a number of workers. These included Manuel Buenacasa, the CNT general secretary. Matters were made worse because the electricity, gas and water companies did not immediately readmit all the strikers, arguing that they needed time to get the services back to normal. In response, the strike committee met to decide what action to take. Seguí's lieutenants, including Piera, opposed a general strike but they were outvoted by one, with the result that the general strike began on 24 March.[20] At the very least Milans del Bosch wished to show that whatever attitude the Government took he would not, as he saw it, capitulate to CRT demands. Although there is no concrete evidence of this, his actions might well have constituted a deliberate provocation, aimed at scuppering the accords and paving the way for a thoroughgoing repression. Amongst the Barcelona officers it was a widely shared view that the Romanones' Government both wished to reach an agreement with the Catalanists and was encouraging the rise of syndicalism through its irresoluteness. The latter belief was also fervently held by the majority of substantial employers.[21]

The declaration of the general strike was to prove a very serious blunder. In Barcelona province, martial law was now reimposed, all CNT union headquarters were closed and, in the following weeks, large numbers of union activists, including Pestaña, along with a number of labour lawyers, were arrested. Seguí, on the other hand, escaped and would spend the next seven months in hiding. Moreover, in the rest of Spain, constitutional guarantees were suspended, prior censorship of the press instituted, and well-known anarchist-syndicalist activists arrested.

The operation of the military-employer front soon made itself felt. Immediately the Sometent began to operate. It quickly enrolled 8,000 volunteers, and, armed by the military, played a key role in breaking the strike. It provided transport, drove trams and patrolled the streets, stopped and search those considered suspicious, and, along with the army, forced shops and cafés to open. The force's social base again emphasises the importance of the neighbourhood in the identitarian construction of Barcelona. It recruited above all in upper and middle-class quarters, from whence it attracted the support of a broad social mix, including industrialists, the liberal professions, shopkeepers, and some white-collar workers. It also seems to have enrolled a small number of industrial workers opposed to the CNT, most particularly foremen and Carlists.[22]

At the same time, the military authorities now overtly set up their own parallel police force under, incredibly, Manuel Bravo Portillo, despite the fact that he had lost his job in the police upon being detained in June 1918 and had only been released from prison on bail in December. It was funded by Catalan industrialists, who channelled the money through the Catalan captain-generalship (Capitanía). It drew part of its membership from Bravo Portillo's old gang, and also recruited actively in the Barcelona underworld. All the indications are that cash from the Employers' Federation was provided by its treasurer, the construction contractor, Joan Miró i Trepat. However, other members of the social elite were also involved, including, it was claimed, 'Muntadas' (one presumes, either the director of La España Industrial, Maties Muntadas, or his brother, Lluís Muntadas), Bertran i Musitu, and the Marquis of Foronda (the father of Mariano, who ran the Barcelona trams). The latter was particularly significant because he was a personal friend of the King.[23]

In subsequent months this parapolice force would take the lead in detaining anarchist-syndicalists with the backing of elements within the official police and also worked closely with the Barcelona Sometent, which set up its own 'office for special services' in the captain-generalship, which both employed informers and set up a file on anarchist activists (the origin of the infamous 'Lasarte file', discovered at the beginning of the Second Republic). Bravo Portillo also collaborated in the Sometent's formation and worked under the hard-line *españolista*, Emili Vidal-Ribes i Güell, an important figure within elite Barcelona society, who was commander of the Sometent in the Fourth District.[24]

During the general strike the CRT was seriously weakened. Shop stewards were still by and large able to collect dues, but amongst some workers there was resentment that they had been led into a strike whose objectives were not altogether clear.[25] By the second week enthusiasm began to flag, with workers starting to go back in. In response, Seguí and his supporters convinced the organisation's committees that they should call a return to work for Monday 7 April.[26] In many industries, employers took advantage of the strike's failure to sack shop stewards and circulate blacklists, while in construction and parts of the metal industry, where a number of boycotts were in operation, they imposed lock-outs from the following week. Only non-CRT workers, they stressed, would henceforth be readmitted. The leading FTN industrialist and Lliga politician, Lluís Sedó, informed the FTN's leadership that Milans del Bosch had given a green light to the sackings. In the newly mobilised sectors, like the trams, and the gas, water and electricity industries, they were largely successful; activists were fired and the back of the unions broken. In industries like metal and construction, on the other hand, worker resistance was greater, and the spring and summer were to see a series of long-running and bitter disputes.[27]

As a result of these events many leading activists were never again to find work in their own trades. Seguí was lucky in that he was able to paint the houses of colleagues and of union headquarters, but, for example, Camil Piñón, who was emerging as a leading figure in the Metalworkers' SU, ended up working in a fishmongers in the central market. Nevertheless, with their reputations secure they remained leading union organisers.[28]

Throughout these weeks the Government continued negotiating with the CRT. Yet, all the indications are that the military garrison had no desire to relinquish power and was determined to crush the CNT. This led it directly to take on the authorities. The spark which provoked the crisis was a conflict between Montañés and Doval, on the one hand, and Milans del Bosch and the Juntas de Defensa, on the other. The military's support for Bravo Portillo's parapolice force had provoked enormous tension with the civil authorities. The crisis exploded on 6 April 1919 when the leading textile unionists, the brothers Josep and Jaume Roca, were arrested by Bravo Portillo while they were negotiating the end of the general strike. Doval asked for them to be freed to continue negotiations and the request was supported by Montañés. This provoked uproar in the Barcelona garrison and Milans del Bosch demanded that they be returned.

Matters were made worse when the Government tried to get Bravo Portillo removed from the captain-generalship, again producing a violent reaction from the Juntas de Defensa and demands that Montañés and Doval be forcibly put on a train to Madrid. The captain-general again threatened to resign, warning that this would provoke 'lamentable demonstrations' in the garrison, while the Juntas' representatives put pressure on Montañés to step down, provoking Romanones' resignation on 14 April. Once again a civilian administration had been unable to stand up to the military. The latter were helped by Alfonso XIII, who was very close to the officer corps, increasingly concerned by the threat of subversion, and backed a tough response.[29]

The new Conservative Government was presided over by Antonio Maura with the arch election-manipulator, and close ally of the Juntas de Defensa, Juan de la Cierva, as Finance Minister. Maura had come to the conclusion that to quash the revolutionary threat was now the top priority, and he was seen by the King as the man to keep the syndicalists in check and recapture the support of both the military and Catalan industrialists.[30] Maura, under the influence of Milans del Bosch, decided to keep martial law in place until the police had been reorganised in order to deal with syndicalist 'terror', with the result that in the summer about 6,000 workers were being held in prison and many more had been forced to flee.[31] Of the former, by the end of July, thirty-one had been convicted by military courts and 120 were still awaiting trial.[32] Those convicted included Buenacasa and Pestaña. The latter had got four years because he was in charge of *Solidaridad Obrera* when Peiró wrote his article following the Badalona massacre, deemed to have 'insulted the

Civil Guard'. At the same time, the FTN began preparing a worker and employer census as a first step towards the introduction of 'compulsory unionisation'. Hence, despite claiming to be a devout constitutionalist, Maura was in reality sanctioning the abdication of the liberal state in Catalonia, and allowing the creation of an authoritarian ambit in which the military and business were tacitly given wide-ranging powers to pursue their own agenda.

Most brazenly, Bravo Portillo's parapolice force was tacitly authorised – no doubt by Milans del Bosch – to carry out attacks on CNT activists. In the force's first action, on 23 April 1919, they shot and wounded the secretary of the Construction Workers' SU, Pere Masoni. However, their next outing had far greater resonance. On the night of 19 July, Pau Sabater ('El Tero'), a key figure in the dyers' section of the Textile Workers' SU, was picked up, supposedly by the police, and his bullet-riddled body turned up on the road to Montcada the following morning. It was an event which produced widespread anger in trade-union circles, with several thousand workers accompanying his funeral cortège.[33] Sabater was murdered because of suspicion that he had financed an 'action group', or even formed part of such a group himself. The message the military wished to send out was that this could no longer be done with impunity.

As was the case of previous shootings, information on the involvement of Bravo Portillo's force soon emerged. The CNT labour lawyer, Josep Ulled, was given a tip-off. This led to the arrest of one of those involved, Luis Fernández, who implicated Bravo Portillo. Ulled was later to state that he was informed that the car used in the murder was the property of the car-maker, Artur Elizalde, and was being driven by his son. Two members of the police force, including a police inspector, were involved in the crime.[34]

The CRT was able to weather this bout of repression relatively well. Most of its leadership, along with a whole raft of intermediate union officials, were imprisoned, but they were held in the Barcelona Modelo prison and were able to keep in contact with the organisation through sympathetic prison officials. Youngsters, and on occasion women and children, little known to the authorities, became union delegates and secretly collected dues, which were held, often very reluctantly, by sympathetic republican tradesmen. By this means they were able to raise large sums to aid the prisoners.[35] Overall, the organisation was greatly weakened in those areas in which it had gained a foothold from 1918, but, with the economic climate still favourable, in the key industries of metal, construction and textiles, it remained quite strong. In these industries it was even able to maintain a number of boycotts, including that of the Girona Foundry.[36] It was unable to publish *Solidaridad Obrera* in Barcelona, but a new Valencia edition of the paper went on sale in March. In addition, from the spring of 1919 it paid Rodrigo Soriano, a leftist republican of dubious financial probity, so that information on the organisation would appear in his Madrid-based paper, *España Nueva*.[37]

It was during these months that ties between union leaders and the action groups became closer. Following the March repression, and once the actions of Bravo Portillo's associates were revealed, most CNT activists believed that the organisation should respond in kind. This illustrates a key feature underlying the growth of terrorism in Barcelona: an action and counter-action spiral had been set in motion in which attacks by one side elicited demands for reprisals. Furthermore, it appears that the number of would-be terrorists increased. During the spring and summer of 1919 many activists lost their jobs, and, the indications are, some were employed as 'special delegates', who were given a pistol and paid 70 pesetas a week to collect dues. This swelled the number of activists who were willing to carry out assassinations on behalf of the organisation. In addition, during these months they began to form neighbourhood groups. The new general secretary of the CNT, Evilio Boal, seems to have responded positively to demands for revenge. A printer who was already on the CNT Committee, he was appointed on the advice of Buenacasa, who was still in jail. Boal was originally from Valladolid. He was wizened and taciturn, and, perhaps to counteract his natural shyness, also worked as an actor. During the war years, he became the director of the theatre group in the CRT's headquarters, the Barcelona Workers' Centre. He enjoyed a night out and drank too much, but after becoming the typographers' representative on the National Committee in August 1917, he showed himself to be a meticulous organiser.[38]

Yet for most of the year the pattern of attacks remained similar to those of 1917 and 1918. There were several shootings of employers and foremen combined with attacks on Bravo Portillo's parapolice force. As we shall see, it was only from December 1919 that there would be a clear qualitative and quantitative transformation. It was in their fight against the employer-sponsored 'dirty war' that the CRT gunmen had their greatest success. After Ulled was tipped-off, the targets were identified relatively quickly and stalked. Finally, on 5 September 1919 Bravo Portillo was gunned down by three men while on the way to visit his mistress. This was a murder of which everyone could approve. There was great rejoicing in working-class circles, with kiosks located outside the city's workshops and factories selling out of cigars.[39] Yet, in the Barcelona military garrison, calls for revenge must have been deafening. Twelve days later his close collaborator, the former secretary of the Metalworkers' Union, Eduard Ferrer, met the same fate. This was not the end of Bravo Portillo parapolice force. It was taken over by a German swindler and adventurer who used the fake title, Baron Koëning, but with most of its members known was never very effective.[40] This highlighted the weakness of the employer-military strategy. Hitmen with only shallow roots in the society in which they operated were vulnerable to reprisals. It was a problem which they would try and correct from late 1921 onwards.

The organisation's ability to resist and counterattack sustained revolutionary illusions. They were further buoyed up by the CNT's rapid growth in much of Spain, by the survival of the Russian Revolution, and by what seemed like the revolutionary opportunities opening in much of western and central Europe. In anarchist-syndicalist circles this fuelled admiration for the Bolsheviks. In rather unanarchist terms, those most convinced of bright revolutionary prospects enthused that it had put 'power in the hands of the proletariat', and even backed the need for a transitory dictatorship of the proletariat (as long as it was the unions who administered it).[41] In this climate, even had they wanted to, Seguí and his supporters could not have sold a programme based on transitional democracy. On the contrary, emphasis was placed on revolutionary preparations. Thus, in the spring of 1919 delegates were chosen to establish contact with other European labour organisations. However, given the mixed response it was decided to concentrate on Spain. As part of this effort, 'Laville' (Pere Foix), a young activist from the Shopworkers' SU, visited Russia, and on his return, together with a Russian friend and explosives expert, set about manufacturing bombs in a flat in Barcelona. This illustrates how within the CNT syndicalism remained overlaid by older insurrectionary anarchist currents.[42]

This led to further tensions within the CNT. According to an anonymous informer, who was clearly very well informed, divisions opened up between the more cautious Seguí and his supporters, and figures like Pestaña, the Roca brothers, Miranda and Buenacasa. In organisational terms this was reflected in tensions between the CRT Regional Committee, controlled by Seguí, and the CNT National Committee, under Buenacasa's protégé Evilio Boal.[43] This was serious because during the First World War the more inflexible anarchist-syndicalists had largely allied with Seguí against the anarchist *enragés*. In subsequent months it would become clear that the space for violent, insurrectionary politics was widening.

The New Attempt at Conciliation, August to November 1919

Yet the CRT was being worn down by repression and by the late summer revolutionary hopes had begun to fade. I have no figures for union membership at this time, but it is clear that some less committed workers were either refusing to pay their dues or paying them reluctantly.[44] Hence, it remained the desire of figures like Seguí to return the CRT to legality. The chance was provided by the fall of the Maura Government. Despite the outrageous manipulation of the elections of 1 June 1919 it faced heavy opposition in parliament and was replaced by another Conservative administration under Eduardo Dato's ally, Joaquín Sánchez de Toca, on 20 July, with the social reformer, Manuel de Burgos y Mazo, as Minister of the Interior. This gave the CRT hope, as Dato's wing of the party favoured integrating independent unions and employers' organisations into state-sponsored collective bargaining machinery. Furthermore, Burgos y Mazo aimed to extend social legislation and implement the eight-hours day.[45]

Seguí no doubt felt that with the revolutionary road blocked it was necessary to adopt a more defensive position, and under his influence the anarchist-syndicalists responded positively and played down any revolutionary objectives. Thus, in early August, leading CNT figures, from Seguí to Buenacasa, produced a manifesto aimed specifically at parliament, in which they affirmed that, if the organisation were legalised, strikes would be peaceful. They even went so far as to suggest that a future transition to socialism could be attained without recourse to revolution. Furthermore, they distanced themselves from terrorist acts, their key message being that state repression and terrorism went together.[46] This was timed to coincide with an intervention by Francesc Layret in parliament, in which he not only defended the right of the CNT to operate openly, but also lifted the veil on the causes behind the fall of the Romanones Government. In a blistering attack on the armed forces he accused them of constantly intervening in politics rather than actually serving the country.[47] One can only imagine the reaction in the Juntas de Defensa.

Over the following weeks the Government's strategy became clear. It wished to open a new dialogue between employers and the CNT, but did not want to be seen as weak. Hence, the CNT would have to meet a series of conditions in return for being allowed to operate openly. The man chosen to deliver an agreement was Julio Amado, a military regenerationalist who was close to the Juntas de Defensa.

The Government's initiative came at a time when, despite the operation of martial law, industrial conflict remained intense. By August it focused on two areas in particular. First, in textiles negotiations had been taking place regarding the implementation of the eight-hours day or forty-eight-hours week. On the Pla, employers largely accepted the cut in working hours, but in the Muntanya they would accede only to a nine-hours day, with the result that the National Textile Federation launched strikes in the industrial textile towns on the Ter and Freser and, where possible, in the Alt Llobregat. By mid-August about 30,000 textile workers were on strike, to which some Alt Llobregat employers responded with lock-outs.

Even more dramatically, after the Barcelona construction workers had presented a series of new demands at the beginning of April, they were met with a lock-out in mid-August, which the Employers' Federation threatened to extend to other sectors of the economy. By 19 August, about 25,000 construction workers were affected. This was indicative of a strategy that industrialists were increasingly employing: the use of industry-wide lock-outs to break worker resistance and, indeed, intimidate the authorities. As we shall see, they were soon to contemplate taking this a step further. Other disputes were to follow. On 22 August, Barcelona's sailors came out as part of a broader nationwide dispute. Then, at the end of the month, the Barcelona Metalworkers' SU presented new demands, the key elements of which were an eight-hours day, wage increases and the 'regulation' of apprenticeship.[48]

In late August, Amado made contact with the CRT and business representatives. On the syndicalist side, Carlos Madrigal acted as the go-between, with Seguí, once again, leading negotiations. Amado's proposal was that the CNT should lift its strikes and demands and the employers their lock-outs, and that state-sponsored arbitration boards would then be established in each Catalan town. This was very much the blueprint for the Juntas Locales de Reformas Sociales, except that an effort was now made explicitly to incorporate the anarchist-syndicalists. In return for their compliance Amado would lift martial law, release the CRT leadership, decree an amnesty for all prisoners held from the March general strike (except those who had committed violent crimes) – of which there were still several thousand – and put the eight-hours day into effect.[49]

For the CNT such a course, which many would see as an abrogation of the tenets of direct action, would not be easy to accept. Yet Seguí – a pragmatist above all else – valued the ability to operate freely and no doubt understood that the establishment of collective bargaining procedures could, in fact, entrench the organisation's power. Hence, on 5 September he provisionally agreed that strikes and lock-outs should be lifted from 9 September, with a period of seventy-two hours set aside for the return to normality. From 11 September a provisional arbitration board (*Comisión Mixta*) would then operate, chaired by the civil governor or his deputy, to try and find a negotiated settlement to the disputes in progress. Union elections would take place at a later date, allowing the arbitration boards definitively to be established.

However, the accord had to be sold to the membership. This was made more difficult because hard-line anarchist-syndicalists, such as Buenacasa, now came out against Seguí. As seen, relations had become increasingly frayed during the year, and state-sponsored arbitration boards were seen by them as a step too far. But crucially Seguí was backed by Pestaña, who retained a strong following within more *enragé* circles.[50] Hence, the alliance of the years 1917 to 1918 was consolidated and, although Pestaña was inclined to place the revolution in a shorter time frame, it would remain intact until 1923. They were able to bring most CRT leaders on board, with the result that the agreement was approved in an assembly on the night of 6 September. Then, on the following day, the various CNT committees published a manifesto in which they stated that given the special circumstances they had agreed to a 'short armistice' in order to show their sense of responsibility.[51]

Both Seguí and Pestaña were quick to deny that they had in any way compromised direct action, arguing that they had only discussed political questions, such as the release of prisoners and the re-establishment of constitutional guarantees, with the authorities. They had dealt with labour relations 'directly' with employers.[52] This, however, ignored two points. First, syndicalist union strategy was based on mass mobilisation against the state and bourgeoisie. Yet they were helping to diffuse tensions. Second, the authorities would organise the union elections and be present on the arbitration boards. This showed how in the right political context the CRT union leadership could be weaned away from their confrontationalist strategy. The key requirement was that the state both allow them to operate freely and make the accords stick with the industrialists.

Moreover, following the assassination of Bravo Portillo and Eduard Ferrer, on 5 and 17 September respectively, leading CRT figures also tried explicitly to rein in their own gunmen. As the manifesto published on 7 August indicated, they were aware that terrorist acts were damaging the organisation's image and the Government may well have demanded an end to the shootings in return for their being allowed to operate legally. At some point in September, a meeting was held by the committees of the CRT and Barcelona local federation in which it was agreed to bring such attacks to a halt. A number of Barcelona syndicalists, including Pestaña and Seguí, then visited Madrid between late September and early October 1919, giving talks and holding meetings, and also discreetly establishing contacts with the authorities. Their principal aim was to capture support for the CNT, but both Seguí and Pestaña also specifically repudiated terrorism. Pestaña's comments may not only have been aimed at public opinion. Until that point there had been some ambiguity in his stance, and although he denied any CNT involvement he was sending out the message that within the organisation itself it was not only Seguí's backers who opposed terrorism.[53]

Indeed, the CRT leadership was, until a new offensive was launched against the organisation, able to take control of the situation. Following the assassination of Ferrer, there would be no assassinations involving CNT gunmen until 16 December. A member of the Sometent was shot at on 13 October, but there would be no similar incidents until 9 December.[54] This is important because it questions claims made at the time, and since repeated by historians, that the CNT and the terrorists were inextricably bound together and that, although Seguí and company may have wanted to rein them in, this was an impossible undertaking. It is a position which, of course, implicitly serves to justify state repression.[55]

Seguí's policy of bringing the CRT into the open was part of a broader strategy aimed at turning the CNT into Spain's most powerful labour organisation. In order to achieve this both he and Pestaña were keen for the CRT to shake off its reputation as an organisation made up purely of industrial workers and integrate 'technical workers', who would not only broaden the organisation's appeal but also aid in the transition to a future syndicalist society. A Union of the Liberal Professions was set up under the auspices of Josep Viadiu during September. Two years later Seguí, like Viadiu before him, went further and rather optimistically expressed the hope that the struggle against the abuses of landlords might serve to build bonds between workers and the middle classes. Furthermore, he developed the idea – already discussed in anarchist circles during the first decade of the century – that the unions should transcend their role as the defenders of workers as producers, and also fight for consumer rights. Thus, the Food Processing SU was called on to ensure that industrialists did not adulterate their products, while the Construction Workers' SU was asked to check that quality raw materials were used.[56] This can be read at a number of levels. Given the experience of the previous years, Seguí was probably convinced that in order to prosper the CNT needed to build a broad front to struggle against the authoritarian Right. Yet he still maintained a longer-term revolutionary syndicalist perspective. By taking on such altruistic functions, unions would be showing their capacity to lead the society of the future.

The aim of converting the CNT into Spain's major labour confederation seemed realistic. In terms of affiliates it was now considerably larger than its Socialist rival, even establishing a base in the Socialist strongholds of Vizcaya and Asturias. This led Seguí to state that the CNT could 'win the battle' against the UGT.[57] By this he did not mean that the UGT would simply be absorbed. As shown in the previous chapter, from 1918 Seguí and his followers were probably aiming at unification on favourable terms. He was no doubt encouraged by the continued growth of a left-wing within the PSOE and UGT, which was keen to link up with the CNT. Hence, Seguí may well have envisaged a new independent labour confederation comprising the syndicalists and Socialist Left, with a UGT rump allied to the Socialist party. Prodded by its own left-wing, the UGT once again approached the CNT in the summer to negotiate possible unification. The CNT National Committee, however, took a more intransigent stance than Seguí would have wished and informed the UGT that no decision could be taken before the proposed CNT congress that winter. As in 1918, therefore, relations with the UGT remained a focus of tension between pragmatists and hardliners.

It was above all in order to challenge the Socialists in their heartland that the Catalan CRT leaders visited Madrid in the late autumn (giving one talk in the Socialist Casa del Pueblo, invited by the leftist intellectuals of the New School). The message they put across, despite the pact with Amado, was that the CNT provided a more combative and revolutionary alternative than its Socialist counterpart, and that it did not waste time and money on 'politics'. Nevertheless, as against the position taken by the anarchist Left, Seguí and Pestaña argued that any such revolution would be the culmination of the CNT's growing power, not the result of a general strike and insurrection declared at the first opportunity. Pestaña was optimistic as to when such a revolution might take place. An informer reported him as commenting in Madrid that, 'partial strikes should be fomented and constant agitation maintained until the time for the definitive battle is reached, which, if the present state of the CNT's progress is maintained, should be next summer'. Seguí, on the other hand, was much more cautious, arguing in a speech on 4 October, which raised hackles on the CNT Left, that if the proletariat were offered power it would have to turn it down because the unions were not yet prepared to organise production. It was also this line of reasoning that led him to distance himself from adulation of the Russian revolution, even questioning whether it could be consolidated.[58]

Seguí therefore envisaged a long haul in which the organisation would grow and strengthen and during which the unions would prepare themselves to take over production after the transition to communism. Yet over the next months both internal and external obstacles would, in fact, become more intractable. In Catalonia, most serious was military and employer hostility to the new Government's attempt at conciliation. From the very beginning, despite Amado's links with the Juntas, he was cold-shouldered by Milans del Bosch. Widespread opposition to the Government's new line was also clear within employer circles. This opposition was captained by the Employers' Federation. In August it threatened to declare a general lock-out if the Government did not treat the CNT with a firm hand. Then, sensationally, after the assassination of Bravo Portillo, in an open letter to the King, its sister organisation, the Spanish Employers' Confederation, called for military intervention. This discontent was further intensified by Burgos y Mazo's plans to put the eight-hours' day into effect and introduce more social legislation.[59]

Nevertheless, at first the industrialists drew back from a direct confrontation and agreed, the indications are very reluctantly, to end their lock-outs and join the arbitration board for its first meeting on 11 September. Amado was helped by the fact that he seems to have enjoyed the tacit support of the Lliga, which opposed the continued operation of martial law and came to consider a domesticated CRT, under Seguí's more responsible leadership, a possible alternative to repression.[60] Nevertheless, from the outset the road would be a rocky one. Large numbers of workers returned to work and the prisoners were released, but a lot of conflicts remained unresolved. The CNT accused the Employers' Federation of not totally lifting the lock-outs and of sacking union representatives. This, it seems, was the case in bottlemaking and lithography. In construction, the atmosphere was further soured because the contractor of the Colón Hotel had capitulated to a boycott, and the Employers' Federation was now refusing to supply him with raw materials. Union activists were also angered because, although martial law had been lifted, constitutional guarantees were not restored and prior censorship remained in place.

However, the CRT leadership was not only faced with the opposition of many employers. Given past experience of government promises, and in a context in which the economic context remained largely favourable, it was difficult to bring sectors of the rank-and-file on board. Hence, the Employers' Federation complained that, despite the guarantees given by the CRT, strikes continued and unions were making new demands. This was the case in parts of construction and in a number of smaller trades, while metalworkers were operating a go-slow. The case of the tanners is a good example of the problems that the CRT leadership faced. They had made a series of demands in August. When the arbitration board was set up they agreed to take their case to it. However, no settlement was reached and so they began to operate a go-slow, which was followed by an employer lock-out.[61]

These difficulties gave the Employers' Federation an excuse to abandon the arbitration board on 25 September. This represented a continuation of the offensive which they had launched against the Government following the assassination of Bravo Portillo earlier in the month. Once again they threatened a lock-out and railed against CNT terrorism. In employer and broader right-wing circles there was talk of the need for a tougher government, possibly headed by La Cierva. Alfonso XIII was also approached. Miró i Trepat was received by him and given a sympathetic hearing, and over the coming month the military and employers would enjoy his tacit support. On the night that Bravo Portillo was assassinated, Amado specifically warned the CNT leadership that forces in both Madrid and Barcelona wished to renew their attack on them. This is confirmed by discussions taking place in military circles. The Barcelona garrison was in contact with the senior general, Miguel Primo de Rivera, and the need for drastic measures to deal with the syndicalist threat, including executions, was discussed.[62]

The employers' nerves were further tested from the beginning of October. The unions no longer felt bound by the 5 September agreement and new strikes were declared. On the port sailors once again took action. Violent strikes of waiters and cooks erupted, under the auspices of the new Food Workers' SU. This was another example of how the CRT was reaching into new sectors of the labour force. It was even more forcefully demonstrated on

19 October, when the Girona Foundry, which had been boycotted since late 1918, capitulated. Tactics used had included the poisoning of its water source, leading to the deaths of two workers in August. Furthermore, strikes and lock-outs continued in the textile industry. In Manresa, and on the Ter and Freser, a compromise was reached in early September and a fifty-two hours week agreed upon, and, on the Pla textile workers forced the industrialists, under pressure, to sign a labour contract covering the entire area. In Barcelona this was followed, on 10 October, with the demand for a 2 peseta wage rise by the Barcelona Construction Workers' SU. Employers were given ten days to respond. Subsequently, the Metalworkers' and Woodworkers' SUs would also make new demands.

Simultaneously, the CRT once again began to reorganise. Unions rapidly strengthened, the end of the month saw *Solidaridad Obrera* reappear in Barcelona, now edited by Salvador Quemades, and the organisation launched a Catalan-wide recruitment drive. Many workers were no doubt keen to unionise voluntarily, but intimidation was again used. An editorial in *Solidaridad Obrera* indeed complained that workers who had stopped paying dues not only had to pay the months they owed but were also being fined. As it noted, this was hardly the best way to make the unions attractive.[63]

The Employer Lock-Out and the New Repressive Onslaught, November 1919 to January 1920

The Government reacted by trying to maintain a firm image, drafting an extra 1,300 civil guards into Barcelona during September. It also proceeded with its reforming programme and managed to gain the explicit backing of the Lliga and also, briefly, involve the FTN in negotiations. Like the Employers' Federation, the FTN had opposed the Government's initiative, but Amado convinced it to draw up plans for a new arbitration board. The position of the Lliga was probably important in this respect, as was the fact that the FTN's leadership formed part of elite Barcelona society, met regularly with the civil governor, and would have found it difficult to totally reject his advances. It was under the auspices of the FTN that the Government promulgated a Royal Decree on 11 October, outlining details of a new Labour Commission to deal within industrial disputes. It now envisaged that there would be one Catalan-wide arbitration board based in Barcelona, whose president would be a government appointee. Elections to the commission were to take place on 7 December after the elaboration of a worker and employer census. In the meantime, a provisional arbitration board would be set up to discuss a formula by which the strikes and lock-outs might be called off and the measures needed to lay the basis for the Labour Commission. For the FTN this went some way towards meeting employer demands for 'compulsory trade-unionism', and it may have hoped that the CRT could be marginalised from the new bargaining machinery. At the same time, the Lliga president of the Mancomunitat, Josep Puig i Cadafalch, established contact with the CRT, and Lluís Sedó began discreetly to advise Amado.[64]

In subsequent negotiations Seguí showed himself favourably disposed, but argued that he would only be able to win over the base if the formation of the Labour Commission were preceded by a conference of Catalan worker and employer representatives that established a 'minimum programme'. Amado had no objection to this as long as the timetable that the Government had outlined was respected and strikes in progress were called off. Seguí intended to hold a CRT congress before this conference in order to sell the Labour Commission to the rank-and-file. Simultaneously, negotiations proceeded regarding current disputes. Workers' representatives demanded a series of concessions, while the Employers' Federation stated that all strikes and boycotts should be lifted before any negotiations could take place.[65]

The Employers' Federation also stated that it would back the Royal Decree, but was still determined to break the back of the CRT. Faced with the prospect of the Government introducing new social legislation, the Spanish Employers' Confederation rapidly organised its second conference, which was held in Barcelona between 20 and 26 October. In a secret session held on 25 October it announced that, if all strikers had not returned to work by 31 October, it would call a general lock-out in Barcelona from 3 November, which it threatened to extend to the rest of Catalonia and Spain. This was followed by a great demonstration of support for Milans del Bosch outside the headquarters of the captain-generalship, in which cries of support for the army, the King and Spain, were heard. In their communiqués the employers claimed that they were taking action because the CNT had never complied with the 5 September accord to lift all strikes in progress, while also attacking what they saw as government weakness in the face of the terrorist and revolutionary threat. Not to act, they maintained, 'would lead us down the road that in other countries was taken by Kerensky'.[66]

Employers were exasperated by the number of strikes and boycotts. The fear of revolution was also genuine, but by stressing this danger they also aimed to galvanise the military and conservative opinion. Moreover, although terrorist attacks had embittered relations they must have realised that Seguí was now effectively containing them. Hence, the re-imposition social control in their factories, combined with the desire to provoke the fall of the Government, emerge as the key elements in explaining their strategy. Both Sánchez de Toca and Burgos y Mazo denounced the latter goal.[67]

Faced with this challenge, Amado did all he could do re-establish the arbitration board in a series of meetings with the political and business elite, the Employers' Federation and the CRT. Crucially, he was, at least on the surface, to maintain the support of the Lliga and FTN. To head off the Employers' Federation, Seguí led further discussions with Amado at which he agreed to work within the framework of the 11 October Royal Decree, as long as they could put forward modifications (a government-appointed president was particularly difficult for the CRT to accept). Given that it was a Catalan matter, the more intransigent CNT National Committee could be sidelined. Instead, Seguí managed to gain the backing of the CRT, the Barcelona local federation, and the SUs. Then, on 2 November, along with Josep Molins, the secretary of the local federation, he signed up to the decree in the civil governor's headquarters. This meant accepting that, in future, wages and working conditions would be fixed centrally by the Labour Commission and that shop stewards could not undertake independent initiatives. Henceforth their only function would be to ensure that agreements reached by the commission were adhered to. This was seen by Amado as crucial in order to ensure that 'discipline' was restored in the factories.[68] In addition, Seguí's team did all they could to keep the lid on industrial conflict. They managed to get a number of go-slows called off. More importantly, after a warning by Amado that his standing would be seriously eroded, Simó Piera, the general secretary of the Construction Workers' SU, headed off the declaration of a new general strike in the industry.[69]

At first these concessions were to no avail. In its first days the lock-out centred on construction and the metal industry. These were the key industries within the Employers' Federation. However, it gathered strength as the week progressed. Shops did not shut but the shopkeepers' association, the Unió Gremial, gave its support. Moreover, elite cultural associations expressed sympathy. The lock-out was, therefore, backed by a broad social alliance, which stretched from the city's 'good families' to at least sectors of the lower-middle class, united in the face of the working-class threat. Under pressure, in the words of the modest industrialist, Gual Villalbí, 'all those who had something to keep' had united. For Amado there was a 'state of spiritual conformity' with the actions of the Employers' Federation amongst the 'employer classes', the 'socially conservative class', and 'most of the garrison'. Reflecting elitist thinking in ruling circles, he referred to this conglomerate as 'the opinion of Barcelona'.[70] On the other side was the industrial working class: on 14 November, according to official figures, 48,473 workers were locked-out.

In response, the CRT called for calm. Seguí realised that to react violently would be to play into the employers' hands. This strategy at first appeared to bear fruit. The Employers' Federation refused to lift the lock-out but, with a broad political spectrum now seemingly behind Amado, it agreed to negotiate. As a result, Amado was able to establish a new arbitration board, chaired by the Lliga mayor, Antonio Martínez Domingo, with the liberal Catalanist, Felip Rodés, and the 'autonomist monarchist' Josep Roig i Bergadà, advising the workers and employers respectively. They reached a new accord on 12 November. In the first phase, it was decided that all strikes and lock-outs would be lifted on 14 November and that no further disputes could be declared until the Labour Commission had been officially set up. In the meantime, the arbitration board could discuss demands relating to wage rises, but agreements could only be reached in the case of unanimity.[71]

This represented a further concession by Seguí. The Employers' Federation seemed at first to go along with this, but from its perspective the agreement was seriously flawed. Rather than the new statist bargaining machinery signifying the eclipse of the CRT, it would in all probability legitimise it. Hence, there is little doubt that it was looking for a reason to pull out. This became clear on 14 November when armed employers, many enrolled in the Sometent, waited on the factory gates and prevented union activists from going back in. This led a group of workers, representing the local federation and a 'permanent commission', to visit the arbitration board and denounce events on the ground. Eight-hundred workers, they maintained, had been sacked. In response, the CRT representatives had no alternative but to walk out.[72]

The Employers' Federation then announced that the lock-out would end on 17 November. Following the dismissal of large numbers of activists the aim was to reorder internal relations in the factories without reference to the CRT. The Government restarted negotiations from 14 November, with employer and worker representatives meeting Sánchez de Toca in Madrid between 21 and 22 November. The Employers' Federation saw the Government's determination to maintain a dialogue with hostility. Graupera, the president of Employers' Federation, warned Sánchez de Toca that if he could not maintain social peace then matters should be left in the hands of the employers. It was in this atmosphere that Amado went so far as to state that, in his view, the workers' representatives were now the 'true guardians of order'.[73]

Meanwhile the Barcelona SUs tried to maintain their organisations intact through all possible means. In a meeting of union delegates on 16 November the decision was taken not to return to work until back-wages had been paid. Moreover, in an indication of how the employers' stance was radicalising the union activists, a mass meeting on 19 November agreed that if the Employers' Federation failed to accept the accord of 12 November, reemploy those sacked within twenty-four hours and pay back-wages, the organisation would break with the arbitration board and the SUs would once again be at liberty to negotiate working conditions directly with the employers.[74] As a result, the situation remained conflict-ridden, with over 13,000 workers still either locked-out or on strike on 21 November.[75] Construction, where up to 5,000 workers were not readmitted, remained the focus of tension. With no prospect of a solution in sight, the Construction Workers' SU decided to increase the pressure. In a meeting on 25 November it agreed once again to put forward the demands first made in July, and on the following day 25,000 construction workers came out.

It was this inability to reimpose social control that led the Employers' Federation to take more drastic measures. On 1 December it called a new lock-out, which, starting in the textile industry, was extended throughout much of industrial Catalonia from the beginning of the following week. Already, by 4 December, in Barcelona over 63,000 workers were once again locked out.[76] On this occasion industrialists were determined that it should be maintained until the back of the CRT was broken, and were also hopeful that they could force the Government's fall. Its response was rather passive. Sánchez de Toca denounced the employers, but did nothing to break the lock-out. Rather, armed Sometent were allowed to operate and troops patrol the streets. This can no doubt be read in the context of a warning by Amado that to take action against the employers would bring the Government into direct conflict with the military.[77] Matters were made worse because Amado was deserted by his supposed allies within the Lliga and social elite. While they were more discreet and cautious than the leaders of the Employers' Federation, when forced to take sides they backed it. Sedó now maintained that the lock-out should be maintained until the CRT was destroyed. In the following year the FTN claimed that it had never supported the arbitration board and eulogised the leaders of the Employers' Federation, 'those brave men who, faced by great danger, took the lead in the campaign against foreign-inspired Bolshevism'. Similarly, in February 1920, Cambó argued that Catalonia was in the midst of a confrontation between 'those who propose and work to destroy present-day society' and 'those who defend the essential bases of our ... civilisation'.[78]

Once again, the CRT leadership attempted to rein in the activists. *Solidaridad Obrera* called for resistance to be 'exclusively peaceful'.[79] Their position was to quietly support the Government with the hope, as previously, that if they remained disciplined employers would finally have to call off the lock-out and come back to the negotiating table. However, they would find it increasingly difficult to hold the line. Hard-line anarchist-syndicalists like Buenacasa believed that the workers should take over the factories. An attempt by the armed forces to dislodge them would then, it was hoped, spark off a revolution. Elements within the CNT also called for terrorist attacks in response. According to an informer, at some point in early December a circular was distributed asking whether they should assassinate the leaders of the Employers' Federation, Miró y Trepat and Graupera. This seems genuine. Seguí and his supporters had to call a clandestine meeting on 30 November in which they persuaded the organisation not to take violent countermeasures. The decision was immediately published by *Solidaridad Obrera*. Correctly they foresaw that such attacks would simply strengthen the forces of counterrevolution. Nevertheless, despite Seguí's opposition, after the lock-out was declared the local federation authorised the planting of bombs. Most were left in the street or in, or near, commercial establishments, although several were aimed specifically at employers or the security forces. Four civil guards and three soldiers suffered minor injuries, but no one was killed. The idea was no doubt to make the employers and military ponder the consequences of their actions, but the effect was to weaken the Government.[80]

The re-imposition of the lock-out therefore made the position of Seguí's 'team' more vulnerable. From September anarchist *enragés* set up a couple of publications in part at least with the specific objective of attacking the Catalan CRT leadership. In mid-September 1919 *Espartaco* came out in Madrid. It asserted that syndicalism had 'absorbed' anarchism and that it was time for the anarchists to reassert themselves, while criticising the 'caudillos of Catalan syndicalism' for having abandoned anarchist ideals, failed to employ direct action in September and then refused to meet the lock-out with an uprising. It was backed by such Catalan figures as Fortunato Barthe, E. Mateo Soriano and Pere Jul, who were active in the anarchist groups and the rationalist education movement rather than in the unions. This indicates that it was rather narrowly based on the opinions of the anarchist critics of anarchist-syndicalism.

This was soon to change. In October the editor of *Espartaco*, Plácido de Valle Jover, travelled to Barcelona, where he helped set up *Bandera Roja*, which, over the next months, was able to gain a broader base, connecting with young anarchist-syndicalists who combined union militancy with recourse to terrorism. It operated out of the Sants Rationalist Athenaeum, run by Joan Roigé, and nearby maintained a clandestine printing press and an arms cache. This further rarefied the atmosphere within the Catalan CNT. *Solidaridad Obrera* fulminated at the 'coffee-table revolutionaries', and even Evilio Boal, according to an informer, bitterly criticised the divisive role *Espartaco* was playing, while rumours began to circulate that attacks were being planned on Seguí's supporters. Seguí's gradualist strategy and his tendency to stray from anarchist-syndicalist orthodoxy was leading support amongst the activists to haemorrhage. *Bandera Roja*'s tone was both violent and elitist, appealing not only to committed anarchists but also to youngsters who both saw themselves as the vanguard of the struggle against employers and the state, and who desired a more active response. In the context of the employer-military offensive, insurrectionary tendencies within the anarchist-syndicalist movement, which drew on Bakunin and Malatesta, were once again coming to the fore.[81]

The movement's increasingly radical temper came through in what was referred to as the CNT's Second Congress (or Congreso de la Comedia), held in Madrid between 10 and 18 December. The congress highlighted the extraordinary growth of the organisation over the past year. There were over 400 delegates present, who claimed to represent 756,101 workers, of whom 699,369 were affiliated. There were 427,086 Catalan members, 226,487 from Barcelona alone. There was no doubt some exaggeration involved here; one wonders, for example, how many of these supposed members were actually paying their dues. Nevertheless, what is clear is that the CRT had integrated much of the Catalan industrial working class into its unions. Moreover, growth in other parts of Spain had been dramatic. In Levante there were now over 100,000 members, in Andalusia about 90,000, while significant union centres had also been built up in Aragón, Galicia and in the towns of Gijón and La Felguera in Asturias. However, the great organisational boom had in fact taken place in late 1918 and early 1919. In Andalusia the movement had not fully recovered from repression meted out in May, while the seriousness of the Catalan lock-out was not appreciated.[82]

Hence, the congress was conducted in a rather unrealistic climate of euphoria, further stimulated by the example of the Russian Revolution. This helps explain the inflexible resolutions approved. Many Catalan delegates, perhaps carried away by a mixture of revolutionary dreams and hatred for the employer-military alliance, lent their support. Furthermore, most delegates from outside Catalonia came from areas in which workers had been rapidly mobilised in little more than a matter of months. As against the situation in Catalonia there was little experience of the realities of running labour unions, which might lead theory to be modified by harsh practical realities. The one exception was Asturias, where a anarchist-syndicalist labour movement had grown up alongside, and sometimes in alliance with, the Socialists. Significantly, the Asturian delegation, headed by Eleuterio Quintanilla, would be close to the positions defended by Seguí in most of the debates.

Overall, however, it would be the hard-line anarchist-syndicalists – Buenacasa and Boal, the leading figures on the National Committee; the fiery figure of Eusebi Carbó, now editing *La Guerra Social* from Valencia; and the virulently anti-Socialist Madrid-based anarchist, Mauro Bajatierra – who dominated proceedings. This could be seen in a number of areas. The commission charged with producing a report on union strategy stated that the decision to enter the arbitration board had been an 'error', but that 'the Catalan organisation has understood this and has happily returned to its normal practice, that is direct action'. The report was approved without even being debated. Presumably Seguí and his supporters felt that they could not defend their actions in the present climate.

Moreover, a long debate on unity with the Socialists concluded with victory for the radicals, who were staunchly opposed to the CNT courting any possible 'political' contagion. Proceedings began with the debate of two rival resolutions championed by Quintanilla and Pestaña. Quintanilla's resolution was the most open, calling for a unity congress. Pestaña, with an eye to the radicals, defended a tougher resolution, which affirmed that the new confederation should be both apolitical and based on SUs, and which gave the UGT just seventy-two hours to accept. Seguí supported Quintanilla, but suggested both resolutions should be combined. It was when Pestaña acceded to this and agreed that a unification congress should be held that the National Committee, along with the Andalusian delegates, supported a narrow and sectarian resolution proposed by Enric Valero, which baldly stated that the UGT should be declared 'yellow' if it did not enter the CNT within three months. The size of the victory, by 325,995 to 169,225 votes (with the National Committee not using the 180,000 votes at its disposal), shows that the dizzy growth of the previous year had gone to the heads of many. Indeed, Valero, a stucco plasterer by trade, was a close friend of Seguí, and enjoyed the explicit support of the Barcelona Construction Workers' SU.[83]

The more 'trade unionist' sectors of the confederation were also defeated in the debate on organisational structure. Several delegates, including Quintanilla and Peiró, argued that the SUs should be the building blocks of Spanish-wide industrial federations, but the proposal was massively outvoted by 651,431 votes to 14,008. A key difference between the CNT and UGT was, as a result, confirmed. While the CNT focused on mobilisation at a local level, the UGT, in key industries at least, was increasingly concerned with 'regional' and 'national' bargaining.

In other areas, however, compromise was reached. This was the case in the debate on international alliances. In previous months the Bolsheviks had set up the Communist or Third International in opposition to what they saw as the incorrigible reformism of the European Social Democrats. As already seen, it was anarchist-syndicalist hardliners who had been particularly attracted. Nevertheless, it was a suggestion by Seguí that was actually taken up. He maintained that they should join the Third International in order not to be isolated, but then call on the 'syndicalist organisations of the world' to construct the genuine workers international. In what seems like a play to the gallery and attempt to reassert his revolutionary credentials, he also affirmed that should the Spanish authorities send troops to Russia (hardly a likely scenario) they should rise up in rebellion. The approval of the resolution reflected the belief that the Russian Revolution had shown the bankruptcy of the parliamentary electoral road to socialism. The leadership was also keen to avoid any repetition of the pre-war situation in which syndicalists and anarchists were isolated, while the Social-Democratic Second International became dominant.

A spirit of compromise could also be seen in a final resolution, which was unanimously approved and which affirmed that the CNT's goal was libertarian communism. Despite claims that this represented another victory for hardliners, in fact Seguí and his supporters would have no problem with this declaration as long as the actual content of libertarian communism was left in the air. This is shown by the fact that, although Simó Piera had, earlier in the congress, rejected any declaration of anarchist principles, he was happy to put his name to the resolution. A debate on whether the unions or anarchist groups should run the communist utopia would, on the other hand, have been extremely divisive.[84]

Yet while the Catalan delegates had been engaged in abstract organisational and theoretical considerations, the situation on the ground was made far worse by the fall of the Sánchez de Toca Government. It was under pressure from the Barcelona garrison, while in Madrid it was under attack from La Cierva for supposedly being soft on anarchism and it did not enjoy the sympathy of the King. Furthermore, the Prime Minister's position cannot have been helped by the fact that, although Dato disapproved of the lock-out, he overtly sympathised with the employers. Officially the Government resigned because of a dispute with the Juntas de Defensa over a question of corporate power, but few doubted that events in Barcelona were behind its fall. Alfonso XIII was then able to engineer a new coalition government under the Maurista, Manuel Allendesalazar, who took power on 11 December.[85] The Employers' Federation could once again draw the lesson that intransigence paid and that reforming elements within the regime could be destabilised. The CRT leadership was appraised of the possible consequences when, on their return from the CNT congress in Madrid, they met Amado, who had just been replaced as civil governor, on the train: 'Be very careful', he warned, 'those gentlemen want blood and I wasn't willing to spill it'.[86]

Immediately, the climate became more adverse. Tight censorship was imposed, a number of syndicalists were arrested and several centres closed down. Meanwhile, troops and the Sometent continued to patrol the streets. Nevertheless, the Government refused to declare martial law as this would have put the repression totally in the hands of the employer-military alliance. The indications are that it wanted to meet the employers short-term demands, but at least partly on its own terms. In response, the Employers' Federation maintained its tough stance, explicitly stating that it would not lift the lock-out until the SUs had been destroyed and they had imposed individual contracts on the workforce. New bargaining structures, it made clear, could not stand in the way of its members hiring whom they wanted.[87] This increasingly reduced Seguí's room for manoeuvre. The committees of the

CRT and local Barcelona federation maintained that they would not return to work until back-wages had been paid, locked-out workers re-employed and the employers had indicated their willingness to negotiate. Nevertheless, they continued to advocate peaceful resistance. Only on one occasion, on 21 December, was a general strike threatened. Yet at the end of the month, in order to gain public sympathy, they stated that their short-term aims were 'rather modest'; and that while their long-term goal was libertarian communism, this did not mean that 'we are immediately going to organise a revolution'. On the contrary, although they held revolutionary ideas their 'procedures were more conservative than those of the employers'.[88]

Yet it was at this point that Seguí lost control of the more radical elements within the organisation. It was amongst the anarchist and anarchist-syndicalist youth that the 'action groups' had emerged and some of them, at least, were now willing to defy the CRT leadership and strike back at employers and the state. They were to take the lead from the metalworker, Ramon Archs. As seen in Chapter Six, he had already been involved in an attempt to murder the director of the Maquinista Terrestre i Marítima in 1910. He was based in France from 1911, but returned in 1918 and quickly re-established himself as a leading figure within the Metalworkers' SU. He was to mastermind a series of attacks in December 1919, and then went on to lead the organisation's terrorist apparatus in the city.[89]

The counterattack began on 16 December when two civil guards were gunned down. This was the first time that the security services had been cold-bloodedly targeted. The Unió Gremial ordered a shut-down of the city's commercial establishments for their funerals on the following day, another indication of the broad nature of the anti-CRT coalition.[90] A week later a foreman, who was enrolled in the Sometent, was also murdered. Simultaneously, several employers were attacked in quick succession, on 19 December 1919, and on 3, 4 and 5 January 1920. In qualitative and quantitative terms these shootings represented a new departure. In the first, third and fourth attacks, groups of gunmen riddled passing cars with bullets. Furthermore, three of the attacks were not related to specific industrial disputes. The first and second targets, the car-maker, Artur Elizalde, and the son of the owner of a dying factory, Joan Serra, were shot at in revenge for the murder of 'El Tero', in which they were believed to have been involved (the latter, it seems, without foundation). Elizalde was unhurt though his chauffeur was killed; Serra, on the other hand, was shot in the side. In the third attack, a car was shot at as it left the La Bohemia brewery, which had been involved in a long-running labour conflict, leaving an employee dead. The final target was the president of the Employers' Federation, Félix Graupera. It was a spectacular shooting, with between twenty and thirty gunmen involved. One of the two policemen in the car was killed and the other four occupants, including Graupera, badly injured.[91]

Yet this strategy was quickly to prove totally counterproductive. After the Graupera shooting, letters flooded in from employers throughout Spain demanding that the Government take tough action. It was seemingly looking for a reason to move decisively against the CRT and now had to act. The organisation was illegalised, its centres closed down and over 1,000 activists detained, along with a number of labour lawyers. A big blow came on 15 January when the police swooped on a clandestine meeting and made sixty-two arrests. Amongst them were many of the organisation's leading figures, including the CNT general secretary, Evilio Boal. From December in particular prisoners were also moved outside Barcelona. By 1 January 1920 fifty-seven people had suffered this fate (twenty-five of whom were being held outside Catalonia).[92]

At the same time, the lock-out continued unabated. This was producing enormous hardship in working-class quarters. Cats were hunted down and eaten, and workers begged (aggressively) in the streets. Many simply stopped paying rent and the most daring took to eating in restaurants and then simply refusing to pay. It was in this climate that a culture in which small illegal actions would be condoned as legitimate means of redressing exploitation could extend itself in anarchist circles. A sense of strong communal solidarity developed, in which cooperatives played an important role in maintaining a supply of food to workers' families.[93] Yet the CNT was being weakened to a far greater extent than during the repression masterminded by Milans del Bosch earlier in the year. Many less committed workers, who had sometimes been forced to join the CRT in the first place, resented the hardship that they had been forced to endure. The tanner, Joan Ferrer, a young activist at the time, recalled that of all the workers locked-out only about 5,000 actually played an active role in supporting the CNT.[94] This reinforces a point already made; it was an organisation composed of a relatively small core of committed activists which, when conditions were right, mobilised much more widely.

Unfortunately, at the beginning of 1920 conditions were anything but propitious. The Allendesalazar Government finally forced the employers to lift the lock-out on Monday 26 January. It wished to outlaw the CNT but to ensure that this was done on its own terms. The CNT tried to maintain the strike until workers were paid and to prevent any sackings, but many began to go in at the end of the week. In response, in a meeting on 12 February, the CRT took the decision to return to work and leave it to the individual SUs to deal with the situation as they saw best. Faced with overwhelming odds, the organisation had inevitably succumbed to defeat. Many employers imposed individual contracts and sacked the union activists with the result that disputes continued into February. Other workers, bitter at the privations they had had to endure for no benefit, ripped up their union cards. According to Joan Ferrer, only about one third of the membership would continue to pay their dues.[95]

Conclusions

Between 1917 and 1919 the CNT had shown an astonishing capacity to mobilise. This, and the fear it provoked, would, ironically, be at the root of its downfall. Unlike the situation in the summer of 1917, it would not subsequently be in a position to seriously threaten the regime. In 1917 it had both strategically and ideologically maintained a rather ambiguous stance, many of its activists pushing for an anti-capitalist general strike, while its leadership was willing to support some form of transitional liberal democracy in which the CNT and the union movement played a key role. Yet neither option was to be on the table between 1919 and 1923. The growth of labour organisation in Spain, the August general strike, plus the revolutionary challenge in Russia and in central Europe, was pushing elite and much middle-class opinion to the Right. Hence, the broad democratic front of the summer of 1917 could not be re-created, with the result that no democratic transition was viable. At the same time, the anti-capitalist revolutionary road was also blocked. Unlike in Russia, the military remained intact, and the officer class had made it abundantly clear that they would suppress any revolutionary threat.

In these circumstances, the CRT was very quickly thrown onto the defensive. Radicals within the organisations still tried desperately to pursue a revolutionary course, but more moderate figures around Salvador Seguí would, ironically, end up tacitly supporting reforming elements within the administration in order to continue operating in the open. Yet despite Seguí's farsightedness, the objective factors he faced determined that in 1919 he would go down to defeat. The CRT, therefore, went into 1920 in a highly precarious situation. Seguí's hopes of building a powerful organisation that could dominate the Spanish labour movement had suffered a massive setback. Furthermore, the revolutionary tide in Europe had began to recede and the storm clouds of counterrevolution were beginning to gather. To cap these problems, within the ranks of the CRT hard-line anarchist-syndicalists were questioning Seguí's policies and the gunmen were taking hold. It was a context in which holding the movement together and reopening a legal space in which it could operate would prove an enormously difficult task.

Notes

1. See the telegrams that crossed between Milans del Bosch, the Minister of the Interior and Minister of War in Archivo del Conde de Romanones (hereafter, AR), 12/31 (1), and 96/38 (6). The employers' role is discussed in Mauro Bajatierra, *¿Quiénes mataron a Dato?*, 98–103. On Milans del Bosch see Boyd, *Praetorian Politics*, 123. For more details on 'compulsory unionisation' see Chapter Seven, 231–2.
2. Archivo Antonio Maura Montaner (hereafter, AMM), 53/1.
3. *La Correspondencia Militar*, 13, 14, 26 January 1919.
4. The quotation is from the right-wing Catalanist Maurista, Gustavo Peyrá. Peyrá to Rovira, 18 Jan. 1919, AMM 82/29.
5. See, for example, *Segundo congreso patronal de la Confederación Patronal Española, Memoria general*, 13–14.
6. Peyrá to Rovira, 18 Jan. 1918, AMM, 82/29.
7. AR, 12/31 (1). Outrageously, a letter from the civil governor's office (presumably by Rothwos) also suggested that they should take advantage of the suspension of constitutional

guarantees to dismiss the charges against Bravo Portillo, given the 'services he has undertaken in the maintenance of public order'. The court would do this 'on the merest suggestion'. AR, 96/60 (2).

8. A short overview is to be found in Albert Balcells, *El sindicalisme a Barcelona, 1916–1923*. I have also consulted *España Nueva* (hereafter, EN) and used the following accounts: Instituto de Reformas Sociales, *Estadística de huelgas, 1919*, 37–60; Vidiella, 'Lluita', 15–16; Ferrer, *Simó Piera*, 78–96; Lladonosa i Vall-llebrera, *Sindicalistes i llibertaris*, 28–31; Plaja, 'Memorias', 41; Baratech, *Sindicatos libres*, 51–62; Angel Pestaña, in *El Socialista*, 3 Oct. 1919, reproduced in Angel Pestaña, *Trayectoria sindicalista*, 376–412.

9. For which see the telegraphic correspondence between the civil governor, captain-general and the Minister of the Interior in AR, 20/5, 6 and 18. The note by the British Ambassador is in Archivo Histórico Nacional, Gobernación, Serie A (hereafter, AHN), 57/10.

10. EN, 17 March 1919; Sastre y Sanna, *Esclavitud moderna*, 37–8.

11. The letter to Romanones is in AMM, 219/16. This fear of revolution is, for example, expressed in Pedro Güal Villalbí, *Memorias de un industrial de nuestro tiempo*, 163. In my view Fernando del Rey Reguillo exaggerates the impact of terrorism as a causal factor in explaining the construction of the reactionary alliance with the military: see Fernando del Rey Reguillo *Propietarios y Patronos*, 514–25.

12. On the formation of the Barcelona Employers' Federation see Bengoechea, *Organització patronal*, 191–5. First-hand information on employers' attitudes and the employer-military alliance is to be found in Hurtado, *Quaranta anys*, vol. 1, 362–4.

13. On the UMN see Joaquinet Puy, 'La Unión Monárquica Nacional frente al catalanismo de la Lliga, 1918–1923'.

14. See AHN, 57/10, and the speech by Guerra del Río in Diario de las Sesiones de las Cortes (hereafter, DSC), 10 Feb. 1921, 363–7.

15. See the comments by Luis Morote in DSC, 26 Jan. 1920, 2020–2. For the FTN's position see, Arxiu del Foment del Treball Nacional, Llibres d'Actes de la Junta Directiva (hereafter, LAJD), 9 April 1919, 299, and the letter sent to Romanones by leading Catalan businessmen on 9 April in AMM 219/16.

16. For Romanones' rejection of 'compulsory unionisation' see, *Memoria de la Junta Directiva del Fomento del Trabajo Nacional correspondiente al ejercicio próximo pasado del 1919–20*, 32. The increasingly radicalised confrontation between business and the Restoration regime over social legislation is dealt with in Rey Reguillo, *Proprietarios y patronos*, 315–417.

17. See the correspondence between Milans del Bosch and Romanones in AR, 20/5, 98/131 (3), and 96/38 (6).

18. Foix, *Apòstols*, 70; Bueso, *Recuerdos*, 111; Porcel, *Revuelta*, 133.

19. A description of the meeting is to be found in Porcel, *Revuelta*. The quotation is taken from EN, 20 Oct. 1919.

20. Ferrer, *Simó Piera*, 96. The best overall account of the general strike is to be found in Instituto de Reformas Sociales, *Estadística de huelgas, 1919*, 60–84.

21. For the Juntas' views see Peyrá to Rovira, 27 Jan. 1919, AMM, 219/10. The Minister of War affirmed that Morote had agreed only to release prisoners held by the Government without charge: see, AR, 96/38 (12). This was, no doubt strictly true, but syndicalist sources insist that Morote promised to try and convince Milans del Bosch to release his prisoners. It may well have been the case that Seguí originally calculated that given the scale of the victory he could sell the agreement even without every prisoner being released. He then made his remarks regarding the liberty of all prisoners at Las Arenas because he saw it as necessary in order to ensure a return to work and because he hoped that he could prevail on the authorities, faced with a general strike, to release everyone.

22. Jesús Pabón, *Cambó*, vol. 2, *Primera Parte, 1918–1930*, 112; León-Ignacio, *Pistolerismo*, 50–2; González Calleja and Rey Reguillo, *Defensa armada*, 71–103.

23. More details on Bravo Portillo's parapolice force are given in the interview with Doval in Bajatierra, *¿Quiénes mataron?*, 155–6, and Manuel Casal Gómez, *Orígen y actuación de los pistoleros*, 48. Casal Gómez was a police captain employed in Barcelona at the time. On Muntadas and Miró y Trepat see Pestaña, *Lo que aprendí*, vol. 1, 81, and Pestaña, *Terrorismo*, 105. The Barcelona correspondent of *El Sol*, Carlos Madrigal ('Francisco Madrid'),

states that a member of the group, Bernardo Armengol, had told him in early 1920 that Foronda and 'a lawyer of his, a regionalist former minister' (presumably Bertran i Musitu) were involved, and maintains that Bravo Portillo, 'enjoyed the support of the King and of the Marquis of Foronda'. Francisco Madrid, *Ocho meses y un día en el gobierno civil de Barcelona*, 30 and 55. Soledad Bengoechea reproduces a letter from José Pallejá, secretary of the Employers' Federation, which proves they supported the parapolice force. *Organització patronal*, 210–11. Manuel de Burgos y Mazo, Minister of the Interior from July 1919, was also informed that the employers had handed over 35,000 pesetas. *El verano de 1919 en Gobernación*, 462.

24. Rey Reguillo, *Propietarios y patronos*, 639–50; Eduardo González Calleja, *El máuser y el sufragio*, 224; Pestaña, *Terrorismo*, 110.

25. Alfaro Baratech, *Sindicatos Libres*, 57–8.

26. Foix, *Apòstols*, 80.

27. On the employers' actions see, EN, 1 Sept. 1919; Instituto de Reformas Sociales, *Estadística de huelgas, 1919*, 77–84. Milan del Bosch's position is outlined in, LAJD, 1 April 1919, 277–86.

28. Baratech Alfaro, *Sindicatos Libres*, 58–9; Lladonosa i Vall-llebrera, *Sindicalistes i llibertaris*, 41.

29. Key correspondence is to be found in Archivo de Eduardo Dato, 83, and AMM 219/16. See also Doval's own accounts in Bajatierra, *¿Quiénes mataron?*, 155–65, and in AR, 96/60 (2), along with Burgos y Mazo, *Verano*, 456–7.

30. Tusell, *Antonio Maura*, 198–207; Javier Moreno Lujón, 'Partidos y parlamento en la crisis de la Restauración', and Fernando del Rey Reguillo, 'Las voces del antiparlamentarismo conservador', in *Con luz y taquígrafos*, ed. Mercedes Cabrera, 91 and 306.

31. Maura to Milans del Bosch, 23 May 1919, AMM, 361/4; EN, 7, 9, 20 Aug. 1919. The president of the FTN, Jaume Cussó, also supported the maintenance of martial law so that the employers could deal effectively with the CNT: see, LAJD, 9 April 1919, 296–7. Burgos y Mazo and Pestaña gave the unbelievable figures – which have often been repeated – of 43,000 and 45,000 arrested respectively.

32. 'Relación nominal de los prisioneros sentenciados con motivo de los actuales sucesos', in AMM 263/16.

33. EN, 27 July 1919.

34. See Madrid, *Ocho meses*, 26–32; Pestaña, *Lo que aprendí*, vol. 1, 81–5; *El Diluvio*, 12 May 1922. Already by July 1919 the CNT had a very clear idea of the gang's membership and modus operandi: see EN, 24, 25 July, 28 Aug. 1919.

35. Bueso, *Recuerdos*, 119–21; Foix, *Apòstols*, 135–6. See also the reports by government informers in Burgos y Mazo, *Verano*, 353–4.

36. 'Informe sobre el sindicalismo en Barcelona, 8.6.1919', in AR, 96/38 (11); Soledad Bengoechea, *El lockaut de Barcelona, 1919–1920*, 62–4.

37. EN, 15 March 1919; Bueso, *Recuerdos*, 119–21.

38. Pestaña, *Terrorismo*, 110–16; Baratech Alfaro, *Sindicatos Libres*, 60–1. There are portraits of Boal in Buenacasa, *Movimiento obrero*, 62, and 195–9, and, less flatteringly, in Bueso, *Recuerdos*, 159–60. Pestaña states that Boal authorised shootings but gives no date, *Terrorismo*, 195–9.

39. Vidiella, 'Lluita', 18; Bueso, *Recuerdos*, 127; Lladonosa i Vall-llebrera, *Sindicalistes i llibertaris*, 33.

40. Madrid, *Ocho meses*, 54–67; Casal Gómez, *Orígen*, 17–107.

41. See the speeches by Buenacasa and Carbó in Confederación Nacional del Trabajo, *Memoria del congreso celebrado en el Teatro de la Comedia de Madrid, los días 10 al 18 de diciembre de 1919*, 342–4 and 363–7. Quemades and Piera were later to stress that any such dictatorship should be based on the unions. EN, 27 Aug., 23 Oct. 1920.

42. Ferrer, *Simó Piera*, 99–101.

43. 'Informe sobre el sindicalismo'; Meaker, *Revolutionary Left*, 151–3.

44. 'Informe sobre el sindicalismo'.

45. Conservative strategy is discussed in Gómez Ochoa, 'Partido conservador', 278.

46. EN, 7, 8 Aug. 1919.

47. DSC, 6, 7 Aug. 1919, 814–19 and 837–48.
48. For these disputes our major source is EN. See also Gual Villalbí, *Memorias*, 171–80; Marquès i Mir, *Radium*, 53–5; Bengoechea, *Lockaut*, 62–4.
49. For Amado's own testimony see Burgos y Mazo, *Verano*, 479–80. Burgos y Mazo states that there were still 15,000 prisoners, but this was no doubt an exaggeration (p. 461). The text of the agreement is reproduced in EN, 27 Aug. 1919.
50. On these negotiations see Manent i Pesas, *Records*, 255–6; Buenacasa, *Movimiento obrero*, 55–7; Ferrer, *Simó Piera*, 157–73.
51. EN, 6, 7 Sept. 1919.
52. EN, 12 Sept., 4 Oct. 1919.
53. Camil Piñón states that Pestaña had not previously rejected terrorism. This is denied by Pestaña in his memoirs: see, Lladonosa i Vall-llebrera, *Sindicalistes y llibertaris*, 34; Pestaña, *Lo que aprendí*, vol. 1, 72.
54. Sastre y Sanna, *Esclavitud moderna*, 132–6.
55. This was the argument put forward by Severiano Martínez Anido, the commander of the Barcelona garrison during 1919, after the brutal repression he orchestrated between 1921 and 1922: see, 'El señor Martínez Anido habla del problema catalán'. It is echoed in Meaker, *Revolutionary Left*, 342.
56. EN, 29 Sept., 5 Oct. 1919; *Vida Nueva*, 27 April 1922; Santiago Oria, 'Habla Salvador Seguí'.
57. EN, 12 Sept. 1919.
58. Burgos y Mazo, *Verano*, 355; EN, 5 Oct. 1919.
59. Burgos y Mazo has provided us with an inside account: see *Verano*, 196–8 and 317–18. On the threat of a lock-out see González Calleja, *Máuser*, 147–8. The letter to the King is discussed in Rey Reguillo, *Propietarios y patronos*, 799–800. Simó Piera stated subsequently that within the Employers' Federation it was only a group of more liberal small-scale employers really wished to negotiate with the CRT: see Ferrer, *Simó Piera*, 173–5.
60. See the comments by Guerra del Río in DSC, 10 Feb. 1921, 365.
61. For these strikes I have used EN.
62. For the CNT's perspective see the articles by Quemades in EN, 16, 19, 30 Sept. 1919. Details of the employers' actions are given in González Calleja, *Máuser*, 148–51. The warning by Amado is found in Ferrer, *Simó Piera*, 178. Links between the Barcelona garrison and Primo de Rivera are described in Javier Tusell, *Radiografía de un golpe de estado*, 41–3.
63. As well as EN see also the supplement to SO, 22 Nov. 1919. This is unfortunately the only number of the paper we have for these months.
64. For these discussions see the speeches by Lerroux and Cambó in DSC, 4 Feb. 1920, 2260–5, and 6 Feb, 2330. For the FTN's role see the comments by Cussó in LAJD, 16 and 18 Oct. 1919, 387, and, *Memoria de la Junta Directiva del Fomento del Trabajo Nacional ... 1919–1920*, 38. Sedó's role is mentioned in Pabón, *Cambó*, vol. 2, *Primera Parte*, 158.
65. Amado to Burgos y Mazo, 3 Nov. 1919, in AHN, 45/13.
66. Gómez Ochoa, 'Partido conservador', 280; Federación Patronal, 'La federación patronal y el lock out', in the file 'El lock out de Noviembre de 1919', Arxiu Històric de la Cambra de Comerç i Navegació de Barcelona (hereafter, AHCCINB), 657/19. This file contains a very useful collection of press cuttings centred on the lock-out.
67. Bengoechea, *Lockaut*, 68–79; González Calleja, *Máuser*, 155–6. The CRT also stated on 3 November that the employers' aim was to provoke a crisis and the rise to power of 'a reactionary government, a strong-arm government': see the note in AHCCINB, 'El lock out'.
68. For these negotiations see Amado to Burgos y Mazo, 2 and 3 Nov 1919, in AHN, 45/13.
69. Amado to Burgoz y Mazo, 2 Nov. 1919, AHN 45/13; Burgos y Mazo, *Verano*, 500–9; Ferrer, *Simó Piera*, 181.
70. Gual Villalbí, *Memorias*, 163; Amado to Burgos y Mazo, 2 Nov. 1919, AHN, 45/13.
71. See the comments by Felip Rodés in DSC, 27 Jan. 1920, 2064–70.
72. Bengoechea, *Locaut*, 99–122. The 12 November agreement is reproduced in AHCCINB, 'El lock out'. The Employers' Federation was to claim that the agreement foundered because not all the strikes had ended, but Amado correctly pointed to the attitude of employers on the factory gates as the key problem: see Madrid, *Ocho horas*, 43.

73. Graupera to Sánchez de Toca, 22 Nov. 1919, and Amado to Burgos y Mazo, 23 Nov. 1919, in AHN, 45/13.

74. Amado to Burgos y Mazos, 19 and 21 Nov. 1919, AHN, 45/13.

75. Arxiu del Govern Civil de Barcelona (hereafter, AGCB), 269.

76. AGCB, 269.

77. Amado to Burgos y Mazo, 2 Nov. 1919, AHN, 45/13.

78. Civil governor to the Minister of the Interior, 17 Dec. 1919, in AHN, 45/13; *El Trabajo Nacional*, 20 May 1920, 36. The FTN quotation is to be found in, *Memoria de la Junta Directiva del Fomento del Trabajo Nacional ... 1919–1920*, 45–6; the comments by Cambó in, DSC, 3 Feb. 1920, 2235.

79. EN, 3 Dec. 1919.

80. Buenacasa, *Movimiento obrero*, 58; Martínez, *Mártires*, 58–60; Foix, *Apòstols*, 222–4; León-Ignacio, *Pistolerismo*, 98–100; Pestaña, *Lo que aprendí*, vol. 2, 80–3; Sastre y Sanna, *Martirología*, 142–8; Burgos y Mazo, *Verano*, 43–44 and 356–7.

81. *Espartaco*, 15, 31 Oct., 9 Nov, 23 Dec. 1919, 22 Feb. 1920; *Bandera Roja*, 7 Dec. 1919; Martínez, *Mártires*, 56–7; Burgos y Mazo, *Verano,* 356–7; García Oliver, *Eco*, 83, 120–1 and 635; Baratech, *Sindicatos Libres*, 62. The 9 November issue of *Espartaco* is to be found in, AHN, 2/16. Seguí particularly upset the 'pure' anarchists when he asserted, in his Madrid speech on 3 October 1919, that the unions, not the anarchist groups or the Socialists, would build the new society.

82. CNT, *Memoria del congreso*, 9–34. It should in fact have been referred to as the CNT's Third Congress. This has generated a good deal of confusion. For Andalusia see Díaz del Moral, *Agitaciones*, 314–63.

83. CNT, *Memoria del congreso,* 75–172.

84. CNT, *Memoria del congreso*, 340–73.

85. For Dato's stance see AD, 83. On the Government's fall, see Burgos y Mazo, *Verano*, 200–8; Gómez Ochoa, 'Partido conservador', 283; Bengoechea, *Locaut*, 127–9; González Calleja, *Máuser*, 156.

86. Ferrer, *Simó Piera*, 181.

87. Note by the Employers' Federation, 20 Dec. 1919, in AHCCINB, 'El lock out'.

88. CRT and Local Federation, 'A los sindicatos de todos los ramos de todas las poblaciones de Cataluña', 21 Dec. 1919, and Los Comités, 'Manifiesto de los sindicatos', 31 Dec. 1919, in AHCCINB, 'El lock out'.

89. Porcel, *Revuelta*, 121–2; García Oliver, *Eco*, 30–1.

90. *Boletín de la Federación Patronal*, 19 Dec. 1919.

91. On these attacks see Bueso, *Recuerdos*, 129; Sanz, *El Sindicalismo y la política*, 60; Porcel, *Revuelta*, 117. There was also an attempt to assassinate Seguí on 4 January 1920, which was probably carried out by Baron Koëning's gang.

92. AGCB, 270; EN, 7 Jan.–5 Feb. 1920; *El Comunista*, 14 Feb., 13 March 1920.

93. AGCB, 269; Pérez Baró, *Feliços*, 26; Bueso, *Recuerdos*, 123.

94. Pestaña, *Terrorismo*, 162; Porcel, *Revuelta*, 115–22.

95. EN, 29, 30 Jan., 9, 12 Feb., 23 March 1920; Buenacasa, *Movimiento obrero*, 58; Juan Ferrer, *Conversaciones libertarias*, 17–18; Porcel, *Revuelta*, 115–22.

10

THE ROAD TO DICTATORSHIP

The Destruction of the Catalan CNT and the Fall of the Restoration Regime, 1920 to 1923

Under escalating pressure from both the employers and the military, the years between 1920 and 1923 were to see a massive offensive against the CNT. The Restoration regime finally fell in September 1923 and would be replaced by a right-wing dictatorship, which, in the following year, illegalised the CNT. It would not resurface until the dictatorship's fall in 1930. It is on these events that this chapter will focus. Attention will, in the first place, centre on the repressive mechanisms used to undermine the CNT, on the circumstances in which the regime allowed them to be implemented, and on the overall consequences for the Spanish polity. I shall, at the same time, be looking, more specifically, at the consequences for the Catalan CNT itself. As we shall see, it was a dramatic and tragic story in which Seguí's dream of building a powerful syndicalist confederation was lost and with it all hopes of integrating the CNT into state-sponsored collective bargaining. Furthermore, within this context, young hotheads, who did not shy away from shootings and hold-ups, and who championed a mix of urban guerilla warfare and insurrectionism, became increasingly prominent within the organisation.

The Catalan CNT under Allendesalazar, January to May 1920

Following the CNT's illegalisation in January 1920, in Catalonia it had to operate clandestinely until the autumn. In this context divisions within the movement remained deep. Salvador Seguí stayed on as CRT general secretary until July but he and other leading figures, like Piera and Pestaña, had to work in Tarragona province, from where they kept in touch and tried to pass on orders. On the ground, it was very much the young gunmen who were in charge. Ramon Archs was arrested after the Graupera shooting, but many who were determined to wage what was starting to look like an urban guerrilla war against the employers and authorities remained at large. The multiplication of groups of young syndicalists who turned to the gun was encouraged by the fact that a large number of activists were left without work and blacklisted after the employer lock-out. This generated a heartfelt desire for revenge.

Hence the escalation in shootings, which began in response to the lockout, continued. While thirty-four people had been killed and wounded in shootings during 1919, forty-nine suffered the same fate in the first half of 1920. Foremen and employers continued to be targeted. In addition, because increasing numbers of men refused to pay their dues and support industrial action, shootings of recalcitrant workers would also grow rapidly over the year. Finally, there were clashes with Baron Koëning's gang and attacks were launched on a new right-wing and employer-friendly union organisation known as the Sindicatos Libres (Free Trades Unions). Shoot-outs between these rival organisations would, over the next three years, give Barcelona and surrounding industrial towns something of the flavour of the Wild West, with bar staff and clients frequently having to fly for cover in the midst of a hail of gunfire.

As seen in the previous chapter, in the autumn of 1919 the so-called Baron Koëning replaced Bravo Portillo and took up the fight against the CNT. The group's most spectacular action also highlighted its limitations. On 23 April a turncoat within the CNT's ranks laid a trap for one of its action groups and in the ensuing gun battle Progreso Ródenas, the brother of the female anarchist textile union organiser, Libertad Ródenas, was wounded. However, one of the Baron's most active operatives, Bernat Armengol, the former secretary of the Woodworkers' SU, was also imprisoned and subsequently abandoned by his protectors. While in prison, to save his skin he confessed, giving the CNT a very precise knowledge of the Baron's gang and its procedures. This allowed the CNT journalist, Antonio Amador, to write a pamphlet denouncing its activities and made it possible for the organisation's gunmen to launch an offensive. On 28 April, another shoot-out left a CNT gunman and a member of the Koëning gang wounded. Over the following two months the action groups would be much more successful, gunning down three members of the gang. It was these events, together with the revelation that Koëning had actually been behind the blackmail of several employers, that led the Dato Government to expel him from the country in the June 1920.[1]

Much more important, in the long term, would be the growth of the Sindicatos Libres and it is, therefore, worth focusing on them in some detail. The Libres were officially founded on 19 October 1919 by a group of workers with links to Carlism. In Barcelona and some other Catalan towns they began building a small union base during 1920. They were favoured by employers, who gave members of the Libres jobs at the expense of the CNT activists, and, with the disappearance of the Koëning group, some industrialists also took to using Libres as bodyguards. This, not surprisingly, led the CNT to declare that they were simply a 'yellow' Catholic union in the service of the employers and the state.

Recent research has, however, allowed a more complex picture to emerge. It is the contention of Colin Winston that the Libres were born independently. The founders, he points out, largely comprised working-class Carlists, who had adopted a reactionary populist ideology, which vaguely called capitalism into question and justified worker demands. Although, de-Christianisation had proceeded apace in Barcelona, groups of workers who maintained the Catholic faith were by no means absent in the city, and were replenished by migration from the peasant interior. Some Carlists had previously joined the CNT, but rebelled against the anarchist-syndicalist tutelage. They were then able to construct their own alternative in a context in which the CNT had alienated large numbers of workers in the course of the great conflicts of 1919.[2]

However, the most accurate picture is probably to be found somewhere between the claims of the CNT activists and Winston's revisionist position. As Soledad Bengoechea has shown, a military commander, Bartolomé Roselló, had originally taken the initiative to found the Libres in February 1919, although on this occasion it did not bear fruit. It seems likely that this move met with the approval of Milans del Bosch, Martínez Anido and the Barcelona garrison. A nexus was provided by the Liga Patriótica Española, in which Carlist workers, including the future head of the Libres, Ramon Salas, were highly active.[3]

Although there is no documentary proof, the indications are that the military played a role in the Libres final launch in October. Moreover, as Winston recognises, at first relations between the Libres and the Employers' Federation were close, and they were not involved in any industrial disputes. There is no concrete evidence of employer funding, but it would certainly be no surprise to learn that they provided financial aid. With respect to the state, the Sánchez de Toca administration showed no sympathy, but under Allendesalazar, through the Barcelona delegate for labour affairs, Pere Roselló, they were given preferential treatment. Nor is it true that the Libres' unions were totally independent. There were a number of foremen in their ranks, as we have seen, a strata of workers who worked closely with the employers. Furthermore, their largest union, the waiters, had 'protecting affiliates'. As seen in the case of the Ateneus Obrers, these were wealthier citizens who supported the organisation by paying dues. To sum up, while it seems that impetus to form the Libres was in part autonomous, elements within the military along with the Employers' Federation were also to use them to weaken the CNT.[4]

The appearance of the Libres was to lead to a new cycle of violence. The offensive was launched by CNT gunmen, who murdered one of the Libres' founders, Tomàs Vives – a foreman in Fabra i Coats – at the beginning of April 1920. Four more members of the Libres were to fall in the following three months. The justification was that they were simply tools in the hands of the employers. Yet the Libres were far from willing to take these attacks lying down. Within Carlist ideology, as seen in Chapter Nine, there was a strong militarist component, and they now began to spawn their own gunmen. Until November the CNT gunmen still retained the upper hand;

between April and October only one CNT activist was shot dead by members of the Libres as against seven members of the Libres murdered by the CNT's action groups. This was to lead to a meeting in November in which the possibility of winding the organisation up was considered but finally rejected.[5]

The new spiral of violence appalled the CRT union leadership, who in the spring tried to retake control. In order to achieve this end, Seguí called a clandestine assembly of 300 union delegates on 18 March, including members of the action groups. Amongst those present was Angel Pestaña, who was informed by Seguí that he had been chosen by the CNT National Committee to go to Russia to report on the revolution along with Carbó and Quemades. No doubt under Seguí's guidance, the decision was taken not to undertake any revolutionary activities which they might later regret and to put an end to terrorism.[6] The problem would be that in the present climate neither he nor his lieutenants had much leverage over the action groups.

The Dato–Bas Opening, May to November 1920

Despite these difficulties, the anarchist-syndicalist leadership could hope that with the fall of Allendesalazar and his replacement, on 5 May, by an administration under Eduardo Dato, matters might improve. As already noted, amongst Dato's supporters there were elements who favoured dialogue. These included the social reformer Francisco Bergamín, who became Minister of the Interior. In addition, the Government showed its concern for social problems by setting up a Ministry of Labour.

Throughout the following months it seemed unsure of its step. At first the CNT remained illegal, but sensing a new political alignment it began to press for the release of its prisoners and to be allowed to reopen. In mid-May it announced that it was to undertake a campaign of meetings. At the same time, the 450 prisoners still held in the Barcelona Modelo prison decided to launch a hunger strike. This called forth a remarkable reaction from the city's female textile workers. On 21 May large numbers of them downed tools and formed large groups, who marched through the city demanding freedom for the 'governmental prisoners'. By mid-day about 10,000 had congregated outside the prison walls. In the afternoon there were new demonstrations, with a group of women finally being allowed in to see the civil governor. These actions again draw our attention to the linkages between the female and male workers. Many of those imprisoned were, of course, the sons, husbands and fathers of the women, and their arrest brought not only emotional distress but also great economic hardship to many working-class homes. The organisation was also able to launch a number of either twenty-four or forty-eight hour strikes to protest at detentions in Barcelona, Manresa and Sabadell, centred on textiles, in late May.[7]

These strikes and demonstrations showed that despite the severe repression suffered by the Catalan CNT over the previous six months working-class resistance still had considerable vitality. But the organisation was no longer strong enough to shake the authorities off course. With gatherings in Catalonia banned, they were only able to hold one meeting in Madrid on 27 May, and the strikes and protests fizzled out from the end of the month. Yet the decision to replace the Count of Salvatierra as civil governor by the more flexible figure of Federico Carlos Bas in late June did indicate that the Government was contemplating some kind of controlled opening. Bas was a friend of Cambó and close to the leading Madrid daily *El Sol*. This meant that through its Barcelona offices, and particularly Carlos Madrigal, he could contact the anarchist-syndicalists.[8] In the following three months, rather like Julio Amado in the previous year, he was to develop a good working relationship with Seguí's 'team'. Constitutional guarantees remained suspended but the 'governmental prisoners' were quickly released, with only sixty remaining by early August. Large meetings also remained banned but individual unions also began to operate more freely.

Seguí and his supporters hoped to use this chink of light to bring the CRT to the surface. Even though he had stepped down as its general secretary in July he remained the key figure in determining strategy. His focus was, as one would expect, on the need to rebuild the organisation. In defiance of the resolution at the CNT's Second Congress to declare the UGT 'yellow' if it did not enter the CNT, from August he again tried to ally with the Socialist union. Along with considerations outlined in previous chapers, such an alliance, he probably hoped, would provide greater protection against government repression. With the left-wing current still strong in the UGT's ranks, in its June 1920 congress it renewed its agreement to work towards unity with the CNT. The CNT National Committee, as was to be expected, at first expressed little interest, but in the wake of the fall of Bergamín, the reform-minded Minister of the Interior, on 30 August, Seguí persuaded the CNT general secretary, Evilio Boal, to accompany him, with Quemades, to Madrid to reach a new pact with the UGT. It was signed on 2 September. The joint manifesto stated that its short-term aim was to fight for the reestablishment of constitutional guarantees, which had been suspended throughout Spain since March 24 1919, but that they would also discuss the question of unity. Furthermore, it echoed the interclass language of July 1917, asserting that although enemies of bourgeois society, 'we have become the defenders of its laws'.[9]

Over the following two months the Government began to authorise union meetings in Catalonia. A big syndicalist meeting was held on 14 September – the first since the Allendesalazar repression – demanding the reestablishment of constitutional guarantees and the release of the remaining prisoners. Joint Socialist-syndicalist meetings were then held in Barcelona, Madrid and Bilbao between late September and November. Again, the emphasis was on the right to operate openly, although this was accompanied by references on the need to cooperate in the future revolutionary process. One of the Barcelona speakers, Julián Martínez, stressed the example of the factory take-overs in Italy. Yet the Barcelona local federation sounded a very conciliatory note, stating that 'we want a period of peace', although, it maintained, supposed Libre violence was making this difficult.[10] Simultaneously, Seguí made favourable noises with respect to unification. For all syndicalists the *sine qua non* was that the new organisation should be independent of any political party, but Quemades (who was now strongly in favour of unification) stated that within it he envisaged there being two main tendencies, 'a party of government .... And another critical and oppositional [party]'. Hence, given the weakness of the CNT, figures close to Seguí now recognised that a unified confederation could not operate under libertarian tutelage. Seguí still maintained that the unions would lead the revolution, but his close colleague, Simó Piera, argued that such a body would not be 'specifically Socialist, syndicalist or anarchist'.[11] This was very much the language of the CGT's Chartre d'Amiens.

This outraged both the most orthodox anarchist-syndicalists, like Buenacasa, and the young gunmen within the action groups. Seguí had in fact resigned as CRT general secretary in the heat of the debates over whether to sign a new pact. Around the same time he was 'judged' in one of the workers' centres by a group of young radicals and stayed away from union meetings for some time.[12] Discontent over the pact then led to the celebration of a CNT plenary in Catalonia at the end of October. Here it seems that while most of the Spanish delegates were hostile, Seguí and his Catalan colleagues were able to hold off any public criticism. He was also faced with renewed calls for revolutionary action. A massive strike, led by local anarchist-syndicalists, had blown up in the Río Tinto mines near Huelva in Andalusia, raising revolutionary hopes. In the plenary there was talk of occupying the mines. Once again, however, Seguí was able to diffuse that situation, with the agreement that he should visit the mines and liaise with the UGT (which was dominant overall in the mining sector) *in situ*.[13]

Seguí's position was, therefore, under threat from the anarchist and anarchist-syndicalist Left. It was further weakened because, unlike the situation in late 1919, the CNT's return to the surface was not accompanied by any abatement in the number of shootings. Between 1 July and 8 November, twenty-five people were killed and another sixty wounded, including five employers and four foremen. All indications are that the action groups were now totally embedded within the organisation and outside the control of the CRT leadership. For the Government it must have seemed as if matters were running out of control.

This perception was heightened by the assassination of the former civil governor of Barcelona, the Count of Salvatierra, in Valencia on 4 August. While the demise of the man who had orchestrated the repression of the first half of the year may have been viewed with sympathy in CNT circles, the murder of a member of the Spanish nobility strengthened support for repression in elite circles outside Catalonia.[14] Perhaps not unrelatedly, during August the Government gave way to lobbying by Catalan industrialists to suspend trial by jury. Then, at the beginning of September, as already noted, Bergamín was replaced as Minister of the Interior by Count Galino Bugallal, a well-known hardliner. Although the Government's stance did not immediately change, the likelihood of a new crackdown was much increased. Tension was further maintained by the continued explosion of small bombs in the city: twenty-seven such devices had gone off between January and March and, after a lull, another fifteen exploded between July and October. Most of these incidents were linked to industrial disputes, although there were instances in which they seem simply to have been left in the street. No doubt the activists who planted them believed that by intimidating the industrialists they could force them to submit. Operating at a local level, they did not factor in the broader political impact of their actions.

The most mysterious bombing took place on 12 September in the Pompeya, a popular Fifth District music hall, leaving six dead and eighteen badly wounded. The reaction in Barcelona was of horror and outrage. The CRT's local federation denied any involvement and all the organisation's committees issued a statement repudiating terrorism. Up to 150,000 people, mostly workers, attended the funeral procession, including all the leading CRT figures.[15] However, syndicalist sources later revealed that the person who planted the bomb was, Inocencio Feced, a young anarchist, originally from Huesca, who was working for the local federation.[16] It was such events which, despite syndicalist denials, firmly established the linkage between the CNT and terrorism in the minds of much of elite and middle-class society, and even, to a degree, amongst sectors of the working-class, swelling the number of those who would view its suppression and a return to 'peace' and 'order' with satisfaction.[17]

Tensions further increased because industrial strife began to grow from the late autumn. As repression eased, the anarchist-syndicalists showed that they still retained a considerable ability to mobilise within the city's key industrial sectors. They were aided by the fact that, although 1920 saw an economic downturn, Catalan industry had not yet been hit by a severe economic crisis. As in the past, activists used coercion. In construction, for example, workers who had stopped paying their dues were subject to heavy fines if they wanted to work. The SU justified this because of the money needed to support its prisoners.[18] A major conflict blew up amongst the carters in mid-September. Bas's response was similar to that of Amado before him. He set up a committee of employer and worker representatives, over which he himself presided, and managed to force a solution. Much more serious was a strike which broke out in the metal industry after the SU presented demands for across-the-board wage increases it had first made the previous year.

Again industrialists took an intransigent line. The dispute provided the Employers' Federation with the opportunity, in Bas's words, to 'take the battle' to the CNT.[19] The CRT leadership did not wish to declare an industry-wide strike. Sectors of the metal industry were already in crisis and they were uncertain that they could win. However, as was so often the case, they were pushed on by rank-and-file frustration and by radicalised activists. At first, the strike committee brought the three worst paid sections out one by one, but on 20 October it declared a general strike across the industry. It then brought out metalworkers employed by the textile factories, railroad workshops and on the trams, with the result that by the end of the month other sectors of Barcelona industry were coming to a standstill. Subsequently, it threatened to extend the dispute to the rest of the province. The Employers' Federation once again railed against the CNT, accusing the carters' and metalworkers' strikes of being revolutionary in intent. This was denied by Quemades, though a statement by Francisco Arín, the president of the Metalworkers' SU, that if the 'metal magnates' did not negotiate they might have to imitate their Italian colleagues and occupy the factories, did rather play into their hands.[20]

Nevertheless, the Government at first agreed to negotiate. On 30 October, workers and employers were called on to name twelve representatives each to hold discussions under the presidency of the under secretary of the new Ministry of Labour, José Joro Miranda, the Count of Altea. In some respects this looked rather like a replay of events in late 1919, and, as can be imagined, within the Catalan CNT there was great opposition. Yet Seguí was able to confirm his standing within the Barcelona organisation when, in a meeting on the night of 31 October, he played a leading role in convincing those present to participate in the discussions. Yet that very night the president of the Association of Electrical Industries, Jaume Pujol, was assassinated. This was without doubt the work of an action group. Whether or not it was aimed at putting pressure on the industrialists or actually undermining the position of Seguí, the result was to strengthen the hand of hardliners in the military and Employers' Federation.

He was the second employer who had been murdered during the dispute and the industrialists now refused to negotiate. Subsequently, the major business associations sent the Prime Minister a telegram lamenting the Government's supposed indifference in the face of 'crime and terror'.[21] In addition, they put as much pressure as possible on the King and Government to have Bas replaced by a military figure. The person they had in mind was the governor of the Barcelona garrison, Severiano Martínez Anido, who had replaced Milans del Bosch (who had been forced to step down in February 1920) as their saviour in waiting. It was a role in which he felt comfortable. Along with another military general, at the beginning of November, he had presented a horrified Bas with the list of eighty syndicalists whom he wanted to see either shot or deported. Meanwhile Cambó, who was now convinced of the need for an thorough-going repression of the CNT, met with Dato, while the Marquis of Foronda held discussions with the King.[22]

As early as 3 November, the metalworkers' committee sounded a note of alarm, revealing that through 'a reliable source' they had been alerted that an all-out assault on the organisation was being planned. This source was Carlos Madrigal, who had contacted Seguí. In response, Seguí and his supporters were able to impose themselves and negotiate an end to the dispute, even though this meant largely accepting the employers' terms. Intense negotiations were held by the strike committee and Seguí with the Count of Altea and Bas in the Ritz Hotel, at which they accepted the employers' offer of a small pay rise and the Government's promise to sponsor the formation of a committee of experts who would look at wages in the industry. The local federation explicitly acknowledged that they had given way in order to 'make fail unspeakable plans to exterminate us'. This was the position taken in a meeting of the strikers held on Sunday 7 November, which successfully argued for a return to work on the following day.[23]

The Martínez Anido Repression,
November 1920 to October 1922

It was, however, too late. The city's political and cultural elites held a meeting on 5 November in which they demanded Bas's resignation. In response he stood down and was replaced by Martinez Anido on 8 November. In an echo of events after the fall of Amado, Bas then called leading anarchist-syndicalists into his office to voice his concern at what was about to occur.[24] Seguí still tried to maintain the organisation in the open. On his way to Río Tinto he stopped off in Madrid on 13 November and attempted to contact Dato, but was rebuffed. The cards had, in fact, already been dealt. On being offered the appointment Martínez Anido demanded and was given virtual *carte blanche* to destroy the CNT through any means he saw fit. As a result, over the next two years Catalonia was basically to function as an autonomous military dictatorship within the Spanish liberal state.

Martínez Anido was quick to claim that he aimed to decapitate the terrorist hydra and there is little doubt that CNT gun attacks had both radicalised the military's stance and made the mass repression that followed justifiable. For men like Martínez Anido, a gruff barrack-room general who had made his name in the colonies, the experience of anti-insurgency campaigns made ruthless solutions thinkable. As he bluntly stated on taking up his post: 'I have worked in Cuba and the Philippines. I should have been in Africa. The Government decided to send me to Barcelona and I will act as through I were on active service'.[25] CNT activists, the implication was, were to be treated like anti-colonial rebels.

Mass detentions and searches of union headquarters began as soon as Martínez Anido came to power. Seguí himself was apprehended when he returned from Andalusia on 22 November, and the labour lawyer and leading figure within the PRC, Lluís Companys, followed on 28 November.[26] But it soon became clear that there were other arrows in Anido's repressive bow. The last day of November would see the inauguration of a policy of both sending activists to jail outside Catalonia and military-sponsored assassinations. During the day rumours circulated that a number of leading anarchist-syndicalists were to be imprisoned on the island of Fernando Po. Fearing that Companys would be among them, his wife asked the Sabadell MP, Francesc Layret, to intercede in his favour. As Layret left his home that evening with Companys' wife to pick up the mayor of Barcelona, before going on to see Martínez Anido, he was gunned down. Later that evening, thirty-five leading syndicalists, including Seguí, along with Companys, set sail for the military fortress of Mahón on Menorca.

All the indications are that the murder was organised by Martínez Anido together with the Libres, with the funding provided by 'Muntadas'.[27] As noted in Chapter Six, from 1913 some industrialists appear to have started funding a 'dirty war' against the CNT. We also know that there were contacts between the Libres and the military from 1919, which were to strengthen as soon as Martínez Anido came to power. The indications are that this funding now began to be challenged to the Libres via the captain-generalship. There were probably two interrelated motives for the murder of Layret. On the one hand, according to Artigas, the former director of the Barcelona Modelo prison, military figures close to Martínez Anido regarded Layret as the 'soul of syndicalism', and believed that only by taking out its top echelon could the organisation be decapitated.[28] Elements within the business community no doubt held similar views. On the other hand, as shown in the previous chapter, Layret had outraged military opinion through his speeches in the Spanish parliament, attacking the army's political interventionism.

Controversially, it has been suggested that before Layret's death Seguí was contemplating allying with him and taking the Catalan CNT into the political arena.[29] As seen in Chapter Eight, the PRC – with Layret at the head – aimed to create a Catalan workers and peasants' party based on the CNT rank and file. Yet, despite Seguí's friendship with Layret, until Martínez Anido became civil governor there is no evidence that the anarchist-syndicalist leadership had considered any such move. The suggestion that CNT members participate in elections had first been mooted by Marcel·lí Domingo in April 1919, two months before the general elections, but he was quickly rebuffed by the CNT National Committee. This was ratified by Seguí, who, in typical syndicalist terms, argued that the 'useless' electoral process was being eclipsed by the CNT.[30]

With elections again due in December 1920, rumours once again began to surface that the Catalan CNT was to put candidates forward. At the end of October this was denied by Simó Piera in a big meeting of the Metalworkers' SU with Seguí present.[31] However, the rise of Martínez Anido certainly saw a change of gear. Layret was planning to form an electoral alliance, called the Proletarian Union, which included the PRC, the Socialists and figures within the Catalan CNT. Although moderates grouped around Largo Caballero retained control of the UGT, radicals in favour of the Third International had taken over the PSOE's National Committee following the party's Twelfth congress held in June 1920 and they seem to have been willing to sanction such a pact in Catalonia. Two leading members of the PSOE's executive committee, Antonio García Quejido and Ramón Lamoneda, were in Barcelona to discuss the plan when he was assassinated. He held discussions with them on 29 November and then held a meeting with Seguí and Companys in the Modelo prison on the morning of the following day. He then met up with García Quejido and Lamoneda, who were in his house when he was murdered.[32]

There is no concrete evidence as to how far Seguí was willing to go. He would have known that his candidature would have irredeemably split the CNT. Moreover, there is no evidence that, at any point in his life, he abjured his anarchist-syndicalist views. Hence the most accurate portrait is probably that of Simó Piera, who later stated that while Seguí would not have entered the political arena he may well have given Layret support from outside.[33] This fitted with Seguí's longer-term vision. He aimed to forge a unified syndicalist movement as the major revolutionary force in Spain, but had no problem in discretly working with political parties when he saw this as necessary and positive. As it was, any chance of building a coalition was undermined by the repression. When the elections finally took place on 19 December in Barcelona, only 29 percent of the electorate voted. This represented by far the lowest turnout since 1905. Clearly, by this time few people believed that the major political parties could deal with the city's problems.[34]

Following the death of Layret and deportation of Seguí, repression further intensified. It was made more effective by the high level of coordination between the officers of the captain-generalship, the police (under Manuel Arlegui, a colonial veteran and a colonel in the Civil Guard) and the Sometent's Office for Special Services. Informers in the pay of both the police and Sometent, and the latter's file of CNT suspects, were used to carry out arrests and provide gunmen with the information necessary to launch attacks. Two informers and agent provocateurs who operated within CNT ranks, the labour lawyer, Pere Mártir Homs, and Inocencio Feced, were particularly important.[35]

The repression took several main forms. First, detentions of CNT activists continued unabated. These focused on everyone who had held a union post, however small, within the Catalan CNT. It is impossible to know how many workers were arrested in all, but by the spring the figure was probably over 1,000.[36] Many more fled Barcelona, with, ironically, 200 ending up in the Spanish Foreign Legion in Morocco.[37] A number of leading anarchist-syndicalists were held in Montjuïc. These included Angel Pestaña, who was picked up on 17 December after he had returned from Russia. However, the authorities were quickly confronted with the problem of where to house the rest. This was, at least in part, the root of the decision taken in mid-December, to put into practice a policy of mass internal deportation to prisons distant from Barcelona. Moreover, it had the additional advantages that it broke any link between the union activists and the rank and file. Each week, groups of about forty men, half common and half political prisoners, were taken out of the Modelo prison and marched on foot (*conducción ordinaria*) to remote parts of the territory where they were held in jails at the government's pleasure. Banishment had been used before (most notably after Tragic Week, when a policy of internal exile was implemented) but never on this scale. It was a degrading and gruelling ordeal. The men were tied and had to walk to their destination, usually between four pairs of civil guards. They walked 60 kilometres a day, and were handed on to a new group of civil guards half way through each stage. For food they were given just 50 céntimos a day. Luckily, in more liberal areas they received the support of workers from the local unions and cooperatives, who would provide them with additional food and visit them. Many ended up in small towns in backward provinces like Teruel, Cuenca and Guadalajara. Overall, about three quarters of the CNT activists imprisoned were affected.[38]

Most of these workers were never tried, but with trial by jury curtailed and constitutional guarantees still suspended convictions became far easier. This was further aided because, for the first time since the Montjuïc trial, under the supervision of Arlegui, torture was widely used in police cells. He was by all accounts a violent and cruel man, who did not disdain from actively participating. In addition, there was widespread complicity within the legal system.

Accordingly, 1921 would see a steady stream of CNT activists convicted of assassination (and two syndicalists from Sabadell executed). By May 1922, 145 had been prosecuted and were awaiting trial.[39]

Even more shocking than the forced marches, after the death of Layret the authorities stepped up their 'dirty war' against the CRT. Their preferred instrument were gunmen close to the Libres, who enjoyed the support of the military, police and Sometent. This included both the provision of arms and documentation, and police back-up after assassinations. Indeed, in order to maintain their cover some were actually integrated into the Sometent.[40] Inocencio Feced was later to claim that payment for their activities came from the employers. Miró i Trepat and 'Muntadas' acted as the key go-betweens in Barcelona, although employers from a particular area on occasion paid for the murder of someone on their patch. In addition, the car-manufacturers, La Hispano Suiza, also maintained their own hit squad.[41]

This led to a dramatic rise in the number of shootings of CNT activists. Out of a total of twenty-seven workers shot dead and seventy wounded between 1 January 1919 and 9 November 1920, I have only been able to positively identify six (possibly seven) CNT activists assassinated and thirteen wounded. Until this date, it is clear, most of the attacks were carried out by the CNT action groups. However, between 10 November 1920 and 18 January 1921, at least six CNT activists were killed and nine wounded, almost all by the Libres. Moreover, a dynamic of attack and counterattack was established, leading the authorities further to radicalise their methods. On 19 January the police inspector, Antonio Espejo 'Espejito', the chief of the Special Brigade, was gunned down by a CNT action group. He was a corrupt former member of the Bravo Portillo and Koëning gangs, but was close to Arlegui. In response, the police and military instituted what came to be known as the *ley de fugas*, whereby CNT prisoners were shot 'trying to escape'.[42] It was not, as CNT sources later indicated, almost a daily occurrence, but there were a number of instances. The first to suffer this fate were four activists from Valencia, who were detained on 18 January and accused of being behind the murder of the Count of Salvatierra, and of coming up to Barcelona to plan the assassination of Martínez Anido and Arlegui. Only one survived to tell the tale. Over the next four days the same procedure was applied to nine more CNT activists, of whom seven were killed outright. Four of these were accused of murdering 'Espejito' and two were caught preparing an assassination attempt on Martínez Anido at the former's funeral.[43] The procedure continued to be used on occasion through to the end of June. At least seven more CNT members were killed in this way, and two more were left for dead but survived.[44]

A variant on this theme was used to eliminate the general secretary of the CNT, Evelio Boal. He had been arrested on 3 March, and on 17 June, along with the CNT treasurer, Antoni Feliu, he was freed in the dead of night. Gunmen were, however, waiting around the corner to shoot them down. After these events activists refused to leave the prison at night and family members camped outside the prison gates. Given the bad publicity generated, there were no further cases between the end of June and the last day of Martínez

Anido's reign in Barcelona. Nevertheless, it seems that several activists were subsequently murdered and then dumped in the sea.[45]

Meanwhile Libre attacks continued unabated. The first half of 1921 was to see an intense offensive designed to spread terror in the CNT's ranks and eliminate the organisation's own gunmen. Thus from 19 January through to the end of June, excepting the cases of the *ley de fugas* mentioned above, at least forty-eight syndicalists were gunned down and killed, and another twenty-five wounded. With the organisation virtually dismantled, attacks would, thereafter, continue on a much reduced scale, with another ten activists killed and three wounded in the second half of the year.[46] In addition, labour lawyers were both intimidated and targeted, with the Lerrouxists, Josep Lastra and Josep Ulled, shot and wounded in April. Overall, with the CNT making desperate attempts to strike back, a total of 113 persons were killed and 95 wounded over the course of 1921. This made it easily the most violent year in post-war Catalonia.

The CNT was enormously weakened by these events. The number of union activists was decimated and the collection of dues strictly outlawed, with the result that the organisation found it impossible to support all of its prisoners. This encouraged a new departure: the use of robberies in order to replenish its coffers. The gunmen were paid for their services and, on one occasion at least, kept part of the booty, and this helped to further professionalise them and create a separate strata within the CNT.[47] Matters were made worse for the CNT by the fact that a full-blown recession hit Catalan industry from the end of 1920, further increasing the power of employers on the shop floor. Hence, during the year the number of strikes plummeted and, in the key sectors of textiles, the metal industry and transport, unemployment rose rapidly.[48]

The generational and political composition of the CNT was also drastically recast. Only a few more experienced activists remained free, with the result that the organisation increasingly fell into the hands of youngsters of between about fifteen and twenty-one years of age. Seguí and his supporters were not inactive, trying to develop contacts with Liberal and republican politicians in order to negotiate their return to the surface. Seguí, in a letter to someone seemingly close to the Liberal party, assured him that if the CNT were legalised there would be no resurgence of terrorism and that they would remove the 'irreflective elements and some low-down adventurers who have, most directly, led us to the present situation'.[49] He was supported by Pestaña, who for the first time openly admitted that there had been links between the CNT unions and gunmen and stated that this must stop.[50]

But they were very much out of touch with feelings on the ground in Barcelona. The murder of Layret and deportations to La Mola were met by a general strike. It was remarkably successful, but inevitably faltered when troops were brought onto the streets on 7 December.[51] The repression also resulted in links with the UGT being severed. The CNT National Committee called for the UGT to support a general solidarity strike and when it refused accused it of 'manifest betrayal' and broke off the pact.[52] This emphasised the distance which separated the CNT and UGT. Despite the fact that leftist *terceristas* had briefly taken over the executive of the PSOE, the UGT was still in the hands of figures such as Largo Caballero, who were not about to risk its integrity by seconding such a strike. The gulf was widened by the jailing of Seguí and most of his followers, which allowed hardliners within the CNT, who had always opposed the pact, to engineer its demise.

On a strategic plane, the strike again emphasised the limitations of a weapon on which so much hope had been laid. If employers and authorities were prepared to sit it out solidarity had finally to crumble. Perhaps envisaging this outcome the CNT's general secretary, Evelio Boal, who at first managed to evade capture, gave the green light for insurrectionary activities. Most determined in following up this advice was Joan García Oliver, a young union activist and gunman from Reus. Like many youngsters from small-town Catalonia, he had migrated to Barcelona as a teenager and gravitated towards the CNT. He helped unionise the waiters, became involved in anarchist cultural activities, and then, in 1919, integrated into an 'action group', which used strong-arm tactics to maintain a big strike of cooks and waiters', finally ending up in prison. In the spring of 1920, upon being released, he was sent back to Reus by the CNT to help organise workers in Tarragona province, and here he would link up with gunmen working for the organisation. Following an interview with Boal and Martí Barrera, he then tried to set off an uprising in the area. It was a total failure, whose ineptitude puts one in mind of similar adventures launched by the anarchist umbrella group, the FAI, during the Second Republic.[53] But the shift to an insurrectionary strategy was indicative of the fact that opposition to the state through union organisation was no longer a viable option.

The rise of Martínez Anido also had another effect. Virtually no one who remained free would now oppose terrorism. Rage and bitterness engendered a desire for revenge at all costs. Once his intentions became clear, the CNT agreed to respond by a number of high-profile assassinations. It was the youngsters in the action groups who made the running. The key figures were the metalworkers, Ramon Archs (released from prison when Bas took over), who became the general secretary of the CRT in March 1921, and Pere Vandellós. As in the case of Archs, Vandellós's father had been executed in the 1890s, and his son had had almost certainly been involved in terrorist activities since the time of the First World War. They restructured the action groups, which were formed along neighbourhood lines and held their own separate meetings, and built a network of bombers. However, the few older activists not already captured also participated. These included Medi Martí, an important figure in dyers' trade unionism; the carpenter Joan Pey, who had acted as the organisation's treasurer and who, despite being a friend of Seguí, had already, it seems, been involved in planning bombings; and the metalworker, Genaro Minguet, a veteran of the Teatro Español *tertulia*, who had married a cousin of Seguí's.[54] Recourse to the gun and the bomb became a central feature of these years. Although there were, no doubt, professionalised gunmen of dubious ideological commitment in the organisation's ranks (whose names are very illusive), a key feature of war-time and post-war Barcelona was the emergence of gunmen who was also insurrectionists and committed anarchist activists. In fact, anyone close to the organisation who remained free would find it difficult not to become involved in some way or another in terrorist activities.

An early initiative of Archs and Vandellós was the murder of the police inspector, 'Espejito'. However, top of the list were, not suprisingly, Martínez Anido, and the Prime Minister, Eduardo Dato. The assassination of Dato was planned by Archs and entrusted to an action group which operated within the metal industry. After meticulous planning he was shot dead from a motorcycle and side-car while being driven home along Madrid's Alcalá Street on 8 March 1921. The police, however, would soon be on the perpetrators' trail. One of those involved, Pere Matheu, was captured on 13 March and a second participant, Lluís Nicolau, would be picked up along with his girlfriend in Berlin several months later. This left only one of the team, Ramon Casanelles (who ended up in Russia), and a mystery figure who had helped stalk Dato, free.[55] As might have been expected, it made no difference to government policy. The Maurista, Manuel Allendesalazar, took over as Prime Minister and kept Martínez Anido in post. The same policy was followed by the 'government of national unity', headed by Maura, which included Cambó and the former head of the Barcelona Sometent, Bertran i Musitu, and came to power in September 1921, after the appalling military catastrophe at Annual in northern Morocco in which around about 9,000 Spanish soldiers were massacred.

Various unsuccessful plots were hatched to murder Martínez Anido. In addition, during 1921, several teams of bombers also began to operate. The most important was the group centred on the lovers Vicenç Salas and Roser Benavent, whose flat in Toledo Street in Sants became a bomb-making factory. Their most daring action was the failed attempt to blow up the authorities present at a review of the Sometent, on 24 March, with a taxi equipped with a home-made mortar. Their limitations were confirmed on 2 May when they blew themselves up while assembling bombs in their flat. Through interrogating the survivors the police learned much about the CNT's terrorist apparatus. Furthermore, the presence of informers in CNT ranks further undermined the organisation. On 27 and 28 May the authorities managed to capture Ramon Archs and Pere Vandellós. Both were tortured in police custody before being assassinated.[56]

Hence, by the end of June 1921, the CNT's terrorist apparatus had largely been dismantled, and in subsequent months Martínez Anido was able to boast that he had brought peace to the citizens of Barcelona. The number of shootings and bombings was rapidly to decline from this month. Yet the price was high. Quite apart from the issue of the morality of the methods employed, as has been stressed, a subculture was being consolidated within CNT ranks, based on the action group, whose modus operandi would be the bomb, the gun and violent insurrection. As experience in other contexts has shown, once this occurs, its transmission from one generation to the next is difficult to break, even if the socio-political context in which it first took root should change. The problem of CNT insurrectionism would plague the Second Republic in the 1930s.[57]

The crisis of the CNT and the persecution of its activists provided the opportunity for rival organisations to make inroads. Although they were not actively persecuted it was not a gap that the Socialists could fill. In the summer of 1922, they claimed the modest figure of 19,000 members in Catalonia. They retained points of influence outside the Catalan capital (Calella–Mataró, Sitges and Tortosa), but in Barcelona they only made significant inroads within the printing trades.[58]

Rather, it would be the Sindicatos Libres who would mount the most formidable challenge. As already seen, during 1920 they remained a small organisation but by January 1922 they claimed 150,000 members, and even syndicalist sources admitted that 100,000 workers had affiliated.[59] This meant that, on paper at least, the clandestine CNT had been eclipsed. In order to understand this remarkable growth, several factors need to be taken into account. First, of course, the total support of Martínez Anido, combined with the backing of at least some employers. In addition, workers faced intimidation. Libre activists were just as willing as their CNT counterparts to force workers, gun-in-hand, into their unions. But, as Angel Pestaña admitted, the growth of the Libres also took place in a context in which less ideologically committed workers had become tired of the constant strife and instability of the previous two years.[60]

There were, in this respect, some positive reasons to join. Martínez Anido argued, probably sincerely, that he was not against the welfare of 'honourable workers', and, in 1921, allowed the Libres to negotiate on the workers' behalf. He was ably assisted in this respect by Pere Roselló, the Ministry of Labour's Barcelona Delegate for Social Affairs, who promoted trade-wide arbitration boards, on which the Libres monopolised labour representation.

The Libres were able to take advantage of this policy because they drew a line between their ideology and the actions of their gunmen, on the one hand, and their union organisation on the other. They very much emphasised that their aim was to build a professional union, which would cooperate where possible with employers and the state, but also defend workers' interests. Alhough they did little to threaten employers with strike action until mid-1922, through the arbitration boards they were able to defend working conditions. In 1921 this led to a crisis in their relations with the Employers' Federation, which, according to Feliciano Baratech, one of the organisation's founding members, called on Martínez Anido to outlaw them. In response, from the summer the Libres launched a ferocious attack on the Employers' Federation, warning it that they intended to be even more combative than the CNT.[61]

It was in this context that, between 1921 and 1923, some differentiation became apparent in the Libre's working-class base. They took a strong hold in large factories, such as La España Industrial, Fabra i Coats, La Maquinista Terrestre i Marítima, Girona Foundry, El Vulcano and La Hispano Suiza, where, as already seen, strenuous efforts had in the past been made to try and keep unions out. Here, the employers' support was the key factor. At the same time, they recruited well amongst foremen, white-collar workers, and workers distant from the world of the SUs and the great strikes. Amongst shop and office workers, they found their way blocked by the CADCI and a number of independent unions – which, in April 1920, had negotiated with Carlos Bas the formation of a independent arbitration board – but they were able to affiliate bank clerks, built up a strong union of waiters and cooks, and also recruited well amongst bakers and barbers. They were able to make inroads amongst workers in some skilled trades which had experienced intense social conflict, most notably the printers and workers in the textile finishing trades. Finally, during 1921 and 1922 they started to recruit more strongly within the major trades in the construction, metal, and textile industries.[62]

This indicates that the Libres' more moderate union strategy appealed above all to groups of workers uncomfortable with the CNT's class-confrontationist stance, but that they were also able to reach out to some skilled workers in more conflict-ridden trades, opposed to the CRT's decision to impose SUs. Support amongst skilled workers was enhanced because the Libres never insisted on industrial unions, and were happy to allow independent craft unions to operate. It is interesting, in this respect, to note that this put them on the same terrain as the Catalan Socialists (indeed, they insisted that they wished to operate *la base múltiple*). They were more successful because of official support and because they were prepared much more aggressively to carve out a niche for themselves. At the same time, while many workers from the major industries of metal, construction and transport, along with female factory hands in textiles, were either forced in to the Libres or opportunistically joined, as Colin Winston emphasises, they were also the first to leave once constitutional guarantees were restored and the CNT once again legalised. Subsequent events would confirm that it was in these industries that the Catalan CNT's power-base rested.

The Sánchez Guerra Opening, March to December 1922

With Martínez Anido firmly in control and the Libres growing rapidly the Catalan CNT faced a very uncertain future. However, a chink of light was provided when the anti-Maurista Conservative, José Sánchez Guerra, became Prime Minister on 8 March 1922. His rise to power was a consequence of the changing face of Spanish politics in the aftermath of the military catastrophe at Annual. The disaster once again galvanised popular opposition to the war and breathed new life into the republican-Socialist alliance, the *Conjunción*. Discontent now spread to the middle classes whose children, following the 1912 reforms, were now liable to be involved in the fighting. In Restoration regime circles this heightened awareness of the need to control the military and respond more readily to public opinion. In February 1922 the Socialists and republicans had launched a campaign for the restoration of constitutional guarantees, with Liberal support in parliament, thereby provoking Maura's fall.[63]

As a gesture to the Left, Sánchez Guerra restored constitutional guarantees (a decision which led to the resignation of the Lliga representative in his

Government, Bertran i Musitu) and restored trial by jury in Catalonia. At first
he kept Martínez Anido in post. Nevertheless, by the beginning of April most
of the La Mola prisoners were free and Spanish jails had begun to empty. The
evolution of the CNT over the previous year was not to the old leadership's
liking. I have already stressed that the Catalan organisation had turned to
urban guerrilla warfare. Furthermore, a group of youngsters had begun to
take it closer to the Bolsheviks. The key figures were Andreu Nin and Joaquín
Maurín, the only members of a generation of young, radicalised, Catalan
intellectuals who affiliated to the CNT rather than Left Catalanism or Socialism. These were the kind of people who Seguí wanted to see join. Yet in the
light of the Russian revolution both Nin and Maurín began to feel that the
CNT by itself could not offer a coherent revolutionary strategy.

Nin first joined the organisation in 1918. Articulate, with a sharp mind, he
quickly made his mark in the new Union of Liberal Professions. He became a
member of the CRT Regional Committee sometime in 1920, took over as its
general secretary following the rise of Martínez Anido, and became CNT general secretary after the arrest of Evelio Boal on 2 March 1921 (with Archs taking over as CRT general secretary). Maurín, who was originally a schoolteacher
in Aragón, established his power base in Lleida, from where he built up the
provincial CNT federation. Then in late 1920 he transferred to Barcelona and
joined the CRT Committee in the spring of 1921. As a result, within the
Catalan CNT a division of labour briefly operated whereby Nin and Maurín
focused on ideology, while Archs and Vandellós directed military operations.[64]

In anarchist circles Nin and Maurín have been presented as leading a plot
to hand the CNT over to the Bolsheviks. In fact their evolution was very
much rooted in the context of the years 1917 to 1921. As already seen,
amongst the anarchist-syndicalists there was considerable sympathy for the
Russian revolution. Nin and Maurín built on these foundations. They were
convinced that a revolutionary opening existed, but argued that, for this to be
possible, a revolutionary union front (which should include anarchists, Communists and Left Socialists) should be put together, linked to the Bolsheviks
via the new Moscow-based Red International of Labour Unions or Profintern. At this point, therefore, their ideas bore no similarity to the centralised
revolutionary vanguard party envisaged by Lenin. From the end of 1920 they
were able to publicise these views through the mouthpiece of the Lleida
provincial federation, *La Lucha Social*, which was out of range of Martínez
Anido, and became the unofficial mouthpiece of the CRT and CNT committees.[65]

At this time the decision was taken in a small CNT plenary conference held
in Barcelona in late April 1921 (usually referred to as the Lleida plenary, presumably to throw the authorities off the scent) to send four delegates to
Moscow – including Nin and Maurín – to attend the Profintern's inaugural
congress. At this conference they accepted the need for an organic link
between the Communist parties and the revolutionary union front but still
believed that in Spain the unions would undertake the revolution. However,
the attempt to unseat anarchism from its vanguard role within the CNT and
the realisation that it was the intention of Moscow to subordinate the union

movement to Communist parties drew the fire of the anarchist-syndicalists. Criticism intensified as reports came through that the Russian Communist Party, the PCUS, was building a one-party state and that Russian anarchists were themselves being persecuted.

Important in this respect was the Madrid-based weekly, *Nueva Senda*, which was edited by Mauro Bajatierra and included Salvador Quemades, who had managed to escape the Martínez Anido repression, amongst the editorial team. The opposition of Quemades was important in that it signalled that Seguí's supporters would not compromise with Bolshevism and would instead work for a return to the status quo ante of 1919. Not only were they concerned at the growing influence of Bolshevik Communism in the movement. They also shied away from the revolutionary adventurism of the young activists, whatever its ideological inspiration.

Disquiet was voiced in a plenary in Madrid in August 1921 in which the delegates reaffirmed the total independence of the CNT and its libertarian communist goals.[66] But the decisive shift in the balance of power came in March 1922, when the pro-Profintern leadership was displaced from the CNT National Committee. Nin had stayed in Moscow and had been replaced as CNT general secretary by Joaquín Maurín. However, Maurín was captured by the authorities on 22 February 1922, and, early in the following month, in what looks very much like a palace coup, a meeting in Madrid decided to replace him by Joan Peiró, who had just been released from prison. Over the next year Peiró would become the dominant organisational figure within the CNT. Many anarchists had been alienated by Seguí's leadership between 1919 and 1920 and under Peiró the organisation tried to reestablish unity within the anarchist camp. The National Committee stressed that the CNT was essentially anarchist and emphasised that no pact with the reformist Socialists could be contemplated. Likewise, Seguí affirmed that, given their divergent conception of the state, there could be no common ground between syndicalist or libertarian communists, on the one hand, and Socialists (whether linked to Moscow or Amsterdam) on the other.[67]

This call to unity was no doubt rooted in the dire threat posed to the very existence of the CNT over the previous year and a half. The feeling amongst the old anarchist-syndicalist leadership was that they needed to bring all anarchists on board in order to save the organisation. But this sat very uneasily with the practical policies they pursued, which aimed to negotiate its return to legality and establish a 'progressive' front against the increasingly powerful, authoritarian, militaristic currents within the Spanish polity.

Given his controversial past Seguí was given no official post within the organisation, but he was once again the leading figure. From La Mola he had already stressed the need for a liberal alliance against reaction. Then, in a number of large meetings it held in Valencia and Andalusia in the spring and early summer of 1922, he urged a united liberal campaign, and, taking the offensive, affirmed that the responsibility for the disaster of Annual lay at the feet of the entire Restoration system.[68] In mid-April he also held meetings with a number of leading political figures in Madrid. Publicly he emphasised that while they would not enter the parliamentary arena they sympathised with 'those groups which operate seriously and support liberal values'. Privately he went further, apparently offering to observe a certain benevolence towards a new Liberal government, which included Lerroux, in return for the CNT being allowed to operate openly. Subsequently, in a CNT meeting held in Madrid on 1 May, he affirmed that the interviews had gone well and that a liberal opening was on the horizon. The CNT National Committee officially denied any involvement, but it is difficult to believe it was not fully appraised of developments.[69] The organisation's leadership was, therefore, once again pursuing the policy, inaugurated in 1917, of working with liberal democrats, except that it now sought a defensive alliance against the authoritarian Right, in which it was (albeit secretly) disposed to compromise with the Left of the Restoration regime.

The new CNT National Committee called a national conference in Zaragoza between 11 and 14 June 1922 to affirm the new orthodoxy. At this conference two major questions were debated. First, Pestaña (who had only been released in late May) was finally able to present his report on the Bolshevik regime. His view was that it was totally incompatible with libertarian values and, in response, the delegates agreed in principle to separate from the Profintern (although this needed to be ratified in a referendum by the affiliated unions) and send delegates to an anarchist-syndicalist international congress to be held in Berlin.

Second, the conference approved what became known as the 'political proposal', apparently written by Peiró and supported by Seguí, Pestaña and Josep Viadiu. The language was opaque, stating that while the CNT rejected parliamentary politics it was 'absolutely political' because it demanded the right to 'review and supervise all the evolutionary values in national life'. Subsequent comments by the anarchist-syndicalist leaders indicate that this meant that they should engage in such campaigns as they saw fit as well as criticising and petitioning the public authorities.[70] This highlights the almost insuperable difficulties in establishing unity within the anarchist-syndicalist camp. As can be imagined, the realisation that they were in a 'political' organisation caused a considerable brouhaha in more 'puritanical' anarchist circles. But the CNT leadership put the resolution forward because they did not wish to be open to accusations of treachery each time that they stood on a platform with a republican or had dealings with government. According to Joan García Oliver, the anarchist Left was further enraged by a speech by Seguí in which he stated that libertarian communism should be seen as a 'social possibilism', whose realisation would be the result of experience. By this he meant, no doubt, that it would be a long, evolutionary process. The obstacles to unity were further highlighted by the fact that a stormy debate was held on Seguí's actions in 1920, his conduct finally being approved.[71]

The desire to operate openly could also be seen in comments by the Barcelona Local Committee in April that it wanted a 'period of peace and truce' (although the price had to be the resignation of Martínez Anido and Arlegui), and its call on CNT activists not to provoke the Libres, combating them in print only.[72] Yet all of these hopes were very much contradicted by events on the ground in Barcelona. Martínez Anido remained firmly in control. It seems that the Prime Minister wished to remove him, but was concerned at the reaction of the military and Catalan elites. Hence, while from April many union activists returned home, the CNT remained banned. They were able to relaunch the publication of *Solidaridad Obrera*, but had to edit it from Valencia, and the only major union meeting they held took place in the town of Blanes in the province of Girona, outside Martínez Anido's reach.

In this atmosphere, despite the local federation's pleas, on the ground the situation did not improve. Martínez Anido had by no means totally smashed the action groups. In the early months of 1922 they began to reorganise and launch revenge attacks on members of the Libres. Between January and March one was killed and two were wounded. Then, after the reestablishment of constitutional guarantees, the Libres' gunmen once again began to target CNT activists, as well as attacking workers who had left the Libres or who had stopped paying their dues. There is little doubt that this was a calculated strategy aimed at stoking up conservative opposition to government policy. Hence tit-for-tat killings continued through to October, with at least eight CNT and five Libre activists assassinated.

The most outrageous shooting was that of Angel Pestaña. Since being released from prison he had given the only talk by a CNT leader in Barcelona province in the elitist Barcelona Athenaeum. On the 25 August, along with the Sabadell activist, Bru Lladó, he was invited to a CNT meeting in Manresa. Events during the day indicate that although the Employers' Federation had broken with the Libres, some employers at least were still financing Libre gunmen. According to Feced, 'Muntadas' had put a price on Pestaña's head, and Martínez Anido and the Libres were keen to quash a CNT revival. Hence, Pestaña was gunned down on arriving in town. He was badly wounded and taken to the local hospital, and the Libres then sent over a hit-squad with the aim of finishing him off in his bed. This was to further exacerbate tensions between the Prime Minister and Martínez Anido. The Madrid press got hold of the story and the Socialist leader, Indalecio Prieto, questioned the Government in parliament, with the result that in order to avoid a scandal Sánchez Guerra actually posted civil guards around the hospital to protect Pestaña's life.[73]

Within Barcelona one can talk of two separate levels within the CNT. On the one hand were to be found the old union leaders, free but unable to operate, and on the other the younger activists and gunmen. The latter were little inclined to listen to talk of liberal alliances. Their position was strengthened because they found common ground with intransigent anarchist-syndicalists critical of the 'reformists'. Very important in this respect was Manuel Buenacasa. He fled Barcelona at the end of 1919 or beginning of 1920 and set up in San Sebastián in the Basque Country. Here he became linked to an anarchist group called Los Justicieros, who were engaged in trade-union work and also, the suspicion is, in shootings, and who became involved in a plot to blow up the King. Although the main focus of terrorism was Catalonia, there was another centre in the Basque Country, and it was within this milieu that Los Justicieros emerged. One of their number was the young anarchist from León, Buenaventura Durruti, who had already played the role of link-man between French and Spanish anarchists while on the run in France, and would subsequently become a central figure in Catalan insurrectionary politics.

The plot was discovered and Los Justicieros fled to Zaragoza in early 1921, where a nucleus of anarchist gunmen also operated. Over the following year they tried to set up a Spanish federation of anarchist groups, whose aim would be to organise a revolutionary uprising, carrying out a hold-up in the Basque Country in order to procure money for arms. In September 1922 Los Justicieros, now also including the anarchist gunman from Aragón, Francisco Ascaso, then transferred to Barcelona. Here they would link up with an action group led by Joan García Oliver, to form Los Solidarios. They were apparently drafted into Barcelona to counter an anticipated offensive by Martínez Anido.[74]

The formation of this group was indicative of a new trend within the CNT. Gunmen would now operate in a small number of so-called affinity groups and under the aegis of Los Solidarios develop their own insurrectionary strategy. In the spring of 1923 the group was even able to produce its own publication, called *Crisol*. Amongst its collaborators were not only Fortunato Barthe, a key figure in Catalan anarchist circles, but also Felipe Aláiz and Liberto Calleja. Both had written for *Solidaridad Obrera* in Valencia, and were considered leading intellectual lights in the anarchist camp. As in the case of Buenacasa, this was indicative of the alliance between the gunmen and broader sectors of the anarchist and anarchist-syndicalist movement.[75]

Deep divisions within the CNT would break to the surface in 1923. However, in late 1922 a semblance of unity was provided by the whole organisation's desire to rid itself of Martínez Anido. This was one assassination of which almost everyone could approve. Plots to murder the Barcelona civil governor had been thick on the ground from the end of 1920. The need to assassinate him was apparently ratified in a secret meeting held in the woods near Mataró in early October 1922. However, through his informers Martínez Anido got wind of the plot and decided to engineer a 'failed assassination', which would both strengthen his position and allow him once again to accentuate repression. The informer and agent provocateur, Inocencio Feced, who was still active in the CNT, volunteered to take the lead, and suggested a plan to gun-down Martínez Anido as he was driving back from the theatre in the early hours of 23 October. The set-up resulted in a gun battle in which two anarchists and a police inspector who had infiltrated the group were killed. Two anarchist gunmen escaped. One of them, Amalio Cerdeño, was subsequently captured and the *ley de fugas* applied. However, before dying he was able to speak to the public prosecutor (*fiscal de su majistad*). He informed the Prime Minister, who then ordered Arlegui be dismissed.[76] Martínez Anido's refusal to support the move also led him to step down. Sánchez Guerra had for some time wanted to be rid of Martínez Anido. The fact that the upper echelons of the army, with the support of the King, had undertaken an offensive against the Juntas de Defensa – which whom Martínez Anido was closely identified – over the previous year made it easier for the Prime Minister to take action. Nevertheless, the result would not be a full return to civilian rule; the posts of Barcelona civil governor and police chief both remained in military hands.

1923: The Reorganisation of the CRT and the Primo de Rivera Coup

The dismissal of Arlegui and Martínez Anido provided an excellent opportunity for the CRT to reorganise. Matters appeared to improve further in December when the Liberals returned to power under Manuel García Prieto, the Marquis of Alhucemas. Again Annual was the key factor. Sánchez Guerra stepped down on 10 December, after a violent parliamentary debate in which Liberals, Reformists and Socialists called for the investigation into the politicians and military men responsible for the debacle to be stepped up.[77] Over the following months the Government would revert to a more liberal approach, trying to create state-sponsored arbitration boards in which all independent unions – including the CNT – would participate, and setting up a delegation of the Ministry of Labour which covered Catalonia and the Balearic Islands.[78]

Immediately, the Catalan CNT showed that it still retained a considerable following. At the first big meeting of the Barcelona organisation on 5 November, over 10,000 workers were present.[79] However, to rebuild the great movement of the spring of 1919 would be another matter. Events in the first few months saw Seguí's generation seemingly reaffirming their control. The local federation and SUs reiterated that they wished to operate peacefully and legally, while there were calls in meetings of the SUs for the strike weapon to be used carefully. Seguí, back in Barcelona from late November 1922, went further, and in a meeting of the construction workers reminded the audience that the role of shop stewards was merely to inform the union committee of any conflict which arose.[80] Clearly the aim was not to antagonise the authorities. As part of this effort a tacit truce with the Libres came into effect. Its basis was, no doubt, that the CNT union leaders did not wish to be sidetracked from the task of union-building, while the Libres feared reprisals now that Martínez Anido was no longer protecting them.[81]

It is extremely difficult to calibrate the growth of the CRT during 1923. There are no official statistics and the data that I have been able to compile is very impressionistic.[82] Expansion was boosted by the fact that the year was to see a patchy economic recovery following the post-war slump, but also held back by continued crisis in some sectors of industry, competition from the Libres, and a reluctance to enrol amongst a significant number of workers. The revival followed the classic CNT pattern, with the SUs once again pursuing an aggressive course. Several SUs considered all the workers in their industry to be union members and gave them until 1 May to join (after which they would have to pay dues from 1 January 1923). They made limited headway in textiles, but enjoyed greater success in the construction, metal and transport industries. The Construction Workers' SU emerged as the largest, claiming 20,000 members in August. Glass and textile unions also set up

Spanish 'coordinating committees'. This was not to the liking of many radicals, but was pushed by Peiró and reflected a clear necessity.

This recruitment drive meant that Barcelona was able to reclaim its place at the heart of the CNT. In the rest of Catalonia, as in the past, they began attracting membership from the surrounding industrial towns, in the textile strongholds of Manresa and the Ter, and also reasserted their dominant position in Tarragona province. However, while a certain recovery could be seen in Catalonia, in other areas the situation remained difficult. In Spain as a whole, the CNT National Committee claimed that 250,000 workers were in the orbit of the organisation. On the back of this growth the Barcelona edition of *Solidaridad Obrera* reappeared in February 1923. By August it was selling about 30,000 copies a day. This was, in fact, close to its post-war peak.[83]

More than ever, outside the union sphere, campaigns for the freedom of the 'social prisoners' were what attracted most sympathy. After the barbarous repression of the Martínez Anido years it was a subject dear to the hearts of many. Given that over 1,000 union activists had been rounded up, close to 100 murdered, and that around 100 had either been charged or sentenced and were still in prison, it touched the lives of many Barcelona working-class families. Emotions were running very high at the turn of the year. The first meeting calling for the prisoners' release, in Barcelona on 19 November 1922, attracted several thousand, and between January and March 1923 a large number of meetings were held throughout Catalonia. Yet, with the Government determined not to grant a new amnesty, as in the past, keeping the issue alive became a problem. Meetings petered out and the campaign was only revived in late August.

The CRT also had grandiose plans for the reconstruction of its unions. In a regional assembly held on 31 December, Seguí's vision of the unions transcending their function as the defenders of the producer and becoming the guardians of consumer interests was revived; the Construction Workers' SU was asked to prepare a report on the housing shortage and the Chemical Workers and Food-Processing SUs were called on to report on rising prices of basic necessities and the adulteration of foodstuffs. In addition, Seguí continued to pursue the strategy of forging a broad alliance against the Right. In a large meeting in Valencia in January, he stressed the need to launch a campaign for withdrawal from Morocco in which, he affirmed, the CNT would be prepared to work with the Socialists.[84]

As previously, he was opposed by the anarchist hardliners. Federico Urales had 'returned to active service' in the spring of 1922, supported by younger CNT activists with whom he had established contacts, and, in the following months, criticised the supposed centralism and bureaucratisation of the SUs.[85] In 1923 he re-launched *La Revista Blanca* in Barcelona, although it remained largely concerned with cultural and artistic matters. By this year *Tierra y Libertad* had broken with the CNT and some anarchists announced that they no longer cooperated with the labour movement.[86] But within the CNT Seguí and his followers also remained under pressure. The hardliner's anger was further fuelled by a meeting between Seguí and the Prime Minister in December 1922 and by speculation in the press that he wished to take the CNT into the parliamentary arena. New attempts were made to marginalise him within the CNT. At a plenary in February 1923, accusations were made that in late 1920 he had sent a letter to the republican, Rodrigo Soriano, agreeing to form part of a candidature in the general elections. This led to a hearing in front of the CNT National Committee on 18 February in which E. Mateo Soriano presented 'proof' that Seguí and Quemades had sold out. Seguí was vindicated but he was so disillusioned he refused to go on a propaganda tour of Andalusia.[87]

Had they been allowed a period of calm, the triumvirate of Peiró, Pestaña and Seguí could no doubt have seen off the insurrectionaries and consolidated the organisation. Yet the new balance of socio-political forces in the city would make this a vain dream. Most employers were unwilling to countenance a revival of the CNT and were able to reactivate their alliance with the military. Of key importance in this respect was the decision by the Sánchez Guerra Government, on 14 March 1922, to name Miguel Primo de Rivera captain-general of Barcelona. The choice was, it seems, linked to internal army politics, but given his extreme hostility towards the CNT and close relationship with Martínez Anido it would undermine the renewed attempt to integrate the CNT into any state-sponsored collective bargaining apparatus. Matters were further complicated because youngsters within the CNT ranks were itching to renew the war with the Libres, and any such resurgence in shootings would once again strengthen calls for repression.

The leadership faced its first crisis when the labour war with the Libres again exploded into life in March 1923. The first assassination which took place was that of Amadeu Campí, a key figure in the Libres' textile finishing trades, on 24 February. The finger of suspicion pointed to the action groups, but *Solidaridad Obrera* accused the Libres themselves. This was later confirmed by Feced, who claimed that Ramon Salas had himself carried out the shooting. Campí, it seems, had distanced himself from the organisation and had stolen incriminating evidence from its headquarters.[88] Two days later two workers who had recently left the Libres were gunned down. However, the shooting which sparked the crisis was that of Salvador Seguí, along with his close friend, Francesc Comes, on 10 March. Seguí was to die at the site and Comes passed away several days later. This was an enormous blow to any attempt to reconstruct industrial relations along peaceful lines. In its aftermath men such as Pestaña and Peiró tried to prevent an all-out war.[89] This was to little avail. Until the end of May there were a spate of attacks and counterattacks which were to leave at least twenty-six men dead (sixteen CNT activists as against ten members of the Libres) and twenty-one injured.

The Libres broke the ceasefire for two reasons. On the one hand, they felt under pressure from the CNT revival and members of their unions had been subject to intimidation. In an extremely violent fly-sheet, probably produced in February, they stated that they had maintained a truce for two or three months but that they were now going to hit back because they were being 'coerced, insulted and attacked'.[90] On the other hand, it seems most likely that within the Libres a group led by Homs, and which included Feced, was paid by a number of industrialists (the name of Muntadas again emerges) to target major CNT figures. All the indications are that they were behind Seguí's murder. Subsequently, they targeted other CNT activists who had opposed terrorist violence. Most notably, Joan Peiró, who remained CNT general secretary until the end of July, was subject to two assassination attempts. The only logical inference to be drawn is that this group within the Libres aimed to re-ignite the labour wars in order to justify a return to repression.[91] As expected, in employer circles the upsurge in shootings resulted in calls for a new clamp-down.[92]

In order to stress their opposition to the shootings, the CNT leadership joined in a campaign launched by the Left-Catalanist cultural association, the Ateneu Enciclopèdic Popular, at the beginning of April. The campaign chimed with their efforts to reach out to the liberal Left and bring the labour wars to a halt. Conveniently, emphasis was laid by all the participants on the role of the police and on the 'unmentionable connivance in the upper reaches of the public administration'.[93]

Yet, in the aftermath of Seguí's murder it was difficult to maintain a cool head. In a secret meeting the local and regional committees held off demands for an indefinite general strike, limiting the organisation's immediate reaction to a one-day strike on Monday 12 March. Its success indicated that whatever their number of affiliates on paper they were still the territory's most powerful labour confederation. Events over the following week confirmed that they still retained an important core of support. Seguí was buried surreptitiously in the early hours of Monday. In response, exasperated and under pressure, when Comes died the CNT committees threatened an indefinite strike if his body were not handed over for them to organise the funeral. On this occasion the civil governor relented. It went off peacefully with nearly 10,000 workers present.[94]

In addition, in the secret meeting they formally agreed to try and construct a broad revolutionary movement with the republicans. More ominously, they also decided to respond to the attacks on the CNT by striking 'at the top'. A committee was then formed, which included Peiró and Pestaña, which chose as their targets the Carlist pretender, Jaime de Borbón, who, according to Feced, was helping to finance the Libres (and whom *Solidaridad Obrera* suspected would be at the forefront of a possible authoritarian coup), Martínez Anido, and Faustino González Regueral, the civil governor of Bilbao under the previous Dato administration. In April the secret committee contacted Los Solidarios to carry out the assassinations.[95] The desire for revenge is understandable. Yet such a move could not benefit the CNT cause. By legitimising the action groups it weakened the position of the union leadership and made more likely a renewed bout of repression.

In response to the request, in May three members of the group, under Buenaventura Durruti, travelled to Paris to try and track Jaime de Borbón down, but had no success. Another team – complete with machine pistols in violin cases – sought out Martínez Anido, first in San Sebastián and then in La Coruña. They had to return home empty-handed. A third team travelled to León, where they managed to assassinate Regueral on 17 May. Even more outrageously, two members of Los Solidarios, Francisco Ascaso and Rafael

Torres Escartín, on their way through Zaragoza, decided, with the help of local sympathisers, to gun-down the well-known Traditionalist cardinal, José Soldevila Romero.[96]

The murder of Soldevila in particular caused an enormous outcry in conservative circles and led to a crackdown on the CNT. It also provided the employers with ammunition. On the same day as the murder, all the Barcelona business associations sent García Prieto a petition calling on the Government to deal with the terrorist threat and impose order.[97] In a meeting between García Oliver, Pestaña and Peiró, a furious Peiró accused the group of not following orders and of risking a military coup. He stated that the secret committee was to disband and urged Los Solidarios to do likewise. They had no intention of making such a move. On the contrary, they forged ahead with plans to form a revolutionary anarchist federation, and from June carried out a number of audacious hold-ups aimed at financing a putsch. These plans received support from older, intransigent anarchist-syndicalists like Manuel Buenacasa, who argued that a small minority could spark off the revolution. They pushed ahead with the preparations, stepping up the number of armed robberies over the summer, leading Primo de Rivera to bring troops and the Sometent onto the streets.[98] In response *Solidaridad Obrera*, with the support of Joan Peiró, became increasingly outspoken in its criticisms of the gunmen in their own ranks. It called for anyone in the organisation linked to shootings to be expelled and argued that the murder of a glass manufacturer on 24 August would serve only to stiffen the Government's revolve to keep the CNT on a tight leash.[99]

Just as difficult for the CNT leadership as the re-ignition of the labour wars was the resurgence of industrial conflict from the spring. This highlighted the contradiction between its attempts to keep the rank and file in check and the practice of the CNT unions. The SUs remained fighting machines, whose locus of support was, as has been emphasised, skilled workers under pressure and the unskilled in the major sectors of the economy. These workers had been adversely affected by the inability of the unions to operate openly over the previous two years and in order to mobilise them the CNT needed to offer tangible benefits. It was a scenario that had often been repeated in the past. From the new year the Barcelona organisation was involved in escalating social conflict, culminating in a general strike in the transport industry, which then spread to other sectors of the economy.

From the outset, construction was once again a focus of tension. The first big dispute which flared up in mid-January affected workers on the new Barcelona underground railway system. Its origin was to be found in the discrimination suffered by a number of shop stewards. The union responded, first with a walk-out and then with the presentation of new demands. Again several key traits which ran through post-war social conflict were revealed. The contractor was aggressively anti-union and the CNT's Barcelona committee tried to put intolerable pressure on him by escalating the dispute, bringing out auxiliary workers and paralysing the project. After negotiations with the mayor it seemed that the dispute had been solved at the end of the month, but it erupted again in March and – with the CNT focused on the transport strike – fizzled out in late June. In February a new conflict blew up amongst building labourers working for an old adversary, Joan Miró y Trepat, after a shop steward had been fired. On this occasion the SU was able to force a compromise settlement.

However, in the spring conflict in construction was overshadowed by what was to become the biggest strike in Barcelona since the La Canadenca dispute. It began at the port on 1 May. As usual, the CNT called a one-day strike and was able to halt production across much of the city's industry, but two coal unloaders who took the day off were then fired. As the civil governor confided to the Minister of the Interior, it was a deliberate provocation, backed by the Employers' Federation, whose aim was to 'take the battle [to the workers' organisations] and destroy the SUs'. The employers were concerned at the advances made by the CNT and determined to push back the tide.[100] The workers' colleagues called a solidarity strike and in response, on 12 May, the employers declared a lock-out of coal unloaders. In subsequent days the dispute continued to escalate, culminating in a general transport strike. This even included refuse collectors, with the result that, from 16 May, great mounds of rubbish built up in the streets. Union activists also attempted to prevent peasants from the surrounding countryside from bringing food into town, and attacked any carters who continued working. The result was a heavy police presence, with members of the security forces protecting food and coal supplies.

As seen in previous chapters, the recourse to solidarity strikes and the attempt to put pressure on consumption was a frequent tactic. It certainly served to concentrate the authorities' minds, but it also had a downside, the disruption and discomfort could easily alienate large swaths of middle-class opinion. The piles of uncollected rubbish symbolised for many a situation that had become intolerable. This sense of loss of order and stability was further accentuated by the resurgence of shootings and by the rise in the number of hold-ups.[101] Looking back, Joan Ferrer admitted that the impact of the strike was 'all too heavy'.[102]

The key difficulty for the leadership was that the employers took advantage of this situation to undermine the Government and could count on the backing of Primo de Rivera, who from the outset wanted to declare martial law and bring the Sometent out onto the streets. Already on 7 April the Employers' Federation had sent the Prime Minister a telegram complaining at the authorities' supposed inability to 'end a situation which is improper in a civilised country'.[103] The employers' were further angered by the Government's social programme and especially the discussion of legislation on labour contracts and on union representation on company boards within the Institute for Social Reforms. For the FTN the result would be 'a soviet system of the worst kind'.[104]

Criticism was further to intensify during the dispute. At first the Government defied them and tried to reach a compromise. At the beginning of June it brought in a new civil governor, Francisco Barber, whose brief was to reach a negotiated settlement with the help of a team from the Institute for Social Reforms. In response, protest by business, the political Right and middle-class and elite cultural associations, reached a crescendo. Meetings were held and manifestos signed. The most pointed, which greeted Barber on his arrival, affirmed that if the Government could not guarantee order then it should allow 'the city' to set up it own body.

Primo de Rivera's support became clear in June. Conservative opinion was outraged by the shooting of a number of Sometent by anarchist gunmen. In late May two members of the Sometent were gunned down (and five bystanders wounded) while they were watching a football match. Then, on 4 June (the same that day Cardinal Soldevila was murdered) Josep Franqueza, an employer in the transport industry, who was also a member of the Sometent and president of the Sant Martí Traditionalist Association (and who, according to Feced, had links with the Libre gunmen), was shot dead. The business associations organised a big protest at his funeral. Barber was jeered and jostled, to shouts of 'down with the governor!', 'Out with the representative of the SU!', 'long live Spain!', and 'long live Primo de Rivera!'.[105] This protest pointed to the fact that part of the employer class, at least, was looking to some form of authoritarian solution to social strife in Barcelona. Significantly, during 1923, in the publication of the Employers' Federation, there were articles favourably inclined towards Mussolini, who was seen as having successfully reimposed order.[106]

As in the past, the Catalan elite bypassed the Government to appeal directly to the King. Sixty economic and cultural associations wrote a letter to him calling for help. Barber ignored this clamour and tried to push home a solution broadly favourable to the workers. It was at this point that Primo de Rivera intervened directly. On 14 June the employers sent an uncompromising proposal to him (rather than to Barber) and, in discussions held the following day, with one minor amendment he backed their demands. As Barber was later to state, this totally undermined his position. Both Barber and Primo de Rivera were then called to Madrid for consultations. The Government wanted to relieve Primo de Rivera of his post but under pressure from the King and army had to back down and remove Barber. Critically, this once again showed that the King preferred to back hard-line military men rather than his own administrations.[107]

When a new civil governor, Manuel Portela Valladares, was appointed on 28 June, it quickly became clear that his function was to oversee the defeat of the strikers. This was exactly the same role that he had played when he took over during the 1910 metalworkers' strike. Indeed, during this earlier period as civil governor he had set up a business in Barcelona and for a time had belonged to the FTN. He stated that he would combat shootings and hold-ups with the aid of the 'functionaries of the civil governor's office, the Sometent and the army'. He also claimed that he would deal with both the Libres and CNT equally and that his only objective was to 'limit them to their union business'.[108] In the following weeks a number of members of the Libres were arrested, but more attention was paid to the CNT. He refused to negotiate and placed a heavy police and army presence on the streets. In addition, union headquarters were searched, several leading anarchist-syndicalists arrested and *Solidaridad Obrera* faced with prosecution. On 12 July it was picked up by the police before it reached the stalls. Under these conditions the strike began to crack. In a last throw of the dice the strike committee called new solidarity strikes for 5 July, but several days later had to throw in the towel. In a big meeting in which the leadership explained why they had called off the strike, Peiró correctly pointed out that the military and industrialists had allied in order to undermine the civil authorities. In these circumstances, he argued, it was pointless to go on strike and suggested that the workers pursue on-the-job strategies such as sabotage.[109] This was indicative of the way that even the more 'moderate' union leaders could be pushed to taking an extremist stance when faced with the impossibility of reaching negotiated settlements to disputes.

Soon after, the organisation suffered two further debilitating defeats. At the end of August, glassworkers in a number of large factories went back empty-handed after six months on strike and in early September the brickmakers followed suit after twenty-six weeks out. Furthermore, Portela Valladares kept up the pressure on the CNT. Troops patrolled the streets and carried out frequent searches, and the Sometent was allowed to operate at night. Union headquarters were searched and after bomb-making equipment was apparently found thirty-three arrests were made. Moreover, about seventy workers were also arrested in relation to the spate of armed robberies. Although constitutional guarantees remained in force, a ruse to keep CNT activists locked up was to use archaic legislation passed by the Barcelona Provincial Diputació, which allowed suspects to be kept for fifteen days without being charged (and rearrested and kept for another fifteen days, and so on). There were also several prosecutions of union leaders, the charges brought again emphasising the catch-all nature of the law. Two leaders of the Transport SU found themselves charged with 'uttering concepts which infringe the right to work', and Peiró was charged for an article 'which slanders the civil governor'. Overall, the impression is that the Government was under no illusion that its position rested on it being able to keep the CNT muzzled.

The blows suffered by the organisation weakened the leadership and gave new impetus to the insurrectionists. In two meetings held in July, the affinity groups and intransigent anarchist-syndicalists were able to break the hold that Peiró and his supporters had over the organisation. First, in a CNT plenary held in Valencia on 13 July, highly radicalised resolutions were put forward by García Oliver, calling for preparations for an uprising and justifying bank robberies. These were not approved, but the CNT National Committee was moved to Seville. Where the new leadership's sympathies lay was indicated by the fact that the new general secretary, Manuel Adame, was arrested soon after, accused of being involved in a hold-up.[110] Then, in an acrimonious regional plenary on 29 July, the CRT leadership was once again attacked for abandoning anarchist principles and, given the 'animosity which reigns amongst the Barcelona activists', it was agreed to move the Regional Committee to Manresa. The choice was not fortuitous. The new general secretary was Joan Espinalt, a friend of García Oliver and close to the affinity groups.[111] The more flexible anarchist-syndicalists then mobilised their forces and, in a new regional plenary held on 9 September, managed to get the CRT Regional Committee returned to Barcelona.[112] They were surprised by Miguel Primo de Rivera's military coup four days later. The CNT had been so weakened by the events of the previous four months, and the Restoration regime was so unpopular, that the leadership took no action to oppose it.

Conclusions

In the aftermath of the coup, repression would slowly tighten, forcing the CNT underground in 1924. It had been a long fall since the giddy heights of 1919. The destruction of the CNT was championed by much of the business class, which enjoyed the sympathy of elite and middle-class Barcelona. As such they spurned the difficult but by no means impossible task of building a more stable pattern of labour relations with the 'team' of Salvador Seguí.

Crucially, they were supported by the military, who at least in part shared their concerns. For the Barcelona-based officer corps the two bêtes noires were Catalan 'separatism' and the revolutionary threat posed by the CNT. Crucially, post-1917, these were worries shared by the King. They could also coincide on the remedy. The officers showed an increasing disdain for liberal institutions which, they believed, were responsible for Spain's 'decline', and no longer able to provide order and stability. Within military circles, especially from 1919, there was also talk of the need for them to play a more active role in government. Similarly, in conservative Catalan circles demands for strong-arm governments to crush the CNT were increasingly heard. Moreover, this was combined with fierce criticism of the socially reforming projects of post-First World War Restoration governments. The Employers' Federation was grateful to the Portela Valladares for breaking the transport strike, but was concerned that in the present institutional context sooner or later they would face a renewed CNT offensive.[113]

Such attitudes were not limited to Barcelona, but it was from this city above all that the military and employers cajoled and broke governments. Already, under Martínez Anido, Catalonia had lived for almost two years under what was, in effect, a non-institutionalised military dictatorship. So it was no surprise that it was from Barcelona that the offensive against the Restoration regime came. When Primo de Rivera began to conspire in June 1923, he allied with a number of so-called Africanista Generals based in Madrid. This was crucial in that it assured military unity. They were angry at the Government's over-defensive stance over Morocco and wanted to bury the whole issue of responsibilities. However, it was Primo de Rivera who took the lead and who, in the aftermath of the coup, was in charge of policy, and he made clear that labour conflict, centred on Barcelona, was his main concern.[114] Moreover, while plotting his coup he was buoyed up by the support he received in the city. He was backed by leading political figures in both the UMN and Lliga, and by the business associations.[115]

More specifically, these years had a massive impact on the development of the Catalan CNT. The labour wars and repression provoked a schism within its ranks, with the emergence of a new tendency, which began to develop a revolutionary strategy based on terrorist attacks, guerrilla warfare and insurrectionism. It was at daggers drawn with Seguí's supporters, but received ideological cover from hard-line anarchist-syndicalists. This division cannot be seen as pitting Catalan workers against migrant *murcianos*. In part it was generational. Seguí's 'team' had overseen the building of the SUs, and came to believe that through increasing their power within capitalist society they would finally force revolutionary change. The gunmen-cum-insurrectionaries emerged out of the hard-fought struggles in which unions engaged in order to gain a foothold within the major industrial sectors, but they came to the fore in the bitter post-war labour wars, and, inspired by the anarchist traditions of Bakunin and Malatesta, they put their faith in the vanguard role of the revolutionary elite.

In part this divide can also be seen as being related to the individual's position within the anarchist-syndicalist movement. Although one cannot draw any hard and fast rules, while Seguí's men were above all committed union organisers, a great many of the movement's journalists and writers, and men closely linked to its cultural institutions, tended to side with the hardliners. While for the union organisers the pragmatic need to defend the unions was often paramount, for the latter doctrinal matters loomed larger. One of Seguí's problems was that, within the movement, there never developed a strong intellectual current which justified his policies. No doubt this can be related to the historical circumstances in post-war Spain. The Russian revolution gave encouragement to the revolutionary Left, and the subsequent repression of the CNT did not lend itself to the emergence of writers and journalists who called for pragmatism. Divisions between these two tendencies would remain dormant under the Primo de Rivera dictatorship, but they would once again burst to the surface during the Second Republic. In the process not only would the CNT be torn asunder but the Republic itself also considerably weakened.

Notes

1. For the Koëning gunmen in 1920 see, León-Ignacio, *Pistolerismo*, 112–27; Casal Gómez, *Orígen*, 135–54; Madrid, *Ocho meses*, 45–77. Already in May 1920, the Barcelona local federation was able to give an outline of the gang's activities, including several names. *España Nueva* (hereafter, EN), 10 May 1920.

2. Winston, *Workers and the Right*, 38–139. This interpretation largely follows that of F. Baratech Alfaro, the only leading Libre figure to write a history of the organisation: see, *Sindicatos Libres*, 68–83.

3. Pestaña, *Terrorismo*, 110; Bengoechea, *Organització patronal*, 216–19; Soledad Bengoechea and Fernando del Rey, 'Militars, patrons i sindicalistes "libres"'.

4. Syndicalist assertions that the Libres were receiving official support in EN, 1 April, 3 May, 28 Oct. 1920. For the waiters see EN, 20 April, 3 Nov. 1920. The Libres subsequently sub-

stantiated some CNT claims. The Libre activist 'Bárano' noted that at first the employers 'thought that the Libres would act like a Civil Guard to keep red syndicalism at bay'. *Unión Obrera*, 16 July 1921. Joan Laguía Literas, the Libres' secretary, later admitted that the workers at first joined, 'with great suspicion'. Baltasar Domínguez Ramos, *El sindicalismo en la banca y en la bolsa y la futura revolución social*, Barcelona, 1923, 29. Severiano Martínez Anido, during 1919 the commander of the Barcelona garrison, stated in the spring of 1924 that 'the precise reason for their formation was to counteract the intrigues of the Sindicato Unico [i.e., the CNT]'. Quoted in Javier Tusell, 'La dictadura de Primo de Rivera', 236.

5. My key sources of statistical data are Sastre y Sanna, *Esclavitud moderna*; Farré Morego, *Los atentados sociales en España*; and Ramon Rucabado, *Entorn del sindicalisme*, supplemented by information from the press.

6. On the assembly see, Salvador Quemades, 'Una asamblea sindicalista en Barcelona', EN, 27 March 1920; Pestaña, *Lo que aprendí*, vol. 2, 83.

7. See EN, 14, 18, 22, 24, 29 May 1920; 'Estadística de huelgas y conflictos habidos en Cataluña de mayo a diciembre de 1920', in Federación Patronal de Cataluña, *Memoria de los trabajos realizados por la Federación Patronal de Cataluña en su primer periodo activo*; Buenacasa, *Movimiento obrero*, 77–8.

8. Madrid, *Ocho meses*, 78.

9. EN, 1, 3, 4 Sept 1920; Balcells, *Sindicalisme*, 139.

10. EN, 14, 21 Sept., 5 Oct. 1920; *Solidaridad Obrera* (hereafter, SO) (Bilbao), 1, 15 Oct. 1920.

11. EN, 4, 20 Sept, 25 Oct. 1920.

12. Lladonosa i Vall-llebrera, *Sindicalistes i llibertaris*, 37; Manent i Pesas, *Records*, 258–60.

13. Buenacasa, *Movimiento obrero*, 77–8. The celebration of plenaries, to be held at least once every three months, in which delegates from the various regions would hold discussions with the National Committee, was instituted by the CNT's Second Congress: see Confederación Nacional del Trabajo, *Memoria*, 378.

14. León-Ignacio, *Pistolerismo*, 134.

15. EN, 14, 17 Sept. 1920. Statistical data on bombings is to be found in Sastre y Sanna, *Martirología*, 148–73.

16. Lladonosa i Vall-llebrera, *Sindicalistes i llibertaris*, 33; Manent i Pesas, *Records*, 265. The revelation that the waiters at the music hall were refusing to pay union dues could provide a motive: see EN, 15 Sept. 1920. Feced was later to become an informer and agent provocateur. It is generally believed that this occurred after he was detained in October 1920. However, León-Ignacio maintains that he was turned during the December 1919 lock-out and that the bombing was a deliberate act of provocation paid for by a group of industrialists. Later, when he was abandoned by his protectors, Feced also claimed that it was a provocation by elements within the Koëning gang designed to undermine Bas (though he covered up his own involvement): see León Ignacio, *Pistolerismo*, 102 and 138, and *Informaciones*, 26 May 1931. Yet, when detained in October 1920, he was armed and cornered by the police: see *El Diluvio* (hereafter, ED), 23 Oct. 1920. If he was already an agent provocateur, it was a very elaborate ploy.

17. Pestaña, *Lo que aprendí*, vol. 2, 86–8.

18. *Boletín Oficial del Sindicato Unico del Ramo de la Construcción*, 15 Aug., 20 Oct. 1920.

19. Madrid, *Ocho meses*, 83.

20. For this strike I have used above all EN and ED along with Bas's account in Madrid, *Ocho meses*, 79–93. For Quemades, Arín and the Employers' Federation see, EN 4, 27 Oct. 1920.

21. J. Oller Piñol, *Martínez Anido: su vida, su obra*, 45. In a telegram to Bugallal on 4 November Bas explicitly recognised that the shootings were making it difficult to 'deal with the employers' intransigence' and fend off demands for martial law to be declared. Archivo Histórico Nacional, Gobernación, Serie A. (hereafter, AHN), 60/12.

22. Madrid, *Ocho meses*, 100–2; Rey Reguillo, *Propietarios y patronos*, 530; Soledad Bengoechea, 'Martínez Anido, la patronal y el pistolerismo'. Bas subsequently justified the repression, but it should be remembered that he was a Dato Conservative and was defend-

ing Government policy: see, Diario de las Sesiones de las Cortes (hereafter DSC), 11 Feb. 1921, 393–5.

23. Madrid, *Ocho meses*, EN, 3, 5, 6, 7, 9 Nov. 1920.

24. Bueso, *Recuerdos*, 131.

25. Ramon Xuriguera, *La repressió contra els obrers a Catalunya*, 12.

26. On this offensive see, Confederación Nacional del Trabajo, *Páginas de sangre, 1920–1921*.

27. This is the claim made by Inocencio Feced in, *De la España Trágica*, 11. These confessions were offered to the CNT by Feced from his prison cell in 1924, in exchange for cash, and, given the impossibility of publishing in Spain, were published by the organisation's anarchist colleagues in Argentina. Further confessions were published in *Informaciones* between May and June 1931. Feced was, by 1924, bitter that his protectors had abandoned him, while also anxious to cover his own tracks. While, therefore, extremely important they also need treating with great caution. Crucially, however, a letter from Artigas (the director of the Barcelona prison in early 1919) to Romanones, dated 12 March 1923, confirms that the Layret assassination was planned by Martínez Anido: see Archivo del Conde de Romanones (hereafter, AR), 70/31. León-Ignacio, for his part, maintains that Layret's assassins were hired directly by the military and that the military only supported Libre gunmen from the following month: see *Pistolerismo*, 156. However, he fails to pick up on the links already established between the military and Libres from early 1919. It may well have been the case that Libres gunmen were already discreetly supported by the military in 1920 before Martínez Anido became civil governor. We also know that the Libres held a key meeting with Martínez Anido as soon as he came to power on 19 November: see Baratech, *Sindicatos Libres*, 91.

28. This is the claim made by Artigas in AR, 70/31.

29. Foix, *Apòstols*, 97.

30. EN, 30 April, 2, 15 May 1919.

31. EN, 23 Oct. 1920.

32. Francisco Madrid, *Las últimas veinticuatro horas de Francisco Layret*, EN, 1 Dec. 1920.

33. Ferrer, *Simó Piera*, 113.

34. Balcells, et al., *Les eleccions generals*, 386.

35. Rey Reguillo, *Propietarios y patronos*, 630–42, González Calleja, *Máuser*, 224. A sense of how the repressive machinery operated can also be gleaned from Pedro Foix, *Los archivos del terrorismo blanco*; and Feced, *España trágica*. Foix was given access of the Lasarte file at the beginning of the Second Republic. The published result is extremely disappointing, but one letter does show that Emili Ribes-Vidal i Güell, a member of the Catalan social elite and important figure in the Sometent, was involved in the payment of informers.

36. This is Pestaña's estimate in *Terrorismo*, 154. Official statistics are contradictory. In March 1921, data from the civil governor's office indicates that thirty-five prisoners were being held in Mahón, twenty-five in Montjüic and eighty-one in Barcelona prison. In addition, 160 had been sent to jails outside Barcelona and thirty-eight confined to their home town. However, in August 1921 government statistics indicate that there were 581 'governmental prisoners' in Barcelona Province and 633 in the rest of Spain (many of whom had presumably been sent from Barcelona): see Arxiu del Govern Civil de Barcelona (hereafter, AGCB), 270; Archivo Antonio Maura Montaner, 267/10.

37. Gabriel Cardona, *El poder militar en la España contemporánea hasta la guerra civil*, 37.

38. Pestaña, *Terrorismo*, 153–4; Bueso, *Recuerdos*, 139; Bajatierra, *¿Quiénes mataron?*, 182 and 262–91. In addition, Albert Pérez Baró provides a valuable first-hand account in *Els feliços anys vint*, 52–179.

39. Bajatierra, *¿Quiénes mataron?*, 284–92; *La Lucha Social*, 27 May 1922.

40. Members of the Libres were given licences to carry arms by the police under Arlegui: see the telegram from the civil governor to the Minister of the Interior on 18 July 1923 in AHN, 58/13. This same file also reports that three Libre gunmen detained in 1923 were members of the Sometent.

41. Feced, *España trágica*. Pestaña also claimed that 'Muntadas' (presumably Maties Muntadas, the director of La España Industrial) was an intimate friend of Martínez Anido. *Lo que aprendí*, vol. 1, 81.

42. As noted in the previous chapter, this strategy had already been debated in correspondence between the Barcelona garrison (with Martínez Anido to the fore) and Miguel Primo de Rivera in late 1919. During 1920 the military continued to push strongly for such action. Miguel Primo de Rivera, who had taken over as captain general of Valencia – and who no doubt remained in close contact with Martínez Anido – stated in a letter to the Prime Minister just before the first cases that 'a round up, a transfer, an attempt to escape and a few shots would begin to resolve the problem [of the shootings]'. González Calleja, *Máuser*, note 263, 187.

43. Bajatierra, *¿Quiénes mataron?*, 236–8; Pestaña, *Terrorismo*, 134–6; SO, 26 April 1923.

44. It is difficult to build up an accurate picture. Along with Sastre y Sanna, Farré Morago and Rucabado, I have used information from *Páginas de Sangre*, *El Diluvio*, and other syndicalist sources.

45. Bajatierra, *¿Quiénes mataron?*, 253–6 and 268.

46. Anarchist-syndicalist sources claim that between 200 and 300 CNT activists were murdered under Martínez Anido's rule: see Pestaña, *Terrorismo*, 143; Manent i Pesas, *Records*, 60; Bajatierra, *¿Quiénes mataron?*, 199–204. This is, no doubt, an exaggeration. Between January 1920 October 1922 I have been able to positively identify ninety-seven CNT activists killed and fifty-one wounded. If we add those CNT activists killed and wounded between the fall of Anido and the military coup of September 1923 the figure comes to 117 killed and fourteen wounded. However, there are gaps in these figures. The Syndicalist sources name forty-seven CNT activists killed and seventeen wounded who I have not been able to identify.

47. Pestaña, *Terrorismo*, 181–9.

48. Gual Villalbí, *Memorias*, 210–20; 'El movimiento social en el año 1921'.

49. 'Carta de Salvador Seguí, "Noi del Sucre" a', AR, 98/7. The recipient of the letter is unknown, but, significantly, it found its way into the Romanones Archive.

50. In articles published in EN, 25 April–5 May 1921, and reproduced in the pamphlet, *Sindicalismo y terrorismo*.

51. EN, 2 Dec. 1920; Buenacasa, *Movimiento obrero*, 77–8; León-Ignacio, *Pistolerismo*, 164–5.

52. SO (Bilbao), 10, 17 Dec. 1920, 7 Jan. 1921.

53. García Oliver, *Eco*, 22–57; Plaja 'Memorias', 28–30.

54. For the involvement of these figures see, García Oliver, *Eco*, 51–4 and 625. On the evolution of the 'action groups', Sanz, *Sindicalismo español*, 51–2.

55. Accounts by anarchist-syndicalists are to be found in Bueso, *Recuerdos*, 140–5; Sanz, *El sindicalismo y la política*, 73. There is a detailed reconstruction in León-Ignacio, *Pistolerismo*, 180–95.

56. Martínez, *Mártires*, 137–40.

57. An interesting parallel is provided by the continuation of ETA terrorism after the consolidation of democracy in the mid 1970s. See, for example, John Sullivan, *ETA and Basque Nationalism*.

58. For Socialist union membership see ED, 8 June 1922.

59. Baratech, *Sindicatos Libres*, 96–100; Bueso, *Recuerdos*, 139.

60. Pestaña, *Terrorismo*, 161–2.

61. Baratech, *Sindicatos Libres*, 127–8; *La Unión Obrera*, 16 July 1921. Several months later the Libres clarified their position. They would use strikes and boycotts, but, unlike the CRT, not undertake general strikes or practise sabotage. *La Veu de Catalunya*, 18 Jan. 1922, *Morning Edition*.

62. On the Libres' union base, along with Winston, *Workers and the Right*, 193–203, see also the comments in Baratech, *Sindicatos Libres*, 72–3 and 120–3, and Bueso, *Recuerdos*, 130.

63. Boyd, *Praetorian Politics*, 183–208.

64. Joaquín Maurín, 'Hombres e historia. Terror y contraterror'.

65. These ideas were expounded in *La Lucha Social*. For an overview of the development of this group over this period see Meaker, *Revolutionary Left*, 385–402, and Andrew Durgan, *El Bloque Obrero y Campesino*, 21–33.

66. *La Lucha Social*, 27 Aug. 1921.

67. *La Lucha Social*, 8 March 1922; *Nueva Senda*, 16 March 1922; *Cultura y Acción* (Zaragoza), 22 Oct. 1922.
68. *Vida Nueva*, 23 Dec. 1921, 19 April, 1 May, 12 June 1922; Vidiella, 'Lluita', 19. Quemades also stressed the need to ally with the 'bourgeois Left'.
69. ED, 19 April, 2 May 1922; Meaker, *Revolutionary Left*, 439.
70. *Vida Nueva*, 11 July, 3 Aug. 1921; ED, 1 Dec. 1922.
71. On the conference see *Vida Nueva*, 12–15 July 1922; *Lucha Social*, 24 June 1922; Buenacasa, *Movimiento obrero*, 83–8; García Oliver, *Eco*, 68–9.
72. *La Lucha Social*, 15 April 1922.
73. Manent i Pesas, *Records*, 78–9; Foix, *Apòstols*, 188–90; Feced, *España trágica*, 11.
74. Hence, their geographical background was very mixed, comprising four members from Catalonia, three from León and Aragón respectively, and one affiliate from each of Valencia, Asturias, the Basque Country and Castile: see, above all, García Oliver, *Eco*, 630; Sanz, *El sindicalismo y la política*, 97–8.
75. For the formation of Los Solidarios see, García Oliver, *Eco*, 634–5; Abel Paz, *Durruti en la revolución española*, 68–93.
76. It is extremely difficult to piece together a coherent picture of events in late 1922. Fragmentary evidence from anarchist-syndicalist sources is to be found in the memoirs of Manent i Pesas, *Records*, 79–100; Bueso, *Recuerdos*, 172–4; Sanz, *El sindicalismo y la política*, 56–7. Feced published an apologia, *Por qué no maté a Martínez Anido*, in return for Primo de Rivera releasing him from prison. See also, León-Ignacio, *Pistolerismo*, 225–36.
77. Mª Teresa González Calbet, *La dictadura de Primo de Rivera*, 29.
78. ED, 16 Feb., 23 March 1923.
79. ED, 7 Nov. 1922.
80. ED, 28 Oct., 14, 28 Nov. 1922.
81. León-Ignacio states that the Libre secretary, Joan Laguía, met Seguí in late November and proposed an armistice. Seguí would not go that far but a tacit ceasefire held. *Pistolerismo*, 248–9. *El Diluvio* picked up on this dialogue on 12, 14 Nov. 1922. On 27 December the Libre leadership wrote to the civil governor expressing their desire for an end to the shootings. AGCB, 270.
82. The Barcelona edition of *Solidaridad Obrera* reappeared in late February 1923, but the only numbers of this newspaper that have been conserved are for March and April and August onwards. I have used information in this daily paper along with references in *El Diluvio*.
83. *Acta de las sesiones del pleno de la CN del T los días 17, 18 y 19 de febrero de 1923*, in AR, 70/31 (6); SO, 26 Aug. 1923.
84. ED, 2 Jan. 1923; Salvador Seguí (Noi del Sucre), *La guerra de Marruecos y las responsabilidades*.
85. *Nueva Senda*, 4 May 1922; Montseny, *Mis primeros cuarenta años*, 37–9.
86. *Tierra y Libertad*, 30 May 1923; *La Revista Blanca*, 15 July 1923.
87. ED, 16, 30 Jan., 13 March 1923; *Acta de las sesiones del pleno*; Vidiella, 'Lluita', 20.
88. SO, 8 March 1923; *Informaciones*, 8, 9 June 1931.
89. SO, 27, 28 March 1923.
90. El grupo reparador de injusticias, 'Se ha agotado la paciencia de los Libres', in AR, 70/21. In May, in a note to the Barcelona civil governor, the Minister of the Interior expressed his concern at coercion by the CRT against the Libre affiliates. 'As you know, the Libres promised to end their actions if the coercions ended and the SU accepted that such methods should not be used in order to gain members.' Minister of the Interior to the civil governor, 11 May 1923, AHN, 58/13.
91. Feced (although, of course, suppressing his own involvement) affirmed that the Libres were paid to kill Seguí and that the shooting was authorised by Primo de Rivera. *Informaciones*, 1 June 1931. The belief that it was the 'Homs gang' and that Feced was prominently involved was general in CNT circles. Joan Manent states that two former Libres confessed this in 1932. *Records*, 272. On the assassination attempts on Peiró see the work by his son, *Juan Peiró*, 31–2.

92. Rey Reguillo, *Propietarios y patronos*, 616–17.

93. SO, 18 April 1923.

94. Foix, *Apòstols*, 114–16; ED, 20 March 1923.

95. García Oliver, *Eco*, 628–32; Paz, *Durruti*, 93.

96. Sanz, *El sindicalismo y la política*, 104–17; García Oliver, *Eco*, 630–1; Paz, *Durruti*, 94–106.

97. *Reseña Ilustrada de la Industria y el Comercio de Cataluña, 1923*, 100–1.

98. García Oliver, *Eco*, 634–5, León-Ignacio, *Pistolerismo*, 297–8; SO (Gijón), 20 July 1923; Buenacasa in *Cultura y Acción* (Zaragoza), 30 Sept. 1922.

99. SO, 4, 20, 24, 29 Aug. The civil governor stated 'I believe this to be sincere as it coincides with information I have received from informers'. Civil governor to the Minister of the Interior, 24 Aug., AHN, 58/13.

100. Civil governor to the Minister of the Interior, 28 May, AHN 58/13. Amadeu Hurtado, who was privy to inside information, came to the same conclusion. *Quaranta anys*, vol. 1, 444. For the strike as a whole, I have relied on the account in *El Diluvio*.

101. This feeling was picked up by Hurtado, *Quaranta anys*, vol. 1, 443. Similar comments, though focused more on the impact of terrorism, can be found in Pestaña, *Lo que aprendí*, vol. 2, 86–8.

102. Porcel, *Revuelta*, 154.

103. Civil governor to Minister of the Interior, 28 May, AHN 58/13; ED, 8 April 1923.

104. *Memoria de la Junta Directiva del Fomento del Trabajo Nacional correspondiente al ejercicio 1923–24*, 49–50.

105. For the funeral see Hurtado, *Quaranta anys*, vol. 1, 444, and ED, 10 June 1923.

106. Soledad Bengoechea and Fernando del Rey Reguillo, 'En vísperas de un golpe de estado.'

107. For the role of the King see Bengoechea, *Organització patronal*, 273–5; González Calleja, *Máuser*, 224.

108. Civil governor to Minister of the Interior, 1 July, AHN, 57/13.

109. ED, 26 July 1923.

110. León-Ignacio, *Pistolerismo*, 291.

111. SO, 24 Aug. 1923; García Oliver, *Eco*, 73.

112. *La Veu de Catalunya*, 11 Sept. 1923.

113. *Producción, Tráfico y Consumo*, June, July 1923.

114. González Calbet, *La dictadura de Primo de Rivera*, 53–94; Tusell, *Radiografía*, 71–83 and 94.

115. Shlomo Ben-Ami, *Fascism from Above*, 45–6 and 75–82.

BIBLIOGRAPHY

Primary Sources

i) Archives

Archivo de Antonio Maura Montaner, Fundación Antonio Maura (AMM)
Archivo de Eduardo Dato, Biblioteca de la Real Academia de la Historia (AD)
Archivo del Conde de Romanones, Biblioteca de la Real Academia de la Historia (AR)
Archivo Histórico Nacional, Gobernación Serie A (AHN)
Arxiu del Foment del Treball Nacional, Llibre d'Actes de la Junta Directa (LAJD)
Arxiu del Govern Civil de Barcelona (AGCB)
Arxiu Històric de la Cambra de Comerç, Indústria i Navegació de Barcelona (AHC-CINB)
Arxiu Municipal de Manlleu (AMM)
Arxiu Municipal de Sabadell (AMS)
Arxiu Municipal de Torelló (AMT)
Arxiu Municipal de Vic (AMV)
Arxiu Nacional de Catalunya, Fons de la Maquinista, Terrestre y Marítima
Diario de Las Sesiones de Las Cortes, Congreso de los Diputados, 1900–1923 (DSC)
Max Nettlau Archive, Internationaal Instituut voor Sociale Geschiendenis

ii) Newspapers, Bulletins and Journals

Anarquía, 1906
Avenir, 1905
Bandera Roja, 1919
Boletín de la Cámara de Industria y Comercio de Sabadell, 1912–1914
Boletín de la Federación Patronal, 1919
Boletín de la Industria y Comercio de Sabadell, 1910–1912
Boletín Oficial del Sindicato Unico del Ramo de la Construcción, 1920
Boletín de la Sociedad del Arte de Imprir de Barcelona, 1899–1909
Boletín de la Unión Obrera del Arte de Imprimir de Barcelona, 1910–1913
Butlletí del Museu Social, 1915–1917

El Comunista, 1920
La Correspondencia Militar, 1919
Cultura y Acción, 1922
La Cuña, 1899–1913
El Diluvio (ED), 1909–1923
El Eco de los Toneleros. Organo de la Federación de Toneleros de la Región Española, 1887–1890
España Nueva (EN), 1919–1920
Espartaco, 1904
Espartaco, 1919–1920
Gaceta Municipal, 1935
La Guerra Social, 1902–1903
La Hormiga de Oro, Ilustración Católica, 1916
La Huelga General (LHG), 1901–1903
La Ilustración Obrera, 1904–1905
La Industria Metalúrgica, 1922–1923
La Internacional, 1908–1909
El Intransigente, April–May 1912
La Justicia Social (LJS), 1909–1916
El Liberal, 1902
La Lucha Social, 1921–1922
El Mismo, 1905
Natura, 1903–1905
Las Noticias, 1902
Nuestro Programa, 1902–1903, 1914
Nueva Senda, 1922
El Pintor, 1904
La Plana de Vich, 1899–1904
El Poble Català (EPC), 1909
Producción, Tráfico y Consumo, 1923
El Productor (EP), 1901–1906
El Progreso, 1909
La Protesta, 1899–1902
La Publicidad (LP), 1899–1903, 1909–1913
El Rebelde, 1907–1908
La República Social, 1897–1898
Reseña Ilustrada de la Industria y el Comercio, 1921–1923
Revista del Ateneo Obrero de Barcelona, 1886–1908
La Revista Blanca, 1898–1902, 1923
Revista Fabril. Organo de la Federación de la Industria Textil Española (RF), 1900
El Sindicalista, 1912
El Socialista (ES), 1898–1917
Solidaridad Obrera (Barcelona) (SO), 1907–1911, 1913–1919, 1923
Solidaridad Obrera (Bilbao) (SO), 1920
Solidaridad Obrera (Gijón) (SO), 1923
Suplemento de La Revista Blanca, 1899–1902
El Ter, 1899–1900
Tierra y Libertad, 1906–1918, 1923
El Trabajo (ET), 1899–1912
El Trabajo Nacional (ETN), 1899–1919
La Tramontana, 1907

La Unión Ferroviaria. Sección Reus Norte, 1913–1914
Unión Obrera, 1921
La Veu de Catalunya, 1922–1923
Vida Nueva, 1921–1922
El Vidrio, 1916

iii) Pamphlets, Books, Diaries and Memoirs Written by the Protagonists

Abad de Santillán, D. *Memorias, 1877–1936*, Barcelona, 1977.

Ametlla, C. *Memòries polítiques, 1890–1917*, Barcelona, 1963.

Bajatierra, M. *¿Quiénes mataron a Dato?*, Barcelona, 1931.

Baratech Alfaro, F. *Los Sindicatos Libres en España. Su orígen – su actuación – su ideario*, Barcelona, 1927.

Bertrán, L. *Yo acuso. El testamento de Ferrer*, Barcelona, 1911.

Bonafulla, L. *La revolución de julio*, Barcelona, n.d. [1910].

Buenacasa, M. *El movimiento obrero español*, Madrid, 1977[1928].

———. *¿Qué es el Sindicato Unico?*, 2nd edn Bilbao, n.d.

Bueso, A. *Recuerdos de un cenetista*, Esplugas de Llobregat, 1976.

———. 'Angel Pestaña: "Caballero de la triste figura" del anarcosindicalismo español', *Historia y Vida*, no. 29, 1970: 52–63.

Burgos y Mazo, M. de. *Vida política española. Páginas históricas de 1917*, Madrid, 1917.

———. *El verano de 1919 en Gobernación*, Madrid, n.d.

Cánovas del Castillo, A. *Discursos parlamentarios*, Introductory study by Diego López Garrido, Madrid, 1987.

Casal Gómez, M. *Orígen y actuación de los pistoleros*, Barcelona, 1931.

Catalunya, J. de (pseudonym of Joan Codina). 'Los obreros de la industria textil, I–X', *Justicia*, 30 January–19 April 1930.

Clarià, I. 'Mi asesinato', *La Huelga General*, 20 February 1903: 5.

Comaposada, J. 'Los Sucesos de Barcelona, I–IX', *El Socialista*, 29 October–24 December 1909.

———. *La organización obrera en Cataluña*, Reus, 1910.

———. *La Revolución de Cataluña*, Barcelona, 1910.

———. 'El movimiento fabril', *La Justicia Social*, 9 August 1913: 2.

———. 'La vida de los obreros en La comarca de Ter, I–X', *La Justicia Social*, 4 November–23 December 1916.

Comaposada, J. and P. Iglesias, 'Epistolario inédito', *Leviatán*, June 1934: 52–6.

Comité Pro Castellví. *La verdad en marcha*, Barcelona, 1916.

El Congreso Revolucionario Internacional de París. Septiembre de 1900, Buenos Aires, 1902.

Coromines, P. *Diaris i records*, vol. 2, *De la solidaritat al catorze d'abril*, Barcelona, 1974.

Cortiella, F. *El Morenet. Drama en tres actes*, Barcelona, 1905.

Domingo, M. *En la calle y en la carcel. Jornadas revolucionarias*, Barcelona, 1921.

Domínguez Ramos, B. *El sindicalismo en la banca y en la bolsa y la futura revolución social*, Barcelona, 1923.

Estévanez, N. *Resumen de la historia de España*, Barcelona, 1904.

Fabbri, L. *Anarquismo y socialismo*, Valencia, n.d. [1906–7].

Fabra Ribas, A. *La Semana Trágica. El caso Maura. El Krausismo*, prólogo de Antonio Pérez Baró, Madrid, 1975.

Feced, I. *De la España Trágica. Revelaciones de un confidente*, Buenos Aires, 1925.

———. *Por qué no maté a Martínez Anido*, n.p., n.d. [1925?].

———. *Informaciones*, 21 May–12 June 1931.

Ferrer, J. *Vida sindicalista*, Paris, 1957.

———. *Conversaciones libertarias*, Paris, 1965.

———. 'Leyendo "Els Altres Catalans". El problema de la inmigración en Catalunya', *Umbral*, no. 45, 1965: 13.

Ferrer Guardia, F. *La Escuela Moderna*, Madrid, 1976 [1910].

Ferrer y la Huelga General. Consideración previa por Anselmo Lorenzo, Barcelona, n.d.

Foix, P. *Los archivos del terrorismo blanco. El fichero Lasarte*, 2nd edn, Barcelona, 1931.

———. *Apòstols i mercaders*, 2nd edn, Barcelona, 1976.

García Oliver, J. *El eco de los pasos*, Barcelona, 1978.

Gironella, M. 'Eusebio Carbó y Carbó (Datos biográficos)', Unpublished manuscript, Biblioteca Arús, n.d.

Güal Villalbí, P. *Memorias de un industrial de nuestro tiempo*, Barcelona, n.d. [1922].

Herreros, T. *Lerroux tal cual es. Historia de una infamia. Reductada por el mismo obrero que ha sido víctima de ella*, Barcelona, 1907.

———. *El obrero moderno*, Logroño, 1911.

La Huelga General (6 postales), Barcelona, 1903.

Hurtado, A. *Quaranta anys d'advocat. Història del meu temps 1894–1930*. vol. 1, Barcelona, 1969.

Iturbe, L. *La mujer en la lucha social y en la guerra de España*, México D.F., 1974.

Leone, E. *El sindicalismo*, Valencia, n.d. [1906/7].

Leroy, C. (pseudonym of José Sánchez González), *Los secretos del anarquismo*, México D.F., 1913.

Lidia, P. de (pseudonym of Adrián del Valle), 'Evocando el pasado (1886–1891)', *La Revista Blanca*, 15 July–15 September 1927.

López Montenegro, J. *La huelga general*, Barcelona, n.d. [1902?].

Lorenzo, A. *El obrero moderno*, Barcelona, 1903.

———. *El proletariado emancipador*, Barcelona, 1911.

———. *La masa popular*, Barcelona, 1913.

———. *El proletariado militante: Memorias de un internacionalista*, Prologue and notes by José Alvarez Junco, Madrid, 1977 [vol.1, 1901; vol. 2, 1923].

Madrid, F. *Sangre en Atarazanas*, Barcelona, n.d. [1926].

———. *Ocho meses y un día en el gobierno civil de Barcelona (confesiones y testimonios)*, Madrid/Barcelona, 1932.

———. *Las últimas veinticuatro horas de Francisco Layret*, n.p [Argentina], n.d.

Manent i Pesas, J. *Records d'un sindicalista llibertari català*, Paris, 1976.

Martínez, L. *Los mártires de la CNT*, Barcelona, 1923.

Maurín, J. 'Hombres e historia. Terror y contraterror', *España Libre*, no. 28, 1960: 1–2.

Montseny, Federica. *Anselmo Lorenzo*, Toulouse, 1970 [1938].

———. *Mis primer cuarenta años. Bibliografías y memorias*, Barcelona, 1987.

Morato, J.J. *El Partido Socialista Obrero*, Madrid, 1976 [1918].

Negre, J. *¿Qué es el sindicalismo?*, Barcelona, 1919.

———. *Recuerdos de un viejo militante*, Barcelona, n.d.

Nin, A. '¿Por qué nuestro movimiento obrero ha sido anarquista?', reproduced in, *El arraigo de anarquismo en Cataluña. Textos de 1926/27*, ed. A. Balcells, Barcelona, 1973: 106–9.

Oria, S. 'Habla Salvador Seguí', *La Voz*, 4 September 1920: 1.

Pataud, E, and E. Pouget. *Cómo haremos la revolución*, 2 vols, Barcelona, n.d. [1913/14].

Peiró, J. *Trayectoria de la Confederación Nacional del Trabajo (páginas de crítica y de afirmación)*, Mataró, n.d. [1925?].

———. *Juan Peiró: Teórico y militante del anarco-sindicalismo español*, Barcelona, 1978.

Pérez Baró, A. *Els feliços anys vint. Memòries d'un militant obrer*, 1918–1926, Palma de Mallorca, 1974.

Pestaña. A. *Sindicalismo y terrorismo*, Madrid, 1923.

———. *Lo que aprendí en la vida*, 2 vols, Algorta, 1970 [1933].

———. 'Historia de las ideas y luchas sociales en España, I–XVI' *Orto*, nos. 2–20, April 1932–January 1934.

———. *Trayectoria sindicalista*, prologue Antonio Elorza, Madrid, 1974.

———. *Terrorismo en Barcelona*, edition and prologue by Xavier Tusell y Genoveva Queipo de Llano Barcelona, 1979 [manuscript, 1923].

Plaja, H. 'Mis memorias', Unpublished manuscript, Biblioteca Arús, n.d.

———. 'Eusebi Carbó Carbó. Bibliografia', Unpublished manuscript, Biblioteca Arús, n.d.

———. 'Salvador Seguí, hombre de la CNT', in *Salvador Seguí, su vida, su obra*, Paris, 1960: 49–78.

Portela Valladares, M. *Memorias. Dentro del drama español*, Madrid, 1988.

Pouget, E. *Bases del sindicalismo*, Barcelona, 1904.

———. *El sindicato*, Barcelona, 1904.

———. *La Confederación General del Trabajo en Francia*, Barcelona, n.d. [1914].

Por qué de la Huelga General, Barcelona, 1903.

Prat, J. *A las mujeres*, Barcelona, 1904.

———. *Necesidad de asociación*, Barcelona, 1904.

———. *La burguesia y el proletariado*, preface by Anselmo Lorenzo, Valencia, n.d., [1909].

———. *Orientaciones*, Barcelona, 1916.

Prat, J. 'Sindicalismo y Socialismo' and R. Mella, 'Sindicalismo y anarquismo', La Coruña, n.d.[1912?].

Recasens i Mercadé, J. *Vida inquieta. Combat per un socialisme català*, Edition and notes by Pere Anguera and Albert Arnavat, Barcelona, 1985.

Rosell, A. *Recuerdos de educador*, unpublished memoirs: Montevideo, 1940.

Salut, E. *Vivers de revolucionaris. Apunts històrics del districte cinqué*, Barcelona, 1938.

Salvador Seguí, su vida, su obra, Paris, 1960.

Samblancat, A. 'A los 37 años del asesinato de Salvador Seguí', in *Salvador Seguí, su vida, su obra*, Paris, 1960: 107–10.

Sanz, R. *El sindicalismo y la política. Los 'Solidarios' y 'Nosostros'*, Toulouse, 1966.

———. *El sindicalismo español antes de la guerra civil*, Valencia, 1976.

Seguí, S. *Anarquismo y sindicalismo. Conferencia pronuncinada en el Castillo de Mahón el día 31 de diciembre de 1921*, Barcelona, 1923.

———. *La guerra de Marruecos y las responsabilidades*, Barcelona, 1923.

'El señor Martínez Anido habla del problema catalán', *El Sol*, 15 February 1922: 1.

Serge, Victor. *Memoirs of a Revolutionary, 1901–1941*, London, 1961.

———. *Birth of our Power*, London, 1968.

El trabajador y la huelga general, Madrid, 1902.

Urales, F. *Mi vida*, vol. 2, Barcelona, 1930.

Vidiella, R. 'Salvador Seguí', *Justicia Social*, 8 March 1924: 2.

———. *Los de ayer*, Madrid, 1938.

———. 'La lluita de classes i la repressió a Barcelona del 1917 al 1923', *Nous Horitzons*, no. 4, 1964: 13–22.

Viadiu, J. 'Nuestro "Noi del Sucre"', in *Salvador Seguí, su vida, su obra*, Paris, 1960: 1–48.

Vilà, P. 'Records d'un treballador', *L'Avenç*, no. 9, 1978: 26–30.

Viladomat, F., 'Els anarquistes i els sindicats', in *Justicia Social*, 19 April–31 May 1924.

Yvetot, G. *ABC sindicalista*, Barcelona, n.d. [1908].

iv) Other Contemporary Sources

Aguilera, J. 'Solución a la crisis', *El Trabajo Nacional*, 1 July 1904: 257–9.

———. 'La crisis de la industria algodonera', *El Trabajo Nacional*, 16 September 1909: 307–9.

Albó y Martí, R. *Barcelona caritativa, benéfica y social*, vol. 1, Barcelona, 1914.

Anuari de Catalunya, 1917, Barcelona, 1918.

Anuari d'Estadística Social de Catalunya, 1912–1915, vols. 1–4, Barcelona, 1913–1917.

Anuario Estadístico de España, 1922–1923, Madrid, 1924.

Anuario Estadístico de la Ciudad de Barcelona, vols. 1–13, 1902–1920, Barcelona, 1903–1921.

Arbón, C. 'Angel Pestaña', *Siluetas*, August 1923: 1–8.

Asociaciones de Fabricantes de las Cuencas del Ter y del Freser. *Los jurados mixtos en España. Datos y consideraciones acerca de la conciliación y el arbitraje en los conflictos entre patrones y obreros*, Barcelona, 1902.

Balaguer, M.M. 'La industria química', in *Reseña Ilustrada de la Industria y Comercio de Cataluña*, 1921, Barcelona, 1923: 112–19.

Barret, J.A. 'Raquitismo metalúrgico nacional. Sus causas y consecuencias', in *Primer Congreso de industriales metalúrgicos celebrado en Barcelona el 13 de abril de 1913*, Barcelona, 1913: 139–49.

Bartolí, E. 'Aprovechamiento de la fuerza hidráulica en la provincia de Barcelona', *El Trabajo Nacional*, 11 July 1898: 44–6.

Bastos Ansart. F. *Pistolerismo*, Madrid, 1935.

Bertrand i Serra, E. 'Un estudio sobre la industria algodonera', in *Boletín del Comité Regulador de la Comisión Textil Algodonera*, no. 33, 1931: 81–98.

Brissa, José. *La revolución de julio en Barcelona. Su represión, sus víctimas. Proceso de Ferrer*, Barcelona, 1910.

Cámara Oficial de Industria de Barcelona. *Memoria reglamentaria del año 1919*, Barcelona, 1920.

Canals, Salvador. *Los sucesos en España en 1909. Crónica documentada*, vol. 1, Madrid, 1909.

Carreras y Candi, F. 'La ciutat de Barcelona', in F. Carreras y Candi, ed. *Geografia general de Catalunya*, vol. 4, 2, Barcelona, 1980 [1913–1918].

Casals, P. 'L'habitació obrera ahir i avui', *La Nació*, 2 October 1915: 5–6.

———. 'El crecimiento de las sociedades anónimas', *Reseña Ilustrada de Industria y Comercio de Cataluña*, 1922, Barcelona, 1924: 44–51.

Causa contra Francisco Ferrer y Guardia instruida y fallada por la jurisdicción de guerra de Barcelona, año 1909, Madrid, 1911.

Causa por el delito de rebelión militar, 1909–1910, 2 vols, Madrid, 1911, vol. 1.

'Censo obrero de 1905', in *Anuario Estadístico de la Ciudad de Barcelona*, 1905, Barcelona, 1907: 599–632.

Cerdá, I. 'Monografía estadística de la clase obrera en Barcelona en 1856', in I Cerdá, ed. *Teoría general de la urbanización*, vol. 2, Madrid, 1867.

Colonia Güell y Fábrica de Panos y Veludillos. *Breve reseña escrita con motivo de la visita hecha a dicha colonia por los señores congresistas de la semana social*, Barcelona, 1910.

La Confederación Nacional del Trabajo a La Opinión Pública de España. *A toda conciencia honrada, manifestaciones y orígen del terrorismo en las luchas sociales; quienes somos y adonde vamos*, Alicante, n.d.

Confederación Nacional del Trabajo. *Páginas de sangre, 1920–1921*, Marsailles, n.d.

———. *Memoria del Congreso celebrado en el Teatro de la Comedia de Madrid, los días 10 al 18 de diciembre de 1919*, Barcelona, 1932.

Confederación Regional de Oficiales y Peones Albañiles de Cataluña. *Reglamento*, Barcelona, 1913.

———. *Memoria de actas del primer congreso celebrado en Villanueva y Geltrú, en el local del ateneo vilanovés los días 28 y 29 de julio de 1914*, Barcelona, 1914.

Confederación Regional de Sociedades de Resistencia Solidaridad Obrera. *Estatutos*, Barcelona, 1909.

Confederación Regional del Trabajo de Cataluña. *Memoria del congreso celebrado en Barcelona los días 28, 29, 30 de junio y 1 de julio del año 1918*, Barcelona, 1918.

Congreso de Constitución de la CNT. Prologue by José Peirats. Notes and bibliography on anarchosyndicalism in Spain by Francesc Bonamusa, Barcelona, 1976.

Congreso de la Federación de Trabajadores de la Región Española Celebrado en Sevilla los días 24, 25 y 26 de setiembre de 1882, Barcelona, 1882.

Coroleu, J. *Barcelona y sus alrededores. Guía histórica, descriptiva y artística del forastero*, Barcelona, 1887.

Díaz del Moral, J. *Historia de las agitaciones campesinas andaluzas. Córdoba* Madrid, 1967 [1929].

Elías de Molins, J. *La obrera en Cataluña, en las ciudades y en el campo. Orientaciones sociales*, Barcelona, 1913.

Escarra, Edouard. *El desarrollo industrial de Cataluña, 1900–1908*, Barcelona, 1970 [1908].

La España Industrial en su 82 aniverario, 1847–1929, Barcelona, 1929.

Fabra i Coats. *Memoria de las obras sociales a favor de los trabajadores de la Compañía Anónima Hilaturas de Barcelona*, Barcelona, 1916.

Farré Morego, J.M. *Los atentados sociales en España*, Madrid, 1922.

Federación Internacional de Industrias Algodoneras. *Memoria del congreso celebrado en Bremen los días 25 al 29 de julio de 1906*, Barcelona, 1907.

Federación de Oficiales Toneleros de la Región Española. *Actas de la conferencia verificada en San Martín de Provensals los días 26, 27 y 28 de enero y el congreso XXII celebrado el la misma localidad los días 9 al 16 de abril de 1894*, Barcelona, 1894.

Federación Patronal de Cataluña. *Memoria de los trabajos realizados por la Federación Patronal de Cataluña en el primer periodo activo*, Barcelona, 1921.

Federación Regional Catalana de Sindicatos Obreros Metalúrgicos. *Memoria del congreso obrero metalúrgico celebrado en el Palacio de Bellas Artes los días 12 y 13 de abril de 1914*, Barcelona, 1914.

Ferrer Vidal, J. 'La indústria tèxtil d'ahir. Càlcul de les diferències en el preu de cost de la filatura de cotó en diversos paisos', *Economia i Finances*, no. 21, 21 November 1928: 3–5.

Gil Maestre, M. 'El anarquismo en España y en especial en Cataluña', *Revista Contemporánea*, vol. CVII, 1897.

Graell, G. 'La industria catalana', *El Trabajo Nacional*, 30 July 1902: 65–6.

Guia Diamante. *Barcelona*, Barcelona, 1896.

Guitart de Cubas, A. *Barceloneta*, 1921.

La huelga general de Barcelona: Verdadera relación de las sucesos desarrollados con motivo del paro general de Barcelona durante la octava semana de este año por un testigo, Barcelona, n.d [1903].

La huelga sangrienta de Barcelona. Relato de los sucesos por un testigo presencial, Barcelona, n.d.

La Iglesia, G. *Caracteres del anarquismo en la actualidad*, 2nd edn, Barcelona, 1907.

Instituto de Estadística y Política Social. *Estadísticas sociales: Monografía estadística de las clases trabajadoras de la ciudad de Barcelona*, Barcelona, 1921.

Instituto de Reformas Sociales. *Estadística de Huelgas, 1905–1923*, Madrid, 1906–1926.

———. *Conflicto de obreros y empleados en la compañía de ferrocarriles, septiembre–octubre 1912*, Madrid, 1913.

———. *La jornada de trabajo en la industria textil, Trabajos preparatorios del reglamento para la aplicación del Real Decreto de 24 de agosto de 1913*, Madrid, 1914.

———. *Suplemento de la información sobre la regulación de la jornada en la industria textil*, Madrid, 1915.

———. *Memoria de la inspección del trabajo correspondiente al año 1909–1914*, Madrid, 1911–1916.

———. *Encarecimiento de la vida durante la guerra: precios de las subsistencias en España y en el extranjero, 1914–1918*, Madrid, 1918.

———. *Movimiento de precios al por menor en España durante la post-guerra*, Madrid, 1923.

Juicio ordinario ante los tribunales militares en la plaza de Barcelona contra Francisco Ferrer Guardia, Prologue by Enric Olivé Serret, Palma de Mallorca, 1977 [1911].

Lerulot, C. *La gran jornada obrera (huelga general de Barcelona, 1902)*, Barcelona, 1907.

Marvaud, Angel. *La cuestión social en España*, Madrid, 1975 [1910].

Memoria de la Junta Directiva del Fomento del Trabajo Nacional correspondiente al ejercicio próximo pasado de 1919–1920, Barcelona, 1920.

Memoria de la Junta Directiva del Fomento del Trabajo Nacional correspondiente al ejercicio 1923–1924, Barcelona, 1924.

Ministerio de Fomento. *Memoria acerca del estado de la industria en la provincia de Barcelona en el año 1907*, Madrid, 1910.

Ministerio de Instrucción Pública y Bellas Artes. *Censo de población, 1900*, vol. 3, Madrid, 1907.

Ministerio de Trabajo y Previsión, *Censo de población de 1920*, vol. 5, Madrid, 1929.

Mira, E. 'Barracópolis: La vida de les barraques de Barcelona', *Justicia Social*, 23 November 1923–14 April 1924.

'El movimiento social en el año 1921', in *Reseña Ilustrada de la Industria y el Comercio, 1921*, Barcelona, 1922: 134–7.

Nadal, J.M. de. *Aquella Barcelona*, Barcelona, 1933.

Negre, L. 'Encuesta sobre las condicions econòmic-socials a les conques del Ter i Fresser', *Anuari d'Estadística Social de Catalunya*, 1915, Barcelona, 1917: 102–50.

Nomenclatura de España, 1900, Madrid, 1904.

Nomenclatura de las ciudades, villas, lugares, aldeas y demás entidades de la población de España formado por la dirección general de estadística con referencia al 31 de diciembre de 1920, vol. 1, Madrid, 1924.

Piñol, J.O. *Martínez Anido: su vida, su obra*, Madrid, 1943.

Planas, A. 'La industria metalúrgica', *in Revista Ilustrada de Industria y Comercio de Cataluña 1921*, Barcelona, 1923: 106–9.

Playá, J. *Estado y estadística de las industrias mecánicas y elécticas en la provincia de Barcelona en el año 1913*, Barcelona, n.d.

Pons Freixa, F., with the collaboration of J.M. Martino. *Los aduares de Barcelona*, Barcelona, 1929.

Prades, P. de. 'Els jornals i las subsistencias', *La Nació*, 2 October 1915: 9–10.

Primer Congreso Nacional de Industrias Metalúrgicas. *Exposición del cuestionario*, Barcelona, 1913.

Rahola y Trémols, F. 'Del comerç y de la industria de Catalunya', in F. Carreras y Candi, ed. *Geografia general de Catalunya*, vol. 1, Barcelona, 1980 [1913–18]: 322–464.

Regàs i Ardèvol, M. *Confessions, 1880–1936*, Barcelona, 1960.

Reglamento de la Sociedad de Obreros Canteros de la Montaña de Montjuich, Barcelona, 1899.

Renté i Casola, M. *La abolición del salario por la participación en los beneficios*, Barcelona, 1899.

Reparaz (fill), G de. *La Plana de Vic*, Barcelona, 1928.

Riera, A. *La Semana Trágica. Relato de la sedición e incendios en Barcelona y Cataluña*, Barcelona, 1909.

Rucabado, R. *Entorn del sindicalisme*, Barcelona, 1925.

Rusiñol, A. *Bases para la creación y funcionamiento de los jurados mixtos en Manlleu. Proyecto de montepío reductado por D. Federico Rahola por encargo de la Junta de Conciliación con un prólogo de D. Joaquín Aguilera*, Barcelona, 1902.

Rusiñol, S. *L'auca del senyor Esteve*, Barcelona, 1979 [1907].

Sallarés i Pla, J. *El trabajo de las mujeres y de los niños. Estudio sobre las condiciones actuales*, Sabadell, 1892.

Sastre y Sanna, M. *Las huelgas en Barcelona y sus resultados durante el año 1903–1909*, 7 vols, Barcelona, 1904–1911.

———. *Las huelgas en Barcelona durante los años 1910 al 1914 ambos inclusive*, Barcelona, 1915.

———. *La esclavitud moderna. Martirología social (Relación de los atentados y actos de 'sabotaje' cometidos en Barcelona, y bombas y explosivos hallados desde junio de 1910 hasta junio de 1921)*, Barcelona, 1921.

Serrat y Bonastre, J. 'De la formación del maestro de taller en la industria metalúrgica', *La Industria Metalúrgica*, May 1923: 1–6.

Suñol Gros, J. *Guia de San Martín de Provensals*, Barcelona, 1918.

Tallada, J.M. *Demografia de Catalunya*, Barcelona, 1918.

Torrent i Garriga, D. *Manlleu: Croquis para su historia*, Vic, 1893.

Valdour, J. *L'ouvrier espagnol. Observacions vécues, Tome 1 Catalogne*, Lille/Paris, 1919.

Vives, S. 'L'obrer malalt', *La Nació*, 2 October 1915: 13.

Xuriguera, R. *La repressió contra els obrers a Catalunya*, Paris, 1937.

Secondary Sources

Albareda i Salvadó, J. *La industrialització a la Plana de Vic, 1770–1875*, Vic, 1981.

———. 'Les colònies industrials a la conca del riu Ter', *El 9 Nou* (Osona), 28 May 1985 (El suplement, economia): 4.

———. 'L'escola laica a la Plana de Vic a principis del segle XX', in J. Monés and P. Solà, eds. *Actes de les cinquenes jornades de la història de l'educació als Països Catalans*, vol. 1, Vic, 1994: 187–210.

Alvarez Junco, J. *La ideología política del anarquismo español, 1868–1910*, Madrid, 1976.

———. *El emperador del Paralelo. Lerroux y la demagogia populista*, Madrid, 1990.

Arnavat, A. *Classe contra classe. El conflicte social de 1915 a Reus*, Reus, 1985.

Avilés, J. 'Republicanismo, librepensamiento y revolución: la ideología de Francisco Ferrer i Guardia', *Ayer*, no. 49, 2003: 249–89.

Balcells, A. *El sindicalisme a Barcelona, 1916–1923*, Barcelona. 1963.

———. 'Introducción', in A. Balcells, ed. *El arraigo del anarquismo en Cataluña. Textos de 1926/1932*, Barcelona, 1973: 5–40.

———. 'La mujer obrera en la industria catalana durante el primer cuarto del siglo XX', in A. Balcells, ed. *Trabajo industrial y organization obrera en la Cataluña contemporánea*, Barcelona, 1974: 7–121.

Balcells, A., J. Culla and C. Mir. *Les eleccions generals a Catalunya, 1900–1923*, Barcelona, 1982.

Balfour, S. *The End of Spanish Empire, 1898–1923*, Oxford, 1997.

Ben–Ami, S. *Fascism from Above: The Dictatorship of Primo de Rivera in Spain, 1923–1930*, Oxford, 1983.

Benaul i Berenguer, J.M. '*La industria tèxtil llanera a Catalunya, 1780–1870. El procés d'industrialització de Sabadell i Terrassa*', unpublished Ph.D. thesis, Universitat Autònoma de Barcelona, 1991.

———. 'Dues ciutats i dues polítiques. Sabadell i Terrassa, 1900–1923', in Conxita Mir ed. *Actituds polítiques i control social a la Catalunya de la Restauració*, Lleida, 1989: 131–46.

Bengoechea, S. *Organització patronal i conflictivitat social a Catalunya*, Barcelona, 1994.

———. *El lockaut de Barcelona, 1919–1920*, Barcelona, 1998.

———. 'Martínez Anido, la patronal y el pistolerismo', *L'Avenç*, no. 224, 1998: 6–11.

———. 'Els dirigents patronals i la Setmana Tràgica', *Quaderns del Seminari d'Història de Barcelona*, April 2000: 3–55.

———. 'The Barcelona Bourgeoisie, the Labour Movement and the Origins of Francoist Corporatism', in A. Smith ed. *Red Barcelona: Social Protest and Labour Mobilization in the Twentieth Century*, London, 2002: 167–84.

Bengoechea, S. and F. del Rey Reguillo. 'Militars, patrons i sindicalistes "libres". Sobre el sindicalisme de ghetto a Catalunya', *L'Avenç*, no. 166, 1993: 8–16.

———. 'En visperas de un golpe de estado. Radicalización patronal e imagen del fascismo en España', in J. Tusell et al. *Estudios sobre la derecha española contemporánea*, Madrid, 1993: 301–26.

Berger, S. 'The British and German Labour Movements Before the Second World War. The Sonderweg Revisited', *Twentieth-Century British History*, vol. 3, no. 2, 1992: 219–48.

Berger, S. and A. Smith. 'Between Scylla and Charybdis: Nationalism, Labour and Ethnicity Across Five Continents', in S. Berger and A. Smith eds. *Nationalism, Labour and Ethnicity*, Manchester, 1999: 1–30.

Bookchin, M. *The Spanish Anarchists. The Heroic Years, 1868–1936*, New York, 1977.

Borderías, C. 'Women Workers in the Barcelona Labour Market, 1856–1936', in A. Smith ed. *Red Barcelona. Social Protest and Labour Mobilization in the Twentieth Century*, London, 2002: 142–66.

Boyd, C.P. *Praetorian Politics in Liberal Spain*, Chapel Hill, 1979.

Brenan, G. *The Spanish Labyrinth. An Account of the Social and Political Background of the Spanish Civil War*, Cambridge, 1942.

Burges, K. 'New Unionism for Old? The Amalgamated Society of Engineers in Britain', in W.J. Mommsen and H. Gerhard Husung, eds. *The Development of Trade Unionism in Great Britain and Germany, 1880–1914*, London, 1985: 169–81.

Cabañas Guevara, L. *Biografía del Paralelo, 1894–1934*, Barcelona, 1945.

Calvo, A. 'Estructura industrial i sistema productiu a Catalunya durant la Primera Guerra Mundial', *Reçerques*, no. 20, 1988: 1–44.

Camps, E. *La formación del mercado de trabajo en la Cataluña del siglo XIX*, Madrid, 1995.

Capdevila, M.D. 'Aportació a la història del socialisme català, nos. I–IV', *Revista del Centro de Lectura de Reus*, September 1973–February 1974.

Capdevila, M.D. and R. Masgrau. *La Justicia Social. Organ de la Federació Catalana del PSOE, 1910–1916*, Barcelona, 1979.

Cardona, G. *El poder militar en la España contemporánea*, Madrid, 1983.

Carr, R. *Spain, 1808–1939*, Oxford, 1966.

Carreras, A. 'El aprovechamiento de la energía hidráulica en Cataluña. Un ensayo de interpretación', *Revista de Historia Económica*, no. 2, 1983: 31–63.

———. 'La producción industrial catalana y vasca, 1844–1935. Elementos para una comparación', in M. González Portilla, J. Maluquer de Motes and B. de Riquer, eds. *Industrialización y nacionalismo. Análisis comparativos*, Barcelona, 1985: 197–210.

Castellanos, J. 'Aspectes de les relacions entre intel·lecuals i anarquistes a Catalunya al segle XIX (a propòsit de Pere Coromines)', *Els Marges*, no. 6, 1976: 7–28.

Castells, A. *Informe de l'oposició*, vol. 2, *Republica i acció directe, 1868–1904*, Sabadell, 1977.

———. *Informe de l'oposició*, vol. 3, *O tot o res, 1904–1918*, Sabadell, 1978.

Casterás, R. *Actitudes de los sectores catalanes en la coyuntura de los años 1880*, Barcelona, 1985.

Castillo, A. del. *La Maquinista Terrestre y Marítima: Personaje histórico, 1855–1955*, Barcelona, 1955.

Castillo, S. 'La implantación del PSOE hasta su IV Congreso (1886–1894)', *Estudios de Historia Social*, nos. 8–9, 1979: 197–206.

———. Los orígenes de la organización obrera en España: de la Federación de Tipógrafos a la UG de T', *Estudios de Historia Social*, nos. 26–27, 1983: 19–256.

———. *Historia del socialismo español*, vol. 1, *1870–1909*, Madrid, 1989.

———. *Historia de la Unión General de Trabajadores*, vol. 1, *Hacia la mayoría de edad*, Madrid, 1998.

Centenario de la fundación de la compañía Fabra i Coats, Barcelona, 1944.

Child, J. *Industrial Relations in the British Printing Industry: The Quest for Security*, London, 1951.

Connelly Ullman, J. *La Semana Trágica, Estudio sobre las causas socioeconómicas del anticlericalismo en España*, Barcelona, 1972.

Coromines, P. *Diaris i records*, 3 vols, *De la solidaritat al catorze d'abril*, vol. 2, Barcelona, 1974.

Crew, D. *Town on the Ruhr. A Social History of Bochum, 1860–1914*, New York, 1979.

Cruells, M. *Salvador Seguí, el Noi del Sucre*, Barcelona, 1974.

Cuadrat, X. *Socialismo y anarquismo en Cataluña, 1899–1911. Los orígines de la CNT*, Madrid, 1976.

Cucurull, F. 'De la revolució monàrquica al "tancament de caixes", 1875–1900', in A. Balcells, ed. *Història de Catalunya*, vol. 5, Barcelona, 1978: 237–54.

Culla i Clarà, J.B. *El republicanisme lerrouxista a Catalunya, 1901–1923*, Barcelona, 1986.

Deu i Baigual, E. 'La indústria llanera de Sabadell en el primer quart del segle XX', unpublished Ph.D. thesis, Universitat Autònoma de Barcelona, 1986.

Deu Baygual, E. 'Republicanisme i obrerisme a Sabadell de 1900 a 1914', *Perspectiva Social*, no. 4, 1974: 47–97.

Dolgoff, S., ed. *Bakunin on Anarchism*, Montreal and New York, 1980.

Dorel-Ferré, G. *Les colònies industrials a Catalunya. El cas de la colònia Sedó*, Barcelona, 1992.

Duarte i Montserrat, A. *El republicanisme catala a la fi del segle XIX*, Vic, 1987.

———. *Pere Coromines: del republicanisme als cercles llibertaris, 1888–1896*, Barcelona, 1988.

———. 'Mayordomos y contramaestres: jerarquía fabril en la industria algodonera catalana, 1879–90', *Historia Social*, no. 4, 1989: 3–20.

Dubief, H. ed. *Le syndicalisme révolutionnaire*, Paris, 1969.

Durgan, A. *El Bloque Obrero y Campesino*, Barcelona, 1996.

Eley, G. and K. Nield. 'Why Does Social History Ignore Politics?', *Social History*, vol. 5, 1980: 249–71.

Ellis, H. *The Soul of Spain*, London, 1937.

Elorza, A. *Artículos madrileños de Salvador Seguí*, Madrid, 1976.

Enrech, C. 'La Llano contra la Montaña. La descualificación del trabajo en la hilatura catalana a finales del siglo XIX', in S. Castillo, and J.M. de Oruña, eds. *Estado, protesta y movimientos sociales a finales del siglo XIX*, Bilbao, 1998: 581–96.

———. 'L'ofensiva patronal contra l'ofici. Estructures laborals i jerarquies obreres a la indústria tèxtil catalana, 1881–1923', unpublished Ph.D. thesis, 2 vols, Universitat Autònoma de Barcelona, 2000.

———. 'la ofensiva contra el oficio en la industria textil catalana (1881–1923). La destrucción de un modelo de sociedad urbana', in S. Castillo, and R. Fernández eds. *Campesinos, artesanos, trabajadores*, Lleida, 2001: 567–82.

———. 'Les colònies no neixen es construeixen', in L. Virós, ed. *Actes de les jornades d'arqueologia industrial de Manresa*, Barcelona, 2002: 201–23.

———. *Entre Sans i Sans. Història social i política d'una població industrial a les portes de Barcelona, 1839–1897*, Barcelona, 2004.

E.R.A. 80. *Els anarquistes, educadors del Poble: 'La Revista Blanca', 1898–1905*. Prologue by Federica Montseny, Barcelona, 1979.

Essenwein, G. 'Anarchist Ideology and the Spanish Working-Class Movement (1880–1900): With Special Reference to Ricardo Mella', unpublished Ph.D. thesis, University of London, 1987.

La España Industrial en su 82 aniversario, 1847–1929, Barcelona, 1947.

La España Industrial S.A. Fabril y Mercantil: Libro de centenario, Barcelona, 1929.

Fàbregas, X. 'El teatre anarquista a Catalunya', in *L'Avenç*, no. 22, 1979: 29–35.

Ferrer, J. *Francesc Layret, 1880–1920*, 2nd edn, Barcelona, 1972.

———. *I .Simó Piera: Perfil d'un sindicalista. II. Simó Piera: Records i experiències d'un dirigent de la CNT*, Barcelona, 1975.

Ferrer, S. *Vida y obra de Ferrer*, Barcelona, 1980 [1962].

Florez Beltrán, L. *La industria algodonera española*, Barcelona, 1943.

Forcadell, C. *Parlamentarismo y bolchevización. El movimiento obrero español, 1914–1918*, Barcelona, 1978.

Fusi, J.P. *Política obrera en el País Vasco, 1880–1923*, Barcelona, 1975.

Gabriel, P. *Joan Peiró. Escrits, 1917–1939*, Barcelona, 1975.

———. 'Sindicats i classe obrera a Catalunya, 1900–1923', unpublished Ph.D. thesis, Universitat Central de Barcelona, 1982.

———. 'El marginament del republicanisme i l'obrerisme', in *L'Avenç*, no. 85, 1985: 34–8.

———. 'La població obrera catalana, una població obrera industrial?', *Estudios de Historia Social*, nos. 32–33, 1985: 192–259.

———. 'Sous i cost de la vida a Catalunya a l'entorn dels anys de la primera guerra mundial', *Reçerques*, no. 20, 1988: 61–92.

———. 'Sindicalismo y huelga. Sindicalismo revolucionario francés e italiano. Su introducción en España', *Ayer*, no. 4, 1991: 15–46.

———. 'Espacio urbano y articulación política popular en Barcelona, 1890–1920', in J.L. García Delgado, ed. *Las ciudades en la modernización de España*, Madrid, 1992: 61–96.

———. 'Red Barcelona in the Europe of War and Revolution, 1914–30', in A. Smith, ed. *Red Barcelona. Social Protest and Labour Mobilization in the Twentieth Century*, London, 2002: 44–65.

García Delgado, J.L. 'Nacionalismo económico e intevención estatal, 1900–1930', in N. Sánchez Albornoz, ed. *La modernización económica de España*, Madrid, 1985: 176–95.

Garrabou, R. 'La crisi agrària espanyola desde finals del segle XIX: Una etapa del desenvolupament del capitalisme', *Reçerques*, no. 5, 1975: 161–216.

Geary, D. *European Labour Protest, 1849–1939*, London, 1981.

Golden, L. 'Les dones com avantguarda. El rebombori de pa del gener de 1918', *L'Avenç*, no. 44, 1981: 45–50.

———. 'Barcelona 1909: las dones contra la quinta i l'església', *L'Avenç*, no. 109, 1987: 48–54.

Gómez Ochoa, F. 'El partido conservador y el problema social durante la crisis final de la Restauración: la sindicazión profesional y obligatoria', in J. Tusell et al. *Estudios sobre la derecha española contemporánea*, Madrid, 1993: 269–88.

González Calbet, M.T. *La dictadura de Primo de Rivera. El Directorio Militar*, Madrid, 1989.

González Calleja, E. *El máuser y el sufragio. Orden público, subversión y violencia política en la crisis de la Restauración, 1917–1931*, Madrid, 1999.

González Calleja, E. and F. del Rey Reguillo. *La defensa armada contra la revolución*, Madrid, 1995.

Hanagan, M.P. *The Logic of Solidarity. Artisans and Industrial Workers in Three French Towns, 1871–1914*, Ilinois, 1980.

Harrison, J. 'The Failure of Economic Reconstruction in Spain, 1916–1923', *European Studies Review*, vol. 13, no. 1, 1983: 63–88.

———. 'The Agrarian History of Spain, 1800–1960', *Agricultural History Review*, vol. 37, no. 2, 1989: 180–7.

Harrison, R.J. 'The Spanish Famine of 1904–1906', *Agricultural History*, vol. 47, no. 4, 1973: 300–7.

———. 'Catalan Business and the Loss of Cuba, 1898–1914', *Economic History Review*, 2nd Series, vol. 37, 1974: 431–41.

Hennessy, C.A.M. *The Federal Republic in Spain. Pi i Margall and the Federal Republican Movement in Spain, 1868–1874*, Oxford, 1962.

Hobsbawm, E.J. 'The Machine Breakers', *Past and Present*, vol. 1, 1952: 57–90.

———. *Primitive Rebels. Studies in Archaic Forms of Social Movement in the Nineteenth and Twentieth Centuries*, Manchester, 1959.

———. 'Religion and the Rise of Socialism', in E.J. Hobsbawm. *Worlds of Labour. Further Studies in the History of Labour*, London, 1984: 33–48.

———. 'The Aristocracy of Labour Reconsidered', in E.J. Hobsbawm. *Worlds of Labour. Further Studies in the History of Labour*, London, 1984: 227–51.

Ibarz Gelabert, J. 'Sociedades y montepíos. Asociacionismo laboral de los cargadores y descargadores del puerto de Barcelona', *Sociología del Trabajo*, no. 18, 1993: 119–38.

Izard, M. *Industrialización y obrerismo. Las Tres Clases de Vapor, 1869–1913*, Barcelona, 1973.

———. 'Entre la impotencia y la esperanza. La Unión Manufacturera (7–V–1872 a 4–VIII–1873)', *Estudios de Historia Social*, no. 4, 1978: 29–105.

Jennings, J. *Syndicalism in France. A Study in Ideas*, Basingstoke, 1990.

Juliá, S. *Madrid, 1931–1934. De la fiesta popular a la lucha de clases*, Madrid, 1984.

Kaplan, Temma. *Anarchists of Andalusia, 1868–1903*, Princeton, 1977.

———. 'Other Scenarios: Women and Spanish Anarchism', in R. Bridenthal, and C. Koonz, eds. *Becoming Visible: Women in European History*, Boston, 1977: 401–21.

———. 'Female Consciousness and Collective Action: The Case of Barcelona, 1900–1918'. *Signs*, vol. 7, no. 3, 1982: 545–66.

Kern, R. *Red Years, Black Years. A Political History of Spanish Anarchism, 1911–1937*, Philadelphia, 1978.

Lacomba, J.A. *La crisis española de 1917*, Madrid, 1970.

Lannon, F. *Privilege, Persecution and Prophecy. The Catholic Church in Spain, 1875–1975*, Oxford, 1987.

La legislación social en la historia de España. De la revolución liberal a 1936, Madrid, 1987.

León-Ignacio. *Los años del pistolerismo*, Barcelona, 1981.

Lida, Clara E. 'Literatura anarquista y anarquismo literario', *Nueva Revista de Filología Hispánica*, no. 19, 1970: 360–81.

Litvak, L. *Musa Libertaria. Arte, literatura y vida cultural en el anarquismo español, 1880–1913*, Barcelona, 1981.

Lladonosa i Vall-llebrera, M. *Catalanisme i moviment obrer: el CADCI entre 1903 i 1923*, Barcelona, 1988.

———. *Sindicalistes i llibertaris: l'experiència de Camil Piñón*, Barcelona, 1989.

Madrid Santos, F. 'La prensa anarquista y anarcosindicalista en España desde la Primera Internacional hasta el final de la guerra civil', 2 vols, unpublished Ph.D. thesis, Universidad de Barcelona, 1989.

———. 'Los grupos anarquistas en España: un estudio sobre la organización', in *Col·loqui internacional revolució i socialisme*, Barcelona, 1989: 153–76.

———. 'Racionalismo pedagógico y movimiento obrero en España: Ferrer Guardia y "La Huelga General"', *Educació i Història*, no. 1, 1994: 61–5.

Magraw, R. 'Socialism, Syndicalism and French Labour', in D. Geary, ed. *Labour and Socialist Movements*, Exeter, 1989: 74–86.

———. *A History of the French Working Class*, vol. 2, *Workers and the Bourgeois Republic*, Oxford, 1992.

Marfany, J.L. *Aspectes del modernisme*, 3rd edn, Barcelona, 1979.

Marquès i Mir, J. *Història de l'organitzacio tèxtil 'Radium'*, Barcelona, 1988.

Martín Ramos, J.L. 'L'expansió industrial', *L'Avenç*, no. 69, 1984: 34–42.

———. 'Anàlisi del moviment vaguístic a Barcelona (1914–1923)', *Reçerques*, no. 20, 1988: 93–114.

———. 'De la tregua a la expansión reivindicativa. El arranque de la explosión huelguística en Barcelona (1914–1916)', *Historia Social*, no. 5, 1989: 115–28.

Marx, K, F. Engels, and I. Lenin, *Anarchism and Anarcho-Syndicalism*, Moscow, 1972.

Mayer, A.J. *The Persistence of the Old Regime*, New York, 1974.

Mayol, A., ed. *Boletín de La Escuela Moderna*, Barcelona, 1977.

McDonogh, G.W. *Good Families of Barcelona. A Social History of Power in the Modern Era*, Princeton, 1986.

Meaker, G. *The Revolutionary Left in Spain, 1914–1923*, Stanford, 1974.

———. 'A Civil War of Words', in H.A. Schmitt, ed. *Neutral Europe between War and Revolution, 1917–1923*, Carlottesville, 1988: 1–66.

Miralles, C., and J.L. Oyón. 'De la casa a la fábrica. Movilidad obrera y transporte en la Barcelona de entreguerras 1914–39', in J.L. Oyón, ed. *Vida obrera en la Barcelona de entreguerras*, Barcelona, 1998: 159–202.

Moreno Lujón, J. 'Partidos y parlamento en la crisis de la Restauración', in M. Cabrera, ed. *Con luz y taquígrafos. El parlamento en la Restauración, 1913–1923*, Madrid, 1998: 65–102.

Muñoz, V. 'Correspondencia selecta de Francisco Ferrer Guardia', *Supplement au Cent*, no. 198, 1971: 9–11.

Nadal, J. 'La formació de la indústria moderna', in J. Nadal, and J. Maluquer de Motes. *Catalunya. La fàbrica d'Espanya, 1833–1936. Un segle d'industrialització catalana*, Barcelona, 1985: 44–111.

———. 'Un siglo de industrialización española, 1833–1930', in N. Sánchez Albornoz, ed. *La modernización económica de España, 1830–1930*, Madrid, 1985: 89–101.

———. 'La industria fabril española en 1900: una aproximación', in J. Nadal, A. Carreras, and C. Sudrià, eds. *La economía española en el siglo XX. Una perspectiva histórica*, Barcelona, 1987: 23–61.

———. 'La metalúrgia', in *Història econòmica de la Catalunya contemporània*, vol. 3, Barcelona, 1991: 161–202.

———. 'La transformación del zapato manual al zapato "mecánico" en España', in J. Nadal and J. Català, eds. *La cara oculta de la industrialización española*, Madrid, 1994: 321–39.

Nadal, J. and C. Sudrià. *Història de la caixa de pensions*, Barcelona, 1979.

Nadal, J. and X. Tafunell. *Sant Martí de Provencals, pulmó industrial de Barcelona, 1847–1992*, Barcelona, 1992.

Nettlau, M. *La Première Internationale en Espagne, 1868–1888*, Amsterdam, 1969.

Olivé Serret, E. 'El moviment anarquista català i l'obrerisme, 1900–1909', unpublished Ph.D. thesis, Universitat Autònoma de Barcelona, 1977.

Oliveras Samitier, J. *Desenvolupament industrial i formació urbana a Manresa, 1800–1870*, Manresa, 1985.

Oyón, J.L. and C. García Soler. 'Las segundas periferias, 1918–1936: una geografía preliminar', in J.L Oyón, ed. *Vida obrera en la Barcelona de entreguerras*, Barcelona, 1998: 47–83.

Pabón, J. *Cambó, 1876–1918*, Barcelona, 1952.

———. *Cambó*, vol. 2, *Primera parte: 1918–1930*, Barcelona, 1969.

Papayanis, N. *Alphonse Merrheim. The Emergence of Reformism within Revolutionary Syndicalism, 1871–1925*, Dordrecht, 1985.

Paz, A. *Durruti en la revolución española*, Madrid, 1996.

Pérez Ledesma, M. 'La primera étapa de la UGT (1888–1897): planteamiento sindical y formas de organización', in A. Balcells, ed. *Teoría y práctica del movimiento obrero en España, 1900–1936*, Valencia, 1977, 113–71.

———. 'Partido y sindicato: unas relaciones no siempre fáciles', in M. Pérez Ledesma, *El obrero consciente. Dirigentes, partidos y sindicatos en la II Internacional*, Madrid, 1987: 222–38.

Pérez Moredo, V. 'La modernización demográfica, 1800–1930. Sus limitaciones y cronología', in N. Sánchez Albornoz, ed. *La modernización económica de España 1830–1930*, Madrid, 1985: 25–62.

Phillips, G. 'The British Labour Movement Before 1914', in D. Geary, ed. *Labour and Socialist Movements in Europe before 1914*, Exeter, 1989: 38–41.

Piqué i Padró, J. *Anarco-col·lectivisme i anarco-comunisme. L'oposició de dues postures en el moviment anarquista català, 1881–1891*, Barcelona, 1989.

Porcel, B. *La revuelta permanente*, Barcelona, 1978.

Prats, L. *La Catalunya rancia. Les condicions de vida materials de les classes populars a la Catalunya de la Restauració segons les topografies mèdiques*, Barcelona, 1996.

Preston, P. *The Coming of the Spanish Civil War. Reform, Revolution and Reaction in the Second Republic*, 2nd edn, London, 1994.

Puy, J. 'La Unión Monárquica Nacional frente al catalanismo de la Lliga, 1918–1923', in *Estudios de Historia Social*, nos. 28–29, 1984: 467–73.

Radcliffe, P.B. *From Mobilization to Civil War. The Politics of Polarization in the Spanish City of Gijón, 1900–1937*, Cambridge, 1997.

Ramos, G. and S. Bengoechea. 'La patronal catalana y la huelga de 1902', *Historia Social*, no. 5, 1989: 77–95.

Rey Reguillo, F. del. *Propietarios y Patronos. La política de las organizaciones económicas en la España de la Restauración, 1914–1923*, Madrid, 1992.

———. 'Las voces del antiparlamentarismo conservador', in M. Cabrera, ed. *Con luz y taquígrafos. El parlamento en la Restauración, 1913–1923*, Madrid, 1998: 273–328.

Richardson, J. *A Life of Picasso*, vol. 1, *1881–1906*, London, 1991.

Ridley, F.F. *Revolutionary Syndicalism in France. The Direct Action of its Time*, London, 1970.

Riquer, Borja de. *Lliga Regionalista. La burgesia catalana i el nacionalisme, 1898–1904*, Barcelona, 1977.

———. 'Burgesos, polítics i caçics a la Catalunya de la Restauració', *L'Avenç*, no. 85, 1985: 16–33.

———. 'Los límites de la modernización política: el caso de Barcelona, 1890–1923', in J.A. García Delgado, ed. *Las ciudades en la modernización de España. Los decenios interseculares*, Madrid, 1992, 21–60.

Robles Egea, A. 'La conjunción republicano-socialista', in S. Juliá, ed. *El Socialismo en España*, Madrid, 1986: 109–30.

Roig, M. *Rafael Vidiella, l'aventura de la revolució*, Barcelona, 1976.

Romero Maura, J. 'Terrorism in Barcelona and its impact on Spanish politics, 1904–1909', *Past and Present*, no. 41, 1968: 149–61.

———. *La Rosa del Fuego*. *Republicanos y anarquistas: La política de los obreros barceloneses entre el desastre colonial y La Semana Trágica*, Barcelona, 1975.

Romero Salvadó, F.J. *Spain 1914–1918: Between War and Revolution*, London, 1999.

Rosal, A. del. *Historia de la UGT de España, 1901–1939*, vol. 1, Barcelona, 1977.

Sales, N. 'Servicio militar y sociedad en el siglo XIX', in N. Sales. *Sobre esclavos, reclutas y mercaderes de quintas*, Barcelona, 1974: 209–46.

Sans Ortega, M. *Els treballadors mercantils dins el moviment obrer català*, Barcelona, 1975.

Santacana i Torres, C. 'La configuració dels municipis periferics: l'impacte cultural i sociopolític', in J.L. Oyón, ed. *Vida obrera en la Barcelona de entreguerras*, Barcelona, 1998: 85–98.

Scott, J.W. *The Glassworkers of Carmaux. French Craftsmen and Political Action in a Nineteenth Century City*, Cambridge Mass., 1974.

Scott, J. and L. Tilly, 'Women's Work and the Family in Nineteenth Century Europe', in C.E. Rosenberg, ed. *The Family in History*, Philadelphia, 1975: 145–78.

Serra i Carné, J. 'La vaga de 1900 a Manresa', in Centre d'Estudis del Bagés, ed. *L'activitat industrial a la Catalunya interior*, Manresa, 1989: 109–31.

Serrano, C. 'Anarquismo fin de siglo', in C. Serrano. *El turno del pueblo. Crisis nacional, movimientos populares y populismo en España, 1890–1910*, Barcelona, 2000: 125–68.

Serrano Sanz, J.M. *El viraje proteccionista de la Restauración. La política comercial española, 1875–1895*, Madrid, 1987.

Shubert, A. *A Social History of Modern Spain*, London, 1990.

Simpson, J. *Spanish Agriculture: The Long Siesta, 1765–1965*, Cambridge, 1985.

Smith, A. 'Social Conflict and Trade-Union Organisation in the Catalan Cotton Textile Industry, 1890–1914', *International Review of Social History*, vol. 36, no. 3, 1991: 332–76.

———. 'Los tipógrafos de Barcelona (1899–1914). Relaciones laborales, desarrollo sindical y práxis política', in S. Castillo, ed. *El trabajo a través de la historia*, Madrid, 1996: 437–47.

———. 'Industria, oficio y género en la industria textil Catalana, 1833–1923' *Historia Social*, no. 45, 2003: 79–99.

Solà i Gussinyer, P. *Francesc Ferrer i Guardia i L'Escola Moderna*, Barcelona, 1978.

———. *Las escuelas racionalistas en Cataluña, 1909–1939*, Barcelona, 1978.

Solé Tura, Jordi. *Catalanismo y revolución burguesa*, 2nd edn, Madrid, 1974.

Soler y Becerro, R. 'La evolución del salario en una empresa textil algodonera. La fábrica de la Rambla de Vilanova i la Geltrú, 1891–1925', *Revista de Historia Económica*, vol. 15, no. 2, 1997: 400–11.

Suárez Cortina, M. *El reformismo en España. Republicanos y reformistas bajo la monarquía de Alfonso XIII*, Madrid, 1986.

Stedman Jones, G. *Languages of Class: Studies in English Working Class History, 1832–1982*, Cambridge, 1983.

Sudrià i Triay, C. 'La exportación en el desarrollo de la industria algodonera española, 1875–1920', *Revista de Historia Económica*, vol. 1, no. 2, 1983: 369–86.

———. 'Una societat plenament industrial', in *Història econòmica de la Catalunya contemporània*, vol. 4, Barcelona, 1988: 11–97.

Sullivan, J. *ETA and Basque Nationalism: the Fight for Euskadi, 1890–1936*, London, 1988.

Tatjer Mir, M. 'Els barris obrers del centre històric de Barcelona', in J.L. Oyón, ed. *Vida obrera en la Barcelona de entreguerras*, Barcelona, 1998: 13–45.

Tavera, S. *Solidaridad Obrera. El fer-se i desfer-se d'un diari anarco-sindicalista (1915–1939)*, Barcelona, 1992.

Termes i Ardévol, J. *Anarquismo y sindicalismo en España. La Primera Internacional, 1864–1881*, Barcelona, 1971.

———. 'El nacionalisme català: per una nova interpretatió', in J. Termes, *La immigració a catalunga i altres estudis d'història del nacionalisme català*, Barcelona, 1984: 63–99.

———. 'Els Ateneus Populars: un intent de cultura obrera', *L'Avenç*, no. 104, 1987: 9–11.

Terrades, I. *Les colònies industrials. Un estudi entorn del cas de L'Ametlla de Merola*, Barcelona, 1979.

Thompson, E.P. 'The Moral Economy of the Crowd in the Eighteenth Century', *Past and Present*, no. 50, 1971: 76–136.

Tilly, C. *From Mobilization to Revolution*, Reading Mass., 1978.

Tortella, G. 'Producción y productividad agraria, 1830–1930', in N. Sánchez Albornoz, ed. *La modernización económica de España*, 1830–1930, Madrid, 1985: 63–88.

———. *El desarrollo de la España contemporánea*, Madrid, 1994.

Tuñón de Lara, M. *El movimiento obrero en la historia de España*, 3 vols, Madrid, 1977.

Turner, H.A. *Trade Union Growth, Structure and Spread. A Comparative History of the Cotton Unions*, London, 1962.

Tusell, J. *Radiografía de un golpe de estado. El ascenso al poder del General Primo de Rivera*, Madrid, 1987.

———. *Antonio Maura. Una Biografía Política*, Madrid, 1994.

———. 'La dictadura de Primo de Rivera', in *Historia de España Menéndez Pidal*, vol. XXXVIII, 2, *La España de Alfonso XIII. El Estado y La Política*.

Tusell, J. and J. Avilés. *La derecha española contemporánea. Sus orígenes: el maurismo*, Madrid, 1986.

Ucelay Da Cal, E. *La Catalunya populista. Imatge, cultura i política en L'etapa republicana, 1931–1939*, Barcelona, 1978.

Vicens i Vives, J. 'El moviment obrerista català (1901–1939)', *Reçerques*, no. 7, 1978: 9–31.

Vicens i Vives, J. and M. Llorens. *Industrials i polítics del segle XIX*, Barcelona, 1983 [1958].

Vilar, P. *Historia de España*, Barcelona, 1978.

Winston, C.M. *Workers and the Right in Spain, 1900–1936*, Princeton, 1985.

INDEX

A

ABC *syndicaliste* (Yvetot, G.) 129
Adame, Manuel 352
ADM (shopworkers' union) 85, 115, 132, 201
agriculture 3, 16–18
L'Aguila (company) 24, 63n12, 230
Aguilar, Angel 110
Aguilar, Joaquín 82
Aixerit (factory) 228
Aláiz, Felipe 344
Alcalá del Valle 124, 128, 135, 162, 166, 169
Alfonso XIII 129, 151, 153, 163, 181, 270, 275, 277, 299, 315
Alhucemas, Marquis of 277, 345, 349
Allendesalazar, Manuel 315, 317, 337, 349
    climate of violence under Allendesalazar Government 323–6
Alt Llobregat 14, 39, 71, 73–4, 210, 229, 254, 303
Altea, Count of 330
Alvarez, Ernesto 115–16
Alvarez Junco, José 166, 178, 186n49
Amado, Julio 303–4, 306–7, 309, 310, 311–12, 327, 329, 331
Amador, Antonio 237, 324
L'Ametlla de Merola company town 73–4, 97n18
anarchism 2–4
    4 de Maig group 128–9, 135, 145n123, 153, 162, 166, 172, 185n31, 186n75, 199
    anarchism, liberal rationalism and
    positivism 6–7, 151, 157–9, 164–6
    anarchist culture 150–62
    anarchist groups 107–8, 115–18, 128–9, 135, 145n123, 151–8, 162, 171, 185n31, 186n75, 187n93, 196, 199, 233, 235–7, 251, 273–4, 276, 312, 315, 322n81, 344
    anarchist ideology 104–5, 118–19, 128–9, 150–2
    anarchist terrorism 108–9, 134–5, 154–5, 250–3, 328–9, 330, 337, 348–9
    anarcho-communism 107
    anticlericalism and 150–1, 179
    anticolonialism and 148, 170, 175–82
    antimilitarism and 151–2
    'antipoliticism' and 2, 150–2, 164–6
    appearance in Spain 103–4
    attitude towards women 40, 90, 121, 143n58, 158, 207–8, 243–5, 247, 268–9, 287n28, 326
    Avenir (and Avenir group) 153, 157, 171, 187n93
    Barcelona Federation of Anarchist Groups 236
    Barcelona labour movement and (1870–1909) 104–8, 112–27, 132–4, 139–40
    Catalan Federation of Anarchist Groups 196, 274
    Catalanism and 131–2, 153, 170–2
    consumer cooperatives, attitude towards 126

'direct action' 96, 129–30, 136, 138, 161, 183, 197–9, 212, 214, 239–40, 243, 265, 269, 304, 312, 314
  see also mobilising practice of; union strategy
eight-hours day, support for 107, 130–1
Ferrer, Lorenzo and the rise of 117–18, 128
FRE (Spanish branch of the First International) 104–7, 130, 142n43
'free love' 161
FRESR (pro-anarchist labour federation), 121–2, 124–5, 128, 131, 143n61, 162
FTRE (pro-anarchist labour confederation) 105–7, 116, 130, 142n43
gender relations within *see* attitude towards women
the General Strike as a revolutionary tool 3, 107–8, 118–19, 122–5
growth in Andalusia and Catalonia of 2
individualist anarchism 107–8, 128, 153
mobilising practice of 90, 107, 120, 161–2
OARE (federation of anarchist groups) 107
Pact of Union and Solidarity (Anarchist labour confederation) 107
press and pamphlets 153, 155–6, 185n31
prisoners (*presos sociales*), campaigns to free 115–6, 124, 128, 135, 162, 166, 169, 189, 211–12, 215, 262
'propaganda by the deed' 107, 129, 153
republicanism and 115–16, 149–50, 159–60, 163–73
SO (Catalan labour confederation) and 128–40
Socialists, criticisms of 127, 205, 336–7
soirée meetings 157
syndicalism and 118, 129–30, 134, 136, 142n44, 155–8

textile workers and 106, 108–28, 153
theories of anarchism 2–5
Tierra y Libertad 116, 128, 131, 135, 138, 156, 172, 185n31, 196, 232–3, 235, 241, 262, 265, 273–4, 280, 346
La Tramontana (and Tramontana group) 153, 169, 172, 185n31, 186n74
union strategy 194–5, 118–20, 128–9, 131–2, 138–9
vegetarianism 161
  see also Bonafulla, Leopoldo; Claramunt, Teresa; CNT; CRT; Ferrer, Francesc; Herreros, Tomás; Lorenzo, Anselmo; Modern School; SO
Andalusia 1–2, 105, 107, 122, 183, 200, 249, 292, 313, 328, 341
Andreu, Manuel 196, 232, 236–9, 261, 263, 271, 273–4, 287–8n34
Angiolillo, Michele 108, 174
Anònima Tram Company 92
anti-*caciquista* language 277
anticlericalism 150–1, 155, 178–9
  see also Tragic Week
anti-union rhetoric and strategies *see* employers
L'Anuari de l'Exportació (factory) 50
Aragón 3, 38, 44, 47, 200, 292, 313, 340, 344
Archs, Ramon 192, 251, 316, 323, 336–7, 340
Arín, Francisco 330
Arlegui, Manuel 333, 342, 344
Armengol, Bernat 324
Arrow, Charles 154, 167
L'Art d'Imprimir 114, 120, 167–8
  see also printing
artisanal trades, changes in 27–9
Ascaso, Francisco 344, 348
Association of Catalan Foundry Owners 92–3
Associations Law (1887) 124
Asturias 122, 200, 215, 305, 313–14
Ateneu Enciclopèdic Popular 271, 348
Ateneus Obrers (Workers' Athenaeums) 169, 172, 181, 325
Avenir (and Avenir group) 153, 157, 171, 187n93
Azcárate, General Manuel 80

B

Badalona 14, 200
Badia Matamala, Antoni 132–3, 135, 13–18, 144n101, 145n121
Bajatierra, Mauro 264, 314, 341
Bakunin, Mikhail 104–5, 107, 129, 170, 274, 313
Balcells, Albert 319n8
Bandera Roja 313
Baratech, Feliciano 221n75, 338, 354n2, 256n27
Barber, Francisco 350–1
Barcelona
    Chinatown 45, 53, 58, 60, 154, 236
    Fifth District 22, 53–4, 56, 58–9, 65n62, 87, 157, 177–8, 180, 235, 266, 280, 282, 329
    industrial power house 12, 19–22
    labour movement and anarchism (1870–1909) 104–8, 112–27, 132–4, 139–40
    'Mediterranean Chicago' 7
    Montjuïc 50, 54, 108, 174, 248
    physiognomy of the city, changes in 53–7
    Pla 12, 16, 48, 208–9, 213, 303, 308
    the Rambla 45, 48, 53, 56, 59, 176, 281
    skilled trades in 84–95
    'Spanish Manchester' 12
    Special Brigade of police 155, 204, 211, 241, 252, 334
    see also La Barceloneta, El Clot, Hostafrancs, Gràcia, Poble Nou, Poble Sec, Sant Andreu, Sant Martí, Sants
Barcelona Athenaeum 343
Barcelona Bricklayers and Bricklayers Labourers' Union 228, 245
Barcelona Bricklayers Labourers' Federation 117
Barcelona Construction Workers' Federation 207, 213, 217, 236, 245, 256n68
Barcelona Federation of Anarchist Groups 236
Barcelona Federation of Bricklayers and Bricklayers' Labourers 245
Barcelona Metalworkers' Federation (1901–03) 90, 93, 120, 122–3

Barcelona Metalworkers' Federation (1913–16) 207–12, 228
Barcelona Metalworkers' Union (1905–10) 190, 192, 207
Barcelona Metalworkers' Union (1916–18) 245, 248, 253
Barcelona Woodworkers' Federation
La Barceloneta 23, 44–5, 53, 55–6, 59, 75, 93, 191, 211, 248
    Rationalist Centre 260
Bargalló, Carles 210
Barrera, Martí 336
Barret, Josep 250, 252–3, 258n103
Barrio, Vicente 264, 276
Barthe, Fortunato 288n35, 312, 344
la base múltiple see el sindicalismo a base múltiple
Bausà, Jaume 171
Baygual, Esteve Deu 187n99
Benavent, Roser 337
Bergamín, Francisco 326–8
Bertran i Musitu, Josep 194, 296, 298, 320n23, 337, 339
Besteiro, Julián 234, 264, 275
Bilbao 19
Bisbe, Jaume 135–6, 144n101, 222n92
blackleg labour 193–4
blue-collar workers, unionisation centred on 85
    see also organised labour; trade unions, trade and industrial federations; working-class community
Boal, Evilio 301–2, 313–14, 317, 320n38, 327, 334, 336, 340
Bolshevik Revolution in Russia, impact of 284–6
Bonafulla, Leopoldo ('Joan Baptista Esteve') 117–20, 123–4, 128, 138, 142n45, 143n73, 152, 157, 163–4, 166, 185n21, 187n93, 218n2
Borbón, Jaime de 348
Borobio, José 232, 240, 261, 271, 274, 276, 280, 287–8n34, 288n50
Botella, Francesc 236
bottlemaking *see* glassblowers
Bravo Portillo, Manuel 252–3, 261, 267, 298–301, 304, 306–7, 318–9n7, 319–20n23
    assassination of 304, 306–7

bricklayers 24, 30, 42–3, 50, 85, 89,
91, 116–17, 120–1, 126, 157,
206, 212–13, 220n48, 228, 231,
235–6, 245–6, 248, 255n9,
256n68, 257n86
see also construction
brickmakers 35n59, 30, 201, 246, 352
see also construction
Brossa, Jaume 171, 283
Buenacasa, Manuel 232, 238–9, 297,
299–302, 312, 320n41, 232, 239,
343–4, 349, 355n13
on CRT membership 249
major commentator on events in
Russia 284
on PSOE-UGT alliance 286
against Seguí 304
Bueso, Adolfo 190, 216, 250
Bueso, Joaquín 51, 187n101, 195–7,
200, 202, 221n59, 237, 279,
282–3
building *see* construction
Bulffi, Lluís 153
Burgos y Mazo, Manuel de 277, 302,
306, 309, 321n59
businesses *see* companies and factories
businessmen *see* industrialists

C

caciques 2, 68, 71, 76, 79, 137, 139,
182, 262, 269
caciquismo 68–9, 71, 76, 79, 97, 146,
149, 151, 161, 269
CADCI (association of shop and office
workers) 85, 99n61, 172, 220n46,
231, 246, 339
Café Suizo *tertulia* 281
Calella 14, 145n113, 338
Calleja, Liberto 344
Calvet, Eduard 209
Cambó, Francesc 270, 277, 280, 283,
290–1, 312, 327, 330, 337
Campalans, Rafael 234
Campí, Amadeu 347
Camprubí, Amadeu 221n75
La Canadeca (company) 290–7, 350
See also Ebro Power and Irrigation
Canalejas, José 128, 152, 192, 194,
206, 214
Cánovas del Castillo, Antonio 68, 108,
174, 182

Cánovas Restoration 68–9
see also Restoration regime
Capdevila, Dolors 142n33, 145n113
capitalism
capitalist transformations 30
modernisation through 18–19
Caralt i Cia (factory) 22
Carbó, Eusebi 232, 264, 271, 273,
314, 320n41, 326
Cardenal, Ernest 159, 217
Cardener River 14, 73
Carlism 80, 163, 291, 298, 324–5, 348
Carlos Bas, Federico 327, 329–31,
338–9
and CNT conciliation hopes
327–30
Carpenters' Federation of the Catalan
Region 89, 99n68, 121
carpentry
industrial structure and the labour
process 20, 24, 30
unions and strikes 85–6, 89,
98n68, 120–1, 207, 227–8, 232
See also construction; woodworking
Casanelles, Ramon 337
Cases, Llorenç 251
Castellà, Agustí 237, 289n60
Castellote, Marià 117, 145n123, 153,
176
Castellví, José 262
Castilians 47, 171
Castillo, Santiago 141n25
Catalan Confederation of Barcelona
Bricklayers and Bricklayers'
Labourers 50, 212–13, 245
Catalan Diputacions Provincals 215
Catalan Federation of Anarchist Groups
196, 274
Catalan Federation of Glassworkers 43
Catalan Nationalism *see* Catalanism
Catalan Regional Metalworkers'
Federation 64–5n41, 207, 212,
222n80, 263
Catalan Regional Textile Federation
208–10, 213, 216
Catalan Section (railway workers'
union) 190, 201, 214, 216
Catalan Socialist Federation 127, 132,
197, 214–15
Catalana de Gas (company) 29, 75, 230
Catalanism

anarchism and 131–2, 159, 170–2
the Left and 169–73
see also CRT; Layret, Francesc;
Lliga Regionalista; PRC; UFNR
Catalonia
Catholic unions, promotion of 75
company towns 72–4
economic development 12
high energy costs due to lack of
coal and iron ore 14
industrial boost of World War I 19
industrial diversification 70–1
and labour agitation 72
protection of industry 17
subordination of labour 71, 72–3
urbanisation 12
Catholic Church 147–8
Catholic
anti–liberalism 69, 147
schools 60, 147–8
unions, promotion of 75
Church attendance 59, 148
paternalism of 148
the upper classes and 147–8
and women 38, 61, 147–8, 178–9
see also anticlericalism; Catalonia;
Comillas, Marquis of; Unions
Professionals
cement manufacture 25
Centre for Social Studies 153, 156–7,
166
Centre Fraternal de Cultura 157
Cerdà, Ildefons 26, 41
Cerdeño, Amalio 344
CGT (French labour confederation)
129–32, 134, 136, 196, 198–9,
203, 217, 274
Chartre d'Amiens (1906)
CGT and 130
Impact in Catalonia 196, 241, 328
chemicals industry 19–23, 87, 226
children, working–class 60
Chinatown 45, 53, 58, 60, 154, 236
Ciencia Social 171
Cierva, Juan de la 176, 299
Claramunt, Teresa 90, 117, 121, 129,
151–2, 170, 179, 181, 185n21
Clarià, Ignaci 167
class boundaries 56, 58
clientalism 68, 147
Climent, Josep 212

El Clot 22, 53–4, 60, 90, 158, 190,
200, 229, 260
clothing industry 18–21, 24, 48, 137,
230
CNT (anarchist–syndicalist
confederation) 1
Adame as general secretary 352
Allendasalazar coalition and climate
of violence 323–6
Andalusian Regional Federation 235
Boal as general secretary 301–2,
327, 334, 340
Buenacasa as general secretary 239,
286, 297
La Canadeca strike 290–97
Carlos Bas and conciliation hopes
327–30
CNT committees, joint agreements
by 216–17, 249, 298, 304, 317,
329, 348
conciliation hopes (1920–23)
326–30, 339–44
culture of protest and growth of
259–69
Dato administration and
conciliation hopes 326–30
destruction of (1920–23) 323–53
detention and assassination of
activists 333–4
'dirty war' by authorities against 334
employer lock–out and repressive
onslaught (1919–20) 308–17, 318
failure to develop (1910–14)
195–206, 211–18
Federal Committee 199, 217
First Congress 195, 204, 214,
219n18, 221n41
foundation of 195–206
general strike (1920) and
limitations of weapon 335–6
general strike (1919) and
repression of 297–302, 318
conciliation attempt 302–8
generational
composition, recasting of 335
conflict within 343–4
growth and development of
Catalan CNT (CRT) (1916–19)
241–50, 259–69
illegalisation of 205 (1911), 317
(1920), 323 (1924)

Jordán as general secretary 274,
276, 288n44
Martínez Anido, violent repression
by 331–9
Maurín as general secretary 341
migrants, supposed radicalising
impact of 3, 44, 247–8, 250,
254n1, 257n79, 354
Miranda as general secretary 239,
276
National Committee 235, 249,
273, 285, 288n43, 289n61,
301–2, 306, 326, 332, 335,
341–2, 346–7, 352, 355n13
Negre as general secretary 197, 217
Nin as general secretary 340–1
Peiró as general secretary 341, 348
persecution of activists 333–4,
337–8
political composition, recasting of
335
reorganisation, hope of (1923)
345–8
repression and military coup
(1923) 349–53
Sánchez Guerra and possibility of
conciliation 339–44
Second Congress (Congreso de la
Comedia) 313–15, 335n13
Seguí and reorganisation of 232–41
Sindicatos Libres attacks on 335,
338–9, 347
Socialists and 273–6, 327–8, 335–6
terrorism and 250–3, 328–9, 312,
323–4, 330, 337, 348–9
see also Boal, Evilio; Buenacasa,
Manuel; Negre, José; Peiró, Joan;
Prat, Josep
Codina, Joan 241
Coll, Jaume 204
Colomer, Antoni 144n101
colonial
losses 76
trading 17–18
Comaposada, Josep 74, 106, 112–13,
127, 141–2n28, 176–7, 186n66
Comes, Francesc 347–8
Comillas, Marquis of (Claudio López
Bru) 58, 70, 75, 281, 283
Comillas-Güell dynasty 70, 175, 248
Compañía del Norte (railway company)
229

companies and factories
L'Aguila 24, 63n12, 230
Aixerit 228
L'Ametlla de Merola company
town 73–4, 97n18
Anònima Tram Company 92
L'Anuari de l'Exportacío 50
La Canadenca 290–97, 350
see also Ebro Power and Irrigation
Caralt i Cia 22
Catalana de Gas 29, 75, 230
Compañía del Norte 229
Coromines company town 73
Costa 242
Ebro Power and Irrigation 230,
248–9, 292
see also La Canadenca
La España Industrial 22, 24, 74,
90, 181, 209, 230, 248, 298, 338
Fabra i Coats 22, 73–4, 78, 325,
338
La Fabril Cotonera 230
Foment d'Obres i Construccions
(FOCSA) 24, 206
Gas Lebón 75, 99n63, 230
Girona Foundry 23, 229, 248,
251, 300, 308, 338
Godó Germans 22
Güell company town 22, 72–3, 82
Harmel Germans 83
Joan Girall Laporte 29
Madrid-Zaragoza-Alicante (MZA)
214
La Mambla company town 73
La Maquinista Terrestre i Marítima
14, 23–4, 32, 93, 100n79 and 81,
192, 229, 316, 338
La Niotipia 16–18
Noves Filatures company town
('Els Anglesos or Borgonyà') 73
see also Fabra i Coats
Pirelli 25
Rosal company town 22, 71, 73
Sedó company town 22, 71, 73,
82, 97n18
El Segle 230
Sert Germans 22
Seydoux i Cia 83, 194
Societat Material per a
Construccions i Ferrocarrils see
Girona Foundry

La Transatlántica 75, 175
Trinxet 230
Vapor Vell 72
Vilaseca company town 75
Vilella 242
El Vulcano 23, 229
company towns 22, 72–4, 97n16, n18, 147
    paternalism, social control and 72–4, 78, 80, 82, 139, 229
Companys, Lluís 270–1, 331–2
competition
    foreign 70, 100n79, 191
    pressures of on workers 26, 28–30, 32, 71, 83
compositors *see* printing industry
'compulsory trade unionism' (*sindicalización forzosa*) 231–2, 308
conciliation
    CNT hopes (1920–23) 326–30, 339–44
    compromise and, even-handedness in 81–2
    Dato administration and hopes for 326–30
    general strike (1919) and repression of CNT, conciliation attempt 302–8
    of liberal opinion in Spain 68
    Sánchez Guerra and possibility for CNT of 339–44
Confederation of Spanish Metalworkers 212
The Conquest of Bread (Kropotkin, P.) 118
Conservative Party and Conservative administrations 68–71, 76, 79, 80–1, 88, 92–3, 95, 124, 134, 173–4, 181, 210, 269, 277, 281, 284, 288n35, 290, 299, 302, 324, 339, 345, 348–9, 351
La Constància 208–11, 213, 216–17, 229–30, 243–4, 252, 260, 267, 288n35
constitutional guarantees, suspension and restoration of 80, 88, 90, 98n43, 134, 174, 181–2, 227, 241, 243–4, 248, 284, 292, 297, 307, 319, 327, 333, 339, 343, 352
construction
    industrial

development 14, 18–19
    structure 23–4, 35n64, 43, 194
    labour process 30, 42
    strikes and union development 50, 85–6, 89, 91, 106–7, 116–7, 120–1, 126, 157, 206, 212–3, 220n48, 228, 235, 245, 248, 255n9, 256n68, 257n86, 300, 303, 307–8, 310–11, 314, 345–6, 349–50
Construction Workers' Federation *see* Barcelona Construction Workers' Federation
Construction Workers' SU 245, 257n86, 292, 300, 308, 311, 314, 345–6
consumer cooperatives 73, 76, 104, 107, 126, 143n74, 150, 167, 211, 222n81, 317, 333
coopers and cooperages
    Coopers' federation (Federation of Journeyman Coopers of the Spanish Region) 30, 89
    industrial structure and the labour process 29–30, 44, 50, 201
    unions and strikes 89, 134, 201, 249
cork-producing industry 24–5
Cornet i Mas, Josep 93
Coromines, Pere 171
Coromines company town 73
corporations *see* companies
El Corsario 156
Cortiella, Felip 64n34, 157, 171, 260, 287–8n34
La Coruña 119, 131
El Cosmopolita 156
Costa (factory) 242
costs
    administrative 121–2
    energy 14, 16
    labour 14, 27, 139
    pressures on 18, 22–3, 25, 28, 30–31, 75, 83, 91, 139
    transport 16
cotton textiles
    employer labour strategies and paternalist-disciplinarian regimes 71–5
    industrial
        development 13–19, 226
        structure 22–3

the labour process, community, gender and family relations 25–7, 37–41, 55, 59, 63n5

trade unionism and strikes 40, 63n22, 71–2, 76–82, 85, 87, 89–91, 105–6, 109–13, 120–1, 125, 127, 129–30, 139–40, 141n17, 169–70, 172, 194, 207–11, 213, 216, 229–31, 241–4, 246–8, 250–2, 257n86, 263, 267, 274, 294, 300, 303, 308, 311, 326, 339, 345–6

working conditions and unemployment 27, 37–9, 55, 63n22, 74, 77, 208–9, 308

see also company towns; trade unions, trade and industrial federations

craft federations *see* trade unions, trade and industrial federations

Criminal Investigation Office 154

Cristina, María 151

CRT (Catalan regional confederation) 211

ambition of leadership 251, 254

Andreu as general secretary 232, 234

Archs as general secretary 336, 340

Barcelona focus of 217, 235, 239, 249, 290

Catalanism and 215, 270–2

CNT-UGT pact and 273–6

coordinating body 245–6

CRT-CNT 217, 259–69, 286, 302–8

contacts with republicans 215

cultural base, smallness of 259–60

development (1916–19) phases of 242–3

'dirty war' against 334

dues for membership 240

eight-hours day, campaign for 248

employers 'crusade' against 254

Espinalt as general secretary 352

FTN and 308–17

growth and development (1916–19) 241–50, 259–69

gun attacks by 218, 301

ideology and praxis following Bolshevik Revolution in Russia 284–6

industrial action by 235, 292–3

leadership, difficulties of life for 242, 300

Lerrouxists and 215, 272, 274, 296, 328

Lleida local federation 249

lock-out and 308–17

La Lucha Social 340

manifesto (June, 1917) 245

membership 218, 234, 237–9, 247, 249

migrant workers 247

mobilising tradition 239

neutralist, anti-imperialist stance 275

organisation (1913–14) 211, 216–17

Pestaña as general secretary 240, 276

political crisis of 1917 and role of 277–83

Pompeya music hall bombing 329

powerful industrialists, sights on 248

Regional Committee 211, 216–17, 222n93, 235, 240, 245, 302, 352–3

reorganisation and Primo de Rivera coup 345–53

Sants Congress (1918) 240–1, 244–5, 251, 256n70, 285

Seguí as general secretary 236, 240–1, 323, 328

Sindicats Unics and 216, 238, 240, 246

single union card 247

UNFR and 270

union-building efforts 274

violence, leadership appalled by 326

weakening of 298–9, 302, 318

white-collar workers, inability to integrate 218

women workers, unionisation amongst 247

see also Pestaña, Angel; Seguí, Salvador; Sindicats Unics

Cruells, Manuel 186n74

La Cuña 222n81

Cussó, Jaume 295

D

Dalmau, Josep Maria 167
Dato administrations 76, 88, 281, 284, 290, 324, 348
  and CNT conciliation hopes 326–30
Dato, Eduardo 210, 277, 281, 315, 326–30, 331, 337
El Diluvio 191
Els Desheretats (anarchist group) 162
Dolcet, Roser 244
domestic service, employment of women 38
domestic sphere, women and 36–8
Domingo, Marcel·lí 270, 280, 282–3, 332
Doval, Gerardo 295, 299
Durruti, Buenaventura 343, 348

E

Ebro Power and Irrigation (company) 230, 248–9, 292
  See also La Canadenca
economics
  economic crises, effect on working-class community 48–9
  economy of Spain 16–17
  social revolution and economic equality, fight for 150
education
  Catholic Church and 147–8, 151
  deficiencies in 60
  see also Ateneus Obrers; Modern School
La Efusió (labourers' union) 243
Elizalde, Artur 300, 316
Ely, Geoff 1
employers
  'compulsory trade unionism' (*sindicalización forzosa*) 231–2, 308
  employer-sponsored terrorism 211, 252, 298–301, 319–20n23, 331–4, 324–5, 334, 343, 347–8, 356n36, 358n91
  employers' ideology and policy towards labour 69–75, 82, 92–5, 98n26, 139, 191–2, 207, 218, 231–2, 252, 258n103, 298, 308
  lock-outs, use of 79–82, 111, 114, 194, 207, 209, 215, 229–30, 243, 298, 303–4, 306–18, 350

  wealth and power of industrial elites 70
employers' organisations
  Association of Catalan Foundry Owners 92–3
  Employers' Federation 207, 248, 254, 338, 350–1, 353
    foundation of 192
    intransigence of 329–30
    lock-out by 303–4, 306–18
    reorganisation of 294
    Sindicatos Libres and 325, 343
    social elite, involvement with 298
  Federation of Textile Industrialists 209
  FTN (employers' confederation) 69, 79–82, 88, 181, 191–2, 209, 312, 350–1
    La Canadenca strike 290–7
    repression of Catalan CNT and 297–302
    Labour Commission, promulgation of 308–9
  Mutua de Contratistes 228
  National Association of Metallurgists 207
  Society of Machine Constructors 92–4
  Society of Metallurgists and Machine Constructors 94, 250
Engels, Friedrich 169
Escorza, Manuel 278–9
Escudé Bartolí, Manuel 48
La España Industrial 22, 24, 74, 90, 181, 209, 230, 248, 298, 338
España Nueva 300
Espartaco 185n31 (1905), 312–3 (1919)
Espejo, Antonio ('Espejito') 334, 337
Esperanto 170, 260, 271, 286n1
Espinalt, Joan 352
Esteve, Joan Baptista *see* Bonafulla, Leopoldo

F

Fabra i Coats (company) 22, 73–4, 78, 325, 338
Fabra Ribas, Antoni 132–3, 136, 176, 178, 197–8, 215
La Fabril Cotonera (factory) 230
factories *see* companies and factories

factory size 19–25
'family wage,' lack of 49
Fanelli, Giuseppe 104–5
Faure, Sebastian 273
Feced, Inocencio 329, 333–4, 343–4,
    347–8, 351, 355n16, 356n27,
    n35, 358n76, n91
Federal Republicans 172–3
Federation of Spanish Railwayworkers
    (UGT) 214, 229
Federation of Textile Industrialists 209
Federation of Waterfront Unions 190–1
Feliu, Antoni 334
Fernández, Luis 300
Ferrer, Eduard 253, 301, 304–5
Ferrer, Francesc 117, 119, 128, 133,
    150–3, 158–60, 163–6, 168,
    170–1, 177–8, 181–2, 185n21,
    186n49, 217, 221n58
    see also 4 de Maig group; Modern
    School
Ferrer, Joan 39, 66n65, 159, 208, 240,
    254n5, 257n80, n91, 317, 350
Ferrer, Lola 244
Ferrer Vidal, Josep 26, 34n42
Fifth District 22, 53–4, 56, 58–9,
    65n62, 87, 157, 177–8, 180, 235,
    266, 280, 282, 329
Foix, Pere ('Laville') 54, 56, 58,
    187n93, 257n80 and 91,
    287–8n34, 302, 356n35
Foment d'Obres i Construccions
    (FOCSA) 24, 206
Fontanals, Ramon 110, 187n88
FORA (Argentinian labour
    confederation) 237
Fornells, Ricard 239, 261
Foronda, Mariano 92, 229, 293
Foronda, Marquis of 298, 330
Franco, Francisco 7
Franqueza, Josep 351
La Fraternal Obrera (mutual-aid
    society) 9
FRE (Spanish branch of the First
    International) 104–7, 130, 142n43
'free love' 161
Freser Valley 14–16, 71, 73–4, 78–9,
    81–2, 111, 210, 303, 308
FRESR (anarchist labour confederation)
    121–2, 124–5, 128, 131, 143n62,
    162

friendship networks see working-class
    community
FTE (textile workers federation) 78–81,
    109–13, 127, 130, 141n17
FTN (employers' confederation) 69,
    79–82, 88, 181, 191–2, 209, 312,
    350–1
    La Canadenca strike 290–7
    Labour Commission, promulgation
    of 308–9
    repression of Catalan CNT and
    297–302
FTRE (pro-anarchist labour
    confederation) 105–7, 116, 130,
    142n43
Fuentes, Juan see Peiró, Joan
fuerzas vivas 68–9

G
Galino Bugallal, Count 328
García, Adrián 203
García Oliver, Joan 336, 342, 344, 349,
    352
García Prieto, Manuel see Alhucemas,
    Maquis of
García Quejido, Antonio 127, 143n77,
    332
Gas Lebón 75 (company) 99n63, 230
gender inequalities
    within anarchism 40, 90, 121,
    143n58, 158, 207–8, 243–5, 247,
    268–9, 287n28, 326
    gender relations 6
    public and domestic spheres 36–7,
    39, 121
    sexual division of labour 25–6,
    36–41
    subordination of female workers by
    industrialists 27, 39, 63n12
Genollà, Josep 110, 141n17
Germandat de Sant Pere Pescador 193
Gil Mestre, Manuel 141n13
Girall Laporte, Joan 29
Girona Foundry 23, 229, 248, 251,
    300, 308, 338
Gironès 14
glassblowers 29, 34n56, 44, 242
glassworks, industrial structure and the
    labour process 29, 34n56, 242
glassworkers, strikes and union
    organisation 43, 227, 237–8, 242,
    247, 345–6, 352

see also Catalan Federation of
Glassworkers; National Federation
of Glass workers; Peiró, Joan
Godó Germans (company) 22
Golden, Lester 178, 268
Gràcia 54–6, 128, 152, 157, 229, 260
Grau, Josep 172
Graupera, Félix 311–12, 316–17,
322n73, 323
Grave, Jean 118
Güell company town 22, 72–3, 82
Güell, Eusebi 70, 82
Guerra del Río, Rafael 295
La Guerra Social (Barcelona) 127,
(Valencia) 314
Guesde, Jules 113
Guiteras, Josep 110, 141n18

H
Harmel Germans (factory) 83
heirarchies
within industry 11, 19–25, 32
within the working class 41–3, 62
Herreros, Tomás 129, 167, 186n75,
196, 198, 221n56, 232, 260, 273
historiography 5
Hobsbawm, Eric 3, 96, 183
Homades, Ramon 94, 122
Homs, Pere Mártir 333, 347, 358n91
L'Hospitalet 22, 54, 230
Hostafrancs 14, 54–5, 187n79
housing quality 49–50
La Huelga General 117, 119, 121, 129,
142n48
Humanitarian Association of Workers at
La Maquinista Terrestre i Marítima
93

I
Ibsen, Henrik 171
La Idea Libre 115
Iglesias, Emiliano 205, 221n57, 266,
295
Iglesias, Pablo 111–13, 115, 141–2n28,
160, 165, 178, 186n66, 198, 202,
234, 281
Igualada 72, 119, 200, 211
Igurbide, Fola 163
illiteracy 42
individualism 153
anarchist 107–8, 128, 153

of industrialists 20–1
industrial action
La Canadeca strike 290–7
company towns, strikes in 78
employer lock-out and repressive
onslaught on CNT (1919–20)
308–18
general strike (1919) and
repression of CNT 297–302, 318
conciliation attempt 302–8
general strike (1920), and
limitations of weapon 335–6
general strikes in Barcelona
(1898–1903) 112–27
generalisation of 90–1
hard fought and violent 231
in Manlleu 80–2
May day strikes (1890–93) 108
organised labour and 81–2, 87–94
in Poble Nou 191, 248, 267
in Sants 208–9, 230, 267
strikes (1912–14) and union
organisation 206–11
in the Ter Valley 77, 80–2, 106,
210, 303
textile workers (1913) 208–10
working days lost through strikes
84, 86
industrial structure and the labour
process
'aristocracy of labour' 29
artisanal trades, changes in 27–9
atomisation of industry 22–3
carpentry 20, 24, 30
capitalist
modernisation 18–19
transformations 30
cement manufacture 25
chemicals industry 23
clothing industry 18–21, 24, 48,
137, 230
competition, pressures of 26
construction 23–4, 30, 35n64,
42–3, 194
cooperage 29–30, 44, 50, 201
cork–producing industry 24–5
costs, pressures on 30
cotton textiles 22–3, 25–7, 37–41,
55, 59, 63n5
differences between industries 22
division of labour 25–6

factory size and 19–25
glassworks 29, 34n56, 242
hierarchies of 11, 19–25, 32
individualism of industrialists 20–1
labour
    availability 21
    processes 25–32
    productivity 26
    relations 11
male employment levels 27
medium-sized enterprises,
    importance of 24, 84–5
Metal industry 23, 31, 35n64, 43,
    91, 219n6
port of Barcelona 27
printing industry 30–1, 42, 59–60,
    63n22
sexual division of labour 25–6,
    36–41
shoemaking 24, 31
tailoring 31
technological
    deficiencies 20–1
    modernisation 26, 27, 30–1
urbanisation and labour agitation 72
woodworking 19–21, 42, 60, 86
woollen textiles 22–3, 83
work structures, reorganisation of
    27, 28–9
workers per production unit 21
industrial unions *see* trade unions, trade
    and industrial federations; Sindicats
    Unics
industrialists *see* employers
Institute for Social Reforms 76, 80,
    192, 210, 213, 226
La Internacional 132, 197
International Working Men's
    Association 104

J
Jaurés, Jean 198, 263
Joan Girall Laporte (factory) 29
Jordán, Francisco 273–4, 276, 288n44
Joro Miranda, José 330
Jouhaux, Léon 274, 281
journeymen, masters and 41–2
    see also working-class community
Jul, Pere 265, 272, 312
Juntas de Defensa 277–8, 283–4,
    291–2, 299, 303, 306, 315,
    319n21, 344

Juntas Locales de Reformas Sociales 76,
    82, 136–8, 303
La Justicia Social 197–9, 202, 210,
    215, 248, 264, 285

K
Kaplan, Temma 143n58, 175
Kerensky, Alexander Fyodorovich 309
Koëning, Baron (and Koëning gang)
    301, 322n91, 324, 355n16
Kropotkin, Pyotr 118, 220n29, 272

L
La Iglesia, Gustavo 151–2
labour organisation *see* organised labour;
    trade unions, trade and industrial
    federations; working-class
    communities
labour process *see* industrial structure
    and the labour process
labour productivity 26, 91
    see also employers
Lacort, Angel 264, 275
Laguía Literas, Joan 354–5n4
Lamoneda, Ramón 332
Largo Caballero, Francisco 264, 276,
    279, 281, 332, 335–6
Lastra, Josep 335
'Laville' *see* Foix, Pere
Law of National Protection (1907) 19
Lawton, Fraser 293
Layret, Francesc 270–1, 303, 331–5,
    356n27
League in Defence of the Rights of
    Man 166, 215
Lenin, Vladimir Ilyich 169
Lerroux, Alejandro 112, 116, 135,
    149–50, 159, 163–8, 178, 199,
    215, 272, 277, 282–3,
    proposal by Seguí for inclusion in
    new Liberal government 342
Lerrouxism 162, 167, 185n25, 186n74,
    202, 214, 221n55, 236, 295, 335
    activism of 164, 176–7, 272, 282
    anarchism and 112, 116, 149–50,
    159, 163–6
    anti-Catalanism of 169–70, 173
    'classing' of Lerrouxist ideology
    150
    CRT and 215, 272, 274, 296, 328
    electoral

participation of 270
  strength of 168, 173
  food riots and 267–8
  influence of 199, 215, 247
  League in Defence of the Rights of
    Man 166, 215
  moderation of ideology and decline
    199, 215, 272
  power relations within 175
  propaganda of 180
  Seguí and 271, 281
  SO and 166, 168–9, 177–8, 182–3
  Socialists and 165
  Tragic Week and 176–8, 182,
    189–90
  vulnerability to syndicalist challenge
    167–8
  youth movement, leadership and
    204
El Liberal 274
Liberal Party and Liberal
  administrations 68, 70–1, 81, 88,
  95, 105–6, 128, 173, 175, 182,
  190, 192, 209, 277, 291, 340,
  342, 345
living standards, inadequacy of 48–50
Lladó, Bru 194, 343
Lliga Regionalista 82, 150, 173, 215,
  270, 294–5, 307–8, 339, 353
  Amado deserted by 312
  CRT hostility towards 279–80,
    282, 309
  foundation of 149
  integration into government 290–1
  nationalism and 271
  reform attempt of 277
  right-wing bias of 170, 173
  see also Cambó, Francesc
Llobregat Valley 14, 22, 72–4, 78–82
Local Transport Federation 90, 92
lock-outs 79–82, 111, 114, 194, 207,
  209, 215, 229–30, 243, 298, 350
  Employers' Federation and 303–4,
  306–18
López Montenegro, José 117, 119,
  142n48, 158, 184n16
Loredo, Antonio 198–9, 232, 273,
  288n41
Lorenzo, Anselmo 104–5, 117–18,
  123, 128–9, 131–3, 143n73,
  144n77, 152–3, 158–61, 171–2,
  181, 196–8, 216, 236, 273

austere figure 160–1
Catalanism, hostility towards 170
cooperation with Ferrer 117, 128,
  158–9
exile in France 117
imprisonment of 123 (1902), 181
  (Tragic Week)
key anarchist figure 104–5, 129,
  152–3
Kropotkin's *Conquest of Bread*,
  importance for 118
political awareness in workers,
  importance for 196
SO, support for 133
sympathy with Allies in World War I
  273
syndicalism, attitude towards 129
'worker solidarity,' recognition of
  need for 131–2
Lorraine in France 69
La Lucha Social 340

M
Macià, Francesc 283
Madrid-Zaragoza-Alicante (MZA)
  (railway company) 214
Madrigal, Carlos 303, 327, 330
4 de Maig group 128–9, 135,
  145n123, 153, 162, 166, 172,
  185n31, 186n75, 199
Malatesta, Errico 129, 274, 313
La Mambla company town 73
Mancomunitat 215, 309
Manent, Joan 159, 358n91
Manlleu 72, 77–8, 110, 139
  industrial action in 80–2
Manresa 14, 78, 106, 109–10, 136,
  200, 263, 343, 352
  destruction of unions in 81–2
  industrial action in 79–80, 308,
  326
  major urban centre 72–3
  radical action in 180
  textile stronghold 346
Maqueda Mateo, Estanislao ('E. Mateo
  Soriano') 265–6, 312, 347
La Maquinista Terrestre i Marítima 14,
  23–4, 32, 93, 100n79, n81, 192,
  229, 316, 338
Maresme area 14, 112, 135, 137, 200,
  213

Marina, José 282
Martí, Joan 213, 216
Martí, Medi 336
martial law 193, 291, 296–7, 303, 307, 315, 350
    invoked against industrial action 80, 88, 94, 123, 177, 264–5, 269, 282, 293–4, 297
    response to terrorist activity 158, 205, 299
Martín Ramos, Josep Lluís 84, 227
Martín Rodríguez, Basilio 113, 141–2n28
Martínez, Julián 327
Martínez Anido, Severiano 321n55, 325, 330–4, 336–48, 353, 354–5n4, 356n27, n41, 357n42, n46
Martínez Campos, General Arsensio 108
Martínez Domingo, Antonio 310
Martorell, Francisco 211, 262, 283
Marx, Karl 169
Marxism 3, 169
    Marxist Socialists 4, 103–5, 115, 164
Mas, Lluís 221n75, 252, 294
Mas Gomeri, Josep 172, 274
masculinity
    battle against replacement by female labour 27, 39–40, 77
    'honourable trades', conception of 42–3, 50–1
    male opposition to the employment of women in 'male' jobs 27, 30–1, 39–40, 77–82
    male primacy in organised labour 77
    'masculine values', exaltation of 39–40
    primary 'bread winner', conception of male as 25–6
    public sphere, as male preserve 36–37
    sexual division of labour 25–6, 36–41, 63n5
Masoni, Pere 300
Matamala, Joan 111–12
Mataró 14, 136–7, 213
Mateo Soriano, E. *see* Maqueda Mateo, Estanislao
Matheu, Pere 337

Maura, Antonio 134–5, 173–5, 181–2, 189, 277–8, 290–1, 296, 299–300, 302, 337, 339
Maurín, Joaquín 340–1
May First, importance of 161–2
Meaker, Gerald 247, 254n1, 257n79, 321n55
medium-sized enterprises, importance of 24
Mella, Ricardo 153
Mercadell, Antonio 81
Mestre, Miguel 240, 243, 285
metal industry 23–4, 31
    economic development 14, 17–20, 70, 100n79, 226
    employer labour strategies 70, 75, 92–4, 191–2, 207, 218, 252, 258n103, 298
    family structures and migrant labour 41, 59
    industrial structure and the labour process 23, 31, 35n64, 43, 91, 219n6
    unions and strikes 42, 64–5n41, 85–6, 90, 92–5, 114–15, 119–23, 127, 190–2, 198–202, 206–7, 212, 217–18, 220n80, 228–9, 231, 235, 242, 245–8, 250–3, 260–1, 263, 298–300, 303, 307–8, 310, 316, 329–30, 332, 335–7, 339, 345
    see also employers; trade unions, trade and industrial federations
migrant labour
    marginalisation and integration 43–7
    migration into Barcelona 43–7, 54, 148, 325
    murcianos 3, 54, 250, 354
    settlement patterns of 45–7, 49–50, 54, 59, 62
    southern and eastern Spanish migrants, supposed radicalising impact on Catalan labour movement 3, 44, 247–8, 250, 254n1, 257n79, 354
Miguel, Josep 129
Milans del Bosch, Joaquín 291, 293–4, 296–300, 306, 309, 317, 319n21, 325, 330
militancy 156, 216, 265, 282, 293, 295, 324, 335–6

industrial and labour militancy 44,
82, 85, 88, 95, 134, 170, 195,
208, 237, 242, 245, 247, 252,
296, 313
rank-and-file 132, 140, 214
roots of industrial 11–32
of women 91
Minguet, Genaro 336
Miranda, Francesc 153, 176, 186n52,
217, 264, 273, 276, 278–9, 281,
287–8n34, 302
'bourgeois politicians,'
denouncement of links with 279
Catalan identity, attitude towards
271
CNT reorganisation, leading role in
232, 239
prisoners' association representative
297
Miró i Trepat, Joan 248, 298, 307,
312, 334, 349
El Mismo 185n31
Modelo prison 123, 262, 300, 326,
332–3
Modern School movement 117, 150,
158–60, 163–4, 166, 168, 170–1,
200
See also Ferrer, Francesc
modernista movement 170–1
Molins, Josep 236, 310
monarchist *caciques* 294
Montañés, Carlos 295, 299
Monteagudo, Félix 196, 244
Montjuïc
campaign of judicial review of
Montjuïc trial 115–16, 149–50, 165
imprisonment at 108, 293–4, 333
repression at as mobilising tool
141n13, 162
Montjuïc trial 108
and slum housing 50, 54
Montseny, Joan *see* Urales, Federico
Moreno, Miguel V. *see* Sánchez
González, José
Morocco
war in 6, 203, 215
Morato, Juan José 113
Morote, Luis 295–6, 319n15
Morral, Mateo 163
El Motín 178
'Muntadas' 70, 211, 298, 331, 334,
343, 348, 356n41

Muntadas, Josep 209
Muntadas, Lluís 181, 298
Muntadas, Maties 75, 298, 356n41
Muntanya 12, 48, 71–2, 84, 88, 90, 93,
97n11, 208
employers' offensive, launch of 80
industrial expansion 14
strikes and union organisation
76–83, 106, 208–10, 213, 229,
303, 346
technological development 26
Murcia 44
Mussolini, Benito 351
Mutua de Contratistes 228
mutual-aid societies 48, 64n40, 74–6,
83, 85, 92–3, 98n26, 126, 150

N
Naken, José 178, 186n49
National Association of Metallurgists
207
National Bricklayers' Federation (UGT)
212–13
National Confederation of Spanish
Metalworkers 207
National Council of Catholic Workers'
Corporations 75
National Federation of Carpenters and
Similar Workers (UGT) 121
National Federation of Glassworkers
242
National Federation of Pasta Makers 40
National Federation of Woodworking
Unions 89, 201, 212, 232
National Maritime Transport Federation
(UGT) 229
National Metalworkers' Federation
(UGT) 212
National Textile Federation 40, 210,
229, 243–4, 247, 251, 259n86,
274, 303
National Woodworkers' Federation
(UGT) 212
Natura 142n44, 153
El Naval (stokers union) 202, 229, 242,
248
Negre, José 197, 199, 214, 217,
222n79, 232, 237, 239, 276, 284
Neighbourhoods *see* working-class
community
neo-Malthusianism 153

Nicolau, Lluís 337
Nield, Keith 1
Nietzsche, Friedrich 128
Nin, Andreu 3, 340–1
La Niotipia (factory) 167–8
Noves Filatures ('Els Anglesos or
    Borgonyà') 73
Nuestra Palabra 286
Nueva Senda 341

O
El Obrero Moderno 156
organised labour 67–8, 95–6
    additional (and simultaneous)
    demands of organised labour 87–8
    alliances and coordinated action
    89–90
    anarchism, syndicalism and 211–17
    Barcelona and the skilled trades
    84–95
    blue-collar workers, unionisation
    centred on 85
    CNT-UGT Alliance and (1916–17)
    growth of 273–6
    community solidarity 77
    conditions for revival of union
    organisation 76–7
    culture of protest and development
    of CNT 259–69
    difficulties
        in company towns 72–4
        in organising 87
    family solidarity 77
    gender differences within 77,
    89–90
    generalisation of industrial action
    90–1
    growth
        (1915–18) and wartime
        economy 225–32
        (1910–14) of union organisation
        217–18
        and development of CNT
        241–50
    independent labour movement,
    articulation of (1868–98) 103–8
    industrial
        action 81–2, 87–9, 90–1, 92–4
        fronts, building up 90
    labour relations, differences
    between industries 91

male primacy in 77
    and mutual-aid 83
    negotiation with independent
    unions 70
    paternalist-disciplinarian regimes
    against 70–5
    political crisis of 1917 and role of
    CRT 277–83
    proliferation of unions 88–9
    rapid union organisation
    (1916–18), 226–50, 269–76
    reconciliation machinery, attempts
    at 82
    Sabadell's union organisation 83
    skill, gender and unionisation,
    relationship between 77–9
    skilled trades in Barcelona 84–95
    social strife and union organisation
    189–94
    strikes
        (1912–14) and union
        organisation 206–11
        in company towns 78
        working days lost through 84, 86
    textiles and the Muntanya 76–83
    trade federations, development of
    89
    trade-union revival in cotton
    textiles (1898–1900) 109–12
    transport, organisation within 91–2
    union
        organisation, conditions for
        revival of 76–7
        power in Ter Valley 78, 213,
        229, 346
        proliferation 88–9
        recruitment 78
    women, role of 91–2
    see also carpentry; construction;
    metal industry; printing industry;
    railways; Sindicats Unics,
    waterfront; woodworking
Orís 73
Osona 14
Ossorio y Gallardo, Angel 143n68, 176
Ovejero, Andrés 264

P
Palau, Father Gabriel 75
Paris Commune 161
paternalist-disciplinarian regimes 70–5

patronage 68, 147
Peiró, Joan ('Juan Fuentes') 43, 161,
  237–42, 244, 249, 314–15, 341–2,
  346–7, 349, 352
  Seguí assassination, dealing with
    aftermath 347–8
Pelloutier, Fernand 118–19, 129
Perezagua, Facundo 140, 205
Perlasio, Constantí 213
Pestaña, Angel 156, 232–3, 240–1,
  261–6, 271, 273, 275–6, 278–9,
  297, 299–300, 302, 305–6, 314,
  323, 349
  anarchist 'purist' and key figure
    156, 240–1
  and anarchist terrorism, 251, 305,
    320n38, 321n53, 335, 347–9,
    356n41, 359
  arrest and imprisonment of 297,
    299–300 (March 1919), 333
    (December 1920)
  assassination attempt on 343
  attitude towards Catalan and
    Catalanism 233–4, 271, 287–8n34
  Bolshevik regime, report on 342
  chosen to travel to Russia 326
  on economic crisis, CRT action
    over 262–3
  editor of *Solidaridad Obrera* 240,
    261–2, 287–8n34
  editor of *Tierra y Libertad* 274
  and employer-sponsored terrorism
    319–20n23, 343, 356n41
  Peiró and 347–9
  'political proposal' support for 342
  price on head of 343
  secretary general of the CRT 240,
    276
  Seguí and 240, 278–9, 302,
    304–6, 326, 335, 342, 347
  Seguí assassination, dealing with
    aftermath 347–9
  Sindicatos Libres and 338
  on Sindicats Unics 238
  UGT-CNT alliance and general
    strike (1916–1917) 264, 275–6,
    278–9, 283, 297–9
  on women's employment 244
Pey, Joan 196, 236, 336
Piazza, Carles 116, 124
Picasso, Pablo 171

Piera, Simó 236, 256n38, 288n44, 292,
  297, 300, 310, 315, 320n41,
  321n59, n62, 323, 328, 332
Piñón, Camil 299, 321n53
Piqué, Camil 210
Pirelli (factory) 25
Pla 12, 16, 48, 208–9, 213, 303, 308
Pla i Armengol, Dr Ramon 234
Plaja, Hermoso 159, 286n1, 288n54
Playá, José 23–4
El Poble Català 176
Poble Nou 22, 49, 53–6, 58–61, 75,
  93, 158, 242
  bottlemaking in 29
  cooperages in 29
  CRT in 259–60
  industrial action in 191, 248, 267
  metalworking in 23
  migration to 47
  radical action in 178
  rationalist culture in 200, 211
  UGT in 190
  woodworkers in 60
Poble Sec 50, 54–5
Polo, Emili 216, 222n16
Port *see* Waterfront
Portela Valladares, Manuel 193, 351–3
post-colonial economic environment
  17–18
post-structuralism 4–5
Pouget, Emile 129, 142n44, 144n89,
  186n50, 219n24
poverty 39, 55, 62, 96, 175, 235, 242
  income inadequacies 48–9
  working-class community and 49
Prat, Josep 100n76, 129, 134, 136,
  138, 142n42, 143n54, 144n90,
  153, 171, 197–8
PRC (left-Catalanist party) 270–1,
  278–80, 283, 331–2
Prieto, Indalecio 343
Primo de Rivera, Miguel 307, 347,
  349–53, 357n42, 358n76 and n91
printing industry
  industrial structure and the labour
    process 30–1, 42, 59–60, 63n22
  unions and strikes 40, 42, 89, 91,
    99n68, 114, 116, 120, 127,
    167–8, 247, 249–50, 293, 338–9
El Productor 109, 117, 119, 128,
  155–6, 163, 166, 172

El Progreso 116, 150, 163, 167–8
El proletariado militante (Lorenzo, A.)
　105
protection of industry in Spain 17–19,
　88, 169
La Protesta 116–17, 124
PSOE (Spanish Socialist Party) 2–4,
　105, 127, 176, 197–8, 112–14,
　200, 202
　anti-state nationalisms and 271
　appearance in Spain 103–4
　campaign for judicial review of
　Montjuïc trial in Catalonia 149–50
　Catalan 'Pablista' Socialists 198,
　202
　Catalan Socialist congress (1908)
　132
　Catalan Socialist Federation 127,
　132, 197, 214–15
　Catalan Socialists and SO 133–4,
　138, 176, 195, 197–8
　Catalan Socialists' 'syndicalist'
　strategy in Catalonia 132–6, 215
　Conjunción with republicans 203,
　205, 214–15
　criticism of anarchist strategy
　107–8, 111–12, 127
　eight-hours day, call for 107–8
　general strikes in Barcelona
　(1898–1903) 112–27
　Grup de Corporacions Obreres
　112–3
　leadership of UGT and 205, 281,
　286
　left wing within UGT and 215,
　285, 306, 335–6
　local/central tensions 109–30
　Madrid base of 105
　National Committee 112, 234, 332
　offensive against TCV, effect on
　106
　political strategy of 165
　pragmatism of 203
　PSOE-UGT link 108, 127, 164,
　176, 198, 202–3, 205, 234, 275
　republican-anarchist 'alliance',
　concern over in Catalonia 164–5
　in Reus 197
　Revolution contemplated by 303
　Second International Socialism 136
　stimulus for change 132

　strikes, attitudes towards 108
　support in Catalonia 105–6
　tensions with Barcelona-based
　UGT 112–14
　toleration of by authorities of 124
　See also Comaposada, Josep;
　Iglesias, Pablo; *La Justicia Social*;
　Ribas, Fabra; UGT
La Publicidad 199
Puig, Jacinto 202
Puig, Maurici 252
Puig d'Asprer, Josep 166
Puig i Cadafalch, Josep 309
Pujol, Jaume 330

Q
Quemades, Salvador 236, 285–6, 308,
　320n41, 321n62, 326–8, 330,
　341, 347, 358n68
Queraltó, Dr 215
Quintanilla, Eleuterio 314

R
Radcliffe, Pamela B. 267
Radical Republican Party *see* Lerroux,
　Alejandro; Lerrouxism; Radicals
Radicals
　CRT and 215, 272, 274, 296, 328
　food riots and 267–8
　Foundation of Party, 167
　moderation of stance and decline
　199, 215, 272
　SO and 166–9, 177–8, 182–3
　Tragic Week and 176–8, 182,
　189–90
　see also Lerroux, Alejandro;
　Lerrouxists
El Radium 230, 246
Rahola, Federic 82
Railways 14, 226
　railway companies 22, 75, 87
　Unionisation and strikes 87, 190,
　201–2, 206, 214, 216, 229, 249,
　264, 281, 285
Railway workers' Federation (UGT)
　201–2
the Rambla 45, 48, 53, 56, 59, 176,
　281
Rationalist Athenaeum in Sants 240,
　244, 260, 286n1, 313
Recasens i Mercadé, Josep 137, 243

regionalist identity, development of in working class 47
Regueral, González Faustino 348
Reoyo, Toribio 110–11, 113, 127, 141n28, 165, 186n66
Republican Union 149–50, 166–7
republicanism 5, 103–4, 106, 113, 149–50, 270
  anarchism and 163–9
  Catalan nationalism and 169–73
  see also Lerrouxism; PRC; Radicals; Republican Union; UFNR
Restoration regime 1, 6, 68–9, 203
  attempt by Left to overthrow 277–83
  colonial losses, effect on 148–9
  common enemy for republicans and anarchists 164
  fall of 350–3
  political challenge to 146–50
  public attitude towards 147
  Socialist opposition to 149–50
  see also caciquismo; conciliation; Conservative Party and administrations; constitutional guarantees, suspension and restoration of; Liberal Party and administrations; martial law; state repression of labour and the Left
Reus 14, 29, 124–7, 200, 213
  Socialists in 197
Revista del Ateneo Obrero de Barcelona 28
La Revista Blanca 115–16, 119, 156, 163, 165, 185n31, 346
Revista Social 80, 110
Ribalta, Pere 214
Riera, Agustí 178
Ripoll 72, 80–1
Ripollés 14
Roca, Jaume 228, 237, 299, 302
Roca, Josep 216–17, 237, 302
Roda 72–3, 77, 81–2, 136
Ródenas, Libertad 244, 324
Ródenas, Progreso 324
Roig i Bergadà, Josep 310
Roigé, Federic 221n75, 252
Roigé, Joan 260, 313
Romà, Jaume 110
Romanones, Count of 264, 291, 293–4, 296–7, 299, 303, 319n11

Rosal company town 22, 71, 73
Rosell, Albà 28
Roselló, Bartolomé 325
Roselló, Pere 325, 338
Rothwos, González 291–2, 319n7
Rueda, Enrique 233–4, 287n28
Ruhr in Germany 69
Rull, Joan 154, 167, 185n25
Rusiñol, Albert 82
Rusiñol, Santiago 171

S
Sabadell 2, 14, 153, 208, 211, 213, 263
  Anarchism and the labour movement in 116–17, 124–5, 130–1, 137, 142n36, 155–6, 187n99, 194–5, 200–1, 211, 213
  anarchist weekly *La Protesta* in 116–17
  artillery fire in (1917) 282
  congress of Catalan unions in 128–9
  execution of anarchists from 334
  Federal Republicans in 172–3
  FOS (Sabadell Labour Federation) 83, 116–17, 124–5, 130, 137, 194, 198
  metalworkers in 31, 207
  social federal republic declared in (1909) 177
  union organisation and strikes 42, 83, 116–17, 194, 208, 215n15, 263, 293, 326
  see also woollen textiles
Sabanés, Jaume 211, 221–2n75, 252
Sabater, Pau ('El Tero') 300
Salas, Ramon 325, 347
Salas, Vicenç 337
Salmerón, Nicolás 167
Salut, Emili 22, 53, 60, 65n55, n62, 141n13, n15
Salvatierra, Count of 328, 334
Salvochea, Fermín 166
Sánchez de Toca, Joaquín 302, 309–11, 315, 325
Sánchez González, José ('Miguel V. Moreno') 176, 204
Sánchez Guerra, José 343–4, 345, 347
  and CNT conciliation hopes 340–4
  rise to power of 339–40

Sant Andreu 22, 54–5, 60, 74, 200, 260
Sant Hipòlit de Voltregà 77, 82
Sant Joan de les Abadesses 25
Sant Martí de Provençals 14, 45, 53–6, 74, 109, 200
  La Constància in 208
  coopers in 30, 249
  radical action in 211
  textile unions in 110
  Traditionalist Association 351
  woodworkers in 60
  Workers Centre in 200, 211, 216
Sant Quirze 73
Sants 14, 22, 45, 54–6, 58, 72, 75, 90, 248, 259
  brickmakers in 201
  centre for rationalist education 211
  La Constància in 229
  CRT congress in 244–6, 251, 285
  industrial action in 208–9, 230, 267
  radical action in 282, 337
  Rationalist Atheneum in 240, 244, 260, 313
Sanz, Marià 221n75
Sanz Escartín, Eduardo 76, 78, 80
Sastre i Sanna, Miguel 84, 86, 90, 91, 283
Second International Socialism 136
Sedó company town 22, 71, 73, 82, 97n18
Sedó, Lluís 298–9, 309, 312
El Segle (company) 230
Seguí, Salvador 7, 153–4, 157, 161, 167, 204, 217, 235–42, 245–7, 251, 253, 262–4, 271, 278, 295–7, 299, 302, 318, 326–7, 330, 341
  anarchist hardliners and 'purists', opposition to 161, 263–4, 273–4, 276, 281–3, 304, 313–15, 316, 322n81, 323–4, 326, 328, 330, 341, 346–7
  anarchist-syndicalist ideology of 237
  anarchist terrorism and 251, 305, 312, 326
  arrest and imprisonment of 292 (January 1919), 331 (November 1920)
  assassination of 347–8

  assassination attempt (1920) 322n91
  attempts to broaden social base of CRT 266, 274, 305
  La Canadenca and general strikes (1919) 292, 295–8, 319n21
  Catalan identity and Catalanism, attitude towards 271
  caution of 302, 328
  Contacts with Restoration politicians 335, 341–2
  CRT
    reorganisation and (1917–18) 235–42, 245–7, 253
    general secretary (1916–17, 1917–20) 236, 240–1, 323, 328
  deportation of 332–3
  escape and hiding (1919) 297
  gradualist strategy of 313, 328
  intellectual support for policies, lack of 354
  key figure 217, 295–7, 330
  Labour Commission, favourable disposition to 309–11
  marginalisation of, attempts at 346–7
  Negotiations
    with Francisco Carlos Bas (1920) 327, 330–1
    with Julio Amado (1919) 303–5, 309–10
  obstructions to objectives, intractability of 306
  opposition to Lerrouxism 167
  'orthodox' anarchist syndicalists, tensions with 217, 239, 276, 279, 284, 302, 313–15
  Pestaña and 240, 278–9, 302, 304–6, 326, 335, 342, 347
  'political proposal' support for 342
  pragmatism of 278–9, 283, 284, 286, 295–7, 304, 306
  the PRC, Layret and 279–80, 331–3
  reaffirmation of control by Seguí's generation 345
  reforming current at CNT under leadership of 7
  responsible leadership of 307, 310, 312, 331, 335

revolutionary strategy 278–9
(1917), 306 (1919)
the Rull gang and 154
setback and defeat for 318
(1919–20)
Socialists and 262–4, 266, 275–6,
284, 305–6, 327–8, 335–6, 341
sympathy with Allies in World War
I 273, 278
the Teatro Español *tertulia* and
153, 157
undermined by young gunmen
(1919–20) 323–4
unification of labour movement,
ultimate aim 262, 274–5, 281,
284–5, 305–6, 327–8, 346
unions fight for consumer rights,
advocacy of 305, 346
work, difficulty in finding post
1919 strikes 299
Semblancat, Angel 283
Sendra (assassinated CNT activist) 211,
221–2n75
Serra, Joan 316
Sert Germans (factory) 22
Sexenio Democrático 68
Seydoux i Cia (factory) 83, 194
SFIO (French Socialist Party) 132
shoemaking 24, 31, 42, 127
Silvela, Francisco 76, 80, 88, 178
el sindicalismo a base múltiple 108,
196–8, 220n48, 339
El Sindicalista 211
Sindicatos Libres (Free Trade Unions)
324–7, 331–2, 334–5, 338–9,
342–3, 345, 347–8, 351
Military's role in 325, 331,
354–5n4
violence and appearance of 325–6
Sindicats Unics (SUs) 216, 225–54,
314–17, 329–30, 338–9, 345,
349–52
Bureaucratisation, criticism of 346
Construction Workers' SU 292,
300, 305, 308, 310–11, 314, 345,
346
fighting machines 349, 354
Food Processing Workers' SU 305,
308, 346
Gas, Water and Electricity Workers'
SU 293

maintaining organisations in
Barcelona 311
Metalworkers' SU 246–7, 299,
303, 308, 316, 330, 332
Shopworkers' SU 302
Textile Workers' SU 247, 300
Woodworkers' SU 245, 257n86,
292, 308, 324
Sitges 200
skilled trades in Barcelona 84–95
skilled workers, attitudes *see* working-
class community
slum housing 49–50, 54
SO 154–5, 158
anarchism and 128–40
Catalan Socialists and 131–8, 197–8
Colomer, general secretary of
144n101
Federal Commission 136, 138,
144, 172, 176, 195, 197
formation of 128–40
ideological divisions within 135–9,
195–200
Lerrouxists and 168–9, 177–8,
182–3
National Confederation,
transformation into 200
Negre, general secretary of 197
'non–political' nature of 138
terrorism, attitude towards 154
unitary aspirations of 134
see also Prat, Josep; *Solidaridad
Obrera*
Social Democratic Alliance 104
social legislation 76, 137
El Socialista 112
Socialists *see* PSOE
Societat Material per a Construccions i
Ferrocarrils *see* Girona Foundry
Society of Machine Constructors 92–4
Society of Metallurgists and Machine
Constructors 94, 250
El Sol 327
Soldevila Romero, Cardinal José 348–9,
351
Soler Gustenech, Josep 40
Solidaridad Obrera 151, 156, 172, 199,
239–40, 250, 252–3, 260–3,
266–8, 271–2, 274, 276, 278,
281–2, 292–3, 299–300, 308,
312–13, 344, 347–8, 351–2,
358n82

Andreu as editor 232, 237, 274, 287–8n34
anti-clericalism of 42
Bisbe as editor 136
Borobio as editor 232, 261, 274, 276, 288n50
Bueso as editor 195–6
circulation of 196, 234, 260–1, 300, 346
criticism of gunmen (1923) 349
first page of first number 133, 136
hostility towards 'bourgeois' Catalanism 215
ideological divisions within anarchist-syndicalism and 196–9, 216–17, 273–4, 276, 285, 312–3, 349
launch of 132–3
Libres, accusations against 347–8
peaceful resistance, call for 312
Pestaña as editor 240, 261–2, 287–8n34
reappearance of in Barcelona of 211 (May 1913), 280 (August 1917) 308 (October 1919), 346 (February 1923)
republican-Socialist alliance, attitude towards 276, 285
Restoration regime, attacks on 278
support for industrial federations 216, 237–8
suspension of publication 280 (July 1917) 292 (January 1919)
union structural reform, campaign for 237–40
Valencia edition 300 (1919), 343 (1922)
violent tone of 281–2
World War I crisis for 234
Solidaritat Catalana 173
Sometent (private security) 94–5, 174, 180, 296, 297–8, 305, 311, 315–16, 333–4, 337, 349–52
The Sons of Whores 153–4, 236
Soriano, Rodrigo 300, 346–7
Spain
    agriculture of 16–17
    anarchism, appearance in 103–4
    anti-*caciquista* language 277
    Associations Law (1887) 124
    caciques 2, 68, 71, 76, 79, 137, 139, 182, 262, 269, 294

caciquismo 68–9, 71, 76, 79, 97, 146, 149, 151, 161, 269
Cánovas Restoration 68–9
Catholic anti-Liberalism 69
clientalism 68, 147
colonial
    losses 76
    trading 17–18
conciliation of liberal opinion 68
defeat by United States (1898) 76
economy of 16–17
fuerzas vivas 68–9
Law of National Protection (1907) 19
limited size of market in 20
modernisation calls in 76
patronage 68
political
    crisis (1917) 277–83
    system 67–8
post-colonial economic environment 17–18
poverty-stricken state 90
privatisation of power in hands of local elites 69
protection of industry 17
Sexenio Democrático 68
social laws in 76
Socialism, appearance in 103–4
state
    and Catalan industrialists 67–75
    security 67
universal suffrage 68
Spanish Metalworkers' Federation 95, 120
Special Brigade of police 155, 204, 211, 241, 252, 334
state repression of labour and the Left 67–8, 80–1, 88, 91, 94–5, 105–7, 112, 115, 119, 123–4, 126, 128, 134–5, 143n68, 149–51, 155, 157–8, 168, 171, 173, 176, 181–2, 193–5, 205–6, 217, 235, 342, 269, 297–300, 313, 315–17, 321n55, 228–9, 331–9, 344–6, 351–2
status, gender differences in 40–41
Stirner, Max 128
strikes *see* industrial action
Suplemento de la Revista Blanca 116, 119, 163, 165

syndicalism 5, 118–19, 129–30, 211–17
  anarchism and 118, 129–30, 134,
    136, 142n44, 155–8
  anarchism, syndicalism and the
    general strike 3, 107–8, 118–19,
    122–5
Syndicalist Athenaeum 158, 195, 200,
  233, 260, 273

T
tailoring industry
  industrial structure and the labour
    process 31
  unions and strikes 230
Tallada, Josep María 20
Tarragona 29, 135–7, 213, 323
TCV (cotton textile labour federation)
  declared 'yellow' 213
  offensive against by industrialists
    105–6
  organised labour and 71–2, 76,
    78–9, 112–13, 121, 127, 140,
    141n17, 169–70, 172, 213
  relations with Socialists 105–6,
    112–13, 127
  republicanism of 106
  resurrection and integration into
    FTE 109–12
Teatro Español *tertulia* 153, 156–7,
  200, 236, 336
technological
  deficiencies 20–1
  modernisation 26–7, 30–1
  effect on working–class 50–1
Los Templarios 156
Ter Valley 2, 14–16, 22, 109–10, 135,
  137, 200, 308
  industrial action in 77, 80–82, 106,
    210, 303
  spinning industry in 39–40, 71–4,
    79, 139
  union
    power in 213, 229, 346
    recruitment in 78
Termes, Josep 4, 172
'El Tero' *see* Sabater, Pau
Terrassa 14, 72, 83
terrorism 324, 325–6
  anarchist terrorism 108–9, 134–5,
    153–5
  CNT and 250–3, 328–9, 330, 337,
    348–9

employer-sponsored terrorism 211,
  252, 298–301, 319–20n23, 331–4,
  324–5, 334, 343, 347–8, 356n36,
  358n91
  repudiation of terrorism by Seguí
    305
Tierra y Libertad 116, 128, 131, 135,
  138, 156, 172, 185n31, 196,
  232–3, 235, 241, 262, 265,
  273–4, 280, 346
Tilly, Charles 6, 96
Torelló 22, 72–3
Torquemada, Tomás de 151
Torres Escartín, Rafael 348
Tosas, Joan 185n25
Tous, Ernesto 192
El Trabajo 125, 129–30, 156, 194
trade federations, development of 89
  see also organised labour; trade
    unions, trade and industrial
    federations
trade unions, trade and industrial
  federations
  ADM (shopworkers' union) 85,
    115, 132, 201
  L'Art d'Imprimir 114, 120, 167,
    168
  Barcelona Bricklayers and
    Bricklayers Labourers' Union 228,
    245
  Barcelona Bricklayers Labourers'
    Federation 117
  Barcelona Construction Workers'
    Federation 207, 213, 217, 236,
    245, 256n68
  Barcelona Federation of Bricklayers
    and Bricklayers' Labourers 245
  Barcelona Metalworkers'
    Federation (1901–1903) 90, 93,
    120, 122–3
  Barcelona Metalworkers'
    Federation (1913–1916) 207–212,
    228
  Barcelona Metalworkers' Union
    (1909–1910) 190, 192, 207
  Barcelona Metalworkers' Union
    (1916–1918) 245, 248, 253
  Barcelona Woodworkers'
    Federation 222n81
  CADCI (association of shop and
    office workers) 85, 99n61, 172,
    220n46, 231, 238, 246

Carpenters' Federation of the Catalan Region 89, 99n68, 121
Catalan Confederation of Barcelona Bricklayers and Bricklayers' Labourers 50, 212–13, 245
Catalan Federation of Glassworkers 43
Catalan Regional Metalworkers' Federation 64–5n41, 207, 212, 222n80, 263
Catalan Regional Textile Federation 208–10, 213, 216
Catalan Section (railwayworkers' union) 190, 201, 214, 216
Confederation of Barcelona Bricklayers 50, 212–13, 228
Confederation of Spanish Metalworkers 212
La Constància 208–11, 213, 216–17, 229–30, 243–4, 252, 260, 267, 288n35
Construction Workers' Federation 207, 228
Construction Workers' SU 245, 257n86, 292, 300, 308, 311, 314, 345–6
Coopers federation (Federation of Journeyman Coopers of the Spanish Region) 30, 89
La Efusió (labourers' union) 243
Federation of Spanish Railway Workers (UGT) 214
Federation of Waterfront Unions 190–1
Food Processing Workers' SU 305, 308, 346
FTE (textile workers federation) 78–81, 109–13, 127, 130
Gas, Water and Electricity Workers' SU 293
Glassworkers' National Federation 242
Local Transport Federation 90, 92
Metalworkers' SU 246–7, 299, 303, 308, 316, 330, 332
National Bricklayers' Federation (UGT) 212–13
National Confederation of Spanish Metalworkers 207
National Federation of Carpenters and Similar Workers (UGT), 121

National Federation of Glassworkers 242
National Federation of Pasta Makers 40
National Federation of Woodworking Unions 89, 201, 212, 232
National Maritime Transport Federation 229
National Metalworkers' Federation (UGT) 212
National Textile Federation 40, 210, 229, 243–4, 247, 251, 259n86, 274, 303
National Woodworkers' Federation (UGT) 212
El Naval, stokers union (UGT) 202, 229, 242, 248
El Radium 230, 246
Railwayworkers' Federation (UGT) 201–2
Shopworkers' SU 302
Spanish Metalworkers' Federation 95, 120
TCV (cotton textile labour federation)
    declared 'yellow' 213
    offensive against by industrialists 105–6
    organised labour and 71–2, 76, 78–9, 112–13, 121, 127, 140, 141n17, 169–70, 172, 213
    relations with Socialists 105–6, 112–13, 127
    republicanism of 106
    resurrection and integration into FTE 109–12
Textile Workers' SU 247, 300
Union of Carpenters, Cabinetmakers and Similar Workers 227, 245
Unión Fabril Algodonera (UGT) 109, 113
Union of Gas, Water and Electricity Workers 243
Union of the Woodworking Industry 245
Woodworkers' SU 245, 257n86, 292, 308, 324
trades, congregation in particular areas 59–60

Tragic Week, anticlerical riots 173–5,
179, 181, 183, 189–90, 282–3, 333
aftermath of 195–7, 204, 207,
218n2
religious buildings attacked 178
La Tramontana (and Tramontana
group) 153, 169, 172, 185n31,
186n74
La Transatlántica (shipping company)
75, 175
Trinxet (factory) 230
Tusell, Javier 143n68

U
Ucelay Da Cal, Enric 4–5
UGT (Socialist labour confederation) 2,
4, 190, 201–2, 212–13, 229, 249,
263, 332, 335
affiliates 106, 111–13, 121, 217,
264, 285
bureaucratic nature of 4
Catalan affiliates *see* union base in
Catalonia
cautious practice of 106, 108, 115,
140, 238–9, 243, 279, 314, 327
*See also el sindicalismo a base
múltiple*
centralisation, criticisms of 202
Centre de Societats Obreres 112
CNT (anarchist-syndicalist
confederation) and 189, 203, 205,
214–15, 217–18, 234, 236,
239–40, 263–5, 305–6, 314
CNT-UGT Alliance 269–76, 281,
284–6, 314, 327–8
foundation of 106
FTE and 109–12
links with PSOE, criticisms of 202
reformist policy 127, 140, 205
relations with TCV 105–6,
112–13, 127
el sindicalismo a base múltiple 108,
196–8, 220n48, 339
SO (Worker Solidarity) and 133–4,
138, 176, 195, 197–8
tensions between Catalan UGT and
PSOE 109, 111–14
union base in Catalonia 106,
112–15, 127, 139–40, 144n82,
190, 201–2, 212–18, 229, 249
union dues 219n19, 220n53

see also Comaposada, Josep;
Iglesias, Pablo; PSOE; Reoyo,
Toribio; trade unions, trade and
industrial federations
Ulled, Josep 335
Ulled, Pau 300
Ullman, Joan Connelly 61n31, 176,
178
UNFR (Left-Catalanist Party) 270
Unión Fabril Algodonera (UGT) 109,
113
Union of Carpenters, Cabinetmakers
and Similar Workers 227, 245
Union of Gas, Water and Electricity
Workers 243
Union of the Woodworking Industry
245
see also Union of Carpenters,
Cabinetmakers and Similar Workers
unions *see* organised labour; trade
unions, trade and industrial
federations
Unions Professionals 75, 210
United States, Spain's military defeat by
76, 148–9
universal suffrage 68
Urales, Federico ('Joan Montseny')
115–16, 122, 153, 165, 171, 272,
274, 346
urbanisation 12
labour agitation and 72
Usón, Joan 172

V
Valdour, Jacques 45, 75, 148
Valencia (and Valencia Region) 38, 44,
47, 122, 124, 156, 197, 200, 236,
240
Agricultural Workers, congress in
249
CNT in 264, 276, 292, 334, 341,
346, 352
industrial action in 205, 281
Salvatierra assassination in 328
Valero, Enric 236, 314
Valladolid 116–17, 301
Valle Jover, Plácido de 313
Vallina, Pedro 163, 165–6
Vandellós, Pere 336–7
Vapor Vell (factory) 72
Vega, Jesús 262

Viadiu, Josep 234, 236, 238, 266, 305, 342
Vicens i Vives, Jaume 3
Vidal-Ribes i Güell, Emili 298, 356n35
Vidiella, Rafael 251
Vilafranca del Penadés 29
Vilanova i la Geltrú 14, 25, 109, 200, 211, 213
Vilella (factory) 242
Vilesca company town 73
Villafranca 200, 211
Villalbí, Gual 310
Viñolas, Gaspar 109–10
Vives, Tomàs 325
La Voz del Pueblo 156
El Vulcano (factory) 23, 229

W
wages 17, 26–7, 31, 37–8, 74–5, 80, 330
    back-wages, payment of 311, 316
    gender differences in 40–1, 77
    working-class living standards and 47–50
    working conditions and 82–3, 231, 249, 310
the waterfront 27, 43, 45, 86, 91–2, 95, 190–1, 193–4, 199–201, 206, 229
Weyler, Valeriano 193
white-collar workers 41, 56, 58, 62, 85, 172, 201, 210, 227, 246, 249, 338
Winston, Colin 8n14, 221n74, 325, 339, 354n2
Women
    anarchists attitude towards women 40, 90, 121, 143n58, 158, 207–8, 243–5, 247, 268–9, 287n28, 326
    burden of domestic as well as paid work for 39
    and the Catholic Church 38, 61, 147–8, 178–9
    domestic
        service, employment of women 38
        sphere, women and 36–8
    male opposition to the employment of women in 'male' jobs 27, 30–1, 39–40, 77–82
    quantitative importance of women's work 38

    sexual division of labour 25–6, 36–41, 63n5
    socialisation within working–class community 61
    and strike action 78–82, 91–2, 94, 174, 176, 208–10, 231, 243–5
    subordination of female workers by industrialists 27, 39, 63n12
    women's
        Anarchist Group 244
        protests 6, 48, 175–9, 265–9, 326
        unionisation 77, 90, 99n70, 121, 208, 269, 300
    see also gender inequalities; masculinity
Woodworking
    industrial structure and the labour process 19–21, 42, 60, 86
    unionisation and strikes 89, 91, 116, 201, 206, 212, 217–8, 222n81, 232, 245, 247, 257, 292, 308, 324
Woollen textiles
    economic development 13–14, 18
    industrial structure 22–3, 83
    unions and strikes 42, 83, 116–17
    working hours 99n57
work structures, reorganisation of 27, 28–9
Workers' Athenaeums *see* Ateneus Obrers
Worker Solidarity *see* SO
workers' organisations *see* organised labour; trade unions, trade and industrial federations
working-class community
    bullying 42
    children within 60
    Church attendance 59
    class boundaries, hardening of 56, 58
    in company towns 72–4
    craft workers, perception of higher status 37, 43
    disease 49
    economic crises, effect on 48–9
    educational deficiencies 60
    family networks 41, 44–5, 47
    'family wage,' lack of 49
    forging of a 51–61

friendship networks, 56, 58, 60
hierarchies within the working class 41–3, 62
housing quality 49–50
illiteracy 42
journeymen and masters 41–2
living standards, inadequacy of 48–50
marriage and cohabitation 61
migrant labour, marginalisation and integration 43–7
problems in common 47–51
regionalist identity, development of 47
sanitation, lack of 49–50
sexual division of labour 25–6, 36–41, 63n5
skilled trades,
    restrictions to entry 26–30, 37, 44
    solidarity within 44–5, 60, 85
slum housing 49–50, 54
socialisation within 60–1
socio-cultural divisions between neighbourhoods 58–9
solidarity within 77–8
status, gender differences in 40–1

ties within working-class communities 60–1
technological change and de-skilling, attitude towards 28, 50–1
trades, congregation in particular areas 59–60
unemployment, risk of 48, 51
wages, gender differences in 40–1
white-collar workers 41
working-class
    life, harsh nature of 60
    neighbourhoods, growth of 53–7
working conditions 50–1
World War I 29, 49, 59
    labour relations and wartime economy 225–32

Y
Young Barbarians 163
Yvetot, Georges 129

Z
La Zorrilla Theatre, Gràcia 157
Zurdo Olivares, Lluís 120